International Business

Second edition

Stuart Wall

Bronwen Rees

FT Prentice Hall
FINANCIAL TIMES

An imprint of **Pearson Education**
Harlow, England • London • New York • Boston • San Francisco • Toronto • Sydney • Singapore • Hong Kong
Tokyo • Seoul • Taipei • New Delhi • Cape Town • Madrid • Mexico City • Amsterdam • Munich • Paris • Milan

Pearson Education Limited
Edinburgh Gate
Harlow
Essex CM20 2JE
England
and Associated Companies throughout the world

Visit us on the World Wide Web at:
www.pearsoned.co.uk

First published 2001
Second edition published 2004

© Pearson Education Limited 2001, 2004

ISBN 0 273 68591 0

British Library Cataloguing-in-Publication Data
A catalogue record for this book is available from the British Library

Library of Congress Cataloging-in-Publication Data
Wall, Stuart, 1946–
    International business / Stuart Wall, Bronwen Rees. -- 2nd ed.
        p. cm.
    Rev. ed. of: Introduction to international business / Stuart Wall and Bronwen Rees. 2001.
    Includes bibliographical references and index.
    ISBN 0-273-68591-0
    1. International business enterprises. 2. International economic relations. 3.
Globalization. I. Rees, Bronwen. II. Wall, Stuart, 1946– Introduction to international
business. III. Title.

    HD62.4W343 2004
    658'.049--dc22

                                                2004045153

10 9 8 7 6 5 4 3 2
08 07 06 05 04

Typeset in 10/12.5 pt Sabon by 30
Printed by Ashford Colour Press Ltd, Gosport

The publisher's policy is to use paper manufactured from sustainable forests.

Contents

5 The political, legal, economic and technological environment   134

Website resources

For Students:
- Learning objectives for each chapter
- Multiple choice and other interactive questions to test students' learning
- Further case study material and updates
- Links to relevant sites on the web

For Lecturers:
- A secure, password-protected site with teaching material
- Complete, downloadable Instructor's Manual with additional question material and answers
- PowerPoint slides that can be downloaded and used as OHTs

Also: This site has a syllabus manager, search functions, and email results functions.

Preface: using this book

This book is primarily written for students taking modules in *international business* on a range of undergraduate, HND and postgraduate programmes. Any text on international business must, of necessity, span a wide variety of topic areas and embrace a number of different subject disciplines. In that sense it is clearly difficult to locate its boundaries precisely. What we can be sure about is that we are studying a vibrant, ever-changing set of issues and relationships, which will almost certainly have major impacts on all our lives. It could hardly be otherwise when almost one-quarter of the world's recorded output is exported and when changes in business practices or technology in Seoul (South Korea) can have major implications for a workforce as far away as Dagenham (Essex, UK)! It has become increasingly clear that a proper understanding of worldwide patterns and trends in international business must draw upon far more than the conventional economic discipline of 'international trade and finance', or the in-depth analysis of 'multinational firm activity', or even the study of key functional areas such as marketing, management, finance and accounting. Important though all these contributions undoubtedly are, attention is increasingly being paid to the often subtle, but highly significant, organisational and cultural characteristics that underpin production and trade in a globalised economy. In fact, today's study of international business draws heavily on disciplines as diverse as law, sociology, anthropology, psychology, politics, history and geography, as well as those previously mentioned.

The first chapter of this book identifies some current patterns and trends, which are of key concern to those engaged in international business, whether from a corporate or national perspective. Chapters 2 to 7 then concentrate on issues that affect most types of international business, whatever their sector of activity, nature of operations or stage reached in the internationalisation process. The principles, practices and institutions underpinning international trading relationships are reviewed, as are a wide variety of external 'environmental factors', which play a key role in determining both the direction and outcome of international business activity. These include political, legal, sociocultural, ethical, ecological, economic and technological factors, all of which shape the environment in which the international business must operate. After considering these 'universal' aspects of international business, the more 'firm-specific' aspects are investigated in Chapters 8 to 12 with an in-depth analysis of the alternative courses of action facing the international business, whether in terms of corporate strategy, human resource management, marketing, accounting and finance, operations management or logistics.

Throughout the book you will find up-to-date case materials to illustrate many of the international issues involved. A number of questions will help direct your thoughts to some of the principles underpinning the facts and events presented in each case study. In a similar vein, you will also find a number of 'pause for thought' sections within the text of each chapter, to which you will find outline responses at the end of the book to self-check your lines of reasoning. A number of 'Boxes' are presented to take further some of the analysis presented in the text. Each chapter concludes with a brief review of further sources of reading and information, including useful websites.

If you turn to the *companion website* to this book, some interactive questions (with solutions) can be found to help you self-check the content of each chapter, together with further up-to-date factual and case study materials on the topics contained in that chapter. You will also find a selection of *articles* on the companion website, which will be updated from time to time to keep you at the forefront of contemporary developments in the subject matter of that chapter.

For this second edition all data, empirical and case study materials have been thoroughly updated and revised with a number of entirely new cases integrated within the text. On occasions the text has been further developed to reflect contemporary debate, as with the more detailed scrutiny of the integration – responsiveness framework in Chapter 8 and the focus on international business activity post 9/11 in Chapter 1.

Acknowledgements

We should like to thank Geoff Black, who has contributed Chapter 11. We would also like to thank Alan Griffiths for contributing important case materials at various parts of the text and Jonathan Wilson for much helpful advice and useful additional content on China.

We would also like to express our gratitude for all the help received from Eleanor and Suzannah Wall in preparing the book. We wish also to thank Suzannah for her important contribution in devising case study materials. Thanks also to Paul Weekes for helpful advice in the marketing chapter.

Our thanks to all those who have given permission for the use of material in the book.

Stuart Wall
Bronwen Rees

Publisher's acknowledgements

We are grateful to the following for permission to reproduce copyright material:

Figure 1.2 from *Global Shift: Transforming the World Economy*, Sage Publications Ltd (Dicken, P. 2003); Figures 2.1 and 3.5 from 'The Multinational Corporation' in *Applied Economics*, Pearson Education (Healey, N. 2001, 2004); Figure 8.4 from 'Changes in the Competitive Battlefield' in *Mastering Strategy*, Pearson Education (Prahalad, C.K. 1999); Figure 8.11 from 'Horizontal Acquisitions: The Benefits and Risk to Long-Term Performance' in *Mastering Strategy*, Pearson Education (Capron, L. 1999); Figure 8.13 from *The Knowledge-Creating Company: How Japanese Companies Create the Dynamics of Innovation*, Oxford University Press, Inc. (Nonaka, I. and Takeuchi, H. 1995) Used by permission of Oxford University Press, Inc.; Figure 8.14 from 'Game Theory in the Real World' in *Mastering Strategy*, Pearson Education (Gertner, R. and Knez, M. 2000); Figure 9.1 from *Policy and*

Practice in Human Resource Management, Thomson Learning (Brewster, C. and Hegewisch, A. 1994); Figure 9.2 from 'Human Resource Management: An Agenda for the 1990s' in *International Journal of Human Resource Management*, Taylor & Francis (Hendry and Pettigrew 1990); Figure 10.1 from *International Business: Theories, Policies and Practices*, Pearson Education (Tayeb, M. 2000); Figure 11.1 from 'Total strategies for risk control' © *Financial Times*, 9 May 2000; Table 5.2 from 'Country Risk ratings' in *Management International Review*, Universität Hohenheim (Dichtl, E. and Koeglmayr, H.G. 1986); Table 11.1 from *Statement of Principles for Financial Reporting*, Accounting Standards Board, (Accounting Standards Board 1999); Tables, 11.2, 11.3 and 11.4 from *Tesco plc Annual Report 2003*, Tesco Stores Limited; Table 12.1 from *International Business: Theories, Policies and Practices*, Pearson Education (Tayeb, M. 2000); Table 12.2 from *Operations Management*, Pearson Education (Slack *et al.* 1998).

The Economist Newspaper Limited for extracts from 'Milberg's Mission', 'Sweatshops to Body Scans' and 'Politics of Scale' all published in *The Economist* 1 April 2000, 29 April 2000 and 24 June 2000 © The Economist Newspaper Limited, London 2000; Edward Elgar Publishing Limited for extracts from *Dimensions of International Competitiveness: Issues and Policies* by L. Lloyd-Reason and S. Wall, 2000; Pearson Education Limited for extracts from 'The Multinational Corporation' published in *Applied Economics* edited by Alan Griffiths and Stuart Wall, 'Digital Buccaneers Caught in a Legal Web' published in *Mastering Risk* by James Pickford, 'Game Theory: How to Make it Pay' by L. Garicano and 'Game Theory in the Real World' by R. Gertner and M. Knez published in *Mastering Strategy*; Sage Publications, Inc. for an extract from 'Ethics and Cultures in International Business' by J. Beyer and D. Nino published in *Journal of Management Inquiry*, Vol. 8, No 3, 1999; and Jonathan Wilson, senior lecturer at the Ashcroft International Business School, Cambridge, for an extract from his thesis 'Inter-Partner Relationships and Performance in UK-Chinese Joint Ventures: An Interaction Approach'; Jagdish Bhagwati and Arvind Panagariya for Case study 4.4 'Bilateral trade treaties are a sham' *Financial Times*, 14 July 2003.

We are grateful to the Financial Times Limited for permission to reprint the following material:

Case Study 1.3 Preparing to compete in the wider world, © *Financial Times*, 28 March 2000; Case Study 1.4 Happy Birthday, globalisation, © *Financial Times*, 6 May 2003; Case Study 2.1 India plans special economic zones, © *Financial Times*, 18 March 2003; Case Study 3.3 CBI battle lines are drawn for tax showdown, © *Financial Times*, 29 April 2000; Case Study 4.1 Trade ruling takes WTO into realm of domestic taxation, © *Financial Times*, 25 February 2000; Case Study 4.2 Cambodia set to join world trade body, © *Financial Times*, 23 July 2003; Case Study 4.3 US steel tariffs illegal, rules WTO, © *Financial Times*, 27 March 2003; CS 4.5 World Bank may help fund small companies in Africa, © *Financial Times*, 25 June 2003; Case Study 5.2 Kraft cuts pack sizes to avert obesity lawsuits, © *Financial Times*, 2 July 2003; Case Study 5.3 Break for Nestlé as trademark case goes to Europe, © *Financial Times*, 26 July 2003; Case Study 5.6 China's banks face a cultural revolution, © *Financial Times*, 27 April 2000, and China tries new attack on bad loans, © *Financial*

Times, 10 July 2003; Case Study 6.4 In European countries, there are three or four competitors. In the US, there are 10 or 20, © *Financial Times*, 25 February 2003; Case Study 6.5 Organisations, too, can be put on the couch, © *Financial Times*, 20 June 2003; Case Study 7.3 Bribery has long been used to land international contracts. New laws will make that tougher, © *Financial Times*, 8 May 2003; Case Study 7.4 Growing pains, © *Financial Times*, 27 June 2000; Case Study 8.1 Crossing the Atlantic can end in oblivion, © *Financial Times*, 25 February 2003; Case Study 8.2 Carlsberg to take second look at China, © *Financial Times*, 9 July 2003; Case Study 8.4 Smaller chips, bigger stakes: how new monster plants will transform the industry, © *Financial Times*, 11 June 2003; Case Study 10.3 Will the world lose its taste for US brands?, © *Financial Times*, 27 March 2003; Case Study 10.4 Love in a warm climate, © *Financial Times*, 24 July 2003; Case Study 11.2 VW switches accounting model, © *Financial Times*, 21 February 2000; Case Study 11.3 An end to make-believe accounting, © *Financial Times*, 5 April 2000; Case Study 11.4 A sting in the tail, © *Financial Times*, 10 March 2003; Case Study 12.2 Outsourcing providers: Trend towards 'bundles' services, © *Financial Times*, 30th June 2003.

In some instances we have been unable to trace the owners of copyright material and we would appreciate any information that would enable us to do so.

Abbreviations

APEC	Asia-Pacific Economic Corporation
ART	alternative risk transfer
ASB	Accounting Standards Board (London)
ASEAN	Association of South East Asian Nations
BIT	bilateral investment treaties
B2B	business-to-business
CCFF	Compensatory and Contingency Financing Facility
CFF	Compensatory Financing Facility
CIMA	Chartered Institute of Management Accountants (London)
DTT	double taxation treaties
EAGGF	European Agricultural Guarantee and Guidance Fund
ECU	European Currency Unit
EPZ	export processing zone
EFF	Extended Fund Facility
ERP	enterprise resource planning
fdi	foreign direct investment
FSC	foreign sales corporation
GATT	General Agreement on Tariffs and Trade
GDP	gross domestic product
GM	genetically modified
GNP	gross national product
HICPs	Harmonised Indices of Consumer Prices
HRM	human resource management
IASs	International Accounting Standards
IBRD	International Bank for Reconstruction and Development
IDA	International Development Association
IFC	International Finance Corporation
IHRM	international human resource management
ILO	International Labour Office
IMF	International Monetary Fund
IPLC	international product life cycle
LDC	less-developed country
MAI	multilateral agreement on investment
M & A	mergers and acquisitions
MGQ	Maximum Guaranteed Quantity
MNE	multinational enterprise
NAFTA	North American Free Trade Association
NGO	non-governmental organisation
OECD	Organisation for Economic Co-operation and Development
PEST	political, economic, social and technological environmental analysis

RTA	regional trading arrangement
RULC	relative unit labour costs
SAF	Structural Adjustment Facility
SAL	Structural Adjustment Lending
SDR	Special Drawing Right
SEC	Securities and Exchange Commission (USA)
SFF	Supplementary Financing Facility
SME	small to medium-sized enterprise
UNCTAD	United Nations Conference on Trade, Aid and Development
UNIDO	United Nations Industrial Development Organisation
VER	voluntary export restraint
WOFE	wholly-owned foreign enterprise
WTO	World Trade Organisation

Chapter 1

Introduction to international business

By the end of this chapter you should be able to:

■ outline some of the key patterns and trends in international business activity;

■ explain the various dimensions of the term 'globalisation';

■ examine the role and importance of the multinational enterprise (MNE) in the global economy;

■ discuss the contribution of different disciplines to an understanding of international business activity.

Introduction

A useful starting point for a book on international business will be to identify some of the more recent patterns and trends in business activity worldwide. Of course, these patterns and trends are in part the *result* of some of the strategic choices taken by firms with an international orientation and in part the *stimulus* for future changes of direction by such firms. We shall examine each of these perspectives in later chapters of this book.

Patterns and trends in international business

Let us first identify some of the more important and measurable trends in international business activity.

■ Rapid growth in world trade and investment

Figure 1.1(a) indicates some aspects of the growth in international trade and capital flows using *index numbers* based on 1980 = 1 for exports and foreign direct investment (fdi) respectively. (The term fdi refers to international investment in productive facilities such as plant, machinery and equipment.) Between 1980 and 2003 *world exports* of goods and services have more than doubled in real terms, reaching over $7,500 billion in 2003 and accounting for over 23% of world gross domestic product. Over the same time period flows of *world foreign direct investment* have almost quadrupled in real terms, reaching around $700 billion in 2003, though this is some $400 billion less than in the peak year 2000.

Put another way, global exports of goods and services have increased at the astonishing rate of almost 5% per year in real terms between 1978 and 2002. It is worth noting that, while the 'high-income economies' (GNP of $9,206 per capita or more) have accounted for most of this growth in absolute value of global exports, the 'developing economies' (GNP of $745 or less) have increased their share of global exports, with the developing economies' exports rising at an above average 6% per annum in real terms between 1978 and 2002. This trend has resulted in the *exports–to GDP ratio* of the 'developing economies' rising much faster than that of the 'high income economies'. As can be seen from Table 1.1 exports accounted for some 33% of GDP in developing economies in 2002, but only some 22% of GDP in high-income economies at that date. The contribution of developing economies to international business is an issue we return to at various parts of this book.

■ Rapid growth in cross-border mergers and acquisitions

A rapid growth in cross-border mergers and acquisitions (M & A) since 1990 is indicated in Figure 1.1(b), despite the decline over the 2000/02 period. Much of this activity has been concentrated in financial services, insurance, life sciences, telecommunications and the media, with M & A being a key factor in accounting for the rise in fdi noted in Figure 1.1(a). Since 1990 the value of cross-border M & A has risen fourfold from around $150 billion per annum in 1990 to over $600 billion per annum in 2002, increasing its share of world fdi from 42% to 60%, though falling by some $300 billion on the peak year in 2000. Largely as a result of cross-border mergers, the 100 largest MNEs increased their foreign assets by 20% in 2000 alone, their foreign employment by 19% and their sales by 15%.

■ More liberalised markets on a global scale

We have already seen the relevance of foreign direct investment (fdi) to cross-border merger and acquisitions by multinational enterprises. Table 1.2 uses data from the United Nations Conference on Trade and Development (UNCTAD 2002) to indicate the progressive increase in regulatory changes affecting fdi by national governments, with the overwhelming majority of these changes being 'more favourable' to fdi flows.

Table 1.1 **Exports–to GDP ratios (%), 1978–2002**

Economy classification	1978	1981	1984	1987	1990	1993	1996	1999	2002
High-income economies	18	20	20	21	20	19	21	23	22
Developing economies	16	18	19	19	20	23	24	27	33

Source: Adapted from *Global Economic Prospects and the Developing Economies* (2003) World Bank, UNCTAD (various)

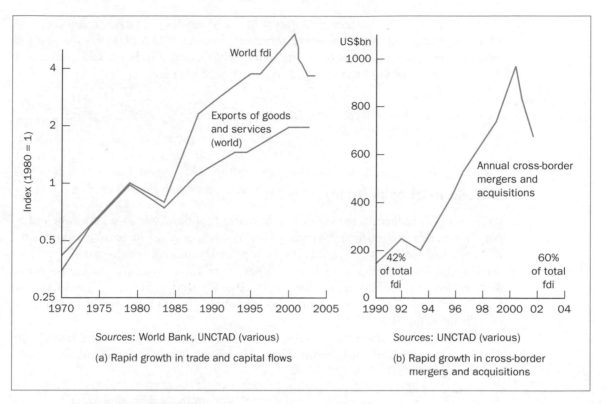

Figure 1.1 **Trends in the global economy**

■ More globally-dispersed value chains

With more market liberalisation comes increased worldwide competition which, together with rapid technological change, has placed increased pressures on large firms to adopt the most efficient and appropriate production and marketing locations if they are to survive and prosper. With improved international communications helping MNEs to coordinate and control geographically-dispersed activities, including service functions, the result has been an increased propensity for MNEs to shift

efficiency

Table 1.2 **Increasing liberalisation of markets on a global scale**

	National regulatory changes in fdi regimes		
Date	Number of regulatory changes	Number more favourable to fdi	Number less favourable to fdi
1991	82	80	2
1993	103	100	3
1995	107	102	5
1997	158	144	14
1999	146	138	8
2001	206	194	12

Source: Adapted from *World Investment Report*, UNCTAD (2002) certain production and service activities to low-cost centres overseas. Put another way, MNEs are engaged in an unending search for increased competitive advantage in terms of costs, resources, logistics and markets and are increasingly willing to reconfigure the geographical locations of their activities accordingly.

pause for thought 1	Can you give a recent example of an MNE adjusting the geographical location of its production or support activities?

■ Bi-polar to tri-polar (triad)

As Figure 1.2 indicates, the old *bi-polar* world economy, which was dominated by North America and Europe, has moved on to a *tri-polar* world economy dominated by the 'triad' of North America, the European Union and South-East Asia. These three regions now account for around 80% of the total value of world exports and 84% of world manufacturing value added. The importance of the economies of East and South-East Asia to both world manufacturing production and world trade is clear from Figure 1.2.

The importance of the triad economies can also be gauged from the fact that in 2002 around 90% of all fdi inflows into the developed economies went into the

Manufacturing value added

(= 28% of world MVA)

Total exports

(= 35% of world exports)

Manufacturing value added

(= 27% of world MVA)

Total exports

(= 19% of world exports)

EU

Manufacturing value added

(= 29% of world MVA)

Total exports

(= 26% of world exports)

North America

East and South-East Asia

Figure 1.2 **The changing global map of production and trade: the 'triad' of economic power**

Source: Adapted from Dicken (2003). Reprinted by permission of Sage Publications Ltd from © Peter Dicken, *Global Shift: Transforming the World Economy* (4th edn), 2003

'triad' economies, which were also the source for some 93% of all fdi outflows from the developed economies.

Changing area patterns of international income

The inclusion of the third leg of the triad in Figure 1.2, namely East and South-East Asia, is further reinforced by projections into the future. It is estimated that between 2002 and 2012 world GDP will nearly double from its present level of just over $32,000 billion to around $58,000 billion, with Figure 1.3 providing some World Bank projections for changes in national contributions to the world economy over the period 1992–2020. Although in terms of market size the global economy is currently dominated by the rich industrial economies of the USA, Japan, Germany, France, Italy and the UK (Figure 1.3(a)), it is projected that by 2020 economies such as China, India, Indonesia, South Korea, Thailand and Taiwan will all have moved into the 'top ten' (Figure 1.3(b)). This is an important pattern, suggesting that the attention of market-orientated companies will be increasingly drawn to these regions.

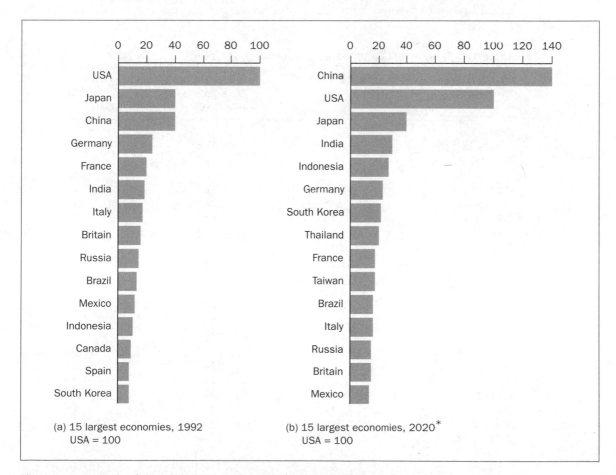

(a) 15 largest economies, 1992
USA = 100

(b) 15 largest economies, 2020*
USA = 100

Figure 1.3 Growth of the global economy, 1992–2020 (index numbers, USA = 100)

*Forecasts assume countries grow at regional rates projected in the World Bank's *Global Economic Prospects* report.
Source: World Bank

■ Changing area patterns of international costs

Of particular interest to international business location is the area pattern of *international labour costs*, both wage and non-wage (employers social security contributions, holiday pay, etc.). Comparable data is notoriously difficult to derive, both within broad geographical regions and between such regions. In any case it is not just overall labour costs that are important but these costs in relation to labour productivity, as can be seen from Table 1.3.

pause for thought 2	Using the data in Table 1.3 how do France and the Netherlands compare as possible locations for a labour-intensive production process? What other factors might be taken into account?

Table 1.3 indicates considerable variation in overall labour costs per hour worked in 2002, from $2.3 per hour in Mexico to $22.9 per hour in Germany. The second column expresses this same data as an index number (UK = 100) and suggests that overall labour costs per hour are 85.7% less in Mexico than in the UK but 42.2%

Table 1.3 Labour costs and labour productivity, 2002

Country	Total labour costs* ($ per hour)	Total labour costs ($ per hour Index: UK = 100)	Labour productivity** (Index UK = 100)
Mexico	2.3	14.3	40.3
Brazil	3.0	18.6	n/a
Portugal	4.8	29.8	n/a
Taiwan	5.7	35.4	n/a
New Zealand	7.7	47.8	77.4
Singapore	7.8	48.4	n/a
Korea	8.1	50.3	43.5
Greece	8.8	54.6	n/a
Spain	10.9	67.7	90.3
Australia	13.2	82.0	99.8
Ireland	13.3	82.6	132.2
Italy	13.8	85.7	122.6
Canada	15.6	96.9	103.2
France	15.9	98.8	135.5
UK	16.1	100.0	100.0
Netherlands	19.3	119.9	129.0
Austria	19.4	120.5	123.1
Japan	19.6	121.8	92.0
Finland	19.9	123.6	108.8
US	20.3	126.1	125.9
Belgium	21.0	130.4	137.1
Switzerland	21.8	135.4	111.3
Denmark	22.0	136.6	124.9
Germany	22.9	142.2	127.4

Sources: *Adapted from US Department of Labour (2002), Bureau of Statistics, September; **Adapted from *The Economist*, 22 February, 2003, p.122

more in Germany than the UK. However, international firms must sometimes be careful not to be unduly influenced by such data alone. For example labour productivity data is also of vital importance to location decisions, and the third column expresses labour productivity data as an index number (UK = 100). South Korea now looks relatively less attractive compared to the UK than if we concentrated on overall labour costs alone. Although it has overall labour costs as low as 50.3% of those in the UK its labour productivity is an even smaller proportion of that recorded in the UK (43.5%) so that overall *labour costs per unit of output* are arguably higher in South Korea than in the UK.

By way of contrast Belgium has overall labour costs 30.4% higher than those recorded in the UK but labour productivity that is an even higher proportion of that recorded in the UK (37.1%), so that overall *labour costs per unit of output* are arguably lower in Belgium than in the UK.

Table 1.4 provides some interesting international comparisons when wage costs are adjusted for productivity differentials. Although the top ten most competitive

Table 1.4 Ranking of countries in terms of labour cost competitiveness*

Country	Rank	Country	Rank
Russia	1	Denmark	30
Ukraine	2	Malaysia	31
Vietnam	3	Hong Kong SAR	32
Bulgaria	4	Spain	33
China	5	United Kingdom	34
Iceland	6	Switzerland	35
Czech Republic	7	Germany	36
Singapore	8	Korea	37
Slovakia	9	United States	38
Hungary	10	Thailand	39
Belgium	11	France	40
Austria	12	Venezuela	41
Israel	13	Costa Rica	42
New Zealand	14	El Salvador	43
Ireland	15	Zimbabwe	44
Norway	16	Indonesia	45
Portugal	17	South Africa	46
Mauritius	18	Poland	47
Luxembourg	19	Peru	48
Greece	20	Turkey	49
The Netherlands	21	Chile	50
Jordan	22	India	51
Taiwan	23	Colombia	52
Italy	24	Egypt	53
Sweden	25	Argentina	54
Japan	26	Bolivia	55
Finland	27	Brazil	56
Australia	28	Mexico	57
Canada	29	Philippines	58

Note: *Gross wages adjusted for productivity differences

Source: World Economic Forum (1999), Global Competitiveness Report (adapted)

countries in terms of the labour market are perhaps largely unsurprising, including mainly the 'transition' economies (*see* Chapter 5) and some low-wage East and South-East Asian economies, we can see how important the productivity issue really is. For example, Belgium (11th), Austria (12th), New Zealand (14th), Norway (16th) and Luxembourg (19th) are hardly low-wage economies, yet their relatively high levels of productivity give them a ranking in the 'top 20' economies in terms of labour cost competitiveness.

A more complete assessment of true labour costs would use the idea of relative unit labour costs (RULC), which are explored further in Box 1.1.

When RULCs are perceived to move in a less favourable direction (that is, rise) then this may have important implications for the location of international business (*see* Case Study 1.1).

■ Growth of regional trading arrangements

As we note in Chapter 3, there has been a rapid growth in regional trading blocs and in associated regional trading arrangements (RTAs), which give preferential treat-

---

Box 1.1   Relative unit labour costs (RULC)

Labour costs per unit of output (unit labour costs) are determined by both the wages of the workers and the output per worker (labour productivity). International competitiveness, in terms of unit labour costs, is also influenced by exchange rates. For example, depreciation of the currency makes exports cheaper in terms of the foreign currency (see Chapter 3) and therefore can even compensate for low labour productivity and high money wages. When we bring all these three elements together and express each of them relative to a country's main competitors, we can derive the most widely used measure of labour cost competitiveness, namely relative unit labour costs (RULC).

The calculation of RULC is as follows:

$$\frac{\text{Relative labour costs}}{\text{Relative labour productivity}} \times \text{Exchange rate} = \text{RULC}$$

This formula emphasises that lower RULC for, say, the UK could be achieved either by reducing the UK's relative labour costs, or by raising the UK's relative labour productivity, or by lowering the UK's effective exchange rate, or by some combination of all three.

Between 1999 (the launch of the Euro) and 2002 the sterling exchange rate rose significantly relative to the euro. Clearly we can see from this analysis that the UK's RULC, other things being equal, would then rise as compared to its EU competitors. Only by reducing UK relative labour costs and/or raising UK relative labour productivity could this rise in the sterling exchange rate be offset and UK exporters remain competitive with their European rivals. Multinational companies located in the UK have sought to offset the adverse impact of the sharp rise in the sterling exchange rate (relative to the euro) on their cost competitiveness. For example, they have supplied an increasing proportion of their EU market from other overseas plants (rather than from those located in the UK), and have forced suppliers to their UK plants to invoice bills in euros (rather than in sterling), etc.

In 2003, however, the sterling exchange rate began to fall against a stronger euro, bringing renewed hope for UK producers vis-à-vis their EU counterparts.

CASE 1.1 Dyson relocates production to South-East Asia

James Dyson, long associated with manufacturing his innovative products in the UK, announced in 2002 that he was to shift production of his revolutionary dual cyclone bagless vacuum cleaner to Malaysia with the loss of over 800 jobs at his factory in Malmesbury, Wiltshire, which had produced some 8,000 vacuum cleaners per day. He argued that the globalisation of manufacturing industry had left Dyson with two ways of surviving in the cut-throat consumer market. The first is to become a low-cost producer making a cheap product that follows the rest of the market. The second is to invest much more than its competitors in technology, design and performance. He argues that it is his determination to follow the second approach that has led him to relocate production to Malaysia. The 54-year-old design engineer made his name by eventually overcoming the scepticism of banks and venture capitalists to bring his revolutionary product to market some 15 years after his breakthrough invention. By 2002 some 32 separate models of vacuum cleaner were in production. Dyson is keen to point out that since the day the first Dyson dual cyclone vacuum cleaner went on sale in 1993, the company has been operating in a price-cutting market in which it has faced the further problems of rises in labour costs, land prices, taxation and other overhead costs while still trying to substantially increase its investment in new technology.

Dyson claims that by 2002 the sums no longer added up and the company faced going out of business if it continued manufacturing its product in the UK. As of September 2002 all vacuum cleaner production has taken place in Malaysia. The company argues that its production costs will benefit from the much lower wages in Malaysia, equivalent to £1.50 per hour (despite its intention to pay twice the Malaysian national average to its employees) as compared to the then £4.10 per hour in the UK. Indeed the company estimates that lower wages will reduce its unit production costs by around 30 per cent, though the added cost of transporting vacuum cleaners back to European markets will almost wipe out any cost savings. Nevertheless further cost savings will come from now having most of its component suppliers nearby (South-East Asian component suppliers having progressively replaced those from the UK) and from now being much closer to emerging new markets in Japan, Australia and the Far East. Dyson makes the point that when he first started making high-speed landing craft in the UK thirty years ago, he located in Birmingham where he found 90 per cent of the suppliers he needed all within a few miles of each other. Over the years, however, these have virtually disappeared and the company has had to go abroad to find suppliers for many of its new product ranges.

Dyson goes on to argue that, over the years, successive UK governments have failed to implement the right measures to support manufacturing, such as good R & D related tax incentives, training sufficient apprentices and educating enough engineers and scientists. In addition, successive governments have used high interest rates to control inflation and strengthen the pound – both of which hurt manufacturers, who need low interest rates to borrow, and a low exchange rate to make their exports competitive abroad. Further disincentives, such as the delay of planning applications for factories, rising national insurance contributions and

▶

crippling factory rates are seen by Dyson as also creating barriers to efficient man-ufacturing in the UK. By contrast governments in Asian countries tend to adopt, in his view, policies that smooth the paths for manufacturers.

While lamenting the loss of UK jobs, the consolation to Dyson in moving his vacuum cleaner manufacturing to Malaysia is that it will now generate enough cash to maintain the company's commitment to reinvesting up to 20 per cent of turnover in research and development, keeping the company alive and ensuring that 1,150 other jobs in Malmesbury are safe, more than 300 of which involve engineers, scientists, designers and testers – the brains that ensure Dyson products remain a step ahead of the rest. Dyson claims to have exported the brawn, keeping the higher level value-added parts at home since Dyson's comparative advantage lies in researching and designing new products to ensure the company stays two steps ahead of its rivals, most of whom manufacture in the Far East. Indeed he claims that to have followed the rest of British industry, which invests an average of only 2 per cent of turnover, would have been to neglect Dyson's engineering and technological heritage and to follow in the footsteps of Britain's car, television and other domestic appliances. Dyson believes that his is the target company to beat for every manufacturer of vacuum cleaners worldwide. Rivals try to copy Dyson, and with the competition so fierce and widespread, Dyson believes his company has to invest much more in research and development than the international norm to retain its competitive advantage.

Questions

1 How can Dyson argue that it is in the interest of his British workforce that he relocates pro-duction to Malaysia?

2 Can you suggest any implications of this study for developed and developing countries?

3 Can you apply the idea of relative unit costs (RULCs) in Box 1.1 to this situation?

ment to trade in goods and services between members of those blocs. Only countries *within* the particular regional trading bloc (e.g. the EU, NAFTA) benefit from these RTAs, which have increased substantially in number over the past decade or so. For example over 100 RTAs were identified by the World Bank in the period 1990–2000, compared to only 14 RTAs in the previous decade. This has led to the growth of 'insiderisation', that is, attempts by MNEs to locate productive facilities inside these various regional trading blocs in order to avoid the protective and discriminatory barriers which would otherwise face their exports to countries within these blocs.

Certainly there is evidence to support the belief of MNEs that being inside such blocs confers considerable advantages. For example, Frankel (1997) noted that during the early 1990s, intra-regional trade within one such bloc – the Andean com-munity of Bolivia, Colombia, Ecuador, Peru and Venezuela – was 2.7 times higher than the levels of national income and geographic separation of those economies would have led us to expect.

■ Growth of bilateral trade and investment treaties

Nor is it only within the broad based regional trading blocs that preferential treatment is available to participating countries and companies. For example there has been a rapid growth in *bilateral (two country) trade treaties*, with around 300 such treaties having been notified to the World Trade Organisation (WTO) by the end of 2003. We consider the impact of these in more detail in Chapter 4, together with that of the rapidly growing *bilaterial investment treaties* (BITs). Over 2,200 BITs had been notified to the WTO by the end of 2003 which, while they may encourage foreign direct investment (fdi) flows between the two countries concluding the investment treaty, arguably discriminate against fdi flows involving countries that are not signatories to the BIT.

■ Growth of 'defensive techniques' to combat global insecurity

The global growth of foreign direct investment and the increasingly 'footloose' activities of MNEs have already been documented as widely-used indicators of globalisation. Many commentators have also drawn attention to parallels between the rapid growth in formal, legal cross-border relationships and the rapid growth in a wide range of illegal cross-border relationships including, at one extreme, activities more commonly associated with terrorism. Some of the characteristics of globalisation reviewed in Box 1.2 (p. 15) are seen as conducive to such growth, especially the weakening of power and control by nation states and the proliferation of new, less detectable methods of communication.

Whilst a proper investigation of so complex an issue is beyond the scope of this section, we can perhaps draw attention to what many believe is a new global business environment since 11 September 2001 (9/11), which is perhaps the date most closely associated with the advent of global insecurity. The additional insurance premiums required since 9/11 is one important indicator of the costs to international business of such 'defensive techniques'. In the airline industry alone it has been estimated that global insurance premiums rocketed from $1.7 billion in 2001 to over $6 billion in 2002 (Kaletsky 2002). When we factor these extra insurance premiums across *all* industries and include monetarised values for the increased time costs to business of additional security-related delays as well as the extra costs associated with more security-related personnel and equipment, then the sums involved rapidly escalate. For example, it has been estimated that the *actual* growth of global GDP has fallen since 9/11 by around one per cent per annum relative to the previously *projected* growth. If so, the impact of 9/11 cost the global economy some £250 billion in 2002 alone.

pause for thought 3 Can you suggest which sectors/industries have been the main 'losers' since 9/11 and which the main 'beneficiaries'?

■ Other international patterns/trends

As well as the factors already discussed, a number of other patterns and trends are likely to be relevant to different types of international business activity.

- *International communications.* There have been dramatic rises in various modes of international communication. For example, the time spent on international telephone calls has risen from 33 billion minutes in 1990 to over 90 billion minutes by the end of 2002. Internet usage is also rising exponentially, with the 2003 *Human Development Report* noting that the number of Internet hosts per 1,000 people worldwide rose from a mere 1.7 in 1990 to 17.8 in 2000, with cellular mobile phone subscribers per 1,000 people worldwide also rising from only 2 in 1990 to 153 in 2001. Various studies have found a strong and positive correlation between the extent of the telephone network and Internet usage. From this perspective it is important to note that the number of telephone mainlines per 1,000 people has more than quadrupled in *developing countries* over this period from 21 per 1,000 people in 1990 to over 87 per 1,000 people in 2001.
- *International travel.* The number of international tourists more than doubled from 260 million travellers a year in 1980 to over 600 million travellers a year in 2002. The growth of tourism is closely correlated with the growth of world GDP and is an important source of income and employment for many developed and developing countries alike. However increases in the perceived and actual risks associated with travel and tourism since 11 September 2001 and its aftermath have been linked to a drop in worldwide tourism of 2.2% from its peak in 2001.
- *International growth in leisure pursuits.* In 1880 some 80% of the time left over after necessities such as sleeping and eating were attended to was used for earning a living. Today that percentage has fallen to below 40% over the average lifetime of an individual in the advanced industrialised economies and is projected to continue falling to around 25% over the next decade (Fogel 2000). This dramatic increase in leisure-time availability in the higher-income advanced industrialised economies clearly has major implications for consumption patterns and therefore for the deployment of productive resources.
- *International growth in ageing populations.* Between 1950 and 2000 the median age (at which 50% of the population is below and 50% above) of the world's population rose by only 3 years, from 23.6 years in 1950 to 26.4 years in 2000. However over the next 50 years the UN projects that the median age will rise dramatically to 37 years by 2050, with 17 advanced industrialised economies having a median age of 50 years or above. This has major implications for international business in terms of productive location (e.g. adequate supply of labour of working age) as well as the range of products likely to be in global demand.
- *International growth in currency transactions.* The daily turnover in foreign exchange markets has dramatically increased from $15 billion in the mid-1970s to over $1,800 billion in 2002. This has contributed to greater exchange rate volatility, on occasions putting severe pressure on national economies and currencies (e.g. Argentina's peso in 2001/2).
- *International growth in countertrade.* When conventional means of payment for international transactions are difficult, costly or not available, then a range of barter (swap)-type transactions may be used instead. Whereas such 'countertrade'

only accounted for 2% of world trade in 1975, by 2003 over 20% of world trade involves some element of barter, with the former Soviet Union and the Eastern European economies particularly active in using countertrade.

pause for thought 4 Can you think of any other patterns and trends that might be of interest to a multinational enterprise? Explain your reasoning in each case.

Globalisation

Globalisation is much talked about in the media. Of course the term 'globalisation' is by no means the preserve of economists alone. Indeed it has been approached from the perspective of at least four academic disciplines, within each of which it tends to take on different characteristics:

- *economists* focus on the growth of international trade and the increase in international capital flows;
- *political scientists* view globalisation as a process that leads to the undermining of the nation state and the emergence of new forms of governance;
- *sociologists* view globalisation in terms of the rise of a global culture and the domination of the media by global companies;
- *international relations experts* tend to focus on the emergence of global conflicts and global institutions.

Globalisation as a multi-dimensional process

Certainly the world is seen as becoming increasingly interconnected as the result of economic, political, sociological and cultural forces. A one-dimensional view of globalisation, which thinks purely in terms of market forces, is likely to result in only a partial picture at best.

> Globalisation is a complex process which is not necessarily teleological in character – that is to say, it is not necessarily an inexorable historical process with an end in sight. Rather, it is characterised by a set of mutually opposing tendencies. (Giddens 1990)

McGrew (1992) has tried to identify a number of these opposing tendencies.

- *Universalisation versus particularisation.* While globalisation may tend to make many aspects of modern social life universal (e.g. assembly-line production, fast food restaurants, consumer fashions), it can also help to point out the differences between what happens in particular places and what happens elsewhere. This focus on differences can foster the resurgence of regional and national identities.
- *Homogenisation versus differentiation.* While globalisation may result in an essential homogeneity ('sameness') in product, process and institutions (e.g. city life, organisational offices and bureaucracies), it may also mean that the general must be assimilated within the local. For example, human rights are interpreted in different ways across the globe, the practice of specific religions such as Christianity or Buddhism may take on different forms in different places, and so on.

- *Integration versus fragmentation.* Globalisation creates new forms of global, regional and transnational communities that unite (integrate) people across territorial boundaries (e.g. the MNE, international trade unions, etc.). However, it also has the potential to divide and fragment communities (e.g. labour becoming divided along sectoral, local, national and ethnic lines).

Some argue that globalisation is a long-standing phenomenon and not really anything new, pointing out that world trade and investment, as a proportion of world GDP, is little different today from what it was a century ago and that international borders were as open at that time as they are today with just as many people migrating abroad.

However, those who believe that globalisation really is a new phenomenon tend to agree that at least three key elements are commonly involved.

- *Shrinking space.* The lives of all individuals are increasingly interconnected by events worldwide. This is not only a matter of fact but one which people increasingly perceive to be the case, recognising that their jobs, income levels, health, and living environment depend on factors outside national and local boundaries.
- *Shrinking time.* With the rapid developments in communication and information technologies, events occurring in one place have almost instantaneous (real time) impacts worldwide. A fall in share prices in Wall Street can have almost immediate consequences for share prices in London, Frankfurt or Tokyo.
- *Disappearing borders.* The nation state and its associated borders seem increasingly irrelevant as 'barriers' to international events and influences. Decisions taken by regional trading blocs (e.g. EU, NAFTA) and supranational bodies (e.g. IMF, World Trade Organisation) increasingly override national policy making in economic and business affairs as well as in other areas such as law enforcement and human rights.

pause for thought 5 How might events in the aftermath of 9/11 relate to these three elements? Would this be evidence for or against the view that globalisation really is a new phenomenon?

■ Different perspectives on globalisation

Of course there are different schools of thought among even those who do accept the reality of globalisation.

- *Hyperglobalists* envisage the global economy as being inhabited by powerless nation states at the mercy of 'footloose' multinational enterprises bestowing jobs and wealth creation opportunities on favoured national clients. National cultural differences are largely seen by these progressively powerful multinationals as merely variations in consumer preferences to be reflected in their international marketing mix.
- *Transformationalists* recognise that globalisation is a powerful force impacting economic, social and political environments, but take a much less prescriptive stance as to what the outcomes of those impacts might be. Predictions as to any end-state of a globalised economy can only be tentative and premature. Rather globalisation involves a complex set of intermittent, uneven processes with unpredictable outcomes rather than a linear progression to a predictable end-state.

It is this more pragmatic transformationalist approach that is most commonly encountered in debates on globalisation. While there may be many theories as to the causes of globalisation, most writers would agree that globalisation is a discontinuous historical process. Its dynamic proceeds in fits and starts and its effects are experienced differentially across the globe. Some regions are more deeply affected by globalisation than others. Even within nation states, some sectors may experience the effects of globalisation more sharply than others. Many have argued that globalisation is tending to reinforce inequalities of power both within and across nation states, resulting in global hierarchies of privilege and control for some, but economic and social exclusion for others.

Box 1.2 attempts to capture some of the features that currently underpin the use of the term 'globalisation' as being something different from what has gone before.

Box 1.2   Globalisation

New markets

- Growing global markets in services – banking, insurance, transport.
- New financial markets – deregulated, globally linked, working around the clock, with action at a distance in real time, with new instruments such as derivatives.
- Deregulation of antitrust laws and growth of mergers and acquisitions.
- Global consumer markets with global brands.

New actors

- Multinational corporations integrating their production and marketing, dominating world production.
- The World Trade Organisation – the first multilateral organisation with authority to force national governments to comply with trade rules.
- A growing international network of non-governmental organisations (NGOs).
- Regional blocs proliferating and gaining importance – European Union, Association of South-East Asian Nations, Mercosur, North American Free Trade Association, Southern African Development Community, among many others.
- More policy coordination groups – G-7, G-8, OECD, IMF, World Bank.

New rules and norms

- Market economic policies spreading around the world, with greater privatisation and liberalisation than in earlier decades.
- Widespread adoption of democracy as the choice of political regime.
- Human rights conventions and instruments building up in both coverage and number of signatories – and growing awareness among people around the world.
- Consensus goals and action agenda for development.
- Conventions and agreements on the global environment – biodiversity, ozone layer, disposal of hazardous wastes, desertification, climate change.
- Multilateral agreements in trade, taking on such new agendas as environmental and social conditions.

▶

Box 1.2	Continued

■ New multilateral agreements – for services, intellectual property, communications – more binding on national governments than any previous agreements.

■ The (proposed) Multilateral Agreement on Investment.

New (faster and cheaper) tools of communication

■ Internet and electronic communications linking many people simultaneously.

■ Cellular phones.

■ Fax machines.

■ Faster and cheaper transport by air, rail, sea and road.

■ Computer-aided design and manufacture.

Source: Adapted from UNDP *Human Development Report* (1999)

Globalisation and the nation state

It has been argued that one of the major effects of globalisation is to threaten the notion of the territorial nation state, in at least three key respects; its competence, its autonomy and, ultimately, its legitimacy.

■ *Loss of competence.* In a global economic system, productive capital, finance and products flow across national boundaries in ever-increasing volumes and values, yet the nation state seems increasingly irrelevant as a 'barrier' to international events and influences. Governments often appear powerless to prevent stock market crashes or recessions in one part of the world having adverse effects on domestic output, employment, interest rates and so on. Attempts to lessen these adverse effects seem, to many citizens, increasingly to reside in *supranational bodies* such as the IMF, World Bank, EU, etc. This inability of nation states to meet the demands of their citizens without international cooperation is seen by many as evidence of the declining *competence* of states, arguably leading to a 'widening and weakening' of the individual nation state.

■ *Loss of autonomy.* In such a situation, the *autonomy* and even *legitimacy* of the nation state are also subtly altered. The increased emphasis on international coop- eration has brought with it an enormous increase in the number and influence of inter-governmental and non-governmental organisations (NGOs) to such an extent that many writers now argue that national and international policy formulation have become inseparable. For example, whereas in 1909 only 176 international NGOs could be identified, by the year 2003 this number exceeded 30,000 and was still growing! The formerly monolithic national state, with its own indepen- dent and broadly coherent policy, is now conceived by many to be a fragmented coalition of bureaucratic agencies each pursuing its own agenda with minimal cen- tral direction or control. State autonomy is thereby threatened in economic, financial and ecological areas.

■ *Loss of legitimacy.* Of course any loss of competence or autonomy for the nation state is, to many, an implied loss of legitimacy. However, proponents of an alleged 'loss of legitimacy' in the UK often point more directly to the new EU constitutional arrangement proposed in 2003 and earlier adjustments of UK law and practice into conformity with the European Court of Justice and other supra-national bodies.

However, as we saw earlier, globalisation consists of a series of conflicting tendencies. While there is some evidence that the relevance of the nation state is declining, other writers claim the alternative view. Some argue that the state retains its positive role in the world through its monopoly of military power which, though rarely used, offers its citizens relative security in a highly dangerous world. Further, it provides a focus for personal and communal identity and finally, in pursuing national interest through cooperation and collaboration, nation states actually empower themselves. The suggestion here is that international cooperation (as opposed to unilateral action) allows states simultaneously to pursue their national interests and at the same time, by collective action, to achieve still more effective control over their national destiny. For example, the international control of exchange rates (e.g. the EU Single Currency) is seen by some as enhancing state *autonomy* rather than diminishing it, since the collective action implicit in a common currency affords more economic security and benefits for nationals than unilateral action.

Globalisation is therefore redefining our understanding of the nation state by introducing a much more complex architecture of political power in which authority is seen as being pluralistic rather than residing solely in the nation state.

Pro and anti-globalisation issues

Announcements and data such as those in Case Study 1.2 below help to fuel the impression that globalisation equates with job losses for many countries. It is hardly surprising therefore that many trade union representatives and their members swell the numbers in the broad based coalition sometimes referred to as the 'anti-globalisation movement'. Since this often finds expression in protests against *global institutions* (such as the WTO, World Bank, IMF, Group of 7/8 etc.), the basis of these anti-globalisation protests is considered in more detail in Chapter 4, where these institutions are reviewed (see for example discussions of the WTO in Chapter 4, pp. 106–15) along with arguments in favour of globalisation. Here we merely note that the picture painted in Case Study 1.2 is, at best, only partial. For example later in this chapter (p. 27) we document the fact that the UK is host to many affiliates (subsidiaries) of overseas multinational companies, which provide numerous jobs directly and, via component and services suppliers, indirectly.

Rules and norms in globalised economies

Not only are new international institutions and trading blocs characteristic of a more globalised economy in which nation states have progressively less influence, but so too are the 'rules and norms' by which they seek to operate (*see* Box 1.2 above). Market-oriented policies, democratic political frameworks, consensus goals involving social and environmental responsibility, and growing multilateral applications of agreed rules were all identified as characteristics of globalisation in Box 1.2. Here we note the importance of good governance and transparency, an absence of corruption and appropriate property rights to the establishment of a sustainable globalised economic environment.

CASE 1.2   Keeping jobs in a globalised economy

In 2003, a large number of press reports announced job losses for UK firms in both manufacturing and service sectors. Many of these announcements were accompanied by statements indicating that these UK-based jobs would be transferred overseas, with the competitive needs of a global marketplace forcing the companies to outsource parts of their operations or face closure. The list below indicates just some of the companies in the manufacturing sector using global competitiveness arguments for UK job losses in 2003.

Waterford Wedgwood	1,058 jobs to China
Black and Decker	950 jobs to Czech Republic
Dyson	800 jobs to Malaysia
Compaq	700 jobs to Czech Republic
Sara Lee Courtaulds	500 jobs to China
Raleigh	300 jobs to Vietnam and South Korea
Alexandra Workwear	170 jobs to Morocco

Waterford Wedgwood, the china and crystal maker, provides a useful example of the issues typically underlying such job losses. Waterford is to close two of its factories near Stoke-on-Trent in an attempt to revive its loss-making Johnson Brothers division, which makes mid-price tableware in patterns such as Willow, Blue Denmark and Old Chelsea. Redmond O'Donoghue, Waterford's chief executive, argued that if the company had not taken such a painful decision there was a serious danger that Johnson Brothers could bring the whole Wedgwood business down. He went on to suggest that outsourcing production to China will bring unit-cost savings of at least 70% without which it would be unable to compete in the mid and lower-priced tablewater market segments. However, Wedgwood would continue to produce its more up-market, higher value-added tableware in the UK, as low costs and low prices were less important in this market segment.

Similar announcements were made in 2003 in the *service sector*, as with BT's plans to open two call centres in India employing 2,200 people. While BT itself denies that UK jobs will actually be lost, unions point out that the 2,200 new jobs in India exactly correspond to the number of jobs BT announced it was cutting from its UK call centre staff exactly a year ago. If this trend continues a major UK sector will be put at risk, since around half a million people work in call centres in the UK.

BT is not the only service sector company seeking to cut costs by outsourcing their back-office jobs abroad. With Indian labour costing as little as £5 a day compared to £5.40 an hour in the UK, savings of up to 20% on running costs for back-office services are widely claimed for such outsourcing. HSBC, Prudential, Royal and Sun Alliance, Citigroup, ABN Amro and Fidelity Investments are all financial services firms that have outsourced back-office and support staff to the sub-continent.

The call centre industry itself has become big business in India, with more than 100,000 people employed in Delhi, Bombay and Bangalore alone. National Rail Enquiries employs 2,000 workers in the UK and handles 60 million calls a year, but announced in 2003 that it will consider transferring its operations to India when its call centre contracts fall due for renewal in 18 months time. Critics argue that the more complicated enquiries cannot be dealt with in India by workers who lack the tacit cultural and linguistic knowledge to deal with them. However, almost all Indian call centre workers are graduates, compared to less than a third in the UK, and the quality of their spoken English is high. New recruits in India also undergo intensive courses in British culture, including watching episodes of *Eastenders* and *Blackadder*.

Questions

1 How might the arguments in this study be used by: a) anti-globalisation protestors b) pro-globalisation protestors?

2 Can you identify any strategic directions which might underlie the events recorded in the case study?

3 If you were a trade union leader of workers employed by Waterford Wedgwood, what points might you make in advising them on their possible responses?

Benefits of good governance

The World Bank (World Development Report 2002) has pointed out that *good governance* – including independent agencies, mechanisms for citizens to monitor public behaviour, and rules that constrain corruption – is a key ingredient for growth and prosperity. In an early study Barro (1991) had found a positive correlation between economic growth and measures of political stability for 98 countries surveyed between 1960 and 1985. More recent empirical research points in a similar direction, for example confirming that fdi inflows are *inversely* related to measures of corruption, as with Lipsey (1999) observing a strong negative correlation between corruption and the locational choice of US subsidiaries across Asian countries. Similarly Clague *et al.* (1999) and Zak (2001) found that productivity and economic growth will improve when governments impartially protect and define property rights. Underpinning these findings is the perception by firms that a non-transparent business environment increases the prevalence of information asymmetries, raises the cost of securing additional information, increases transaction costs (e.g. risk premiums) and creates an uncertain business environment which deters trade and investment. For example Wallsten (2001) found a strong inverse relationship between investment intentions and the threat of asset expropriation, as well as a propensity for firms to charge higher prices to help pay back their initial capital outlays more rapidly when they felt less secure about the intentions of host governments, the higher prices often inhibiting the penetration and growth phase of product life cycles.

Knowledge and information in globalised economies

Management specialist Stephen Kobrin (1994) describes globalisation as driven not by foreign trade and investment but by information flows. It is this latter perspective, which sees globalisation as a process inextricably linked with the creation, distribution and use of knowledge and information, which is the focus here. Many contributors to the globalisation debate regard the technological convergence of information, computer and telecommunications technologies in the late twentieth century as having acted as a key catalyst in the rapid growth of these information-based activities, seen here as the hallmark of the globalised economy (Held *et al.* 1999).

International communications have grown dramatically, as we noted earlier (p. 12). Contemporary discourse often seeks to express globalisation in terms of the exponential growth in the creation, processing and dissemination of knowledge and information. For example, an 'index of globalisation' recently compiled jointly by the Carnegie Foundation and ATKearney (a global consultant) gives considerable weight to the proportion of national populations online as well as to the number of Internet hosts and secure servers per capita. These indicators of access to information technology and associated information flows are seen here as proxy variables for 'global openness', to be used in association with the more conventional indicators of investment, capital flows, foreign income as a proportion of national income and convergence between domestic and international prices when compiling the overall globalisation index (Walker 2001). Singapore was recorded in the 2000 index as the 'most globalised' country, helped by the fact that its recorded outgoing telephone traffic at 390 minutes per head per year was some four times as much as in the US. Sweden (ranked third) recorded some 44% of households online while Finland (ranked fifth) had over 70 web-connected servers (Internet hosts) per 1000 people while Swiss citizens (ranked fourth) spent 400% more time on international phone calls than Americans.

Case Study 1.3 uses Singapore as its particular context and looks at some of the broader implications of the globalisation process.

CASE 1.3 Preparing to compete in the wider world

Goh Chok Tong, Prime Minister of Singapore, sounded uncharacteristically insecure in 2000. His economy was ranked among the most competitive in the world, his political party was firmly entrenched, and his people remained deferential. So what was unsettling him? The absolute control that has enabled the government to make Singapore so successful was about to be wrested from it by the demands of the new global economy. If Singapore was to compete effectively in the wider world, it would have to wean the industries, companies and even the people away from some of the approaches it had so painstakingly nurtured in what is arguably the world's most successful social engineering programme. This meant that the business, political and cultural components of society might have to be transformed so profoundly that even Mr Goh was unsure how they would evolve. But he could not turn away from the new realities of a globalised world.

'We have no choice. This is becoming a smaller and smaller world, and if Singapore is to survive into the future in this new economy, new world, it's got to embrace the cultures of the world.' Mr Goh said, 'We are embracing globalisation and the IT revolution, convinced that they present more opportunities than costs.'

This pragmatism is what sets Singapore's policymakers ahead of many in the world. Although they have spent four decades since independence perfecting the current system, they refuse to cling to it now that the Internet and other such information technology cannot be kept out by borders, and freewheeling risk-takers rule the day. That realisation must have come as a shock to Singapore, whose closely guarded perimeter has for years rebuffed even *Cosmopolitan* magazine, and whose conservatism has bred companies so cautious they sit on billions in cash. But Lee Kuan Yew, the man who created the system, first as Prime Minister and then in his current capacity as Senior Minister, is enough of a visionary to see it is unsuitable. Despite the personal fame that the rich and stable Singapore of today has brought him, the Senior Minister recently explained in California's Silicon Valley that, unlike Japan, Singapore did not have 'that same irreversible attachment' to the blueprint by which it was built.

So the authorities are hustling to change it. In 1999 they lifted foreign ownership restrictions on banking, in 2000 they brought forward, by two years, the total liberalisation of telecommunications and announced plans to deregulate the power and insurance sectors. Analysts believe the media, healthcare, education and transportation will follow as the authorities force their protected industries to fight for survival.

'Sometimes creative destruction is necessary', says Barry Desker, chief executive officer of the Trade Development Board. 'If an industry has succeeded only because it has been protected, then there is no case to continue to protect it.' Singapore is not simply opening its markets but also making sure that they conform to best international practices. The stock exchange is moving from a merit-based regulatory environment to one requiring full and timely corporate disclosure. The authorities have started allowing dealers in Singapore government bonds to trade directly with each other instead of through the central bank, and foreigners are being invited to head banks and companies to change the guarded business culture. The government hopes these efforts will prepare Singapore's companies to compete on the world stage. But to get them to do so effectively it must first rewrite their scripts. The failure of Singapore Telecommunications (SingTel) in 2000 to secure Cable & Wireless HKT was the first major attempt by a Singapore company to expand into the region through merger and acquisition and its failure demonstrated how far they had to go. SingTel never considered there might be another competitor with enough cash to steal Asia's biggest corporate takeover from its grasp. When one arose in the form of a ten-month-old Internet start-up, SingTel trusted in its reputation and careful planning to win. But the world of business now belongs to freewheeling risk-takers acting on instinct.

To encourage this mindset in executives it has raised on a diet of conservatism and rigidity, Singapore revised its listing requirements to permit loss-making companies onto its main stock market board, and changed bankruptcy rules to encourage those who fail to try again. It is also establishing an award for entrepreneurs who rise from failure to build prosperous businesses, and is teaming up with private-sector professionals to provide venture capital funds.

Poorly dressed 'twenty-somethings' are taking advantage of these changes, raising millions of dollars on little more than concepts. There is the risk that the older generation, particularly those with minimal education, will be unable to adapt, so the authorities are offering them training in skills needed in the new

▶

knowledge-based economy. The authorities are guarding against a political back-lash through nation-building concessions, including plans to offer people discounted shares in government-owned companies and lower fees to upgrade the subsidised homes that nine out of ten Singaporeans can afford.

But the government knows it will take time to bring around the established entrepreneurs. First, they have to shed the perception many hold that government ownership means they are controlled by the political leadership. SingTel's chief executive officer, Lee Hsien Yang, insists his company is commercially run despite being almost 80% government-owned. Yet, when SingTel and Singapore Airlines tried to buy notable assets abroad, objections were raised to the very idea that the Singapore government would own another country's strategic industries. The government must sell down its stakes in such companies, if they are to serve significantly more than Singapore's 3.5 million people. But dumping its stakes in the open market would undermine the value of its holdings, so it will take time to achieve that goal. In the meantime, the authorities hope their entrepreneurs will at least lose their reputation as awkward government servants by assuming the freer, more modern thinking they are trying to instil in all Singaporeans. This is being done through the modification of the school curriculum to encourage innovation instead of memorisation, and the emphasis on technology through initiatives such as providing e-mail addresses and personal websites to those aged five and over. The government-influenced media are providing an outlet for criticism through 'forum' pages, where a debate on calls for a more civil society recently raged for weeks. Singaporeans note responses are now received in accommodating tones from ministers who once might have issued a strong rebuke.

Perhaps most significant of all, Mr Goh has reversed the objection he made to establishing a Speakers' Corner, like that in London's Hyde Park, so activists can openly voice objections that until now have been bound by closed doors. The government hopes that by taking such steps to loosen its grip over the people, it will inculcate the more independent, creative thinking needed to compete with the outside world. Mr Goh knows it could go terribly wrong: 'Can we be more entrepreneurial, more innovative, more creative within that model which we decide to have for Singapore? I think that's a basic question. Can you do it? I won't have the answer. Ten years from now, you can come back and ask me if we succeeded.'

Source: Sheila McNulty, *Financial Times*, 28 March 2000.

Questions

1 On what basis does Mr Goh argue that globalisation would create more opportunities for Singapore than costs?

2 What arguments might someone who opposes globalisation use to counter Mr Goh's views?

3 How does this case study point to globalisation as being a multi-dimensional phenomenon? You might check back to the points raised in Box 1.2 (p. 15).

The multinational enterprise (MNE)

Put simply, a multinational (sometimes called a transnational) is a company that has headquarters in one country but has operations in other countries. It is not always obvious that a firm is a multinational. The growth in alliances, joint ventures and mergers and acquisitions, means that consumers tend to recognise the brand, rather than know who the parent company is. Who, for example, now owns Jaguar or Land Rover? The answer in this case is Ford.

> **pause for thought 6**
>
> Can you think of brands for three different types of product and identify the multinational company that owns those brands in each case?

Dunning (1993) defines the multinational as a firm 'that engages in foreign direct investment and owns or controls value-adding activities in more than one country'. Typically the multinational would not just own value-adding activities, but might buy resources and create goods and/or services in a variety of countries. While the central strategic planning takes place at the headquarters, considerable latitude will usually be given to affiliates (subsidiaries) to enable them to operate in harmony with their local environments.

■ Ranking multinationals

Healey (2004) points out that from a statistical point of view, there are two main methods of ranking the world's top multinationals. First, ranking them according to the amount of foreign assets they control and second, ranking them in terms of a 'transnationality index'.

- *Foreign assets*. Table 1.5 ranks the top ten multinationals according to the *value of foreign assets* they control and we can see that three of the top ten are from the

Table 1.5 World's top ten multinationals ranked by foreign assets (and transnationality index), 2000

Ranking					
Foreign assets	*Transnationality index*	*Company*	*Country*	*Industry*	*Transnationality index (%)*
1	15	Vodafone	UK	Telecommunications	81
2	73	General Electric	USA	Electronics	40
3	30	Exxon/Mobil	USA	Petroleum	68
4	42	Vivendi Universal	France	Diversified	60
5	84	General Motors	USA	Automotive	31
6	46	Royal Dutch/Shell	UK	Petroleum	57
7	24	BP	UK	Petroleum	77
8	80	Toyota Motor	Japan	Automotive	35
9	55	Telefonica	Spain	Telecommunications	54
10	47	Fiat	Italy	Automotive	57

Source: Adapted from UNCTAD (2002), p. 86

USA, three from the UK and one from each of France, Japan, Spain and Italy. They are primarily based in the telecommunications, petroleum, electronics/computing and motor vehicle sectors.

- *Transnationality index*. However, Table 1.5 also provides each company's transnationality index and its transnationality ranking. The *transnationality index* takes a more comprehensive view of a company's global activity and is calculated as the average of the following three ratios:
  - foreign assets/total assets;
  - foreign sales/total sales;
  - and foreign employment/total employment.

For example, we can see that the second largest multinational company is General Electric in terms of the foreign assets it owns. However, its transnationality index of 40% means that it is only ranked 73rd in terms of this criteria. The reason for this is that even though it has large investments overseas in absolute value, in *percentage* terms most of its assets, sales and employment are still located in the USA. This is in contrast with Exxon Corporation where 68% of its overall activity in terms of the three ratios is based abroad, and Vodafone where this figure rises as high as 81%.

If we wanted to find the companies that operate mostly outside their home country, we would have to look at the ten top multinationals in terms of the transnationality index only. These are shown in Table 1.6 and here we see the dominance of EU companies in sectors such as mining, food/beverages, pharmaceuticals/chemicals and electrics/electronics. The companies with the highest transnationality index are often from the smaller countries as a more restricted domestic market creates incentives to operate abroad if they are to maximise their growth in terms of revenue or profits.

Technical definitions of multinationals, however, fail to convey the true scope and diversity of global business, which covers everything from the thousands of medium-sized firms that have overseas operations to the truly gigantic multinationals like IBM,

Table 1.6 **World's top ten multinationals ranked by the transnationality index (and foreign assets), 2000**

Ranking					
Transnationality index	Foreign assets	Company	Country	Industry	Transnationality index (%)
1	39	Rio Tinto	UK	Mining	98.2
2	49	Thomson Corporation	Canada	Media	95.3
3	24	ABB	Switzerland	Machinery/equipment	94.9
4	18	Nestlé SA	Switzerland	Food/beverages	94.7
5	31	BAT	UK	Tobacco	94.7
6	91	Electrolux AB	Sweden	Electrical/electronics	93.2
7	86	Interbrew	Belgium	Food/beverages	90.2
8	26	Anglo American	UK	Mining/quarrying	88.4
9	52	AstraZeneca	UK	Pharmaceuticals	86.9
10	25	Philips Electronics	The Netherlands	Electrical/electronics	85.7

Source: UNCTAD (2002), p. 97 adapted

General Motors and Ford. Some multinationals are *vertically integrated*, with different stages of the same productive process taking place in different countries (e.g. British Petroleum). Others are *horizontally integrated*, performing the same basic production operations in each of the countries in which they operate (e.g. Marks & Spencer). Many multinationals are household names, marketing global brands (e.g. Rothmans International, IBM, British Airways). Others are holding companies for a portfolio of international companies (e.g. Diageo) or specialise in capital goods that have little name-recognition in the high street (e.g. BTR, Hawker Siddley, GKN).

How important are the multinationals?

In 2002 the United Nations Division on Transnational Corporations and Investment estimated that there are almost 65,000 multinationals, collectively controlling a total of over 850,000 foreign affiliates (subsidiaries) and employing over 35 million people worldwide. Table 1.7 provides an overview of multinational activity. It shows that in 2001 the sales of multinationals' foreign affiliates (subsidiaries) exceeded the total global export of goods and services, and amounted to 58% of world gross domestic product (GDP). It also shows that foreign direct investment has grown much faster than the rate of growth of exports for much of that period.

Although not shown in Table 1.7, the gross output of the world's largest 100 MNEs alone was $4.8 trillion (i.e. $4,800 billion) in 2000, accounting for around 15% of world GDP and providing employment for over 14 millipn people, i.e. around 14% of world employment. Ranked by either turnover or GDP, half of the world's largest economic 'units' are multinationals, rather than countries. Only 14 nation states have a GDP that exceeds the turnover of Exxon, Ford or General Motors.

Historically, the bulk of multinational activity has been concentrated in the developed world. Indeed, as recently as the mid-1980s, half of all multinational production took place in only five countries – the United States, Canada, the UK, Germany and the Netherlands. This pattern is now changing rapidly. The rapid industrialisation and economic growth in the newly-industrialising nations of the world has led to a sharp increase in multinational investment in Asia and (to a lesser extent) Latin America. Some of these countries, notably the 'four tigers' (Taiwan,

Table 1.7 Multinational activity in a global context

	2001 ($bn)	Average annual growth rates (%)		
		1986–90	1991–95	1996–2000
fdi outflows	621	24.3	15.8	36.7
fdi outward stock	6,582	19.8	10.4	17.8
Sales of foreign affiliates of MNEs	18,517	16.9	10.5	14.5
World gross domestic product	31,900	11.5	6.5	1.2
World gross fixed capital formation	6,680	13.9	5.0	1.3
Total exports of goods and services	7,430	15.8	8.7	4.2

Source: Adapted from UNCTAD (2002), Table 1.1 and previous reports

South Korea, Hong Kong and Singapore), now have per capita GDP levels that exceed those of most European nations and their indigenous companies are now beginning to establish production facilities in the 'old world', although the 1997 'Asian crisis' slowed down this process.

Figure 1.2 has already shown that the old bi-polar world economy has now been replaced by the 'triad' of North America, the European Union and East and South-East Asia, with these three regions accounting for approximately 80% of the world's exports and 84% of world manufacturing output and almost all multinational activity.

■ Multinationals and fdi

Table 1.8 shows the changing pattern of *foreign direct investment* (fdi) by which domestic companies acquire control over productive facilities overseas. While there is a strong cyclical pattern evident, with foreign direct investment in the rich industrial countries higher during the world boom years of the mid to late 1990s than in the recessionary years of the early 1990s, investment in the developing countries shows a sustained increase over the period 1990–2001, which is less dependent on fluctuations in national income.

Table 1.8 also reflects the reintegration of the former centrally-planned economies of central and eastern Europe into the world economy. These former centrally-planned economies are included in the category 'developing countries'. Although the total volume of inward foreign investment is still relatively low (central and eastern Europe attracted only 2.4% of total global inflows in the period 2000–01) inflows have increased strongly since the transition process began in 1989. In this region, 60% of the inflows are associated with the privatisation of former state-owned enterprises (compared with 8% in the other developing countries).

Unsurprisingly, countries that have pushed ahead with market reform and privatisation in particular, have attracted the bulk of the foreign investment, both by creating international confidence in their future economic and political stability and by providing the opportunities for foreign companies to buy local production and distribution facilities. Poland and the Czech Republic, for example, have been highly successful in attracting multinationals like Ford, Volkswagen and Philip Morris. Countries that have resisted or delayed market reform, notably many of the states of the former Soviet Union have, in contrast, found foreign companies less willing to risk large-scale inward investment.

Table 1.8 Inflows of foreign direct investment ($ billion)

Region	1990–95 (annual average)	1996	1997	1998	1999	2000	2001
Developed countries	145.0	219.9	267.9	484.2	837.7	1,227.5	503.1
Developing countries	74.3	152.7	191.0	187.6	225.1	237.9	204.8
Central and eastern Europe	6.0	13.5	19.1	22.6	25.4	26.6	27.2

Note: Figures are rounded

Source: UNCTAD (2002) Annex Table B.1 (modified)

Multinationals and globalised production

Table 1.9 throws further light on the increasing globalisation of productive activity by showing the progressive growth in the Transnationality Index (TNI) for the world's largest 100 MNEs in their home economies between 1990 and 2000. The TNI has been defined above as the average of the three ratios: foreign assets/total assets; foreign sales/total sales; and foreign employment/total employment. A rise in the TNI index suggests still more international involvement of the top 100 MNEs outside their home country, which is certainly a pattern strongly supported by the data in Table 1.9.

The European Union (EU) is home to almost half of the world's largest MNEs and we can see from Table 1.9 that the average transnationality index (TNI) for the EU has risen from 56.7 to 67.1 over the 1990–2000 period alone. A still more rapid growth in the TNI is indicated for MNEs with North America as their 'home' base, with Japan alone showing only modest growth. For 'all economies' the greater internationalisation of production is indicated via the TNI rising from 51.1 to 57.8 in the 1990–2000 time period. Closer scrutiny of this data reveals that the driving forces behind these observed increases in the TNI have been the growth in the foreign sales/total sales and in the foreign employment/total employment components of the TNI.

Multinationals and the UK economy

Multinationals play a central role in the UK economy. Table 1.10 gives one indication of their importance. The UK still ranks as a major home to multinationals, reflecting its colonial past and the vast assets accumulated pre-1914. Although Table 1.10 suggests that the number of *home-based multinationals* is smaller in the UK than in the other countries represented, the value of their contribution to multinational activity is substantially greater, with *outward* foreign investment from Britain often higher by value from home-based multinationals in the UK than from the other countries represented in Table 1.10. Moreover, despite the UK's increasingly close

Table 1.9 Transnationality Index for the world's largest 100 MNEs in their home economies, 1990 and 2000

Economy	Average TNI (%)		Number of MNEs	
	1990	2000	1990	2000
European Union	56.7	67.1	48	49
France	50.9	63.2	14	13
Germany	44.4	45.9	9	10
UK	68.5	76.9	12	14
North America	41.2	62.9	30	25
US	38.5	43.0	28	23
Canada	79.2	82.9	2	2
Japan	35.5	35.9	12	16
All Economies	51.1	57.8	100	100

Source: Adapted from *World Investment Report* (2002)

Table 1.10 Home and host to multinationals

	Parent corporation based in country: home	Foreign affiliates based in country: host
France	1,922	9,473
Germany	8,522	13,267
United Kingdom	3,203	8,609
Japan	3,786	3,359
United States	3,263	15,699
Total (five countries)	20,696	50,407
Developed countries	50,250	100,825

Source: UNCTAD (2002) Annex Table 1.3 (modified)

economic and political ties with other member states of the EU, the bulk of outward foreign direct investment still goes to the United States where UK multinationals retain a pre-eminent position in terms of the value of US assets controlled.

As a *host country*, the UK is also an important destination for inward direct investment by foreign multinationals. Of the *Financial Times* top 500 companies operating in the UK, 313 are foreign owned, with Germany (87), France (77), Switzerland (28) and the Netherlands (17) being the most important European nations. Just as UK multinationals dominate foreign direct investment in the United States, however, so US multinationals account for the lion's share of foreign direct investment in the UK; and led by Nissan, Sony, Toyota and Honda, Japanese and Korean multinationals are also increasing their stake in the UK economy. In the last few years, 120 major Japanese companies have set up in the UK. Over 30% of all Japanese foreign direct investment in the EU to date has been in the UK and the Confederation of British Industry (CBI) estimates that, by the year 2010, subsidiaries of Japanese multinationals could produce as much as 20% of the UK's industrial output.

The UK economy is thus particularly affected by the globalisation of business, being simultaneously home of, and host to, a large number of multinationals producing a rapidly growing proportion of UK output. Multinational companies (both UK companies and foreign companies in the UK) account for an estimated 30% of GDP in the UK and almost half of total manufacturing employment. Most activity is concentrated in capital-intensive, high-technology sectors – computers, automobiles, electronics, pharmaceuticals and chemicals.

One third of UK exports and imports by value are estimated to be *intra-firm* (within firm) transactions, as multinationals import and export the intermediate products, which tie together production processes that are vertically integrated across national frontiers.

■ Types of MNE

The wide variety of strategies embraced by MNEs has led some writers to distinguish between different types.

■ *Global corporations* that view the whole world as their marketplace, with goods and services standardised to meet the needs of consumers worldwide

- *Multidomestic corporations* that comprise a relatively independent set of sub-sidiaries, each producing goods and services focused on a particular local market.
- *Transnational corporations* that integrate a geographically dispersed set of specialised activities into a single production process.

For the purposes of this book we will use the term 'multinational enterprise' (MNE) to apply to all three categories discussed above. However, from time to time we will apply terms such as 'market oriented' or 'cost oriented' to different multinationals, but only to indicate the broad strategic thrust behind their activities rather than the 'type' of multinational. The nature of many of today's MNEs will reflect, in part, the methods the company has used in its attempts to internationalise in the past. We discuss these different approaches to internationalisation in more detail in Chapters 2 and 8 respectively.

However, the nature of many of today's MNEs and of their activity in the UK and elsewhere also reflects broader changes in a globalised economy, including changing patterns of consumer behaviour and technological changes, as is illustrated in Case Study 1.4.

CASE 1.4   Happy birthday, globalisation

Marketing guru Theodore Levitt, a professor at Harvard Business School, was never a man given to understatement. But even by his standards, the prophecy he made on 1 May 1983 was bold. 'The globalisation of markets is at hand,' he declared in a *Harvard Business Review* article, written at a time when the word 'globalisation' was virtually unknown. Prof Levitt's message was simple. As new technology extended the reach of global media and brought down the cost of communications, the world was shrinking. As a result, consumer tastes everywhere were converging, creating global markets for standardised products on a previously unimagined scale.

His theory was colourfully illustrated. 'In Brazil, thousands swarm daily from pre-industrial Bahian darkness into exploding coastal cities, there quickly to install television sets in crowded corrugated huts and, next to battered Volkswagens, make sacrificial offerings of fruit or fresh-killed chickens to Macumban spirits' he wrote. And again 'During Biafra's fratricidal war against the Ibos, daily televised reports showed soldiers carrying bloodstained swords and listening to transistor radios while drinking Coca-Cola.'

Globalisation meant that old-fashioned 'multinational' companies that made different products to suit local tastes were doomed. They would be undercut by 'global corporations' that offered the same products in the same way everywhere, benefiting from 'enormous economies of scale' in production, distribution, marketing and management. 'The world's needs and desires have been irrevocably homogenised,' Prof Levitt proclaimed. 'This makes the multinational corporation obsolete and the global corporation absolute.'

Was he right? He was certainly influential. Sir Martin Sorrell, Chief Executive of WPP, well remembers the day the article appeared. At the time – April 1983 – he was Finance Director of Saatchi & Saatchi, then a relatively small outfit that was briefly to become the world's biggest advertising and marketing conglomerate. 'I read the piece and I remember giving it to Maurice (Saatchi) saying "this is a key article". We distributed it to all our key clients and said "this is the way the world's going and this is the way the Saatchi agency will be positioning itself".' Maurice Saatchi became a passionate believer in Prof Levitt's theory and set about establishing Saatchi as a global operation that would market the new global brands with global advertising campaigns.

Soon after the article appeared the agency put theory into practice with its 'Manhattan' advertisement for British Airways, a science fiction-style spectacular that appeared to show the whole of New York's Manhattan Island coming in to land at London's Heathrow airport. Describing British Airways as 'The world's favourite airline', the same advertisement was dubbed into 20 languages and shown in every country in the world with a developed television network – 35 in all.

Partly as a result of Maurice Saatchi's advocacy, Prof Levitt's prophecy reverberated in boardrooms around the world. Even so, in 1983 it looked a bit of a futuristic fantasy. Many of the world's markets were still closed and nearly a third of its population lived under communism. By the end of the 1980s, however, as the barriers to world trade came down, Prof Levitt was beginning to look more right than he could ever have imagined. People in former communist countries celebrated their freedom by cracking open cans of Coca-Cola, MTV embraced the globe's youth and, in 1990, McDonald's opened in Moscow.

In the 1990s the share prices of global brand-owners such as Coca-Cola, McDonald's and Walt Disney soared as investors savoured the companies' growth prospects. Another sign of the times was the trend for companies to brand or rebrand themselves with global sounding names seemingly plucked from Esperanto, such as Diageo, Novartis and Invensys.

Then, something unexpected happened: a reaction set in. People around the world started demanding more local sovereignty and more protection for their cultural identities. Most worryingly for global brand-owners, consumers in newly opened markets started expressing a desire for local products – which, as local manufacturers adopted western business methods, were simultaneously showing a big improvement in quality.

By the end of the 1990s, most global brand-owners were switching chief executives as their share prices plummeted in response to slowing growth rates. In March 2000 in a signed article in the *Financial Times*, Douglas Daft, Coca-Cola's new chief executive, offered a startling analysis of what had gone wrong. Coca-Cola, Mr Daft wrote, 'had traditionally been a "multi-local" company but as globalisation had gathered pace, it had centralised its decision-making and standardised its practices. We were operating as a big, slow, insulated, sometimes even insensitive "global" company and we were doing it in a new era when nimbleness, speed, transparency and local sensitivity had become absolutely essential to success,' he wrote. But Coca-Cola had learnt its lesson, Mr Daft said. It was that 'the next big evolutionary step of "going global" now has to be "going local". In other words, we have to rediscover our own multi-local heritage.'

Astonishingly, it was almost the opposite of what Prof Levitt had advocated. Yet now it is the almost universally accepted wisdom. The one-size-fits-all approach is out; 'think local, act local' is in. Coca-Cola owns not one brand but more than 200, mostly local; McDonald's varies its menu to suit local tastes; MTV has different programming to suit different countries and regions.

While homogenisation has affected some product categories – mainly in the technology sector, where there are no cultural barriers to overcome – the paradox of globalisation is that it has led not to a convergence of tastes but to a vast increase in the number of choices available to consumers. People can now buy products from all over the world: global, regional and local.

Another paradox is that technology is aiding the fragmentation. 'Prof Levitt was assuming that the only way to get scale was through standardisation. It was essentially the Henry Ford argument,' says Lowell Bryan, a McKinsey director and former student of Prof Levitt. 'But technology has changed the economics of production. Now, you can have both economies of scale and also deliver very discrete, specialised products.'

Prof Levitt has retired and does not give interviews. But through an intermediary, he indicates that he stands by his story. 'Global consumer products like Coke, Pepsi, McDonald's and Fuji and Kodak film are not fashioned to meet the needs of certain markets. They are simply sold in those markets about the same way they're successfully sold at home,' he says.

Few would agree that Prof Levitt's prophecy has been entirely borne out. But 20 years after its publication, his article is still widely quoted and read. And you do not have to be right to be interesting. 'Sometimes, even if they are wrong, ideas can set off a chain of debate that results in greater knowledge,' says Richard Tedlow, professor of business administration at Harvard Business School.

Source: Richard Tomkins, *Financial Times*, 6 May 2003.

Questions

1 Identify the policy implications for MNEs who fully believe in the globalisation scenario of Professor Levitt.

2 Why do others dispute the validity of this scenario?

3 How does the experience of Coca-Cola support or conflict with the Levitt scenario?

Useful websites

Now try the self-check questions for this chapter on the companion website at www.booksites.net/wall. You will also find further resources as well as the following useful weblinks:

Many interesting articles can be found in periodicals and newspapers on international business issues. Check the following sites:

www.economist.co.uk
www.ft.com
www.telegraph.co.uk
www.timesonline.co.uk

www.guardian.co.uk
www.Virgin.com
Procter & Gamble's website is at *www.pg.com*
Coca-Cola is *www.cocacola.com*
McDonald's website is *www.mcdonalds.com*

This next site has a wealth of detail about the EU, its institutions and the euro:

www.europa.eu.int
The IMF website is *www.imf.org*
The World Bank website is *www.worldbank.org*
The UN's Food and Agriculture Organisation is at *www.fao.org*

Other websites relevant to international business can be found at the end of each topic-based chapter.

Useful key texts

Daniels, J., Radebaugh, L. and Sullivan, D. (2004) *International Business* (10th edn), Pearson Prentice Hall, especially Part I.

Dicken, P. (2003) *Global Shift: Transforming the World Economy* (4th edn), Paul Chapman Publishing Ltd, especially Chapter 1 and Parts I and II.

Hill, C. (2003) *International Business: Competing in the Global Marketplace* (4th edn), McGraw-Hill Irwin, especially Chapter 1.

Morrison, J. (2002) *The International Business Environment*, Palgrave, especially Chapter 2.

Rugman, A. and Hodgetts, R. (2003) *International Business* (3rd edn), FT Prentice Hall, especially Chapter 1.

Tayeb, M. (2000) *International Business: Theories, Policies and Practices*, Financial Times Prentice Hall, especially Chapters 5–8 and 18.

Woods, M. (2001) *International Business*, Palgrave, especially Chapter 1.

Other texts and sources

Barro, R. (1991) 'Economic Growth in a Cross-Section of Countries', *Quarterly Journal of Economics*, 106, 20, pp. 407–43.

Claugue, C., Keefer, P., Knack, S. and Olson, M. (1999) 'Contract – Intensive Money: Contract Enforcement, Property Rights and Economic Performances', *Journal of Economic Growth*, 4, pp. 185–211.

Corkhill, D. (2000) 'Internationalisation and Competitiveness: the Portuguese Experience', in *Dimensions of International Competitiveness*, Lloyd-Reason, L. and Wall, S. (eds), Edward Elgar.

Dunning, J.H. (1993) *Multinational Enterprises and the Global Economy*, Addison-Wesley.

Fogel, R. (2000) *The Fourth Great Awakening*, University of Chicago Press.

Frankel, J. (1997) *Regional Trading Blocs in the World Economic System*, Institute for International Economics, Washington, DC.

Giddens, A. (1990) *The Consequences of Modernity*, Polity Press.

Healey, N. (2004) 'The Multinational Corporation', in *Applied Economics* (10th edn), Griffiths, A. and Wall, S. (eds), Financial Times Prentice Hall.

Held, D., McGrew, A., Goldblatt, D. and Perraton, J. (1999) *Global Transformations: Politics, Economics and Culture*, Polity Press.

Kaletsky, A. (2002) 'If Leaders Persist with Failed Economic Policy they will be Doing Bin Laden's Work for him', *The Times*, 10th September.

Kobrin, S.J. (1994) 'Is There a Relationship Between a Geocentric Mind-set and Multinational Strategy?', *Journal of International Business Studies*, 3, pp. 493–511.

Lipsey, R.E. (1999) 'The Location and Characteristics of US Affiliates in Asia', *National Bureau of Economic Research* (NBER) Working Paper, Cambridge, Mass.

McGrew, A. (1992) 'A Global Society', in *Modernity and its Futures*, Hall, S., Held, D. and McGrew, A. (eds), Open University Press.

United Nations Conference on Trade and Development (UNCTAD), *World Investment Report* (annual publication).

United Nations Development Programme (UNDP), *Human Development Report* (annual publication), OUP.

Walker, D. (2001) 'Global's Good Side', *Guardian*, 2nd May.

Wallsten, S. (2001) 'Ringing in the 20th Century', World Bank Research Working Paper, Washington, DC.

World Bank, *World Development Report* (annual publication).

World Economic Forum, *Global Competitiveness Report*, OUP.

Zak, P. (2001) 'Institutions, Property Rights and Growth', *The Gruter Institute Working Papers*, 2(1): Article 2.

Chapter 2

Internationalisation process

By the end of this chapter you should be able to:

- explain the pressures for internationalisation and why firms move production facilities abroad;

- outline the various methods available to firms seeking to enter foreign markets;

- assess the advantages and disadvantages of each method;

- discuss some of the principles that may contribute to successful international alliances;

- evaluate the different theoretical approaches to internationalisation.

Introduction

As we note in Chapter 3, there has been a rapid growth in international trade in both goods and services. Such global competition has forced corporations to seek new markets, both at home and abroad, and to speed up the cycle of product development. The costs of entry into these new markets can be formidable. The days of large corporations working solely by themselves would seem to be numbered. Few firms can afford to be sophisticated in all areas of technology or to develop distribution channels and new markets in numerous countries. In addition, rapid technical change and newly emerging patterns and locations of international specialisation place continual pressure on the cost base of the modern corporation. As a means of meeting these challenges, many firms realise that they must find partners to share the risks of expansion. Partnership and collaboration are the order of the day. This in turn creates new and difficult challenges for international managers. The choice of direction is almost infinite. Which markets to expand into? Which products to develop? How much can we afford to invest? Which partners to choose? Which areas of business to keep as core competencies and which to develop with others?

But why and how do firms internationalise? The reasons for going international and the conditions under which firms choose to do so are complex and have been the subject of much debate. In this chapter we examine the history of internationalisation, the reasons firms choose to internationalise, the ways in which this has been done and the theoretical frameworks that seek to explain this process. Chapter 8 looks further into international strategic choice and Chapter 9 considers the types of international organisational structure often adopted by MNEs during the internationalisation process.

Once a firm has decided to go international, this may take place in a wide variety of ways, most of which fall into three broad categories:

- export-based methods;
- non-equity methods;
- equity methods.

Export-based methods for internationalisation

This is the most common way in which a firm begins to go international. It continues to produce its product in the domestic market, but exports a proportion of this output to foreign markets. This may involve physical movements of products by air, sea, road or rail, but it increasingly involves the cross-border transfer of less tangible items such as computer software, graphics, images and the written word.

Exporting is the oldest and most straightforward way of conducting international business. Its growth can be put down to the liberalisation of trade that has taken place globally and within regional trading blocs over recent decades, with the World Trade Organisation significantly reducing tariff rates and quotas imposed on most imports (*see* Chapter 4, p. 106). Other protectionist measures are gradually being phased out or lowered at the *regional* level in free trade areas such as NAFTA (North American Free Trade Association), ASEAN (Association of South East Asian Nations) and the APEC (Asia-Pacific Economic Corporation), and in customs unions such as the Andean Pact and Mercosur, and in economic unions such as the European Union (EU). In addition to these regional arrangements a host of *bilateral* free trade treaties have been concluded, providing further direct exporting opportunities. At the same time, international transportation costs are still falling and cultural barriers to trade are now more readily recognised and overcome than has previously been the case. Governments may further stimulate trade by providing export-promoting initiatives in order to improve the country's balance of payments.

These export-based methods of internationalising are sometimes broken down into 'indirect exporting' and 'direct exporting'.

■ Indirect exporting

Indirect exporting happens when a firm does not itself undertake any special international activity but rather operates through intermediaries. Under this approach the exporting function is outsourced to other parties, which may prepare the export documentation, take responsibility for the physical distribution of goods and even set up the sales and distribution channels in the foreign market. The role of the intermediary may be played by export houses, confirming houses and buying houses:

- *an export house* buys products from a domestic firm and sells them abroad on its own account;

■ *a confirming house* acts for foreign buyers and is paid on a commission basis, brings sellers and buyers into direct contact (unlike an export house) and guarantees payment will be made to the exporter by the end-user;

■ *a buying house* performs similar functions to those of the confirming house but is more active in seeking out sellers to match the buyer's particular needs.

The advantages of such an approach clearly involve the fact that no additional costs need be incurred or expertise acquired in order to access the overseas market. However, there are disadvantages of resorting to indirect exports, which include having little or no control over local marketing issues and little contact with the end-user, so that there is no feedback for marketing.

Such indirect exporting may take different forms. For example, independent export management companies will sometimes handle the export arrangements for a number of clients, providing them with purchasing, shipping, financing and negotiation services (e.g. setting up contracts, providing localised overseas knowledge, etc.) as regards dealing with foreign orders. This is more likely to be the approach adopted by small and medium-sized businesses to indirect marketing. However, larger companies, such as MNEs, will sometimes set up their own subsidiary export management companies to deal with the overseas sales of their entire range of products and brands – as in the case of Unilever, which has established Unilever Export to deal with all its exports from the UK. This enables any scale economies within the exporting function to be gained on behalf of all the products and brands of the MNE.

Hill and O'Sullivan (2003) point out that indirect exporting sometimes involves unexpected alliances rather than competition between firms. 'Piggybacking', for example, is where different companies share resources in order to access foreign markets more effectively. Here a firm with a compatible product (known as the 'rider') pays to get on board the distribution system already being operated by a firm active in the overseas market (known as the 'carrier'). The 'rider' thereby gains immediate access to the network of outlets operated by the existing 'carrier' while the 'carrier' can reduce various costs by operating closer to full capacity as well as add more value to its activities by offering its clients a greater product range.

■ Direct exporting

Direct exporting would typically involve a firm in distributing and selling its own products to the foreign market. This would generally mean a longer-term commitment to a particular foreign market, with the firm choosing local agents and distributors specific to that market. In-house expertise would need to be developed to keep up these contacts, to conduct market research, prepare the necessary documentation and establish local pricing policies. The advantages of such an approach are that it:

■ allows the exporter to closely monitor developments and competition in the host market;

■ promotes interaction between producer and end-user;

■ involves long-term commitments, such as providing after-sales services to encourage repeat purchases.

pause for thought 1   You are the managing director of a manufacturing firm, which currently sells all its product on the domestic market. What factors might encourage you to consider exporting abroad (whether directly or indirectly)?

Export processing zones (EPZs)

Direct exporting has been encouraged in recent years by the establishment of export processing zones by countries. These are designated geographical areas within a country that provide appropriate infrastructure and incentives to encourage inward fdi that is focused on direct exporting from the EPZs. Case Study 2.1 considers seventeen EPZs announced in India in 2003. The *World Investment Report 2002* notes that most of the countries identified as 'winners' in terms of their export competitiveness within designated product groups, used EPZs or their equivalents to promote the export-oriented inward fdi which has underpinned their subsequent export performance. Successful EPZs can be found, for example, in China, Costa Rica, the Dominican Republic, the Philippines and Singapore. However the effective performance of EPZs depends not only on the incentives provided but on other policies directed towards enhancing human resources and other aspects of the infrastructure needed to attract and develop export-oriented fdi.

CASE 2.1   India plans special economic zones

India is planning an aggressive drive to create special economic zones that would enable the country to compete better with China for foreign investment, say senior government sources. The move coincides with India's decision to play a more constructive role in global trade negotiations, following its opposition to the launch of a new round at the World Trade Organisation's meeting in Doha in 2001.

Senior officials say New Delhi is planning to forego India's restrictive labour laws within the country's planned 17 special economic zones. This would be designed to allay foreign investor concerns about India's low labour productivity. In addition, New Delhi would remove remaining bureaucratic obstacles to creation of the zones.

India, which has roughly half the per capita income of neighbouring China, aims to increase its share of world trade to 1 per cent by 2007, up from 0.7 per cent this year. In 2002 India attracted roughly one-tenth the foreign direct investment that went to China. 'We need to create success stories in trade so that we can move forward in India,' said a senior government figure. 'We also need to increase foreign direct investment. The SEZs are key to this.'

India's increasingly positive approach to trade liberalisation follows the appointment of Arun Jaitley – an economic reformer – as minister for trade and commerce in 2003. However, Mr Jaitley told Pascal Lamy, the European Union's trade negotiator, in Delhi last week that India would continue to oppose any moves towards significant progress in the 'new areas' of the Doha Round. These are competition policy, investment, labour standards and the environment.

▶

Mr Jaitley also said India remained firm in its insistence that the US implement clauses within the previous world trade agreement that permitted patent laws to be relaxed where public health issues were involved. India, which has led the developing world in exporting generic drugs that fight HIV/Aids and other diseases, argues that large parts of the 1995 Uruguay round remain unimplemented.

Mr Lamy and Mr Jaitley also agreed on the need to improve access for India's manufacturing exports to developed-country markets and on the fact that agriculture had a special 'social' significance that made it unlike other economic sectors. 'We have 700 million farmers,' said an Indian official.

Mr Lamy assured India he would lobby EU governments to address New Delhi's complaints about tough restrictions on the movement of labour, in particular to relax visa policies for Indian workers in information technology and other service sectors. India has long accused the EU of inconsistency by promoting free movement of labour. 'I will try my best to convince EU member states that their attitude of reluctance (over visas) should change,' said Mr Lamy.

Source: Edward Luce and Martin Wolf, *Financial Times*, 18 March 2003.

Questions

1 Why is India seeking to establish these 'special economic zones' and what features will they have?

2 What other policies does India believe will help increase its exports?

3 Why does India oppose implementing the 'new areas' of the Doha Round?

Exporting by either indirect or direct methods is considered less risky than other methods of internationalisation and can be a 'way in' for firms testing out the waters before making the more resource-intensive fdi decision. Of course, some risks are still present when exporting, for example, exchange rates may change unexpectedly, affecting the anticipated profitability of the export transactions. However, the majority of today's international trade (and therefore exporting activity) takes place between firms that are themselves part of a single MNE. In fact, over a half of all world trade takes place *within* the company (*intra-trade*) (*see* Chapter 3). As regards this 'intra-trade', approximately 50% consists of exports by the MNE or its affiliates of *finished products* to its own distribution affiliates for sale in the host country or neighbouring markets. Around a further 50% involves the export of *intermediate products* for final assembly by the MNE's own production affiliates in other countries.

Besides exporting, the firm can internationalise by *investing* in foreign markets. A distinction is often made between *non-equity* and *equity*-based methods of fdi.

Non-equity-based methods for internationalisation

In this form of internationalisation, firms sell technology or know-how under some form of contract, often involving patents, trademarks and copyrights. These are often referred to as *intellectual property rights* and they now form a major part of international transactions, having grown enormously since the 1980s. These non-equity methods of internationalisation often take the form of licensing, franchising or other types of contractual agreement.

■ Licensing

At its most simple, *licensing* can mean permission granted by the proprietary owner to a foreign concern (the licensee) in the form of a contract to engage in an activity that would otherwise be legally forbidden. The licensee buys the right to exploit a fairly limited set of technologies and know-how from the licensor, who will usually have protected the intellectual property rights involved by a patent, trademark or copyright. This tends to be a low-cost strategy for internationalisation since the foreign entrant makes little or no resource commitment. The licensor benefits from the licensee's local knowledge and distribution channels, which would otherwise be difficult and time consuming to develop and maintain. Such agreements are often found in industries where R & D and other fixed costs are high, but where aggressive competition is needed at the local level to capture market share. The pharmaceutical and chemical industries provide licensing agreements as do the industrial equipment and defence industries. For example, McDonnell-Douglas and General Dynamics have licensing arrangements with different Japanese and European governments to produce jet fighters.

In *manufacturing industries* the patent is the most common form of protecting intellectual property rights and licensing is often used as a means of controlling industry evolution: for example, Japanese manufacturers have successfully cross-licensed VHS-formatted video recorders to one another as well as to foreign firms that produce them under licence. This helped the VHS standard become dominant worldwide and displaced the competing Sony and Philips' versions. In high-tech industries, where breakthroughs tend to occur discontinuously, licensing helps firms avoid excessive costs from expensive plant and product obsolescence. IBM, for example, has linked up with Motorola Communications and Electronics Inc. to advance the state of X-ray lithography for making superdense chips. Licensing can be costly, however, if a firm transfers its core competencies into those of a competitor. RCS licensed its colour television technologies to Japanese firms during the 1960s only to be leapfrogged by new but related technologies emanating from those competitors. Licensors (the granters of licences) may therefore find themselves under pressure to continuously innovate in order to sustain the licensee's dependence on them in the relationship. Microsoft's Windows '98 system has been widely criticised as having been introduced primarily as a means of maintaining the dependence of licensees on Microsoft itself, rather than as a source of new capabilities for existing users.

In general, the use of licensing, with its technological associations, has tended to be less readily adopted by the *service industries*.

pause for thought 2	In 2002 the US alone issued 86,659 patents, more than double the number it issued twenty years ago. Despite the rapid growth of patents worldwide, many observers believe that because of 'global shift' we should pay less attention to this particular indicator of intellectual property rights than we used to. Can you explain their reasoning?

■ Franchising

In *franchising* the franchisee purchases the right to undertake business activity using the franchisor's name or trademark rather than any patented technology. The scale of this activity varies from so-called 'first-generation franchising' to 'second-generation franchising' in which the franchisor transfers a much more comprehensive business package to the franchisee to help establish a 'start-up position'. This may include detailed guidance on how to operate the franchise, even extending to specialist staff training.

In *first-generation* franchising, the franchisor usually operates at a distance. However, in *second-generation* franchising, the franchisor exerts far more control on the day-to-day running of the local operations. This type of franchising is common in the hotel, fast-food restaurant, and vehicle rental industries, such as Holiday Inn, McDonald's and Avis respectively. Mature domestic service-based industries have chosen franchising as a means of internationalising because:

■ it establishes an immediate presence with relatively little direct investment;
■ it employs a standard marketing approach helping to create a global image;
■ it allows the franchisor a high degree of control.

For instance, Coca-Cola's franchising arrangements with its numerous partners would seem to have given it an advantage over its arch rival PepsiCo. Franchising also helps build up a global brand that can be cultivated and standardised over time. Before opening its first restaurant in Russia, McDonald's flew all key employees to its 'Hamburger University' for a two-week training session. During these sessions, Russian employees learned the McDonald's philosophy and the McDonald's way of addressing customers and maintaining quality standards.

Benefits to the franchisee include the guarantee of a high level of support (promotion, merchandising, a tried-and-tested business idea) as well as the absence of immediate competition.

■ Other contractual modes of internationalisation

Besides licensing and franchising, non-equity forms of internationalisation may involve activities such as *management contracting*, where a supplier in one country undertakes to provide to a client in another country certain ongoing management functions, which would otherwise be the responsibility of the client. Other examples include *technical service agreements* that provide for the supply of technical services across borders, as when a company out-sources the operation of its computer and telecommunications networks to a foreign firm. As we noted in Chapter 1 (p. 18) India, with its highly educated and inexpensive labour force, is winning many such contracts in many types of teleworking. *Contract-based partnerships* may also be formed between firms of different nationalities in order to share the cost of an investment. For example, agreements between pharmaceutical companies, motor vehicle companies and publishing houses may include cooperation, co-research and co-development activities.

Equity-based methods for internationalisation

These essentially refer to the use of fdi by the firm as a means of competing internationally in the modern global economy. The major advantage of this method is that the firm secures the greatest level of control over its proprietary information and therefore over any technological advantages it might have. In addition, profits need not be shared with any other parties such as agents, distributors or licensees.

In practice, firms can use different approaches to fdi by acquiring an existing firm, by creating an equity joint venture overseas, by establishing a foreign operation from scratch ('greenfield' investment) or by creating various consortia.

◼ Joint ventures

Unlike licensing agreements, *joint ventures* involve creating a new identity in which both the initiating partners take active roles in formulating strategy and making decisions (*see also* Chapter 8). Joint ventures can help:

- to share and lower the costs of high-risk, technology-intensive development projects;
- to gain economies of scale and scope in value-adding activities that can only be justified on a global basis;
- to secure access to a partner's technology, its accumulated learning, proprietary processes or protected market position;
- to create a basis for more effective future competition in the industry involved.

Joint ventures are particularly common in high-technology industries. For instance, Corning Incorporated of the USA has numerous global joint ventures, such as those to produce medical diagnostic equipment with CIBA-Geigy, fibre optics with Cie Financière Optiques and Siemens, colour television tubes with Samsung and Asahi and ceramics for catalytic converters with NGK Insulators of Japan.

Joint ventures usually take one of two forms, namely specialised or shared value-added.

- *Specialised joint ventures*. Here each partner brings a *specific competency*; for example one might produce and the other market. Such ventures are likely to be organised around *different functions*. One specialised joint venture has involved JVC (Japan) and Thomson (France). JVC contributed the specialised skills involved in the manufacturing technologies needed to produce optical and compact discs, computers and semi-conductors, while Thomson contributed the specific marketing skills needed to compete in fragmented markets such as Europe.
- *Shared value-added joint ventures*. Here both partners contribute to the *same function* or value-added activity. For example, Fuji-Xerox is a case of a shared value-added joint venture with the design, production and marketing functions all shared.

The major benefits of *specialised joint ventures* include an opportunity to share risks, to learn about a partner's skills and proprietary processes and to gain access to new distribution channels. However, they carry risks as well, perhaps the greatest being that one partner's exposure of its particular competencies may result in the other partner gaining a competitive advantage, which it might subsequently use to become a direct competitor. This happened to GE when it entered into a specialised joint venture with Samsung to produce microwave ovens. Samsung now competes with GE across the whole range of household appliances. Another risk relates to the high co-ordination costs often involved in assimilating the different types of value-added activity of each partner. Sometimes a partner can be relegated to a position of permanent weakness. For example, the GM–Fanuc venture was originally intended to co-design and co-produce robots and flexible automation systems, but GM was unable to learn the critical skills needed from its partner and has ended up as little more than a distributor.

Shared value-added joint ventures pose a slightly different set of risks: partners can more easily lose their competitive advantage since the close working relationships involve the same function. If the venture is not working, it may be more difficult to exit since coordination costs tend to be much higher than they are in specialised joint ventures, with more extensive administrative networks having usually been established.

'Success factors' for joint ventures

Critical success factors for joint ventures might include the following:

- *Take time to assess the partners.* Extended courtship is often required if a joint venture of either type is to be successful; Corning Incorporated of the USA formed its joint venture with CIBA-Geigy only after two years of courtship. Being too hurried can destroy a venture, as AT & T and Olivetti of Italy discovered when they formed a joint venture to produce personal computers that failed because of an incompatibility in management styles and corporate cultures as well as in objectives.
- *Understand that collaboration is a distinct form of competition.* Competitors as partners must remember that joint ventures are sometimes designed as ways of 'de-skilling' the opposition. Partners must learn from each other's strengths while preserving their own sources of competitive advantage. Many firms enter into joint ventures in the mistaken belief that the other partner is the student rather than the teacher.
- *Learn from partners while limiting unintended information flows.* Companies must carefully design joint ventures so that they do not become 'windows' through which one partner can learn about the other's competencies.
- *Establish specific rules and requirements for joint venture performance at the outset.* For instance, Motorola's transfer of microprocessor technology to Toshiba is explicitly dependent on how much of a market share Motorola gets in Japan.
- *Give managers sufficient autonomy.* Decentralisation of decision making should give managers sufficient autonomy to run the joint venture successfully. Two of the most successful global value-adding joint ventures are those between Fuji-Xerox and Nippon-Otis, which are also among those giving management the greatest autonomy.

It has been found that extensive training and team building is crucial if these joint ventures are to succeed. There are three ways in which effective human resource management (HRM) is critical (*see also* Chapter 9):

- developing and training managers in negotiation and conflict resolution;
- acculturation (i.e. cultural awareness) in working with a foreign partner;
- harmonisation of management styles.

Problems with international joint ventures in China

When the first Sino-foreign joint venture, the Beijing Aviation Food Co., was established in 1980, it led to the beginning of intensive foreign direct investment (fdi) into China, which in turn has contributed to China's continuous growth of 8% every year for the last 15 years. World Trade Organisation (WTO) entry is also expected to lead to a surge in fdi in forthcoming years. Combine this with Beijing hosting the Olympics in 2008 and a population of nearly 1.3 billion and it soon becomes evident why so many foreign firms are hurriedly trying to gain a presence in China. With Chinese people having a well-earned reputation for thrift, holding savings of more than US$1 trillion, nowhere is this desire more apparent than in the finance sector. For example, in 2002, Newbridge Capital, the US-based multinational finance corporation sought to tap into this huge savings stockpile and paid US$1.8 billion for nearly 20% of Shenzhen Development Bank, while HSBC paid US$600 million for 10% of Pingan Insurance (Webb 2003).

Many foreign companies turn to the *international joint venture* (IJV) as their chosen mode of entry into China. To foreign investors there exist three modes of foreign entry, the first two of which are types of IJV – *equity joint venture* (EJV), *co operative joint venture* (CJV) and *wholly-owned foreign enterprises* (WOFE). However, IJVs continue to experience high rates of dissolution.

The problems associated with IJVs in China have been well documented (Child 1991; Lu and Bjorkman 1998). Harrigan (1986) states that 'Alliances fail because operating managers do not make them work, not because contracts are poorly written.' One reason for foreign investors to shy away from IJVs is their fear of leaking proprietary technology and know-how to Chinese partners and thus losing long-term competitive advantages (Deng 2001). To the Chinese partner gaining invaluable knowledge is a main strategic objective for entering into an IJV. For the Western partner, the problem is knowing how much of their technical expertise should be shared with their partner. A key factor that allows for sharing information is the establishment of trust between parties. In Chinese culture, trust is very much built on personal relationships and involves socialising and working together in order to build trust. In Western society, trust between business partners is underlined by the contract, therefore there is likely to be less importance placed on building relationships. It is often very difficult to build trust between two companies that originate from very different cultural backgrounds. Lack of cultural understanding and different strategic objectives are two of the main reasons why IJVs continue to experience high failure rates.

China's WTO entry and changes to market entry methods

In recent years *wholly-owned foreign enterprises* (WOFEs) have exceeded IJVs to become the favoured market entry method for foreign firms entering China. Factors such as Chinese partners competence, joint venture management control, and frustration from IJV failure examples, have been cited as reasons why a strict adoption of WOFE for conducting business in China might be preferable (Yan and Warner 2001). There are two key reasons for this. First, changing government policy towards foreign investment. Second, established foreign firms not perceiving any value through having their IJV partner are now considering doing business independently

(Wilson 2003). The IJV entry method will continue to be an attractive form of entry for SMEs, however, although larger companies already firmly established or those considering entering for the first time, are more likely to opt for mergers, acquisitions or WOFEs.

Deng (2001) identifies three key factors driving foreign firms to choose WOFEs: (1) the disappointing performance of too many EJVs, (2) the inherent advantages of WOFEs, and (3) changes in government regulations and a less uncertain environment. Yan and Warner (2001) suggest that as foreign companies keep acquiring practical experience in China, they are increasingly likely to 'go it alone' to pursue success in the Chinese market. They go on to argue that although China's WTO entry appears to favour WOFE formation, the situation can be multi-faceted. Reasons why a WOFE may not be appropriate include the nature of the industry and geographical region. The Chinese government is actively encouraging foreign companies to invest in its western regions. However western cities such as Kunming are far less developed than Shanghai, Guangzhou and Beijing. A major stumbling block for foreign companies entering western regions is the lack of government experience of handling fdi. Given this situation, initially an IJV may be the preferred option.

| *pause for thought 3* | How might you expect China's WTO entry to influence the prospects of doing business in China? |

Case Study 2.2 suggests a continuous and ongoing search for economically, culturally and politically appropriate means of joint venture development in China.

CASE 2.2 Market entry into China

For well over a decade China has presented itself as an attractive venue for market entry, with over 2.6 billion consumers in a progressively deregulated marketplace experiencing high (if somewhat unverifiable) rates of economic growth. The provisional accession of China into the World Trade Organisation (WTO) in 2000 has provided a still further stimulus to firms seeking market entry as has the rapid diffusion of Internet-related technologies. Nevertheless, the experience of companies seeking to enter the Chinese market in recent years has been less than encouraging. However, these disappointments may have had much to do with Western companies using inappropriate methods in their attempts to internationalise their operations into the Chinese market.

In fact, most Western companies have sought to enter China via the joint-venture route, sharing day-to-day control of the business with a local partner. Having a local partner in a joint venture does provide certain advantages, as in securing contracts that often depend on political linkages and being better able to use guanxi-type relationships (*see* Chapter 6). However, sharing operational control with the local partner can paralyse decision making. Lucent, for example, has seen its share of the market for optical-fibre equipment in China fall from 70% to 30% largely because, in the view of analysts, it has had to negotiate each technological change in its product base with the local partner. Such time delays in rapidly evolving high-technology markets can be extremely adverse.

Worse still, Chinese regulations are often geographically and product specific, forcing Western companies to have separate local partners in different Chinese regions and for different product groups. This restricts the benefits available to joint ventures in terms of economies of scale and scope. For example, Unilever has separate joint ventures in Shanghai for making soap, skin cream and laundry detergent. Adopting a uniform strategy across all these product groups and across different geographic regions has proved difficult to implement as individual partners fear that such coordination may be at the expense of their particular joint venture.

In recognition of these problems, some Western companies have established wholly-owned foreign enterprises (WOFEs). Unfortunately, while this has helped avoid the lengthy decision-making process of joint ventures, it has proved a difficult vehicle for securing contracts and for establishing the local alliances and networks so important in a guanxi business culture.

Vanhonacker (2000) has suggested that a more appropriate vehicle for Chinese market entry than either joint venture or WOFE is the foreign investor shareholding corporation (FISC). In fact, this has many of the characteristics of the Western joint-stock company and Eastman Kodak is currently successfully pioneering an FISC in China. The FISC grants local partners in different geographic regions or product groups, minority stakes in return for their business assets, such as factories, offices and vehicles. Since local partners have lost direct ownership of these assets, they can be removed from day-to-day decisions involving their use. Nevertheless, as part owners of the corporation they have a vested interest in its overall success. They are therefore motivated to help the FISC secure contracts and make best use of local networks and relationships to further its business interests. The FISC can now coordinate activities across many such local partners to exploit any available economies of scale and scope in ways precluded to the joint venture. A further benefit of the FISC is that it has allowed the Chinese political authorities to encourage industrial reform through the back door, with no 'loss of face'. So far Kodak has created two FISCs, Kodak (China) being one of these, in which it holds an 80% share. Kodak (China) has purchased the assets of two domestic photofilm manufacturers (Xiamen Finda and Shantou Era), giving to each of these a 10% shareholding stake and the right to one board member, with Kodak naming the remaining eight board members. Chinese law requires at least five shareholders, so Kodak (China) has invited two further shareholders to take small stakes in the FISC, namely the Guangdong and Fujian international trust. Kodak itself has made available some $380 million as investment capital for Kodak (China). Similar arrangements are in place for the other Kodak FISC, Kodak (Wuxi), though with different shareholders.

The Chinese authorities have welcomed these Kodak initiatives, and the new FISCs are quoted on the Shanghai and Shenzhen stock exchange making it easier for them to raise capital. Having seen its photo industry almost collapse due to lack of investment and slowness to adopt new high-technology operations, no less than five central government organisations, including three ministries, were willing to cooperate with Kodak in establishing these FISCs. Indeed, Vanhonacker reports

▶

that the China State Development Planning Commission, which had been involved in creating Kodak's FISCs, released a research report in 1999 supporting the Kodak model. This is an especially important development since many of China's previously highly protected domestic industries have problems of inefficiency and overcapacity and are in urgent need of investment and modernisation by Western companies willing to transfer technology. For example, in the pharmaceuticals industry alone there are some 1,800 domestic manufacturers, 80% of which have sales of less than $1 million with the result that they are internationally inefficient, being currently unable to exploit the large economies of scale and scope typically available in the pharmaceutical industry.

Questions

1 Why are the Chinese authorities receptive to the FISC as a method of internationalisation?

2 What are the benefits to Western companies of using this method rather than the more traditional joint-venture approach?

■ Acquisitions and 'greenfield' investment

Some of the problems of joint ventures (especially those involving decision making and culture clashes) can be avoided by wholly owning the foreign affiliates (pp. 51–7). This can be achieved through acquisition of an existing firm or through establishing an entirely new foreign operation ('greenfield' investment).

Acquisition of an existing foreign company has a number of advantages compared to 'greenfield' investment; for example, it allows a more rapid market entry, so that there is a quicker return on capital and a ready access to knowledge of the local market. Because of its rapidity, such acquisition can pre-empt a rival's entry into the same market. Further, many of the problems associated with setting up a 'greenfield' site in a foreign country (such as cultural, legal and management issues) can be avoided. By involving a change in ownership, acquisition also avoids costly competitive reactions from the acquired firm. Strategic aspects of mergers and acquisitions policies are considered in more detail in Chapter 8 (pp. 248–59).

Consortia, keiretsus and chaebols

In the USA and Europe there has been little success in building cross-industry consortia, largely as a result of the difficulties involved in getting firms to pool their resources into an integrative organisational design. The one exception in Europe is perhaps the Airbus Industrie. In the Far East, on the other hand, consortia such as the Japanese *keiretsus* and the South Korean *chaebols* are much more commonplace.

The Japanese *keiretsu* is a combination of 20–25 different industrial companies centred around a large traditional company. Integration is achieved through interlocking directorates, bank holdings and close personal ties between senior managers. Group members typically agree not to sell their holdings. Examples include Sumitomo, Mitsubishi, Mitsui and Sanwa. Case Study 2.3 looks at the impact of the *keiretsu* in supporting the post-war Japanese export drive, which has largely been based on the competitive advantages of Japanese firms.

The South Korean *chaebols* are similar agglomerations, which are also centred around a holding company. These are usually dominated by the founding families. While a *keiretsu* is financed from group banks and run by professional managers, *chaebols* usually get their funding from government and are managed by family members who have been groomed for the job. Prominent examples include Samsung, Daewoo and Sunkyong. Such alliances are usually initiated by merchant and industrialist families and the company keeps the stock in family hands.

Consortia of these types are essentially sophisticated forms of strategic alliances designed to maximise the potential benefits of joint ventures – namely risk sharing, cost reductions, economies of scale, etc. Both in Japan and South Korea governments have played an important role in encouraging such developments. Such consortia tend to have a long-term focus and are uniquely positioned to share the risks of investing in high fixed-cost projects in order to stay at the forefront of technology-based industries. At the same time, risk is diversified because the different companies are involved in many different industries. This encourages investment in the more volatile industries such as satellites, biotechnology, microelectronics and aerospace. The members of the consortia also benefit from strong buyer–supplier relationships, with costs reduced by bulk purchase discounts, etc. It often means extensive resource sharing of components and end products that can produce fast responses to changed consumer requirements, so essential when employing mass customisation techniques (*see* Chapter 12).

pause for thought 4	Conglomerate mergers have been widely used in Western economies. (a) Give some examples. (b) Suggest the benefits they confer. (c) Consider why they have become less popular in recent times.

It is worth noting that the *keiretsus* and *chaebols* benefit from government in the form of preferential interest rates and capital allocations that, arguably, only a managed economy can deliver. They are also characterised by close ties and shared values leading to mutual understanding and sacrifices that cannot easily be duplicated in the West. These organisations are linked together by networks and personal relationships, so the corporate culture needs to be able to embrace both hierarchical and horizontal integration. Fraternal relationships, mutual long-term commitment and pride in membership are characteristics that are less commonly found in the individualised cultures of the USA or UK (*see* Chapter 6).

CASE 2.3 The Japanese keiretsu

Whereas macro environmental factors have provided the direction and stability needed to underpin Japan's rapid post-war growth in competitiveness, the actual mechanisms underpinning many of its efficiency gains have involved the dynamic behaviour of companies at the corporate level. To understand this process we need to look at the structure of Japanese industry, which consists of two key dimensions.

▶

First, there is the large-firm sector dominated by six major groupings of firms (*Kigyo Shudan*). Second, there is the important sector of small and medium-sized firms (*Chusho Kigyo*) whose members often act as sub-contractors to the larger firms.

The six major groupings are Mitsubishi, Mitsui, Sumitomo, Fuyo, Dai-ichi Kangyo (DKB) and Sanwa. The 'core' of each group consists of a number of large enterprises from different sectors of the economy, e.g. metals, oil, electrical, automobiles, etc., together with at least one major bank. Each group maintains its internal cohesiveness through regular meetings of the presidents of the larger companies and by the exchange of shares and directorships between member companies of the group (interlocking directorships). In addition, the various companies within the group would hold each other's shares as a means of affirming their relationship. Such shares would not be actively traded, making it difficult for companies to be taken over under this system as buying sufficient shares to gain control would be extremely difficult. In other words, the corporate governance of Japan was of a type that encouraged stable, long-term relationships between the members of large industrial groupings. However inter-group rivalry was often intense – for example, Mitsubishi motors (Mitsubushi Group) competed actively with Toyota (Mitsui Group) and Isuzu motors (DKB Group) so that the market was often oligopolistic in nature. Surveys in the 1990s that asked Japanese companies for the reasons that motivated them to introduce new technology found that 36% of companies cited domestic competition with other Japanese companies as a major motivating factor.

However, the success of these large exporting firms depends ultimately on the numerous small and medium-sized firms that act as primary, secondary and tertiary sub-contractors to the large firms. Many of the large Japanese companies, such as Toyota, are basically assemblers of parts produced by sub-contractors. For example, Toyota has 158 primary sub-contractors and 4,700 secondary sub-contractors and almost 31,600 tertiary sub-contractors – most situated in relatively close proximity to the main parent company. This vertically organised production group or keiretsu provides a vital source of competitiveness for Japanese industry. Cost savings derive from the fact that the major firms can save on overheads while, at the same time, also asking the various layers of small companies to trim their costs. As a result, the potential total cost reduction throughout the keiretsu can be substantial. The nature of the contractual relationship between companies in Japan is based more on unwritten, long-term contracts based on trust, rather than the more legally framed, one-off 'spot' contracts more prevalent in Europe and the USA.

In terms of production and innovation, Japanese managers began concentrating on the 'focused factory', i.e. on fewer product lines with a view to maximising benefits from economies of scale and scope. Together with these cost benefits, came those based on the learning curve that measured the savings made year after year as a result of increases in cumulative output. For example, between 1984 and 1990 the CD-player market grew very rapidly and Sony, Sharp and Rohm produced their low-powered laser diodes for the CD player. Over this time the costs per unit for the diodes fell from 2,000 yen to 200 yen each, showing clearly how cumulative production helps companies to learn how to produce laser diodes more efficiently.

In their continuous quest for lower costs and increased competitiveness, Japanese production managers also concentrated on some basic but important factors:

■ First, the Japanese concept of *kaizen* (i.e. the constant search for small incremental improvements in all aspects of company behaviour) was a powerful tool for improving competitive behaviour, especially when economic conditions were relatively difficult and when introducing new technology was expensive. For example, in the 1980s Toyota workers were providing 1.5 million suggestions a year for small improvements in production.

■ Second, Japanese production managers, led by those at Toyota Motors, concentrated on the development of the just-in-time or *kanban* system whose aim was to create a continuous process flow both within large firms and also between large assemblers and their various sub-contractors. This meant that each workstation supplied a component to the next station ahead of it on the production line only when needed, saving the costly build up (both purchase and storage) of inventories. The perfection of this process took Toyota over 25 years to achieve.

■ Third, the management of quality was also critical for Japanese competitiveness and here the approach was based very much on the ideas of William Edwards Deming who visited Japan in the 1950s and who helped Japan to reverse the usual American approach to quality management by stressing that 85% of the responsibility for quality should be in the hands of plant workers and only 15% should be dependent on line managers. In other words, the Japanese identified in their approach to *total quality management* that the individual worker was the main quality controller and not the manager, as is often thought to be the case in a high proportion of US and European firms.

It would seem that these approaches by Japanese production managers are continuing to yield productivity gains. For example a recent study (Oliver *et al.* 2002) shows that Japanese car component makers are still more efficient than their US or European counterparts: over the period 1994–2001, the average change in labour productivity for car components was 20% for Japan, but only 12% for the US and still lower figures for most EU member countries.

Source: Griffiths (2003 updated and 2000). Reprinted with permission.

Questions

1 As well as helping Japanese export performance, what other impacts might you expect the keiretsu system to have in the internationalisation process?

2 Can you identify any factors in today's global economy that might put this system under strain?

Table 2.1 provides a useful summary of some of the benefits and costs of the various types of global alliances previously discussed.

Table 2.1 Characteristics of different types of global alliance

Type of global alliance	Benefits	Costs	Critical success factors	Strategic human resources management
Licensing – manufacturing industries	■ Early standardisation of design ■ Ability to capitalise on innovations ■ Access to new technologies ■ Ability to control pace of industry evolution	■ New competitors created ■ Possible eventual exit from industry ■ Possible dependence on licensee	■ Selection of licensee likely to become a competitor ■ Enforcement of patents and licensing agreements	■ Technical knowledge ■ Training of local managers on-site
Licensing – servicing and franchises	■ Fast market entry ■ Low capital cost	■ Quality control ■ Trademark protection	■ Partners compatible in philosophies/ values ■ Tight performance standards	■ Socialisation of franchisees and licensees with core values
Joint ventures – specialisation across partners	■ Learning a partner's skills ■ Economies of scale ■ Quasi-vertical integration ■ Faster learning	■ Excessive dependence on partner for skills ■ Deterrent to internal investment	■ Tight and specific performance criteria ■ Entering a venture as 'student' rather than 'teacher' to learn skills from partner ■ Recognising that collaboration is another form of competition to learn new skills	■ Management development and training ■ Negotiation skills ■ Managerial rotation
Joint ventures – shared value-adding	■ Strengths of both partners pooled ■ Faster learning along value chain ■ Fast upgrading of technological skills	■ High switching costs ■ Inability to limit partner's access to information	■ Decentralisation and autonomy from corporate parents ■ Long 'courtship' period ■ Harmonisation of management styles	■ Team-building ■ Acculturation ■ Flexible skills for implicit communication
Consortia, kairetsus, and chaebols	■ Shared risks and costs ■ Building a critical mass in process technologies ■ Fast resource flows and skill transfers	■ Skills and technologies that have no real market worth ■ Bureaucracy ■ Hierarchy	■ Government encouragement ■ Shared values among managers ■ Personal relationships to ensure coordination and priorities ■ Close monitoring of member-company performance	■ 'Clan' cultures ■ Fraternal relationships ■ Extensive mentoring to provide a common vision and mission across member companies

Source: Adapted from Lei and Slocum (1996)

Why invest abroad?

Of course, the 'bottom line' may simply be an estimated higher present value of future profits from establishing a production facility in a foreign country as opposed to the alternatives (e.g. continuing to export to the foreign country). Nevertheless, an fdi decision is a complex process that may be influenced by social relationships within and outside the firm and for which there may be a whole array of other motivating factors. Some approaches seek to classify these *motivating factors* into supply factors, demand factors and political factors.

■ Supply factors

A number of *supply factors* may encourage the firm to resort to foreign direct investment. These may be particularly important for those firms sometimes described as *cost-orientated multinationals*, i.e. those for which the major objective is to reduce costs by internationalising their operations.

Production costs

Foreign locations may be more attractive because of lower costs of skilled or unskilled labour, lower land prices, tax rates or commercial real-estate rents. Of course, particular locations can vary in terms of their popularity as low-cost centres of production. For example, South Korea was once a production centre for low-priced training shoes, but as the country began to prosper, wages rose and this market is now dominated by China. At the moment, Ireland is attractive as a result of its low labour costs, English-speaking population, tax abatement opportunities and an infrastructure containing modern fibre-optic telephone networks. McGraw-Hill publishers moved the maintenance of the circulation files of its 16 magazines to Loughrea, Ireland, while retaining a direct link to its mainframe computers at its New Jersey headquarters.

This type of globalised production decision may often involve *vertical integration*. For example, many US and European companies have integrated forwards by establishing assembly facilities in South-East Asia in order to take account of the relative abundance of cheap, high-quality labour. Companies like America's ITT ship semi-manufactured components to the region, where they are assembled by local labour into finished products, which are then re-exported back to the home market. Such host countries for foreign direct investment are sometimes termed 'production platforms', which underscores their role as providers of a low-cost input into a global, vertically-integrated production process.

Of course, even when looking solely at the factor of labour, we have already noted in Chapter 1 that it is not only labour costs that are important but also labour productivity. Table 1.3 (p. 6) usefully pointed out that sometimes countries with low labour costs may be less attractive because of low labour productivity, and vice versa for high labour-cost countries. In fact, the most revealing overall statistic is relative unit labour costs (RULC) as outlined in Box 1.1 (p. 8).

Distribution costs

Where transportation costs are a significant proportion of total costs, firms may choose to produce from a foreign location rather than pay the costs of transportation. Heineken, whose products are mainly water-based, finds it cheaper to brew in locations geographically closer to the foreign consumer. International businesses may find it cheaper to establish distribution centres in the foreign location, rather than to send individual consignments directly to sellers. For example, Citrovita, a Brazilian producer of orange concentrate operates a storage and distribution centre in Antwerp, Belgium, so that it can benefit from low shipping rates when transporting in bulk. Mechanisms for minimising distribution costs are considered in more detail in Chapter 12.

Availability of natural resources

This is very important in certain industries such as oil and minerals. Indeed, this reason has often led to *backwards vertical integration* in search of cheaper or more secure inputs into the productive process. Oil companies, such as Exxon, Shell and BP, have provided well-known examples of this approach. In order to secure control of strategic raw materials in oil fields around the world, they established overseas extraction operations in the early years of the twentieth century with the aim of shipping crude oil back to their home markets for refining and sale.

pause for thought 5	Can you give two further examples of backwards vertical integration by MNEs?

Access to key technology

Many firms find it cheaper to invest in an existing firm rather than put together a new team of research specialists. Many Japanese pharmaceutical manufacturers have invested in small biogenetics companies as an inexpensive means of finding cutting-edge technology. Mitsubishi Electronics took over (and is now profitably running) Apricot in the UK, while Fujitsu is now the second-largest computer corporation in the world, after acquiring ICL, at that point the largest UK computer company.

■ Demand factors

A number of *demand factors* may also encourage the firm to resort to foreign direct investment. These may be particularly important for those firms sometimes described as *market-orientated multinationals*, i.e. those for which the major objective is to internationalise with a view to accessing new markets and greater sales. In this case the internationalisation process is more likely to take the form of *horizontal* (rather than vertical) *integration* into new geographic markets. Figure 2.1 presents a stylised version of this process with companies gradually switching from exporting (or licensing) to establishing first a sales outlet and finally full production facilities overseas (*see* Healey 2004). Underpinning this process may be a number of identifiable motivating factors of a demand type.

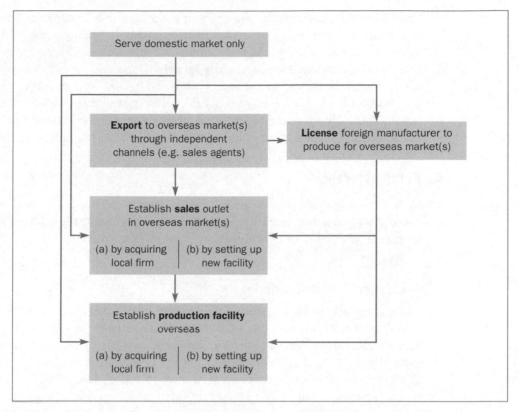

Figure 2.1 Evolution of a market-orientated multinational
Source: Adapted from Healey (2001)

Marketing advantages

There are several types of marketing advantage that may be reaped from investing in overseas enterprises or setting up foreign affiliates. The physical presence of a factory may give a company visibility and the company may also gain from a 'buy-local' attitude.

Preservation of brand names and trademarks

In order to maintain control over its brands, an established firm may choose to manufacture in the host country rather than merely license its name and run the risk of licensees using inferior materials. Levi-Strauss, for example, manufactures approximately half of its clothing in its own domestic and overseas factories and closely monitors the production of its carefully selected independent contractors.

Customer mobility

A firm may be motivated to move its operations close to a business customer if that customer sets up operations elsewhere, in order to reduce the possibility that a host-based competitor might step in and replace it as the supplier. For example, Japanese firms supplying parts to the major Japanese automobile companies have responded to the construction of Japanese automobile assembly plants in the USA and UK by building their own factories, warehouses and research facilities there. This need to move abroad was heightened by the fact that Japanese automobile companies use just-in-time techniques, and it is difficult to be just-in-time when the parts suppliers are thousands of miles away. Of course, subsequently the Japanese car firms have helped to develop the abilities of local firms to supply the quality and frequency of parts and components compatible with their manufacturing practices.

■ Political factors

At least two reasons with a 'political edge' may influence an fdi decision: one is to avoid trade barriers erected by governments (or regional trading blocs) and the other is to take advantage of economic development incentives offered by the government in the host country.

Avoidance of trade barriers

Firms often set up facilities in foreign countries in order to avoid trade barriers (*see also* Chapter 3). For example, US automobile companies have placed consistent pressure on their government to restrict Japanese imports of cars into the USA. At the same time, the Japanese government has itself imposed a voluntary export restraint (VER) on the number of cars exported to the USA. To get around these restrictions, many Japanese companies have set up factories in the USA, not only avoiding the VER but also helping to reduce US consumer opposition to Japanese cars since US jobs are now directly involved.

Taylor (2000) used a measure of 'trade openness' in seeking to estimate the impact of host country government policies on US multinational investment decisions. He found a positive and significant relationship between the two variables, showing that the more 'open' a country's trading regime (e.g. low tariff and other barriers) the more inward fdi from American MNEs it attracted. In actual fact, as Box 2.1 indicates, there are circumstances in which a negative (rather than positive) relationship might be anticipated between trade openness and fdi.

Economic development incentives

Most governments see fdi as creating new employment opportunities, raising the technological base and generally increasing the economic welfare of its citizens. Governments have therefore been ready to offer various incentives to firms to induce them to locate new facilities in their countries, including tax reductions or tax holidays, free or subsidised access to land or buildings (e.g. zero business rates), specially constructed infrastructure (road, rail, air links) and so on. In Case Study 2.1 earlier we noted that in 2003 India joined an increasing number of countries when developing 17 of its own 'export processing zones' (EPZs) providing various incentives to encourage inward fdi that can help India to improve its export competitiveness.

Box 2.1	Government policies, exporting and fdi

There is a considerable body of evidence (e.g. Markusen 1995) to suggest that imposing higher tariff barriers and other trade restrictions results in MNEs substituting exports to that country by fdi into that country. In other words, in order to overcome these barriers, MNEs invest in production facilities within the country, i.e. 'tariff-jumping' investment. In such circumstances we might expect exports from the multinationals home country to fall and affiliate sales generated by fdi activity in the host country to rise. The suggestion here is there is a *negative* relationship whereby countries with less open trade policies attract more inward fdi from MNEs. Such a negative relationship has indeed been found in a number of studies; for example, Brainard (1997) found that a 1% increase in tariffs resulted in a rise in affiliate sales via fdi of between one-third to one-half of 1%.

Taylor (2000), however, found quite the opposite, namely a *positive* relationship with countries having more open trade policies (less trade restrictions) attracting more rather than less inward fdi from the USA. In this study a 1% increase in tariffs resulted in a fall in affiliate sales via fdi of slightly over 1%. Some of the reasons for these findings may involve the strategy of MNEs in situating their factories wherever the combination of labour, component suppliers and transport is most efficient, then exporting from these 'production platforms' to the rest of the world. In other words, Taylor's findings might be expected where MNEs see fdi as part of a global exporting perspective (see Case Study 2.3) rather than merely as an attempt to sell to a local market protected by tariff barriers. In this sense 'trade openness' would assume a greater importance than 'tariff jumping' in their strategic thinking as regards fdi decisions.

In fact, the most important variable in increasing fdi investment was found to be not 'trade openness' but 'fdi openness'. Here fdi is regarded as being more 'open' the easier it is for the MNE to hire and fire labour, change prices, use the justice system, protect intellectual property, engage in cross-border ventures, understand and comply with regulations, and so on. Taylor (2000) found that a 1% increase in a country's 'fdi openness' leads to a 3% to 4% increase in the flow of fdi to that country.

■ Other factors

The decision to internationalise is complex and the reasons cannot always be neatly contained in the supply, demand and political categories already considered. Other concerns include:

- *The role of management*. The ambitions of management are often crucial in the first stages of the decision to go international. Often a change of chief executive can prompt activity in this area.
- *Motives of the organisation*. Some commentators identify three broad motivations for internationalisation; namely *market seeking* (the lure of additional revenue and profit from new overseas markets), *efficiency seeking* (the lure of lower production costs) and *resource seeking* (the lure of access to specific types of natural resource).
- *Saturation of the home market*. Restrictions in the size of the home market may mean that further growth requires the firm to gain access to overseas markets.
- *The bandwagon effect*. Intense rivalry can mean that a decision by one firm to enter an overseas market tends to be followed by other firms. The bandwagon effect has doubtless played some part in inducing some firms to enter the Chinese, Eastern European and ex-Soviet markets.

- *International product life cycle*. The internationalisation process may be more than simply an attempt to start new product life cycles elsewhere or to extend the maturity stage of an existing product life cycle. The suggestion here is that there may exist an *international product life cycle* for many products which will govern the geographical location of production in each stage (*see* Chapter 3).

Case Study 2.4 indicates the impact of a range of factors on decisions by car making firms to invest in Thailand and other parts of South-East Asia.

CASE 2.4	Car making in Asia

They are cheap, educated, friendly and fastidious, and Ralph-Rainer Ohlsen loves them. He smiles benignly at the women and men assembling BMW 318s and 328s in the light-flooded, squeaky-clean factory in Thailand's Rayong province that he opened last month. 'Those Thais even take their shoes off when they get in the cars', he enthuses. 'It's great.' That sort of thing never happens at BMW's South African factory, which he previously ran; nor, for that matter, at its Dingolfing plant in Bavaria.

After Ford in 1999 and GM in 2000, BMW is the latest Western car maker to set up in Thailand. This might seem odd in a country where car sales plummeted by 70% during the Asian crisis and production is still well below pre-crisis levels. Indeed, a new study of the car market in the Association of South-East Asian Nations (ASEAN) by the Economist Intelligence Unit, a sister company of *The Economist*, suggests that car sales in the region will return to pre-crisis levels only after 2005.

The Americans and Europeans come to Thailand with a vision that differs from that of the Japanese companies which dominate the region. Whereas the Japanese treat each ASEAN country as a distinct market, the Americans and Europeans are planning for a day when trade is free across the region.

According to Jochen Legewie, a car expert at the German Institute for Japanese Studies in Tokyo, this 'power shift' away from the Japanese, who today make nine out of ten cars and trucks sold in ASEAN, towards Western producers will prove the biggest force for change in the economics and politics of car making in Asia. The goal for Westerners is global economies of scale. If they reach it, the Japanese will lose out.

Visit, for instance, the factory of Toyota in Samrong, an hour north of Bangkok, and you see trucks unloading Thai parts from Thai suppliers for assembly lines that make cars for Thai consumers. At Toyota's plants in the Philippines, Indonesia and Malaysia, it is the same story. Everywhere in the region, Toyota and other Japanese car makers have, in effect, re-created a whole supply chain in order to serve the local market.

This is inefficient, and Toyota, for one, is losing money in the region. But the Japanese have had little choice, because politics has dictated their Asian strategy. ASEAN countries used to subscribe to import substitution as a development philosophy, and to burden foreign investors with onerous local content requirements. Some also have their own 'national' car projects, such as Malaysia's Proton, and are hostile to foreign competition. Tariffs on cars and car parts, high to begin with, went higher still during the crisis of the late 1990s, as countries tried in vain to conserve hard currency. Having watched American trade unionists bash Japanese cars in Detroit in the 1980s, says Yoshiaka Muramatsu, president of Toyota in Thailand, the Japanese decided to follow a strategy of 'harmonious growth' in the region, in effect sacrificing bigger economies of scale to national politics.

But hopes of liberalising trade in ASEAN have revived. Since 1996, companies in ASEAN have been able to apply for a reduction in tariffs on parts traded within the region. But the bureaucracies empowered to grant the reductions have tended to block any applications. The biggest hope now is for an Asian Free-Trade Area (AFTA) to take effect in January 2002. If it goes ahead, tariffs on cars and parts will be limited to a ceiling of 5%, low enough to allow the development of a genuine pan-regional marketplace.

It is this prospect that so excites the Western companies. GM, for instance, plans to export up to 90% of the Zafira vans that it makes at its Thai factory to the rest of the region, and the world. Ford now makes several models with sub-optimal efficiency, but it has designed its plant to convert to making one model highly efficient for export around the region. As for BMW, it sees three phases for its Thailand plant. In the first, it makes cars for Thailand, in the second it expands production and starts exporting to neighbouring countries, and in the third it sources from, and exports to, anywhere in the world. Of course, it all depends on AFTA going ahead, says Mr Ohlsen. 'If phases two and three happen, it's a hat-trick', he says. 'I'm convinced it won't go pear-shaped.'

Because so much rides on trade liberalisation, Westerners are lobbying hard for it. Kitcha Minakan, a director at Thailand's ministry of industry, says 'the Japanese come and ask what our laws are and then try to please us. The Europeans look at our laws, say they cannot abide by them entirely, but then try as much as possible. But the Americans come in and say, "This is all wrong, you have to change everything."'

In fact, Mr Minakan, and Thailand will not be the biggest obstacles to AFTA, because Thailand, as the production base of choice for the Westerners, has the most to gain from liberalisation. The main foot-dragger will be Malaysia, which fears for its Proton. But the Westerners are undaunted. They look forward to being able to put their factories wherever the combination of labour, suppliers and transport works best, and to export from them to the world. 'This is a critical point. Their way is different from ours', says Toyota's Mr Muramatsu. 'We must study how we, too, can enjoy further liberalisation.' That is as close as a Japanese executive ever comes to saying, 'We are worried.'

Source: *The Economist*, London, 24 June 2000. Reprinted with permission.

Questions

1 Consider some of the implications of this case study for the internationalisation process.

2 Why is it suggested that the Japanese 'are worried' about recent developments in the Asian car market?

Theoretical explanations

Attempts have been made to bring together various arguments to form theories or models of the internationalisation process. Some of these theories are taken further in Chapter 3.

■ Ownership-specific advantages

Here the focus is on the assets owned by the firm which might give it a competitive edge vis-à-vis other firms operating in overseas markets. Such ownership-specific advantages might include superior technology, a well-known brand name, economies of scale or scope (*see* Box 8.1, pp. 249–51), managerial or organisational skills, etc.

■ Internalisation

The focus here is on the costs of entering into a transaction, e.g. the costs of negotiating, monitoring and enforcing a contract. The firm decides whether it is cheaper to own and operate a plant or establishment overseas or to contract with a foreign firm to operate on its behalf through a franchise, licensing or supply agreement. Foreign direct investment is more likely to occur (i.e. the process to be *internalised*) when the costs of negotiating, monitoring and enforcing a contract with a second firm are high. On the other hand, when such transaction costs are low, firms are more likely to contract with outsiders and internationalise by licensing their brand names or franchising their business operations.

■ Location-specific advantages

These theories have mainly sought to answer the 'where' question involving MNE activity outside the home country as well as the 'why'. The availability and price of natural and human resources in overseas territories, of transport and communications infrastructure, market-size characteristics and other locational attributes are the focus of attempts by these theories to explain the internationalisation process.

■ Eclectic theory

John Dunning (1993) has sought to bring together all three of these theories, namely ownership, internalisation and locational factors in one combined approach. His so-called 'eclectic paradigm' suggests that firms transfer their *ownership-specific* assets to *locational settings* which offer the most favourable opportunities for their sector of activity while seeking wherever possible to *internalise* these processes in order to retain control of the subsequent revenue generation.

Dunning concluded that companies will only become involved in overseas investment and production (fdi) when the following conditions are all satisfied:

1 companies possess an 'ownership-specific' advantage over firms in the host country (e.g. via assets which are internal to the firm, including organisation structure, human capital, financial resources, size and market power);

2 it must be more profitable for the multinational to exploit its ownership-specific advantages in an overseas market than in its domestic market. In other words, there must additionally exist 'location-specific' factors which favour overseas production (e.g. special economic or political factors, attractive markets in terms of size, growth or structure, low 'psychic' or 'cultural' distance, etc); and

3 these advantages are best exploited by the firm itself, rather than by selling them to foreign firms. In other words, due to market imperfections (e.g. uncertainty), multinationals choose to bypass the market and 'internalise' the use of ownership-specific advantages via vertical and horizontal integration (such internalisation reduces transaction costs in the presence of market imperfections).

The decisions of multinationals to produce abroad are, therefore, determined by a mixture of motives – ownership-specific, locational, and internalisation factors – as noted above.

Under 'eclectic theory' other theories of internationalisation are more concerned with the *processes* that a firm must go through.

Sequential theory of internationalisation

Adherents of this approach (sometimes called the 'Uppsala model') include Johanson and Widersheim-Paul who examined the internationalisation of Swedish firms. They found a regular process of gradual change involving the firm moving *sequentially* through four discrete stages: (1) intermittent exports; (2) exports via agents; (3) overseas sales via knowledge agreements with local firms, for example by licensing or franchising; (4) foreign direct investment in the overseas market.

This particular sequence is sometimes called the *establishment chain*, the argument being that each of these stages marks a progressive increase in the resource commitment by the firm to the overseas markets involved. There is also a suggestion that as firms move through these sequential stages, the knowledge and information base expands and the 'psychic distance' between themselves and the overseas markets involved contracts, making progression to the next stage that much easier. In this sense the model is dynamic, with the stage already reached by the firm in the internationalisation process helping determine the future course of action likely to be taken. Put another way, the greater the resource commitment to the overseas market and the information and knowledge thereby acquired, the smaller the uncertainty and the perceived risks associated with further internationalisation, leading eventually to foreign direct investment and the establishment of a production affiliate overseas. Firms will move initially to countries that are culturally similar to their own (a close psychic distance) and only later move into culturally diverse geographical areas.

Simultaneous theory of internationalisation

Other writers have put forward a *simultaneous view* of internationalisation, based on global convergence. For example, they suggest that customers' tastes around the world are becoming progressively homogeneous, citing the success of such global products as Coca-Cola, Levi jeans or Sony Walkman. This approach contends that the economies of scale and scope available for standardised products in such global markets are so substantial that a gradual, sequential approach to internationalisation is no longer practicable. Proponents of this approach point to studies such as that by Reisenbeck and Freeling (1991) which suggest that the global awareness of brands has fallen dramatically over time, with less than two years now needed for making consumers worldwide aware of high profile brand images. Critics, however, suggest that there is little evidence for the notion of 'homogenisation' of consumer tastes, indeed quite the opposite with sophisticated customers demanding greater customisation (*see* p. 316). Further, although simultaneous entry into a variety of overseas markets may be possible for highly resourced and established firms, it may be out of the question for smaller or less experienced firms.

■ Network theory

In a network perspective the process of internationalisation is seen as building on existing relationships or creating new relationships in international markets, with the focus shifting from the organisational or economic to that of the social. It is *people* who make the decisions and take the actions.

The series of networks can be considered at three levels.

- *Macro* – rather than the environment being seen as a set of political, social and economic factors, network theory would see it as a set of diverse interests, powers and characteristics, which may well impinge on national and international business decisions. To enter new markets a firm may have to break old relationships or add new ones. A new entrant may find it difficult to break into a market that already has many stable relationships. Those firms better able to reconfigure their existing networks or which are seeking to enter overseas markets with few existing networked relationships, may be more successful in the internationalisation process.
- *Inter-organisational* – firms may well stand in different relationships to one another in different markets. They may be competitors in one market, collaborators in another and suppliers and customers to each other in a third. If one firm internationalises, this may draw other firms into the international arena.
- *Intra-organisational* – relationships within the organisation may well influence the decision-making process. If a multinational has subsidiaries in other countries, decisions may well be taken at the subsidiary level that increases the degree of international involvement of the parent MNE, depending on the degree of decentralisation of decision making permitted by the firm.

The network approach would suggest that internationalisation can be explained, at least in part, by the fact that the other firms and people who are involved in a particular national network themselves internationalise.

■ International product life cycle (IPLC)

The suggestion here is that the pattern and extent of internationalisation achieved by the firm, and future prospects for continuation of that process, will depend in part on the stage in the IPLC reached by the firm. This approach also sees internationalisation as a process and is considered in more detail in Chapter 3 (p. 75).

Case Study 2.5 reviews the internationalisation experience of Portugal and provides an opportunity to consider the different approaches to internationalisation.

CASE 2.5 Internationalisation: the Portuguese experience

Multinationals chose to locate in Portugal for reasons that included a stable political environment, the commitment to European integration, and an adaptable and inexpensive labour force. Texas Instruments, Inlan, Ford, Siemens, Pioneer, Blaupunkt and other multinationals had already established a presence in Portugal during the 1960s, but the high-water-mark came in the late 1980s with the largest-ever foreign direct investment in a leading sector, namely motor vehicles. The VW/Ford joint venture to produce their new multi-purpose vehicle, the Sharan/Galaxy, was located at Palmela in the Setúbal peninsula south of Lisbon. The project undoubtedly helped to transform Portugal's economic profile, not least because a number of countries had hoped to be chosen as the location for the project and it gave a much needed boost to the local car components suppliers. However, it has proved hard to build on this success because, among other factors, the European economy experienced a downturn during the 1990s, the motor vehicles market became intensely competitive, and eastern Europe emerged as a rival, competing with Portugal as a location in terms of low labour costs, generous firm incentives, etc. An indication of just how fierce this 'place competition' can be came in September 1999 when the decision was taken to locate production of VW's new Porsche model at Bratislava in Slovakia where hourly wage costs are 60% lower than at Palmela.

Indeed, an important recent development has been the strong surge in Portuguese investment abroad. During the 1990s Portugal's outward foreign direct investment multiplied at an impressive rate. By 1998 Portugal was among the leading 15 countries that invest overseas, with most of the fdi taking the form of cross-border acquisitions or partnerships. Internationalisation efforts have followed a distinct pattern in terms of their economic geography. Typically the first moves were made into the neighbouring economy, Spain. An example of this 'toe in the water' stage was the acquisition by Cimpor, the leading Portuguese cement maker, of Corporación Noroeste, a Spanish cement maker based in Galicia. The next move was for Portuguese firms as diverse as Cenoura, Petrogal, Transportes Luis Simões and Caixa Geral de Depósitos to penetrate the wider Spanish market. A survey conducted among Portuguese companies in 1997 found that the priority markets for internationalisation were Spain (69.9%), the former Portuguese African colonies or PALOPs (47.3%), the rest of the EU (38.7%) and Brazil (35.5%).

A clear pattern and trajectory is discernible in Portugal's internationalisation efforts. Typically the first moves, as indicated above, are made into the neighbouring economy. As a result of these rapidly expanding two-way flows, an EU regional bloc based in the Iberian peninsula came into existence during the 1990s as a buoyant new trading area. Using Spain as a springboard, the next natural step was into North Africa and the countries that were formerly Portugal's African colonies. The latter were attractive because they were undertaking privatisation programmes, while Brazil became a focal point for economic relations with Mercosur. The most recent stage has involved investments in the more advanced EU economies. In some cases, a presence has also been established in eastern Europe, notably Poland, Hungary and Russia.

▶

The Portuguese expansion strategy is driven by the need to stay competitive in order to survive by 'growing' multinationals. The problem of scale is important. Given the country's dimensions, large nationally based groups are inevitably thin on the ground. World-ranking tables, for instance, placed Portugal's largest bank, CGD, in 146th place. In such circumstances, there exists an ever-present danger that Portuguese firms will fall prey to foreign, perhaps Spanish, transnationals. This poses a dilemma for public policy with regard to the industrial and service sectors. If size contributes to competitiveness, is it the state's role to support these groups and to encourage mergers and expansion when the ultimate beneficiaries may be the shareholders of foreign groups? Indeed, some economists argue that the priority should be given to tackling the structural problems confronting Portuguese businesses which, in some cases, reveal deficiencies in human resources at both management and workforce levels.

There is also the problem of location and specialisation. In a recent study David Owen, economist at Dresdner Kleinwort Benson, predicted that there will be greater industrial specialisation across Europe with individual countries concentrating on fewer products. Using trade flow data he identified the winners and losers for each EU member state. In Portugal's case the best positioned industries turned out to be alcoholic beverages, paper and packaging, household goods and mining. He concluded that most other industries suffered from a comparative disadvantage, with general engineering, chemicals and pharmaceuticals emerging as the chief losers. According to this study, tourism and leisure along with clothing and footwear are likely to retain their importance in Portugal's economic profile well into the new millennium.

In the past Portugal's export clusters were based on natural resource or labour-intensive activities. According to Owen, in future the advantages to be gained as a low-wage location may be less than assumed by the conventional economic wisdom. This is because investors are likely to focus their attention on clusters that have a comparative advantage, rather than simply seeking out locations that can offer cheap labour. In this scenario, they will normally favour clusters that can offer an excellent infrastructure, specialist components suppliers and other factors that serve to offset the wage savings of alternative locations (Owen 1999: 6–7). One such cluster recommended for Portugal involves the motor components sector.

The region has been identified as an important level for promoting economic development and improving competitiveness. There is evidence that local authorities and regional organisations are beginning to seek alternatives to mergers and acquisitions. An example is support for the 'association' (associativismo) whereby new firms are created while maintaining the autonomy of the individual member units. The Minho Industrial Association, for example, is seeking to build on the fierce individualism among the local business community through a new competitiveness programme, CompeteMinho, which benefits from both European and government funds. It acts as an 'incubator', encouraging 'círculos de negócio' (business districts) based on clusters of firms which possess neither the scale nor the organisation to compete effectively in the global marketplace. The majority are SMEs, microfirms in particular, that wish to co-operate whilst still retaining their own identity. The experience to date has been positive, notably in the footwear industry. Mastershoe was established under the programme, involving partners from various parts of the country including a consultancy and investment firm, with the aim of exporting to the central and eastern European markets. Although still at the experimental stage, the innovative promotion of predominantly regionally based 'clusters' holds out the prospect that SMEs and microfirms might begin to compete in international markets.

Source: Corkhill (2000). Reprinted with permission.

Questions

1 How does the Portuguese experience relate to the various theories of internationalisation?

2 What policies might be used to encourage further internationalisation by Portuguese firms?

Useful websites

Now try the self-check questions for this chapter on the website at www.booksites.net/wall. You will also find further resources as well as the following useful weblinks:

Sources of information on international trade and payments, international institutions and exchange rates include:

www.wto.org
www.imf.org
www.un.org
www.dti.gov.uk
www.europa.eu.int
www.eubusiness.com

Useful key texts

Daniels, J., Radebaugh, L. and Sullivan, D. (2004) *International Business* (10th edn), Pearson Prentice Hall, especially Chapter 1.

Dicken, P. (2003) *Global Shift: Transforming the World Economy* (4th edn), Paul Chapman Publishing Ltd, especially Chapter 1 and Parts I and II.

Hill, C. (2003) *International Business: Competing in the Global Marketplace* (4th edn), McGraw-Hill Irwin, especially Chapters 14 and 15.

Morrison, J. (2002) *The International Business Environment*, Palgrave, especially Chapter 2 and Chapter 5 (pp. 142–6) and Chapter 11 (pp. 331–6).

Rugman, A. and Hodgetts, R. (2003) *International Business* (3rd edn), FT Prentice Hall, especially Chapter 2.

Tayeb, M. (2000) *International Business: Theories, Policies and Practices*, Financial Times Prentice Hall, especially Chapters 5–8 and 18.

Woods, M. (2001) *International Business*, Palgrave, especially Chapter 5 and Chapter 8 (pp. 195–204).

Other texts and sources

Bennett, R. (1999) *International Business* (2nd edn), Financial Times Pitman Publishing, especially Chapters 1 and 9.

Brainard, S.L. (1997) 'An Empirical Assessment of the Proximity–Concentration Trade-off between Multinational Sales and Trade', *American Economic Review*, 87.

Child, J. (1991) 'A Foreign Perspective on the Management of People in China', *International Journal of Human Resource Management*, 2, pp. 93–107.

Corkhill, D. (2000) 'Internationalisation and Competitiveness: the Portuguese Experience', in *Dimensions of International Competitiveness*, Lloyd-Reason, L. and Wall, S. (eds), Edward Elgar.

Deng, P. (2001) 'WFOEs: the Most Popular Entry Mode into China', *Business Horizons*, July–Aug.

Dunning, J.H. (1993) *Multinational Enterprises and the Global Economy*, Addison-Wesley.

Griffiths, A. (2000) 'Cultural Determinants of Competitiveness: the Japanese Experience', in *Dimensions of International Competitiveness: Issues and Policies*, Lloyd-Reason, L. and Wall, S. (eds), Edward Elgar.

Harrigan, K.R. (1986) *Managing for Joint Venture Success*, Lexington, MA: Lexington Books.

Healey, N. (2004) 'The Multinational Corporation', in *Applied Economics* (10th edn), Griffiths, A. and Wall, S. (eds), Financial Times Prentice Hall.

Hill, E. and O'Sullivan, T. (2003) *Marketing* (3rd edn), Longman.

Johanson, J. and Wiedersheim-Paul, F. (1975) 'The Internationalisation of the Firm – Four Swedish Cases', *Journal of Management Studies*, 19, 3.

Lei, D. and Slocum, J. (1996) *Organizational Dynamics*, vol. 24, no. 4.

Lu, Y. and Bjorkman, I. (1998) 'Human Resource Management in International Joint Ventures in China', *Journal of General Management*, 23, pp. 63–74.

Markusen, J. (1995) 'The Boundaries of Multinational Enterprises and the Theory of International Trade', *Journal of Economic Perspectives*, 9.

Oliver, N., Delbridge, R. and Barton, H. (2002) 'Lean Production and Manufacturing, Performance Improvements in Japan', *ESRC Centre for Business Research*, University of Cambridge, Working Paper No. 232.

Owen, D. (1999) 'Economic Geography Rewritten', *Economic Focus*, January, Dresdner Kleinwort Benson, London, pp. 6–7.

Reisenbeck, H. and Freeling, A. (1991) 'How Global are Global Brands?', *McKinsey Quarterly*, 4.

Taylor, C.T. (2000) 'The Impact of Host Country Government Policy on US Multinational Investment Decisions', *Harvard Business Review*, March/April.

United Nations Conference on Trade and Development (UNCTAD) *World Investment Report* (annual publication).

United Nations Development Programme (UNDP) *Human Development Report* (annual publication), OUP.

Vanhonacker, W.R. (2000) 'A Better Way to Crack China', *Harvard Business Review*, July/August.

Webb, A. (2003) 'China and the M&A Boom', *Accounting & Business*, February.

Wilson, J. (2003) 'Inter-Partner Relationships and Performance in UK–Chinese Joint Ventures: an Interaction Approach', unpublished Ph.D. thesis, University of Middlesex.

World Bank, *World Development Report* (annual publication).

Yan, D. and Warner, M. (2001) 'Sino-foreign Joint Ventures versus Wholly Foreign Owned Enterprises in the People's Republic of China', Research papers in management studies, University of Cambridge, October.

Chapter 3

International business: theory and practice

By the end of this chapter you should be able to:

- outline the arguments used to support free trade between nations;

- identify the sources of comparative and competitive advantage between nations;

- discuss the nature and importance of both inter-industry and intra-industry trade in a global economy;

- assess the arguments and practices used to support protectionism;

- examine the impacts of a range of government policies and practices on international business;

- evaluate the contribution of the EU and its associated institutions to international business activity.

Introduction

Most international business is conducted in a context in which the major players believe such business to be of benefit to themselves, to the nation states they represent and even to the broader international community. It would therefore seem appropriate to review the theoretical basis for trade at the outset of this chapter before moving on to discuss some of the issues and practices involving protectionism. Since the European Union (EU) plays such a key role in the UK's international business environment, it is considered in some detail in this chapter. The next chapter discusses the institutions and markets that underpin the present system of global trade and payments and consider some recent proposals for reform.

Gains from trade

■ Absolute advantage

As long ago as 1776, Adam Smith in his *Wealth of Nations* suggested that countries could benefit from specialising in products in which they had an *absolute advantage* over other countries, trading any surpluses with those countries. By 'absolute advantage' Smith meant the ability to produce those products at lower resource cost (e.g. fewer labour and capital inputs) than the other countries.

This was an essentially limited view as to the benefits of international business. For example, in a simple two-country, two-product model, each country would have to demonstrate that it was absolutely more efficient than the other in one of these products if specialisation and trade were to be mutually beneficial.

■ Comparative advantage

David Ricardo sought, in 1817, to broaden the basis on which trade was seen to be beneficial by developing his theory of *comparative advantage*. Again, we can illustrate by using a simple two-country, two-product model. In this approach even where a country has an absolute advantage (less resource cost) over the other country in *both* products, it can still gain by specialisation and trade in that product in which its *absolute advantage is greatest*, i.e. in which it has a *comparative advantage*. Similarly, the other country that has an absolute disadvantage (higher resource cost) in both products can still gain by specialisation and trade in that product in which its *absolute disadvantage is least*, i.e. in which it also has a *comparative advantage*.

Ricardo's theory can be illustrated using Table 3.1 where, for simplicity, we assume each country to have the same amounts of resources (e.g. labour and capital) available for producing two products, CDs and videos. Initially the analysis will also assume constant returns in producing each product. Table 3.1 shows the production possibilities if each country devotes all its (identical) resources to the production of either CDs or videos.

From Table 3.1 we can see that country A has an absolute advantage in both products (greater output for the same resource input) but a *comparative advantage in videos*. This is because although A is twice as efficient as B in CDs, it is four times as efficient as B in videos. Therefore, according to the principle of comparative advantage, country A should specialise in videos and trade these for the CDs that B produces.

By similar reasoning, from Table 3.1 we can see that country B has an absolute disadvantage in both products (less output for the same resource input) but *a comparative advantage in CDs*. This is because although B is only one-quarter as efficient as A in videos it is one-half as efficient as A in CDs. Therefore, according to the principle of comparative advantage, country B should specialise in CDs and trade these for the videos that A produces.

Table 3.1 **Production possibilities in a two-product, two-country model**

Country	Output of CDs	Output of videos
A	2,000	800
B	1,000	200

A country has a *comparative advantage* (in a two-product model) in that product in which its *absolute advantage is greatest* or in which its *absolute disadvantage is least*.

This idea of comparative advantage can be expressed in terms of *opportunity cost* (*see* Table 3.2), defined here as the output foregone by producing one more unit of a particular product. In country A, for example, the production of an extra video has an opportunity cost of only 2.5 CDs whereas for country B the production of an extra video has an opportunity cost of 5 CDs. In other words, country A has a lower opportunity cost in video production than country B, and therefore has a *comparative advantage* in video production, even though it has an *absolute advantage* in both products.

Similarly, country B can produce an extra CD at an opportunity cost of one-fifth (0.2) of a video, whereas country A can only produce an extra CD at an opportunity cost of two-fifths (0.4) of a video. In other words, country B has a lower opportunity cost and therefore *comparative advantage* in CD production even though it has an *absolute disadvantage* in both products.

A country has a *comparative advantage* (in a two-product model) in that product in which it has a *lower opportunity* cost than the other country.

Whichever approach we adopt, we would conclude that country A has a comparative advantage in videos and country B a comparative advantage in CDs.

Gains from specialisation and trade

We can show the potential benefits from specialisation and trade according to comparative advantages in a number of different ways. Clearly a country will benefit if, by specialisation and trade, it can reach a consumption situation better than that which would result from being self-sufficient. Suppose that initially each country tries to be self-sufficient, using half its resources to produce videos and half to produce CDs. This gives us the *self-sufficiency* consumption bundles of C_A (1,000 CDs, 400 videos) and C_B (500 CDs, 100 videos) respectively. Provided that the *terms of trade* (i.e. the rate at which videos exchange for CDs) are appropriate, each country can be shown to benefit from specialisation and trade according to comparative advantages.

In Figure 3.1(a), with terms of trade of 1 video : 3 CDs, country A specialises in videos and trades 250 of its 800 videos for 750 CDs (from B), ending at the consumption bundle of C'_A (750 CDs, 550 videos). Since C'_A is *outside* its production possibility frontier, country A could not have achieved this consumption bundle by being self-sufficient.

Table 3.2 **Opportunity costs in a two-product, two-country model**

Country	Opportunity cost of 1 extra CD	Opportunity cost of 1 extra video
A	0.4 videos	2.5 CDs
B	0.2 videos	5.0 CDs

In Figure 3.1(b), with the same terms of trade of 1 video : 3 CDs, country B specialises in CDs and trades 750 of its 1,000 CDs for 250 videos (from A), ending at the consumption bundle of C'_B (250 CDs, 250 videos). Since C'_B is *outside* its production possibility frontier, country B could not have achieved this consumption bundle by being self-sufficient.

> If the *terms of trade* are appropriate, both countries can gain from *specialisation and trade according to comparative advantages*.

You should be able to see from Figure 3.1(a) that at terms of trade of *less than* 1 video : 2.5 CDs, country A will be better off by being self-sufficient than by specialis-

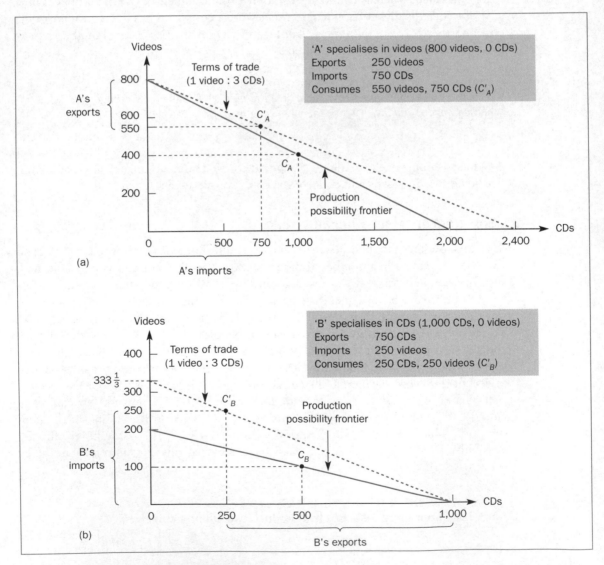

Figure 3.1 **Gains from specialisation and trade**

ing in videos and trading them for CDs. In other words, the slope of A's production possibility frontier represents the 'worst' terms A is prepared to accept if it is to engage in specialisation and trade according to comparative advantages. Similarly, from Figure 3.1(b) we can see that at terms of trade of *less than* 1 CD : 0.2 videos, country B will be better off by being self-sufficient than by specialising in CDs and trading them for videos. In other words, the slope of B's production possibility frontier represents the 'worst' terms B is prepared to accept if it is to engage in specialisation and trade according to comparative advantages.

pause for thought 1

(a) If the terms of trade for A are less than 1 video : 2.5 CDs, namely 1 video : 2 CDs, what would be the result of A exporting 250 videos in Figure 3.1?

(b) If the terms of trade for B are less than 1 CD : 0.2 videos, namely 1 CD = 0.1 videos, what would be the result of B exporting 750 CDs in Figure 3.1?

(c) Can you re-express the terms of trade for B of 1 CD : 0.2 videos into a relationship between videos : CDs?

(d) What would be the outcome if the terms of trade for A and for B were exactly as represented by their respective production possibility frontiers?

We can therefore say that the terms of trade which will enable *both* country A and country B to gain from specialisation and trade, must lie between 1 video : 2.5 CDs and 1 video : 5 CDs (i.e. 1 CD : 0.2 videos).

The *terms of trade* which will enable both countries to gain from specialisation and trade must lie between the slopes of their respective production possibility frontiers.

An alternative approach to demonstrating the gains from trade is shown in Box 3.1. This approach makes use of the ideas of consumer and producer surplus.

Box 3.1 Gains from trade

Figure 3.2 shows that free trade could, in theory, bring welfare benefits to an economy previously protected. Suppose the industry is initially completely protected. The domestic price P_D will then be determined solely by the intersection of the domestic supply ($S_D - S_D$) and domestic demand ($D_D - D_D$) curves. Suppose that the government now decides to remove these trade barriers and to allow foreign competition. For simplicity, we assume a perfectly elastic 'world' supply curve $P_W - C$, giving a total supply curve (domestic and world) of S_DAC. Domestic price will then be forced down to the world level P_W with domestic demand being $0Q_3$ at this price. To meet this domestic demand, $0Q_2$ will be supplied from domestic sources, with Q_2Q_3 supplied from the rest of the world (i.e. imported). The *consumer surplus*, which is the difference between what consumers are prepared to pay and what they have to pay, has risen from D_DBP_D to D_DCP_W. The *producer surplus*, which is the difference between the price the producer receives and the minimum necessary to induce production, has fallen from P_DBS_D to P_WAS_D. The gain in consumer surplus outweighs the loss in producer surplus by the area ABC, which could then be regarded as the net gain in economic welfare as a result of free trade replacing protectionism.

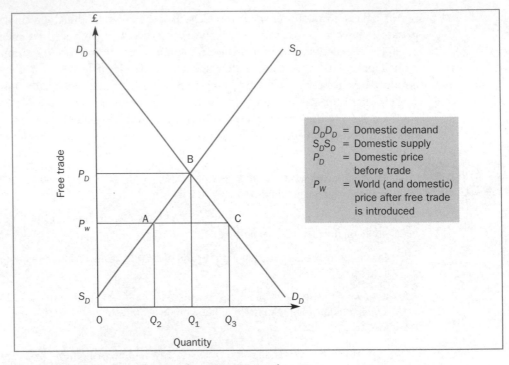

Figure 3.2 **Gains from free trade versus no trade**

pause for thought 2   In the analysis above, what has happened to the area P_WP_DBA?

Sources of comparative and competitive advantage

We have seen that countries can gain from trade by specialising in those products in which they have a lower opportunity cost (i.e. a comparative advantage) vis-à-vis other countries and trading surpluses with those countries. An obvious question then presents itself, namely, what is it that gives one country a comparative advantage in certain products over other countries? We briefly review a number of theories that have sought to answer this question.

Factor endowments: Heckscher-Ohlin

Named after two Swedish economists, the Heckscher-Ohlin (HO) theory suggests that *factor endowments* will broadly determine the pattern of trade between nations. The idea here is that those countries with an abundance of certain types of factor (labour, capital, natural resources, etc.) will be able to produce products that embody those abundant factors relatively more cheaply than other, less well endowed, countries. In its simplest form a labour abundant country will be able to produce (and export) labour intensive products relatively more cheaply than a labour scarce country, and so on.

Empirical testing of the HO theory, however, has provided little support for it being a major explanation of observed patterns of trade, even when more complex forms of the theory have been devised. For example, international trade is larger in volume and value terms between the *similar* developed (advanced industrialised) economies rather than between the *dissimilar* (in terms of factor endowments) developed and less developed economies. This is, of course, the opposite to what we might have expected from the HO theory.

Possible reasons for these 'disappointing' empirical results might include the following:

1 Factors of production – such as labour, capital, etc. – are hardly homogeneous so aggregate statements such as 'labour abundant' may be relatively meaningless. For example, labour can be broken down into many different skill levels, capital into different levels of technological intensity (e.g. high, medium and low technology), etc. In this case it may make little sense to regard a country as having a comparative advantage in, say, labour-intensive products merely because it is labour abundant vis-à-vis some other country. To compare 'like with like' we may need to disaggregate labour (and any other factor) into its component parts. Only then might we be able to say that a country is labour abundant in, say, highly-skilled labour and might therefore be expected to have a comparative advantage in those products which intensively embody high-skilled labour inputs.

2 Products may exhibit *factor intensity reversal* in different countries. For example, producing certain types of car in Japan (with higher real wages) is likely to be a more capital-intensive process than producing the same car in, say, Spain (with lower real wages). The suggestion here is that the higher *relative* price ratio of labour: capital in Japan than in Spain may provide greater incentives to substitute capital for labour in Japan than would be the case in Spain. Where substantial differences in such factor price ratios exist, there might even be factor intensity reversal, with a given product using relatively capital intensive processes in one country but relatively labour intensive processes in another.

3 Factor and product markets must be competitive if differences in factor endowments and therefore factor productivities are to be reflected in differences in product costs. In reality, imperfections in factor markets (existence of unions, large employers, employer confederations, etc.) and in product markets (monopoly or oligopoly, public-sector involvement, etc.) may well result in prices diverging markedly from actual marginal production costs.

4 The *terms of trade* between the potential exported and imported products may lie outside the limits which would permit trade to be beneficial to both parties (*see* pp. 67–9). For example, the export : import price ratio may be influenced in arbitrary ways by unexpected fluctuations in relative exchange rates, etc.

5 A host of other market imperfections may distort the linkage between factor endowment, actual production costs and the relative prices at which products are exchanged on international markets. Differences between countries in the degree of multinational or governmental involvement in a given sector, in the market structure of production in that sector or in terms of other types of 'market failure', can be expected to break any simple linkage between relative factor endowment and relative product prices.

For all these reasons it may be unsurprising that little empirical evidence exists to suggest that different national factor endowments have played a major part in explaining the observed patterns of international trade flows.

Disaggregated factor endowments

More refined versions of HO have tried to disaggregate the factors of production into units that are more homogeneous for purposes of comparison between countries.

- *Efficiency units.* Here labour and capital inputs are adjusted to take account of productivity differentials. So if American workers are twice as productive in manufacturing as, say, Thai workers, the number of American workers should be multiplied by two when comparing labour factor endowment between the two countries in terms of 'efficiency units'.
- *Human capital.* Workers can be disaggregated by *level* of human capital (e.g. years of education, experience, etc.) and by *type* of human capital (e.g. vocational/non-vocational, marketing/non-marketing, etc.). Again, we can then apply 'weights' to any raw data we might have when comparing labour factor endowment between countries.

Revealed comparative advantage

The suggestion here is that the sources of comparative advantage can be determined indirectly by *observing* actual trade flows between countries. For example, it is interesting to note that in the more dynamic sectors of UK industry, there are signs of a shift towards the higher end of the quality market for both UK manufacturing exports and for the production of substitutes for manufacturing imports. In other words, the data arguably suggests a *revealed comparative advantage* for the UK in terms of more technologically intensive manufacturing exports and imports (substitutes).

Competitive advantage: Porter

Michael Porter (1990) has attempted to explain the critical factors for success in both national and international production and exchange in terms of *competitive advantages*.

Competitive advantage: corporate

In the *corporate* context, the competitive advantages of a company are defined in terms of the 'marginal' company in that sector of economic activity. In other words, they are the collection of reasons that allow the more successful companies to create positive added-value (profits) in that sector of economic activity as compared to the 'marginal' company, which is just managing to survive. Reasons for such competitive advantages could include some or all of the following:

- *architecture*, benefits to the company from some distinctive aspect of the set of contractual relationships the company has entered into with suppliers and/or customers;
- *innovation*, benefits to the company from being more innovative than rivals (perhaps reinforced by legal structures, e.g. patent laws);

■ *incumbency advantages*, benefits to the company from being an early 'player' in that field of activity (reputation, control over scarce resources, etc.).

pause for thought 3 Can you give examples of these sources of competitive advantage using major international businesses?

The essential feature about many of these sources of competitive advantage is that they are usually *temporary*. Distinctive contractual relationships that prove to be successful (e.g. franchising arrangements) can be replicated by other firms, patents that protect innovation eventually expire and even incumbency advantages may not last. New sources of raw materials or other factor inputs may be found, technical change may alter production possibilities and even reputations can be transposed from other fields of economic activity (e.g. Virgin taking its reputation for quality/efficiency in entertainment/transport, etc. into financial services operations). Companies must continually seek new sources of competitive advantage if they are to avoid becoming themselves the 'marginal' firm in any sector of economic activity.

Competitive advantage: national

In the *national* context, Porter has again used this perspective of a dynamic, ever-changing set of competitive advantages as a basis for explaining trade patterns between countries. Porter sees both *product innovation* and *process innovation* as key elements in determining national competitive advantages. In his view these dynamic elements far outweigh the more static elements of 'factor endowments' in determining success in international trading relationships. Still more so when technology is constantly changing the optimal combination of capital/labour/natural resource inputs for a product, when multinationals are so 'footloose' that they can readily relocate across national boundaries and when capital markets provide investment finance on an increasingly global basis.

Porter identifies six key variables as potentially giving a country a competitive advantage over other countries:

1 *demand conditions*: the extent and characteristics of domestic demand;
2 *factor conditions*: transport infrastructure, national resources, human capital endowments, etc.;
3 *firm strategies: structures and rivalries*: the organisation and management of companies and the degree of competition in the market structures in which they operate;
4 *related and supporting industries*: quality and extent of supply industries, supporting business services, etc.;
5 *government policies*: nature of the regulatory environment, extent of state intervention in industry and the regions, state support for education and vocational training, etc.;
6 *chance*.

Porter's diamond

The first four of these variables form a *diamond* shape, as shown in Figure. 3.3, when mapped as the most important determinants of national competitive advantage.

In Porter's view, the four determinants are interdependent. For example favourable 'demand conditions' will only contribute to national competitive advantage when combined with appropriate 'factor conditions', 'related and supporting industries' and 'firm strategies: structures and rivalries' so that companies are *able* and *willing* to take advantage of the favourable demand conditions. To sustain national competitive advantages in modern, high-technology industries and economies, Porter argues that all four determinants in the 'diamond' must be favourable. However, in less technology intensive industries and economies, one or two of the four determinants being favourable may be sufficient for a national competitive advantage: e.g. natural resource dependent industries may only need favourable 'factor conditions' (presence of an important natural resource) and appropriate infrastructure to extract and transport that resource.

The last two determinants 'government policies' and 'chance' outlined above can interact with the four key determinants of the diamond to open up new opportunities for national competitive advantage. For example government policies in the field of education and training may help create R & D and other knowledge–intensive competitive advantage for a nation. Similarly 'chance' events can play a part, as in the case of Russia supporting a greater US presence in Uzbekistan during the War in Afghanistan in 2001/02, thereby creating new opportunities for US oil companies to exploit the huge oil resources in that country.

pause for thought 4	Can you identify some possible impacts of 9/11 in terms of national competitive advantage?

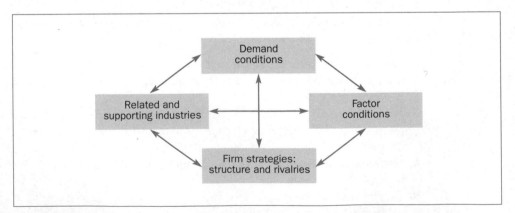

Figure 3.3 **Porter's diamond: the determinants of national competitive advantage**

Source: Adapted from Porter, M. (1998) *The Competitive Advantage of Nations*, Palgrave, p. 72

International product life cycle (IPLC)

The suggestion here (e.g. Vernon and Wells 1991) is that the pattern of products traded between countries will be influenced by the stage of production reached in the international life cycle of a variety of knowledge-intensive products. The *new product stage* (invention/development) will typically occur in the (advanced industrialised) innovating country but then the balance between production and consumption (and therefore between export and import) may shift *geographically* as different stages of the product life cycle are reached. In Figure 3.4 we can see a stylised IPLC for a knowledge-intensive product over three stages of the product life cycle (new product, mature product, standardised product) and for three broad geographical regions (innovating country, other advanced countries, less developed countries – LDCs).

■ *New product stage.* Here production is concentrated in the *innovating country*, as is market demand. A typical scenario for this stage would be where the (initially) relatively low output is sold at premium prices to a price-inelastic domestic market segment (with few, if any, exports). There may be a small amount of production via subsidiaries in 'other advanced countries' but little or none in the LDCs.

■ *Mature product stage.* Both production and consumption typically continue to rise in the *innovating country*, with scale economies beginning to reduce costs and price to a new, more price sensitive mass market segment. Exports to other countries become a higher proportion of total sales. Output of the generic product also rises in the 'other advanced countries', via the output of subsidiaries or of competitors in these countries which have the knowledge-intensive capability of developing close substitutes. These countries typically import a high proportion of their sales from the innovating country, as do the LDCs.

■ *Standardised product stage.* At this stage the technology becomes more widely diffused and is often largely 'embodied' in both capital equipment and process control. Low-cost locations become a more feasible source of quality supply in this stage, often via MNE outsourcing and technology transfer. The LDCs may even become net exporters to the innovating country and to other advanced countries.

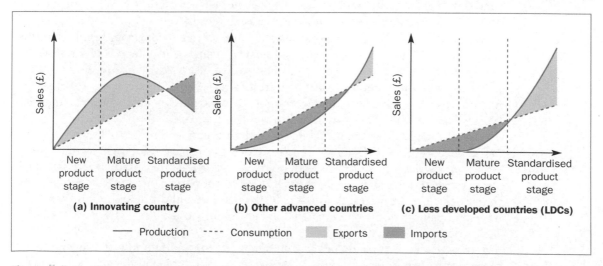

Figure 3.4 The international product life cycle (IPLC) for knowledge-intensive products

Some of the issues previously discussed are raised in Case Study 3.1, which looks at some of the impacts on the US textile and garment industry of moves towards free trade.

CASE 3.1   Impacts of freer trade

The epitaph for America's textile and garment industry was written decades ago. Clothes making is labour intensive, and ten Chinese will work for the price of one American. Everyone knows that sunset industries are best left to developing countries hoping to pull themselves out of poverty; and that only tariffs, quotas and other barriers have sustained America's enormous textile and garments industries, which together employ 1.4 million workers, account for nearly 10% of all American manufacturing, and produce more than $100 billion of goods each year.

Now the end of the free ride is in sight. By 2005 when the trade liberalisation agreements of the World Trade Organisation kick in, most of these barriers will be gone. By then China will also have joined the WTO, bringing its huge textiles and apparel industry to the same open party. An industry that has been protected almost as long as the country has existed (George Washington wore a dark brown domestically made suit to his first inauguration as a 'buy-American' statement) will for the first time be fully exposed to the harsh winds of globalisation.

Each week brings news of another factory closure, the jobs sent to Latin America or Asia where they belong. As go garments, so go textiles – fabric-making tends to 'follow the needle', and over the past few years dozens of American textile makers have moved mills to Mexico to be near to the border-located clothes-making factories, a trend accelerated by the North American Free-Trade Agreement which lowered tariffs.

But despite the defections to Mexico, American textile exports are still rising. And total employment in the garment and textile business is expected to drop just 100,000 or so, to 1.3 million, by 2006, according to industry projections. Trevor Little, a professor at the North Carolina State University college of textiles, reckons that the domestically made share of the American clothing business will fall to about 25%, but stabilise there for the foreseeable future.

Why not zero? Because labour costs do not matter so much in textile making these days. It has become a capital-intensive business, in which a few relatively skilled workers watch over huge mechanical looms. Moreover, America remains the world's second largest grower of cotton (after China), and in many cases it still makes sense to weave near the farms, most of which are in such southern states as North Carolina and Mississippi, rather than to ship cotton abroad.

There is more to garment making, too, than boatloads of cheap T-shirts. At the top end there is high fashion, which is price-insensitive: globalisation has little effect on the designers of Paris, Milan or New York. More broadly there is mainstream style, which changes by the week; speed to market there often counts more than rock-bottom prices. And there is always a demand for high quality, a safe haven for small domestic garment makers from London's Savile Row to New York's Seventh Avenue.

But as strong as these domestic niches may be, they add up to just a few per cent of total sales. To keep a full quarter of the industry at home in the absence of trade barriers will take a lot more. What that will be, reckon the industry bulls, is technology. Those who view the global garment and textile industries through the prism of labour costs see it as an industry dominated by commodities. If the Gap is going to sell a million blue polo shirts year in and year out, Mexico or China is the place to make them. Lead times may be long and the supply chain inflexible, but you can't beat the price.

But today's Internet-driven retail trends go in the opposite direction: mass customisation, 'lots of one', rapid product changes and just-in-time manufacturing. Retailers such as Levi's and Brooks Brothers are already experimenting with the Dell Computer model, where customers order products that are made specially for them. In a black-curtained cube at [TC]^2 the textile industry's research consortium, technicians show how this future might work. A customer walks in, closes the curtains, strips and dons special disposable undergarments that do not distort her body shape. Then she grabs two ski pole-like handles, presses a button and waits as beams of light trace over her body. Within seconds, a computer generates a 3-D body scan with every possible measurement precisely quantified. The scan booth could be in a clothing store or a stand-alone service. [TC]^2 even imagines chains of 'tan and scan' parlours in shopping malls.

A body scan is a handy thing. It could be stored on a personal password-protected Website, with temporary access granted to any e-tailer (e-commerce retailer) a customer chooses. Select a Brooks Brothers shirt online, let the site 'measure' your body scan, and get a robot-tailored custom garment by post a week or two later, cut to fit (unless you have put on weight since your last scan). No more size shortages, or settling for standard or idiosyncratic sizes. And, since the garment is custom-made, it can be custom-designed with any combination of material, colours and styles the manufacturer can handle.

This is an extreme view of the future of the clothing industry, and one still years away. There is only a handful of body-scanning booths in use today (the army is using a few to outfit its recruits), and the technology is still too bulky and expensive for all but a few adventurous retailers. But it hints at a day where America can preserve a relatively healthy textile and clothing business without artificial barriers.

In a recent book,[1] Janice Hammond, a Harvard Business School professor, and three co-authors argue that the trend of 'lean retailing' is already having this effect. 'Although it is true that the American apparel industry could have given up in the early 1990s, with only distribution centres and designers remaining in this country, it did not', they write. Instead, companies moved upstream, using technology to help solve the clothing retailer's biggest problem – stocks of garments that are unsold, and, if they go out of style, unsaleable.

American garment makers increasingly offer electronic ordering, automated distribution centres and inventory-management systems tied into those of their customers. The best manufacturers have learned how to deliver orders at a few days' notice, something their offshore competitors cannot match. It is, the authors claim, 'a triumph of information technology, speed and flexibility over low labour rates'.

What this suggests is a natural division of labour: a trouser maker could assemble average-sized khakis in volume in Mexico, but make special sizes such as narrow waists or long inseams in the United States, offering fast turnaround for retailers and less risk of overstocking. As the technology advances, the balance

▶

between custom and bulk manufacturing may become quite fine. If this comes to pass, the high-tech firms that remain may wonder why they fought so long to keep trade barriers when innovation worked even better.

[1] Abernathy, Frederick, Dunlop, John, Hammond, Janice, and Weil, David (1999) *A Stitch in Time: Lean Retailing and the Transformation of Manufacturing – Lessons from the Apparel and Textile Industries,* Oxford University Press.
Source: Adapted from © *The Economist,* London, 29 April 2002. Reprinted with permission.

Questions

1 What does this case study suggest in terms of the factor endowment theory of international trade?

2 Briefly outline the factors that might permit the USA to retain a sizeable textile and garment industry.

Trade and the world economy

The rapid growth of world trade over the last century reflects, at least in part, the fact that nations have become more interrelated as they have attempted to gain the benefits of freer trade. Table 3.3 compares the *relative growth* of world trade and world output from 1870 to the present day. It shows that the growth rate of world merchandise trade (exports) has exceeded the growth of world output (GDP) in four of the five periods. The only exception to this pattern occurred in the period 1913 to 1950 when two world wars and a major world depression resulted in the widespread adoption of protectionist trade policies. The post-Second World War period (1950–73) saw an unprecedented growth of world trade which far outstripped the growth of world production. While such data cannot prove causation, we can at least say that growth in world trade is consistent with rising economic prosperity.

It may be useful at this point to consider the *type* of trade flow which underlies the recorded growth in world trade.

■ Type of trade flow

A distinction is frequently made between inter- and intra-industry trade.

■ *Inter-industry* trade refers to situations where a country exports products that are fundamentally different in type from those that it imports. The UK exporting com-

Table 3.3 **Growth in world GDP and merchandise trade 1870–2001 (average annual % change)**

	1870–1900	1900–13	1913–50	1950–73	1973–2001
GDP	2.9	2.5	2.0	5.1	2.7
Trade (exports)	3.8	4.3	0.6	8.2	4.2

Source: Adapted from WTO, International Trade Statistics (various) and Annual Reports (various) puter software to Switzerland but importing precision watches from Switzerland would be an example of inter-industry trade between two countries.

■ *Intra-industry trade* refers to situations where a country exports certain items from a given product range while at the same time importing other items from the same product range. The UK exporting certain types of car to Germany but importing other types of car from Germany would be an example of intra-industry trade.

Clearly the likely explanations will be different for each type of trade flow. Factor endowment and other comparative advantage theories are often used in attempts to explain *inter-industry* trade patterns whereas the activities of multinationals, the international product life cycle and various types of competitive advantage theories are more usually used to account for *intra-industry* trade patterns.

Most empirical studies suggest that it is the growth in *intra-industry* trade flows that have made the greatest contribution to the recorded growth in world trade. The experience of Honda provides a useful case study of the role the multinationals often play in promoting such patterns of trade.

CASE 3.2   Intra-industry trade: Honda

Figure 3.5 shows the Honda motorcycle network in Europe together with its outside supply links. Honda is very much a multinational company with a transnationality index of over 50%. In other words, the average of the following ratios exceeds 50% for Honda: foreign assets/total assets, foreign sales/total sales and foreign employment/total employment. Honda began its operations by exporting motorcycles from Japan to Europe, but this was quickly followed by its first European overseas production affiliate in 1962. This affiliate, Honda Benelux NV (Belgium) was set up to provide a 'learning' opportunity before Honda brought its motorcycle and automobile production to Europe. Figure 3.5 shows that, by 2003, Honda's operations had widened significantly, with its affiliates in Germany acting as its main European regional headquarters. Honda Deutschland GmbH coordinates the production and marketing side, while Honda R & D Europe is engaged in research, engineering and designing for all the affiliates in Europe.

Honda's key assembly affiliates are Honda Industriale SpA (Italy), which is wholly owned, and Montessa Honda SA (Spain) which is majority owned (88%). These companies were originally designed to concentrate on the assembly of specific types of motorcycle model appropriate to the different European locations in order to benefit from various economies of scale. At the same time, each assembler exported its own model to the other Honda locations in Europe in order to gain economies in joint production and marketing; in other words, any given model is produced in one location, but a full range of models is offered for sale in all locations. Finally, in the international context, Honda's European models are also exported to subsidiaries in the USA, Brazil and Japan, while its European network imports large and medium-sized motorcycles from its US and Brazilian affiliates.

As far as motorcycle parts are concerned, engines and key parts were initially supplied from Japan. However, in 1985 Honda acquired a 25% stake in Peugeot

▶

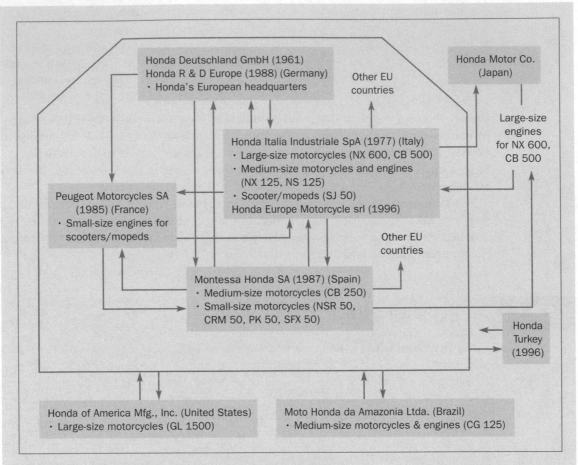

Figure 3.5 Honda: EU motorcycle networks and supply links
Source: Adapted from Healey (2001)

Motorcycles SA and began producing small engines in France for scooters and mopeds. These engines were then supplied to its Italian and Spanish assemblers of scooters and mopeds. Following this, medium-sized engines began to be produced in Honda Italia Industriale SpA, both for its own models and for Montessa Honda, while the latter began producing frames and other parts locally. Large-sized engines were still, however, supplied from Japan.

This study of Honda illustrates the types of motives underlying multinational activity in a globalised economy and the reasons for the consequent growth in intra-industry trade between countries. The traditional technical economies of scale were exploited to reduce average costs as were the more market-based economies from producing and selling within the EU with its 370 million consumers in 2003 rising to around 450 million consumers with the 10 new entrants in 2004. Some non-technical economies of scale have also been exploited with R & D activities concentrated in the UK, Germany and Italy as well as Japan. In addition, the improved communications within the EU and the rise of more sophisticated corporate structures enabled Honda to integrate operations both horizontally, through affiliate specialisation in particular models, and vertically, through specialisation of affiliates in the production of parts. Honda was able to capitalise on its well-known ownership-specific advantages of excellent quality engineering and sound business skills, and to combine this with an intelligent strategy for locating production within the largest consumer market in the world.

The Honda experience helps to illustrate the nature of multinational inter-firm activity within a sophisticated market dominated by product differentiation, which in turn is the basis for much of the growth in the intra-industry trade already noted.

Source: Healey (2004). Reprinted with permission.

Questions

1 How might the Honda case study relate to the various theoretical explanations of the basis for trade?

2 What benefits to Honda might result from integrating its operations both horizontally and vertically?

■ Intra-regional trade

It may be useful to enquire at this stage whether the expanding role of world trade seen in Table 3.3 was accompanied by an increase in the share of that trade conducted on a *regional* basis. It would seem natural that nations would tend to trade more with their immediate neighbours in the first instance, thereby raising the share of world trade occurring between nations within a specific geographical region. This tendency towards *intra-regional* trade can be seen in Table 3.4.

From Table 3.4 it can be seen that the share of intra-regional trade grew most rapidly in Western Europe between 1948 and 2001, while in Asia and North America the share of intra-regional trade also increased but at a slower pace. Intra-regional trade occurring in other regions remained largely unchanged or even declined (i.e. deregionalization of trade), as seen in the early and mid 1990s in Central and Eastern Europe, though some renewed growth in intra-regional trade

Table 3.4 Share of intra-regional trade in total trade 1929–2001 (% of each region's total trade in goods occurring between nations located in that region)

	1928	1938	1948	1968	1979	1996	2001
Western Europe	50.7	48.8	41.8	63.0	66.2	68.3	67.5
Central/Eastern Europe/USSR	19.0	13.2	46.4	63.5	54.0	18.7	26.6
North America	25.0	22.4	27.1	36.8	29.9	36.0	39.5
Latin America	11.1	17.7	17.7	18.7	20.2	21.2	17.0
Asia	45.5	66.4	38.9	36.6	41.0	51.9	48.2
Africa	10.3	8.9	8.4	9.1	5.6	9.2	7.8
Middle East	5.0	3.6	20.3	8.7	6.4	7.4	7.6

Source: WTO, Annual Reports (various)

has occurred since 1996. It is also clear from Table 3.4 that intra-regional trading is not a new phenomenon and that geographically adjacent nations in many areas of the world have been trading with each other for many years.

In Chapter 1 we have already noted the growth in preferential terms given to members of regional trading blocs (via regional trading arrangements – RTAs) which has, of course, been a key factor in the growth of intra-regional trade. Chapter 4 will consider attempts by the World Trade Organisation (WTO) to remove some of the discriminatory effects (i.e. on non-members) of such regional arrangements.

Barriers to trade

Those involved in international business face a number of methods by which individual countries or regional trading blocs (*see* p. 88) seek to restrict the level of imports into the home market. The World Trade Organisation (WTO) plays an important role in seeking to regulate and remove many of these impediments to trade. While aspects of that role are considered in this chapter, a more detailed analysis of the WTO occurs in Chapter 4.

■ Tariff

A *tariff* is, in effect, a tax levied on imported goods, usually with the intention of raising the price of imports and thereby discouraging their purchase. Additionally, it is a source of revenue for the government. Tariffs can be of two types: *lump sum* (or *specific*) with the tariff a fixed amount per unit; *ad valorem* (or *percentage*) with the tariff a variable amount per unit. There is a general presumption that tariff barriers will discourage trade and reduce economic welfare. Box 3.2 considers the possible impacts of a tariff in rather more detail.

Box 3.2 **Impacts of a tariff**

To examine the effect of a tariff, it helps simplify Figure 3.6 if we assume a perfectly elastic world supply of the good S_W at the going world price P_W which implies that any amount of the good can be imported into the UK without there being a change in the world price. In the absence of a tariff, the domestic price would be set by the world price, P_W in Figure 3.6. At this price domestic demand D_D will be $0Q_2$, though domestic supply S_D will only be $0Q_1$. The excess demand, $Q_2 - Q_1$, will be satisfied by importing the good.

If the government now decides to restrict the level of import penetration, it could impose a tariff of, say, $P_W - P'_W$. A tariff always shifts a supply curve vertically upwards by the amount of the tariff, so that in this case the world supply curve shifts vertically upwards from S_W to S'_W. This would raise the domestic price to P'_W which is above the world price P_W. This higher price will reduce the domestic demand for the good to $0Q_4$ while simultaneously encouraging domestic supply to expand from $0Q_1$ to $0Q_3$ and the government will gain tax revenue from the remaining imports which must now pay an import duty (area 3). All these are arguably 'positive' outcomes for governments. However, in terms of resource allocation, the impact of the tariff may be shown to be less favourable. Imports will be reduced from

Box 3.2	Continued

$Q_2 - Q_1$ before the tariff to $Q_4 - Q_3$ after the tariff. Domestic consumer surplus will decline as a result of the tariff by the area 1 + 2 + 3 + 4, though domestic producer surplus will rise by area 1, and the government will gain tax revenue of $P'_W - P_W \times Q_4 - Q_3$ (i.e. area 3). These gains would be inadequate, however, to compensate consumers for their loss in welfare, yielding a net welfare loss of area 2 + 4 as a result of imposing a tariff.

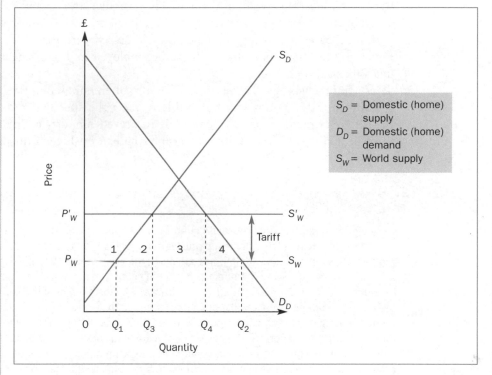

S_D = Domestic (home) supply
D_D = Domestic (home) demand
S_W = World supply

Figure 3.6 **Effects of a tariff**

Non-tariff barriers

In recent years there has also been a considerable increase in trade that is subject to *non-tariff* barriers. The main types of non-tariff barrier in use include the following:

- *Quotas*. A quota is a limit applied to the number of units (or the monetary value) of an imported good that may be sold in a country in a given period.
- *Voluntary export restraints* (VERs). These are arrangements by which an individual exporter or group of exporters agrees with an importing country to limit the quantity of a specific product to be sold to a particular market over a given period of time. VERs are in effect, quotas. An example of a VER involved the import of cars from Japan into the EU. Until phased out in 2000, there was an understanding that Japanese producers would limit their sales into the UK, France, Spain, Italy and Portugal to a maximum of 1.1 million units in total (the figure excluded output from Japanese plants based in the EU).

- *Subsidies.* The forms of protection we have described so far have all been designed to restrict the volume of imports directly. An alternative policy is to provide a subsidy to domestic producers so as to improve their competitiveness in both the home and world markets. The effect of subsidies is considered in more detail in Box 3.3.
- *Exchange controls.* A system of *exchange controls* was in force in the UK from the outbreak of the Second World War until 1979 when, in order to allow the free flow of capital, they were abolished. They enabled the government to limit the availability of foreign currencies and so curtail excessive imports; for instance, holding a foreign-currency bank account required permission from the Bank of England. Exchange controls could also be employed to discourage speculation and investment abroad.
- *Safety and technological standards.* These are often imposed in the knowledge that certain imported goods will be unable to meet the specified requirements. The British government used such standards to prevent imports of French turkey and ultra-heat-treated (UHT) milk. Ostensibly the ban on French turkeys was to pre-

---

Box 3.3 Impacts of a subsidy

Once again, we assume that the world supply curve is perfectly elastic at P_W. Under conditions of free trade, the domestic price is set by the world price at P_W. Domestic production is initially $0Q_1$ with imports satisfying the excess level of domestic demand which amounts to $Q_2 - Q_1$. The effect of a general subsidy to an industry would be to shift the supply curve of domestic producers downwards (by the amount of the subsidy) and to the right. The domestic price will remain unchanged at the world price P_W but domestic production will rise to $0Q_3$ with imports reduced to $Q_2 - Q_3$. If, however, the subsidy is provided solely for exporters, the impact on the domestic market could be quite different. The incentive to export may encourage more domestic production to be switched from the home market to the overseas markets, which in turn could result in an increased volume of imports to satisfy the unchanged level of domestic demand.

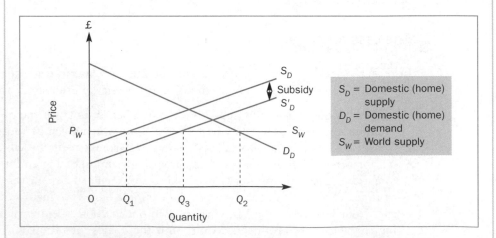

Figure 3.7 **Effects of a subsidy**

vent 'Newcastle disease', a form of fowl pest found in Europe, from reaching the UK. The European Court ruled, however, that the ban was merely an excuse to prevent the free flow of imports.

- *Time-consuming formalities*. During the 1990s the EU alleged that 'excessive invoicing requirements' required by US importing authorities had hampered exports from member countries to the USA. These problems abound in many parts of the world and often involve considerable administrative and capital costs for many companies. A similar problem in China can lead to a two or three weeks' delay.
- *Public-sector contracts*. Government often give preference to domestic firms in the issuing of public contracts, despite EU directives requiring member governments to advertise such contracts. A number of Australian states have continued to give price preferences of up to 20% to domestic bidders for public contracts in the latter half of the 1990s. Public contracts are actually placed outside the country of origin in only 1% of cases.
- *Labour standards*. This bears some resemblance to the point made above concerning safety and technological standards but is rather more controversial. Does the enforcement of minimum labour standards represent a source of support for the poorest workers in the developing world or is it simply a covert form of protection? Low-cost producers, not surprisingly, believe the latter to be the case. The WTO (*see* Chapter 4) is at present reluctant to go down this route but has come under increasing pressure from governments in the industrialised world to take action on what is perceived as 'unfair' competition by countries which have few, if any, effective minimum labour standards.

Protectionist policies

In this section we briefly review the case for and against protectionist policies. Of course our earlier theoretical arguments supporting free trade (pp. 66–70) are themselves arguments against protectionist policies.

The case for protection

Protectionist measures may be applied on a selective or more widespread basis, with most of the measures currently in force falling into the first category. A number of arguments have been used to justify the application of both tariff and non-tariff barriers on a selective basis:

1 to prevent dumping;
2 to protect infant industries;
3 to protect strategically important industries;
4 to maintain employment by preventing the rapid contraction of labour-intensive industries.

Preventing dumping

Dumping occurs where a good is sold in an overseas market at a price below the real cost of production. We note in Chapter 4 that under Article 6, the WTO allows retaliatory sanctions to be applied if it can be shown that the dumping materially affected the domestic industry. As well as using the WTO, countries within the EU can refer cases of alleged dumping for investigation by the European Commission. The Commission is then able to recommend the appropriate course of action, which may range from 'no action' where dumping is found not to have taken place, to either obtaining an 'undertaking' of no further dumping, or imposing a tariff.

The prevalence of dumping is indicated by a significant increase in the number of anti-dumping cases initiated by the WTO during the 1990s, as Table 3.5 illustrates, with 2001 seeing a record number in a single year. The US has consistently been one of the main initiators of anti-dumping investigations and has had such success in securing WTO approval for retaliatory tariffs that the current official figures for average US tariffs on manufactured imports of 6% rises to around 23% when these additional retaliatory tariffs are included. Canada, India and the European Union have also initiated numerous actions. The main targets of anti-dumping probes have been the European Union, China, Chinese Taipai and India. The sectors where anti-dumping measures are most widely applied include chemical products and base metals, in particular steel, which is currently a battleground between the US and the EU. The US steel industry has alleged that financial support from European governments has given the EU steel industry an unfair advantage over US producers. In response the US government imposed tariffs of up to 30 per cent on selected steel products in March 2002.

Protecting infant industries

The use of protection in order to *establish new industries* is widely accepted, particularly in the case of developing countries. Article 18 of the WTO explicitly allows such protection. An infant industry is likely to have a relatively high-cost structure in the short run, and in the absence of protective measures may find it difficult to compete with the established overseas industries already benefiting from scale economies. The EU has used this argument to justify protection of its developing high-technological industries.

Protecting strategically important industries

The protection of industries for *strategic reasons* is widely practised both in the UK and the EU, and is not necessarily contrary to the WTO rules (Article 2). The protection of the UK steel industry has in the past been justified on this basis, and the EU has used a similar argument to protect agricultural production throughout the

Table 3.5 **Anti-dumping: cases initiated**

1987	1989	1991	1993	1995	1997	1999	2001
120	96	228	299	156	233	328	348

Source: WTO, Annual Reports (various)

Community under the guise of the CAP. In the Uruguay round of the then GATT (now WTO) the developing countries used this argument in seeking to resist calls for the liberalisation of trade in their service sectors. This has been one of the few sectors recording strong growth in recent years and is still a highly 'regulated' sector in most countries.

Maintaining levels of employment

There is a small but growing body of opinion that advocates a degree of protection to maintain levels of employment and that questions the benefits to be derived from international trade and is hostile to the drive by the WTO to liberalise trade. This movement, which is quite diverse, comprises environmentalists, trade unions, charities, third-world activists, among many others, and has manifested itself in WTO/IMF demonstrations in Seattle, Prague and many other locations in recent years. Although not necessarily rejecting the theoretical benefits of free trade, opponents of the WTO contend that the gains are largely expropriated by big business, leaving both workers and developing nations no better off and in many cases actually worse off. Groups such as Global Trade Watch suggest that the WTO has little regard for democracy or for environmental standards and almost always acts against the public interest.

Case against protectionism

A number of arguments are often advanced as reasons for avoiding protectionist policies.

Retaliation

A major drawback to protectionist measures is the prospect of retaliation. The consequences of retaliation could be especially serious for the UK, given the importance of trade within its economy. In 2002 UK exports of goods and services totalled 34% of GDP, which is higher than most of its major competitors (e.g. France 28%, Japan 11%, USA 12%).

Misallocation of resources

Protectionism can erode some of the benefits of free trade. For instance, Box 3.2 showed that a tariff raises domestic supply at the expense of imports. If the domestic producers cannot make such products as cheaply as overseas producers, then one could argue that encouraging high-cost domestic production is a misallocation of international resources.

A related criticism also suggests that protectionism leads to resource misallocation on an international scale, but this time concerns the multinational. Multinationals are the fastest-growing type of business unit in the Western economies, and they are increasingly adopting strategies which locate particular stages of the production process in (to them) appropriate parts of the world. Protectionism may disrupt the flow of goods from one stage of the production process to another, and in this sense inhibit global specialisation.

Regional trading arrangements

As we have noted above, the resumption of rapid growth in world trade after the Second World War was tied up with the desire for the resumption of *multilateral trade* under the auspices of the GATT (now WTO). However, this movement towards free trade was accompanied by a parallel movement towards the formation of *regional trading blocs* centred on the EU, North and South America and East Asia. We noted in Table 3.4 that intra-regional trading is not a new phenomenon but one which has been active for at least a century or more. However, there is evidence to suggest that the nations of a given region have begun to create more formal and comprehensive trading and economic links with each other than was previously the case.

There are four broad types of regional trading arrangements (RTAs):

■ *free trade areas*, where member countries reduce or abolish restrictions on trade between each other while maintaining their individual protectionist measures against non-members;
■ *customs unions*, where, as well as liberalising trade among members, a common external tariff is established to protect the group from imports from any non-members;
■ *common markets*, where the customs union is extended to include the free movement of factors of production as well as products within the designated area;
■ *economic unions*, where national economic policies are also harmonised within the common market.

Table 3.6 provides examples of different types of regional trading arrangements across the globe, with the associated percentage of exports to countries within each RTA.

■ The European Union (EU) was founded in January 1958 as a *common market* with six member nations. By 2003 the EU included 15 nations with a combined population of over 370 million and accounted for some 42% of world trade, expanding to 25 nations in 2004 with a population of around 490 million. From Table 3.6 we can see that around 62% of EU exports go to other member countries. This group originated as a *common* market, the majority of members effectively progressing into a type of *economic union* with the Maastricht Treaty of 1992 and the advent of the euro and its related financial arrangements on 1 January 1999.

Table 3.6 **Regional trading arrangements (RTAs): intra-regional export shares (%)**

	1990	1995	2001
EU	64.9	64.0	61.9
NAFTA	42.6	46.1	55.5
MERCOSUR	8.9	20.5	17.3
APEC	67.5	73.1	71.8
ANDEAN PACT	4.2	12.2	11.2
CEFTA	–	14.5	12.4

- In August 1993 the North American Free Trade Agreement (NAFTA) was signed between the US, Canada and Mexico, having grown out of an earlier Canadian–US Free Trade Agreement (CUFTA). NAFTA, as the name implies is a *free trade area* with around 56% of NAFTA exports going to member countries, covering a population of 372 million and accounting for 31% of world output and 17% of world trade.
- MERCOSUR was established in South America in 1991, evolving out of the Latin American Free Trade Area, with the four initial members being Argentina, Brazil, Paraguay and Uruguay. It developed into a partial *customs union* in 1995 when it imposed a common external tariff covering 85% of total products imported.
- In Asia and the Pacific, the rather 'loose' Association of South-East Asian Nations (ASEAN) with a population of 300 million was formed in August 1967. In 1991 they agreed to form an ASEAN Free Trade Area (AFTA) by the year 2003. A Common External Preference Tariff (CEPT) came into force in 1994 as a formal tariff-cutting mechanism for achieving *free trade* in all goods except agricultural products, natural resources and services. In November 1994, the goal of an open trade and investment area was agreed in principle by members of the Asia-Pacific Economic Cooperation Forum (APEC) which includes the members of ASEAN, ANZCERTA (Australia and New Zealand) and NAFTA as well as China, Japan, Korea, Hong Kong, Taiwan, and Papua New Guinea. It is hoped that this arrangement may be realised by 2010 for developed countries and by 2020 for developing countries. This group would account for 38% of the world's population (2.1 billion) and 43% of the world trade in goods.
- On the western side of Latin America, a *free trade area* has been established by Venezuela, Columbia, Ecuador, Peru and Bolivia (ANDEAN PACT).
- In Central and Eastern Europe, a *free trade area* has been established by Poland, the Czech Republic, Slovakia, Hungary, Slovenia, Romania and Bulgaria (CEFTA).

From the above examples it is possible to see that trading blocs have adopted various types of arrangements depending on their specific circumstances. Table 3.6 shows the share of intra-regional exports of each specific bloc as a percentage of the total exports of that bloc. For example, in 2001 the exports of EU members to each other comprised some 61.9% of total EU exports.

Three features have characterised post-war regional integration:

1 Post-war regional integration has been primarily centred in Western Europe. Out of 184 agreements notified to GATT/WTO between 1948 and 2002, more than half involved Western European countries, with most of the post-1990 agreements with the EU involving the Central and Eastern European countries.
2 Only a small number of post-war regional agreements have been concluded by developing countries. This is mainly due to continuing competition between these countries involving trade in similar products (e.g. primary products) together with the difficulty of achieving the political stability in some developing countries, which is so vital to trade.
3 The *type* of economic integration between the parties to agreements has varied quite significantly. Most of the notifications made to GATT/WTO have involved free trade areas, with the number of customs unions agreement being much smaller.

In recent years many of these free trade areas have taken the form of *bilateral trade treaties*, often involving the USA (see p. 113).

Those who favour the regional approach argue that the setting up of trading blocs can enable individual countries to purchase products at lower prices because tariff walls between the member countries have been removed; this is the *trade creation effect*. They also argue that regional trading arrangements help to harmonise tax policies and product standards, while also helping to reduce political conflicts. Others argue that where the world is already organised into trading blocs, then negotiations in favour of free trade are more likely to be successful between these large and influential trading blocs than between a large number of individual countries with little power to bargain successfully for tariff reductions.

On the other hand, the critics of regionalism warn that regional trading blocs have, historically, tended to be inward looking, as in the 1930s when discriminatory trade blocs were formed to impose tariffs on non-members. Some also argue that member countries may suffer from being inside a regional bloc because they then have to buy products from within the bloc, when cheaper sources are often available from outside; i.e. the *trade diversion effect*. Further, it is argued that regionalism threatens to erode support for multilateralism in that business groups within a regional bloc will find it easier to obtain protectionist (trade diversionary) deals via preferential pacts than they would in the world of non-discriminatory trade practices favoured by the GATT/WTO. Finally, it is argued that regionalism will move the world away from free trade due to the increasing tendency for members of a regional group to resort to the use of *non-tariff barriers* (VERs, anti-dumping duties, etc.) when experiencing a surge of imports from other countries inside the group. Such devices can then easily be used by individual countries against non-members from other regional groups.

Government policies and international business

Government policies can influence international business in a variety of ways, some of which have already been considered in Chapter 2. For example, change in fiscal policies (involving government spending/taxation) or monetary policies (involving money supply/interest rates) will influence the macroeconomic environment in which domestic and international businesses operate. However, sometimes government policies can impact upon international business *indirectly*; for example, changes in interest rates may influence the price of currencies on the foreign exchange markets (*see* Chapter 4), which in turn may exert a strong influence on the prospects for exporting and importing products across national boundaries. It is to this issue that we first turn our attention.

■ Exchange rates

We note in Chapter 4 that few governments can now influence their exchange rates directly, via unilateral action. More usually they can only influence such rates indirectly whether intentionally or unintentionally. For example, high interest rates used as part of an anti-inflationary monetary policy may make a country's currency relatively attractive on foreign exchange markets, the extra demand then raises the price of that country's currency.

A *rise* in, say, the UK sterling exchange rate makes UK exports dearer abroad in terms of the foreign currency, and UK imports cheaper at home in terms of the domestic currency. Suppose, for example, sterling *appreciates* against the euro from £1 = €1.60 to £1 = €1.70. An item priced at £1,000 in the UK would have a euro-zone equivalent price of €1,600 prior to the sterling appreciation but €1,700 after that appreciation. Not only will exports be dearer abroad but imports will be cheaper at home. An item priced at €1,600 in the euro-zone would have a sterling equivalent price of £1,000 prior to the sterling appreciation but £941.02 after that appreciation.

The impact of higher export prices and lower import prices on business turnover (and the balance of payments) will depend to some extent on *price elasticities of demand* in the export and import markets respectively.

- If *price elasticity of demand for UK exports is relatively elastic* (greater than one), then any rise in euro-zone prices will reduce total expenditure in euros on those items. Since each euro is now worth less in sterling, this fall in the euro value of UK exports will mean a still more substantial fall in sterling turnover for UK exporters.
- If *price elasticity of demand for UK imports is relatively elastic* (greater than one), then any fall in sterling prices will raise total expenditure in sterling on those items. This is likely to imply a loss of turnover and market share from UK domestic producers to euro-zone producers.

Clearly the more elastic the respective price elasticities of demand for UK exports and UK imports, the greater the disadvantage for businesses located in the UK in trading with the euro-zone after sterling appreciates against the euro, and the greater the advantage for businesses located in the euro-zone in trading with the UK.

pause for thought 5 Can you work through the previous analysis if sterling *depreciates* against the euro? (For example, £1 is now worth €1.50 instead of €1.60.)

Import protection/export support

We have already seen how a variety of *protective trade barriers* (such as tariffs and quotas) can be used to discourage imports into a country, whether imposed unilaterally by a country or collectively as part of a regional trading bloc. An example of the latter would be the Common External Tariff imposed on industrial imports into the EU. Domestic producers can also be helped vis-à-vis overseas producers by a variety of support policies directed towards exporters.

The Common Agricultural Policy (CAP) of the EU provides a useful illustration of government-directed policies involving import protection/export support which exert a strong influence on the operations of farms and agri-businesses, both inside and outside the EU. Box 3.4 considers the operation of the CAP in rather more detail. Other operational and policy aspects of the EU are considered in some detail at the end of this chapter (pp. 96–103).

Box 3.4 Impacts of EU policies on farms and agri-businesses

The formal title for the executive body of the CAP is the European Agricultural Guarantee and Guidance Fund (EAGGF), often known by its French translation of 'Fonds Européen d'Orientation et de Garantie-Agricole' (FEOGA). As its name implies, one of its key roles is in operating the 'guarantee system' for EU farm incomes.

Different agricultural products are dealt with in slightly different ways, but the basis of the system is the establishment of a 'target price' for each product (Figure 3.8(a)). The target price is not set with reference to world prices, but is based upon the price which producers need to cover costs, including a profit mark-up, in the highest-cost area of production in the EU. The EU then sets an 'intervention' or 'guaranteed' price for the product in that area, about 7–10% below the target price. Should the price be in danger of falling below this level, the Commission intervenes to buy up production to keep the price at or above the 'guaranteed' level. The Commission then sets separate target and intervention prices for that product in each area of the Community, related broadly to production costs in that area.

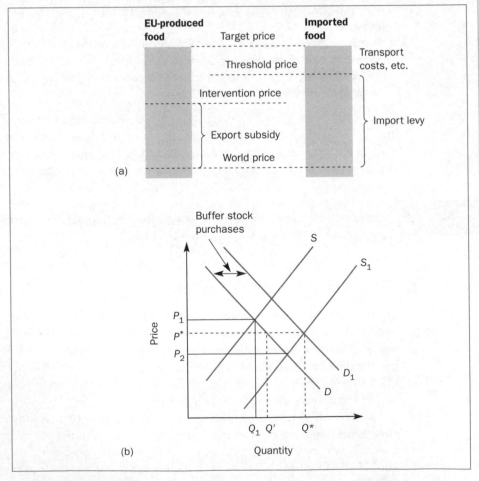

Figure 3.8 (a) CAP system: world price below target price and (b) Guarantee system: maintaining the intervention price ($P*$)

Box 3.4	Continued

As long as the market price in a given area (there are eleven such areas in the UK) is above the intervention price, the producer will sell his produce at prevailing market prices. In effect the intervention price sets a 'floor' below which market price will not be permitted to fall and is therefore the guaranteed minimum price to producers.

In Figure 3.8(b) an increase in supply of agricultural products to S_1 would, if no action were taken, lower the market price from P_1 to P_2 below the intervention or guaranteed price, P^*. At P^* demand is Q' but supply is Q^*. To keep the price at P^*, the EAGGF will buy up the excess $Q^* - Q'$. In terms of Figure 3.8(b), the demand curve is artificially increased to D_1 by the EAGGF purchase.

If this system of guaranteed minimum prices is to work, EU farmers must be protected from low-priced imports from overseas. To this end, levies or tariffs are imposed on imports of agricultural products. If in Figure 3.8(b) the price of imported food were higher than the EU target price then, of course, there would be no need for an import tariff. If, however, the import price is below this, say at the 'world price' in Figure 3.8(a), then an appropriate tariff must be calculated. This need not quite cover the difference between 'target' and 'world' price, since the importer still has to pay transport costs within the EU to get the food to market. The tariff must therefore be large enough to raise the import price at the EU frontier to the target price minus transport costs, i.e. 'threshold price'. This calculation takes place in the highest-cost area of production in the EU, so that the import tariff set will more than protect EU producers in areas with lower target prices (i.e. lower-cost areas).

Should an EU producer wish to export an agricultural product, an export subsidy will be paid to bring his receipts up to the intervention price (*see* Figure 3.8(a)), i.e. the minimum price he would receive in the home market. Problems involving this form of subsidy of oil-seed exports have been a major threat to dealings between the EU and the USA (*see* Chapter 4), with the latter alleging a breach of WTO rules. The system outlined above does not apply to all agricultural products in the EU. About a quarter of these products are covered by different direct subsidy systems, e.g. olive oil and tobacco, and some products such as potatoes, agricultural alcohol, and honey are not covered by EU regulation at all.

Reforms of the CAP over the past decade or so have modified this system which has proved an expensive method of supporting farm incomes. For example, Maximum Guaranteed Quantities (MGQs) have now been set for most agricultural products. If the MGQ is exceeded, the intervention price is cut by 30% in the following year. Further CAP reforms were also agreed in 2003 to come into effect from 2007 onwards. For example 'compulsory modulation' is to be introduced whereby payments directly related to agricultural production are to be progressively replaced by payments for a wide range of environmental protection activities by EU farmers.

Some further aspects of the EU are considered at the end of this chapter.

■ Taxation policies

The ability of 'footloose' multinational enterprises to take advantage of tax discrepancies between countries or regions is well known, as in the examples of 'transfer pricing' (*see* p. 356). Case Study 3.3 shows how proposed tax changes on multinationals in the UK Budget of March 2000 threatened to disrupt patterns of foreign direct investment and the related *intra-industry trade* flows, which we have already noted as making a major contribution to the growth of international trade.

CASE 3.3 CBI battle lines are drawn for tax showdown

The government faces an assault on its measures against multinationals. The dispute between industry and the government over the Budget clampdown on the taxation of multinationals will turn into a showdown next week. On Tuesday the Confederation of British Industry (CBI) will launch a campaign to sabotage the measures, which the government has refused to withdraw despite a month-long attack by business. The CBI assault shows how the issue has made a mockery of talk of a consensual approach between the private sector and the government.

The battle has revealed divisions over the definition of tax avoidance and the calculation of the impact of the changes, with both sides employing questionable statistics to support their cases. The row relates to the strategy used by multinationals to minimise the extra tax paid on profits repatriated from countries with low corporation tax rates. If these profits were remitted directly, the Inland Revenue would impose a levy to bring the effective tax charge up to the British rate of 30%. Companies avoid this by channelling profits through mixer companies, overseas subsidiaries that offset earnings from low-tax countries against those from high-tax regimes.

The Budget proposals will end the practice, which has been used extensively since the abolition of foreign exchange controls in 1979. The government says mixers are a form of tax avoidance that should be abolished as part of a crackdown on artificial tax regimes.

The European Union and the Organisation for Economic Co-operation and Development are both taking action against 'harmful' tax practices. Last year the government ended the practice of designer taxation, whereby havens such as the Channel Islands tailored rates to help British companies avoid tax.

Business says the use of mixers is not comparable to unacceptable regimes such as designer taxation, adding that the Budget changes will cost companies much more annually than the £300 million estimated by the government. Pricewaterhouse Coopers (PWC), the largest accountancy firm, says mixers are used by most of Britain's biggest companies: a survey of 24 of its largest clients suggested that the Budget changes would add £1.9 billion to their tax bills. Companies say the abolition of mixers would cause them to invest more of their profits overseas or even relocate their headquarters abroad.

One reason for the discrepancy in the effects estimated by the government and the private sector is that the two are starting from different points. While official figures are based on tax returns for 1998–99, accountants are looking at their clients' future plans. This means the accountants' forecast will inevitably be higher, reflecting rising profits and the accumulation of overseas assets through mergers and acquisitions. But these trends go only part way to describing the disagreement between two numbers that reflect subjective judgements.

Another aspect is the government's decision to factor in assumptions about how companies will change their behaviour once the rules have altered. The government is in effect guessing at possible strategies without knowing whether these are feasible or desirable from a business point of view.

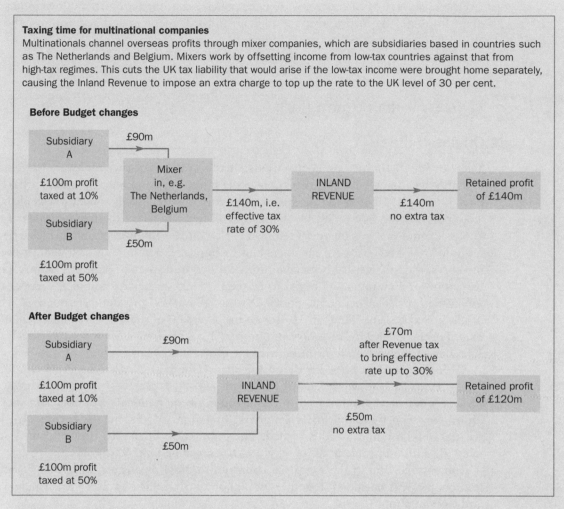

Taxing time for multinational companies
Multinationals channel overseas profits through mixer companies, which are subsidiaries based in countries such as The Netherlands and Belgium. Mixers work by offsetting income from low-tax countries against that from high-tax regimes. This cuts the UK tax liability that would arise if the low-tax income were brought home separately, causing the Inland Revenue to impose an extra charge to top up the rate to the UK level of 30 per cent.

Figure 3.9 **Effects of Budget changes**

Another debatable practice is the use by some companies of estimates of the extra tax loss they would sustain if they remitted all their overseas profits to Britain. This is an overstatement because many companies retain profits overseas for investment purposes.

Business people are reluctant to predict a compromise as long as the government holds its position that mixers are nothing more than vehicles for tax avoidance.

Source: Michael Peel, *Financial Times*, 29 April 2000, p. 4.

Questions

1 Consider the costs and benefits to the UK of allowing 'mixer' practices to continue.

2 Why do estimates of the impacts of these practices vary so widely?

Of course, a host of other government policies can impact on trade flows other than those already mentioned, e.g. policies towards mergers and acquisitions, the granting of patents, establishing industrial 'clusters', etc. We return to some of these in later parts of the book (Chapters 5–7, 8, 11–12).

The European Union (EU)

■ Origins of the EU

The European Union has been in existence in various forms for over 40 years, arguably beginning with the formation of the European Economic Community (EEC) on 1 January 1958 after the signing of the Treaty of Rome. This sought to establish a 'common market' (*see* p. 88) by eliminating all restrictions on the free movements of goods, capital and persons between member countries. By dismantling tariff barriers on industrial trade between members and by imposing a common tariff against non-members, the EEC was to become a protected free-trade area or 'customs union'. The formation of a customs union was to be the first step in the creation of an 'economic union' with national economic policies harmonised across the member countries. The original 'Six' became 'Nine' in 1973 with the accession of the UK, Eire and Denmark, and 'Ten' in 1981 with the entry of Greece. The accession of Spain and Portugal on 1 January 1986 increased the number of member countries to twelve.

With the signing of the Treaty on European Union at Maastricht (*see below*) on 7 February 1992, the now renamed EU went beyond a 'merely' economic institution (if it ever was such) and moved in the direction of the political, economic and social union foreseen by many of its founders. In January 1995 the 12 became 15, as Austria, Finland and Sweden joined. The population of the EU now encompasses over 382 million people in 2002 with a GDP exceeding ECU 9 trillion.

The enlargement of the EU to 25 countries in 2004 means that a further 75 million people will be added, together with another 30 million in 2007 when Bulgaria and Romania join.

Single European Act (SEA)

The Single European Act came into force in July 1987. It constituted a major development of the Community and was based on a White Paper, 'Completing the Common Market', which had been presented by the Commission to the Milan meeting of the European Council in June 1985. It represented the first time that the original Treaty of Rome had been amended. The Act looked towards creating a single European economy by 1993. The objective was not simply to create an internal market by removing frontier controls but to remove all barriers to the movement of goods, people and capital. Achieving a single European market has meant, among other things, work on standards, procurement, qualifications, banking, capital movements and exchange regulations, tax 'approximation', communication standards and transport.

Since 1987 over 600 separate new directives have been created, ranging from common hygiene rules for meat and regulations on the wholesaling, labelling and advertising of medicines, to capital adequacy rules for investment and credit institutions and a common licensing system for road haulage. The SEA also had political ramifications in that it formalised the use of qualified majorities for taking decisions in the Council of Ministers and gave the elected European Parliament greater legislative powers.

Maastricht Treaty

The Treaty on European Union, which was signed at Maastricht on 7 February 1992, represents one of the most fundamental changes to have occurred in the EU since its foundation. Although, legally speaking, merely an extension and amendment to the Treaty of Rome, Maastricht represents a major step for the member states. For the first time many of the political and social imperatives of the Community have been explicitly agreed and delineated. Maastricht takes the EU beyond a 'merely' economic institution and takes it towards the full potential, economic and social union foreseen by many of its founders. Some of its major objectives are as follows:

1 to create economic and social progress through an 'area without internal frontiers' and through economic and monetary union (EMU);
2 to develop a common foreign, security and defence policy which 'might lead to common defence';
3 to introduce a 'citizenship of the Union'.

We look more carefully at the *single currency*, seen as a key element of EMU, later in this chapter (*see* p. 100).

■ Characteristics of the EU

Country-specific data

Table 3.7 presents some of the important characteristics of the 15 member countries. It shows how diverse they are in terms of population, industrial structure, standard of living, unemployment level and inflation rate. In terms of population the UK is the third largest member, with a smaller proportion engaged in agriculture than in other EU countries and the third largest in services. In overall wealth, however, the UK drops down the rankings. It has the second largest GDP in absolute terms, but comes sixth in terms of GDP per capita, some 15% above the EU average.

■ EU enlargement

In October 2002, the EU Commission approved the most ambitious expansion plans in its history when ten countries were told that they had met the 'Copenhagen criteria' for membership. The criteria include such aspects as institutional stability, democracy, functioning market economies, and adherence to the aims of political, economic and monetary union. These ten countries were deemed to be ready to join the EU in 2004 while a further two – Bulgaria and Romania would be due for membership in 2007. Table 3.8 provides some economic data on these countries together with their projected dates of accession.

There have been many arguments regarding the strengths and weaknesses of enlargement. A key academic study by the Centre for Policy Research estimated that the enlargement would bring an economic gain of 10 billion euros (£7 billion) for the

Table 3.7 **The EU 15 in the year 2002: some comparative statistics**

Member country	Economically active population						Share of EU				
	Population (million)	Agriculture (%)	Industry (%)	Services (%)	GDP € (bn)	GDP per capita € (000s)	GDP (%)	Population (%)	Index of GDP per capita	Unemploy- ment (%) 2000	Inflation (%) 2000
Austria	8.2	7.2	33.2	59.6	216.4	26.4	2.4	2.2	111.2	4.3	1.4
Belgium	10.3	2.5	6.1	71.4	261.4	25.4	2.9	2.7	106.0	6.8	1.8
Denmark	5.4	4.0	27.0	69.0	186.6	34.5	2.0	1.4	145.5	4.2	2.3
Finland	5.2	7.1	27.6	65.3	139.5	26.8	1.5	1.4	112.4	9.1	2.0
France	61.2	4.6	25.9	69.5	1,504.0	24.6	16.5	15.8	103.0	8.8	1.6
Germany	82.4	3.3	37.5	59.2	2,107.0	25.6	23.2	21.8	107.2	8.1	1.3
Greece	11.0	20.4	23.2	56.4	139.9	12.7	1.5	2.8	53.5	9.9	3.1
Ireland	3.9	10.7	27.2	61.1	124.8	32.0	1.4	1.0	133.3	4.4	4.7
Italy	58.0	7.0	32.1	60.9	1,252.0	21.6	13.7	15.3	90.5	8.9	2.7
Luxembourg	0.4	2.8	30.7	66.5	21.7	54.3	0.2	0.1	203.6	2.2	1.9
The Netherlands	16.2	3.9	22.4	73.7	446.3	27.5	4.9	4.2	116.0	3.1	3.4
Portugal	10.3	12.2	31.4	56.4	129.7	12.5	1.4	2.6	52.7	4.6	3.5
Spain	40.5	8.7	29.7	61.6	689.8	17.0	7.6	10.5	71.3	11.4	3.6
Sweden	8.9	2.9	26.1	71.0	246.9	27.7	2.7	2.4	116.0	4.9	2.0
UK	60.2	2.0	26.4	71.0	1,645.0	27.3	18.1	15.8	114.8	5.0	0.9
Total EU	**382.1**	**3.9**	**28.2**	**67.9**	**9,111.0**	**23.8**	**100.0**	**100.0**	**100.0**	**7.6**	**1.9**

Notes: 'Total EU' percentages for agriculture, industry and services are weighted averages.
Source: Adapted from European Commission (2003) European Economy, No. 3

Table 3.8 **EU enlargement 2004–07**

	Population (m)	GDP per capita (% of EU average)	General government budget (% of GDP)	Unemployment rate (%)	Inflation (%)
Bulgaria (2007)	7.9	28	1.7	19.9	7.4
Cyprus (2004)	0.8	80	−3.0	4.0	2.0
Czech Rep. (2004)	10.2	57	−5.5	8.0	4.5
Estonia (2004)	1.4	42	−0.4	12.4	5.6
Hungary (2004)	10.2	51	−4.1	5.7	9.1
Latvia (2004)	2.4	33	−1.6	13.1	2.5
Lithuania (2004)	3.5	38	−1.9	16.5	1.3
Malta (2004)	0.4	55	−7.0	6.5	2.5
Poland (2004)	38.6	40	−3.9	18.4	5.3
Romania (2007)	22.4	25	−3.4	6.6	34.5
Slovakia (2004)	5.4	48	−5.6	19.4	10.8
Slovenia (2004)	2.0	69	−2.5	5.7	8.6

Source: European Commission (2002) 'Towards the Enlarged Union COM'

EU 15 and 23 billion euros (£16 billion) for the new members (Baldwin, Francois and Porter 1997). A more recent study of the period 2000-09 by the European Commission's Directorate General for Economic Affairs estimated that enlargement would result in an increase in the annual growth of GDP in the new member countries of between 1.3 and 2.1 percentage points above pre-existing growth-rate levels (European Commission 2001). For the existing members, the annual increase in the level of GDP would be in the region of 0.7 percentage points on a cumulative basis. In 2002, the European Round Table of Industrialists calculated that the new enlargement should create 300,000 jobs in the EU 15. In terms of budgetary consequences, the enlargement should involve only a modest (less than 10%) transfer to the Central and East European countries in the early years after entry. In UK terms, some 14,000 UK firms export to Eastern and Central Europe and the DTI has noted that each enlargement has brought a surge of exports from British companies. It estimated that the new round of enlargement should increase UK's GDP by £1.75 billion.

In the meantime establishing the EU 25 will not be easy since even the optimists believe it will take a decade to fully absorb the ten new nations, whose per capita income is less than 40% of the EU 15 average. This is a much more demanding challenge than the last EU expansion, which admitted three small and wealthy nations Austria, Finland and Sweden in 1995. Demands for larger subsidies for farming from the new entrants will become an inevitable problem; e.g. in Poland, 25% of the population gain some income from farming. Others argue that most of the gains will go to countries such as Germany, Austria and Italy, which are physically closer to the new entrants. It has also been argued that accession countries add less than 5% to EU GDP and are thus more likely to help boost EU competitiveness through cost and labour benefits rather than by stimulating growth of the internal market.

Operations of the EU

Quite apart from the political rationale behind the EU, several economic arguments have been advanced in its support.

1 By abolishing industrial tariff and non-tariff barriers at national frontiers, the EU has created a single 'domestic' market of around 382 million people, with opportunities for substantial economies of scale in production. With the advent of a further 75 million people in 2004, this huge market becomes even larger at almost 460 million people and a further 30 million will be added in 2007 when Bulgaria and Romania join. By surrounding this market with a tariff wall, the Common External Tariff (CET), member countries are the beneficiaries of these scale economies. The Common Customs Tariff is common to all members of the EU and is imposed on imports from non-EU countries. Tariff rates differ from one kind of import to another. For example, raw materials and some types of semi-manufactured goods that are not produced within the EU tend to benefit from low duty rates to stimulate competition within some sectors of the EU. Tariff rates may also be set at a low level for pharmaceutical and IT-related goods.

2 By regulating agricultural production through the Common Agricultural Policy (CAP), the EU has become self-sufficient in many agricultural products (*see* Box 3.4, p. 92).

3 By amending and coordinating labour and capital regulations in the member countries, the EU seeks to create a free market in both, leading to a more 'efficient' use

of these factors (*see* Case Study 3.4 below). A further factor, 'enterprise', is to be 'freed' through increased standardisation of national laws on patents and licences.

4 By seeking to intervene in various monopoly and restrictive practice situations, competition has been encouraged both within and across frontiers. Many European countries have long histories of state intervention in markets so it is hardly surprising that the European Commission accepts the case for intervention by member governments. Apart from agriculture, competition is the only area in which the EU has been able to implement effectively a common policy across member countries. The Commission can intervene to control the behaviour of monopolists, and to increase the degree of competition, through authority derived directly from the Treaty of Rome:

(a) Article 81 prohibits agreements between enterprises which result in the restriction of competition (notably relating to price-fixing, market-sharing, production limitations and other restrictive practices). This article refers to any agreement affecting trade between member states and therefore applies to a large number of British industries.

(b) Article 82 prohibits a dominant firm, or group of firms, from using their market power to exploit consumers.

(c) Article 87 and 88 prohibit government subsidies to industries or individual firms which will distort, or threaten to distort, competition.

5 By creating a substantial 'domestic' market and by coordinating trade policies, the EU hopes to exert a greater collective influence on world economic affairs than could possibly be achieved by any single nation.

Case Study 3.4 looks at the ways in which EU Directives have been used in an attempt to correct 'market failure' in the EU Financial Sector.

Some of these areas in which the EU operates are considered in more detail elsewhere in the book. For example, the CAP has been examined earlier in this chapter and various Directives of the EU involving competition policy are considered in Chapter 5. However, before leaving the EU we consider the issue of the single currency (the euro) with its major implications for international business.

◼ The single currency (the euro)

Eleven countries replaced their national currencies with the euro on 1 January 1999, forming the 'euro-zone'. Greece joined the euro-zone countries in 2000, raising this number to 12.

Harrison (2004) has outlined some of the advantages and disadvantages of membership of the single currency.

Advantages of single currency

- *Lower costs of exchange.* When goods are imported the trader receiving the goods must obtain foreign currency to pay the exporter. Banks will happily supply foreign currency, but they will levy a service charge for the transaction. For the economy as a whole these charges are sizeable and, in general, they will be passed

CASE 3.4 EU directives and regulations

The EU often uses *Directives* in seeking to establish a 'level playing field' to encourage fairer competition within the EU. Although a strict classification of the numerous types of regulation would seem improbable, McKenzie (1998) makes a useful distinction:

- Regulations aimed at *protecting* the consumer from the consequences of market failure;
- Regulations aimed at *preventing* the market failure from happening in the first place.

In terms of the Financial Sector, the *Deposit Guarantee Directive* of the EU is of the former type. This *protects* customers of accredited EU banks by restoring at least 90% of any losses up to £12,000, which might result from the failure of a particular bank. In part this is a response to asymmetric information, since customers do not have the information to evaluate the credit-worthiness of a particular bank, and might not be able to interpret that information even if it was available.

The *Capital Adequacy Directive* of the EU is of the latter type. This seeks to prevent market failure (such as bank collapse) by directly relating the value of the capital a bank must hold to the riskiness of its business. The idea here is that the greater the value of capital available to a bank, the larger the buffer stock which it can use to absorb any losses. Various elements of the Capital Adequacy Directive force the banks to increase their capital base if the riskiness of their portfolio (indicated by various statistical measures) is deemed to have increased. In part this is in response to the potential for negative externalities in this sector. One bank failure can invariably lead to a 'domino effect' and risk system collapse with incalculable consequences for the sector as a whole.

In these ways the regulatory system for EU financial markets is seeking to provide a framework within which greater competition between banks can occur, while at the same time addressing the fact that greater competition can increase the risks of bank failure. It is seeking both to protect consumers should any mishap occur and at the same time to prevent such a mishap actually occurring.

Overall we can say that those who support any or all of these forms of regulation, on whatever sector of the economy, usually do so in the belief that they improve the allocation of resources in situations characterised by one or more types of market failure.

Questions

1 Explain what type of 'market failure' is being tackled by the *Deposit Guarantee Directive*.

2 Explain what type of 'market failure' is being tackled by the *Capital Adequacy Directive*.

3 Can you identify any other types of 'market failure' that the EU seeks to tackle by the use of Directives?

on to consumers through higher prices. For the EU as a whole the transaction costs associated with intra-community trade are estimated at 0.4% of the EU's GDP. These figures give an idea of the resource savings to those countries which adopted the euro and provide an encouraging argument about why these resource savings might be reflected in lower prices within the euro area.

■ *Reduced exchange rate uncertainty*. Inside the euro area, exchange rates are irrevocably fixed and there is no uncertainty over future rates of exchange. This is important because traders often negotiate contracts for delivery and payment stretching six months and longer into the future. Outside the euro area, exchange rate risk exists for traders involved in international transactions. It is, of course, possible for traders to hedge the foreign exchange risk in the forward market where rates of exchange can be agreed today for delivery of currency at some future point in time. However, such arrangements are costly and so raise the cost of a transaction. A different alternative might be for traders to find a domestic producer instead of trading internationally. The implication is that exchange rate risk might raise the cost of trading internationally or discourage international trade altogether. To the extent that this is the case, a single currency will reduce the cost of transacting business across frontiers (because of the costless elimination of exchange rate risk) and will increase international trade with all the associated benefits of comparative advantage. These advantages include the increased variety of products that become available, lower prices due to competition (because price differences between markets will no longer be masked by being quoted in different currencies) and greater economies of scale because of the larger market.

■ *Eliminating competitive devaluations*. Between the two world wars, several European countries engaged in what became known as 'competitive devaluations' when a devaluation in one country was matched by a devaluation in other countries. While such competitive devaluations have been avoided in the latter half of the century, the possibility that they might recur still exists; in fact all devaluations adversely affect inflationary expectations in the devaluing country. Given the increasing scale of intra-European trade, any return to competitive devaluations (or any other form of protectionism) would have devastating effects on Europe's economies. The possibility of these disruptions disappears when a common currency exists.

■ *Preventing speculative attacks*. Where different currencies exist, there is also the possibility of a speculative attack on one or more currencies. The problem is exacerbated when a fixed exchange rate exists because speculators have a one-way bet. If the currency they have bet against is not devalued, all they have lost is their transactions costs on the deal, whereas betting correctly can result in speculator gains. Governments can defend currencies against such attacks, but this often involves raising interest rates, which reduces business investment and hampers economic growth. To the extent that exchange rate disruption is avoided, trade, investment and economic growth will be encouraged, and there will be resource savings (e.g. no longer necessary for the authorities to hold reserves of foreign currency to defend the exchange rate). The latter will again have a positive impact on investment and growth.

Disadvantages of a single currency

The advantages of adopting the euro seem encouraging, but these advantages do not come without costs. It is to a consideration of these that we now turn.

- *Loss of independent monetary policy*. Countries participating in the euro relinquish the right to implement an independent domestic monetary policy. Instead they accept the monetary policy implemented by the European Central Bank (ECB). However, this 'one size fits all' monetary policy might not suit all countries equally, for example, when there is a recession in one country but not in others. If that country is outside the euro area, the country's central bank could reduce interest rates and stimulate economic activity. However, the ECB is unlikely to respond in this way if the recession is only country-specific because this will raise inflation throughout the Union. Monetary policy actions for the ECB, as with the Bank of England, will involve changes in the rate of interest. However, a 'one size fits all' monetary policy might be less effective than the policy an independent country could pursue.

  The ECB has announced that monetary policy will target the rate of inflation. In other words, changes in monetary policy will be initiated whenever the forecast rate of inflation for the euro area as a whole rises above the ECB's target rate of 2%.
- *Loss of an independent exchange rate policy*. Similarly, when a common currency exists, countries lose the ability to devalue the exchange rate to offset a loss of competitiveness. The exchange rate, like the rate of interest, is a powerful weapon for bringing about changes in demand and economic adjustment. In the event of a balance of payments deficit inside a common currency area, the burden of adjustment is thrown on to the domestic economy. For example, cutting aggregate demand to reduce imports and curb any price inflation will be reflected in lower domestic output and employment. This will continue until rising unemployment depresses real wages far enough to restore competitiveness. Adjustment is less painfully achieved when the rate of exchange can be devalued to restore competitiveness.
- *Loss of an independent fiscal policy*. It might be argued that fiscal policy could fill the vacuum left by loss of monetary policy sovereignty and exchange rate policy sovereignty. However, since the maximum allowable budget deficit for any country in the euro-zone is 3% of that country's GDP, scope for an active fiscal policy is clearly limited. It will be limited even further if current thinking on harmonising taxation within the euro-zone is adopted!
- *Loss of convergence*. Loss of policy sovereignty might not be so important if economies are reasonably convergent, in which case country-specific shocks are less likely to occur. Unfortunately not all economies have the same levels of unemployment, inflation, etc. so that a monetary policy that fits one may not fit another.

Useful websites

Now try the self-check questions for this chapter on the website at www.booksites.net/wall. You will also find further resources as well as the following useful weblinks:

Sources of information on international trade and payments, international institutions and exchange rates include:

www.wto.org
www.imf.org
www.un.org
www.dti.gov.uk
www.europa.eu.int
www.eubusiness.com
Honda website is *www.hondamotorcycle.com*
EU statistics can be found at the Eurostat website at *www.europa.eu.int*

Useful key texts

Daniels, J., Radebaugh, L. and Sullivan, D. (2004) *International Business* (10th edn), Pearson Prentice Hall, especially Chapters 5–7.

Dicken, P. (2003) *Global Shift: Transforming the World Economy* (4th edn), Paul Chapman Publishing Ltd, especially Part II.

Hill, C. (2003) *International Business: Competing in the Global Marketplace* (4th edn), McGraw-Hill Irwin, especially Chapters 4, 5 and 8.

Morrison, J. (2002) *The International Business Environment*, Palgrave, especially Chapter 9.

Rugman, A. and Hodgetts, R. (2003) International Business (3rd edn), FT Prentice Hall, especially Chapter 6.

Tayeb, M. (2000) *International Business: Theories, Policies and Practices*, Financial Times Prentice Hall, especially Chapters 1 and 11.

Woods, M. (2001) *International Business*, Palgrave, especially Chapter 2.

Other texts and sources

Baldwin, R., Francois, J.F. and Porter, R. (1997) 'The Costs and Benefits of Eastern Enlargement', Centre for Economic Policy Research (CEPR), *Economic Policy*, no. 24.

European Commission (2001) 'The Economic Impact of Enlargement', Director General for Economic and Financial Affairs, *Enlargement Papers*, no. 4, June.

Harrison, B. (2004) 'Money and EMU', in *Applied Economics* (10th edn), Griffiths, A. and Wall, S. (eds), Financial Times Prentice Hall.

Healey, N. (2004) 'The Multinational Corporation', in *Applied Economics* (10th edn), Griffiths, A. and Wall, S. (eds), Financial Times Prentice Hall.

McKenzie, G. (1998) 'Financial Regulation and the European Union', *The Economic Review*, April.

Porter, M. (1990) *The Competitive Advantage of Nations*, Macmillan.

Rubinsohn, S. (2004) 'Free Trade, Regional Trading Blocs and Protectionism', in *Applied Economics* (10th edn), Griffiths, A. and Wall, S. (eds), Financial Times Prentice Hall.

United Nations Conference on Trade and Development (UNCTAD) *World Investment Report* (annual publication).

United Nations Development Programme (UNDP) *Human Development Report* (annual publication), OUP.

Vernon, R. and Wells, L.T. (1991) *The Manager in the International Economy*, Prentice-Hall, Upper Saddle River, NJ.

World Bank, *World Development Report* (annual publication).

Chapter 4

International business: institutions and markets

By the end of this chapter you should be able to:

■ identify and assess the contribution of those international institutions that play a major role in supporting international trade and investment;

■ examine the role of organisations such as the World Trade Organisation, World Bank and IMF, and be aware of any current proposals for their reform;

■ describe the functions of the main international financial markets (including the foreign exchange market);

■ analyse the impacts of these institutions and markets on international business.

Introduction

Chapter 3 considered some important patterns and trends in the growth of international trade and investment. It also examined the theoretical basis underpinning free trade while acknowledging the reality of protectionist measures in today's global economy. The impacts of these various 'barriers to trade' were discussed from both the standpoint of individual businesses as well as from the broader perspective of 'economic welfare'. This chapter continues the theme of international trade, payment and investment but gives rather more attention to the *international institutional* context within which such activities take place. However, the *markets* in which many of these institutions operate are also considered, especially the currency and money markets. A particularly important 'price', namely the *exchange rate*, is determined on the foreign exchange market and the importance of this rate is examined in some detail.

The WTO and GATT

■ General Agreement on Tariffs and Trade (GATT)

The General Agreement on Tariffs and Trade was signed in 1947 by 23 industrialised nations that included the UK, USA, Canada, France and the Benelux countries. The objectives of GATT were to reduce tariffs and other barriers to trade in the belief that freer trade would raise living standards in all participating countries. Since 1947 there have been eight 'rounds' of trade negotiations with the average tariff in the industrialised nations falling from 40% in 1947 to below 5% in 1995 when the GATT was replaced by the World Trade Organisation (WTO). Supporters of the role of GATT point to facts such as the volume of world trade rising by 1,500% and world output by 600% over the years of its existence.

■ The World Trade Organisation (WTO)

The World Trade Organisation replaced GATT in 1995 and now has 147 members, with the People's Republic of China, Chinese Taipei and Cambodia being the latest to join. The WTO's members in total account for more than 90% of the value of world trade. The objectives of the WTO are essentially the same as GATT's, namely to reduce tariffs and other barriers to trade and to eliminate discrimination in trade, and by doing so contribute to rising living standards and a fuller use of world resources.

■ WTO authority

Trade disputes between member states now come under the auspices of the WTO, which has been given more powers than GATT to enforce compliance, using streamlined disputes procedure with provision for appeals and binding arbitration. Whereas under GATT any single member (including the one violating GATT rules) could block a ruling of unfair trade, the findings of the WTO's disputes panels cannot be blocked by a veto of a member state. Countries found to be in violation of a WTO principle must remove the cause of that violation or pay compensation to the injured parties. If the offending party fails to comply with a WTO ruling, the WTO can sanction certain types of retaliation by the aggrieved party.

Since its creation in January 1995, more than 240 cases have been brought before the WTO against only 200 cases brought before GATT in the 47 years of its existence. More than half of these have involved the USA and the EU while around one-quarter have involved developing countries. The WTO also seeks to provide a forum for further multilateral trade negotiations.

■ WTO principles

Both the GATT and its successor the WTO have sought to implement a number of principles:

- *non-discrimination*: the benefits of any trading advantage agreed between two nations (i.e. in bilateral negotiations) must be extended to all nations (i.e. become multilateral). This is sometimes referred to as the 'most-favoured nation' clause;

- *progressive reduction in tariff and non-tariff barriers*: certain exceptions, however, are permitted in specific circumstances. For example, Article 18 allows for the protection of 'infant industries' by the newly industrialising countries, whereas Article 19 permits any country to abstain from a general tariff cut in situations where rising imports might seriously damage domestic production. Similarly, Articles 21–5 allow protection to continue where 'strategic interests' are involved, such as national security;
- *solving trade disputes through consultation rather than retaliation*: again, certain exceptions are permitted. For example, Article 6 permits retaliatory sanctions to be applied if 'dumping' can be proven, i.e. the sale of products at artificially low prices (e.g. below cost). Countries in dispute are expected to negotiate bilaterally, but if these negotiations break down a WTO appointed working-party or panel can investigate the issue and make recommendations. Should any one of the parties refuse to accept this outcome, the WTO can impose fines and/or sanction certain types of retaliation by the aggrieved party.

The WTO has inherited 28 separate accords agreed under the final round of GATT negotiations (the Uruguay round). These accords sought to extend fair trade rules from industrial products to agricultural products, services, textiles, intellectual property rights and investment.

Case Study 4.1 indicates the growing authority of the WTO and the far-reaching implications of its judgments.

CASE 4.1 Trade ruling takes WTO into new realms

European Union officials appeared to be suffering the consequences of the famous curse of Confucius – may you get what you wish for – as they struggled to play down the impact of winning the biggest case in the World Trade Organisation's five-year history.

As expected, the WTO's appellate body had in 2002 upheld an earlier panel ruling that tax breaks granted to US companies on income from exports channelled through offshore foreign sales corporations (FSCs) constitute illegal export subsidies.

The FSC system: how it works

1 Any US company whose exports have at least 50% US content can set up a foreign sales corporation, a shell company established in a tax haven. Companies with FSCs include GE, Monsanto, Microsoft, Ford, Exxon/Mobil, Motorola, Boeing and Proctor & Gamble.

2 More than 90% of FSCs are in the Virgin Islands, Barbados and Guam. According to the EU, there are 'letterbox' companies that will offer to manage an FSC for $2,000 a year. Estimates of the number of companies with FSCs vary from 3,000 to 7,000.

3 The US company 'sells' its exports to the FSC which then 'exports' them. However, no physical transaction takes place. Instead, the FSC subcontracts the physical handling of the exports and other economic activities back to the parent company.

4 Part of the FSC's income – as much as 65% – is exempt from US tax. The remainder of the income is taxed by the tax haven (minimally). Dividends paid by the FSC to the parent company are also not taxed. Using an FSC can reduce a company's tax bill by between 15% and 30%.

▶

The USA was given until the start of 2001 to bring its FSC measure 'into conformity' with international trade rules.

The amount of trade involved was huge. According to the EU, FSC subsidies assist US exports worth around $250 billion annually, at a cost to the US budget of tax forgone of an estimated $3.5 billion per annum. This dwarfs US retaliation of just over $300 million annually that the WTO authorised in 1999 for the EU's failure to comply with WTO rulings in disputes over bananas and hormone-treated beef.

However, far from trumpeting victory, the EU has been at pains to sound reasonable and non-confrontational while officials on both sides stressed the desirability of an agreed solution that would avoid further WTO action. That, say trade diplomats, is because the case has far-reaching and potentially uncomfortable implications for Brussels as well as for Washington. On a political level the ruling requires Congress to change important tax legislation: a tall order if not an impossible one. Charlene Barshefsky, US trade representative, said that the US respected its WTO obligations and would 'seek a solution that ensures that US firms and workers are not at a competitive disadvantage with their European counterparts'. In these circumstances too much pressure from Brussels could be counterproductive, jeopardising the delicate transatlantic trade relationship and further compromising US congressional support for the multilateral trading system.

In its ruling the appellate body said it was not making a judgement on the relative merits of the 'territorial' and 'worldwide' systems of taxation, used by the EU and USA respectively. But countries were not entitled to use the tax system to provide subsidies contingent on export performance, which are outlawed by the WTO's subsidies accord. Initially the USA continued to maintain that FSCs were consistent with WTO rules, arguing that they did not distort trade and merely granted US companies the same tax benefits as European companies receive through VAT rebates on exports. However by 2003 the US had decided to come into compliance with the WTO decision.

To further encourage the USA to comply, the EU stated that retaliatory tariffs would be levied on imports from the USA of 5% starting in April 2004, and rising by 1% each month to a maximum of 17% by March 2005. Even this was seen as a cautious response, the estimated value of these tariffs being *below* the $4 billion approved by the WTD.

Bill Thomas, of the US Congress, proposed ending this $4 billion per annum tax break provided by the Financial Services Corporation, thereby avoiding the EU imposing retaliatory sanctions of $4 billion per year granted by the WTO. However to make this concession more palatable to Congress and US business he is also proposing even larger domestic tax reductions for US companies.

Source: Frances Williams, *Financial Times*, 25 February 2000.

Questions

1 Consider the benefits and costs to the US of using FSCs.

2 Why might the WTO ruling in favour of the EU nevertheless create some potential problems for the EU?

■ Perspectives on WTO initiatives

Despite its greater authority, not everyone is convinced that the WTO is using that authority effectively or fairly. It may be useful to briefly review the arguments of both critics and supporters of the WTO.

Critics of the WTO

■ *Bias to the 'North'.* Developing countries ('South') exporting to the advanced industrialised countries ('North') face tariffs on their exports that are four to five times higher than those placed on exports from advanced industrialised countries. For example the average tariffs on imports of textiles and garments from developing countries into industrialised countries are 15%–20%, as compared to only 3% on the imports of industrial goods. As a result Bangladesh, one of the world's poorest countries, pays the US $314 million a year in import taxes – about the same as France, the world's fifth richest economy (Walker 2002).

■ *Inability to progress the Doha Round of negotiations.* The most recent round of multilateral negotiations by the WTO to reduce trade restrictions began in Doha, Qatar, in 2001. Promises were made to reduce restrictions on trade in textiles and agricultural products (among others) which together account for around 70% of the exports of developing countries. Little progress has been made in either. For example, industrialised countries promised to phase out an elaborate system of quotas applied to textile imports by 2005 but by late 2003 when more than half the quotas should have been removed, the EU had withdrawn only around 30% of these quotas and the US only 20%. Reducing tariffs on agricultural imports and the subsidies given to agricultural exports was a key element of the Doha Round. Yet little progress has been made as the powerful agri-businesses in the EU and USA lobby effectively against such measures.

■ *Undue pressure on the 'South'.* Critics argue that the WTO is only consistent and effective in pursuing its free trade credentials when it places intense pressures for import liberalisation on the developing ('South') countries, as is suggested by Case Study 4.2 below. The impact of such pressures can be seen from the fact that indices of 'trade openness' currently place 17 African countries as more accessible to import penetration than either the EU or the US. Yet the most successful developing countries have been those of East Asia which have liberalised slowly and in a staged manner, only lowering trade barriers as domestic productivity rises and home industries become more competitive on world markets.

■ *Undue emphasis on protecting trade-related aspects of intellectual property rights.* The 'North' countries account for some 90% of world patents and successfully secured increased protection for intellectual property rights in the WTO 'TRIPS Agreement' (*see* p. 154) in 1995. However, the developing countries insisted before agreeing to the current Doha Round of negotiations, that a declaration be made at Doha confirming their right to 'set aside patents in the interests of public health and to buy or make cheap generic versions of expensive drugs'. While the developing countries see this as applying to any condition which undermines public health, whether diabetes, cancer, asthma, HIV/Aids or whatever the large pharmaceutical companies have sought to limit the list of diseases to which this 'right' applies to malaria, tuberculosis and HIV/Aids, and to give only the poorest countries the opportunity of exercising this 'right'. With no agreement yet reached, critics blame the WTO for being ineffectual in failing to secure a more broad based application of this 'right' enshrined in the Doha Declaration.

■ *Undue emphasis on liberalising trade in services.* Of course many other criticisms have been levelled at the WTO, as for example the suggestion that it is too compliant in seeking to open world markets in *services*, to the benefit of the 'North'. Major proposals for wholesale deregulation of services have been proposed by the EU and US, opening up everything from banking and insurance to energy, water, sanitation and a host of 'public services'.

Case Study 4.2 indicates the pressures on new entrants to liberalise trade in goods and services as a condition of WTO inclusion.

CASE 4.2 Cambodia set to join WTO

Cambodia is poised to become the 147th member of the World Trade Organisation and the first least-developed country to enter the WTO since its inception in 1995. A WTO working party on Cambodia's accession in July 2003 approved its terms of entry, which will now go for formal endorsement by ministers when they meet in Cancun, Mexico, in September.

Cambodia, which applied to join the WTO in December 1994, has agreed to substantial opening of its goods and services markets to trading partners in return for the benefits of WTO membership, most crucially the abolition of import quotas on textiles, Cambodia's main export earner, from 2005.

Nine other least-developed countries are in the queue for WTO membership. Nepal's accession negotiations are the most advanced, the others being Bhutan, Cape Verde, Ethiopia, Laos, Samoa, Sudan, Vanuuta and Yemen.

Source: Frances Williams, *Financial Times*, 23 July 2003.

Questions

1 Why might these conditions of WTO entry be regarded by many as 'unfair' on developing countries such as Cambodia?

2 Consider the reasons for critics suggesting that the 'North' has an overwhelming competitive advantage in services.

3 What policies would you expect to be advocated by those who support the argument of the critics in Question 2 above?

■ *'Localisation' as an alternative doctrine.* Critics of the WTO include adherents of a doctrine opposed to unbridled free trade, namely 'localisation' which proposes that everything that can be produced locally should be produced locally, and to that end nations should protect their economies using trade taxes and legal barriers, though some international trade is still envisaged. The author of the 'localisation' manifesto, Colin Hines, suggests that 'some long-distance trade will still occur for those sectors providing goods and services to other regions of the world that can't provide such items from within their own borders, e.g. certain minerals or cash crops'. However, this is clearly a minimalist world trading environment which, in this view, hardly needs a WTO to regulate and expand it!

pause for thought 1   Outline the arguments that could be used both for and against 'localisation'.

Supporters of the WTO may even accept some of these criticisms, yet focus on its role in preventing still greater excesses in a global environment characterised by grossly unequal power relationships between 'North' and 'South'. We now review a number of counter-arguments presented by supporters of the WTO.

Supporters of the WTO

- *Unilateralism/bilateralism may be the alternative to multilateralism*. We noted (p. 106) that the WTO embodies a *multilateral* approach to trade negotiations, as in the 'most favoured nation' clause extending benefits to all. We also noted the growth of *bilateral* trade treaties and regional trade arrangements in Chapter 1 (p. 8) which threaten this multilateral approach. In seeking to avoid such discriminatory treaties and arrangements, the WTO has won considerable support. Indeed some see powerful nations (e.g. US) or supranational bodies (e.g. EU) as seeking to impose their own *unilateral* rules on world trading practices and regard the WTO as an indispensable bulwark in the fight against such unilateralism.

- *Absence of rules may be the alternative to imperfect WTO rules*. Even critics of the WTO often hesitate to contemplate a world trading regime with no rules whatsoever. As George Monbiot, a previously strong critic of the WTO has admitted: 'The only thing worse than a world with the wrong international trade rules is a world with no trade rules at all' (Monbiot 2003a).

- *WTO has not distorted trade patterns*. Two recent working papers for the National Bureau of Economic Research in the US by Richard Rose (2003) suggest that the World Trade Organisation scarcely merits the demonisation it receives. On the basis of extensive research, he finds the WTO members do not display significantly different trading patterns from non-members. Traditional linkages among countries, such as belonging to the same regional trade pact, or sharing languages, borders or colonial histories, appear to be more powerful factors in explaining variations in trade. Membership of WTO and its predecessor organisation, the GATT, appears to have had no strong or consistent impact on policy either, judged by 64 measures of trade policy openness.

- *WTO is taking more robust action against trade restrictions from the 'North'*. Case Study 4.1 above (p. 107) showed the WTO having an impact on removing trade distortions resulting from implicit subsidies to US exporters via Financial Service Corporations (FSCs). Case Study 4.3 below also shows the WTO taking firm action against further alleged trade distortions from the US, this time involving its impositions of steel tariffs on imports.

CASE 4.3   US steel tariffs illegal, rules WTO

The World Trade Organisation ruled in July 2003 that the US violated international trading rules when it imposed tariffs of up to 30 per cent on steel imports in 2002. The decision, by a dispute settlement panel in a case brought by the European Union and seven other countries, could stoke fresh trade tensions between the US and EU. A US trade official said that if the 900-page interim decision remained unchanged, the US would appeal. 'Safeguard measures are allowed under WTO rules,' the official said. 'We believe the measures comply with international obligations.'

The confidential report has been sent by the WTO to the US and the eight complainants – the EU, Japan, South Korea, China, Switzerland, Norway, New Zealand and Brazil – for comment, but no interim finding has ever been overturned in the WTO's seven-year history.

The US imposed tariffs of up to 30 per cent in March 2002 on many imported steel products, saying that ailing US steel companies needed protection against a flood of cheap foreign steel. The tariffs particularly hit steelmakers in the EU, Japan and Korea, while excluding most developing countries as well as Mexico and Canada.

The tariffs sparked a transatlantic dispute that was only partially defused by the extensive exemptions the US has since offered for many steel products, most recently in March 2003. Brussels argued that the duties were illegal because they failed to meet the basic test for a safeguard action – a recent surge in imports. Under WTO rules, countries can extend temporary protection to industries hit by import competition, but only under strict conditions. The US has previously lost half a dozen WTO cases concerning safeguard measures, including curbs on steel, wheat, gluten and lamb.

While the final appeals could still take another six months the US is likely to be faced with a WTO ruling that it must end the steel tariffs or face sanctions. The US has brought its own WTO case against EU safeguards on imported steel after the US move to prevent steel, that would otherwise have gone to the US, flooding European markets.

Source: Edward Alden and Frances Williams, *Financial Times*, 27 March 2003.

Questions

1 What would seem to be the reasons for the US imposing tariffs on steel imports in 2002?

2 Why does the US believe these to be legal and the WTO believe them to be illegal?

3 What is the basis for the US itself bringing a case to the WTO against the EU policy on steel? What are the prospects for the EU defending its own actions on steel?

■ *'Localisation'* is viewed by free-traders as diminishing the wealth of poorer nations rather than enhancing it. The World Bank (Dollar and Kraay 2000) has argued that increased openness to trade (the opposite of localisation) raises average incomes and the incomes of the poor; i.e. there is no relationship between increased openness to trade and rising inequality, if anything quite the opposite.

Sebastian Edwards of the University of California also concludes in a study of 93 countries that there is a close link between openness to trade and rates of productivity growth. In this view 'localisation' is itself seen as a recipe for increased inequality. George Monbiot, a previous adherent of localisation, observes with some irony that the doctrine itself relies upon enhanced political globalisation.

Colin Hines' model invents a whole new series of global bodies to impose localisation on nation states whether they like it or not. States would be forbidden to pass laws that diminish local control of industry and services. Hines, in other words, prohibits precisely the kind of political autonomy he claims to promote. (Monbiot 2003a)

- *Reformed WTO may have much to commend it.* Even critics of the WTO see the potential for this body undergoing reform to the benefit of the global trading system. Many suggest that greater 'fairness' to the developing countries would result from the WTO placing greater emphasis on the short-term protection of infant-industries and the short-term use of intellectual property rights in the developing countries. Developing countries could then follow the well-trodden path of the now developed countries which, historically, used trade barriers and the acquisition (legally or illegally) of intellectual property to grow themselves. A second 'fairness' might involve extending the rules currently applied by the voluntary 'fair trade' movement to all companies involved in international trade. For example George Monbiot (2003b) suggests that for a company to acquire a (WTO) licence to trade internationally, it would have to demonstrate that it and its suppliers applied certain minimum conditions to the labour force and to environmental protection.

Before leaving our discussions of the hugely important role of the WTO in international trade and business, it will be useful to consider Case Study 4.4 on the rapidly evolving situation of *bilateral free trade areas*. This is a case study that might be used by both critics and supporters of the WTO to advance their point of view.

| CASE 4.4 | Bilateral trade treaties are a sham | |

Pascal Lamy, the European commissioner for trade, recently wrote that 'half the world's economists' were opposed to the epidemic of bilateral free trade agreements (FTAs). That was a splendid example of British understatement from a Frenchman.

The fact of the matter is that nearly all scholars of international economics today are fiercely sceptical, even hostile, to such agreements. By contrast, politicians everywhere have succumbed to a mania that originated in Europe but is now eagerly promoted by Robert Zoellick, the US trade representative, with Asia – the last holdout – now joining in. We are witnessing possibly the biggest divide between economists and politicians in the postwar period. Unfortunately, the economists are right. The politicians' lemming-like rush into bilateral agreements poses a deadly threat to the multilateral trading system. There are three reasons.

First, bilateral trade deals are undermining an essential principle of the World Trade Organisation: that the lowest tariff applicable to one member must be extended to all members (the most favoured nation status rule). While it is true that the architects of the WTO/General Agreement on Tariffs and Trade exempted free trade areas from the 'most favoured nation' (MFN) rule, they surely did not foresee that a proliferation of agreements would fragment the trading system. By the end of 2002, 250 FTAs had been notified to the WTO. If those currently under negotiation are concluded, that number will approach 300. The result is a 'spaghetti bowl' of rules, arbitrary definitions of which product comes from where and a multiplicity of tariffs depending on source.

Second, if the Europeans started this fad, the Americans are now pursuing it with zeal, exploiting their hegemonic power and the lure of preferential access to a multi-billion dollar market. Unlike Brussels, Washington has adopted bilateral FTAs to advance the agendas of domestic lobbies, agendas that are not related to trade. The US is using one-on-one agreements with small countries as models for other multilateral trade agreements, hawking them around the world as the ideal way to further trade liberalisation.

Third, America's tactic is weakening the power of poor countries in multilateral trade negotiations. Bilateral deals fragment the coalitions of developing countries, as each abandons its legitimate objections to the inclusion of extraneous issues in trade treaties. Having abandoned these objections in a bilateral deal with the US, how can those countries pursue them in WTO negotiations?

The process of trade liberalisation is becoming a sham, the ultimate objective being the capture, reshaping and distortion of the WTO in the image of American lobbying interests.

The protection of intellectual property provides a good example of US tactics. Washington has used both inducements and punishments to secure its interests. During negotiations over the North America Free Trade Agreement, Mexico was told that the price of a deal was acceptance of intellectual property protection provisions.

It was a price Mexico was prepared to pay. But the US has also demanded that other countries accept similar provisions or face retaliatory tariffs. Subsequently, during the Uruguay round of trade liberalisation, the US was able to insert the trade-related intellectual property regime (TRIPS) into the WTO, even though no fully argued case had ever been made that TRIPS, which is about royalty collection and not trade, should be included.

Mexico also had to accept provisions on environmental and labour standards annexed to the Nafta treaty. But such standards were put right at the centre of the free trade agreement with Jordan, drafted in the last days of the Clinton administration. And with the Bush administration currently negotiating an agreement with Central America, Democrats are under pressure from the labour and environmental lobbies to demand not just the enforcement of local standards but higher standards altogether.

In the free trade agreements with Chile and Singapore, the US Treasury insisted on inserting a ban on the use of capital controls, even though the International Monetary Fund has finally come round to the view that they might, on occasion, be justified. Chile and Singapore finally gave in, agreeing to a dispute settlement and compensation mechanism should such controls ever be used. Washington has thereby created another precedent.

Thanks to the myopic and self-serving policies of the world's only superpower, bilateral free trade agreements are damaging the global trading system. They are undermining the most favoured nation rule ensuring equal treatment in the WTO. Bilateral deals have become a vehicle for introducing extraneous issues into the WTO for the benefit of narrow US domestic interests. They are thereby distorting the role of the WTO.

Source: J. Bhagwati and A. Panagariya, *Financial Times*, 14 July 2003.

Questions

1 Why are *developed economies* generally supportive of bilateral trade treaties?

2 Why are *developing economies* and their supporters often opposed to the use of bilateral trade treaties?

3 Carefully consider how this case study could be used by both critics of the WTO and by supporters of the WTO.

International Monetary Fund (IMF)

The IMF plays a key role in providing foreign currencies and other sources of world liquidity to support the growth of international trade and payments. It also provides specific packages of financial support for economies in times of need. This latter role involves a variety of 'stabilisation programmes' (*see* p. 119), which provide essential funding but only on condition that the countries receiving funds agree to implement specific programmes of change agreed with the IMF.

■ Foreign currencies and world liquidity

In order to settle balance of payments deficits arising from international trade, theory tells us that deficit countries should be able to run down their foreign exchange reserves or to borrow from surplus countries. Both methods have, in reality, proved next to impossible. The countries most likely to suffer balance of payments deficits are those with low per capita incomes and with few foreign exchange reserves, in other words, countries with low credit ratings on the international banking circuit, making borrowing from surplus countries difficult. It was in order to solve just these sorts of liquidity problems for deficit countries that the IMF was established.

The IMF began in 1946 with just 39 members, but is now a giant international organisation with 171 members. It has an unwieldy board of governors, with one governor from each member country. However, day-to-day decisions are taken by an executive board of twenty-two members, seven of whom are appointed by the USA, Germany, the UK, France, Japan, Saudi Arabia and China, with the remaining 15 elected from geographical constituencies.

Currency quotas

The IMF was originally set up to provide a pool of foreign currencies, which could be used by members to 'finance' temporary balance of payments deficits. This would give deficit countries time to 'adjust' their deficits, i.e. adopt policies which would eventually eliminate them without having to resort to immediate and massive deflations aimed at cutting spending on imports, or to sudden moves towards protectionist measures, or to reductions in the exchange rate to regain price competitiveness. By helping deficit countries to finance their deficits, the IMF was therefore seeking to promote the smooth growth of world income and trade.

Quotas

These have been assigned to each country to determine its access to foreign currency and also its voting rights within the IMF. Critics of the IMF point out that these quotas were allocated *pro rata* to each country's total value of trade, so that in practice the richer countries received much higher quotas than poorer, less trade oriented countries. So for example, in 2002 the US Quota (against which it could access 125%, over 5 years, in foreign currencies) was equivalent to around $40 billion, while that for Tonga and Bhutan was a mere $7 million or so.

Borrowing facilities

There are, however, further facilities for borrowing, with varying degrees of strictness as to the conditions attached. As we shall see, these various facilities and practices, and especially the creation of SDRs (*see* p. 117) have together changed the nature of the IMF. It is no longer the rather conservative institution of its Articles, simply reallocating a *given* pool of world currencies, but one which can intervene actively to find varied sources of finance and even to *create* new world money.

- *Compensatory Financing Facility* (CFF). The CFF was introduced in 1963 to assist primary producing countries in difficulty due to a temporary fall in export earnings (e.g. crop failure or natural disaster).
- *Compensatory and Contingency Financing Facility* (CCFF). This superseded the CFF in August 1988. It has added the possibility of contingency financing to support agreed structural adjustment programmes.
- *Extended Fund Facilities* (EFF). The EFF began in 1974 and was introduced to provide countries with more time to adjust their financial affairs. Most IMF loans had to be repaid in three to five years, but the EFF initially gave up to eight years for repayment, and now even longer.
- *Oil Facilities*. These were temporary facilities established in 1974 to assist countries whose balance of payments had been severely hit by rising oil prices. In theory, the oil facility had an upper limit of 450% of quota (to enable less developed countries with very low quotas to receive significant assistance), but some countries received loans up to 800% of quota. The oil facilities were ended in 1976.
- *Bufferstock Facility*. This was established in June 1969 to finance the building up of bufferstocks by commodity producers at times of falling world prices. Up to 45% of the quota is permitted for this purpose.

In addition to its 'normal' resources, the IMF has a variety of other instruments and facilities at its disposal:

- *Supplementary Financing Facility* (SFF). This is actually a separate trust, established with the IMF as a trustee, in February 1979. It originally borrowed SDR 7.5 billion from the oil producers to assist countries that had exceeded their Credit Tranche borrowing.
- *Enlarged Access Facilities*. Set up in May 1981 after SFF money became fully committed, it allows members to borrow up to 150% of quota in a single year, or up to 450% of quota over a three-year period. The intention is to assist countries with large deficits relative to quota.
- *Structural Adjustment Facility* (SAF). In 1986 a new 'structural adjustment facility' was implemented in order to recycle the loan repayments to some of the Fund's poorer members, the Low Income Developing Countries.
- *Enhanced Structural Adjustment Facility*. At the Venice Summit of 1987 it was agreed to expand the SAF on identical terms but with additional funds. Loans are now determined on need and there is no overall ceiling. However, the IMF operates a policy of 250% of quota as the maximum access unless there are 'exceptional circumstances'. Normal repayments are in ten half-yearly payments, beginning after five-and-a-half years and ending ten years after the date of the loan.
- *Trust Fund Facility*. Between 1976 and 1980 the IMF sold 25 million ounces of gold at market prices. It used most of the revenue to establish a trust fund to assist the lesser developed countries (LDCs). This facility ceased in 1981 when the fund had been exhausted.
- *Systemic Transformation Facility*. Established as a series of initiatives between 1990 and 1993, this facility was designed to channel restructuring funds and support to countries in the former 'Eastern Bloc'.

Intermediation

The role of the IMF does not end with these various facilities. It has been an intermediary in arranging *standby credits* at times when currencies have come under severe strain. These credits have not usually been used, but have helped restore market confidence in a country's ability to withstand speculative pressure, which itself has often eased that pressure. It has also from time to time arranged finance from the Group of Ten (*see* p. 123) countries.

Special Drawing Rights (SDRs)

These were introduced by the IMF in 1969, both to raise the total of world official reserves and to serve as a potential replacement for gold and foreign currency in the international monetary system. Special drawing rights were essentially a 'free gift' from the IMF to its members, which could be used to settle debt between countries. The SDR had no separate existence of its own, being simply a book entry with the IMF. It served as international money since it could be transferred to other countries in settlement of debt. The total of SDRs to be created was at the discretion of the IMF, but the allocation of that total was to be strictly in proportion to quotas. To make this new world currency acceptable it was initially valued in gold, with interest rates paid on credit balances. Special Drawing Rights were later valued in terms of a basket of 16 different currencies, the idea being to move away from depending on gold yet to retain confidence in the value of the SDR by avoiding dependence on any single currency. In 1981 this rather unwieldy basket was replaced by a smaller basket of five major currencies.

The fact that SDRs have been given to members in amounts proportional to the size of their quotas has not been without criticism. It is the major trading countries that (as we have seen) have the largest quotas. There have been eight issues of SDRs to date with the most recent (16.0 billion SDR) being in 2002.

The whole matter of SDRs has become much more controversial in recent years as their shortcomings have become more apparent. Although efforts were made to make them more attractive (in 1981 they were denominated in terms of a basket of five currencies – as above – and market rates of interest were allowed), they still only represent 2% of total liquidity and are, essentially, being held by those who least need them (the richer trading countries).

■ General arrangements to borrow (GAB)

In 1962 the ten largest IMF members plus Switzerland (which is not an IMF member) constructed the GAB. Each of the signatories contributed an amount of its own currency towards a fund which stood at $7 billion in 1982. In January 1983 the fund was increased substantially to $19 billion in order to help alleviate the world banking crisis. Until January 1983 the GAB had been an arrangement available only to signatories, but since then its resources have been available to any country in need.

■ 'Swap' arrangements

In the 1960s the USA instituted a system of currency 'swaps' with other countries, whereby each central bank agrees to lend its own currency, or to acquire currency balances of the other, for a specified time period. Although these are relatively short-term arrangements, there is currently an additional $30 billion to $40 billion that could be added to total reserves under such schemes.

pause for thought 2	Why has the IMF sometimes been termed 'the rich man's club'? Is this criticism fair?

■ Review of the role of the IMF

The IMF has undoubtedly helped to support the growth of international trade and payments through its various and substantial contributions to world liquidity. Nevertheless, where it has been involved in 'stabilisation programmes' in support of particular LDCs and transition economies at times of financial hardship, it has been the subject of some criticism (*see* Box 4.1).

Box 4.1   IMF stabilisation programmes

IMF stabilisation programmes (*see also* p. 122) seek to address adverse balance of payments situations whilst retaining price stability and encouraging the resumption of economic growth. The main components of typical IMF stabilisation programmes include some or all of the following:

- *fiscal contraction* – a reduction in the public sector deficit through cuts in public expenditure and/or rises in taxation;
- *monetary contraction* – restrictions on credit to the public sector and increases in interest rates;
- *devaluation of the exchange rate* (this is often a pre-condition for the serious negotiation of a stabilisation programme, rather than part of the programme as such);
- *liberalisation of the economy* – via reduction or elimination of controls, and privatisation of public-sector assets;
- *incomes policy* – wage restraint and removal of subsidies and reduction of transfer payments.

Criticisms of the IMF's stabilisation programmes in LDCs and the transition economies can be grouped as follows:

1 *IMF programmes are inappropriate*. The criticism here is that its approach to policy has been preoccupied with the control of demand, and too little concerned with other weaknesses stemming from problems with the productive system in LDCs and transition economies. By deflating demand, the IMF has imposed large adjustment costs on borrowing countries through losses of output and employment, further impoverishing the poor and even destabilising incumbent governments.

2 *IMF programmes are inflexible*. The criticism here is that the IMF has imposed its solutions on the country needing to borrow rather than negotiating a more flexible package. This has arguably infringed the sovereignty of states and alienated governments from the measures they are supposed to implement.

3 *IMF support has been too small, expensive and short term*. The programmes have been criticised for having been too small in magnitude and too short term in duration for economies whose underlying problems are rooted in structural weaknesses and who often face 'adverse' terms of trade (fall in export prices relative to import prices).

4 *The IMF is dominated by a few major industrial countries*. The criticism here is that the industrial countries have sometimes used their control of the IMF to promote their own interests, as for example in using the IMF to shift a disproportionate amount of the debt burden onto the debtor countries rather than forcing lenders (e.g. banks) to accept some of the debt burden, given their earlier readiness to lend huge funds at high rates of interest to 'risky' ventures.

Box 4.2 on p. 122 looks further at the principles involved in the IMF stabilisation programmes and contrasts those with some of the World Bank's attempts to support the global economic system.

World Bank

The World Bank is, in effect, a grouping of three international institutions, namely the International Bank for Reconstruction and Development (IBRD), the International Development Association (IDA) and the International Finance Corporation (IFC).

■ International Bank for Reconstruction and Development (IBRD)

The origins of the World Bank lie in the formation of the IBRD in 1946. The IBRD sought to help countries raise the finance needed to reconstruct their war-damaged economies. This often took the form of guaranteeing loans that could then be obtained at lower interest rates than might otherwise have been possible.

■ International Development Association (IDA)

In 1958 a second international institution was created to operate alongside the IBRD, namely the International Development Association. The main objective of the IDA was to provide development finance for low-income nations which had insufficient resources to pay interest on the IBRD loans.

■ International Finance Corporation (IFC)

The International Finance Corporation was established in 1959. Unlike the previous two bodies, the IFC concentrates on lending to *private* borrowers involved in development projects.

Initially much of this lending was for specific infrastructure projects such as dams, power facilities, transport links, etc. More recently, the focus of lending has shifted towards improving the efficiency and accountability of the administrative and institutional structures in the recipient countries.

The role of the World Bank has broadened in recent years to include the private sector as well as governments (*see* Case Study 4.5).

CASE 4.5 World Bank may help fund small companies in Africa

The World Bank is considering using its soft-money arm directly to help finance small companies in Africa, in a break from its usual practice of giving loans and grants to governments. The pilot plan, in June 2003, would mean the International Development Association – the bank's concessional arm, which deals with the world's poorest countries – giving grants of around $100m (£60m) to improve the financial services available to small and medium-sized companies. Together with financing from the International Finance Corporation, the bank's private-sector arm, and other commercial investors, the total programme size would be $225m over three to four years. It marks a continued cultural shift away from the bank's traditional public-sector focus, and has attracted some criticism for subsidising private companies.

'There is always some resistance against giving public money to the private sector,' said Peter Woicke, head of the IFC. 'But this programme does not simply subsidise private companies. The money will aim to commercialise micro-finance institutions, which are often the only source of finance for small companies in Africa, and establish investment vehicles to support medium-sized businesses.' Small companies are thought to play a huge role in many African economies, where the 'informal' sector often makes up 40–60 per cent of the economy, but are often neglected by commercial banks.

In June 2003, a commission of former US government officials and private-sector executives released a study on increasing capital flows to Africa. The commission, chaired by James Harmon, former chairman of the US Export-Import Bank, the credit guarantee agency, said that US trade concessions to Africa should be made more generous and extended beyond their current cut-off date of 2008. It also called for a tax holiday on repatriated earnings on new investments by American companies in Africa. The commission said the US administration should build on the African Growth and Opportunity Act, a set of trade concessions, and seek to complete a free-trade agreement with the continent in 10 years.

Sub-Saharan Africa currently receives less than 1 per cent of global foreign direct investment, much of it in the mining and oil industries.

Source: Alan Beattie, *Financial Times*, 25 June 2003.

Questions

1 What are the reasons for the World Bank changing its lending approach to Africa?

2 Why is this new lending approach of the World Bank attracting some criticism?

3 How useful might the US approach be? Are there any potential problems with the commission's proposals?

■ World Bank 'Structural Adjustment Lending'

Since 1980 the World Bank has been involved in various types of Structural Adjustment Lending (SAL) which accounts for over 20% of the World Bank's lending. These SAL programmes are non-project related, rather they involve lending to support specific programmes or policy which may involve elements of institutional change. These SAL programmes are generally directed towards improving the 'supply side' of the borrowing countries, intending to initiate and fund changes which will ultimately raise productive efficiency in various sectors of their economies.

Box 4.2 provides a rather stereotyped but useful overview of the World Bank's SAL programmes and compares these with the IMF's 'stabilisation programmes' previously discussed (*see* Box 4.1).

Box 4.2   **World Bank structural adjustment and stabilisation**

Structural adjustment. As noted above, most of the World Bank Structural Adjustment Lending (SAL) programmes have sought to improve the supply side of the economy. Where successful this will result in the downward, to the right, movement of the aggregate supply curve (AS) from AS_1 to AS_2 thus reducing the price level (from P_2 to P_3 with AD_2) and increasing output (from Q_2 to Q_3). Clearly the remedies involving structural adjustment are rather more palatable than the remedies which involve deflation (see below) in that both output and employment rise, but only after possibly difficult changes to labour and capital market practices and institutions to improve supply-side conditions.

Figure 4.1 Structural adjustment and stabilisation

It is also worth noting, as we saw in Case Study 4.5, that the World Bank is seeking to offer progressively 'softer' loans to developing countries.

Stabilisation. As was noted earlier (*see* p. 119) most of the policies in the IMF stabilisation programmes have been of a deflationary nature. This results in the downward movement, to the left, of the aggregate demand curve (AD) from AD_1 to AD_2 thus reducing the price level (from P_1 to P_2 with AS_1) but also reducing output (from Q_1 to Q_2). The debtor country may be made more competitive in its exports and import-substitute sectors, benefiting its balance of payments and reducing its debt, but at the cost of lost output and employment.

UN international institutions

Here we consider a number of institutions that operate under the auspices of the United Nations. The UN itself was established by charter in 1945 and consists of 185 member states. Its mission statement is to establish a world order based on peace, prosperity and freedom, and its most visible decision-making body is the UN General Assembly, in which all members participate.

■ United Nations Conference on Trade, Aid and Development (UNCTAD)

The conference first met in 1964 and has met subsequently at three or four-year intervals. All members of the UN are members of the conference, which has a permanent executive and secretariat. UNCTAD seeks to give particular support to the LDCs in their various trade disputes with the more developed economies. An important contribution of UNCTAD has been to support the introduction of the 'Generalised System of Preferences' (GSP) in 1971 which has helped give some of the exports of LDCs preferential access to the markets of the advanced industrialised economies.

■ United Nations Industrial Development Organisation (UNIDO)

This was established in 1966 to provide technical assistance for developing countries seeking to industrialise. It helps countries to undertake industrial surveys, formulate industrial development strategies, conduct project appraisals and implement productivity and marketing strategies.

Organisation for Economic Co-operation and Development (OECD)

The OECD was established in 1961 as a grouping of the advanced industrialised economies. Its main objectives were to encourage high levels of economic growth and employment among its member states, together with a stable financial system. It also seeks to contribute to the economic development in non-member states (including LDCs) and to expand world trade on a multilateral basis.

■ Group of Seven/Eight/Ten

This refers to the seven major industrial countries within the OECD that meet at fairly regular intervals to consider global economic issues, especially those of a macroeconomic nature. The seven countries involved are Canada, France, Germany, Italy, Japan, the UK and the USA (the Russian Federation has been added to this number on an informal basis in recent times when the G7 became G8). The so-called Group of Ten (G10) countries are the G7 countries plus Belgium, the Netherlands and Sweden.

In recent times many of these international institutions and arrangements have become the focus of criticism and their meetings have often been the occasion for large-scale protest.

International financial markets

The international financial markets are usually regarded as those involved in trading foreign exchange and various types of paper assets such as equities (shares), government debt (bills, bonds, etc.) and financial derivatives (options, etc.). They are important to firms, individuals and governments in raising finance to support international production, trade and investment, in reducing risks and in providing a potentially income-generating repository for any surplus funds they might hold.

The foreign exchange market

The foreign exchange market is the market on which international currencies are traded. It has no physical existence: it consists of traders, such as the dealing rooms of major banks, who are in continual communications with one another on a worldwide basis. Currencies are bought and sold on behalf of clients, who may be companies, private individuals or banks themselves. A distinction is made between the 'spot' rate for a currency, and the forward rate. The *spot rate* is the domestic currency price of a unit of foreign exchange when the transaction is to be completed within three days. The *forward rate* is the price of that unit when delivery is to take place at some future date – usually 30, 60 or 90 days hence. Both spot and forward rates are determined in today's market; the relationship between today's spot and today's forward rate will be determined largely by how the market *expects* the spot rate to move in the near future. The more efficient the market is at anticipating future spot rates, the closer will today's forward rate be to the future spot rate.

The spot market is used by those who wish to acquire foreign exchange immediately. Forward markets are used by three groups of people:

- *hedgers* who wish to cover themselves (*hedge*) against the risk of exchange variation. For instance, suppose an importer orders goods to be paid for in three months' time in dollars. All his calculations will be upset if the price of dollars rises between now and payment date. He can cover himself by buying dollars today for delivery in three months' time; he thus locks himself into a rate which reduces the risk element in his transaction;

- *arbitrageurs* who attempt to make a profit on the difference between interest rates in one country and another, and who buy or sell currency forward to ensure that the profit which they hope to make by moving their capital is not negated by adverse exchange rate movements;

- *speculators* who use the forward markets to buy or sell in anticipation of exchange rate changes. For instance, if I think that today's forward rates do not adequately reflect the probability of the dollar increasing in value I will buy dollars forward, hoping to sell them at a profit when they are delivered to me at some future date.

London is the world's largest centre for foreign exchange trading, with an average daily turnover of over US $8,000 billion. The market is growing all the time; indeed, the average daily turnover in 2002 was more than treble the value recorded in 1992. Some 64% of transactions are 'spot' on any one day, 24% are forward for periods not exceeding one month, and 10% are forward for longer than one month. Increasingly, however, more sophisticated types of transactions are being done. For instance, there is a growth in the following types of transactions:

1 *foreign currency futures*, which are standardised contracts to buy or sell on agreed terms on specific future dates (*see* p. 129)
2 *foreign currency options*, which give the right (but do not impose an obligation) to buy or sell currencies at some future date and price (*see* p. 130)
3 *foreign currency swaps* – rather than purchase the foreign currency, countries and films swap agreed values of one currency for another, to be returned at a specified future date (*see* p. 130).

Foreign exchange market business in London is done in an increasingly wide variety of currencies with the £/$ business now accounting for only 11% of activity.

■ Supply and demand for a currency

Prices of currencies are determined, as on any other market, by demand for and supply of the various currencies. Tourists coming to the UK will sell their own currency in order to buy (demand) sterling. Businessmen wishing to import goods will often sell (supply) sterling in order to buy currency with which to pay the supplier in another country. Other types of transactions, too, will have exchange rate repercussions. For instance, if an American company wishes to buy a factory in the UK, it will need to convert dollars into sterling. A similar demand for sterling will result from foreign banks who wish to make sterling deposits in London, or residents abroad who wish to buy UK government bonds.

Another way of saying this is to say that in any given period of time the factors that determine the demand for and supply of foreign exchange are those which are represented in the balance of payments account. For example, demand for sterling results from the export of UK goods and services and inflows of foreign capital into the UK (short and long term). Similarly, a supply of sterling results from imports of goods and services into the UK and outflows of capital from the UK (short and long term).

It is clear from the balance of payments accounts that companies and individuals are not the only clients of foreign exchange market dealers. In the case of the UK the Bank of England buys and sells foreign currency, using the official reserves in the Exchange Equalisation Account. In order to reflect on why this might be the case, we have to remember that governments have an interest in the level of the exchange rate (*see* Chapter 3) and that they may on occasion wish to intervene in the workings of the foreign exchange market to affect the value of their currency. Indeed, it was estimated that on the day sterling was forced to withdraw from the Exchange Rate Mechanism (16 September 1992), the Bank of England spent an estimated £7 billion, roughly a third of its foreign exchange reserves, in buying sterling. In particular, it bought sterling with deutschmarks in an unsuccessful attempt to preserve the sterling exchange rate within its permitted ERM band.

The worldwide demand for and supply of a currency will determine its price (the *exchange rate*) on the foreign exchange market.

The exchange rate

The exchange rate is the price of one currency in terms of another. The exchange rate for sterling is conventionally defined as the number of units of another currency, such as the dollar, that it takes to purchase one pound sterling on the foreign exchange market. In the market, however, it is usually quoted as the number of units of the domestic currency that it takes to purchase one unit of the foreign currency. In general terms the sterling exchange rate is perhaps the most important 'price' in the UK economic system. It affects the standard of living, because it determines how many goods we can get for what we sell abroad. It influences the price of UK exports and hence their sales, thereby determining output and jobs in the export industries. It structures the extent to which imports can compete with home-produced goods, and thereby affects the viability of UK companies. Because the price of imports enters into the retail price index (RPI) any variation in the exchange rate will also have an effect on the rate of inflation.

Figure 4.2 presents a stylised picture of how the sterling exchange rate is determined on the foreign exchange market.

Suppose we start with the supply of sterling S and the demand for sterling D, giving an initial equilibrium exchange rate $0P$ with $0Q$ pounds sterling bought and sold on the foreign exchange market. Anything which shifts one or other of the curves will change the equilibrium price (exchange rate) on the foreign exchange market. Supply and demand curves for sterling can shift for a number of reasons:

- A shift (increase) in supply from S to S_1 might be due to a change in the tastes of UK residents in favour of foreign goods. More expenditure by UK residents on imports will mean more sterling being supplied in order to buy the foreign currencies to pay for those imports (more investment overseas by UK residents will have the same effect).
- A shift (decrease) in demand from D to D_1 might be due to a change in the tastes of overseas residents away from UK goods. Less expenditure by overseas residents on UK exports will mean less sterling being demanded in order to pay for those exports (less investment in the UK by overseas residents – firms and individuals – will have the same effect).

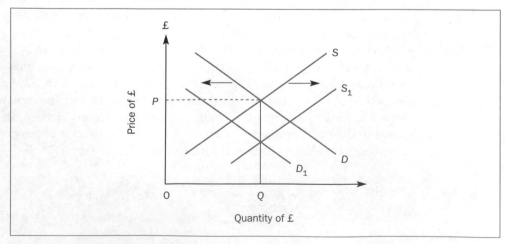

Figure 4.2 **The foreign exchange market**

Each of these changes (increase in supply or decrease in demand) will result in the pound falling in value (depreciating). We have already noted how a fall in the exchange rate then makes exports cheaper abroad and imports dearer at home (*see* Chapter 3).

pause for thought 3

In recent times the pound has been rising in value (appreciating against the US dollar). Can you use Figure 4.2 to explain the factors that might cause the pound to rise above 0*P*?

In actual fact there are different types of exchange rate, as is noted in Box 4.3.

Box 4.3 Types of exchange rate

In a foreign exchange market where exchange rates are allowed to 'float', every currency has a price against every other currency. In order to allow for measurability three different types of exchange rate may be used.

1 *The nominal rate of exchange.* This is the rate of exchange for any one currency as quoted against any other currency. The nominal exchange rate is therefore a bilateral (two country) exchange rate.

2 *The effective exchange rate (EER).* This is a measure that takes into account the fact that each currency (e.g. sterling) varies in different ways against each of the other currencies, some of which are more important than others in the UK's trading relationships. It is calculated as a trade weighted average of the individual or bilateral rates, and is expressed as an index number relative to the base year. The EER is therefore a multilateral (many country) trade weighted exchange rate.

3 *The real exchange rate (RER).* This concept is designed to measure the rate at which home goods exchange for goods from other countries, rather than the rate at which the currencies themselves are traded. It is thus essentially a measure of competitiveness. When we consider multilateral UK trade, it is defined as:

$$RER = EER \times \frac{P(\text{UK})}{P(\text{F})}$$

In other words, the real exchange rate is equal to the effective exchange rate multiplied by the price ratio of home, $P(\text{UK})$, to foreign, $P(\text{F})$, goods. If UK prices rise, the real exchange rate will rise unless the effective exchange rate falls.

In fact there was a sharp upward revision between 1996 and 1998 in nominal sterling exchange rates against individual countries and against the weighted average of 16 major industrial countries (i.e. the sterling effective exchange rate). This appreciation of sterling led to a sharp deterioration in the UK's international competitiveness between 1996 and 1998, making UK exports dearer overseas and imports into the UK cheaper. For example, the sterling effective exchange rate rose as an index from 86.3 to 105.3 (1990 = 100) between 1996 and 1998, a rise of over 22%. A lower price inflation in the UK than in its competitors would help modify any loss of competitiveness, resulting in a smaller rise in terms of real sterling exchange rates.

Since 1998, however, the sterling effective exchange rate has fallen considerably and by mid 2003 was only 100.9 (1990 = 100).

We have already considered the advantages and disadvantages of adopting the euro as a single currency in Chapter 3 (pp 100–3).

International debt financing

Firms can raise short and long-term loans on international as well as domestic financial markets. The term 'money markets' is usually applied to the buying and selling of short-term (less than one year to maturity) debt instruments, whereas the term 'bond markets' refers to trading longer-term (more than one year to maturity) debt instruments.

Here we select a number of important international financial markets by way of illustration.

■ Eurocurrency market

Eurocurrency is currency held on deposit with a bank outside the country from which that currency originates. For example, loans made in dollars by banks in the UK are known as Eurodollar loans. The Eurocurrency market is a wholesale market and has its origins in the growing holdings of US dollars outside the USA in the 1960s. Since that time, Eurocurrency markets have grown rapidly to include dealing in all the major currencies, and have become particularly important when oil price rises have created huge world surpluses and deficits, resulting in large shifts in demand for and supply of the major world currencies.

The major participants are banks, who use the Euromarkets for a variety of reasons: for short-term inter-bank lending and borrowing, to match the currency composition of assets and liabilities, and for global liquidity transformation between branches. However, the market is also extensively used by companies and by governmental and international organisations. Lending which is longer term is usually done on a variable-rate basis, where the interest is calculated periodically in line with changing market rates.

There are two important factors which make Eurocurrency business attractive. The first is that the market is unregulated, so that banks which are subject to reserve requirements or interest rate restrictions in the home country, for instance, can do business more freely abroad. The other factor is that the margin between the lending and borrowing rates is narrower on this market than on the home market, primarily because banks can operate at lower cost when all business is wholesale and when they are not subject to reserve requirements.

■ Euro-paper and Euro-note markets

The Eurocurrency markets have led to the issue of various types of *Euro-paper* and *Euro-note* debt instruments.

- *Euro-commercial papers* (ECPs) are short-term debt instruments usually denominated in dollars. They can be issued by multinational companies with excellent credit ratings, and holders obtain a return by purchasing them at a discount (i.e. paying less than face value at issue and receiving face value on maturity).

■ *Euro notes* are short to medium-term debt instruments (up to five years to maturity) which again can be issued by multinational companies, but with an interest return (rather than discount) to those holding them to maturity. Euro medium-term notes (Euro MTNs) have been growing rapidly in recent years, often being seen as much more flexible than more conventional debt instruments (e.g. more choice in terms of value, maturity date, currency, fixed/variable interest, etc.).

■ Eurobond markets

Longer-term bonds typically have maturity dates ranging up to 30 years. A *Eurobond* is underwritten by an investment bank and can be sold only outside the country from which the bond originates. Eurobonds are usually issued by large multinational firms (of high credit standing), governments and international institutions. The interest paid may be fixed or variable; in the latter case a linkage is made with other interest rates (e.g. the London Interbank Offer Rate – LIBOR). Some Eurobonds are 'convertible' in the sense that holders can convert the bond at a set price ('warrant' price) prior to the maturity date. The Eurobond market has grown substantially, partly because there is less regulation and fewer disclosure requirements than in other bond markets and various tax advantages (e.g. interest on Eurobonds has been exempt from the EU income-withholding tax).

■ Futures and options markets

Exchange rates became highly volatile in the early 1970s as countries moved away from the system of pegging their exchange rates to the dollar. Futures and options markets have therefore developed as a means of reducing the risks of companies requiring foreign currencies for international transactions. Both of these instruments are referred to as 'financial derivatives'. Attempts to avoid future risks of this kind are sometimes referred to as 'hedging'.

Futures markets

A foreign currency futures contract is an agreement to deliver or receive a fixed amount of foreign currency at a future specified time and price. The 'margin requirement' refers to the price the purchaser of the future foreign currency must pay for others taking the risk of exchange rate volatility. Typically such margin requirements are 5% or less. The International Monetary Market (IMM) on the Chicago Mercantile Exchange is the main US market for foreign currency futures. Eurex is the German equivalent and LIFFE (London International Finance and Futures Exchange) the UK equivalent.

■ *Holder* is the purchaser of the option.
■ *Writer (or grantee)* is the seller of the option.
■ *European options* are those which can only be exercised on the specified expiration date.
■ *American options* are those which can be exercised at any time before the expiration date.
■ *Premium* is the initially agreed difference between the selling and buying price of the currencies (i.e. the cost of the option to the purchaser).

Clearly those involved in buying and selling options must negotiate the premium. However, the other avenue for gain/loss is the difference between the exercise (strike) price agreed at the outset and the spot (current) price at the time at which the option is exercised.

Such options can be traded on formal exchanges or on less formal, over-the-counter (OTC) markets. Important formal exchanges include LIFFE in the UK, Chicago Mercantile Exchange and Philadelphia Stock Exchange in the USA, the European Options Exchange in Amsterdam and the Montreal Stock Exchange.

Options markets

There are obvious similarities between the futures and option markets. The main difference, however, is that the forward and future contracts markets involve a legal obligation to buy or sell a fixed amount of foreign currency at a specified point in time (expiration date), whereas the options markets only involve a right to such a transaction.

- A *call option* purchaser has the right to buy foreign currency (sell domestic currency).
- A *put option* purchaser has the right to sell foreign currency (buy domestic currency).

Currency and interest rate swaps

The IMF introduced (in 1961) the idea of 'currency swaps' by which a country in need of specific foreign exchange could avoid the obvious disadvantage of having to purchase it with its own currency by simply agreeing to 'swap' a certain amount through the Bank for International Settlements. The swap contract would state a rate of exchange which would also apply to the 'repayment' at the end of the contract.

Multinational firms as well as governments are now making use of swap facilities, with the swaps arranged by dealers located in various international financial centres. These can involve both currency swaps and interest rate swaps. For example, one multinational may borrow funds in its own financial market in which it has low interest access to funds and swap these loans with those similarly obtained by another multinational located overseas. As well as removing the exchange risk on low-cost borrowings, such swap transactions have the further advantages of not appearing on the firm's balance sheet! Interest rate swaps can also involve changing the maturity structure of the debt. Here one party to the swap typically exchanges a floating-rate obligation for a fixed-rate obligation.

Some of the instruments which are particularly important in the finance of foreign trade are considered in rather more detail in Chapter 11.

International equity markets

As well as raising international finance by trading in various types of debt instruments, business can raise funds by issuing share capital (equity) in financial centres throughout the world. Equities (or shares) are non-redeemable assets issued by companies, and investors are actually buying part-ownership (a share) of a company. Investors in ordinary shares receive dividends if companies are able to pay them, but their major advantage as an asset lies in the possibility of capital appreciation if strong profits growth is anticipated. In the case of *preference shares* the company pays a fixed annual sum to the shareholder, and there is also the possibility of capital appreciation when the share is sold. *Ordinary shareholders* bear the largest risks since if the company goes out of business, the 'preferred' shareholders are entitled to a share of the money raised by selling assets first (although only after the Inland Revenue, Customs and Excise and secured bank borrowers are paid). However, in good times, the ordinary shareholder will earn the greatest returns as dividend payments may be much greater than the fixed return received by preference shareholders. As always in the financial markets, those who bear most risk have highest potential for returns.

A high proportion of equities are traded on the stock exchanges throughout the world. Strictly speaking, 'stock' refers to the issued capital of a company other than that in the form of shares (equities). In more recent times the term 'stock' has become synonymous with the issue of securities of any type (bonds, shares, etc.). The stock exchanges we consider below are markets for all these securities though our main concern here is with equities.

■ London Stock Exchange (LSE)

The London Stock Exchange (LSE) is the second largest market for equities in the world. The largest is in the hands of Euronext, the company that controls the Paris exchange. In recent times the securities markets in Germany, France and Italy have all become 'integrated', i.e. with cash and derivatives trading, settlement and clearing all done under one roof. In contrast the UK securities market on the London Stock Exchange remains fragmented, with different institutions responsible for settlement, clearing and trading.

Individual share prices may move for a whole host of reasons: stockbrokers' reports; bid rumours; executive departures; adverse press reports; results which beat, or fall short of, market expectations. This last factor is one of the most important. Outsiders are often puzzled when a company which reports a 30% rise in profits sees its shares fall.

Markets indulge in what one might call the 'White Queen syndrome', after the character in *Through the Looking Glass*. The White Queen screamed before she pricked her finger and when the injury actually occurred, made only a small sigh, as she had got all her screaming over with in advance. Similarly, stock markets are forever looking to the future and anticipating what will happen. Expectations are built into the market, thus, if a company is expected to increase profits by 40% and only reports a rise of 30%, its shares will fall.

■ FTSE

Because there are so many quoted shares, investors use 'benchmarks', in the form of baskets of representative stocks, to track the market's overall movements. The most commonly used in the UK is the FTSE 100, which stands for the *Financial Times/Stock Exchange 100 index* and is designed to show the UK's 100 largest companies. Broader indices, such as the *FTSE All-Share*, which includes around 800 stocks and the *FTSE SmallCap*, which covers shares in smaller companies, are also used. Companies drop in and out of these indices as their shares rise and fall, or are subject to takeover.

The indices are also used to monitor the performance of fund managers who look after other people's money, whether it be pension funds, charities, or the portfolios of private investors. Experience has found that it is very difficult to beat these benchmarks. In part, this is because the index will inevitably represent the average performance of all shares, and thus all investors; by definition, therefore, half of all investors should not beat the index. On top of that factor is the burden of administrative and dealing costs, which investors have to pay, but the index does not reflect. More fundamentally, it seems as if very few people have the ability to pick successful shares. Academics have argued that this is because markets are efficient; share prices reflect all the available knowledge about a company. What will affect the price, therefore, is future news, which by definition cannot be known.

The main factors which cause the market to rise and fall include the following:

- *Interest rates*. Broadly speaking, rising interest rates are bad news for share prices and falling rates are good. Rising rates increase the cost of corporate borrowing and thereby reduce profits. Higher interest rates also increase the attraction of selling shares to hold funds on deposit. Factors which are likely to lead the government to raise interest rates – rising inflation, strong economic growth – are therefore often bad news for the markets.
- *Profits growth*. Equities represent a share of the assets and profits of a company. The faster profits grow, therefore, the better for the markets. Tax changes which eat into profits hit the market.
- *Supply and demand*. Flotations and rights issues increase the supply of shares in the market and drive prices down (other things being equal); high dividends, share buybacks and takeovers for cash, increase the demand for shares and push prices up.
- *International influences*. Increasingly, stock markets are being dominated by global influences as investors move money round in search of the most attractive havens. There is a tendency for share prices to move up and down together; London, in particular, is heavily influenced by Wall Street and a sharp fall in the US market usually has a knock-on effect in the UK.

Useful websites

Now try the self-check questions for this chapter on the website at www.booksites/net/wall. You will also find further resources as well as the following useful weblinks:

Sources of information on international trade and payments, international institutions and exchange rates include:
www.wto.org
www.imf.org
www.ifg.org
www.un.org
www.dti.gov.uk
www.europa.eu.int
www.worldbank.org/devcom

www.unctad.org
The International Chamber of Commerce website is *www.iccwbo.org*
The OECD website is *www.oecd.org*
The IMF website is *www.imf.org*
The World Bank website is *www.worldbank.org*
The UN's Food and Agriculture Organisation is at *www.fao.org*

Useful key texts

Daniels, J., Radebaugh, L. and Sullivan, D. (2004) *International Business* (10th edn), Pearson Prentice Hall, especially Chapters 6 and 9.
Dicken, P. (2003) *Global Shift: Transforming the World Economy* (4th edn), Paul Chapman Publishing Ltd, especially Part IV.
Hill, C. (2003) *International Business: Competing in the Global Marketplace* (4th edn), McGraw-Hill Irwin, especially Chapters 5 and 9.
Morrison, J. (2002) *The International Business Environment*, Palgrave, especially Chapters 9 and 11.
Rugman, A. and Hodgetts, R. (2003) *International Business* (3rd edn), FT Prentice Hall, especially Chapters 6 and 7.
Tayeb, M. (2000) *International Business: Theories, Policies and Practices*, Financial Times Prentice Hall, especially Chapters 2, 3 and 11.
Woods, M. (2001) *International Business*, Palgrave, especially Chapters 2 and 7.

Other texts and sources

Dollar, D. and Kraay, A. (2000) 'Growth is Good for the Poor', World Bank (unpublished paper), March.
Edwards, S. (2000) 'Trade Development and Poverty Reduction', World Bank, *www.worldbank.org/devcom*.
International Bank for Reconstruction and Development (2003), *Global Economic Prospects and the Developing Countries*.
Monbiot, G. (2003a) 'I was Wrong about Trade', *The Guardian*, 24 June.
Monbiot, G. (2003b) *The Age of Consent: a Manifesto for a New World Order*, Flamingo.
Rose, R. (2003) 'Companies UK: Unsmash the WTO', *Financial Times*, 26 May.
United Nations Conference on Trade and Development (UNCTAD) *World Investment Report* (annual publication).
United Nations Development Programme (UNDP) *Human Development Report* (annual publication), OUP.
Walker, K. (2002) 'Main Development from WTO Talks is a Fine Line in Hypocrisy', *The Guardian*, 26 August.
Wall, S. (2004) 'Exchange Rates', in *Applied Economics* (10th edn), Griffiths, A. and Wall, S. (eds), Financial Times Prentice Hall.
Webb, R. (2004) 'Financial Institutions and Markets', in *Applied Economics* (10th edn), Griffiths, A. and Wall, S. (eds), Financial Times Prentice Hall.
World Bank, *World Development Report* (annual publication).

Chapter 5

The political, legal, economic and technological environment

By the end of this chapter you should be able to:

- assess the effects of globalisation on world political systems;

- explain the various ways in which political risk can be analysed and minimised;

- discuss the implications of different political and regulatory systems for international business;

- outline the issues that MNEs have to consider in relation to the legal environment, including the increasingly important areas of intellectual property rights and e-commerce legal risks;

- consider the main features of the different types of economic system in which international businesses operate;

- identify and explain some of the key economic variables which influence international businesses in the assessment of their economic environment;

- discuss the opportunities and threats to international business of technological change.

Introduction

In Chapters 1–4, we outlined how the internationalisation of business increasingly transcends national barriers. Nevertheless, the basic unit in which the MNE operates is still the nation state, each one of which has its own method of governance, institutional framework and legal environment. It would be folly indeed for any company thinking of going international to be unaware of these different factors, and to have failed to take them into account before making any significant strategic decisions. In this chapter, we look at the various political and legal elements that make up 'governance', highlight areas of political and legal risk, and suggest ways in which businesses may seek to address such risk.

In the widely-used approach of PEST analysis (*see* p. 228) businesses seek to assess the political, economic, social and technological environments in which they must operate. In this chapter, as well as the political and legal variables, we also pay particular attention to the economic and technological variables that may cruci determine the outcomes for international business of individual investment projects or broad strategic initiatives. Further discussions of the economic and technological issues facing the individual business also take place in Chapters 8–12. For example, Chapter 12 looks at the impacts of new technologies on the supply chain and on other logistical operations.

The following two chapters focus on the sociocultural, environmental and ethical aspects of international business decisions which may also play a part in more sophisticated PEST type analyses.

Political environment

At the heart of governance is the notion of 'sovereignty', which implies the power to rule without constraint and which, for the last three centuries, has been associated with the nation state. We live in a world which is organised as a patchwork of nation states within which different peoples live, with their own systems of government exerting authority over the affairs within their territory. Of course, groupings within those territories may arise from time to time which seek a measure of independence from the central authorities, sometimes claiming nation statehood themselves. Many would also argue that the idea of the nation state has itself been challenged by the growth of globalisation. Before turning to this issue it may be useful to highlight some opposing and arguably contradictory tendencies in globalisation (*see also* Chapter 1).

■ *Centralisation versus decentralisation.* Some aspects of globalisation tend to concentrate power, knowledge, information, wealth and decision making. Many believe this to be the case with the rise of the MNE, the growth of regional trading blocs (e.g. the EU), the development of world regulatory bodies such as the WTO, etc. However, such centralising tendencies may conflict with powerful decentralising tendencies as nations, communities and individuals attempt to take greater control over the forces that influence their lives (e.g. the growth of social movements centred on the global environment, peace and gender issues, etc.).

■ *Juxtaposition versus syncretisation.* In the globalisation process, time and space become compressed, so that different civilisations, ways of life and social practices become juxtaposed (placed side-by-side). This can create 'shared' cultural and social spaces characterised by an evolving mixture of ideas, knowledge and institutions. Unfortunately this can also stimulate the opposite tendencies, such as a heightened awareness of challenges to the established norms of previously dominant groups, which can result in determined attempts to avoid integration and instead combine against a 'common opponent' (syncretisation).

While there may be many theories as to the causes of globalisation, most writers would agree that globalisation is a discontinuous historical process. Its dynamic proceeds in fits and starts and its effects are experienced differentially across the globe. Some regions are more deeply affected by globalisation than others. Even within nation states, some communities (e.g. financial) may experience the effects of globalisation more sharply than others (e.g. urban office workers). Many have argued that globalisation is tending to reinforce inequalities of power both within and across nation states, resulting in global hierarchies of privilege and control for some but economic and social exclusion for others.

We have already considered the ways in which globalisation has arguably influenced the notion of the nation state in Chapter 1, suggesting some loss of competence, autonomy, authority and ultimately legitimacy for the nation state (pp. 16–17). We concluded that globalisation is redefining our understanding of the nation state by introducing a much more complex architecture of political power in which authority is seen as being pluralistic rather than residing solely in the nation state.

Political risk

While businesses are largely aware that the political climate in different countries varies enormously, for organisations wishing to go global a far more detailed analysis needs to take place. When considering penetrating or expanding into new markets, organisations need to be able to assess the political risk. Political risk can be defined as: 'uncertainty that stems, in whole or in part, from the exercise of power by governmental and non-governmental actors' (Zonis and Wilkin 2000).

Political risks can be classified into two broad categories, 'macropolitical' and 'micropolitical'.

- *Macropolitical risks* potentially affect all firms in a country, as in the case of war or sudden changes of government. Such risks may even result in expropriation or confiscation, where governments seize the assets of the firm without compensation. Communist governments in Eastern Europe and China expropriated private firms after the Second World War, with the same happening at different times in the post-war period to private enterprises in Angola, Chile, Ethiopia, Peru and Zambia. Higher general levels of inflation or taxation might adversely affect all firms, as might security risks related to terrorism, etc.
- *Micropolitical risks* within a country affect only specific firms, industries or types of venture. Such risks may take the form of new regulations or taxes imposed on specific types of businesses in the country. For example, the indebtedness of countries in South America has meant that many have introduced legislation to encourage certain types of exports and discourage certain types of imports. For firms focused on exporting products into these countries, such practices are extremely adverse. However, for MNEs looking for an international location ('platform') from which to produce and export products to other countries, these government policies may appear very attractive.

It may be useful to disaggregate the types of political risk further, as indicated in Table 5.1.

| *pause for thought 1* | You are the MD of a US-based multinational company considering establishing a major affiliate in the UK. Which types of political risk in Table 5.1 are likely to be of major concern? |

Table 5.1 **Types of political risk and their likely impacts**

Type	Impact on firms
Expropriation/confiscation	Loss of sales Loss of assets Loss of future profits
Campaigns against foreign goods	Loss of sales Increased cost of public relations campaigns to improve public image
Mandatory labour benefits legislation	Increased operating costs
Kidnappings, terrorist threats, and other forms of violence	Disrupted production Increased security costs Increased managerial costs Lower productivity
Civil wars	Destruction of property Lost sales Disruption of production Increased security costs Lower productivity
Inflation	Higher operating costs
Currency devaluations/depreciation	Reduced value of repatriated earnings
Currency revaluations/appreciation	Less competitive in overseas markets and in competing against imports in home market
Increased taxation	Lower after-tax profits

■ Analysing political risk

Analysing political risk has, in the past, been a rather ad hoc affair, but in more recent times it has become increasingly sophisticated. A common criticism of political risk analysis is that it usually takes place too late, when projects are already underway. More management time and effort is now being directed towards appraising political risk at the initiation stage of projects as companies become more aware of its importance to their future operations. For example, organisations seeking to internationalise typically investigate the following factors in countries which might become the focus of fdi activity: the system of government, foreign capital controls, industrial regulations, history of civil unrest, diplomatic tensions, and so on.

Managers or their representatives may well visit the countries under investigation, as well as using information and data sources from libraries, the Internet, industry associations, government agencies, banks and insurers. Country-risk reports are also available from risk assessment companies and specialists in particular business activities, often consisting of a country profile and macro-level market/non-market risk assessment. However, such analyses may not include the fine detail that might be vital for particular ventures, and at best provide only an indication of the sociopolitical background.

Quantifying political risk

There are more sophisticated ways of analysing political risk, of which one is to identify and then *quantify* the various elements involved. Table 5.2 outlines the criteria that might be used for such an analysis. We can see that some of the criteria in Table 5.2 have a wider minimum to maximum range than others, because that particular risk is perceived as varying more widely between different countries. For example, no country is viewed as having perfect 'stability of the political system', hence the minimum risk assessment is three rather than zero. At the other extreme some countries are viewed as extremely unstable in this respect, receiving the maximum risk assessment, for this criterion, of 14. The respective minimum and maximum scores are indicated for some 30 criteria across three major areas: political economic environment, domestic economic conditions and external economic conditions.

Suppose, for example, that an MNE wishes to evaluate the political risk of pursuing a joint venture in a particular country. If the country scores too highly over the selected criteria deemed appropriate to the joint venture or investment project under consideration, then the MNE will look elsewhere unless there is a way of reducing these risks. For some criteria this may be possible. For example, while the MNE may itself be unable to influence the first criterion in Table 5.2 of 'stability of the political system', it might believe that it can reduce the initial risk score ascribed, say, to the eighth criterion of 'labour relations and social peace'. For example, the MNE may well look at an initial risk score on this criterion for a particular country and then re-evaluate that assessment in the light of its own strategic intentions (e.g. adopting widespread worker consultation procedures, paying above the minimum wage, etc.) and any promises made to it by the authorities of a potential host country (e.g. assurances as to no-strike agreements, etc.). However, should the overall risk-assessment score for a particular project still be higher than that in other countries despite taking into account these planned risk-reduction strategies, this may cause the firm to reconsider its location decision.

Of course, these 'risk scores' for the various criteria will to some extent be subjective, based on management perceptions as to the likelihood (probability) of that risk factor actually occurring. These risk scores must continually be reviewed as events and circumstances (and associated probabilities) are ever-changing. For example, investment in Indonesia facilitated by a close confidant of the then President Suharto before 1997, will have very different political risk scores for the various factors after the fall of President Suharto in 1997, the instability induced by various independence movements (e.g. East Timor in 1999), and recent investigations into state corruption in the pre-1997 period.

| *pause for thought 2* | You are the MD of a US-based MNE specialising in heavy equipment (capital goods) manufacture. You are about to decide whether to establish a production platform in either Italy or Russia. Look at Table 5.2 and identify some of the political risk factors that might influence your decision. What other considerations might be taken into account? |

Table 5.2 **Select criteria for evaluating political risk**

Major area	Criteria		Score	
			Minimum	Maximum
Political economic environment	1	Stability of the political system	3	14
	2	Imminent internal conflicts	0	14
	3	External threats to stability	0	12
	4	Degree of control of the economic system	5	9
	5	Reliability of the country as a trading partner	4	12
	6	Constitutional guarantees	2	12
	7	Effectiveness of public administration	3	12
	8	Labour relations and social peace	3	15
Domestic economic conditions	9	Size of the population	4	8
	10	Per capita income	2	10
	11	Economic growth over the last 5 years	2	7
	12	Potential growth over the next 3 years	3	10
	13	Inflation over the past 2 years	2	10
	14	Accessibility of the domestic capital market to outsiders	3	7
	15	Availability of high-quality local labour force	2	8
	16	Possibility of employing foreign nationals	2	8
	17	Availability of energy resources	2	14
	18	Legal requirements regarding environmental pollution	4	8
	19	Infrastructure, including transportation and communication systems	2	14
External economic conditions	20	Import restrictions	2	10
	21	Export restrictions	2	10
	22	Restrictions on foreign investments	3	9
	23	Freedom to set up or engage in partnerships	3	9
	24	Legal protection for brands and products	3	9
	25	Restrictions on monetary transfers	2	8
	26	Revaluation of the currency during the last 5 years	2	7
	27	Balance of payments situation	2	9
	28	Drain on foreign funds through oil and energy imports	3	14
	29	International financial standing	3	8
	30	Restriction on the exchange of local money into foreign currencies	2	8

Source: Adapted from Dichtl and Koeglmayr (1986), p. 6

Expected value and political risk

It is not only the probability of a particular political risk factor occurring but the magnitude of its potential impact on the objectives of the company that must also be taken into account. It is worth remembering that the expected value of an event is the sum of the probability of each possible outcome multiplied by the value (impact) of each outcome.

$$EV = \sum_{i=1}^{n} p_i x_i$$

where p_i = probability of outcome i (as a decimal)
x_i = value of outcome i
n = number of possible outcomes

So if the firm estimated a 60% probability of a 'strike' labour dispute (criterion 8 'labour relations and social peace' in Table 5.2) occurring so that profits are £10 million and a 40% probability of a 'work to rule' occurring so that profits are £20 million, the expected value (EV) should a labour dispute occur would be:

$$\text{EV (£m)} = (0.60 \times 10) + (0.40 \times 20)$$
$$= £14 \text{ m}$$

A change in the firm's assessment of the probabilities of these events occurring or the value of their impact should they occur would, of course, influence the expected value calculation.

Once identified and assessed, such political risks can be prioritised, as in Figure 5.1. The 'gross risks' (expected values) associated with the various political factors or events are sometimes placed by businesses in a two-by-two diagram, giving four 'boxes'. Box A shows risks (high impact/high likelihood) requiring immediate action, resulting in attempts by the firm to reduce either the probability of their occurrence or the impact should they occur. Perhaps it would also be sensible to have in place contingency plans to cover some of the risks in boxes B and C, but those in D would be of lesser concern.

Responses to political risk

Once the risk has been analysed and assessed, an organisation must decide if there are ways in which such risks can be managed. There are two common responses:

- improve relative bargaining power;
- adopt integrative, protective and defensive techniques.

Relative bargaining power

In an attempt to overcome political risk, some MNEs may seek to develop a stronger bargaining position than that of the host country itself. For example, the MNE might attempt to create a situation in which the host country loses more than it gains by taking action against the company. This could be the case when the MNE has propri-

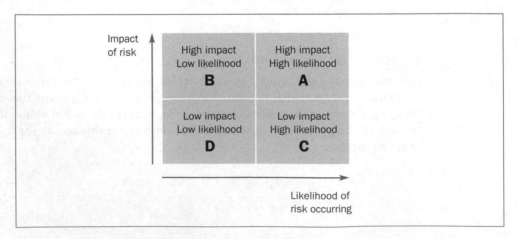

Figure 5.1 Prioritising (political) risk

etary technology that will be lost to the host country if the company is forced to meet certain governmental regulations or where the MNE can credibly threaten to move elsewhere (with significant job losses) to avoid such regulations.

Integrative, protective or defensive techniques

A second approach is to use a set of techniques to prevent the host government interfering with the operations of the MNE.

- *Integrative techniques* ensure that the subsidiary is as fully integrated as possible with the local economy, so that it becomes part of the host country's infrastructure. Techniques here may include: developing good relations with the host government and other local political groups; producing as much of the product locally as is possible; creating joint ventures and hiring local people to manage and run the operation; carrying out extensive local research and development; and developing good employee relations with the local labour force. These techniques raise the 'costs' to the host country economy of unwelcome interference in MNE activities.

- *Protective and defensive techniques* seek to limit, in advance, the 'costs' to the MNE should the host government interfere in its activities. Such techniques may include doing as little local manufacturing as possible, locating all research and development outside the country, hiring only those local personnel who are essential, manufacturing the same product in many other different countries, etc.

A risk management strategy involves adopting a comprehensive and systematic approach to dealing with the factors causing political risk. Clearly prioritising the areas of political risk in the manner of Figure 5.1 (above) is one step in such a process. Zonis and Wilkin (2000) suggest that a business might also try to break down the 'drivers' of political risk into three separate categories, namely external, interaction and internal drivers.

- *External drivers* of political risk involve factors whose probability cannot be influenced by the firm. Examples include political instability (e.g. riots, civil war, coups) and weak public policy (e.g. hyperinflation, currency crisis). Although the company cannot influence these factors itself, it can try to assess accurately their probabilities of occurrence and potential impacts, as a preliminary to taking out appropriate levels of risk insurance.

- *Interaction drivers* of political risk involve factors that are broadly related to company relationships. Examples include relationships with home-country and host-country governments, regional and local authorities, national and supranational institutions and regulatory bodies, pressure groups, local communities, and so on. Unlike the 'external drivers' the firm *can* influence these 'interaction drivers' by its own actions. It can influence both the probabilities and potential impacts of any breakdown in the various categories of relationship. It can seek to manage such risks by investing resources in fostering those relationships it has given the highest priority in terms of their potential for favourable or unfavourable corporate outcomes. For example, given the importance of *guanxi*-type relationships to business activities in Confucian societies, the politically 'risk averse' firm operating in China or Hong Kong might invest substantial resources in fostering such relationships (*see* Chapter 6).

■ *Internal drivers* of political risk involve factors which are specific to the organisation and *operation* of the company itself. Examples might include the extent to which internal incentive structures are aligned with corporate objectives. An executive remuneration scheme which links bonuses to turnover or market share may be less appropriate where the corporate objective is primarily profit related. The Turnbull Report on corporate governance in 1999 called on the directors of all listed companies in the UK to disclose whether there was an ongoing process for identifying, evaluating and managing significant corporate risks. In particular, it called on company boards regularly to receive and review reports on internal control from line managers and, where appropriate, from specialists in areas such as internal audit.

Case Study 5.1 provides an opportunity to consider political issues and political risk analysis in the context of major decisions involving the future of Rover, then owned by BMW.

CASE 5.1   BMW after Rover

Joachim Milberg took over as chief executive of BMW in 1999. The board had fired his predecessor, Bernd Pischetsrieder, who had made a mess at Rover, the British volume car-maker that he had bought in 1994. The new boss soon came to the conclusion that the German company could turn round the ailing British subsidiary. Mr Milberg held to that view until early March 2000, when he concluded that the worsening situation in Britain had become hopeless, a situation not helped by the continuing strong pound damaging Rover group exports.

Hence the decision to sell Rover for a pittance to Alchemy, a group of British venture capitalists who would have ended up making only a small number of sports cars under the MG label. This decision by BMW to sell Rover caused uproar in the British press and among politicians in the West Midlands who feared large job losses in Rover and in the numerous component suppliers located around the region. The West Midlands has many parliamentary seats, often with only small majorities and which regularly change hands at general elections.

In the event Alchemy eventually withdrew from the bidding process and the bulk of Rover was sold to the Phoenix consortium for the princely sum of £10! Over the previous six years BMW had spent a total of DM 9 billion (£34 billion) trying to turn Rover into a car maker with a future, but had posted large losses, as high as £2.5 billion in 1999 as well as writing down Rover assets by £3.2 billion in the same year. The disposal provoked a political storm in Britain, which was still rumbling in April 2000, when BMW bosses were summoned to appear before a parliamentary inquiry.

The British government was furious that it had learnt about the disposal from a leak in the German press. Mr Milberg retorted that the British government had been slow to hear the signals he sent in telephone calls before Christmas as Rover's situation worsened. Even this reply further infuriated the British government as it came under press criticism for failing to 'read' these alleged signals from BMW. BMW had bought Rover because its Board had doubted whether it could survive as a niche firm, then making around 600,000 cars a year. By buying Rover, it secured production of around 400,000 cars, plus the Land Rover business. Having abandoned this strategy, can BMW now survive on its own?

Major losses had resulted from trading Rover group products in the previous years, (e.g. £3.2 billion lost in writing down the value of Rover assets in 1999 alone). The strong pound had provided added problems, making Rover group exports progressively less competitive in its major euro-zone markets. One of Rover group's key assets, Land Rover, was to be replaced by an own-brand product, which was much cheaper to produce (fewer basic platforms required). Land Rover could therefore be sold, raising useful revenue. Underlying all this was the conviction that volume car-production will be increasingly in the hands of only a few producers, given the huge scale economies involved. BMW will increasingly focus on niche markets, selling quality cars (e.g. acquisition of Rolls-Royce label from Volkswagen) at premium prices.

Today, giant firms dominate the industry to an even greater extent than they did in 1994. Only Honda, PSA Peugeot Citroen and BMW remain as smaller independents. Of those, BMW is the smallest, at around a third the volume of the others. BMW plans to remain in Britain, moving production of its new Mini from Birmingham to a modernised plant in Oxford. It also has a brand new factory in the Birmingham area producing engines for BMW models produced in the UK and overseas. Continuing good relations with the UK government, workers and consumers would still seem important for BMW.

Questions

1 What political problems were raised by the sale of Rover?

2 How might a more systematic approach to political risk analysis have influenced the outcome for BMW?

The international legal environment

Legal systems vary enormously throughout the world, and these have a significant impact on the ways in which international business is conducted. While many large organisations will employ their own lawyers to advise and settle any disputes, it is important that international managers themselves have some understanding of the likely impacts of legal systems in the countries in which the firm operates.

■ Types of legal system

The different types of legal system can generally be divided into the following categories: common law; statutory law; code law; religious law; bureaucratic law. These categories need not be mutually exclusive: for example common law can coexist with various types of code law, e.g. civil law.

■ *Common law*. This is the foundation of the legal system in the UK and its former colonies, including the USA, Canada, Australia, India, New Zealand, and much of the Caribbean. Common law is essentially unwritten, has developed over long periods of time and is largely founded on the decisions reached by judges over the years on different cases. When a judge makes a particular decision, a *legal precedent* is then established. Such case law has evolved over the centuries, which means that there will obviously be legal variations between countries. For example, manufacturers of defective goods are more liable to litigation in the USA than they are in the UK.

■ *Statutory law*. Common law countries depend not only on case law but also on statutory law, i.e. *legislation*, the laws passed by government. This can also be a source of legal variation between countries. For example, the US Freedom of Information Act is more far reaching than similar UK legislation, so that transactions between the government and companies have to be more transparent in the USA than in the UK.

■ *Code law*. This is the world's most common system. It is an explicit codification in written terms of what is and what is not permissible. Such laws can be written down in criminal, civil and/or commercial codes, which are then used to determine the outcome of all legal matters. When a legal issue is in dispute, it can then be resolved by reference to the relevant code. Most continental European countries, together with their former colonies, follow this type of legal system.

■ *Religious law*. Religious law is based on rules related to the faith and practice of a particular religion. A country that works in this way is called a *theocracy*. Iran is one such example. Here a group of mullahs (holy men) determine what is legal or illegal depending on their interpretation of the Koran, the holy book of Islam. This can pose interesting dilemmas for firms operating in these countries. For example, the Koran says that people should not charge others interest as this is an unfair exploitation of the poor. Thus banks, rather than charging interest, charge up-front fees, and owners of bank deposits are given shares of the bank's profits rather than interest. The emphasis within countries operating under religious laws tends to be on smaller family-owned businesses since the prohibitions we have mentioned often result in less capital being available through national banking systems, forcing a greater emphasis on borrowing from family members. Companies need to be cautious in countries relying on religious laws as there is often an absence of a due process and appeals procedure; for example, companies operating in Saudi Arabia often find that they need a local representative or sponsor to mediate between themselves and the Royal Family in many business disputes.

■ *Bureaucratic law*. This occurs in dictatorships and communist countries when bureaucrats largely determine what the laws are, even if these are contrary to the historical laws of the land. MNEs operating in such countries have often found it difficult to manage their affairs as there tends to be a lack of consistency, predictability and appeals procedures.

■ Effects of national laws on international business

National laws affect international business in a variety of ways. There may be legal rules relating to specific aspects of business operations such as off-shore investment, the environment, ways in which financial accounts are prepared and disclosed, corporate taxation, employee rights and pension provisions. There may even be legal rules as to the amount of assets and shares companies may own and the proportion of profits they are allowed to remit back to their home country. Countries vary enormously in the amount of control they impose in these different areas.

National laws may also affect aspects of the companies' internal organisation such as its human resource management and health and safety policies. These might include factors such as the provision of maternity and paternity leave, payment of a statutory minimum wage, physical working conditions, protection of employees against hazards at work and pollution, pension and medical provisions and childcare facilities.

Of course, the nature of these rules and regulations may, to some extent, reflect the national government's trade and industrial policies. Some governments positively encourage inward investment (such as the current Eastern European countries) while others may create a whole web of red tape and bureaucracy, which may take months or even years to unravel. Certainly the MNE should be aware of national regulations in the following areas.

- *Trade restrictions*: as noted in Chapter 3, various types of regulations may be imposed to restrict trade, even to the extent of imposing sanctions or embargo's on trade with particular countries. Sanctions can take many forms such as restricting access to high-technology goods, withdrawing preferential tariff treatment, boycotting the country's goods or denying new loans.
- *Foreign ownership restrictions*: many governments may limit the foreign ownership of firms for economic or political reasons. This may sometimes be applied to particular industrial sectors, such as air transportation, financial services or telecommunications. For example, Mexico restricts foreign ownership in its energy sector, while the USA limits foreigners to a maximum 25% ownership of US television and radio stations.
- *Environmental restrictions*: sometimes domestic laws in a country can indirectly affect the competitiveness of MNEs. For example, the extensive legislation involving the environmental packaging of goods in Germany means higher costs if products are to meet these environmental restrictions.
- *Exit restrictions*: international businesses also need to take account of the costs of exiting a country, should they need to. Many countries impose legal restraints on the closing of plants in order to protect the rights of employees. For example, in Chinese law, if a partner in a joint venture wishes for any reason to shut down a factory, this would require not only the approval of the entire board, but also the approval of the Chinese government.

■ Effects of supranational regulations on international business

We have already noted the rapid rise in non-governmental organisations (NGOs) and supranational institutions (e.g. the EU) in Chapter 1. Multinational enterprises must pay careful attention to the regulations imposed by these bodies (and the interpretations placed on them) when devising corporate policy. For example, when companies are offered governmental inducements to retain or initiate production facilities in particular countries within the EU, they must ensure that these inducements are compatible with EU directives on state aid. Otherwise, the aid inducements will be vetoed by the EU, and both the MNE's and host country's policies will be disrupted. An important issue in the initial BMW plan to build new production lines for its Rover Group affiliate in the UK was the 'legality' of a £200 million-plus aid package from the UK government. This part of the 'rescue package' was still being considered by the EU as to its legality when BMW decided instead to dispose of the Rover Group in early 2000 (*see* pp. 142–3). Box 5.1 looks in rather more detail at various EU regulations regarding state aid.

Box 5.1   EU directives and state aid

The reasoning behind European competition policy is exactly that which created the original European Economic Community (EEC) over 45 years ago. Competition is viewed as bringing consumers greater choice, lower prices and higher-quality goods and services. The European Commission has a set of directives in this area which are designed to underpin 'fair and free' competition. They cover cartels (price fixing, market sharing, etc.), government subsidies (direct or indirect subsidies for inefficient enterprises – state and private), the abuse of dominant market position (differential pricing in different markets, exclusive contracts, predatory pricing, etc.), selective distribution (preventing consumers in one market from buying in another in order to maintain high margins in the first market), and mergers and takeovers. The latter powers were given to the Commission in 1990.

State aid

One of the most active areas of competition policy has involved state aid. The Commission has attempted to restrict the aid paid by member states to their own nationals through Articles 87 and 88 (formerly Articles 92 and 93 of the original Treaty of Rome). These Articles cover various aspects of the distorting effect that subsidies can have on competition between member states. However, it is likely that the progressive implementation of single-market arrangements will result in domestic firms increasing their attempts to obtain state aid from their own governments as a means of helping them meet greater Europe-wide competition. Overall the amount of aid given by member states to their domestic industry had been running at around 1.5% of their respective GDPs during the 1990s but has now been cut back to around 1%, though with considerable variation across member countries.

Currently some 860 billion euros per year are spent on state aid to EU manufacturing. Germany tops the league of aid recipients as it tries to help its new *Länder* in the former East Germany to restructure their industry. The main problem with state aid is that the big, industrially powerful countries – Germany, France, UK and Italy – account for some 85% of the total state aid given by EU countries to their domestic industry. This arguably gives such economies considerable advantages over the four 'cohesion' countries – Greece, Portugal, Spain and Ireland – and the ten countries that joined the EU in 2004.

To counter some of these trends, the European Commission began in the 1990s to scrutinise state aid much more closely – especially where the aid seems to be more than is needed to ensure the ultimate viability of the recipient organisations. For example, in April 1998 the Commission decided that aid paid to the German porcelain firm, Triptis Porzellan GmbH, should be recovered because it believed the aid to be more than was needed to restore the firm's viability, thereby distorting competition in the market.

Article 87 determines all state aid to be illegal, unless it conforms to one or more of a number of exceptions:

- aid to promote improvements of a social character;
- aid to promote economic development in areas with high unemployment or low living standards;
- aid to promote a project of common EU interest;
- aid to the former German Democratic Republic;
- aid to disaster areas;
- sectoral aid to assist in the restructuring of an individual sector in structural decline, e.g. shipbuilding.

In recent years the Commission has also recognised the importance of small and medium-sized enterprises (SMEs) within the EU, so that certain grants and low-interest loans for small businesses are now allowed, as is government support for SME start-ups involving innovation and research and development.

As regards the decision as to whether any governmental support constitutes state aid, the Commission uses the 'market investor principle', i.e. would a rational investor get a reasonable return on the investment undertaken? If the answer is 'no', the state support is regarded as aid rather than as an economic investment. Even when a state aid programme is accepted, the Commission will continually review its implementation.

If a new aid scheme is to be introduced by a member state, the Commission must be informed in advance. The commission will apply the concept of 'one time – last time' which means that aid for restructuring an industry or rescue aid should only be granted once.

In all these ways it is clear that both MNE and host government must tread carefully through a complex set of legal directives and rules as regards any support via state aid and many other aspects of EU competition policy.

As can be seen from Box 5.2 below, EU directives on data protection can also have an important influence on international business activities.

Box 5.2   **EU directives and data protection**

The Internet may have greatly facilitated global commerce and communication, but differences in national attitudes to data protection are causing legal problems for companies that wish to operate across national borders. In the EU, there is broad agreement that individuals have certain rights over information concerning them and that companies should be prevented from collecting, using, sharing or selling those data without their permission. The EU directive on data protection, passed in October 1998, laid down four basic principles:

- individuals should be able to obtain and make corrections to information that is held about them by companies or institutions;
- companies must gain their customers' consent before storing or using information about them;

▶

> **Box 5.2   Continued**
>
> - companies must only use data for the original purpose that was expressed at the time of collection, unless the customer agrees otherwise;
> - companies must not obtain more data on individuals than they need to carry out their stated purpose.
>
> Crucially, the directive also provides that data should not be sent to countries that do not follow the same rules. That includes the USA, which has no federal laws governing the 'right to privacy' in commercial transactions and no independent ombudsman for data issues. US attitudes surrounding the use of personal data are generally more relaxed than those of the EU – companies have routinely used transaction records and mailing lists without gaining the permission of the relevant consumers. There are also few restrictions governing the secondary use of data in the USA. Credit-card companies, for instance, are not obliged to ask cardholders if they can use their data for other purposes, nor even to tell them if they have already done so.
>
> These national differences on data privacy have profound consequences for industries that operate in Europe and the USA. When, for example, a European airline wishes to arrange a connecting flight for a passenger via a US airline, compliance with the directive entails that it gains the passenger's permission before using the relevant data to complete the transaction. In theory, any company with subsidiaries in Europe and the USA could face prosecution for exchanging data on individuals without authorisation.
>
> For two years, no agreement could be reached that satisfied both sides. In March 2000, however, EU and US negotiators agreed to recommend a system of self-regulation – the so-called 'safe harbour' principle – under which US companies will sign up to certain standards of privacy on a voluntary basis. These companies would then be deemed to comply with EU privacy rules and would be able to conduct business in Europe. Any violation of the rules would trigger sanctions against the offending company.
>
> *Source*: Randall and Treacy (2000). Reprinted with permission

■ Settling international disputes

The cross-border activities of MNEs can create problems in settling international disputes. At least four issues are often involved:

1 Which country's laws apply to the dispute?
2 In which country should the issue be resolved?
3 What techniques should be used to resolve the conflict – litigation, arbitration, mediation or negotiation?
4 How will the settlement be enforced?

The answers to the first two questions may be written into MNE contracts. If not, companies may seek to initiate the legal process in the country most favourable to their own interests (a process known as 'forum shopping'). For example, since monetary rewards for compensation are higher in the USA than elsewhere, many plaintiffs attempt to use USA courts to adjudicate lawsuits involving US companies.

- *Litigation*. The principle of *comity* provides for a country to honour and enforce within its own territory the decisions of foreign courts. 'Comity' requires three conditions to be met:
  1 reciprocity is extended between the countries;
  2 proper notice is given to the defendant;
  3 the foreign court's judgment does not violate domestic statutes or treaty obligations.
- *Arbitration or mediation*. Court cases can be costly and time consuming, so many companies may prefer the process of arbitration whereby the two conflicting parties agree to abide by the decisions of a third party or mediation whereby a third party attempts to bring the positions of the conflicting parties closer together.
- *Governmental disputes*. Sometimes a company may be in dispute with a national government. There is little legal recourse here for companies. For example, the Foreign Sovereign Immunities Act of 1976 in the USA provides that the actions of foreign governments against US firms are beyond the jurisdiction of the US courts. If Germany, say, chose to nationalise IBM's German operation or impose taxes on IBM, there would be no redress for the company. If, however, a government reneges on a commercial agreement, such as repudiating a contract to purchase, then there is the possibility of legal proceedings.
- *Negotiation*. International negotiations bring with them a whole new set of problems over and above those faced when negotiating domestically. The bargaining power of the MNE with host governments or businesses will depend on factors such as the level of technology, nature of the goods or services, importance of its managerial expertise, value of its capital input, etc. The bargaining power of the host country will depend on factors such as the size of the consumer market, the degree of economic and political stability, etc.

The problems facing multinationals in responding to prospective legal disputes involving legal codes inside and outside the home country are well illustrated by Case Study 5.2.

| CASE 5.2 | Kraft cuts pack sizes to avert obesity lawsuits | |

Kraft Foods acted to fight obesity and avert lawsuits in July 2003, saying it would cut portion sizes, reduce fat and sugar in its foods and stop marketing to schools. The moves by one of the world's biggest food companies – which makes Philadelphia cheese and Suchard chocolate – could put pressure on competitors such as Unilever, Nestlé and Cadbury Schweppes to follow suit.

They are part of a growing industry effort to review products and marketing, fuelled partly by US litigants' attempts to blame foodmakers and restaurants for the obesity 'epidemic'. McDonald's, the world's biggest fast food chain, is fighting a lawsuit from a group of obese teenagers. But a central claim in the case – that some of its foods were unhealthier than the public realised – was dropped in June 2003. Kraft has also been threatened with a lawsuit over levels of artery-clogging trans fats in its Oreo biscuit. The suit was dropped after Kraft said it would try to address the issues.

▶

Separately, Mark McClellan, commissioner of the US Food and Drug Administration, said yesterday he planned to require food labels to include trans fat content. Kraft insisted its latest moves were prompted more by a realisation that obesity was a 'health challenge of global proportions' than by the litigation threat. It said: 'We are making this commitment first and foremost because we think it is the right thing to do for the business and for people who use the products. But if along the way it discourages the plaintiffs' attorneys or an unwarranted piece of legislation that's fine with us.'

Kraft is setting up a committee to advise on obesity and will work with it to set maximum portion sizes for single servings of desserts, snacks and meals, and reduce packages that exceed that limit. It will also set nutritional levels for future products and may trim the calorie, fat or sugar content of some existing products. It will adopt new guidelines on marketing and advertising to children. It is dropping marketing in schools and will review what products it puts in school vending machines. It will also label the nutritional content of its foods in all markets.

Source: Neil Buckley, *Financial Times*, 2 July 2003.

Questions

1 What factors do you believe to be behind these initiatives by Kraft?

2 How does the case study suggest that legal codes in one country can have impacts on international business activity in other countries?

Intellectual property rights

The international economy is becoming a 'knowledge-based' economy, so that questions of intellectual copyright are becoming ever more important. The value of intellectual property can quickly be destroyed unless countries enforce rights in this area. Intellectual property rights (IPRs) can take various forms, with patents, trademarks and copyrights being particularly important.

Patents

Patent law confers ownership rights on the *inventor*. To qualify as the subject matter of a patent the invention must be novel, involve an inventive step and be capable of industrial application. 'Novel' seeks to exclude granting monopoly ownership rights to something which already exists; 'inventive' seeks to establish that a step has been taken which would not be obvious to experts in the field; 'industrial application' seeks to avoid the restrictions which would result from ideas and principles being patentable, instead limiting such protection to specific applications of these ideas. Patents depend upon registration for their validity.

- *Paris Convention 1883*. This was the first major attempt to achieve international cooperation in the protection of patents (as well as trademarks and other intellectual property rights). This convention led to the setting up of the International Bureau for the Protection of Industrial Property Rights (BIRPI). One key provision is to grant reciprocity to foreigners whose countries are members of the convention. Another is to grant a 'period of grace' to patents registered in one country before they need to be registered in other countries. After registration a further 'transition period of protection' is granted before the patent holder has to make use of the patent in a particular market; once this transition period is exhausted with no use having been made of the patent, the patent is deemed to expire. The Uruguay Round of GATT agreed a transition period of one year in developed countries, five years in developing countries and 11 years in the least developed countries.

■ Two other important treaties allow international recognition of patents granted in member countries:
 – *European Patent Convention* (EPC);
 – *Patent Cooperation Treaty* (PCT) of the World Intelligence Property Organisation (WIPO).

These respective treaties allow businesses to make a uniform patent search and application, which is then valid in all signatory countries.

These various methods provide some protection to owners of intellectual property rights, but not all countries have signed them, and enforcement by signatories can be lax. Certainly patents are receiving a much higher profile in terms of international business strategy. For example, the number of patents currently issued in the USA is more than double that of a decade ago. Patents are becoming global in scope with reciprocity agreements and the work of international bodies (e.g. UN, WTO) ensuring that, say, a US patent will restrict attempts to exploit that process or product elsewhere in the world. However, there are international discrepancies, with court decisions in the US making biotechnology and genes (1980), computer software (1981) and business methods (1998) patentable. At present in the EU only biotechnology and genes of these particular categories are patentable. The whole patenting issue is becoming a key part of MNE international business strategy (*see* Box 5.3).

Box 5.3   Strategic patenting

The USA has permitted more aspects of business activity to be patented than has been the case elsewhere and tends to be more supportive of the rights of patent holders when those patents are challenged. 'Strategic patenting' refers to attempts by MNEs to incorporate their approach to patenting into a more coherent strategic approach, which may be broadly defensive or offensive in its direction. Underlying all this is a general recognition that patents are a valuable 'barrier to entry' in an otherwise more open global economy and that intellectual property protected by patent can be a major factor in stock market evaluations.

■ *Defensive patenting* involves the aggressive defence of established patents by holders. Texas Instruments and National Semiconductors aggressively and successfully defended themselves against perceived patent infringements by Japanese and other chip-makers in the early 1990s. Rivette and Kline (1998) argue that without such defence they would have been bankrupted by lower priced but similar quality chips available from other suppliers in their major markets.

▶

> **Box 5.3 Continued**
>
> ■ *Offensive patenting* involves exploiting patents to increase revenue. For example, IBM boosted its revenue from licensing patents threefold, from $500 million in 1994 to over $1.5 billion in 1999, and is reported as applying for ten new patents every working day. Dell Computers now has around 80 patents for process operations involving manufacture and testing. Biotech and dot.com companies which are currently unprofitable have stock market valuations almost entirely dependent on the patents they possess or have applied for. Companies such as Walker Digital in the USA are now specialising entirely in the holding and development of patents, one of which, Priceline, involves 'reverse auctions' (customers set a price they are willing to pay, companies decide whether they are willing to supply) and is worth over $11 billion.

■ Trademarks

Trademarks have been defined as 'any sign capable of being represented graphically which is capable of distinguishing goods or services of one undertaking from those of other undertakings' (*UK, Trade Marks Act 1994*). This is sometimes referred to as the 'product differentiation' function. Such trademarks require less intellectual activity than patents or copyright to be deemed protectable, with the focus instead being on the commercial activity associated with such trademarks. As with patents, trademarks depend on registration for their validity, which gives the holder the exclusive right to use the mark in the UK for ten years, subject to further renewals in periods of ten years. Infringement occurs where others use the trademark without permission.

Trademarks can be a key element of worldwide 'branding' strategies by companies. Failure to register a brand name can be costly. For example, New Zealand growers of Chinese gooseberries began to market the product as 'kiwifruit' in the 1960s but unfortunately neglected to register a trademark, with the result that growers throughout the world can use this as a generic name for the fruit.

■ *Trademark Registration Treaty* (Vienna Convention). Once a trademark has been registered, each signatory country must accept it or provide grounds for refusal within 15 months of registration.

Case Study 5.3 shows how both national and supranational (EU) law can be important in the context of trademarks.

CASE 5.3 Break for Nestlé as trademark case goes to Europe

A trademark battle between confectionery giants Nestlé and Mars over the 'Have a Break' phrase is set to become a test-case for the protection of advertising slogans after three senior judges referred the dispute to the European Court of Justice (ECJ). Swiss-based Nestlé, which makes Kit Kat, has for years had trademark protection over the 'Have a Break, Have a Kit Kat' slogan, as well as over 'Kit Kat' itself. But it wants to gain similar intellectual property rights over the simpler 'Have a Break' tag-line, in respect of all chocolate products.

That, say lawyers, has far-reaching implications. 'If a company can claim monopoly rights because they're using a phrase in an advertising slogan, that's fairly dramatic,' says Emma Riach, intellectual property specialist at Laytons law firm.

Nestlé's initial application to the Trade Mark Registry was turned down last year after Mars, its US-owned rival, objected. However, to bolster its case, the company pointed to consumer research suggesting that use of the phrase 'Have a Break' did elicit the response 'Have a Kit Kat' from consumers.

Even so, a High Court judge in the UK was unpersuaded that the public's association meant 'Have a Break' had actually acquired distinctiveness 'as a result of its use as a mark'. Accordingly, he upheld the registry hearing officer's decision.

The ECJ will be asked to advise whether 'the distinctive character of a mark ... may be acquired following, or in consequence of, the use of that mark ... in conjunction with another mark'. If it says yes, the case will be re-assessed in the domestic courts.

Source: Nikki Tait, *Financial Times*, 25 July 2003. Reprinted with permission.

Questions

1 How might Nestlé benefit by appealing the High Court judge's decision in the UK to the European Court of Justice (ECJ)?

2 How might Mars benefit by the ECJ upholding the previous decision of the High Court judge in the UK?

3 What implications for international business might be drawn by MNEs from this issue, whatever its final outcome?

■ Copyrights

Copyright law prevents the copying of forms of work (e.g. an article, book, play, poem, music score, etc.) rather than the ideas contained within these forms. However, sometimes the copyright can be extended to the 'structure' underpinning the form actually used (e.g. the plot of a book as well as the book itself).

Copyright (unlike patents and trademarks) applies automatically and does not require registration. For copyright to apply, there must be three key conditions:

1 *a recorded work which is 'original'*, in the sense that the work is different from that of its contemporaries;
2 *of an appropriate description*, i.e. literacy, dramatic, music, artistic, sound recordings, films and broadcasts all qualify. Even business letters can receive protection as 'literacy works';
3 *being sufficiently connected to the country in question*, since copyright is essentially national in character, at least in the first instance. So in the case of the UK, the author (or work) must be connected to the UK by nationality, domicile, source of publication or in some other acceptable way.

The period of copyright extends to the life of the author +70 years. Copyright protection is not absolute: for example, limited copying of copyright material is permitted for purposes of research or fair journalistic reporting. Breaching copyright beyond any existing provision can result in an injunction to desist and/or the award of damages.

■ *Berne Convention* and the *Universal Copyright Convention* (UCC) are international agreements which extend the copyright laws of one country to the other signatory countries.

■ Trade-related aspects of intellectual property rights (TRIPS)

The WTO Agreement on *Trade-Related Aspects of Intellectual Property Rights*, the so-called TRIPS Agreement, is based on a recognition that increasingly the value of goods and services entering into international trade resides in the know-how and creativity incorporated into them. The TRIPS Agreement provides for minimum international standards of protection for such know-how and creativity in the areas of copyright and related rights, trademarks, geographical indications, industrial designs, patents, layout-designs of integrated circuits and undisclosed information. It also contains provisions aimed at the effective enforcement of such intellectual property rights, and provides for multilateral dispute settlement. It gives all WTO members transitional periods so that they can meet their obligations under it. Developed-country members have had to comply with all of the provisions of the Agreement since 1 January 1996. For developing countries and certain transition economies, the general transitional period ended on 1 January 2000. For the least-developed countries, the transitional period is 11 years (i.e. until 1 January 2006).

Case Study 5.4 emphasises the growing importance of intellectual property rights to international business and the problems faced by companies that find themselves in breach of those rights.

CASE 5.4 Intellectual property rights in China (IPR): Durex

SSL plc is a major producer of health-related products and is responsible for the famous condom brand 'Durex'. Since its registration as a condom brand in 1929, the name has become well known in many countries. Durex has a 22% global market share, became a premium seller in over 40 countries, and number two in 23 countries. In recent years the company has taken steps to conquer the Chinese market by establishing a 50/50 equity joint venture (EJV) with a Chinese state-owned enterprise. Set up in 1998, the EJV is based in the Chinese coastal city of Qingdao, Shandong Province. The condom market in China is very competitive. Durex's main competitors in China are essentially the other foreign brands. However, one of the company's local competitors is a brand called Jissbon, which in the short term has created a major problem for Durex. The world famous condom producer felt so under threat that it filed a lawsuit against Jissbon on June 24th 2002. Durex is accusing Jissbon of stealing information from Durex's website and printing it word-for-word to describe its own product.

On its website, Jissbon described itself as 'a British-based world famous condom producer with a 70-year history and 20% of the global market share whose products are sold in more than 140 countries.' The description is very similar to that of Durex.

Durex claims the design of Jissbon's website and even the details it provides are copied from Durex. As a result, Durex accused Jissbon of making claims that Durex alone can genuinely make about its own brand. In response to Durex's accusations, Jissbon admitted that some of the information on its website is false but stressed that the website is not for business purposes but intended to change people's ideas of condoms and safe sex. Durex asked for a formal apology and compensation of 5 million yuan (US$602,410) from Jissbon, saying that Jissbon has caused great loss to Durex's valuable image.

Source: Wilson (2003).

Questions

1 Whatever the outcome of the litigation, why has Durex felt it necessary to pursue legal action?

2 What do you consider to be the potential benefits and costs to Durex of this action?

3 How might the WTO TRIPS Agreement be relevant to Durex and to Jissbon and to other situations involving intellectual property rights in China?

Economic systems

■ Free-market economies

Most international business takes place within the context of free-market economies in which the market is the key mechanism for resource allocation. It is here that buyers and sellers interact to determine the prices and quantities of the goods and services exchanged. Of course, the market need not be a particular physical location; for example, foreign exchange is bought and sold worldwide from numerous geographical locations.

Markets yield prices that act as 'signals' to both consumers and producers in resource allocation. For instance, in a situation of excess demand, price will typically rise, acting as a signal to discourage some consumer demand and encourage some additional producer supply, until the quantities bought and sold are once more in balance (equilibrium).

The 'profit motive' is seen as playing a key role here, with higher prices increasing the relative profitability of a product, thereby attracting more resources (labour, capital, land, etc.) into producing that product. In fact profit can be seen as performing at least four key functions:

- acting as a 'signal' to firms in terms of allocating scarce resources;
- rewarding risk taking;
- encouraging productive efficiency (lower costs imply greater profit);
- providing resources for expansion (e.g. 'ploughed back' profits).

Supporters of such a system see the 'invisible hand' of the free market as the most efficient means of coordinating the innumerable individual decisions which must be taken by consumers and producers every day in global markets. Critics of the free market point to the many examples of 'market failures' which often distort its operation. These can include imperfect information, non-competitive market structures and divergences between private and social costs (externalities), among many other types of market distortion. Occasional periods of economic recession, with declining output and rising unemployment, have helped to temper some of the more excessive claims made by free-market adherents.

pause for thought 3	Choose one of these types of 'market failure' and suggest how it might prevent the market from allocating resources efficiently. Can you repeat your analysis for another type of market failure?

Following Heather (1994), Case Study 5.5 shows how shifts in the demand for and supply of shares in Wellcome, a major pharmaceutical company, influenced the market price of these shares during the early 1990s.

CASE 5.5   Market influences on Wellcome share price

Figure 5.2 uses market analysis to explain some of the observed changes in the Wellcome share price during the early 1990s.

(a) American medical opinion expresses doubts over the effectiveness of Retrovir, a new anti-AIDS drug developed at great expense by Wellcome. There is an increased supply of Wellcome shares as people lose confidence and sell them. Price falls from P_1 to P_2.

(b) A major AIDS conference makes favourable comments on Retrovir. Demand for Wellcome's shares increases (shifts to the right). Price rises from P_1 to P_2.

(c) Enthusiasm for pharmaceutical stocks has been growing; Wellcome had benefited from this, being one of the major drugs companies. Demand had previously risen, but now US investors decide they are over-priced. Supply of Wellcome shares increases. Price falls from P_1 to P_2.

(d) The Wellcome shares provide investors with a high dividend. Demand further increases (shifts to the right). However, the supply of shares to the market decreases (shifts to the left) as shareholders speculate on a further rise in price and sell fewer shares than before. Price rises from P_1 to P_2 (but quantity of shares traded is little affected).

(e) The Wellcome trust announces its decision to sell 38% of its shares. The market is taken by surprise. The supply curve shifts sharply to the right at a time when share prices are generally depressed. Wellcome's share price falls from P_1 to P_2.

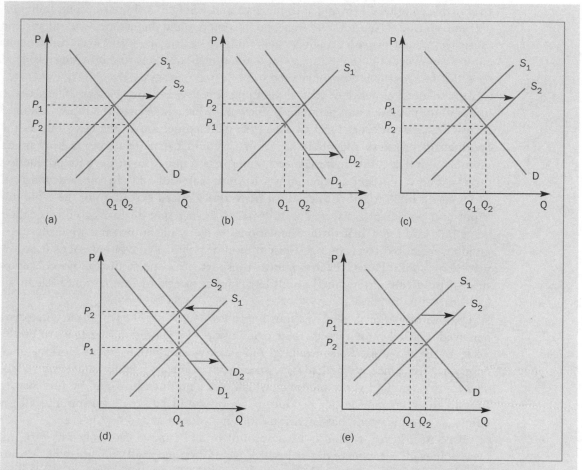

Figure 5.2 Using demand–supply analysis in explanation of specific movements in Wellcome's share price

Questions

Consider the likely impact on the Wellcome share price of each of the following:

1 Wellcome announces that it is to begin production of a best-selling ulcer treatment drug, which is currently produced by a rival whose patent is about to expire;

2 Wellcome introduces a rights issue of shares in order to raise new investment capital.

Command economies

Although few examples of a command economy remain, this structure was previously used by many of the so-called 'transition economies' of Central and Eastern Europe. The command economy dominated every aspect of life, often involving the issue of explicit instructions to factories as to where to buy their inputs, how much to pay their workers, how much to produce and where to sell their output; individuals were trained in specialist schools and universities and directed to work at specific factories, which provided their wages, houses, healthcare – and even holidays in enterprise-owned hotels and sanatoria; the national bank was told how much to lend to which factories and how much cash to print to pay wages.

As a theoretical concept, central planning was very elegant (Healey 2004). Using 'input–output' analysis (a planning framework which calculated the inputs required for each factory in order for it to deliver its planned outputs to the next stage in the production process), the planning ministry could calculate precisely how much labour, capital and raw materials each enterprise required to achieve its production targets. The various production targets for raw materials and intermediate and final products all fitted together to ensure a perfectly balanced expansion of the economy. Input and output prices were carefully set to ensure that all firms could pay their wage bills and repay loans from the national bank, while at the same time consumer goods were priced to encourage consumption of politically favoured goods (e.g. low prices for books, ballet, theatre, public transport, etc.) and to discourage consumption of politically unfavoured goods (e.g. higher prices for international telephone calls, cars, luxury goods).

The overall national plan was thus internally consistent. If each of the enterprises achieved its production targets, there could not be, by definition, shortages or bottlenecks in the economy. There would be full employment, with everyone working in an enterprise for which he/she had been specifically trained at school and/or university. The total wage bill for the economy, which was paid in cash, would be sufficient to buy all the consumer goods produced. There would be zero inflation and all the country's citizens would have access to housing, education and healthcare.

Of course, in reality this stylised account of a command economy was rarely, if ever, achieved. Plans were devised which were often internally inconsistent, leading to massive shortages or surpluses. Output frequently fell below target as workers saw little incentive to meet productivity targets. Poor-quality products often failed to satisfy either home or overseas consumer demands. The process of economic transformation from central planning to a market economy in Eastern Europe is now well underway, though it has been neither smooth nor uniform. States in the vanguard of reform like Poland, the Czech Republic and Hungary quickly succeeded in creating thriving, dynamic private sectors, which are generating new jobs and contributing to economy recovery; together with Estonia and Slovenia, this group are on the verge of entry to the European Union. In contrast, in the 12 states of the former Soviet Union that now comprise the Commonwealth of Independent States (CIS) the slump in economic activity has been much more prolonged and economic recovery more fragile.

Nevertheless, the direction of movement is towards the market economy, as indeed has largely been the case within the People's Republic of China for more than two decades. This process of transition clearly has implications for both domestic firms within these economies and for multinational enterprises seeking to invest in, or trade with, these economies. Case Study 5.6 raises a number of issues with regard to moving the Chinese economy more firmly in the direction of the market economy.

CASE 5.6   China's banks face a cultural revolution   **FT**

When a senior Chinese state banker recommended in 2000 that the country's 'big four' state banks should be floated on the stock market, it may have sounded relatively uncontroversial to outsiders. But in China it was a shocking idea, and not only because making a public proposal of this kind was unprecedented in 50 years of Communist rule. Compelling the big four – which control at least 80% of total banking assets – to obey the diktats of stock market investors rather than government apparatchiks would amount to nothing less than a revolution in China's credit culture.

If credit were one day allocated according to genuine commercial criteria, the wasteful and corrupt state-owned industrial sector that forms the bulwark of the Communist Party's economic power would rapidly become marginalised. In short, the stock market listing of the big four would represent one of the last and largest strides in China's journey from Marxism to market economics. However, 21 years of economic transition have shown that reform is slowest whenever it bumps up against the entrenched interests of the Communist hierarchy.

Among the most compelling reasons for reform is that China can no longer afford to subsidise one of the world's greatest misallocations of credit. Exact statistics are elusive, but according to senior Chinese government economists, the 300,000 strong state-owned enterprise sector produces only one-third of the country's industrial output but swallows at least two-thirds of its credit resources. Such enterprises, which still employ more than 50% of China's urban workers, are generally poorly managed, overstaffed and unprofitable. Their parlous state finds its most notable expression in the rate of return on assets held by their main creditors – the 'big four': it fell from 1.4% in 1985 to only 0.2% in 2002.

Recent estimates by Standard and Poor, the credit rating agency, of 'non-performing loans' (NPLs) by the big four banks were as high as 48% of all loans in mid-2003, though official Chinese estimates are lower at 25%. The misallocation of credit to the economy's least profitable sector is sustainable only for as long as Chinese households are willing to keep pouring most of their savings into the state banks, and the finance ministry is willing to keep writing off bad loans by the big four. There are grounds to believe that neither of these assumptions is any longer safe. More and more competition has emerged for the savings of Chinese households, which in 2002 reached Rmb 7,000 billion (£540 billion). Not only are several Chinese commercial banks wooing savers in increasingly sophisticated ways, but official policies aimed at boosting stock market liquidity are expected to divert funds from bank deposits into portfolio investments.

Another competitive crunch may come when foreign banks are allowed to start taking deposits from and lending to Chinese businesses two years after WTO accession, and again, when they begin to provide the same services for individuals five years after entry.

As for Beijing's willingness to keep on bailing out the 'big four', there are clear signs that patience is wearing thin. Fang Zin-ghai, general manager of the group co-ordination office at China Construction Bank, one of the big four, estimates the finance ministry will have to pay Rmb 1,000 billion to write off bad debts under a

▶

current corporate debt-to equity swap scheme being run by the banks. After forking out this amount to help bring the big four towards international levels of capital adequacy, the finance ministry may be unwilling and unable to give them more free lunches. Indeed a new bank regulation installed in 2002 is insisting that each of the big four banks reduces its non-performing loan (NPL) ratio by 4% per annum to an official level of no more than 15% of all loans by the end of 2005.

Commentators say that given such strains, the banking system can no longer afford to support inefficient state industries. But attempts over the past few years to inculcate a commercially driven lending culture into state banks have only met with limited success. The fundamental reason for this is the lack of incentive. For as long as state banks answer to the state, they will find it difficult to withdraw support from state enterprises. Mr Fang and others see stock market listings as the only solution.

Listing will not only make management accountable to a new master – the market – that will penalise poor lending decisions, it will also allow bank staff to own shares, making them stakeholders in the success of their employers. For China's state banks, these notions are close to revolutionary. As such, the idea of listing will be regarded with suspicion by Beijing's central planners, ensuring that any progress will probably be gradual and fraught with complications. But even slow progress will have significant implications. When household savings are funnelled towards more deserving borrowers in the vibrant non-state sector, the effect on China's competitiveness could be dramatic.

Source: James Kynge, *Financial Times*, 10 July 2003 and *Financial Times*, 27 April 2000.

Questions

1 Consider some of the implications of this 'cultural revolution' in the banking sector for Chinese business.

2 What might be the implications for overseas firms seeking to do business with China?

Economic variables and the business environment

Whatever stylised type of economic structure provides the context for international business, a number of key *economic variables* will shape the environment in which such business is conducted. Managers of international businesses must take into account a number of economic indicators in the countries with which they seek to do business if economic opportunities and threats are to be properly assessed.

■ Real income per head

The gross national product (GNP) is a widely used measure of economic well-being, reflecting the total value of output (or income) attributable to nationals of that country in a given year. To serve as a measure of the *standard of living* this is often expressed 'per head of population' and in 'real terms' (i.e. excluding inflation).

The World Bank and a number of other bodies use annual GNP per head to identify three broad groups of countries, one of which is further subdivided, making four groups in all:

1 *high-income economies*: countries with an annual GDP per head of $9,206 or more (in 2002 values);

2 *middle-income economies*: countries with an annual GNP per head from $746 to $9,205 (in 2002 values).

Because this group is so broad it has been subdivided into:

(a) *upper-middle income economies*: annual GNP per head from $2,976 to $9,205;

(b) *lower-middle income economies*: annual GNP per head from $746 to $2,975.

3 *low-income economies*: countries with an annual GNP per head of $745 or less (in 2002 values).

Of course, it is not just the *absolute* level of income per head of a country or group of countries that is important in assessing the prospects for business, but *changes* in that level.

■ Economic growth

This is often expressed in terms of the percentage change in real national income per head and can be a key indicator for future business prospects. For example, where a business is trading in products which have a high *income elasticity of demand* (*see* Box 5.4), such as air travel, then prospective changes in economic growth rates can have a major influence on projected future profitability. As real incomes rise by a given percentage, demand for these products increases by more than that percentage. For example, estimates for air travel have suggested income elasticities of demand as high as +4, suggesting that a 1% rise in real income will increase the demand for air travel by over 4%.

Box 5.4   Elasticity of demand

Businesses should be aware of at least three types of elasticity of demand if they are to accurately assess prospects for the future.

Price elasticity of demand (PED)

This measures the responsiveness of demand for a product to changes in its own price.

$$PED = \frac{\% \text{ change in quantity demanded of } X}{\% \text{ change in price of } X}$$

When this ratio is greater than 1 (ignoring the sign), we speak of a relatively elastic demand; when smaller than 1, a relatively inelastic demand.

PED > 1 (relatively elastic demand): fall in price raises total revenue, rise in price reduces total revenue.

PED < 1 (relatively inelastic demand): fall in price reduces total revenue, rise in price increases total revenue.

▶

Box 5.4	Continued

Income elasticity of demand (IED)

This measures the responsiveness of demand for a product to changes in the real income of consumers.

$$IED = \frac{\% \text{ change in quantity demanded of } X}{\% \text{ change in real income}}$$

For products with high (positive) values for IED, a rise in real income will shift the demand curve substantially to the right (increase), whereas a fall in real income will shift the demand curve substantially to the left (decrease).

Products, with a negative value for IED are often called 'inferior goods', with a rise in real income causing demand to shift to the left (decrease).

Cross elasticity of demand (CED)

This measures the responsiveness of demand for a product to changes in the price of some other product.

$$CED = \frac{\% \text{ change in quantity demanded of } X}{\% \text{ change in price of } Y}$$

Where X and Y are substitutes in consumption, the sign of CED will be positive. A fall in the price of Y, the substitute, will decrease the quantity demanded of X ($-/- = +$)

Where X and Y are complements in consumption (fit together), the sign of CED will be negative. A fall in the price of Y, the complement, will increase the quantity demanded of X ($+/- = -$).

■ Exchange rate

When comparing the standard of living (e.g. GNP per head) between different countries it is usual to use a common currency such as the US dollar in the World Bank classification above. Even this may be misleading, since converting the value of GNP expressed in the local currency into a $ equivalent using the *official* exchange rate may misrepresent the actual purchasing power in the local economy. This is because the official exchange rate is influenced by a range of complex forces in the foreign exchange markets and may not accurately reflect the purchasing power of one country's currency in another country. A more accurate picture is given if we use *purchasing power parities* (PPPs) rather than official exchange rates when making this conversion. Purchasing power parities measure how many units of one country's currency are needed to buy *exactly the same basket of goods* as can be bought with a given amount of another country's currency.

Quite apart from the role of the exchange rate in making more accurate international comparisons of GNP, we have seen (Chapter 4) that it is a crucial determinant of export/import competitiveness. Indeed, it is sometimes called an 'expenditure switching' economic variable. For example, a *fall* in the exchange rate will make exports cheaper overseas and imports dearer at home, encouraging consumers in overseas markets to switch from domestic to the now relatively cheaper foreign products and consumers in home markets to switch from the now relatively more expensive foreign products to domestic products. The opposite effects can be expected from a *rise* in the exchange rate, exports becoming relatively more expensive and imports relatively cheaper.

International business must clearly take into account actual and prospective changes in relative exchange rates when evaluating the economic environment in which they are doing business.

pause for thought 4 China has pegged the exchange rate of its own currency the renminbi to the US dollar. How will that influence the EU if the euro continues to strengthen against the US dollar?

Inflation

Inflation is a persistent tendency for the general level of prices to rise. A modest rate of inflation is often regarded as 'favourable' by business as in such an economic environment any extra costs can more readily be passed on to consumers in the form of higher prices. Of course, excessive rates of inflation can result in instability and rapid increases in costs, often followed by deflationary macroeconomic measures by governments resulting in sharp decreases in consumer demand.

In the UK the Retail Price Index (RPI) is the most widely reported measure of inflation, measuring the change from month to month in the cost of a representative 'basket' of goods and services of the type bought by a typical household. In the EU the Harmonised Index of Consumer Prices (HICP) has been calculated on a standardised basis to allow more accurate comparisons across countries. The HICP uses the geometric mean in its calculation and gives lower recorded rates of inflation for the UK than the RPI, which uses the arithmetic mean and a different 'basket' of goods and services. However, the UK itself adopted the HCIP as its official inflationary measure in 2003.

For a 'cost-orientated' multinational (*see* p. 51), locations with low and stable rates of inflation might prove more attractive in terms of foreign direct investment. (Aspects of strategic policy for a business are considered in more detail in Chapter 8.)

Taxes and subsidies

Variations in national tax rates and allowances and in the provision of grants and subsidies can have a major influence on international business decisions. These can obviously include decisions as to where to locate particular elements of the globalised production process. They might also include decisions involving the 'transfer pricing' of internal transactions within the multinational enterprise (*see* p. 356).

This section has dealt with a number of economic variables that might influence the decisions taken by international business. Of course, in reality many of these (and other) variables are changing or are about to change, in different directions at the same time.

Technological environment

Technological change can have important effects on the decisions taken by international business. Technological change can involve *new processes* of production, i.e. new ways of doing things which raise the productivity of factor inputs, as with the use of robotics in car assembly techniques which has dramatically raised output per assembly line worker. Around 80% of technological change has been process innovation. However, technological change can also be embodied in *new products* (goods or services) which were not previously available. Online banking and many new financial services are the direct result of advances in microprocessor based technologies.

■ Technology and employment

One important issue to governments, firms, labour representatives (e.g. unions) and indeed society as a whole has been whether such process innovations have generally resulted in job losses. Each case must, of course, be judged on its separate merits. Box 5.5, however, indicates that there need be no presumption that the continuing technical change that often accompanies inward and outward foreign direct investment by multinational enterprises need necessarily result in job losses. In fact, provided that any cost reductions for productivity gains via the new technologies are passed on to consumers as lower prices and that the demands of consumers are sufficiently responsive (price elastic) to those lower prices, job gains can be anticipated. Of course, whatever the impact on the *volume* of labour required, there may also be changes in the patterns of skills required from those who remain, with the often repeated claim that many craft and intermediate levels of skill have been displaced by automated processes.

Box 5.5 Creating or destroying jobs

New technologies have substantially raised output per unit of labour input (labour productivity) and per unit of factor input, both labour and capital (total factor productivity). There has been much concern that the impact of these productivity gains has been to reduce jobs, i.e. to create technological unemployment. We now consider the principles which will in fact determine whether or not jobs will be lost (or gained) as a result of technological change.

Higher output per unit of factor input reduces costs of production, provided only that wage rates and other factor price increases do not absorb the whole of any productivity gain. Computer-controlled machine tools are a case in point. Data from Renault show that the use of DNC machine tools resulted in machining costs one-third less than those of general-purpose machine tools at the same level of output. Lower costs will cause the profit-maximising firm to lower price and raise output under most market forms, as in Figure 5.3. A downward shift of the average cost curve, via the new technologies, lowers the marginal cost curve from MC_1 to MC_2. The profit-maximising price/output combination ($MC = MR$) now changes from P_1/Q_1 to P_2/Q_2. Price has fallen, output has risen.

The dual effect on employment of higher output per unit of labour (and capital) input can usefully be illustrated from Figure 5.3. The curve $Q = F(N)$ is the familiar production function

Box 5.5 Continued

Figure 5.3 Technical change and the level of employment

of economic theory, showing how output (Q) varies with labour input (N), capital and other factors assumed constant. On the one hand the higher labour productivity from technical change shifts the production function outwards to the dashed line $Q' = F(N)$. The original output Q_1 can now be produced with less labour, i.e. with only N_2 labour input instead of N_1 as previously. On the other hand, the cost and price reduction has so raised demand that more output is required. We now move along the new production function Q' until we reach Q_2 output, which requires N_3 labour input. In our example the reduction in labour required per unit output has been more than compensated for by the expansion of output, via lower prices, so that employment has, in fact, risen from N_1 to N_3.

This analysis highlights a number of points on which the final employment outcome for a firm adopting the new techniques will depend:

Box 5.5	Continued

1 the relationship between new technology and labour productivity, i.e. the extent to which the production function Q shifts outwards;

2 the relationship between labour productivity and cost, i.e. the extent to which the marginal cost curve shifts downwards;

3 the relationship between cost and price, i.e. the extent to which cost reductions are passed on to consumers as lower prices;

4 the relationship between lower price and higher demand, i.e. the price elasticity of the demand curve (*see* Box 5.4, p. 161).

Suppose, for instance, that the new process halved labour input per unit output! If this increase in labour productivity (1 above), reduces cost (2 above), and price (3 above), and output doubled (4 above), then the same total labour input would be required. If output more than doubled, then more labour would be employed. The magnitude of the four relationships above will determine whether the firm offers the same, more, or less employment after technical change in the production process.

◼ Technology and competitive advantage

Of course, technological change provides national and international businesses with both opportunities and threats. For example, five new broadband wavelengths were auctioned in the UK in early 2000. Access to such wavelengths has been regarded as vital for the new generation of Wireless Application Protocol (WAP) products, making possible the Internet, television and other interactive applications on the third-generation of mobile phones. The British auction of five broadband (third-generation) licences in April 2000 brought in a staggering £22.5 billion, around £20 billion more than Treasury officials had pencilled into their budgets a few months earlier. The German auction of six such licences in August 2000 raised even more, some £30.8 billion. A key question is: can such high expectations be realised?

The impact of technical change on competitive advantages is also considered in other parts of the book. For example Case Study 8.4 (p. 258) looks at the impacts of new technologies in the manufacture of semiconductors.

Technology transfer

It is widely held that multinational activity by more efficient foreign multinationals promotes technology transfer to the benefit of domestic companies. For example, when Nissan established a car plant in north-eastern England, it demanded much higher standards of UK component suppliers than the incumbent national producers such as Ford and Rover. Nissan's engineers assisted these supplying companies to upgrade their production processes in order to meet their requirements. The result was the creation of a strong positive externality: the international competitiveness of the UK car supply industry was strengthened and, as a direct consequence, the quality of the inputs to the existing domestic car makers improved.

This so-called 'technology transfer' is clearly maximised by such 'direct linkages' with domestic suppliers, which occurs when incoming multinationals like Sony, Nissan, Honda and Toyota work closely with domestic suppliers to raise the standard of UK-produced inputs. Technology transfer may also bring with it some positive indirect 'demonstration effects' as less efficient local producers seek to imitate the superior processes and organisational advantages of the foreign multinationals.

As Healey (2004) points out there are, however, clear limitations to technology transfer. The inward fdi may, for example, reflect the multinational seeking to exploit an ownership-specific advantage over domestic companies. In such circumstances it is unlikely that the foreign multinational will willingly share the technologically-based sources of its competitive advantage over local rivals. Moreover, in the case of Japanese multinationals, their historical advantage was built upon close relationships with Japanese suppliers. For example, the big four Japanese motorcycle companies (Honda, Yamaha, Suzuki and Kawasaki) rely heavily on a very limited number of domestic suppliers (e.g. Bridgestone for tyres, Nippon Denso for electronic components, etc.). Early dissatisfaction with UK suppliers with regard to quality and reliability of deliveries has led to a number of these Japanese suppliers following their major customers into the European market, thereby reducing the potential scope for technology transfer via linkages with local suppliers.

A further obstacle to technology transfer may involve the issue of cultural dissonance. The psychic distance between US and UK companies is relatively small. Both share a broadly common culture, a common language and they have a reasonably high level of mutual understanding. However, the success of multinationals from, say, Japan or other parts of East and South-East Asia is built on a very different set of social and cultural values, which are not easily transferable to the UK setting (*see* Chapter 6). Companies like Sony, Nissan and Honda have all reported difficulties in establishing Japanese-style work practices, which many economists regard as an integral part of that country's corporate success. The operation of 'just-in-time' production processes and 'quality circles' rely on employee loyalty to his/her company, which in Japan is reinforced by lifetime employment and a shared set of values which emphasises collectivism. Such techniques are much less easily transposed to Western cultures with their stress on individualism and self-determination.

An opposing view points to the potential damage to host country's of technology transfer when it enables foreign affiliates to dominate domestic markets and displace domestic producers. This argument holds still greater weight when such foreign affiliates largely import components and other intermediate inputs rather than using domestic suppliers located in the host country.

■ Types of technology transfer

Technology transfer usually occurs in one of two ways:

- *internalised transfer* – this takes the form of direct investment by a parent company in its foreign affiliate. Such intra-firm technology transfer may be difficult to measure;
- *externalised transfer* – this can take a variety of forms: licences, franchises, minority joint ventures, subcontracting, technical assistance, purchase of advanced equipment (embodied technical progress), and so on.

The following factors are widely regarded as increasing the probability of an MNE resorting to 'internalised transfer':

- the more complex and fast moving the technology;
- the larger and more transnational (*see* Chapter 1) the company;
- the more internationally experienced and more technologically specialised the parent company and its affiliates;
- the fewer obstacles placed in the way of fdi by host governments and the more inducements offered;
- the greater the focus of the parent company on utilising advanced technology as rapidly as possible without waiting for host country domestic firms to develop technological capabilities.

Benefits of internalised transfer to host country

The most important benefit to the host country of *internalised technology transfer* is that it gives host country firms access to new, up-to-date and more productive technologies, which are unlikely to be available by any other means. These technologies of the parent company are often based on expensive R & D related to branded products or to complex manufacturing processes, which are part of a globalised pattern of international specialisation. Such technologies would only be shared by the parent company with related parties such as wholly-owned (or majority-stake) affiliates.

Other benefits often follow from access to such technologies, as in the case of the host economy being used by the parent company as a production platform for an export-oriented policy to that region (e.g. Japanese motor vehicle firms using the UK as a production platform to export to the EU). The host country affiliates may also gain access to expensive brand images which further aid overseas sales as well as to substantial financial and other resources owned by the parent company. New operations management and other logistical techniques may be learned by the host country workers, with the general skill base of local labour being raised by exposure to more advanced operations and in-house training methods. In summary, internalised transfer gives the host country, at least in principle, access to the whole range of MNE technological, organisational and skill assets, including those related to tacit knowledge (*see* Chapter 8) as well as explicit knowledge.

Costs of internalised transfer to host country

Local firms may be disadvantaged by being dominated in their home and export markets by the production affiliates of the overseas parent company. This may reduce overall employment and income in the home economy, especially where the parent MNE uses few local resources in component supply or manufacture in its overseas affiliates. Parent companies may, in fact, share little of their tacit or explicit technological, organisational or operational knowledge with the local affiliates, thereby doing little to raise the skill and knowledge base of the local economy.

We consider many other aspects of technological change and their impacts on international business in Chapter 11, especially the impact of Internet-related technologies on business-to-business and business-to-consumer activities.

Useful websites

Now try the self-check questions for this chapter on the website at www.booksites.net/wall. You will also find further resources as well as the following useful weblinks:

Sources of information on international institutions, business and exchange rates include:

www.wto.org
www.imf.org
www.dti.gov.uk
www.europa.eu.int
www.eubusiness.com
www.un.org
The website of the European Central Bank is *www.ecb.int*
The website of the UK Patent Office is *www.patent.gov.uk*
The website for the US Patent and Tradesmark Office is *www.upto.gov*
The European Union's site for intellectual and industrial property is
http://europa.eu.int/comm/internal_market/en/entprop/indprop/index.htm
More information on TRIPS can be found at *www.wto.org/english/tratop*

For information on past decisions of the UK Competition Commission, go to:
www.competition-commission.org

The Business Bureau provides information on legal issues facing business:
www.vianetworks.co.uk

Many interesting articles on labour issues are included in:
www.peoplemanagement.co.uk
www.tomorrowscompany.com
www.croner.co.uk

Pressure group websites include:
www.foe.co.uk
www.greenpeace.org.uk

Useful key texts

Daniels, J., Radebaugh, L. and Sullivan, D. (2004) *International Business* (10th edn), Pearson Prentice Hall, especially Chapters 3 and 4.
Dicken, P. (2003) *Global Shift: Transforming the World Economy* (4th edn), Paul Chapman Publishing Ltd, especially Chapters 4, 5 and 6.
Hill, C. (2003) *International Business: Competing in the Global Marketplace* (4th edn), McGraw-Hill Irwin, especially Chapter 2.
Morrison, J. (2002) *The International Business Environment*, Palgrave, especially Chapters 3, 7, 8 and 10.
Rugman, A. and Hodgetts, R. (2003) *International Business* (3rd edn), FT Prentice Hall, especially Chapters 4 and 13.
Tayeb, M. (2000) *International Business: Theories, Policies and Practices*, Financial Times Prentice Hall, especially Chapters 5, 10 and 12.
Woods, M. (2001) *International Business*, Palgrave, especially Chapter 1 and parts of Chapters 6 and 8.

Other texts and sources

Dichtl, E. and Koeglmayr, H.G. (1986) 'Country Risk Ratings', *Management International Review*, vol. 26, no. 4.

Griffiths, A. and Wall, S. (2004) 'The European Union', in *Applied Economics* (10th edn), Griffiths, A. and Wall, S. (eds), Financial Times Prentice Hall.

Harrison, B. (2004) 'Money and EMU', in *Applied Economics* (10th edn), Griffiths, A. and Wall, S. (eds), Financial Times Prentice Hall.

Healey, N. (2004) 'The Multinational Corporation' and 'Transition Economies', in *Applied Economics* (10th edn), Griffiths, A. and Wall, S. (eds), Financial Times Prentice Hall.

Heather, K. (1994) 'The Stock Market: a Quick Way to Riches', *Modern Applied Economics*, Harvester Wheatsheaf.

Randall, J. and Treacy, B. (2000) 'Digital Buccaneers Caught in a Legal Web', *Financial Times*, 30 May. In *Mastering Risk* (2001) Financial Times Prentice Hall.

Rivette, K. and Kline, D. (1998) *Rembrandt in the Attic*, Sage.

United Nations Conference on Trade and Development (UNCTAD) *World Investment Report* (annual publication).

United Nations Development Programme (UNDP) *Human Development Report* (annual publication), OUP.

Wilson, J. (2003) 'Inter-Partner Relationships and Performance in UK–Chinese Joint Ventures: An Interaction Approach', unpublished Ph.D. thesis, University of Middlesex.

World Bank, *World Development Report* (annual publication).

Zonis, M. and Wilkin, S. (2000) 'Driving Defensively Through a Minefield of Political Risk', *Financial Times*, 30 May.

Chapter 6

International sociocultural environment

By the end of this chaper you should be able to:

- explain the nature of culture and the differences between national, organisational and occupational culture;

- say why it is important to have an understanding of culture in international business;

- define the different dimensions of culture;

- outline the different ways of analysing national culture in business;

- suggest strategies for developing intercultural competence;

- show an understanding of how to develop transnational teams.

Introduction

Over the ages many philosophers, thinkers, novelists, anthropologists, social scientists and latterly management theorists have grappled with the concept of culture. Definitions have been used to try to capture the all-pervasive scope of cultural influence, as in the following example.

> We can liken it to the air: it is everywhere, we cannot see it but we know it is there, we breathe it and we cannot exist without it. Culture is not a biological necessity and we will not die if we are deprived of it. But it is rather improbable if not impossible for a person to be devoid of the traces of his or her cultural upbringing and separated from his or her cultural context. (Tayeb 1994)

While any definition of culture remains necessarily broad, we can at least see some of the processes by which culture is constructed. As human beings we are social animals and it is from a constant interaction with one another that we learn acceptable ways of being, of behaving, of thinking and of acting. In our day-to-day lives we learn how to act in different circumstances, modelling our behaviour on those around us to build up a coherent set of preferences, beliefs, values and meanings that create our cultural context. At least two features help to distinguish culture from other attributes, such as opinion. The first and most important is that it is enduring and changes very little over time. The second is that it has a social context in that it is expressed as part of a community.

National cultural characteristics

Elias, a famous social scientist and thinker, has made significant contributions to our understanding of culture. He suggested that the development of social institutions and accepted ways of behaving become so closely associated with the groups that historically have dominated particular societies that we can, with reason, speak of national cultural values. In his major work, *The Civilizing Process* (1994), Elias identifies gradual but discernible changes in the expectations of people's interpersonal conduct and in the ways in which they approach their emotions and even bodily functions, as being distinctive between different European states such as Britain, France and Germany. He saw many of these national characteristics arising from variations in the routes by which the different bourgeois and courtly societies evolved. In France, for example, by the eighteenth century the most prominent bourgeois groups and the nobility read, spoke and behaved in roughly the same way, with courtesy, eloquence, respect for hierarchical differences and a sense of honour accepted by a broad strata of French society.

Elias has therefore focused on national cultures as being the outcome of historical power struggles between different groups for dominance in different nation states. The ideas and values associated with the 'successful' groups in such power struggles eventually evolve into 'national' cultures. Of course, other factors may also play a part in this process.

- *Religious background.* While the underlying values and assumptions of all world religions may share some common features, there are arguably some important differences. Weber (1930), for example, argued that individualism, expressed as a preference for personal choice, autonomy and the pursuit of personal goals, was the hallmark of Protestantism, with the result that these characteristics have been incorporated into the 'Protestant' work ethic of many northern European countries. He suggested that this work ethic was in part responsible for the creation of many of the attributes we ascribe to modern Western capitalism. In contrast, Confucianism of East and South-East Asia is characterised by family and group orientation, respect for age and hierarchy, a preference for harmony and the avoidance of conflict and competition, and a set of cultural values quite unlike the acquisitive behaviour of Western capitalism.

- *Ecological factors.* The environment may also play a part in the development of cultural characteristics. It has often been argued that harsh and 'unfriendly' climates and poor agricultural conditions can, over time and across generations, result in people who are hardworking, resilient, patient, tough and aggressive. Tayeb (2000) describes how this can happen using the example of the Arian tribes who, thousands of years ago, migrated from central Asia to India and Iran. Those who settled in India found a fertile land with plenty of water and rivers and a relatively mild climate. Those who settled in Iran faced harsh variable seasons, salt deserts and very few rivers. Tayeb suggests that it is hardly an accident that Hinduism and Buddhism took root in India, religions noted for their non-violence and passivity. By way of contrast, those from the same ethnic Arian tribes who settled under the harsher ecological conditions of Iran became aggressive, fought other nations and built up the Persian Empire, which ruled over a vast area for centuries.

High and low context cultures

Whatever their origins, attempts have been made to identify some of the differences in national cultural characteristics. For example, early work by Hall (1976) suggested that the various national cultures could be divided into 'high context' and 'low context' cultures in terms of the ways in which people in that culture communicate with one another. Table 6.1 briefly outlines some of the differences between each type. For Hall, the high context cultures include countries or regions such as Japan, China, the Middle East, South America and the southern European countries.

Geert Hofstede (1980) undertook a major research project to identify different national cultures within the same multinational organisation: IBM. Using the responses of some 116,000 IBM employees in 40 countries, Hofstede identified four important dimensions of national culture, namely individualism, power distance, uncertainty avoidance, and masculinity/femininity, to which he later added a fifth dimension: long-term orientation (*see* Figure 6.1).

Individualism

■ In *individualist* societies, people tend to put their own interests and those of their immediate family before others. People in such societies would have a high degree of self-respect and independence but a corresponding lack of tolerance for opposing viewpoints. Such people may put their own success through competition over the good of others. Hofstede found that people in the United States, the United Kingdom, Australia, Canada, New Zealand and the Netherlands tend to be relatively individualist in their values.

■ In *collectivist* societies there is the belief that the group comes first. Such cultures would contain well-defined social networks in which people are expected to put the good of the group ahead of their own personal freedom, interests or success. Group members try to fit into their group harmoniously with a minimum of conflict or tension. Hofstede found that people from Mexico, Greece, Hong Kong, Taiwan, Peru, Singapore, Columbia and Pakistan tend to be relatively collectivist in their values.

Table 6.1 High context and low context cultures

High context cultures	Low context cultures
Define personality more in terms of the group than the individual	Are more individualistic than group-orientated
Tend to have a high sensory involvement (low boundaries in terms of personal space)	Tend to have a low sensory involvement (high boundaries in terms of personal space)
Initiate and receive more bodily contact when talking	Convey more information via explicit codes which do not rely so heavily on non-verbal language
Are polychronic, i.e. time does not have a totally linear aspect so that punctuality and scheduling have low priority	Are monochronic, i.e. time is viewed in more linear terms involving punctuality and tight scheduling

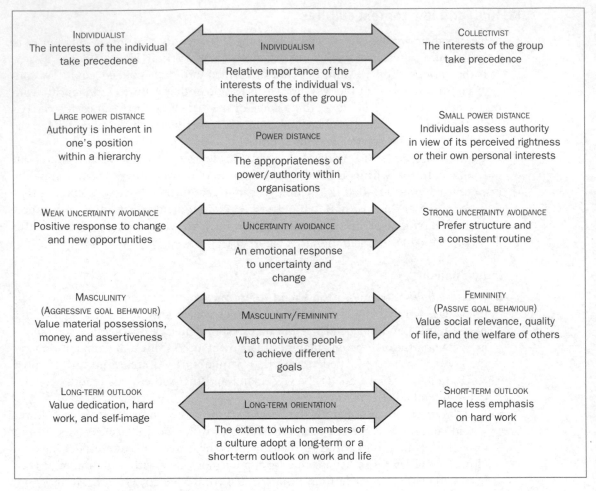

Figure 6.1 Hofstede's five dimensions of culture
Source: Adapted from Griffin and Pustay (1996)

Power distance

Hofstede refers to power distance as 'the extent to which the less powerful members of institutions and organisations within a country expect and accept that power is distributed unequally'.

■ In *large power distance countries* there is considerable dependence of subordinates on bosses, and a preference for clearly demarcated hierarchy. The emotional distance between hierarchies will tend to be relatively large: subordinates will rarely approach and contradict their bosses. People in such a culture tend to accept the power and authority of their superiors simply on the basis of the superior's position in the hierarchy and to respect the superior's right to that power. Hofstede found that people in the Philippines, Mexico, Venezuela, India, Singapore, France, Spain, Japan and Brazil tend to be relatively power respecting.

■ In *small power distance countries* there is limited dependence of subordinates on bosses, and a preference for consultation. The emotional distance between hierarchies will tend to be relatively small: subordinates will quite readily approach and contradict their bosses. People in such a culture are reluctant to accept the power and authority of their supervisors merely because of their position in the hierarchy. Hofstede found that people in Austria, Israel, Denmark, New Zealand, Ireland, Great Britain, Germany, Australia, Canada and the USA have relatively little power respect.

Uncertainty avoidance

Hofstede defines this as 'the extent to which the members of a culture feel threatened by uncertain or unknown situations. This feeling is, among other things, expressed through nervous stress and in a need for predictability: a need for written and unwritten rules'. An important aspect of the level of uncertainty avoidance in a society is the amount of trust between citizens and authorities.

- *Weak uncertainty avoidance* (uncertainty accepting) stands for citizen competence; i.e. a belief that ordinary citizens are able to influence their authorities, and that there is some degree of mutual trust among them. People in cultures characterised by weak uncertainty avoidance tend to be positive in their response to change, which is seen more in terms of providing new opportunities rather than as posing considerable threats. Nordic and Anglo-Saxon countries as well as most other Asian and sub-Saharan countries score below average on this dimension (i.e. they exhibit weak uncertainty avoidance).
- *Strong uncertainty avoidance* implies that decisions should be left to experts; citizens and authorities tend to exhibit mutual distrust for each other. People in cultures characterised by strong uncertainty avoidance will avoid ambiguity whenever possible. These people prefer the structured routine and even bureaucratic way of doing things. Latin, Mediterranean and Central and Eastern European countries tend to score above average on 'uncertainty avoidance', along with Japan, South Korea and Pakistan (i.e. they exhibit strong uncertainty avoidance).

Masculinity/femininity

Hofstede used these labels for a dimension he believed to be the only one on which the scores of men and the women in his sample were consistently and significantly different.

- *Masculinity* refers to cultures in which the social gender roles are clearly distinct; men are supposed to be more assertive and acquisitive, valuing material possessions and money.
- *Femininity* refers to cultures in which social gender roles overlap; both men and women are supposed to be modest, tender and concerned with the quality of life.

In some respects the label for this dimension is somewhat confusing. Griffin and Pustay (1996) relabelled it as 'goal orientation', referring it to the way in which people are motivated towards different types of goal. Those people towards the extreme 'masculine' side demonstrate *aggressive goal behaviour*: they place a high premium on material possessions, money and assertiveness. At the other extreme, people on the 'feminine' side who adopt *passive goal behaviour* place a higher value on social relationships, the quality of life and concern for others.

According to Hofstede, in cultures characterised by extremely aggressive goal behaviour, gender roles are rigidly defined: thus men are expected to work and to focus their careers in traditionally male occupations; women are generally expected not to work outside the home and to focus more on families. If they do work outside the home, they are usually expected to pursue work in areas traditionally dominated by women. Many people in Japan tend to exhibit relatively aggressive goal behaviour, whereas many people in Germany, Mexico, Italy and the United States tend to exhibit moderately aggressive goal behaviour. People from the Netherlands, Norway, Sweden, Denmark and Finland tend to exhibit relatively passive goal behaviour.

Table 6.2 gives a rather more detailed account of the impact of these different cultural dimensions.

Table 6.3 outlines the specific scores obtained by Hofstede (1980) on the first four cultural dimensions.

Table 6.2 Impacts of different cultural dimensions at the workplace

Cultural dimension	Impacts at the workplace
Individualist	Same value standards apply to all: universalism Other people seen as potential resources Task prevails over relationship Calculative model of employer–employee relationship
Collectivist	Value standards differ for in-group and out-groups: particularism Other people seen as members of their group Relationship prevails over task Moral model of employer–employee relationship
Large power distance (power respect)	Hierarchy reflects on existential inequality of roles Subordinates expect to be told what to do Ideal boss is a benevolent autocrat (good father)
Small power distance (power tolerance)	Hierarchy means an inequality of roles, established for convenience Subordinates expect to be consulted Ideal boss is a resourceful democrat
Weak uncertainty avoidance (uncertainty acceptance)	Dislike of rules, written or unwritten Less formalisation and standardisation
Strong uncertainty avoidance	Emotional need for rules, written or unwritten More formalisation and standardisation
Masculinity (aggressive goal behaviour)	Assertiveness appreciated Oversell yourself Stress on careers Decisiveness
Femininity (passive goal behaviour)	Assertiveness ridiculed Undersell yourself Stress on life quality Intuition

Table 6.3 **Scores of cultural dimensions (by country)**

Country	Individualism	Power distance	Uncertainty	Masculinity
Argentina	46	49	86	56
Australia	90	36	51	61
Austria	55	11	70	79
Belgium	75	65	94	54
Brazil	38	69	76	49
Canada	80	39	48	52
Chile	23	63	86	28
Colombia	13	67	80	64
Denmark	74	18	23	16
Finland	63	33	59	26
France	71	68	86	43
Germany (FR)	67	35	65	66
Great Britain	89	35	35	66
Greece	35	60	112	57
Hong Kong	25	68	29	57
India	48	77	40	56
Iran	41	58	59	43
Ireland	70	28	35	68
Israel	54	13	81	47
Italy	76	50	75	70
Japan	46	54	92	95
Mexico	30	81	82	69
The Netherlands	80	38	53	14
New Zealand	79	22	49	58
Norway	69	31	50	8
Pakistan	14	55	70	50
Peru	16	64	87	42
Philippines	32	94	44	64
Portugal	27	63	104	31
Singapore	20	74	8	48
South Africa	65	49	49	63
Spain	51	57	86	42
Sweden	71	31	29	5
Switzerland	68	34	58	70
Taiwan	17	58	69	45
Thailand	20	64	64	34
Turkey	37	66	85	45
USA	91	40	46	62
Venezuela	12	81	76	73
Yugoslavia	27	76	88	21

pause for thought 1   Look carefully at Table 6.3. Compare and contrast the results for Australia, Denmark, Japan and Singapore. What do these differences imply in terms of business practice?

In later studies Hofstede (1991) added a fifth dimension to his national cultural classification, namely 'long-term orientation'.

Long-term orientation

Hofstede defines this as 'dealing with a society's search for virtue'. Long-term orientation means focusing on the future and implies a cultural trend towards delaying immediate gratification by practising persistence and thriftiness. The top long-term oriented countries were found to be China, Hong Kong, Taiwan, Japan and South Korea in that order. Its opposite, short-term orientation means a greater focus on the present and a more immediate gratification of need, such as spending to support current consumption even if this means borrowing money. The short-term oriented countries in Asia included Pakistan, Philippines and Bangladesh. All Western countries showed a short-term orientation.

CASE 6.1 National culture and Japanese competitiveness

Among the many factors contributing to Japan's post-war competitiveness has been the sociocultural underpinnings at the national level of its industrial and commercial activities. For example, during most of the post-war era Japan's workers had a strong preference for work over leisure so that as real incomes rose, a high percentage of the additional income was saved. This, coupled with relatively low inflation and low interest rates, helped stimulate investment.

The social framework of Japanese society also played a part, having been influenced by two powerful ideologies, namely Buddhism and Confucianism. Buddhism taught the importance of harmony and respect, reminding people that they should be prepared for change since this was an endemic part of life. Confucianism taught the importance of the individual's position in society and the vital significance of the interaction between a person and his/her immediate superior/inferior. With this background, Japan became a strongly 'vertical' society based on the household or 'ie'. Individuals were subservient to group interest, whether it was within a traditional family framework or in a 'quasi' family-type situation based on the company. This aspect of Japan's nature has been characterised as a society in which work organisation is *gemeinschaft* rather than *gesellschaft* in nature – that is, one based on natural will and close face-to-face relationships rather than one which is based on rational will and which is more utilitarian and goal directed in nature.

Competitiveness also depends to a great extent on how companies manage their most valuable asset – their workers. Japanese corporate strategy on labour management in the large firm sector is very much about creating an efficient internal labour market. First, they hire individuals straight from school or college and employ them as far as possible until retiring age at about 55 to 58 years. On average Japanese companies tend to hire people with 'neyaka', i.e. an optimistic, open minded and wide ranging set of interests as compared to the more specialist hiring policies of many European companies. Second, they mould workers into 'flexible assets' by rotating them between different departments within the company to ensure a broader perspective and a more flexible attitude. Third, they involve workers in in-company training schemes and stress the importance of on-the-job training. Finally, the pay system varies closely with age around the concept of providing workers in large and medium-sized firms with 'lifetime' employment. Japanese managers work hard at creating a stable internal labour market and treat workers as key resources deserving of attention. If workers feel that the company has a commitment to keep them employed, this gives them the confidence to release the 'tacit' knowledge or basic know-how, which often cannot be easily articulated. In other words, workers have the confidence to share any untapped knowledge they may have because they operate within a secure and dynamic environment.

Source: A. Griffiths (2003 and 2000). Reprinted with permission.

Questions

1 How does the discussion above relate to Hofstede's five cultural dimensions?

2 Comment on the scoring for Japan in Hofstede's investigations in Table 6.3. Are there any surprises?

Cultural impacts on international business

In Chapters 1 and 2 we noted the rapid growth in joint ventures, strategic alliances and mergers and acquisitions in a globalised economy. At such times managers and executives often focus on the business needs of the new operations, such as raising finance, acquiring the capital infrastructure, drawing up operational plans and providing technical training. Unfortunately cultural issues at a national or organisational level have often been ignored during these periods of consolidation, as many firms have subsequently found to their cost. Box 6.1 brings this issue into focus.

Box 6.1 A clash of cultures

Mike Burgess is an operations manager from the USA who is in charge of a multicultural team in Indonesia, which includes a number of Japanese experts on production control. At a team meeting beginning at 9.00 a.m. he is surprised to find that at 9.20 a.m. three of the remaining members of the Indonesian team are still arriving, each bringing with them an additional three uninvited participants. The room has to be reorganised and an extra nine chairs brought in. Four members of the Japanese team have reorganised themselves so that they are sitting together. Mr Budi, the senior Indonesian member, is due to deliver the opening formal comments and eventually arrives at 9.45 a.m. He begins his opening address immediately but exceeds his allotted five minutes, taking ten minutes in all. The meeting itself is finally underway at 9.55 a.m.

Mike presents the agenda and outlines the objectives of the meeting and invites questions. To his surprise, no one volunteers with a first question. He then realises that Mr Budi, as senior member, is expecting to be invited to make comments. After he does so the rest of the team joins in. The meeting is going well, but Mike becomes annoyed by side conversations among the Indonesian team members – as a rule he likes his meetings to maintain their focus on achieving the final results and objectives.

▶

> ### Box 6.1 Continued
>
> Halfway through the meeting, Mike and his marketing director have a disagreement. The openness of the heated debate surprises the Indonesian and Japanese teams. By 10.30 a.m. everyone is irritated and Mike suggests a coffee break, at which point the Indonesians express surprise that Mike has not ordered any snacks. When the meeting reconvenes, Mike wants to reach a decision so he asks Mr Yamaguchi, the senior Japanese team member, to agree to a vote. Mr Yamaguchi replies by asking for a week to consult with his headquarters in Tokyo, which frustrates Mike whose project will now be delayed. Mr Yamaguchi decides this is an opportunity to vent his own frustrations and he questions Mike, who works on the upper floor, about his failure to reply directly to the e-mails he has been sent.
>
> Mr Yamaguchi does not understand why Mike cannot meet with him personally to discuss some of the issues contained in these e-mails.
>
> *Source*: Adapted from Elashmawi, F. (1998) 'Overcoming Multicultural Clashes in Global Joint Ventures', *European Business Review*, vol. 98, no. 4, pp. 211–16. Reprinted with permission.

The situation in Box 6.1 shows the clash between American values of individualism, directness and time consciousness and the Japanese interest in face-to-face discussion and consensus building. At the core of the clash are the differing values underlying task-oriented versus process-oriented cultures. Americans typically come to business meetings well informed, focused and expecting an open dialogue. They also expect to take action and assign responsibilities. However, their Asian and Japanese partners place more emphasis on group harmony, consensus and the need to discuss proposals and actions; they rarely make an immediate decision. Japanese people may come to a meeting, sit as a group, ask ten questions and leave with 20 more in mind. Decisions come later after reaching a consensus. The Indonesian team expects a senior person to open and close important meetings, frequent coffee breaks and snacks and perhaps sufficient time to conduct their daily prayers. Indonesians are used to inviting others to their meetings if they are subject specialists and do not mind side conversations if these are on important points. They also expect seating to be arranged according to seniority, as well as explicit invitations to participate during the course of the meeting. With three sets of competing values, cultural clashes can easily occur and teamwork can be seriously damaged.

It may be useful to briefly review some other possible impacts of Hofstede's analysis of national culture on international business practices.

- *Power distances*: If companies operate with others from nations with different degrees of power distance, misunderstandings can easily arise. For example, a firm from a country with a small power distance, when negotiating in a joint venture, may send a team of experts who are relatively junior. If this team is sent to a large power distance (power-respecting) culture, this may be viewed as an insult. The informality that characterises communication in countries with a small power distance may be misinterpreted by those from a power-respecting culture as an attempt to reduce their authority.
- *Uncertainty avoidance*: Those operating in strong uncertainty avoidance countries tend to adopt more rigid hierarchies and more elaborate rules and procedures for doing business. Risk taking may also be less preferred than in weak uncertainty

avoidance (uncertainty accepting) countries such as the United States and Hong Kong. This can affect the way in which certain benefits are received. For example, Japanese firms operating in uncertainty accepting countries such as Canada and the United States have been forced to modify their pay and promotion policies because North American workers are more oriented towards an individualistic 'pay me what I'm worth attitude' and are less worried about job insecurity.

pause for thought 2	What impacts might result in terms of international business practices if two companies involved with one another originate from countries with sharply different scores for 'individualism' and 'long-term orientation'?

The next section emphasises the types of understanding and awareness that may be needed of national cultural differences if international business negotiations are to be conducted effectively. It emphasises the differences between the collectivist/individualist dimension of national culture, with particular reference to conducting business with Confucian societies, such as China.

■ Doing business in Confucian societies: the importance of *Guanxi* (connections)

Economists forecast that China will be one of the world's four largest economies by the year 2010. The success has often been attributed to Confucianism, which stresses hard work, thrift and perseverance. Confucius lived from 551–478 BC and societies influenced by his thinking include China, Hong Kong, Taiwan, Japan and Korea, all of which have prospects for sustained economic growth in the new millennium. In these societies 'who you know is more important than what you know'. These connections are known in Chinese as *guanxi*; in Japan they are known as *kankei*; and in Korea as *kwankye*. Here we pay particular attention to *guanxi*.

Under the influence of Confucianism these societies share the following characteristics: disdain for institutional law; strong bonds on the basis of blood, ancestral village and school and military ties; a clear demarcation between members of the in versus out-groups; an ability to grasp the interdependent relationship situations, that may not be obvious to Westerners; and a tendency to view matters from a long-term perspective. These characteristics mean that connections in virtually all social functions, including business, are of the utmost importance. In the West, institutional law and contracts establish what can and should be done and largely overshadow the role of connections.

The word *guanxi* contains two characters that make up the term 'gate/pass' or 'to connect'. Thus *guanxi* refers to the establishment of a connection between independent individuals to enable a bilateral flow of personal or social transactions. Both parties must derive benefits from the transaction to ensure the continuation of such a relationship.

How does this differ from 'networking' in the West? Yeung and Tung (1996) analyse these differences along six dimensions.

1 *Motives: role obligation versus self-interest.* Confucianism emphasises the importance of an individual's place in the hierarchy: individuals are part of a social system, not isolated entities. These include such relationships as ruler–subject, father–son, husband–wife, brother–brother and friend–friend. People have responsibility to the role and not merely to their own self-interest, as in the West.

2 *Reciprocation: self-loss versus self-gain.* In Confucianism everyone is encouraged to become a *yi-ren* (righteous person). To do so, a person must repay favours and increase the value of the favour given. There is a Chinese saying: 'If someone pays you an honour of a linear foot, you should reciprocate by honouring the giver with ten linear feet.'

3 *Time orientation: long-term versus short-term perspective.* In Confucian societies people understand all social interaction within the context of a long-term perspective. Their values are based on an understanding of the interdependence of events and of the relationship between events and time. Every *guanxi* relationship is regarded as 'stock' to be put away in times of abundance and plenty. The 'stock' will then be at their disposal in times of need and trouble. *Guanxi* is maintained through continuous, long-term interactions. Social interactions in the West are usually seen as one-offs with the main emphasis placed on immediate gratification from the situation.

4 *Power differentiation: xia versus power.* In Confucianism everyone striving to become a righteous person becomes a *xia* or knight, attempting to right the wrongs in the world. Those in positions of power and authority must assist the disadvantaged; it is their obligation to do so. In return, those in positions of power and authority gain face and reputation. While social conscience may be strong in the West, there is no obligation for the powerful to help the disadvantaged.

5 *Nature of power: personal power versus institutional authority.* Governance by ethics is preferred to governance by law. There is a general aversion to law and litigation in Confucian societies. The focus is on personal power and the importance of *guanxi*, since an individual (rather than authority) defines what is permissible in a given context in a given time.

6 *Sanction: shame versus guilt.* The primary sanction in Confucian societies is that of shame. There is great emphasis on face and face-saving. Face implies more than reputation. There is a Chinese saying that 'face is like the bark of a tree; without its bark, the tree dies'. People who lose face in these societies are more than social outcasts; a loss of face brings shame to the person and to his or her family members. Face can be given and taken away only in the broader context of social interactions. To maintain *guanxi*, extra care needs to be taken in acquiring and maintaining 'face' – often known as 'face works'. In the West, probably due to the influence of Judeo-Christianity, sanctions work on the basis of guilt. Thus, if the behaviour deviates from the norm, it is individuals who are required to internalise their understanding of sin.

To many in the West, *guanxi* can appear to resemble nepotism. For example, someone in authority may make decisions based on family ties instead of being based on an objective evaluation of ability. As with any system, it is open to abuse, though defenders of *guanxi* might also point to the arguably adverse impacts of excessive litigation in the USA!

Although *guanxi* may appear undemocratic, it is embedded in a rich cultural heritage which places a strong emphasis on the family and is drawn from the Confucian background in which most of the key relationships already discussed pertain to the family. In fact, the majority of Chinese businesses are family-run concerns. The importance of *guanxi* cannot be overestimated. In their research of 2000 Chinese businesses surveyed in and around Shanghai, Gordon C. Chu and Yanan Ju (1993) found that 92.4% of those polled affirmed the importance of *guanxi* in their daily lives. Also 84.5% indicated that they did not trust strangers until they had had the opportunities to get to know them better, and 71.7% preferred to use *guanxi* connections rather than normal bureaucratic channels.

The following quotation from the chairman of the Lippo group, an Indonesian conglomerate, usefully summarises many of the above points when he stated that he devotes his time exclusively to cultivating relationships while delegating the daily functioning of the group's business to his two sons. In his words, 'I open the door and others walk through.'

Effective ways of cultivating *guanxi*

Yeung and Tung (1996) reported the results of their survey of executives who identified the following activities as being crucial for cultivating *guanxi*.

- *Group identification/altercasting*. Kinship and locality are the important bases for *guanxi*. Kinship is based on people's immediate and extended families, while locality refers to the ancestral village or province. Such 'ascribed' relationships are based on common or shared experiences, such as going to the same school, serving in the same military unit or working in the same organisation. As most non-Chinese investors cannot do this, 'altercasting' is an alternative possibility. This means rearranging the social network so that individuals can focus on some element of commonality. The most effective way of doing this is through an intermediary. According to Victor Fung, chairman of Prudential Asia, a Hong Kong investment bank: 'If you are being considered for a new partnership, a personal reference from a respected member of the Chinese business community is worth more than any amount of money you could throw on the table.' As another executive put it: 'The China market is like a pond full of hidden delicious food. A new fish in the pond can starve to death because he doesn't know how to locate the food. Your intermediary is an old fish who knows where every plant and plankton is. He can show you the precise location of this food so you can eat to your heart's satisfaction.'
- *Tendering favours*. Another way of establishing relationships is to offer immediate rewards. Gift-giving, entertainment, overseas trips, sponsoring and support for the children of Chinese officials at universities abroad, are common. When a gift has been received, there is a symbolic breaking down of the boundaries between persons, although these cannot be the basis for long-term *guanxi*.
- *Nurturing long-term mutual benefits*. The intent of this approach is to create an interdependence between two parties in the relationship so that there will be a great cost to either side in severing such ties.

- *Cultivating personal relationships. Guanxi* relations that are based exclusively on material benefits are fragile; many respondents felt that it was important to develop a personal relationship with the partner that cannot be readily imitated by others. 'Personal' means sharing inner feelings or secrets for which, in Chinese society, sincerity and frankness are absolutely essential. To do this you would need to acquire an in-depth knowledge of the Chinese business associate and know what appeals to his or her needs.
- *Cultivating trust.* Finally, cultivating trust is crucial. Around 85% of the companies interviewed indicated that this was an essential condition for cultivating *guanxi.* For many this was based on two factors: 'Deliver what you promise' and 'Don't cheat'. Another way is to learn all you can about the Chinese culture, including its language.

Case Study 6.2 casts further light on the relevance of guanxi relationships.

CASE 6.2   East meets West

When East meets West there are clashes with respect to their management practices. For example, in the context of strong global fdi and M & A activity, great demands are placed on joint-venture firms having all their subsidiaries working within a common form of governance, and conforming to the transparency of accounting practices that result from the adoption of GAAP (generally accepted accounting practices). This commonality allows the global management team to measure, contrast and control their operations in a straightforward way – but such operations are anathema to most Eastern managers. In fairness, we should note that opaqueness is not a unique East/West issue since the Channel Islands, Belgium, Spain and Switzerland all practise low levels of financial disclosure. However, research as to the Oriental concept of probability and risk taking indicates that Asian cultures tend to be more 'fate-oriented' and less willing (than Occidentals) to take a probabilistic view of the world. The inclination towards a lack of disclosure in Asian accounting together with a reluctance to adopt management accounting poses serious problems for those seeking goal congruence in joint operations. It may be useful at this stage to consider in more detail some of the key differences between Western and Eastern practices as they may impinge upon international business activity.

- *Rules versus relationships.* In advanced economies, companies do business within a 'rules-based' system, with business generally conducted by using contracts under laws that are widely known and consistently enforced. Although it may not be apparent to those operating in a rules-based system that has grown up over decades or even centuries, such a system carries large fixed costs. These include the establishment of the legislation and the judiciary, the drafting and interpretation of laws, and the implementation of contracts, all of which involve high sunk costs. On the other hand, once such a system is in place, the incremental cost of enforcing an additional contract is minimal.
  China's is not a rules-based economy, at least not yet; it is still an economy based on relationships. Business transactions are made on the strength not of

contracts but of personal agreements. Transactions are purely private, and are neither verifiable nor enforceable in the public sphere. However, the marginal costs of finding, screening and monitoring a potential partner are extremely high. For instance, the relationships have to be managed personally: you cannot afford to delegate the task. A telling difference with the West is that executives in China tend to answer their own phones. Given this marginal cost of cultivating new relationships, it makes sense to do business with close family, then with the extended family, then neighbours from your home town, then former classmates, and only then, reluctantly, with strangers.

■ *Ethical norms*. In Western literature it has only been in relatively recent times that business ethics have impinged explicitly on decision-making techniques and structures. In China, however, there has always been a debate about *yi* and *li* – where *yi* is ethical value (justice) and *li* is economic value (profit). Indeed, both *yi* and *li* have been central concepts within Chinese Confucianism. It is said that one cannot 'have both fish and a bear's paw at the same time'. So man will favour *yi* and discard *li*, and thus it is to be understood that '*xiao-ren* (a mean person) is pushed by *li*, whereas *jun-zi* (a gentleman) is delighted by *yi*'. Of course, such attitudes are being increasingly challenged in an age of globalism as the world is effectively reduced to a single market economy.

■ *Guanxi*. As already noted, Asians tend to deploy rather opaque accounting practices and to adopt 'gift giving' on a scale that seems to many Westerners as little short of bribery though in many cases this may be a misconception. In China there is the universal practice of *guanxi*, the maintenance of which will involve gift giving. In Chinese society the exchanges of favours involving *guanxi* are not strictly commercial, they are also social – involving *renqing* (social or humanised obligation) and the giving of *mianzi* (the notion of 'face'). More recently, as China opens up, *guanxi* has become known as 'social capital' and has been seen in the West as an important element in securing commercial contracts between corporations. Although 'gift giving' and 'banqueting' are both normal facets of Chinese *guanxi*, many Western firms' operations arguably go too far and operate too close to bribery. Western individuals can become known as 'eat and wine friends', defeating the object of true *guanxi* – which is the offering of favours during the development of a personal relationship. Confucianism is sometimes (many would argue unfairly!) accused of promoting corruption in East Asia given that its teachings call for individuals to improve and maintain relationships among relatives and friends through influence and contacts. The World Bank and the International Monetary Fund now seem more vigilant in acting as 'whistle blowers' whenever they detect funding diversions. Similarly, the United States seems more ready to implement its 1977 laws, which declare acts as criminal if national personnel offer commercial payoffs to public servants abroad. Corporations themselves also seem more ready to tackle perceived corruption. For example, the Royal Dutch/Shell Group in its April 1998 annual report said it had fired 23 of its staff and had terminated contracts with 95 firms on ethical grounds. In China, there is a strong history of *guandao*, or official corruption that is more pervasive than in Japan.

In terms of the management of projects and of joint ventures, there have clearly been examples of attempts by negotiators to ask for bribes in some form. From the

Western ethical perspective, giving bribes should be resisted. In an attempt to tackle this issue, the OECD Council adopted in 1996 the 'Recommendation on Bribery of Foreign Public Officials in International Business Transactions' which calls on member countries to act to combat illicit payments in international trade and investment. As part of that recommendation, reference was made to the need 'to take concrete and meaningful steps including examining tax legislation, regulations, and practices insofar as they may indirectly favour bribery' (OECD 1996, C (94) 75). Following this, the OECD Committee on Fiscal Affairs undertook an in-depth review of tax measures that may influence the willingness to make or accept bribes. The committee concluded that bribes paid to foreign public officials should no longer be deductible for tax purposes. They noted that many member countries would have to change their current practices.

Source: Adapted from Kidd and Xue (2000).

Questions

1 Consider some of the differences between a 'rules-based' system and a 'relationship-based' system.

2 How might *guanxi* relationships influence international business activity?

National, organisational and occupational cultures

As well as his major study on differences in national cultures within a given organisation (IBM), Hofstede (1991) undertook a study on variations in organisational culture within the same nation. He compared otherwise similar people in different organisations within the same countries (Denmark and the Netherlands). His results suggested that at the organisational level 'culture' differences consisted mostly of different practices rather than different values (this emphasis was reversed at the national level). Using the word 'culture' for both levels suggested that the two kinds of culture were identical phenomena, but to Hofstede this was clearly false. A nation is not an organisation and the two types of 'culture' are of a different kind.

This conclusion contradicts a popular notion about 'corporate culture' derived from Peters and Waterman's (1982) classic work, *In Search of Excellence*, which assumed that *shared values* represented the core of a corporate culture. Hofstede's work showed that while the values of founders and key leaders may undoubtedly shape organisational cultures, the ways in which these 'cultures' affect ordinary members is through *shared practices*. The fact that organisational cultures are shaped by management practices and not by values explains why such cultures can, to some extent, be managed. As Hofstede points out, values are shaped early in our lives, through family, school and peers so that employers cannot readily change the values of their employees. The only way in which they can affect them is through selecting and promoting employees with the 'desired' values, where appropriate candidates are available. If, in order to change organisational cultures, employers had to change their employees' values, it would arguably be a hopeless task. However, because organisational cultures reside mainly in the more superficial arena of practices rather than values, they are somewhat more manageable.

Table 6.4 provides a brief outline of some aspects of national, corporate (organisational) and occupational cultures. Many of the terms presented are considered further in Box 6.2.

Table 6.4 Aspects of national, corporate and occupational cultures

National culture	Corporate culture	Occupational culture
An individual's orientation towards:	A particular company's:	A given occupation's:
■ universalism v particularism	■ values ■ rituals ■ heroes ■ symbols	■ analytical paradigm ■ work norms and practices ■ code of ethics ■ jargon
■ analysing v integrating	NB: Corporate culture can also refer to the values, systems and practices which influence the corporate behaviour of all firms in a country.	
■ individualism v communitarianism		
■ Inner-directedness v outer-directedness		
■ time as sequence v time as synchronisation		
■ achieved status v ascribed status		
■ equality v hierarchy		

Source: Adapted from Snow *et al.* (1996)

pause for thought 3 Think of any particular company with which you are familiar. Can you identify any distinctive elements in its corporate culture? Can you trace the origin of any of these elements?

Box 6.2 | **National and organisational cultural dimensions**

As well as Hofstede's seminal work, Trompenaars (1993) set out a cultural model consisting of seven dimensions, five of which are grouped under 'relationships with people' and the other two are concerned with time and the environment.

■ *Universalism v particularism*. In universal cultures 'rules' are favoured over 'relationships'. Contractual agreements are considered of the utmost importance, and logical, rational analytical thinking and professionalism are of great importance. In particularist cultures there are greater obligations to friendship and kinship and these are maintained through personalism, saving 'face' and paternalism.

■ *Individualism v collectivism*. This is almost identical to Hofstede's dimension (*see* p. 173).

■ *Affective v neutral*. This relates to the extent to which emotion is displayed in communication.

▶

> ### Box 6.2 Continued
>
> - *Specific v diffuse relationships*. In a diffuse society, aspects of personal, leisure and family life are not necessarily distinct from life at work, and relationships may transcend many or all aspects of life.
> - *Achieving or ascribing*. In ascribing societies achievement is a more collective affair and organisations in these societies often justify a high power distance so that things get done. Power here does not need to be legitimised by title or qualification and abuse is checked by moral responsibilities.
> - *Perceptions of time*. This reflects different attitudes to time: synchronic and circular attitudes allow parallel activities and are less concerned with punctuality. In a 'sequential culture' the focus is on rational efficiency and time is viewed in a more linear fashion.
> - *Relating to nature*. This concerns beliefs about nature's ability to be controlled. 'Inner-directed' cultures want to overcome nature and depend a great deal on technology, while 'outer-directed' cultures see themselves more as a product of the environment.

As noted in Table 6.4, corporate culture can refer both to the individual company's values, rituals, heroes and symbols or to the values, systems and practices which are generally accepted by *all home-country companies* within a given nation. Case Study 6.3 looks at the second of these aspects of *corporate culture*, taking further the material on Japan presented in Case Study 6.1.

CASE 6.3 Corporate culture and Japanese competitiveness

Another important area of debate has been the nature and perceived weaknesses in the much vaunted industrial groupings either of the *Kigyo-Shudan* or *keiretsu* types. The typical corporate governance system in Japan included such attributes as the long-term supply of funds to industry at low interest rates; the monitoring of industry by the main group bank; the extensive cross-holding of shares; the lack of non-corporate shareholders; and the absence of mergers and acquisitions as a means of extracting value from poorly-performing firms. All these attributes arguably created a corporate culture which aided Japan's catch-up process.

However, weaknesses in such a corporate culture began to emerge during the rapidly changing environment of the 1980s, which began to erode the traditional corporate governance system. For example, banks found that large firms began to rely more on the capital market for funds so that a greater proportion of their lending had to be directed to the small and medium-sized companies whose performance was more difficult to monitor. There was also an increasing realisation that the 'old' corporate culture of the *Kigyo-Shudan* form of industrial organisation based on six major industrial groupings (*see* Case Study 2.3) would have to change. Under this system company shares were mostly held by other companies in order to consolidate a relationship rather than as an active form of investment. This would have to change in a globalised environment in which cross-border mergers and acquisitions are increasingly the norm rather than the exception. Further, the changes brought about by financial deregulation will bring new investors into the equity market (pension funds, insurance companies) which are likely to be more active traders of shares.

The other main form of industrial organisation, the *keiretsu* system of parent company and vertically organised subcontracting suppliers, is also changing. For example, the Renault 'revival plan' for Nissan involves a reduction in its capacity by 25% together with the selling of its shareholdings in its affiliated companies where it owns less than 20% of those shares. This will inevitably weaken the vertical *keiretsu* 'relationship' based on long-term 'family' type bonds between large firms and their subcontractors who lie below them in the production 'pyramid'. Infact 36% of sub-contractors surveyed in 2001 stated an intention of reducing their dependence on specific parent companies. The unwinding of cross-holdings also continues, with a survey by Toyo Keizai estimating that cross-holdings have decreased by 10% between 1992 and 2000 with most of those acquiring the released shares being foreigners who are more interested in profits than the previous holders.

If shares become more easily traded as cross-holdings decrease, then the ownership of Japanese companies may change and restructuring through mergers and acquisitions may eventually become more prevalent. In the past, the importance of creating shareholder value has been relatively unimportant in Japan since managers were mostly recruited from the pool of workers within the company so that there was a lack of a pure profit motive. However, the changing industrial system and the banking reorganisation underway will inevitably shift Japanese corporations in the direction of a greater emphasis on raising short-term profits and increasing shareholder value. For example in the past each *keiretsu* group would have its own 'main' bank, but now those banks have themselves been involved in large amalgamations in attempts to rationalise operations, such as the Mitsubishi-Tokyo Financial Group (MTFG), the Sumitomo-Mitsui Financial Group (SMFG), or the Mizuho Financial Group (MFG). These *keiretsu* groups therefore now include banks from different *keiretsu* and this could, of course, change the nature of individual groups identity and funding.

Japanese firms are meeting the challenges of the new millennium by increasingly redeploying their assets, with the numbers of companies announcing restructuring plans increasing from an average of 42 per month in 1998 to 91 per month in 2001. Many firms are also placing relatively less emphasis on sales and total profits and more emphasis on returns on equity and the efficiency of capital use. The much vaunted Japanese car industry is a classical case of the restructuring process, with Toyota creating much closer links with Hino Motors and the Yamaha Motor company, while in March 2000 the German-American company Daimler-Chrysler secured control of 34% of Mitsubishi Motors' equity as a means of combining the companies more effectively in order to cut marketing and production costs. Indeed by 2003, Renault owned 37% of Nissan, Daimler-Chrysler owned 34% of Mitsubishi Motors and Ford owned 33% of Mazda Motors. Corporate restructuring in Japan is being led by dynamic companies such as Toyota, which have begun diversifying into auto insurance and consumer finance and Sony, which is in the process of transforming itself into a fully networked corporation by opening an online store.

▶

On the human resource front, the basic pillars of the Japanese employment system have included employment for life, wages according to age/length of service and company-based unions. These have helped Japan to develop an 'internal' labour market where workers in large companies were 'grown' within the organisation in which they were trained. However, the pressures of competition have begun to slowly modify this system. There has been a lowering of the age of retirement for permanent employees in order to decrease wage bills while at the same time there has been a decrease in yearly hirings. Also the number of mid-term employees (i.e. those who change job in mid-career) has increased as companies try to 'poach' good workers. In addition, wages are now being increasingly determined by merit rather than by age, although it should be remembered that only some 20% of Japanese workers are paid according to merit. Finally, more Japanese companies have been resorting to temporary workers as a way of cutting labour costs. In other words, a number of features more reminiscent of the 'external' labour markets familiar in the West are now gradually developing within large Japanese companies.

Some of these points have been reinforced by recent survey evidence. For example a survey from the Japan Ministry of Health and Labour in 2003 showed that in 2002 only 48.6% of employers attached great importance to the lifetime employment system when hiring emloyees. The same survey also showed that in 2002 some 55.9% of Japanese employers attached greater importance to the merit system of payment when deciding on employees pay. Finally the electronics giant, Matsushita Electric stated that it is planning to change its salary system starting in April 2004 by abolishing automatic pay rises according to age and length of service and introducing instead a system where pay is linked to the category of employment.

It has been argued that the so-called pillars of the Japanese employment system only worked because economic growth was high and that in the present low-growth era restructuring of industry will mean over 1 million workers losing their jobs every year over the next few years – with companies only keeping those with special skills. The change in the system will, however, be relatively slow, as government employment subsidies to firms to encourage the hoarding of labour will continue. Further, the relatively low unemployment benefit and the lack of sufficient private labour agencies will tend to inhibit increased labour mobility. However, in the longer term there will remain a core group of career workers with both general and company specific skills for whom the old lifetime employment pattern will continue. In addition, a somewhat more mobile group of specialised workers will develop who will be better able to meet the 'market' needs of the economy for certain skills. There may even be greater mobility within the group of relatively unskilled workers to help meet the constant shifting demands for these workers.

Source: Adapted from Griffiths (2003 and 2000). Reprinted with permission.

Questions

1 Identify some of the corporate cultural changes underway in Japan and comment on their likely impacts.

2 What factors have been 'driving' these changes in corporate culture?

The linkages between national and corporate/organisational cultures prevalent across the majority of home-country companies is taken further in the next section, using investigatory material from France, the USA and the Netherlands.

■ Interaction of national with organisational cultures

Hofstede has suggested that while management practices differ between organisations and societies they remain remarkably similar within each society. D'Iribane (1996) adopts a similar view and researched this area by carrying out in-depth interviews in the 1980s in three production plants of a French-owned aluminium company, one in France, one in the USA (Maryland) and one in the Netherlands. The plants were technically identical, but interpersonal interactions on the shop floor differed dramatically between them. D'Iribane identified three different 'logics' that controlled the interpersonal interactions at the sites: honour in France; fair contract in the USA; and consensus in the Netherlands. These philosophies represent patterns of thinking, feeling and acting which can be traced back to the national histories of these three societies over the centuries.

In France, for example, D'Iribane argues that the most important feature is that it still is largely a 'class-based' society. Within the plant the different 'classes' coexist on at least three levels: the cadres (managers and professionals), the maitrise (first-line supervisors) and the non-cadres (levels below maitrise). The relationships between these 'classes' are governed by antagonism, yet a sense of respect prevails, for the types of orders a supervisor can give are constrained by a need to respect the honour of the subordinates. In the USA on the other hand, everybody is supposed to be equal and the relationship between management and workers is contractual. While this is less hierarchical than in France, American managers can get away with demanding things from their workers that in France would be impossible. In practice, some people in the USA would seem to be still more equal than others. D'Iribane attributes the US practices to the country's immigrant past: the heritage of the Pilgrim Fathers and other seventeenth- and eighteenth-century white settlers. Since there was no traditional aristocracy as in France, immigrants developed a middle-class society, with relationships governed by contractual agreements. D'Iribane calls them 'pious merchants'. In the Netherlands, while they have pious merchant ancestors, relationships have historically been based on compromise rather than contract. The Republic was borne from a revolt against their Spanish overlords and in order to survive, the former rebels learned to cooperate across religious and ideological lines. The Dutch tradition leaves room for contracts, but negotiations may be re-opened the day after conclusion if new facts emerge. D'Iribane is struck by everybody's respect for facts, which he finds stronger than in either France or in the USA. In France, status and power often prevail over facts; in the USA, moral principles are often seen as superseding facts. Dutch consensus is based on concern as to the individuals' quality of life, which should not be harmed by avoidable conflicts.

However, too simplistic and stereotyped a perspective can sometimes lead to false assumptions as to the national characteristics most closely aligned with 'business success', as Case Study 6.4 suggests.

CASE 6.4 Management gurus might rethink the Dutch approach FT

In 2002, a group of consultants published a book examining 'the extraordinary successes of Dutch companies acquiring abroad, most especially in the USA'. The book, *Leading Cross-Border Mergers*, by Spencer Stuart, the headhunters and the Trompenaars Hampden-Turner, the Amsterdam-based specialists in inter-cultural management, said that if your company was going to be taken over by foreigners, you should pray they came from the Netherlands.

Dutch owners offered 'autonomy, understanding, respect, collegiality, friendship and complementarity, with no nationalistic agendas', the book says. 'It is a very attractive approach.' Among the chief executives interviewed for the book was Cees van der Hoeven, chief executive of Ahold, the Dutch retailer. Mr van der Hoeven boasted that Ahold was a 'real champion' when it came to making the acquisitions that had turned it into the second largest food retailer in the US. 'In all modesty, we can say that we are by far the best integrators in our sector,' he said.

In 2003, Mr van der Hoeven and Michael Meurs, the chief financial officer, resigned after revealing a $500 million overstatement in earnings at Ahold's US unit. Ahold is not the only Dutch company to have run into difficulties since appearing in the book. Others extolled for their skill in integrating foreign acquisitions included Akzo Nobel, the drugs and chemicals group, Buhrmann, the supplier of office products, and information technology company Getronics – all of which have since been hit by trouble at US subsidiaries.

None of this is likely to lead to immediate changes in the way the Netherlands views management and business. Indeed, the Dutch are considered experienced international managers. They are also successful at forging international partnerships; the Anglo-Dutch groups Unilever and Royal Dutch/Shell are the world's longest-standing cross-border companies.

Dutch managers pride themselves, too, on having an outlook that is far removed from the US obsession with shareholder value and quarterly financial reports. 'The Dutch way of management is different from [other countries],' says Karel Waagenaar, chief executive of Dutch-based W&S, an international firm that provides companies with temporary managers.

'The French like dictating. The Germans look to their superiors and are very obedient. The Americans are no-nonsense – if the boss says "we're going ahead" then you go ahead. The Dutch always try to compromise.'

It is a popular portrayal. The authors of *Leading Cross-Border Mergers* cite foreign observers' admiration of the way the Dutch deal with paradox. 'They are a monarchy, but think and behave like republicans. They are thrifts yet generous, blunt yet caring, protesting yet tolerant,' the book says.

Above all, the Dutch encourage the long-term view in business. The US focus on shareholder returns is seen as damaging to a company's future. 'We have a deep reluctance to accept the Anglo-Saxon framework of "shareholders first". Shareholders are people who never share. Holland is the country of the stakeholder. It should not be the analysts who decide how you run a company. We say: "Forget about the analysts. They kill our long-term thinking",' says one Dutch management consultant.

Ahold's financial problems were widely known so there was little shock at yesterday's resignations. But management observers are waiting to see what drove the US operation to behave as it did before drawing conclusions about the need for Dutch managers to change their approach. Some suspect the affair will confirm what happens when you press managers to produce financial performance beyond what the business can manage. Others wonder whether Dutch companies will have to allow foreign subsidiaries less autonomy. All agree that Dutch companies will think harder before buying US companies in future. And there will probably be less bragging about how good the Dutch are at managing them.

Source: Michael Skapinker, *Financial Times*, 25 February 2003.

Questions

1 What are believed to be effective Dutch characteristics for managing cross-border mergers and takeovers?

2 How does the Dutch approach differ from that perceived to be followed by other nationalities?

3 What evidence is there in the Case Study for questioning whether these national cultural assumptions will, or will not, bring international business 'success'?

Strategies for developing intercultural competence

Having established the importance of cultural sensitivities to international business operations, how can managers develop their own intercultural competences as well as those of their subordinates? Snow *et al*.'s research (1996) showed that the development of a healthy group process must take into account at least five major factors reflecting different elements of national and corporate cultures:

- the degree of similarity among the cultural norms of the individuals on the team;
- the extent to which such norms are manifested in the group;
- the level of fluency in the common language used by the team;
- the communication styles and expectations of what constitutes effective group behaviour;
- the management style of the team leader.

Fedor and Werther (1996) have outlined an eight-stage process that can help to create a culturally responsive joint-venture alliance, assuming, of course, that those involved have already accepted the strategic imperatives of such an alliance. By following this multi-step process, decision makers can systematically consider the organisational dynamics of both firms by adding the cultural dimension to the normal strategic, financial and legal considerations. Working through these issues should mean that deeply rooted values are brought to the surface before they damage the prospects of the alliance.

■ Eight-stage process for cultural compatibility

1 *Corporate cultural profiles*. You can't create cultural compatibility unless you first realise where you are coming from. For this reason, it is important to have an idea of the original corporate culture for each of the partners before working out cultural compatibility. There are, of course, many different ways of carrying out cultural audits. Fedor and Werther suggest that the corporate culture can be defined by the unique set of beliefs and methods of problem-solving which underpin each company's activities.

2 *Cultural incompatibility identification*. At this stage, teams can compare profiles and identify problem areas. Such exercises usually reveal ambiguities and inconsistencies that should not be ignored. It could also reveal areas of mutuality that may have gone unnoticed.

3 *Development of a joint business purpose*. Teams need to agree on the nature of their purpose by reaching consensus about business objectives – such as desired rates of return, market shares, salaries, growth and time targets. This should uncover areas where there is any divergence. Reconciling such divergences early might help avoid future misunderstandings.

4 *Operational independence*. Both parties need to agree the degree of operational independence they are hoping to achieve. The degree of independence will depend on how much each party is prepared to reveal about their working practices without making their partners more formidable competitors.

5 *Structural choice*. The legal structure chosen for the alliance must take into account the desired culture. The variety of structures are wide: from open-ended joint ventures with varying ownership splits, through to time-specific technology sharing contracts. The choice is likely to be driven by deep-seated cultural preferences. For example, American-based partners often gain operational control by choosing a structure that gives them the final say in significant decisions, typically secured through majority ownership. This may, however, create obstacles in the design of an international alliance.

6 *Management systems agreement*. It is vital that these factors be taken into consideration. Management systems reflect deeply embedded ways of working that are often manifested in working practices. For example, in the failure of the Colgate–Palmolive/Kao joint venture in shampoo production, it was the Colgate marketing force that set up the marketing and distribution programme. Even the Colgate people questioned whether the market perspectives and practices successful for toothpaste would work for shampoo. In this way, the culture of the joint venture emerged unconsciously from Colgate's desire to maintain control. These were the driving forces creating the international alliance, rather than the unique needs of the shampoo business.

7 *Staffing the international alliance*. Care needs to be taken in selecting the managing director and key senior officers, since corporate cultures tend to be embodied in the values and beliefs of the people who work in them. Careful discussion will also be needed as to the job specifications and responsibilities, which may reveal deep-seated values about how organisations should be run.

8 *Assessing the international alliance's demands on parent company culture*. It is equally important to have a clear picture of what changes may be required in the

parent company's culture. How will those changes be made? By whom? These questions may yield further insights into the cultural expectations and capabilities of the respective companies.

Fedor and Werther suggest that assessing the cultural compatibility of international alliances is critical if failure is to be avoided. This is the fourth dimension, after the financial, legal and strategic deal has been struck. Knowing the cultural match between the partners helps define the type of deal most likely to succeed once the deal makers have gone.

Case Study 6.5 highlights the increasing emphasis being placed on the corporate/organisational culture, even to the extent of adapting psychologically-based personality tests for individuals to the corporate culture. Since, as we note in Chapters 2 and 8, many mergers and acquisitions, joint ventures and alliances fail as much because of *organisational* cultural incompatibility as *international* cultural incompatibility, this new emphasis is receiving much attention by the potential acquirers and acquired.

CASE 6.5 | ## Corporate 'personality' has a big impact on business success

According to a study by the Chartered Institute of Personnel and Development, 30 per cent of the difference in performance between companies can be attributed to differences in culture. That compares with just 5 per cent that can be attributed to differences in strategy. Other studies have repeatedly found that as many as 75 per cent of mergers and acquisitions fail primarily because of cultural clashes.

The idea that organisational culture or personality exists, and profoundly affects performance, raises no eyebrows these days. But can you go one step further and improve performance by analysing corporate personality in the same way as you might analyse that of an individual?

That is the question raised by Cognosis, a management consultancy that has adapted the Myers-Briggs Type Indicator (MBTI), a personality test widely used in the recruitment and personal development of individuals, and is now applying it to organisations. 'It seems bizarre that, given the critical importance of culture to corporate performance, its management isn't taken more seriously,' says Richard Brown, managing partner of Cognosis.

Methods of measuring personality and motivation

MBTI (Myers-Briggs Type Indicator) is a personality questionnaire used worldwide for individual, team and organisational development. Based on more than 50 years of research, the MBTI promotes understanding of an individual's personality, their motivation and their preferred behaviours and an appreciation of differences between people. It has many applications, including team-building and management and leadership development.

Using the averaged responses to a 15-minute paper containing 30 questions, given to as few as a dozen executives, Cognosis claims to be able to use MBTI to identify four organisational character types. The organisation is then profiled on a number of characteristics, such as its approach to problem solving, how it deals with change, innovation and internal communications and how it will react to stress. 'The resulting insights can be used to allow us to make fairly detailed recommendations about a range of development needs,' says Mr Brown.

What sort of person is your company?

The Cognosis method of analysing company personality sorts companies into four types:

- Rational – logical and ingenious, e.g. Diageo
- Sympathetic harmoniser, e.g. EasyJet
- Pragmatic – focused on the here and now, e.g. Nestlé
- Idealistic – enthusiastic and insightful, e.g. Interbrew

While no type is better than any other, some organisational character types are better suited to the markets in which they compete and each character type has its own particular development needs, he says.

So drinks company Allied Domecq is a pragmatic 'fixer' organisation, he says. Fixers are action-oriented, resourceful and realistic but tend to value action over strategy. As a consequence they reorganise constantly and achieve inconsistent results.

'The fixer organisation needs to stop and think. It needs to broaden its perspective, look further into the future and articulate its long-term goals. It needs to introduce some structure into its planning and some discipline into its performance management. It also needs to connect with and articulate its values,' says Mr Brown.

Cognosis' approach has met a mixed reception among organisational psychologists and academics. The idea of a simple way of identifying profound truths about a company sounds attractive. But it also raises suspicions that Cognosis may be selling 'snake oil'.

That is certainly the concern of Angela Baron, an organisational psychologist who advises the Chartered Institute of Personnel and Development. 'I agree that corporations have individual cultures but I am not sure I would describe it as a personality. Myers-Briggs is a useful tool for dealing with individuals but it could be enormously dangerous to use it in a way it wasn't designed for,' she says.

Others are concerned that the Cognosis approach may be to glib. 'You can't just flash a questionnaire to understand a culture. You have to immerse yourself in it and get under the skin. This may be a useful way into complex organisational issues but I wonder whether these are the most appropriate dimensions to assess corporate culture. I suspect there are better tools available than this,' says Nigel Nicholson, professor of organisational behaviour at London Business School.

Nevertheless the Open University, which has been remodelling itself to deal with changes in the distance learning market, says its insights have been invaluable. 'We have been engaged in a major change programme. We used Cognosis' approach to culture mapping to look more deeply inside our organisation, identifying the behaviour and attitude changes needed to improve our customer focus and service. It provided new insights into the underlying character of our organisation, and its constituent parts, and identified specific areas for change,' says Professor Geoff Peters, pro-vice-chancellor for strategy and planning.

Sports and leisure conglomerate The Pentland Group is also sold on the idea. 'We plan to use it to understand our own culture in reference to the culture of any takeover target. Think of it as cultural due diligence,' says Tim Hockings, corporate development director.

Source: Alex Benady, *Financial Times*, 20 June 2003.

Questions

1 Why is such emphasis being placed on cultural aspects of organisational behaviour?

2 If companies could be categorised according to the MBTI test, what benefits might result and to whom?

3 Consider the arguments for and against this organisational approach.

Useful websites

Now try the self-check questions for this chapter on the website at www.booksites.net/wall. You will also find further resources as well as the following useful weblinks:

Many interesting articles on labour issues are included in:

www.peoplemanagement.co.uk
www.tomorrowscompany.com
www.croner.co.uk

For aspects of Asian culture check *www.apmforum.com*

Also *http://english.china.com*
www.japanecho.com
The Commission for Racial Equality is found at *www.cre.gov.uk*

Useful key texts

Daniels, J., Radebaugh, L. and Sullivan, D. (2004) *International Business* (10th edn), Pearson Prentice Hall, especially Chapter 2.

Dicken, P. (2003) *Global Shift: Transforming the World Economy* (4th edn), Paul Chapman Publishing Ltd, especially Chapter 5.

Hill, C. (2003) *International Business: Competing in the Global Marketplace* (4th edn), McGraw-Hill Irwin, especially Chapter 3.

Morrison, J. (2002) *The International Business Environment*, Palgrave, especially Chapter 5.

Rugman, A. and Hodgetts, R. (2003) *International Business* (3rd edn), FT Prentice Hall, especially Chapter 5.

Tayeb, M. (2000) *International Business: Theories, Policies and Practices*, Financial Times Prentice Hall, especially Chapters 4, 13 and 19.

Woods, M. (2001) *International Business*, Palgrave, especially Chapter 4.

Other texts and sources

Chu, G.C. and Ju, Y. (1993) *The Grand Wall in Ruins*, State University of New York Press.

D'Iribane, I., cited in Hofstede, G. (1996) 'Problems Remain but Theories will Change: the Universal and the Specific in 21st Century Global Management', *Organizational Dynamics*, vol. 1, pp. 34–43.

Elias, N. (1994) *The Civilizing Process*, Blackwell.

Fedor, K.J. and Werther, W.B. Jr (1996) 'The Fourth Dimension: Creating Culturally Responsive International Alliances', *Organizational Dynamics*, vol. 1.

Griffin, R.W. and Pustay, M.W. (1996) *International Business: A Managerial Perspective*, Addison-Wesley.

Griffiths, A. (2000) 'Cultural Determinants of Competitiveness: The Japanese Experience', in *Dimensions of International Competitiveness: Issues and Policies*, Lloyd-Reason, L. and Wall, S. (eds), Edward Elgar.

Hall, E.T. (1976) *Beyond Culture*, Anchor Press.

Hofstede, G. (1980) *Culture's Consequences*, Sage.

Hofstede, G. (1991) *Cultures and Organizations: Software of the Mind*, McGraw-Hill.

Hofstede, G., Neuijen, B. and Ohavy, D. (1990) 'Measuring Organisational Cultures: A Qualitative and Quantitative Case Study across Twenty Cases', *Administrative Science Quarterly*, 35.

Kidd, J. and Xue, Li (2000) 'The Modelling of Issues and Perspectives in MNEs', in *Dimensions of International Competitiveness*, Lloyd-Reason, L. and Wall, S. (eds), Edward Elgar.

Peters, T. and Waterman, R.H. (1982) *In Search of Excellence*, Harper & Row, New York.

Snow, C.C., Davison, S.C., Snell, S.A. and Hambrik, D.C. (1996) 'Use of Transnational Teams to Globalize your Company', *Organizational Dynamics*, vol. 24, no. 4, pp. 90–107.

Tayeb, M. (1994) 'Japanese Managers and British Culture: a Comparative Case Study', *International Journal of Human Resource Management*, 5.

Trompenaars, H. (1993) *Riding the Waves of Culture: Understanding Cultural Diversity in Business*, The Economist Books.

United Nations Conference on Trade and Development (UNCTAD) *World Investment Report* (annual publication).

United Nations Development Programme (UNDP) *Human Development Report* (annual publication), OUP.

Weber, M. (1930) *The Protestant Ethic and the Spirit of Capitalism*, Allen and Unwin.

World Bank, *World Development Report* (annual publication).

Yeung, I.Y.M. and Tung, K.L. (1996) 'Achieving Business Success in Confucian Societies: the Importance of Guanxi (Connections)', *Organizational Dynamics*, vol. 1.

International ethical and ecological environment

By the end of this chapter you should be able to:

■ explain why an awareness of ethical issues can be important for international business;

■ outline the different ethical positions that can be adopted;

■ discuss the different ethical approaches that multinationals have taken when trading abroad;

■ examine some of the national/international agreements and regulations that have been adopted in an attempt to instil an ethical awareness into business practices, with particular reference to MNE activity;

■ assess the importance of managing the ecological environment, for both individuals and companies.

Introduction

What is an organisation for? Why does it exist? How are decisions taken within it? People often assume that organisations exist in order to make a profit or to provide a service in the most cost-effective way. In the West businesses have developed under the capitalist ethic, which focuses on the creation of surplus value (profit) and its distribution to shareholders in the form of dividends. Over time, national governments have increasingly sought to remedy aspects of 'market failure' in such economies, by providing minimum levels of public services in education or health or by seeking to prevent private businesses from abusing their market power. As societies become ever more complex, businesses are beginning to exert still more influence over the ways in which the economy is run, so that even social institutions are becoming more intimately linked with economic patterns. In the UK, for example, the powerful lobby of the supermarkets has exerted considerable influence on transport policies, on the types of goods we consume, on trading relationships with domestic and international suppliers and on the ways in which we define our leisure hours. Thus business organisations are carrying more and more responsibility for the ways in which wealth is both created and distributed and the ways in which we organise ourselves. In these various ways the ethical responsibilities of business are arguably growing. But what do we mean by business ethics?

Ethical standards are generally regarded as those ways of acting or being that are deemed acceptable by some reference group at a particular time and place. These standards can be implicit to the group or explicit, as in the case of a 'code of practice'. The objective of making such standards explicit usually involves an attempt to avoid an excess of self-interest that might mitigate against the 'good of all'. Of course, the key question is, what is the good of all? One man's meat may be another man's poison! Further, even if a code of ethics were to be agreed by a reference group it must be flexible and capable of change, otherwise it can easily become institutionalised, dogmatic and ultimately self-defeating.

Business ethics

Too often, in the past, business ethics have been taken for an 'oxymoron' (a contradiction in terms). At the level of business the prevailing view has often seemed to be that as long as the business is profitable, then 'anything goes'. Somewhere along the line business and ethics have become separated out; no one in business talks about ethics and no one in the moral field of actions talks about business.

And yet, if we can define ethics or morality as the 'set of organising principles by which people live together', ethics must surely play a large part in organisational and business activities – based, as they are, on group dynamics and individual interactions. The reason that the process of applying ethical standards to business or management seems to be difficult may be because it might appear to contradict economic perspectives such as 'competition', which sets organisations (communities of beings) against one another.

This is, of course, a misperception: ethics are as much an integral part of business and commerce as they are of specialised functions, such as financing, accountancy, legal practices, etc. The fundamental issue here is that of choice – and in business choices are made each and every moment. Business decisions are choices in which the decision makers could have acted otherwise. Every decision or action affects people or relationships between people such that an alternative action or inaction would affect them differently. What criteria are these decisions based upon? Are they criteria of profit or of 'well-being'? It is far better for everyone concerned if managers are aware of the ethical significance of their actions and decisions and thus consciously, rather than inadvertently, lead and shape their corporate cultures.

A study by Collins and Porras (1994) cited a number of companies that survived major changes in management, new product development and the impacts of various business cycles. The companies that flourished over a long period were found to be companies that pursued a stable core mission, which provided the basis for all corporate activities and drove decision making through all the business changes encountered. According to Collins and Porras, the 'best' (longest lasting and most profitable) business organisations are those that do not focus on profitability as their primary mission. In their rankings, the highest performing corporations tended to be those that were governed by core beliefs, which transcended purely economic pursuits, seeking rather to produce the finest products in the marketplace, to win customer satisfaction, to serve employees, and so on. Such findings are contrary to much of the theory taught in our business schools.

The authors cited a number of international businesses that have thrived through the creation of ethical cultures. For example, Patagonia Inc. has created a strong corporate culture that values its employees and the social and natural environments in which it conducts business. Patagonia gives 1% of its annual sales revenue to environmental groups and grants employees up to two months off with full compensation to work for non-profit environmental groups. Independent human rights organisations have been invited to audit any of their facilities on request. In response to the 1996 public dialogue on 'sweatshops', Patagonia implemented a corporate policy not to contract with any supplier engaging in such practices.

The Body Shop has also adopted overtly 'ethical' aims, which are explained further in Case Study 7.1.

CASE 7.1 The Body Shop

The Body Shop is a publicly quoted manufacturer and retailer of health and beauty products. It began in 1976 with the opening of the first shop in Brighton and is now an international company rapidly expanding throughout the world. Today The Body Shop has over 1,200 shops, operates in 45 countries and trades in 23 languages with over 3,000 staff directly employed and a similar number of staff working in franchised retail outlets. Its founder is a charismatic woman with very firm ideas, particularly about the values involved in business trading. Unlike other companies in this area, they do not use direct marketing or pay for advertising and believe that what differentiates them is not so much the product but 'what they represent as a company' (Head of Corporate Services).

They are a known brand retailer who manufacture their own products, which means that, unlike other retailers, they do not work on short cycles. Traditional problems such as branding and design appear less important since the labels stay the same and the bottles in which the products are sold stay the same. They are the top sellers in their markets and new products are simply extensions of existing ones. Their competitors have had only a marginal impact on their market since their customer profile is that of 20–35-year-old females who have an interest in the environmental and social issues on behalf of which this organisation campaigns.

The Body Shop claims that its values are fundamentally very simple, and represent the initial values of the founders, namely that people, in relating to each other, should act with honesty, care, integrity and respect.

The mission statement of the company seeks to reflect these values.

Our reason for being:

- to dedicate our business to the pursuit of social and environmental change;
- to creatively balance the financial and human needs of our stakeholders, namely employees, customers, franchisees, suppliers and shareholders;
- to courageously ensure that our business is ecologically sustainable, meeting the needs of the present without compromising the future;
- to meaningfully contribute to local, national and international communities in which we trade, by adopting a code of conduct which ensures care, honesty, fairness and respect;
- to passionately campaign for the protection of the environment and human and civil rights and against animal testing within the cosmetics and toiletries industry;
- to tirelessly work to narrow the gap between principle and practice, while making fun, passion and care part of our daily lives.

However, as the general manager for company culture noted, though these basic values appear superficially quite straightforward, they are notoriously difficult to implement.

Question

1 Can you suggest any hypothetical (or actual) ethical problems which The Body Shop might face (or has faced) in implementing its core values?

Ethics and the corporate culture

In all organisations the same principles arguably apply. Organisations need certain 'ways of acting or being' (which can be either explicit or implicit) as a guide to 'acceptable' behaviour by members of the organisation. In the current business press two things stand out. One is the issue of global competitiveness and the other is a list of alleged wrongdoings by business leaders in virtually all countries. For Beyer and Nino (1999):

> It seems likely that the two are related, that the ethical and cultural fabrics of our business communities and whole societies are being weakened, virtually torn apart by the struggles inherent in unprecedented levels of economic competition. Clearly it is time for management scholars and academics everywhere to begin to address the ethical issues associated with the all-out economic war being waged throughout the world.

Beyer and Nino go on to tell a story which, in their view, has a number of parallels with modern international business practice (*see* Box 7.1).

Box 7.1	An ethical dilemma

McCoy was in the mountains of Nepal on his way to a village considered a holy place with an American anthropologist named Stephen, a Sherpa guide and a group of porters. To get to the village they had to climb across a mountain pass at 18,000 feet (about 5,500 metres). The night before the planned climb they camped at around 15,000 feet, near several other groups; four young men from New Zealand, two Swiss couples and a Japanese hiking club.

At 3.30 a.m. the next morning the New Zealanders got the first start up the mountain. The American party left next, followed by the Swiss, while the Japanese lingered in their camp. When the Americans reached about 15,500 feet, Stephen began to feel ill and they stopped to rest. Soon thereafter one of the New Zealanders appeared with a body slung over his back. It was a *sadhu* (old man) he had found on the mountain – almost naked and unconscious, clearly suffering from hypothermia, but still alive. The New Zealander suggested that the porters travelling with the Americans take the old man down the mountain and then went back to join his group. Stephen and the Swiss couples attended to the *sadhu*, stripping off his wet clothes, wrapping him in clothing from their packs and giving him food and drink when he revived.

Meanwhile the businessman McCoy was growing anxious about the delay because he feared that if he waited any longer to resume his climb, the sun would melt the steps carved in the snow that he needed to help him cross the mountain pass. Adding to his worry was the fact that previously he had suffered quite severe altitude sickness even at a lower altitude. Neither of these concerns led him to abandon his goal. He was still determined to cross the mountain pass and reach the sacred village. So he left to catch up with some of the porters who had gone ahead to prepare the way. His friend Stephen, who was still not feeling well, and the Swiss couples stayed behind with the *sadhu*.

An hour or so later, after climbing most of the way, McCoy himself became dizzy and stopped to rest, allowing the Swiss to catch up with him. He asked them about the *sadhu* and was told he was fine and that his friend Stephen was on the way. When Stephen finally arrived he was suffering from altitude sickness and could only walk 15 steps at a time before resting. He was also very angry and accosted McCoy saying, 'How do you feel about contributing to the death of a fellow man?' McCoy was stunned and asked if the *sadhu* had died. 'No', Stephen replied, 'But he will.' He then explained that the Swiss had departed not long after McCoy and that the Japanese, when asked, refused to lend a horse they had with them to carry the man down the mountain to the nearest village. The Japanese then went on their way taking the horse with them. When Stephen asked the Sherpa and the remaining porters if they would take the *sadhu* they also refused, saying they would not have the strength or time to get across the pass if they first carried him down the mountain. Instead, the porters took the old man a short distance down the mountain, where they laid him on a large rock in the sun, and left him there, awake, but weak. No one in the four groups of climbers ever found out whether the *sadhu* lived or died but all got over the pass and on to the holy village that was their goal.

Source: Beyer and Nino (1999). Copyright © 1999 by Sage Publications, Inc. Reprinted by permission of Sage Publications, Inc.

We can usefully use this account to derive a number of ethical implications, which have some parallels in international business. Beyer and Nino pick out the following parallels.

- First, no one assumed ultimate responsibility for the *sadhu*. By focusing on reaching a holy place, they ignored their ethical responsibilities. Trying to reach the mountain top can be compared with the unremitting competition of global business with its elements of social Darwinism, namely the idea of the survival of the fittest. This modern business 'ethic' would see it as natural that others get left behind. 'Doing unto others as you would have them do unto you' would be suicidal in business. Such attitudes encourage people to set for themselves self-interested (organisational goals) and to pursue them relentlessly with little concern for their effects on others. Some forms of winning in business (getting a new product to market, achieving assigned targets, taking over another firm) can overwhelm broader based ethical principles and impulses.
- Second, the groups involved had no prior experience or model for jointly arriving at a consensus about what to do. They came from four different cultures and lacked a commonality of mutually accepted values that would give them guidance as to what to do. Each group passed the problem on to the other group. There was no strong culture to glue their actions together. This 'buck-passing' between departments and multinational divisions is hardly uncommon.
- Third, there was a failure to act which then itself became the decision. This can often happen in business, especially when something has been going on for some time. The lack of guidance given to Nick Leeson, an inexperienced trader in Singapore in 1996, is arguably one such example.
- Fourth, the decision makers were physically and mentally stressed and under time pressures. It is precisely under these conditions in a hyper-competitive world that personal and corporate values are most severely tested.
- The final parallel is that even though one of the people saw through all of these considerations as regards his ethical responsibility, he did not get the support he needed from the others present to rescue the *sadhu*. It was beyond his individual capacity, a circumstance that often occurs in business. Many ethical decisions require the support of the corporate community. Ethically sensitive and courageous individuals cannot often perform ethically without the support of others.

The lesson here is that it is up to management to provide such support as part of the corporate culture. The ethical dilemma previously described was heightened by the fact that people of different cultures were attempting (or not attempting) to reach a decision. With increasing globalisation, such issues are becoming increasingly common as multinational teams attempt to work together.

pause for thought 1 Can you suggest how two MNEs from different national cultures, which are collaborating on a joint venture, may adopt different ethical positions on certain issues?

Different ethical positions

We have already noted that our actions as individuals are determined in part by the values we hold, which can be influenced by our surroundings and our experiences. But what happens in an organisation?

Corporate agency and responsibility

An organisation is neither an individual nor a total social system. It is comprised of individuals in various roles which may be authorised by the larger 'society' to function for specific, often narrowly defined, purposes. The actions of an organisation are often the result of collective, rather than individual decision making. We saw in Box 7.1 how the *sadhu* was left to die because no single group or person was prepared to take responsibility. This can be true within organisations, even more so when that organisation is trading internationally.

But who is acting in an organisation? Can we reduce the group action down to the level of each individual? Or do we treat an organisation as if the organisation itself was an individual directing the activity of its constituents? Ethically and academically many thinkers have sought to understand the nature of corporate responsibility.

The Nobel Prize economist Milton Friedman declared: 'There is only one social responsibility of business – to use its resources and engage in activities designed to increase its profits so long as it stays within the rules of the game, which is to say, engages in open and free competition without deception or fraud' (Friedman 1970: 126).

This does not mean that 'anything goes': law and common morality should guide action. However, there is an assumption here that profit maximisation is the main responsibility of business. This is based on the so-called 'rational actor' theory. In this view when an individual acts rationally, he/she is seeking to maximise his/her own long-term self-interest. In Friedman's view, that self-interest will be allied to making an overt contribution to enhancing corporate profitability.

However, the idea of such a 'unity of purpose' impacting on the values of those who act on behalf of an organisation has been challenged in various ways.

The principal–agent problem

In the case of a sole trader, the principal (owner) and the agent (manager) are one and the same. However, to assume that it is the owners who control the firm neglects the fact that today the dominant form of industrial organisation is the public limited company (plc), which is usually run by managers rather than by owners. This may lead to conflict between the owners (shareholders) and the managers whenever the managers pursue goals which differ from those of the owners. This conflict is referred to as a type of *principal–agent* problem and emerges when the shareholders (principals) contract a second party, the managers (agents), to perform some tasks on their behalf. In return, the principals offer their agents some compensation (wage payments). However, because the principals are divorced from the day-to-day running of the business, the agents may be able to act as they themselves see fit. This independence of action may be due to their superior knowledge of the company as well as their ability to disguise their actions from the principals. Agents, therefore, may not always act in the manner desired by the principals. Indeed, it may be the agents' goals which predominate. This has led to a number of managerial theories on the behaviour of business organisations, such as sales revenue maximisation and growth maximisation, which see the salary and status of managers being more closely related to turnover and company size rather than to its pure profit performance.

Social contract theory

Thomas Hobbes suggested that human beings tacitly agree to laws and regulations on their behaviour so that they can live in harmony and achieve their own ends in relation to others. Donaldson and Dunfee (1999) take this argument further in their 'Integrated Social Contract Theory', by suggesting that there are basic moral minimums (or 'hypernorms') that govern all social relationships on the macro level. These are subject to debate, can be explicit or tacit, but might include:

- not causing gratuitous harm;
- honouring contracts;
- respecting human rights;
- treating people and organisations fairly.

On a micro level, however, there may be a moral 'free space' dictated by the community in question. Here communities can spell out the specific norms deemed acceptable among themselves as long as these are compatible with the hypernorms. These 'consistent norms' tend to be tacit. Figure 7.1 shows a global model of the Integrated Social Contract Theory (ISCT).

Figure 7.1 **Global norms in the Integrated Social Contract Theory (ISCT)**

- *Hypernorms* – these moral minima include, for example, fundamental human rights or basic prescriptions common to most major religions. The values they represent are, by definition, acceptable to all cultures and organisations.
- *Consistent norms* – these values are more culturally specific than those at the centre, but are consistent both with hypernorms and other legitimate norms. The ethical codes and vision value statements of companies would fall within this circle.
- *Moral-free space* – as one moves away from the centre of the circle one finds norms that are inconsistent with at least some of the other legitimate norms existing in other cultures. Such norms often reflect strongly held cultural beliefs, whether at the national, corporate or occupational level (*see* Chapter 6).
- *Illegitimate norms* – these are norms that are incompatible with hypernorms. When values or practices reach a point where they transgress permissible limits (as specified, say, by fundamental human rights) they fall outside the circle and into the 'incompatible' zone. Exposing workers, for instance, to unreasonable levels of carcinogens (e.g. asbestos) is an expression of a value falling outside the circle.

The ISCT model has proved helpful for evaluating ethical behaviour in organisations, especially at the international level (*see* p. 210).

Stakeholder theory

There is an increasing focus by leading organisations on their obligation to *stakeholders*, i.e. the internal and external individuals and groups which relate to that organisation. Stakeholders can be defined as any individual or group which can affect or be affected by the achievement of the organisation's objectives. Such stakeholders might include employees, customers, suppliers, consumers, etc.

While the stakeholder perspective may simply appear to be a way of describing an organisation, in fact it also moves away from the moral assumptions that are made in the 'rational actor' theory. Stakeholder theory challenges the position that the primary purpose of a firm is to maximise the welfare of its stockholders (e.g. dividends), arguing instead that the goal of any firm should be to satisfy the aspirations of all its primary stakeholders. In addition to moral obligations to employees, there are additional responsibilities because of the unique and specifically defined relationships between a particular organisation and its stakeholders.

CASE 7.2 · Ethics and profits

The conventional wisdom has long been that the more ethical the stance of a company, the lower the returns to shareholders. Socially Responsible Investing (SRI) is an organisation in the UK which challenges this view and insists that its members take into account the environmental, ethical and social impacts of their investments. SRI companies point to their share portfolio outperforming the market average. It would seem that events are moving strongly in the direction of these companies.

▶

For example, since 3 July 2000 all pension funds in the UK must, by law, disclose whether or not they will take into account the environmental, ethical and social impacts of their investments.

Indeed, the 10 largest world banking groups (including Barclays and Royal Bank of Scotland in the UK, Citigroup in the US, West LB in Germany) agreed in 2003 to abide by the 'equator principles' when considering future investments. These principles are based on the policies of the International Finance Corporation (p. 120) which advises the banks on major development projects. Banks agreeing to these 'equator principles' will now grant loans only to projects whose promoters can demonstate their willingness and ability to conduct the projects in a 'socially responsible manner' and according to 'sound environmental management practices'. Environmental impact anlayses will be required of projects regarded as high and medium risk in this context, including the impact on involuntary resettlement of local people.

Campaign groups, such as Friends of the Earth, while welcoming such initiatives, are cautious as to what they will mean in practice. For example, the banks have refused to say whether they would have regarded the controversial Three Gorges Dam in China (now nearing completion) as having been in breach of the principle and therefore ineligible for the loans actually made.

The growing corporate acceptance of a need to be more socially responsible is reflected in the launch of a new FTSE 4 Good Index in July 2001 in the UK, using social and ethical criteria to rank corporate performance. All companies in three sectors were excluded, namely tobacco, weapons and nuclear power (representing 10 per cent of all FTSE companies). Of the remaining companies, three criteria were applied for ranking purposes: environment, human rights and social issues. If a company 'fails' in any one of these criteria, it is again excluded. Of the 757 companies in the FTSE All-Share Index, only 288 companies have actually made it into the index.

The FTSE itself has produced figures showing that if this new FTSE 4 Good Index had existed over the past five years, it would actively have outperformed the more conventional stock exchange indices. The same has been found to be true for the Dow Jones Sustainability Group Index in the USA. This is a similar ethical index introduced in the USA in 1999. When backdated to 1993 it was found to have outperformed the Dow Jones Global Index by 46 per cent.

Questions

1 Why is it suggested that the more ethically and environmentally conscious firms might actually be more profitable than those which pay little heed to the environment?

2 For what reasons might we expect UK companies to become more ethically and environmentally aware in the future?

International business ethics

So far we have seen that each organisation, and indeed individual within it, has a role to play in ensuring that decisions have a conscious ethical content. However, how do people deal with one another when the ethical content varies at a cultural level? The cultural differences explored in Chapter 6 have their counterparts in ethical differences. How can managers manoeuvre through the grey areas that exist within and between organisations and cultures. Take, for example, the following illustration. As a director of a joint venture in Hungary you become aware that many of the employees are working long hours on jobs outside the company to supplement their work for the joint venture. You deem this to be not only inefficient but also possibly unethical. When you confront senior managers in the joint venture they defend their workers vigorously. They argue that the wages are not high enough to support families and that there is a tradition of 'moonlighting' which has historically been considered to be ethical. Hungarians, having suffered over 500 years of living with 'oppressors' – the Turks, the Austro-Hungarians and the Russians – typically do not confine their loyalties to any single entity. Clearly, as a director, you have been presented with what is both an efficiency and an ethical dilemma.

Similar dilemmas were highlighted by the work of Turner and Trompenaars (1993) who asked thousands of managers around the world the following question:

> While you are talking and sharing a bottle of beer with a friend who is officially on duty as a safety inspector in the company you both work for, an accident occurs, injuring a shift worker. The National Safety Commission launches an investigation and you are asked for your evidence. There are other witnesses. What right has your friend to expect you to protect him?

The choices offered were these:

1 a definite right;
2 some right;
3 no right.

Fundamental to this question is the ethical tension between a 'right' and the implicit notion of the 'duties' of friendship. The results of the survey were very revealing. To cite only a few figures, approximately 94% of US managers and 91% of Austrian managers answered 3, 'no right', whereas only 53% of French and 59% of Singaporean managers considered there to be 'no right'.

Other studies show striking differences among ethical attitudes towards everyday business problems. One study (Macdonald 1988) revealed that Hong Kong managers considered taking credit for another's work as being at the top of a list of unethical activities; in contrast to their Western counterparts, they considered this to be more unethical than bribery or the gaining of competitor information. The same study showed that 82% of Hong Kong managers thought that additional government regulation would improve ethical conduct in business, whereas only 27% of US managers believed it would.

How then do organisations deal with such ethical and cultural variations? The first step, of course, is to understand that they exist. Many multinationals fail to even acknowledge the ethical implications of cultural differences.

Enderle (1995) has identified four broad types of approach which international business might take to ethical issues, each of which can be compared to a posture taken historically by nation states. These are: foreign country type, empire type, interconnection type and global type.

- *Foreign country type.* This does not apply its own ethical norms to the foreign country but conforms to the local customs, taking its direction from what prevails as morality in the host country. The Swiss are often identified with this approach to business.
- *Empire type.* This resembles the approach of Great Britain in India and elsewhere before 1947. This type of company applies domestic ethical concepts without making any serious modifications to local customs. Empire-type companies export their values in a wholesale fashion, and often do so regardless of the consequences to the host company or its stakeholders.
- *Interconnection type.* This regards the international sphere as differing from the domestic sphere. Companies here do not necessarily see themselves as protecting a national identity or ethical framework. The notion of national interest becomes blurred with that of the supranational (e.g. the EU).
- *Global type.* This abstracts from all national or regional differences, viewing the domestic sphere as entirely irrelevant; citizens of all nations need to become more cosmopolitan. Only global citizenry makes sense from this perspective.

In terms of Integrated Social Contract Theory (*see* p. 206) the danger with the 'foreign country' type is that there is nothing to limit the moral-free space of the host country culture. If government corruption and environmental pollution are accepted in the host country, then the 'foreign country' type of approach to ethical issues might be regarded as colluding with this unethical framework.

The 'empire' and 'global' types fall into the opposite trap. Each acts from a fixed idea of what is right or wrong, and so will suffocate the moral-free space of the host country. The 'empire' type sees itself as the bearer of moral truth. In the same way, though perhaps more subtly, the 'global' type seeks to impose moral truth – namely that since only global citizenry makes sense, the company can be impervious to ethical differences that mark a culture's distinctiveness. The opportunity for host cultures to define their own versions of moral and economic truth is lost.

The 'interconnection' type is consistent with the ISCT approach by acknowledging both universal moral limits at the macro level (hypernorms) and also ethical consideration at the micro level. While the notion of national interest is blurred, it does manage to balance moral principles with moral free space in a way that makes it somewhat more convincing than its three counterparts.

So what are the implications of these findings for the international manager? How can they negotiate the stormy sea of differing ethical values and behaviours? It may be instructive to attempt to use the ISCT global values (Figure 7.1) to consider the ethical problems involved with bribery or sensitive payments.

■ Bribery and corruption

Bribery is a major source of concern to many companies trading globally. Are such payments examples of legitimate norms or are such payments invariably a direct violation of hypernorms and other legitimate norms and hence located outside the circle and in the 'illegitimate' area? Not only does the incidence of bribery vary across nations, so too do perceptions as to its being unethical. Studies have shown Hong Kong and Greek managers to be less critical of bribery in certain scenarios than their American counterparts. An interesting question is whether bribery or 'sensitive' payments are more likely to be considered as an acceptable way of conducting international business (hence a legitimate norm) in countries where such practices are commonplace?

Donaldson and Dunfee (1999) do not think so, arguing that it is a myth to believe that bribery is accepted wherever it flourishes. In fact, there is a surprising amount of agreement to the contention that bribery is unethical. We can suggest at least three reasons for this ethical perspective on bribery using the ISCT approach.

1 Acceptance of a bribe usually violates a microsocial contract specifying the duties of the agent (the bribe recipient) to the principal (the employing body), whether the government or a private company.

2 Bribery is typically not a legitimate norm. All countries have laws against the practice. Some countries, even where the practice is flourishing, have draconian penalties. In China in 1994 the president of the Great Wall Machinery and Electronic High-Technology Industrial group, Mr Shen Haifu, was executed for bribery and embezzlement offences, despite the recorded prevalence of such practices in China. The OECD has increased its efforts to reduce bribery by launching, in March 1994, a campaign aimed at reducing the incidence of bribery in international trade transactions.

3 Bribery may violate the hypernorms of political participation and efficiency. When, in the 1970s, Japan bought planes from the American aircraft manufacturer, Lockheed, Prime Minister Tanaka was subsequently found to have accepted tens of millions of dollars in bribes. The Japanese press and other sources questioned whether he was discharging his duties correctly in the context of established norms of political participation; he resigned shortly after the bribery revelation was made public. Another hypernorm, that of efficiency, may also be brought into this arena. Bribery interferes with the market mechanisms role of using 'price' alone as a signal for efficient resource allocation (see Chapter 5). Interviews with Indian CEOs have borne this out as they explicitly recognised that inefficiencies grow as decisions are made on the basis of how much money people receive under the table rather than on the basis of price and quality.

Box 7.2 looks in more detail at some of these issues involving bribery and corruption.

| Box 7.2 | TI Corruption Perception Index |

Transparency International (TI) is a non-governmental organisation founded in 1993 and based in Berlin. It has developed one of the more comprehensive databases on corruption which it defines as an abuse of public office for private gain. The 'TI Corruption Perception Index' correlates a number of surveys, polls and country studies involving the number of bribe requests which those conducting business in some 102 separate countries perceive to have been made to them. A score of 10 indicates a perception that bribe requests are never made in that country, while a score of 0 indicates a perception that bribe requests are always made. A score of 5.0 indicates a perception that there is an equal chance of a bribe being made as not being made. Of the 102 countries included in the 2002 index, 69 scored 5.0 or below; in other words, businessmen perceive that in two-thirds of these countries it is more likely than not that a bribe request will be made in any given transaction. In 2002 Finland scored 10, UK 8.6, USA 7.8, China 3.9, India 2.7, Pakistan 2.2 and Indonesia 1.9.

Paying bribes carries with it the risk of damaging the company's reputation, both within the country in which the bribes are paid and at home. There is also the risk that the corporate culture of the company itself will become more tolerant of a range of other practices at the margins of legality. There is also evidence to suggest that those host nations with a reputation for bribery and corruption damage themselves. For example, a direct link between high levels of corruption and low levels of fdi has been found, while high levels of corruption resulted in low rates of economic growth.

Case Study 7.3 considers some recent moves to tighten legal restrictions on bribery and their impacts on international business.

CASE 7.3 Bribery and international business

As Mobil Corporation negotiated for a slice of Kazakhstan's prize oil field in 1996, executives probably did not worry too much about paying a $51 million 'success' fee to the government's adviser. The field – Tengiz – was thought to hold more than 6 billion barrels of oil, making it one of the biggest finds in decades. The deal itself was valued at more than $1 billion.

In 2003 that comparatively meagre fee is starting to look a lot more costly. James Giffen, the US consultant who received the money and represented the Kazakh government, has been arrested and charged in what could be the largest ever violation of the Foreign Corrupt Practices Act (FCPA), the US law banning bribery of foreign officials.

In total, authorities have accused him of taking more than $78 million in commissions and fees from Mobil and other western oil companies and then illegally funnelling them to senior Kazakh officials. More ominously for the company, today known as ExxonMobil, US prosecutors have also filed charges against J. Bryan Williams, the former executive who negotiated the deal.

At Mr Giffen's arraignment last month, prosecutors spelt out their intent, stating that ExxonMobil itself was now the subject of their investigation. If prosecutors charge ExxonMobil and it is found guilty of violating the FCPA, the company could be fined tens of millions of dollars. Individual executives could be sentenced to up to five years in prison. In theory, the US government could also bar ExxonMobil from public contracts, withdraw export privileges and suspend investment protection abroad. Just as damaging, such sanctions would almost certainly encourage Kazakh officials to re-examine the terms of the Tengiz deal.

The legal noose is tightening around companies suspected of bribery. Under new legislation in the UK and around the world, companies could face stiff penalties if they do not look carefully at what their executives are doing to win business abroad. Thirty-five nations have now adopted the anti-bribery convention drawn up by the Organisation for Economic Co-operation and Development, under which they undertake to make foreign bribery illegal in their countries. After much foot-dragging, Britain complied with the convention by inserting some last-minute wording into the Anti-Terrorism, Crime and Security Act rushed through parliament in the aftermath of the September 11 attacks. A new UK Corruption Bill, expected to become law in 2004, will formalise the UK law's international grasp.

To complement the OECD convention, other international institutions – including the Organisation of American States, the European Union, the Council of Europe and the United Nations – have passed or are negotiating rules against bribery in business transactions. The change in attitudes toward bribery of foreign officials has come about largely as a result of US diplomatic pressure. Since the FCPA was passed in the aftermath of the Watergate scandal, US companies have complained that it places them at a disadvantage against companies from other countries that pay bribes to win contracts. The US Commerce Department estimates that between May 1994 and April 2002, the outcome of 474 contracts worth $237 billion may have been affected by bribery. It claims US companies lost 110 of these contracts worth $36 billion.

Despite the US protestations, some claim that the rules simply force US companies to bribe more dexterously. A survey last year by Transparency International, the anti-corruption campaign, found that senior international business executives ranked US companies ahead of rivals from France and Germany in their propensity to bribe. Fifty-eight per cent of respondents also said that US companies gained an unfair advantage by enlisting diplomatic or financial pressure, including the tying of foreign aid to a successful result.

The World Bank has identified corruption as 'the single greatest obstacle to economic and social development', hitting the poor and least-politically connected the hardest. Other international financial institutions such as the International Monetary Fund have blamed corruption for economic crises from Asia to Argentina.

Bribes can add substantially to the cost of public works programmes in developing countries. Businesspeople often speak of 10 per cent as a standard 'commission', but a survey by Control Risks, the consultancy, found that more than a third of business managers thought it was higher. Bribes also result in major projects being awarded to contractors that are unable or unwilling to do the job properly, at even greater cost to the public purse. Across the developing world, crumbling motorways, malfunctioning power stations and other sub-standard infrastructure projects stand as testaments to the damage wrought by such corrupt bidding processes. Such white elephants are paid for with public debt – one of the contributing factors to the collapse of many economies in recent years.

▶

Despite this evidence, there has been far less focus on the international companies that fuel corruption by paying officials to win business. The talk has been of bribe-takers rather than bribe-payers. In part, that is because catching companies in the act of bribing is extremely difficult – both sides in the transaction have a powerful incentive to cover it up. And even if a suspect payment can be identified, it is often difficult to prove that there had been a quid pro quo.

Mr Giffen's case could send the clearest signal yet to companies about the importance of vetting consultants and other intermediaries that help broker deals in foreign countries. ExxonMobil has denied knowledge that any improper payments were made. There are, however, at least two features of Mr Giffen's contract with Mobil that raise questions about the purpose of the transaction. For one, the company agreed to pay Mr Giffen's $51 million success fee on top of the agreed purchase price even though he was nominally representing the government in the transaction. Secondly, the criminal indictment against Mr Giffen claims that Mobil paid him £10 million of the fee months before the Tengiz deal was even completed. 'It is only a matter of time before there is a similar case in Europe,' says Brian Stapleton, managing director for Kroll in northern Europe. 'Companies need to take action to ensure it isn't them.'

Source: Thomas Catan and Joshua Chaffin, *Financial Times*, 8 May 2003.

Questions

1 What are the reasons for taking a firm line against bribery and similar practices?

2 Why do businesses sometimes criticise their governments for acting against such practices?

3 Why do some regard this particular case against Mr Giffen as being of particular importance?

The next section looks at some of the national and international measures adopted in an attempt to combat bribery, corruption and other unethical practices.

International efforts to improve business ethics

Clearly the global economy is presenting new ethical challenges as traditional ways in which societies have controlled corporate behaviour are breaking down. While we have seen that being ethical may, in the long-run, produce good business results, managers may not necessarily be motivated by what happens in the long run!

pause for thought 2   Consider some of the problems involved in devising international codes of ethical conduct.

■ International agreements

A number of international bodies have sought to address ethical issues in international business activities.

United Nations Code of Conduct for Transnational Corporations (1983)

This has its origins in earlier UN recommendations and codes of behaviour:

- 1948 Havana Declaration of the UN, calling for host countries to provide security for foreign investments;
- 1952 UN Resolution that nations have permanent sovereignty over their natural resources;
- 1971 Developing Countries Statement of UN members, whereby 77 developing countries stated that fdi in poorer nations should seek to generate inflows and to avoid outflows of foreign exchange, stimulate aggregate investment and result in 'appropriate technology' being adopted;
- 1974 Commission on Transnational Corporations. These recommendations and codes eventually culminated in the 1983 UN Code of Conduct for MNEs, whereby MNEs should seek to:
  - respect the national sovereignty of host countries, and observe their domestic laws, regulations and administrative practices;
  - respect human rights;
  - adhere to the objectives of host nations as regards economic and development goals and sociocultural values;
  - avoid interfering in internal politics or inter-governmental relations;
  - avoid engaging in corrupt practices;
  - disclose relevant information to host country governments.

Organisation for Economic Co-operation and Development Guidelines for MNEs (1976)

The 1976 declaration embodies some of the elements outlined above, while recognising the importance of MNEs in the international economy and as a source of investment. It also declared that 'every state has the right to prescribe the conditions under which multinational enterprises operate within its national jurisdiction, subject to international law and the international agreements to which it has subscribed'.

International Labour Office Tripartite Declaration of Principles Concerning MNEs and Social Policy (1977)

This code was drafted on a tripartite basis involving governments, employers' organisations and trade unions. MNE managers are requested to provide worker representatives in individual countries with all the information needed to pursue meaningful negotiations. Governments are requested to actively promote 'full employment'.

The ILO's international labour code also seeks to standardise conditions of employment and sets out minimum rights and standards in various Conventions. For example, Conventions 87 (freedom of association), 98 (right to organise and collective bargaining), 5 and 138 (minimum age for employment of children), 29 and 105 (prohibition of forced labour), 111 (prohibition of discrimination in employment on the basis of race, sex, religion, political affiliation), etc.

UNCTAD Code on Restrictive Business Practices (1980)

The main aim is to prevent and eliminate restrictive business agreements and practices, with the focus on action at the regional and international levels as well as national. Some of the international aspects of the code involve the responsibilities and rights of both host country government and the MNEs. For example, MNEs should conform to the laws on restrictive practices in the host country as well as avoiding engaging in specified activities listed in the code (e.g. those involving cartels, restrictive pricing practices, etc.).

At least four shortcomings of such agreements have been identified:

■ they are largely agreements between national governments and not between corporations or business leaders;
■ they rely on the voluntary compliance of the signatories;
■ the values represented by these codes may not fit with those of all countries;
■ the agreements are often so broad as to be operationally impractical.

The Multilateral Agreement on Investment (MAI)

The MAI might also be mentioned at this point. This was an attempt to make certain investment rules and associated practices legally binding, some of which had clearly ethical and social implications. The negotiations began in 1995 but were abandoned in 1998. Although these negotiations may be revived under the auspices of the OECD, what has happened in practice has been a wide range of bilateral investment treaties (BITs) between individual countries setting out the rules governing fdi between themselves. A revived MAI would be an attempt to move back to a *multilateral* approach to fdi.

■ Industry-specific agreements

A number of industries have sought to develop codes of conduct for international business practice in specific industries.

■ *International Code of Marketing of Breast-Milk Substitutes (1981)*. This sought to prevent misleading information as to the merits of their product being explicitly or implicitly given by manufacturers of breast-milk substitutes.
■ *Code of Marketing Practices of the International Federation of Pharmaceutical Manufacturers Associations (1984)*. This seeks to ensure accurate rather than misleading marketing of a broad range of pharmaceutical products.
■ *Rugmark Initiative*. This establishes a code of labour practices for producing rugs. This is an attempt to improve labour conditions in this industry, especially to restrict the use of child labour. Manufacturers who comply with this scheme's criteria can use the rugmark label for their products.
■ *World Federation of Sporting Goods Industry*. This also has sought to develop a code of practice with regards to the manufacture of sportswear and equipment.

pause for thought 3 Can you identify and list any other industry-based agreements involving codes of conduct?

As well as these and other industry-specific codes of practice, various individual companies have sought to adopt more ethical practices.

Company-specific agreements

A number of individual companies have drawn up codes of conduct that are meant to apply throughout their organisation. Levi Strauss and Co. has been one of the pioneers in setting out the labour practices that contracting firms are expected to follow, with contracts risking being terminated for breaches of these standards. Reebok and Nike have responded in this way after adverse publicity on labour market practices by suppliers. Mattel Inc., one of the world's largest toy manufacturers, announced its 'Global Manufacturing Principles' in 1997 to establish minimum labour standards in its own plants and those of its major subcontractors. It has even established a Monitoring Council to audit each plant in order to check compliance.

pause for thought 4	Can you identify and list any other company-based agreements involving codes of conduct?

The role of social activists

Social activists have formed various organisations to campaign against particular practices of multinationals.

- *Infant Feeding Action Coalition (INFACT).* This has sought to boycott the Nestlé Corporation as a result of its practice of selling baby formula containing little objective nourishment to underdeveloped countries. After 15 years of lobbying, Nestlé signed an agreement to stop these practices and an independent audit commission was created to monitor its compliance.
- *Coalition for Environmentally Responsible Economies (CERES).* This seeks to engage with investors to promote corporate activities for a 'safe and sustainable future for our planet'. Organisations such as Greenpeace are affiliated to CERES and pays particular attention to the fishing industry.
- *Sullivan Principles.* These principles were devised by the Revd Leon Sullivan, a Philadelphia minister, a black civil-rights activist and board member of General Motors. In 1977 he devised a set of principles that requested companies to improve workplace and social conditions for blacks in South Africa during the apartheid era. At its peak, over 180 companies were signed up to these principles before the programme ceased in 1994.

Bribery and corruption

Following our earlier discussion (*see* pp. 211–14) it may be useful to consider in more detail some of the national/international attempts to reduce this problem. Two important international conventions have required member countries to criminalise transnational bribery:

- *Organization of American States Inter-American Convention against corruption (1994)*;
- *OECD Convention on Combating Bribery of Foreign Public Officials (1999)*. By mid-2000 some 20 countries had already adopted such laws with another 14 close to enacting them. Countries with laws that outlaw the payment of bribes to foreign officials include Austria, Belgium, Canada, Germany, Japan, Korea, the UK and the USA. In fact, the USA was the first country to pass laws to this effect:
- *US Foreign Corrupt Practices Act 1977*. This made certain payments to foreign officials illegal even when these officials are located abroad, with penalties including prison, fines and disqualification from doing business with the US government.

Although attempts to reduce corruption and bribery in these ways have been broadly welcomed, some criticisms still remain. For example while business ventures may be prosecuted for bribing foreign officials, a wide variety of government inducements are still permissible, some of which are arguably akin to bribes. For example, governments may give substantial sums in aid on the understanding that the recipient country will grant economic and political concessions to the donor country and its companies in return.

Ecological/environmental issues

Ecological and environmental issues are of obvious concern to individuals, governments and the global community, as they are to international business.

National and global issues

The environment has become an increasingly important focus of national and international policy makers as global warming, the erosion of the ozone layer and other environmental threats are increasingly linked to worldwide growth in the emissions of harmful substances (e.g. CO_2, chlorofluorocarbons, etc.).

Role of the environment

At a more conceptual level, there is an increasing acceptance of the key role of the environment in business/economic activity in at least three respects:

1 *Amenity Services*: the natural environment provides consumer services to domestic households in the form of living and recreational space, natural beauty, and so on;
2 *Natural Resources*: the natural environment is also the source of various inputs into the production process such as mineral deposits, forests, water resources, animal populations, and so on;
3 *Waste Products*: both production and consumption are activities that generate waste products or residuals. For example, many productive activities generate harmful by-products, which are discharged into the atmosphere or watercourses. Similarly, sewage, litter and other waste products result from many consumption activities. The key point here is that the natural environment is the ultimate dumping place or 'sink' for all these waste products or residuals.

Sustainable development

It is when the environment is regarded as being unable to efficiently fulfil all three functions as the economy grows over a period of time that we use the term 'unsustainable development'. In this view, the earth is a closed system in which a finite set of resources is available for current and future growth. In other words, the capacity of the economy to produce still more products is constrained or limited by the availability of natural resources. Even if resources are sufficient to permit economic growth, the extra production will simply 'draw through' more materials and energy in products, which the environment must ultimately assimilate, since matter and energy cannot be destroyed (Newton's first law of thermodynamics).

Wherever possible, materials must therefore be recycled, renewable energy sources must be used in preference to non-renewable sources, and waste emissions must be limited to the extent that the earth can safely absorb these 'residuals'. This approach has led many economists to propose limiting our demand for goods and services in order to attain a level of economic growth that can be 'sustained' over future generations.

■ Business issues

In this section our main concern will be with the impact of these environmental issues and concerns at the level of national and international business. In today's global economy a number of driving forces are arguably raising environmental concerns to the forefront of corporate policy debate.

- *Environmentally conscious consumers.* Consumer awareness of environmental issues is creating a market for 'green products'. Patagonia, a California-based producer of recreational clothing, has developed a loyal base of high-income customers partly because its brand identity includes a commitment to conservation. As already noted (see Case Study 7.1) a similar successful approach has been used by The Body Shop. However, even when core activities and products have few direct environmental effects, consumer demand may be significantly influenced by the environmental implications of backward or forward linkages. For instance, Shell petrol sales were adversely affected in 1996 when Greenpeace alleged that the proposed disposal of the Brent Spar oil platform (backward linkages) at sea posed a serious threat to the marine environment. Similarly, Asea Brown Boveri, a Swiss-based multinational received extremely adverse publicity around the same time from environmental groups protesting at its alleged destruction of the Malaysian rainforest. Concern for their 'environmental footprint' is now widespread among MNEs engaged in international business.

  Reinhardt (1999) suggests that three key conditions are required for success with 'environmental product differentiation', i.e. segmenting the market so that consumers will pay higher prices for overtly 'environmentally-friendly' products:

  1 the company must have identified a distinctive market segment consisting of consumers who really are willing to pay more for environmentally-friendly products;
  2 the branding/corporate image must clearly and credibly convey the environmental benefits related to the products;
  3 the company must be able to protect itself from imitations for long enough to profit from its 'investment' in the previous two conditions.

- *Environmentally- and cost-conscious producers.* Producers are increasingly aware that adherence to high environmental standards need not be at the expense of their cost base. In other words, they can be environmentally friendly at the same time as reducing (rather than raising) their cost base. For example, between 1975 and 1996 the multinational, 3M, reduced its waste released to the environment by 1.4 billion pounds in weight and at the same time saved over $750 million in costs. Similarly, between 1992 and 1998 the multinational, S.C. Johnson, reduced its waste output by 420 million pounds in weight while saving over $125 million.

  Rank Xerox even adopted an 'Environmental Leadership Programme' in 1990 in an attempt both to regain market share lost in the 1980s and to restore profit margins. This programme included waste reduction efforts, product 'return' schemes (when existing products are overtaken by technologically superior alternatives) and design-for-environment initiatives. Substantial cost savings were reported (several hundred million dollars between 1990–95) together with revenue increases, and by the mid-1990s Xerox executives were hailing the programme as a major success. Case Study 7.4 also considers some of the benefits of environmental association, as does Case Study 9.1 (p. 280).

- *Environmentally- and risk-conscious producers.* Multinational enterprises are increasingly aware that failure to manage environmental risk factors effectively can lead to adverse publicity, lost revenue and profit and perhaps even more seriously a reduction in their official credit rating, making it more difficult and costly (e.g. higher interest rates) to finance future investment plants.

- *Environmentally-conscious governments.* Businesses have a further reason for considering the environmental impacts of their activities, namely the scrutiny of host governments. Where production of a product causes environmental damage, it is likely that this will result in the imposition of taxes or regulations by government. The reasons for this are considered further in Box 7.3.

Environmental codes and regulations

A number of the national/international codes and regulations involving ethical issues already considered (*see* pp. 215–17), have elements dealing with the environment. There are, in addition, some important environment-specific codes and regulations, which are important to international business.

- *ISO 14001.* The International Organization for Standardization has developed ISO 14001 as a means of certifying companies that adopt certain minimum standards of environmental management.
- *Regional Agreements.* Bilateral investment agreements between nations (e.g. Bolivia – USA bilateral investment treaty) often contain minimum environmental standards as do broader based 'regional' treaties such as NAFTA (North American Free Trade Agreement).
- *Multilateral Agreements.* The OECD countries moved towards accepting wide-ranging minimum environmental standards in the MAI draft treaty (*see* p. 216), yet to be ratified. Various *protocols* have been agreed (e.g. Montreal, Kyoto) as to reductions in greenhouse gas emissions, etc.

Box 7.3	Environmental impacts, taxes and regulations

If the production process results in environmental damage that the producer does not (at least initially) have to pay for, then marginal social cost (MSC) will be greater than marginal private cost (MPC). This is the case in Figure 7.2. The private cost to the firm of producing one more unit of output (MPC) is rising, due to extra labour, raw material or capital costs. However, the cost to society of producing that extra unit of output (MSC) is rising by more than the cost to the firm (MSC > MPC). This is because of the environmental damage (e.g. emission of CO_2) caused by producing the last unit, which is a cost to society (e.g. ill health), even if not to the firm. The true cost to society of producing the last unit of output does include the cost to the firm (MPC) of using factor input (since these scarce factors are thereby denied to other firms). However, the true cost to society also includes any environmental damage caused by producing the last unit of output. We call any such damage the marginal external cost (MEC). We can therefore state that:

Marginal Social Cost = Marginal Private Cost + Marginal External Cost
MSC = MPC + MEC

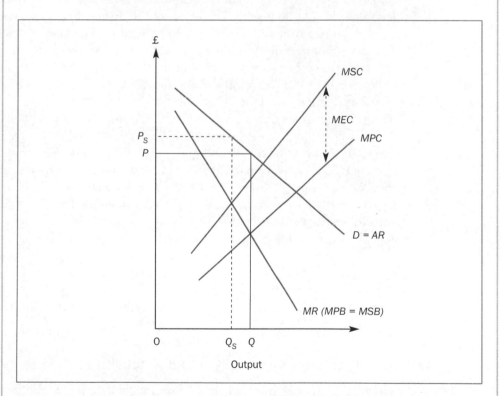

Figure 7.2 Impact of environmental damage (MSC > MPC) on price and output

In Figure 7.2 a profit-maximising firm will equate MPC with MR, producing output $0Q$ and selling this at price $0P$. However, the government may realise that from society's point of view the appropriate output is that which equates MSC with MR (here we assume MR to represent both marginal private benefit and marginal social benefit), producing output $0Q_S$ and selling this at price $0P_S$.

> **Box 7.3   Continued**
>
> To achieve this 'social optimum' solution, the government may try to tax the product (e.g. by raising MPC to MSC). This would be an attempt to 'internalise the externality' by making the producer pay for any damage the producer causes. If MPC is now raised by the tax so that it is equal to MSC, then the profit-maximising firm would itself choose to produce output $0Q_S$ and sell it at price $0P_S$ (at this output and price, MPC = MSC = MR and profits are a maximum). Alternatively, the government might seek to regulate the firm by preventing it producing more than output $0Q_S$. Whatever policy instruments are chosen, business must be aware that production activities that damage the environment are likely to result in adverse impacts on themselves from host governments.

Use of private standards

This approach has been particularly successful in the US chemical industry. In 1984, toxic gas escaped from the plant of a Union Carbide subsidiary in Bhopal, India, and killed more than 2,000 people. The image of the chemical industry was damaged and it faced the threat of punitive government regulation. The industry recognised that it had to act – to forestall government regulations and improve its safety record. As a result, the leading companies in the Chemical Manufacturers Association (CMA) in the USA created an initiative called 'Responsible Care' and developed a set of private regulations that the association's members adopted in 1988.

The US companies that make up the CMA must comply with six management codes that cover such areas as pollution prevention, process safety, and emergency response. If they cannot show good faith efforts to comply, their membership will be terminated. The initiative has enhanced the association's environmental reputation by producing results. Between 1988 and 1994, for example, US chemical companies reduced their environmental releases of toxic materials by almost 50%. Although other industries were also achieving significant reductions during this period, the chemical industry's reductions were steeper than the national average.

The big companies that organised 'Responsible Care' have improved their competitive positions. They spend a lower percentage of their revenues to improve their safety record than smaller competitors in the CMA; similarly, they spend a lower percentage of revenues on the monitoring, reporting, and administrative costs of the regulations.

■ Supporting 'environmentally-friendly' activities

We have already seen how negative environmental activities can be taxed or regulated in Box 7.3. Here we look at how positive environmental activities can be nurtured and supported. Case Study 7.4 looks at some of these issues in the context of organic food.

CASE 7.4 Growing pains

When Iceland announced in 2000 it was 'going organic', at no extra cost to the customer, the UK retailer proclaimed an embryonic movement was coming of age. 'It is time the food industry woke up to the future', declared Malcolm Walker, Iceland's chairman. 'We do not see why organic food should remain a niche product.'

You might have expected the organic industry to have given unqualified support; instead it wavered. The Organic Farmers and Growers group expressed concern. The National Farmers' Union was worried. The Soil Association, it emerged, had already written to the frozen-food chain listing its reservations. 'Exciting, but flawed', was the view of one of the association's directors. 'We have mixed feelings about this.' This is because Iceland's scheme has revealed the British organic industry's predicament. Even as its advocates urge politicians, retailers and the public to embrace sustainable agriculture, they fear heavy-handed attempts to transform organic food from middle-class speciality to mass-market phenomenon could strangle the sector in its infancy.

Few doubted Iceland's good intentions. Mr Walker, the man credited with coining the phrase 'Frankenstein foods' to describe genetically modified ingredients, had made no secret of his dislike of intensive farming methods and what he called 'industrialised agriculture'. Nor, recent studies show, is the organic food sector's potential for expansion in any doubt. While surveys show nearly 80% of consumers, traumatised by a series of food-contamination scandals, would buy organic produce if it cost the same as conventional food, British production falls well short of meeting that demand.

Support from the previous government was paltry – it raised the subsidy to organic farmers to only £571,000 by its last year in office. Although the present administration is promising £140m over the next seven years, Britain remains one of only three EU countries not to offer organic farmers long-term 'stewardship grants' after they have converted to organic methods. Britain lies in only 10th place in terms of land given over to organic production, with less than 2%, compared with Liechtenstein's 17%, Austria's 8.4% and Switzerland's 7.8%. As a result, Britain imported about 75% of the £550m of organic food it consumed last year, much of that – humiliatingly – was root crops, cereals and dairy produce, all ideally suited to the British climate and soil.

With the annual 40% growth rate in British sales of organic foods likely to continue, and every supermarket now offering a range of products, local farmers have, belatedly, been queuing up to fill that vacuum. The government's entire budget for organic subsidies in 1999 and 2000 was allocated in just six months. Extra funds were quickly exhausted, leaving applicants to twiddle their thumbs until the following year. And therein lies the rub. Many of the farmers 'going organic' are not acting out of ideological conviction. Instead, they view organic farming, with its 25–30% premiums and booming demand, as a way of weathering the most serious crisis to hit the agriculture sector since the 1930s.

Becoming organic demands that farmers undertake a laborious two-year 'conversion', which requires switching to natural herbicides and fertilisers, rotating crops and building up populations of natural predators. Additional costs vary according to the kind of food they produce. A chicken farmer who once operated from a hangar will have to rent land to win organic certification; a mixed-livestock farmer may only have to lower herd density and change his feed.

▶

But such costs are real. Indeed, they go to the heart of the organic philosophy. While the intensive farming methods introduced in the 1920s boosted yields and led to cheap food, organic enthusiasts have always argued that this came at a vast hidden cost, in the form of environmental degradation, epidemics such as BSE and medical bills. Those who bought organic produce accepted higher prices, because they were paying for sustainable agricultural techniques and healthier food. 'The pricing mechanisms of any retailer have to reflect the cost of production and there are extra costs involved in organic', says Simon Brenman, of the Soil Association. 'People have to realise you don't get something for nothing.'

In promising customers organically produced food at the prices of intensively produced food, Iceland was challenging the logic of that contract. The company undertook not to pass the price cut on to its suppliers, a gesture it said would cost £8m a year. But there was no guarantee rival retailers, now under pressure to match Iceland's offer, would show a similar readiness to burden their shareholders. This raised the prospect of a price-cutting war on organic produce. And from bitter experience, already pressed British farmers feared they would end up the losers.

In the wake of Iceland's announcement, warning signals were quickly sounded, with rival supermarket Asda promising to cut the prices of organic meat by an average of 8% and the Co-op pledging to slash prices on 100 organic lines. Most supermarkets promised not to make their savings at the growers' expense. However, with the leading retailers engaged in a turf war and conventional farmers already operating at a loss in several sectors, many wondered how long such grower-friendly policies could last. The risk was that farmers taking their first, faltering steps into the organic world would think again. If they saw prices coming under pressure they would tend to stick with intensive agriculture. 'A lot of farmers are going into this sector through duress', says Bill MacFarlane-Smith, of the Scottish Crop Research Institute. 'If that premium disappears, I'd question if they would choose to go down that road. You risk seeing a cycle of boom and bust.'

The pity is that in the long-term, organic producers argue, organic farming could supply the mass-market relatively cheaply. Yields will gradually increase as crop rotation kicks in and soil fertility rises. The gradual transformation of what is, in effect, a cottage industry into a serious commercial concern will allow economies of scale. Steady government support, including aid that recognises the rural 'stewardship' provided by organic farmers would narrow the differences with conventional farming. Only when a certain critical mass has been attained – and many organic advocates believe it must wait until 30% of British land and 20% of British food is organic – can farm prices be expected to fall of their own accord. Until that point, their message will be: please buy organic, but be prepared to pay for it.

Source: Michela Wrong, *Financial Times*, 27 June 2000. Reprinted with permission.

Questions

1 Consider the reasons why the frozen-food retailer, Iceland, was seeking to support organic food.

2 What methods did Iceland use to support this strategy and what impacts have they had on Iceland itself?

3 Why are organic farmers fearful of Iceland's approach?

4 How might the government better support the growth of organic food consumption?

Useful websites

Now try the self-check questions for this chapter on the website at www.booksites.net/wall. You will also find further resources as well as the following useful weblinks:

Pressure group websites include:
www.foe.co.uk
www.greenpeace.org.uk
www.panda.org
The National Environmental Trust is at *www.environet.policy.net/*
The issue of sustainability can be considered at: *www.sustainability.co.uk*
Visit The Body Shop website for material on human rights and environmental issues: *www.bodyshop.co.uk*
The Business Owners Toolkit has a section on pricing and elasticity: *www.toolkit.cch.com*
KPMG has a section devoted to business ethics: *www.kpmg.com/ethics*
Also for cultural specific resources check *www.itp.berkeley.edu/-thorne/HumanResources.html*

Useful key texts

Daniels, J., Radebaugh, L. and Sullivan, D. (2004), *International Business* (10th edn), Pearson Prentice Hall, especially Chapters 3–7.
Dicken, P. (2003) *Global Shift: Transforming the World Economy* (4th edn), Paul Chapman Publishing Ltd, especially Chapter 8.
Hill, C. (2003) *International Business: Competing in the Global Marketplace* (4th edn), McGraw-Hill Irwin, especially Chapters 1 and 2.
Morrison, J. (2002) *The International Business Environment*, Palgrave, especially Chapter 12.
Rugman, A. and Hodgetts, R. (2003) *International Business* (3rd edn), FT Prentice Hall, especially Chapter 5.
Tayeb, M. (2000) *International Business: Theories, Policies and Practices*, Financial Times Prentice Hall, especially Chapters 4 and 19.

Other texts and sources

Beyer, J. and Nino, D. (1999) 'Ethics and Cultures in International Business', *Journal of Management Inquiry*, vol. 8, no. 3.
Collins, J.C. and Porras, J.L. (1994) *Built to Last*, Harper Business.
Donaldson, T. and Dunfee, T.W. (1999) 'When Ethics Travel: The Promise and Peril of Global Business Ethics', *California Management Review*, vol. 41, no. 4.
Enderle, G. (1995) 'What is International? A Topology of International Spheres and its Relevance for Business Ethics', Paper presented at the Annual meeting of the International Association of Business and Society, Vienna, Austria.
Friedman, M. (1970) 'The Social Responsibility of Business', *New York Times Magazine*, 13 September.
Healey, N. (2004) 'The Multinational Corporation', in *Applied Economics* (10th edn), Griffiths, A. and Wall, S. (eds), Financial Times Prentice Hall.
Hornby, W., Gammie, B. and Wall, S. (2001) *Business Economics* (2nd edn), Longman, especially Chapters 10–11.
Macdonald, G.M. (1988) 'Ethical Perceptions of Hong Kong Chinese Business Managers', *Journal of Business Ethics*, 7.

Reinhardt, F.L. (1999) *Down to Earth: Applying Business Principles to Environmental Management*, Harvard Business School Press, Boston, MA.

Stone, M. (2000) 'Scourges that Strike at the Heart of Global Business', *Financial Times*, 30 May.

Turner, C.H. and Trompenaars, A. (1993) *The Seven Cultures of Capitalism*, Doubleday.

United Nations Conference on Trade and Development (UNCTAD), *World Investment Report* (annual publication).

United Nations Development Programme (UNDP), *Human Development Report* (annual publication), OUP.

Wall, S. (2004) 'Economics of the Environment', in *Applied Economics* (10th edn), Griffiths, A. and Wall, S. (eds), Financial Times Prentice Hall.

World Bank, *World Development Report* (annual publication).

Chapter 8

International strategic issues

By the end of this chapter you should be able to:

- examine the meaning and relevance of business strategy in today's corporate and national environment;

- discuss those strategic issues of particular relevance in a globalised economy;

- consider in some detail the strategic issues involved in discrete areas of international business such as mergers, acquisitions and alliances and knowledge management, technology and innovation;

- explain some of the techniques used by international business in developing and reviewing strategic initiatives.

Introduction

Many definitions have been applied to business strategy which, while differing in detail, broadly agree that it involves devising the guiding rules or principles which influence the direction and scope of the organisations activities over the long term. Kenneth Andrews of the Harvard Business School defined corporate strategy as: 'the pattern of decisions in a company that determines and reveals its objectives, purposes or goals, produces the principal policies and plans for achieving those goals, and defines the range of business the company is to pursue'.

Before considering the evolution of business strategy within a global marketplace, it may be useful to briefly review the more conventional ideas and concepts that have dominated business strategy over the past two decades. Many of these ideas originated during the 1970s and 1980s when industrial structures were relatively stable and technical change largely incremental. After reviewing the seminal works of Michael Porter of Harvard University (1980; 1985) which helped to give a more coherent analytical structure to a broad range of managerial practices, we assess the contribution of more recent strategic approaches to international business activity.

Business strategy – ideas and concepts

Techniques such as the following were widely applied to strategic thinking during much of the 1980s and 1990s.

■ SWOT and PEST analysis

During the 1970s Andrews proposed a framework for strategy formulation based on the premise that the final strategy adopted by a company should achieve a 'fit' between its internal capabilities (strengths and weaknesses) and the external situation (opportunities and threats). This is commonly known as SWOT analysis (*see* Figure 8.1 (a)) and involves undertaking (1) an analysis of the external environment within which the firm operates and (2) an objective appraisal of the organisation's current position in order to determine factors that might influence their ability to compete effectively within a particular market.

1 An *external analysis* should highlight the general environmental influences that a firm must cope with, for example, the political, economic, social and technological factors (PEST) already considered in Chapters 5–7. This analysis of the external environment will lead to the identification of a number of *opportunities* and *threats*.

2 An *internal analysis* of a firm should identify those things that the organisation does particularly well (strengths) and those features that inhibit its ability to fulfil its purposes (weaknesses). The features to be assessed may include the organisation, personnel, marketing, finance and logistical features which are considered further in Chapters 9–12.

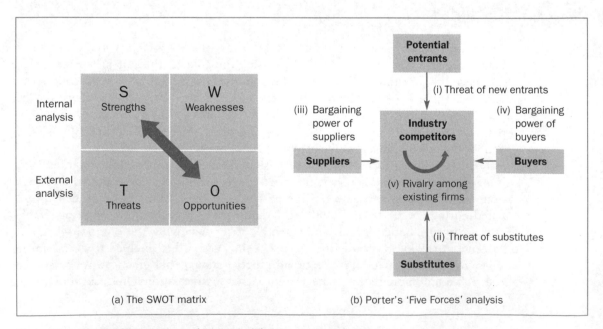

(a) The SWOT matrix

(b) Porter's 'Five Forces' analysis

Figure 8.1 **The SWOT Matrix and Porter's 'Five Forces' analysis**

Strategic alternatives arise from matching current strengths to environmental opportunities at an acceptable level of risk. This framework was further developed during the 1980s by Michael Porter who proposed a more analytical approach to strategy formulation.

■ Porter's Five Forces analysis

Porter argued that 'the essence of strategy formulation is coping with competition' and that in addition to undertaking a PEST analysis, it is also necessary to undertake a structural analysis of the industry to gauge the strengths and weaknesses of the opposition and also determine the competitive structure of a given market. The key elements in Porter's Five Forces analysis (*see* Figure 8.1(b)) can be identified as the threat of (1) potential entrants and (2) substitutes, as well as the power of (3) suppliers and (4) buyers, together with an exploration of (5) the degree of competitive rivalry.

(1) Threat of potential entrants

The threat of new entrants into an industry depends on the barriers that exist in the market and the expected reaction of existing competitors to the entrant. Porter identified six possible sources of barriers to entry, namely economies of scale, differentiation of the product, capital requirements of entry, cost advantages, access to distribution channels and legislative intervention.

(2) Threat of substitute products

The threat of substitute products can alter the competitive environment within which the firm operates. A new process or product may render an existing product useless. For an individual firm the main issue is the extent to which there is a danger that substitutes may encroach on its activities. The firm may be able to minimise the risks from substitutes by a policy of product differentiation or by achieving a low-cost position in the industry.

(3) Bargaining power of suppliers

Suppliers have the ability to squeeze industry profits by raising prices or reducing the quality of their products. Porter states that a supplier is powerful if few suppliers exist in a particular market, there are no substitute products available, the industry is not an important customer of the supplier, or the supplier's product is an important input to the buyer's business. Japanese firms have shown the importance of establishing a strong relationship with suppliers so that they 'become an extension of the firm itself', as in the *keiretsu* approach to industrial organisation (*see* Chapter 6).

(4) Bargaining power of buyers

In general, the greater the bargaining power of buyers, the greater is their ability to depress industry profitability. Porter identified a number of determinants of bargaining power including; the concentration and size of buyers, the importance of purchases to the buyer in cost terms, the costs of switching between suppliers, and the degree of standardisation of products. Buyers should be treated as rivals but should have a 'friendly relationship based on performance and integrity'.

(5) Rivalry among existing firms

Finally, the extent of rivalry between firms can influence the competitive environment within which the firm operates. Rivalry is influenced by the above forces but also depends on the concentration of firms in the marketplace and their relative market shares, the rate of industry growth, the degree of product differentiation, and the height of exit barriers. Porter refers to the tactics used by firms to seek an advantage over their competitors as 'jockeying for position'. This usually takes the form of policies towards pricing, promotion, product innovation and service level.

According to Porter, strategy formulation requires that each of the above forces be carefully analysed in order to successfully:

1 *position the company* so that its capabilities provide the best defence against the competitive forces;
2 *influence the balance* of the forces through strategic moves, thereby improving the company's position;
3 *anticipate changes* in the factors underlying the forces and respond to them.

■ Portfolio analysis

The Boston Consulting Group's portfolio matrix provides a useful framework for examining an organisation's own competitive position. The organisation's portfolio of products is subjected to a detailed analysis according to market share, growth rate and cash flow. The four alternative categories of company (or product) that emerge from the model are given the labels of 'stars', 'cash cows', 'dogs' and 'problem children' (or 'question marks').

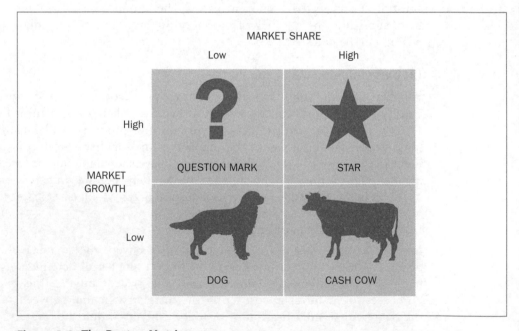

Figure 8.2 **The Boston Matrix**

- *Stars* have high market share, high growth, but limited cash flow due to the substantial amount of investment required to maintain growth. Successful *stars* go on to become *cash cows*.
- *Cash cows* have a high market share but slow growth. They tend to generate a very positive cash flow that can be used to develop other products.
- *Dogs* have a low share of a slow-growth market. They may be profitable, but only at the expense of cash reinvestment, and thus generate little for other products.
- *Problem children* have a low share of a fast-growing market and need more cash than they can generate themselves in order to keep up with the market.

The growth–share matrix is useful in providing a visual display of the strengths of a portfolio and therefore can be helpful in guiding the strategic direction of each business. However, there have been several criticisms aimed at the Boston Portfolio, namely that it is prone to oversimplification and that it takes no account of other key variables such as differentiation and market structure.

Choice of strategy

There have been several theoretical models of strategic choice, each of which seeks to identify the main strategic options open to the business in pursuit of its objectives. The following three approaches to strategic choice are often referred to.

- *product–market strategies* – which determine where the organisation competes and the direction of growth (e.g. Ansoff);
- *competitive strategies* – which influence the action/reaction patterns an organisation will pursue for competitive advantage (e.g. Porter);
- *institutional strategies* – which involve a variety of formal and informal relationships with other firms usually directed towards the method of growth (e.g. acquisition v. organic).

▪ Product–market strategies

Igor Ansoff (1968) presented the various strategic options in the form of a matrix (*see* Figure 8.3(a)).

- *Market penetration* strategy refers to gaining a larger share of the market by exploiting the firm's existing products. Unless the particular market is growing, this will involve taking business away from competitors, perhaps using one or more of the 4 Ps (*see* Chapter 10) in a national or international context.
- *Market development* strategy involves taking present products into new markets, and thus focusing activities on market opportunities and competitor situations.
- *Product development* strategy is where new products are introduced into existing markets, with the focus moving towards developing, launching and supporting additions to the product range.
- *Diversification* strategy involves the company branching out into both new products and new markets. This strategy can be further subdivided into horizontal, vertical, concentric and conglomerate diversification.

Figure 8.3 (a) Ansoff's product–market matrix; (b) Porter's generic strategies

pause for thought 1   Can you define and give examples of each of these four types of diversification strategy?

■ Competitive strategies

Porter (1980) and later writers emphasised the contribution of strategic decisions to achieving some *competitive advantage* over the competition.

Such competitive advantages were often expressed in terms of the additional 'added value' the more successful firms in an industry were able to generate vis-à-vis the most marginal firm in that industry.

> Where no explicit comparator is stated, the relevant benchmark is the marginal firm in the industry. The weakest firm which still finds it worthwhile to serve the market provides the baseline against which the competitive advantage of all other firms can be set. (Kay 1993)

These competitive advantages could be attributed to a host of potential factors:

- *architecture* (a more effective set of contractual relationships with suppliers/customers);
- *incumbency advantages* (reputation, branding, scale economies, etc.);
- *access to strategic assets* (raw materials, wavebands, scarce labour inputs, etc.);
- *innovation* (product or process, protected by patents, licences, etc.);
- *operational efficiencies* (quality circles, just-in-time techniques, re-engineering, etc.).

Our discussion here is primarily in terms of *organisations*. Aspects of *national* competitive advantage (e.g. Porter's diamond) have already been considered in Chapter 3 (pp. 73–4).

Generic strategies

Writing in 1980 in his pioneering book, *Competitive Strategy*, Porter identifies three *generic* strategies open to firms, which may help position the firm to achieve such competitive advantages. These are overall cost leadership, differentiation and focus.

- *Overall cost leadership strategy* requires the business to achieve lower costs than other competitors in the industry while maintaining product quality. This strategy requires aggressive investment in efficient plant and machinery, tight cost controls and cost minimisation in functional areas. An organisation must understand the critical activities in the business' value chain that are the sources for cost advantage and endeavour to excel in one or more of them.
- *Differentiation strategy* is based on creating 'something unique, unmatched by its competitors' which is 'valued by its buyers beyond offering simply a lower price' (Porter 1985). This entails achieving industry-wide recognition of different and superior products compared to competitors, which might result from using superior technology or providing superior customer service.
- *Focus strategy* involves selecting 'a particular buyer group, segment of the product line, or geographic market' as the basis for competition rather than the whole industry. This strategy is 'built around serving a particular target very well' in order to achieve better results. Within the targeted segment the business may attempt to compete on a low cost or differentiation basis.

Mintzberg (Mintzberg and Quinn 1991) examined both Ansoff's and Porter's models of strategic choice and suggested an alternative view of generic strategies. Mintzberg sees such strategies as being divided into five groupings, which can be summarised as locating, distinguishing, elaborating, extending and reconceiving the core business.

Institutional strategies

The focus here is on possible relationships with other firms and organisations. An initial decision for a firm seeking growth is whether to do so using its own endeavours (e.g. *organic growth*) or to short-cut the growth process by some kind of institutional tie-up with other firms. These can, of course, take many forms, including the franchise, joint venture, alliances and mergers and acquisitions considered in Chapter 2. We return to consider mergers and acquisitions in more detail later in this chapter after briefly reviewing what many believe to be the new competitive landscape of a globalised economy within which all strategic choices must now take place.

To the above we can, of course, add many other conventional techniques of business analysis which are well covered elsewhere (e.g. Hornby *et al.* 2001, Chapter 9), such as product life cycle, strategic clock, value chain analysis, barriers to entry and contestable market theory, and so on. However, our main concern here is with international business strategies in a far less stable context than pertained in the 1970s and 1980s when many of these techniques were devised and applied.

Corporate strategy in a global economy

Prahalad (1999) paints a vivid picture of a 'discontinuous competitive landscape' as characterising much of the 1990s and early years of the millennium. Industries are no longer the stable entities they once were:

- rapid technology changes and the convergence of technologies (e.g. computer and telecommunications) are constantly redefining industrial 'boundaries' so that the 'old' industrial structures become barely recognisable;
- privatisation and deregulation have become global trends within industrial sectors (e.g. telecommunications, power, water, healthcare, financial services) and even within nations themselves (e.g. transition economies, China);
- Internet-related technologies are beginning to have major impacts on business-to-business and business-to-customer relationships;
- pressure groups based around environmental and ecological sensitivities are progressively well organised and influential;
- new forms of institutional arrangements and liaisons are exerting greater influences on organisational structures than hitherto (e.g. strategic alliances, franchising).

In a progressively less stable environment dominated by such discontinuities, there will arguably be a shift in perspective away from the previous strategic focus of Porter and his contemporaries in which companies are seen as seeking to identify and exploit competitive advantages within stable industrial structures.

pause for thought 2   Think of the marginal (just surviving) firm in an industry with which you are familiar. Can you identify some of the competitive advantages of the market leader in that industry over the marginal firm?

■ Strategy in the new competitive environment

The more conventional strategic models focused on securing competitive advantages by better utilising one or more of the five factors mentioned above. However, the discontinuities outlined previously have changed the setting in which much of the strategic discussion must now take place. Prahalad (1999) goes on to suggest four key 'transformations' which must now be registered.

1 *Recognising changes in strategic space.* Deregulation and privatisation of previously government-controlled industries, access to new market opportunities in large developing countries (e.g. China, India, Brazil) and in the transitional economies of Central and Eastern Europe, together with the rapidly changing technological environment, are creating entirely new strategic opportunities. Take the case of the large energy utilities. They must now decide on the extent of integration (power generation, power transmission within industrial and/or consumer sectors), the geographical reach of their operations (domestic/overseas), the extent of diversification (other types of energy, non-energy fields), and so on. Powergen in the UK is a good example of a traditional utility with its historical base in elec-

tricity generation which, in a decade or so, has transformed itself into a global provider of electricity services (generation and transmission), water and other infrastructure services. Clearly the strategic 'space' available to companies is ever expanding, creating entirely new possibilities in the modern global economy.

2 *Recognising globalisation impacts.* As we discuss in more detail below, globalisation of business activity is itself opening up new strategic opportunities and threats. Arguably the distinction between local and global business will itself become increasingly irrelevant. The local businesses must devise their own strategic response to the impact of globalised players. Nirula, the Indian fast-food chain, raising standards of hygiene and restaurant ambience in response to competition from McDonald's, is one type of local response and McDonald's providing more lamb and vegetarian produce in its Indian stores is another. Mass customisation and quick-response strategies (*see* p. 368) require global businesses to be increasingly responsive to local consumers. Additionally, globalisation opens up new strategic initiatives in terms of geographical locations, modes of transnational collaboration, financial accountability, and logistical provision.

3 *Recognising the importance of timely responses.* Even annual planning cycles are arguably becoming progressively obsolete as the speed of corporate response becomes a still more critical success factor, both to seize opportunities and to repel threats.

4 *Recognising the enhanced importance of innovation.* Although innovation has long been recognised as a critical success factor, its role is still further enhanced in an environment dominated by the 'discontinuities' previously mentioned. Successful companies must still innovate in terms of new products and processes but now such innovation must also be directed towards providing the company with faster and more reliable information on customers as part of mass customisation, quick response and personalised product business philosophies.

These factors are arguably changing the context for business strategy from positioning the company within a clear-cut industrial structure, to stretching and shaping that structure by its own strategic initiatives. It may no longer be sensible or efficient to devise strategic blueprints over a protracted planning timeframe and then seek to apply the blueprints mechanically given that events and circumstances are changing so rapidly. The direction of broad strategic thrust can be determined as a route map, but tactical and operational adjustments must be continually appraised and modified along the way.

Nor can the traditional strategy hierarchies continue unchallenged – i.e. top management creating strategy and middle management implementing it. Those who are closest to the product and market are becoming increasingly important as well-informed sources for identifying opportunities to exploit or threats to repel. Arguably the roles of middle and lower management in the strategic process are being considerably enhanced by the 'discontinuities' previously observed. Top managers are finding themselves progressively removed from competitive reality in an era of discontinuous change. Their role is rather to set a broad course, to ensure that effective and responsive middle and lower management are in place to exercise delegated strategic responsibilities, and to provide an appropriate infrastructure for strategic delivery. For example, a key role of top managers in various media-related activities may be to secure access to an appropriate broadband wavelength by successfully competing in the UK or German auctions (see Case Study 8.5). Such access is likely to be a prerequisite for competitive involvement in a whole raft of Internet-related products for home and business consumption via mobile telephony.

Figure 8.4 provides a useful summary of the traditional and emerging views of international business strategy.

The emerging view of strategy contrasts dramatically with the traditional view. The difference is shown below:

Traditional view	**Emerging view**
· Strategy as *fit* with resources	· Strategy as *stretch and leverage*
· Strategy as *positioning in existing* industry space	· Strategy as *creating new industry* space
· Strategy as *top management* activity	· Strategy as *total organisational* process
· Strategy as an *analytical* exercise	· Strategy as an *analytical and organisational* exercise
· Strategy as *extrapolating* the past	· Strategy as *creating the future*

Figure 8.4 The new view of strategy
Source: Adapted from Prahalad (1999)

International business and the value chain

We noted in Chapter 1 that international production is dominated by MNEs that are increasingly transnational in operation, including horizontally and vertically integrated activities more widely dispersed on a geographical basis. This brings into focus the *value chain* in Figure 8.5, which breaks down the full collection of activities that companies perform into 'primary' and 'secondary' activities.

- *Primary activities* are those required to create the product (good or service, including inbound raw materials, components and other inputs), sell the product and distribute it to the marketplace.
- *Secondary activities* include a variety of functions such as human resource management, technological development, management information systems, finance for procurement, etc. These secondary activities are required to support the primary activities.

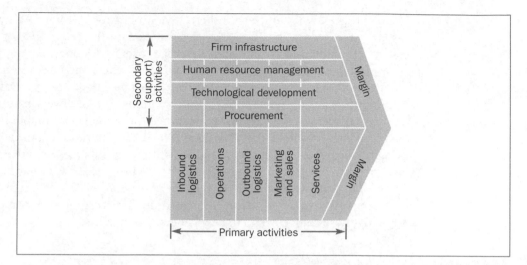

Figure 8.5 **Value chain**

It is useful to remember that an effective international business strategy must encompass *all* parts of the value chain configuration, wherever their geographical location. Later chapters of this book consider the international dimension of these various activities in their own right. Here we concentrate on international strategic approaches that might help the firm maximise the sum of these individual activities. International strategies that yield *global synergies* for the firm over its entire value chain are likely to be of particular interest, where synergies refer to the so-called '2 + 2 > 4 effect' whereby the whole becomes greater than the sum of the individual parts.

A number of sources can be identified as contributing to these global synergies.

■ Sources of global synergies

Expanding internationally may allow firms to reconfigure their value chains and raise overall corporate profitability in ways that would not otherwise be available within a wholly domestic context. International businesses may be able to develop these 'global synergies' from a variety of sources.

- *Localisation on a global scale* where only the international business can disperse individual value-creating activities (both 'primary' and 'secondary') around the world to locations where they can be undertaken most efficiently (at least cost) and effectively. For example we saw in Chapter 1 (p. 6) how labour costs and productivities varied markedly between different geographical locations.

- *Economies of scale* where it is only by becoming an international business that the firm can operate at such a size that all available economies of scale (technical and non-technical) are achieved for a particular activity within the value chain. This is especially important when the 'minimum efficient size' for an activity within the firm's value chain exceeds the maximum level of output achievable within the domestic economy (*see* Box 8.1, p. 249).

- *Economies of scope and experience* where only the international business can configure the most appropriate *mix* of activities (*economies of scope*) within the value chain consistent with efficient and effective production. Or where only by becoming an international business can the firm secure the *economies of experience* essential to minimising (cumulative) average costs (*see* p. 369).

■ *Non-organic growth on an international scale* where the international business recognises that organic growth is insufficient to meet its key objectives and where some form of *institutional arrangement* with one or more overseas firm(s) is seen as the way ahead. The various institutional mechanism's available have already been touched on in Chapter 2 and are considered in more detail in the international context below. Of course these institutional linkages may themselves be a means to achieving one or more of the global synergies already identified.

■ *Increase in geographical reach of core competencies* where the international business seeks to earn a still higher return from its distinctive core competencies by applying those competencies to new geographic markets.

International business strategies

The enormous variety of operations embraced by the term 'multinational' has led some writers to distinguish between four key strategies when competing in the international business environment: a global strategy, a transnational strategy, a multidomestic strategy and an international strategy. The appropriateness of the particular strategy selected will depend to a considerable extent on the pressures faced by the international business in terms of both cost and local responsiveness, as indicated in Figure 8.6. These will become clearer as we discuss the nature of these various strategies and their associated advantages and disadvantages.

■ Global strategy

This is particularly appropriate when the firm faces high pressures in terms of cost competitiveness but low pressures in terms of being responsive to local market conditions. Firms adopting a global strategy focus on being cost competitive by securing

Figure 8.6 Four international strategies

the various economies of scale and scope outlined in Box 8.1 (p. 249) and economies of experience (p. 369). Production, marketing and R & D activities tend to be concentrated in a few (and in extreme cases a single) favourable geographical locations rather than being widely dispersed. The emphasis of the global firm is on a homogenous, standardised product to maximise these various technical and non-technical economies. Of course such a low-cost strategy is only possible where few pressures exist to localise either production or marketing. If localisation pressures were high, then shorter production runs of a locally-differentiated product would invariably raise both technical (production) and non-technical (function/support services) costs.

The global strategy is best suited to industrial products for which there are high pressures for cost reductions but relatively low pressures for the product to be differentiated to meet local market requirements. The semiconductor industry is widely regarded as suitable for this strategy, with global standards placing a premium on firms such as Intel, Motorola and Texas Instruments producing standardised products at minimum cost. A global strategy does not suit many consumer goods markets where product differentiation is a key to local/cultural acceptability.

Transnational strategy

This is particularly appropriate when the firm faces pressures in terms of both cost competitiveness and responsiveness to local conditions. Of course such local responsiveness may involve more than the 'local' market acceptability of a differentiated product. It might, for example, also reflect entry barriers which effectively protect the local market from the import of a standardised product, however locally acceptable to consumers.

Firms adopting the transnational strategy cannot depend on cost reductions via scale economies from producing a standardised product in a few selected geographical locations. Rather, they must seek cost reductions by exploiting *location economies* appropriate to a particular element of the value chain; for example, locating labour intensive component production in countries where relative unit labour costs (RULCs – *see* p. 8) are low. Another cost reduction mechanism open to a transnational strategy might involve benefiting from *experience economies* (*see* p. 369) related to cumulative production across a larger number of geographical locations. *Global learning* may be a further mechanism yielding cost reductions, as when foreign subsidiaries themselves add value to any core competencies transferred from the parent company. The foreign subsidiaries may go on to develop the expertise to become the primary centres for further, initially unforeseen, value added activities, thereby increasing global efficiency. Foreign subsidiaries may then be able to use this 'global learning' to transfer their own (newly acquired) core competencies to other foreign subsidiaries or back to the parent company itself.

These cost reduction outcomes via a transnational strategy must, of course, remain consistent with the high pressure towards local responsiveness. For example, local responsiveness may require product differentiation and non-standardised marketing and HRM approaches appropriate to local sociocultural sensitivities.

Implementing a transnational strategy is likely to require a high degree of complex organisational coordination across geographically-dispersed primary and secondary activities within the global value chain. There is also likely to be an element of conflict between cost reductions via the various mechanisms outlined above and cost increases resulting from an increased local responsiveness which inhibits scale economies of both a technical and non-technical nature. How then can the international business implement a transnational strategy?

There are of course many variants, but a widely-used method for implementing this strategy involves the idea of 'modularity' in both design and production (*see* p. 371). This approach is currently being widely used in the car industry as part of a transnational strategy, whereby production activities are progressively broken down into a number of large but separate elements that can be carried out independently in different international locations, chosen according to the optimum mix of factor inputs (cost and quality) for each element. Final assembly, characterised by local responsiveness in terms of product differentiation involving design and other features, often takes place at, or near to, the intended market.

Ford is following this approach, making many different models but using the same 'platform' – the basic chassis and other standardised internal parts. Design and technological breakthroughs of this kind permit even the transnational strategy to benefit from scale economies, as in the production of the basic platform. However, Ford plans to produce ten different vehicles from this common platform, with differentiated features reflecting the need to respond to localised consumer preferences.

Multidomestic strategy

This is particularly appropriate when the firm faces low pressures in terms of cost competitiveness but high pressures in terms of local responsiveness. This strategy tends to involve establishing relatively independent subsidiaries, each providing a full range of value chain activities (primary and secondary) within each national market. The subsidiary is broadly free to customise its products, focus its marketing and select and recruit its personnel, all in keeping with the local culture and the expressed preferences of its customers in each local market.

Such a strategy is more likely to occur when economies of scale in production and marketing are low, and when there are high coordination costs between parent and subsidiary. A disadvantage of such local 'independence' may also be an inability to realise potential experience economies. A further disadvantage may manifest itself in the autonomous actions of subsidiaries, sometimes paying little regard to broader-based corporate objectives. A classic example in this respect is the decision by the US subsidiary of Philips NV in the late 1970s to purchase the Matsushita VHS-format video-cassette recorders (VCRs) and put its own label on them, when the parent company was seeking to establish its own V2000 VCRs as the industry standard.

International strategy

This is particularly appropriate when the firm faces low pressures as regards both cost competitiveness and local responsiveness. The international strategy places the main focus on establishing the 'core architecture' (e.g. product development and R & D) underpinning the value chain at the home base of the MNE and seeking to translate this more or less intact to the national market overseas. Some localised production and marketing activities may be permitted, but these will be limited in scope. McDonald's, IBM, Microsoft, Wal Mart, Kelloggs and Procter & Gamble are often cited as companies pursuing an international strategy in which head office keeps a tight rein over product strategy and marketing initiatives.

Over time some additional local customisation of product and marketing has tended to accompany the international strategy. Not least because of some well publicised failures from an overly strict adherence to the 'core architecture' at head offices. For example IKEA, the Swedish furniture retailer, transferred its retailing formula developed in Sweden into other nations. While such a transfer has proved successful in the UK and elsewhere, it most certainly failed in the USA, with product ranges proving inappropriate to both the larger American physiques (e.g. beds and sofas were too small), the American preferences for larger storage spaces (drawers, bedroom chests and other containers too confined), and European-sized curtains proving incompatible with the sizes of American windows. After entering the US market in 1985, IKEA had realised by the early 1990s that it would need to customise its product range to the American market if it was going to succeed there, which it has duly done to considerable success.

Such celebrated failures, together with a growing awareness of the benefits of at least a limited amount of local responsiveness, have somewhat diluted the international strategy, though it still remains one in which a centralised core architecture persists. It is most appropriate to situations where the parent firm possesses core

Table 8.1 Characteristics of four international strategies

Strategy	Advantages	Disadvantages
Global	Standardised products become highly cost competitive Economies of scale Economies of experience Emphasise home country core competencies	Less responsive to local conditions Loss of market share if consumer behaviour becomes more responsive to localised characteristics Few opportunities for global learning
Transnational	Economies of location via a geographically-dispersed value chain Economies of experience Global learning stemming from the sharing of core competencies Product differentiation, with production and marketing responsive to local conditions	Complex coordination to implement strategy Possible conflicts between cost competitiveness and local responsiveness
Multidomestic	Highly customised production and marketing, emphasising local responsiveness Most appropriate where the minimum efficient size (MES) is relatively low for key elements of the value chain and strong local/cultural preferences exist.	Loss of location economies (which require a geographically-dispersed value chain) Loss of experience economies Little global learning where core competencies are not transferred between foreign companies Lack of corporate group cohesion
International	Core competencies transferred to foreign markets Economies of scale for centralised markets in 'core architecture' (e.g. product development, R & D)	Less responsive to local conditions Less location economies available, via retention of 'core architecture' Less global learning as few core competencies transferred Less experience economies available

competencies, which are unmatched by indigenous competitors in foreign markets, and where the key characteristics of the product are broadly welcomed by consumers in those markets.

Table 8.1 (p. 241) reviews the advantages and disadvantages of these four international strategies.

Case Study 8.1 investigates the strategies behind a number of the mechanisms adopted for market entry.

CASE 8.1 MNE strategies in the US market

Management theorists have a special rule for companies expanding outside their home markets; never underestimate the liability of foreigners. Ambitious executives, operating on unfamiliar turf, fail to recognise cultural differences. European companies moving into the US are no exception, says Julian Birkinshaw, of the London Business School. 'Too often they say "Oh I know America. This should be straightforward." In more distant countries, they know there are cultural factors to overcome and work hard to overcome them. In the US they are deceived by the cultural proximity.'

In recent decades, the US has proved attractive to many European businesses. Some have prospered but others have been scarred by the process. And for some, crossing the Atlantic has ended in disaster – even oblivion. All went with high hopes. For some, entering the world's largest market is part of a strategy of global acquisitions. Deutsche Telekom, for example, bought Voicestream, the US mobile operator, as part of a portfolio of international telecommunications businesses. France's Vivendi paid $34 billion in 2000 for Universal Studios to build a global media giant. Marks and Spencer bought Brooks Brothers, the upmarket clothing retailer, and King's Supermarkets in 1988 as part of its expansion plans outside the UK.

Some believed a US acquisition alone could turn them into a global business. When Farnell, the UK component distributor, bought Premier Consolidated of the US for $2.8 billion in 1996, Farnell's market value was less than £1 billion ($1.5 billion at the time). Howard Poulson, then chief executive, said the deal was a once-in-a-lifetime opportunity. 'With one move, we have transformed ourselves into a truly global company.' The hubris at what became Premier Farnell was shortlived. Two years later, Mr Poulson had departed after two profit warnings and a slashed dividend. Like many other chief executives, he had underestimated the challenge of a US acquisition. One of his mistakes was to pay too much. His reasoning was that unless Farnell snapped up Premier, a US rival would act and squeeze it out of important markets. This is a common error for European companies entering the US, says Marco Becht of the European Corporate Governance Institute in Brussels – particularly during the stock market euphoria of the 1990s. 'It was hard to resist – everyone was doing it. If you didn't want to look like "old Europe", you did it like the Americans.'

This reflects the difficulty many European executives have in understanding just how competitive the US market is. 'In most European countries, there are three or four significant players,' says Prof Birkinshaw, 'There are often 10–20 competitors in the US in sectors such as retailing.'

Dixons, the UK electronics retailer, discovered this when it bought Silo, a US chain in 1987. A recession followed and Silo, which had over-expanded, was unable to compete with bigger rivals. Eventually Dixons sold the US chain and took write-offs of more than £200 million.

Renault also found it had misunderstood the US consumer after it had attempted to enter the US in the 1970s through a partnership with American Motors. But it chose to launch its assault in small cars, one of the most competitive segments and one with weak profit margins. It also made technical errors, including under-powering its models in the wrong expectation that the energy crisis would end the American love affair with gas-guzzlers. The strategy was supposed to be cheaper than building a presence in the US from scratch, which Renault estimated would have cost at least $1.5 billion. By the time it managed to pull out by selling AMC to Chrysler, the venture had cost it an estimated $730 million – with little to show for it. Indeed, it almost brought the French carmaker to bankruptcy. Renault has yet to return to the US, except through Nissan Motor, its Japanese arm.

Given the competitive intensity of the US market, it is essential to have a clear strategy. But the European companies that fail in the US often lack a clear strategy, says Subi Rangan of Insead, the French management school. 'Global strategy is never a substitute for a good business strategy. International expansion is one of the things companies do to conceal a lack of strategy. The activity gives shareholders the impression that something is being achieved,' says Prof Rangan.

Retail groups can find it particularly hard to stand out in such a competitive market. But that is only one of the problems faced by businesses that are close to consumers. 'They have to capture the local zeitgeist,' says Joanna Waterous, who heads the European retail practice of McKinsey, the consultants. This is not easy when head office is thousands of miles away and may not grasp the subtle cultural differences of the US market.

Whether they can overcome this distance will depend on the skill with which the US businesss is managed, says LBS's Prof Birkinshaw. When Ericsson bought a California company called Raynet, a fibre optics group, in 1996, it adopted its standard integration approach and soon found it had driven out most of the staff whose skills were essential to the business. In subsequent acquisitions, the Swedish group was much more hands-off.

But leaving too much to US management can also be risky, as several European companies have found. When Midland Bank bought a majority stake in Crocker National Corporation of California in 1981, it promised the regulators it would not take control of management. The last UK bank to expand overseas, Midland, was catapulted into the world's top 10 banks by the deal. But within a year, Crocker's local managers had authorised an expansion in the California property market and racked up levels of debt that almost brought Midland to collapse before it sold its US subsidiary to Wells Fargo.

BP is another European company that found its US activities weighing heavily when it took a majority stake in Sohio. It eventually took full control of the US oil group after a series of moves by local managers that weakened Sohio's position. Sohio had squandered much of the cash from its Alaskan field in an unsuccessful effort to build up reserves in the lower 48 US states. And it bought Kennecott, a copper mining company, just as the metal's price was beginning to collapse.

▶

Such failures in management reflect cultural differences, says Marco Becht of the European Corporate Governance Institute. But these gaps can impinge in other ways, including American legal traditions and the liabilities these impose on companies. 'Litigation can begin as soon as the deal is done,' he says. He cites the case launched against DaimlerChrysler by Kirk Kerkorian, who claims that the German company failed to pay enough for control of Chrysler in 1998.

Prof Birkinshaw says that these legal differences penetrate day-to-day management in the US. 'Swedes put trust in the handshake, but the US relies on legal documents.'

Some of the companies that do well are the truly multinational companies such as Unilever and Nestlé that have grown much bigger outside their home countries over long periods. They have little difficulty building their operations in the US, though they often prefer to start from scratch and make acquisitions later.

And whatever the difficulties about entering the US, most observers expect there to be no shortage of candidates to follow where others have gone. On the day that Ahold announced its problems, Egg, the UK-based internet bank said it was exploring venturing into the US market.

Ms Waterous says the answer to why companies still go to the US is the same that Willie Sutton gave for why he robbed banks, 'It's where the money is!'

Source: John Wilman, *Financial Times*, 25 February 2003.

Questions

1 Using the four international strategies shown in Figure 8.6, suggest which companies would appear to have followed one of these strategies in their approach to the US.

2 What can we learn in a *strategic context* from the successes and failures in the Case Study?

3 Apart from strategic issues, what other factors determine success or failure in approaching the US market?

4 What is meant by the suggestion that 'global stategy is never a good substitute for business strategy'?

International business strategies and political perspectives

The broad framework discussed in the last section has been adapted to give further insights into strategic decision making by MNEs. In particular there has been a focus on the alleged trade-off between the need for MNEs to be responsive to the *national* concerns of host countries (or regional groupings) on the one hand, and to be *economically integrated* (globally or regionally) on the other. Following Rugman and Hodgetts (2003) we can use Figure 8.7 to illustrate this so-called *integration–responsiveness* framework.

■ Economic integration–national responsiveness framework

- *National responsiveness*. The horizontal axis of Figure 8.7 corresponds to an essentially political dimension, namely 'national responsiveness'. It refers to the pressures on MNEs to respond to different national or regional (e.g. EU) standards imposed by governments and agencies and to different consumer tastes in segmented national (or regional) markets.
- *Economic integration*. The vertical axis of Figure 8.7 corresponds to an index of 'economic integration' worldwide (i.e. globalisation), or more regionally focused as in the case of increased integration within the EU. It refers to the pressures on MNEs to develop economies of scale, to develop location economies (via global specialisation for appropriate activities within the value chain), to develop experience economies and to seek to benefit from other efficiency advantages from increased coordination and control of geographically-dispersed activities.

Strategies appropriate to the MNE will then depend on the quadrant they inhabit or seek to inhabit.

- *Quadrant 1* (high economic integration, low national responsiveness). Here the MNE operates in a market characterised by high economic integration pressures and its strategy must therefore incorporate a drive for cost and price competitiveness. Typically MNEs in this quadrant will be centralised in structure, often using mergers and acquisitions to achieve economies of scale, scope and experience (Box 8.1 p. 249). However, the MNE in this quadrant need not be unduly concerned with responding to host country national (political, regulatory and cultural) concerns as these are deemed to have a 'low' impact on its operation.
- *Quadrant 2* (high economic integration, high national responsiveness). Here the MNE operates in a market characterised by strong international cost and price competitiveness pressures but it must meet such challenges while paying due regard to the high political sensitivities of host national/regional governments and

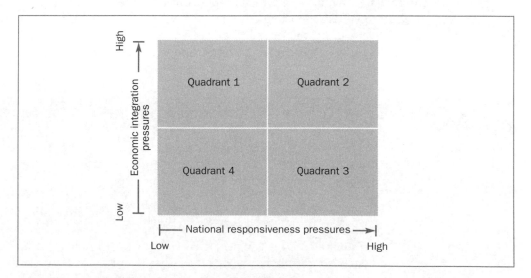

Figure 8.7 **Integration–responsiveness framework**

agencies. The MNE in this quadrant will face a variety of policy options which seek a compromise between these two, somewhat opposing tendencies. The coordination of a variety of flexible responses (*see also* p. 239) may be challenging for the MNE. Rugman and Hodgetts suggest that many MNEs based in one or other of the triad regional groupings face these compromises, and the most adaptive and innovative in terms of policy/organisation are the ones which tend to thrive.

- *Quadrant 3* (low economic integration, high national responsiveness). Here economic integration is less important to the MNE than national responsiveness. Production practices, product specification and support activities (e.g. marketing) must be carefully adapted to the consumer characteristics, standards and regulation of the national/regional grouping. Economic integration is much less important (less cost and price competitive pressures) than a decentralised strategy responsive to national (regional) characteristics. In practice segmented strategies appealing to niche and target groups within the national/regional economies are likely, as in the case of food products and higher-quality (designer) clothes.
- *Quadrant 4* (low economic integration, low national responsiveness). Few scale economies or location economies via a more geographically-dispersed value chain are likely in this quadrant so price competition will tend to be less fierce. Nor are there many benefits from seeking close alignment with national (regional) regulations, standards and consumer characteristics. A broadly standardised product can, however, be sold by MNEs in this quadrant and there may be benefits from a centralised transfer of core competencies to overseas national (regional) subsidiaries.

The high population (380 million rising to over 450 million with enlargement) and high income base of the EU will then permit substantial scale economies for products conforming to clearly demarcated EU specifications. In other words high economic integration within the EU will serve EU 'home' MNEs well in competition with their triad (*see* p. 4) counterparts. By using more stringent directives and other regulations re product specifications, the EU is placing less focus on member state national responsiveness but more focus on EU supranational (regional) responsiveness. To support EU 'winners' the EU competition policy is seen by many as increasingly directed towards supporting cross-border merger activities, strategic partnerships and the achievement of scale economies.

Case study 8.2 looks at integration-responsiveness issues.

CASE 8.2 Carlsberg to take second look at China

It is easy to see why Carlsberg is shaking off the hangover that followed its previous push into China and coming back for another taste of what is one of the world's most challenging beer markets.

By most counts, China last year passed the US as the world's biggest beer consumer. However, per capita consumption remains tiny by international standards. China consumed only around 19.5 litres per person in 2003 (59th ranked) compared to around 122 litres per person in Germany (3rd ranked). Rapid economic development also means many consumers have more money to spend on liquid refreshment than ever before.

Lured by the market's vast potential, Carlsberg acquired two breweries in China's south-western province of Yunnan in 2003 – less than three years after selling its expensively built brewery in Shanghai to Chinese rival Tsingtao.

Carlsberg's Yunnan deals are part of a resurgence of interest in China by foreign brewers, many of which were wary of investment following the embarrassing and costly failure of a string of ventures set up in the 1990s by brewers such as Fosters of Australia and Bass of the UK.

In recent months, Belgium's Interbrew has taken control of a leading brewer in eastern Zhejiang: Anheuser-Busch of the US has raised its stake in Tsingtao to 10 per cent; and Heineken of the Netherlands has signalled it is seeking a suitable Chinese partner. And in July 2003, South Africa's SABMiller announced it would take a 30 per cent stake in China's Harbin Brewery Group for HK$675 million (US$86.5 million). 'The Chinese market remains as interesting and exciting as it has been in the past,' says Jesper Madsen, managing director of Carlsberg Brewery HK, which controls the Danish brewer's Chinese operations. The recent wave of investment is no mere re-run, however.

Like any chastened tippler after an all-night binge, foreign brewers are insisting this time will be different. In the 1990s Carlsberg and many of its rivals spent large sums building breweries to produce high-priced premium brands for China's biggest urban markets. 'We assumed quite aggressive growth in the premium market, which did not really materialise,' says Mr Madsen. 'The local brands responded very aggressively by launching [themselves] in the premium sector and we found ourselves competing not only with other foreigners but also a number of locals.' In Yunnan, by contrast, Carlsberg will focus on promoting the existing brands of its newly-acquired ventures and expanding the undeveloped local market.

Another sign of the new caution is the change of approach by Anheuser, which has spent heavily building a brewery in central China's Wuhan city to produce its Budweiser brand. While the plant is now reportedly profitable, Anheuser last year switched its focus to a partnership with Tsingtao under which it plans eventually to take a 27 per cent stake in the Chinese brand leader.

The more humble strategy of buying local brands or taking minority stakes in local brewers is something of a vindication for SABMiller, the world's second largest beer producer by volume. Unlike its international rivals, it has prospered in China by working through a 49 per cent owned joint venture with local group China Resources Enterprise and now seeks to repeat that success with its new minority stake in Hong Kong listed Harbin Brewery. SABMiller says the approach combines its international brewing savvy with the local market clout and distribution networks of its Chinese partner. 'They are the smartest ones in the market,' agrees one former executive at a rival foreign brewer that once scorned SABMiller's low-profile approach in favour of premium brand building.

Joe Zhang, head of China Research at UBS in Hong Kong, says foreign brewers stand to benefit from structural change in the beer market, which after four years of minimal plant construction is at least resolving the long-standing problem of over-capacity.

But in spite of large-scale consolidation in recent years, China remains a difficult and highly regionalised market, divided between hundreds of small-scale local brewers. Shifting the focus from premium brands and investing through local brewers gives foreign companies access to a much larger pool of drinkers. But also means costs have to be kept under tight control and a lot of beer sold to generate significant returns.

Source: Mure Dickie, *Financial Times* 9, July 2003.

Questions

1 How might you describe Carlsberg's initial and subsequent strategies in terms of Figures 8.6 or 8.7?

2 What is so attractive about China for brewers and what are the problems?

Institutional strategies and international business

To a greater or lesser extent, all four strategies discussed in the previous two sections may involve the firm in devising new *institutional arrangements*, especially where 'green field' foreign direct investment (*see* p. 46) overseas is deemed inappropriate. Mergers and acquisitions and strategic alliances were seen, in Chapter 1, to be an increasingly prominent aspect of international business. In this section we consider these institutional arrangements within the international business environment in rather more detail.

■ Mergers and acquisitions (M & A)

We have already noted (*see* Chapter 2) how globalisation has influenced MNE perspectives of horizontal and vertical integration, with the former particularly relevant to cost-oriented MNEs and the latter to market-oriented MNEs. Laurence Capron (1999) expressed similar views in her assertion that two types of synergy (sometimes described as the '2 + 2 > 4 effect') are typically used to justify mergers and acquisitions, namely cost and revenue based synergies:

■ *cost-based synergies* – horizontal acquisitions have traditionally been considered an effective means of achieving economies of scale in production, in R & D and in administrative, logistical and sales functions;

■ *revenue-based synergies* – horizontal or vertical acquisitions enable companies to develop new competencies, which may in turn enable them to command a price premium (via increased market power, higher innovation capabilities) or to increase sales volume (via increased market leverage – both geographic and product-line extension).

Figure 8.8 provides a still broader classification of the potential synergies from M & A activity, breaking them down this time into 'real term' and 'financial' issues. Box 8.1 looks in rather more detail at some of the synergies commonly ascribed to M & A.

A merger takes place with the mutual agreement of the management of both companies, usually through an exchange of shares of the merging firms with shares of the

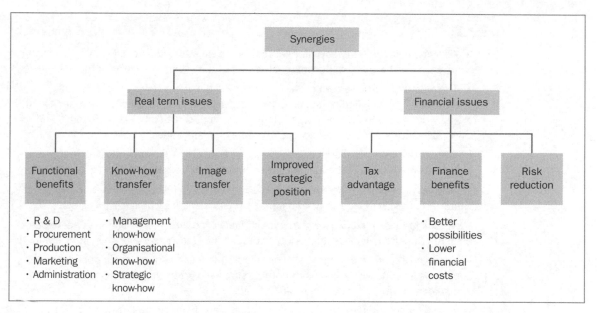

Figure 8.8 Potential synergies from M & A

new legal entity. Additional funds are not usually required for the act of merging, and the new venture often reflects the name of both the companies concerned.

An acquisition (or takeover) occurs when the management of Firm A makes a direct offer to the shareholders of Firm B and acquires a controlling interest. Usually the price offered to Firm B shareholders is substantially higher than the current share price on the stock market. In other words, a takeover involves a direct transaction between the management of the acquiring firm and the stockholders of the acquired firm. Takeovers usually require additional funds to be raised by the acquiring firm (Firm A) for the acquisition of the other firm (Firm B), and the identity of the acquired company is often subsumed within that of the purchaser.

Box 8.1   Mergers and acquisitions incentives

Mergers and acquisitions constitute the main vehicle by which firms grow in size (accounts for around 60% of the increase in industrial concentration in the UK) and provide a more rapid alternative to organic growth via 'ploughed-back' profits. Of course, it also offers benefits in terms of cost efficiencies, risk reduction and market power.

Cost efficiencies

The suggestion here is that growth in firm size can provide economies of scale, i.e. a fall in long-run average costs (*see* Figure 8.9). These can be of a technical or a non-technical variety.

1 **Technical economies.** These are related to an increase in size of the plant or production unit and are most common in horizontal M & As. Reasons include:

– *specialisation of labour or capital*, which becomes more possible as output increases. Specialisation raises productivity per unit of labour/capital input, so that average variable costs fall as output increases;

▶

Box 8.1 Continued

- *the 'engineers rule'* whereby material costs increase as the square but volume (capacity) increases as the cube, so that material costs per unit of capacity fall as output increases;

- *dovetailing of processes*, which may only be feasible at high levels of output. For example, if the finished product needs processes A, B and C respectively producing 10, 20, 30 items per hour, then only at 60 units per hour can all processes 'dovetail' and avoid incurring the unnecessary cost of spare (unused) capacity.

2 **Non-technical (enterprise) economies.** These are related to an increase in size of the enterprise as a whole and are valid for both horizontal and vertical M & As. Reasons include:

- *financial economies* – larger enterprises can raise financial capital more cheaply (lower interest rates, access to share and rights issues via Stock Exchange listings, etc.);

- *administrative, marketing and other functional economies* – existing functional departments can often increase throughput without a pro-rata increase in their establishment;

- *distributive economies* – more efficient distributional and supply-chain operations become feasible with greater size (lorries, ships and other containers can be dispatched with loads nearer to capacity, etc.);

- *purchasing economies* – bulk buying discounts are available for larger enterprises. Also, vertical integration (e.g. backwards) means that components can be purchased at cost from the now internal supplier rather than at cost plus profit.

As can be seen from Figure 8.9, where economies of scale exist for these various reasons, the long-run average cost (*LRAC*) curve will fall as output rises over the range $0 - Q_1$. The more substantial these economies of scale, the steeper the fall in the *LRAC* curve, which

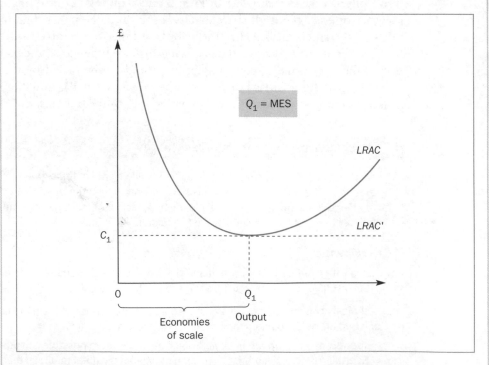

Figure 8.9 **Economies of scale and minimum efficient size (MES)**

Box 8.1	Continued

then means that any firm producing less output than Q_1 is at a considerable cost disadvantage vis-à-vis its competitors. This output (Q_1) at which *LRAC* is a minimum is often called the 'minimum efficient size' (MES). The larger Q_1 is relative to total industry output, the fewer efficient firms the industry can sustain. For example, if Q_1 is 50% of the usual UK output of glass, then arguably the UK can only sustain two efficient glass producers.

Some surveys suggest that if a firm attempts to produce beyond the MES (Q_1), average costs then begin to rise. These are called diseconomies of scale, and are usually attributed to managerial problems in handling output growth efficiently. However, other surveys suggest that while *LRAC* ceases to fall, there is little evidence that it actually rises for levels of output beyond Q_1 (i.e. *LRAC'* in Figure 8.9).

Other cost efficiencies can result from economies of scope via M & A (*see also* p. 379). Here the suggestion is that a more appropriate mix of products or activities in the company's portfolio can help reduce average costs. The joint production of two or more products by the firm or its engagement in two or more activities can bring complementarities which may yield overall cost savings (e.g. heat from energy production by the firm may be available as a by-product to support its other activities).

- *Risk reduction*. This applies particularly to conglomerate M & As, which involve diversifying the firm's existing portfolio of products or activities. Such diversification helps cushion the firm against any damaging movements which are restricted to particular product groups or particular countries.

- *Market power*. The enlarged firm can use its higher market share or capitalised value to exert greater influence on price or on competitor actions/reactions in 'game' playing situations (*see* p. 263). Enhanced market power can be deployed to raise corporate profit or to achieve other corporate objectives.

While it has been widely accepted that successful mergers and acquisitions can create value and add growth, the outcome of such integration has often proved disappointing. Indeed, this has to some extent been anticipated by the short-run stock market return to acquiring companies, which for some time has been approximately zero. Robert Gertner (2000) suggests that at least three reasons underlie these disappointing outcomes: unpredictability, agency problems and managerial error.

- *Unpredictability*. The 'discontinuities' already outlined (*see* pp. 234–6) give ample reasons why linear predictions of the future are unlikely to be realised. Nevertheless, this may not be the whole story. Mitchell and Lehn (1990) found that for acquisitions where the stock market reacts negatively to the merger announcement, the subsequent break-up (divestment) of the new entity was more likely to occur. This suggests that the stock market does in fact have some ability to identify those mergers and acquisitions that are more likely to fail in the future.
- *Agency problems*. Where the principal–agent problem occurs (*see* p. 205), there may well be a separation of interests between those of shareholders (principals) and managers (agents). It may then follow that a merger/acquisition viewed as favourable by one may actually be unfavourable to the other. Buckingham and Atkinson (1999) note that only 17% of mergers and acquisitions produced any

value for shareholders while 53% of them actually destroyed shareholder value. However, there is ample evidence (Fuller 2004) that managers remuneration and perquisites may be more closely related to variables such as corporate turnover and growth rates than to corporate profitability. This misalignment of incentives (agency problem) may be an important factor in the continued drive towards M & A as a strategic focus.

■ *Managerial errors.* Lack of knowledge, errors of judgement and managerial hubris (overconfidence) can manifest themselves in all three phases of M & A activity, i.e. the planning, implementation and operational phases. For example, in the *planning phase* imagined synergy is far more common than actual synergy, as is indicated in Case Study 8.3 using the Daimler-Benz and Chrysler merger. Often the actual estimates of merger benefits prove too optimistic and in reality the enhanced resource base of the company may not add value in the ways planned. In the *implementation phase* culture clashes at corporate or national levels may also occur, preventing potential synergies being realised (*see* Chapter 6). For example, at the corporate level, acquisitions involving a traditional bureaucratic company with an innovative entrepreneurial company will invariably bring conflicts, with the result that for some employees there will be a loss of identification with, and motivation by, the new employer. High-quality human resources are extremely mobile and key knowledge, skills, contacts and capabilities are embedded in these employees, whose loss as a result of the M & A activity will seriously diminish the prospects of the new corporate entity. Finally, in the *operational phase* the hoped for economies of scale and scope outlined in Box 8.1 may fail to materialise, for a variety of logistical reasons.

Case Study 8.3 on the Daimler-Benz and Chrysler merger usefully illustrates some of these aspects of a cross-border merger.

CASE 8.3 Daimler-Benz AG and Chrysler

Karl Benz constructed the first automobile in 1886 at which time Gottlieb Daimler was active in the same field of business. After years of partnership their businesses were formally integrated in 1926 as the Daimler-Benz Company. In the 1980s Daimler-Benz pursued a strategy of diversification, acquiring MTU, AEG, the aeroplane company Dornier, MBB and Fokker, the latter completing the aviation arm of Daimler-Benz. The vision of the chairman (Mr Reuter) was to transform the firm from a car maker into an integrated technology group along the lines of General Electric or the Japanese Mitsubishi conglomerate. His vision included generating cross-border synergies between the automobile, the aeroplane and electronics industry, exchanging skills and knowledge, and spreading the company's risks over the many businesses in its portfolio.

Daimler's first acquisition round

This round of acquisitions soon ran into trouble. The electronics industry was being pressurised by cheap components from Asia, the civil aviation industry was badly affected by the recession of the late 1980s early 1990s and the market for military aeroplanes collapsed after the end of the cold war. Further, many of the acquired businesses had needed restructuring to make them internationally cost competitive. Few of the newly acquired firms had proved to be cash cows for Daimler, quite the opposite, absorbing profits as the company invested heavily in them during restructuring. In terms of Porter's 'parenting advantage' concept it would seem that Daimler provided neither benefits to its acquired businesses nor gained competitive advantages or other benefits from them. For example Daimler proved unable to provide readily transferable skills from its core automobile business to units like AEG or Fokker. The outcome was that AEG – one of the best-known and established German companies – was broken up, with the brand sold to Electrolux, some parts integrated into other Daimler businesses and most others closed. With Fokker (aeroplanes) the outcome was similar – Fokker was on the edge of bankruptcy after Daimler withdrew financial support in 1996. Arguably Daimler not only destroyed shareholder value, but also destroyed whole companies with its attempt to build a conglomerate based on unrealistic expectations of planned synergies.

Daimler's first round of acquisitions ended with the highest loss since its foundation (DM 5.8bn) being announced in 1995, mainly due to restructuring charges. Applying M & A success measurements it would seem that the strategy had failed. Many of the acquired firms had been sold off or closed and in terms of stock market figures the market value of Daimler had plunged during the diversification period from DM 53bn in 1986 to DM 35bn in 1995.

Daimler's merger with Chrysler

On 6 May 1998 a new chapter in Daimler's M & A history began: Daimler-Benz AG and Chrysler Corporation announced their merger and the creation of the new DaimlerChrysler AG. To understand this merger one must first consider all the environmental factors. The automobile industry is becoming increasingly mature, with only certain regions (especially Asia) offering higher than average growth opportunities. If a car maker wants to survive, it must have a global reach and be established in all markets of the triad (for example, the number of independent car producers has halved in the last 30 years). A second factor involves the time dimension. Those who wish to sustain their position must react very quickly to changing demands and must renew their product portfolio more frequently. As a result, they are forced to share expensive fixed overheads (e.g. gain synergies in research and development) and use economies of scale and scope to keep variable costs down. Arguably only large, globalised companies can fulfil these criteria.

The Daimler–Chrysler management engaged international merger experts to assist in all the vital steps of the pre- and post-merger phases. The merger with Chrysler was undertaken with a view to capitalising on core competencies. Both companies, as car producers, sought to keep their core business in the automobile sector. Other expressed reasons involved increasing market power and sharing infrastructure, identified in Figure 8.8 as 'real term' issues. Figure 8.10 outlines some of the product range synergies stated by the participants as relevant to this particular merger.

DaimlerChrysler AG – range of products

	Small class	Medium class	Upper class	Luxury class	Pickup	Minivan	Off-road
High price	A-class ●	C-class ●	E-class ●	S-class ●		Town & Country ●	M-class ● / Grand Cherokee ○
Medium price	Neon ○	Cirrus/ Stratus ○	Intrepid/ Concorde ○	LHS/ 300M ○	Ram ○	Caravan ○	Durango/ Cherokee ○
Low price	Neon ○	Breeze ○			Dakota ○	Voyager ○	Cherokee/ Wrangler ○

● Daimler product range
○ Chrysler product range

Figure 8.10 **Product range synergies in the Daimler and Chrysler merger**

As can be seen in Figure 8.10, except in the 'off-road' segment there were no product overlaps – rather the respective product portfolios complemented one another. This was also the case in terms of their geographical markets, with Chrysler a strong player in the NAFTA region, while Daimler-Benz was a leading company in Europe. DaimlerChrysler AG subsequently moved to acquire a third leg in the Asian market to consolidate its position in all regions of the triad.

Further synergies can be found in fields such as procurement, common use of parts and sales. Synergies totalling DM 2.5 billion were stated as having already been obtained in those fields within one year of the merger. For the future, more synergies have been targeted in sales, production, research and development and sales. For example, Chrysler brands are expected to gain entry into the European market by using the market knowledge acquired by the established Daimler sales network and some of its distribution outlets. Pilot plants in South America are being used as test beds for combining production of Daimler and Chrysler vehicles with standardised parts being used across the different models wherever possible. Common efforts in R & D have also been undertaken in the field of future drive concepts. Further synergies of DM 6.4 billion were expected by 2001. When these projected savings were compared with the actual merger costs of DM 550 million, then the advantages became obvious.

A number of critical success factors were highlighted by the chairman, Mr Barnevik.

- In the pre-merger phase
  - *Act quickly and keep it secret.* The company tried to limit the number of people involved and to act rapidly to achieve surprise and momentum. It is better to concentrate on essentials rather than be distracted by less important details.

- *Approach M & A as a project*. The whole merger and subsequent integration should be done in the form of a series of mini-projects. Therefore, strong project managers are necessary.
- *Negotiation team to be kept as small as possible*. This helps to keep the negotiations secret and to make decisions more quickly.

■ In the post-merger phase

- *Find key people*. They are important for accelerating projects, integrating people and cultures.
- *Walk to talk*. Top management must engage directly with people to make sure they participate in the overall vision.
- *Maintain centralised control*. The use of a centralised control system made information available faster and facilitated quick decisions.

The Daimler–Chrysler merger incorporated many of these factors. The merger was undertaken in a record time, with only six months elapsing between the announcement and the actual flotation of Daimler–Chrysler shares. The whole preparation took place without any leaks from the negotiation team, with the global auto industry caught unawares by the announcement of this transatlantic alliance. Key people were found and more than 90 projects for integration defined.

Daimler–Chrysler installed special post-merger integration (PMI) teams and a PMI network by which all participants had 24-hour worldwide access to an information base, obtaining details on the various integration projects. As well as the PMI teams, issue resolution teams (IRT) were installed. Their objectives included supervising and coordinating the PMI projects. Speed, accuracy, reliable communication, transparency and clear goals were the objectives of these developments. The achievement of synergy potential was monitored all the time. Accordingly the PMI teams encouraged the sharing of existing resources and, if necessary, the raising of new resource allocations. Synergies to the value of more than DM 2.5bn were stated as being achieved overall in the first year of operation.

Daimler–Chrysler also introduced a new Integrated Controlling System (ICS) using common concepts and data to help compare the different businesses. This approach helped to eliminate contradictory rules as regards definition and to foster rationalisation and integration. A vital element for a successful cross-border integration, and arguably the most difficult, is the creation of one common culture and corporate identity, especially where the new business involves different national as well as corporate cultures. Chrysler perceived German companies as being too comfortable, less innovative and less project-orientated than US companies. On the other hand, Daimler-Benz thought its American partner was too capitalistic and insensitive towards the German social security system.

In an attempt to combine these different cultures and mentalities, a conscious effort was made to create a culture of discussion. A senior management figure was appointed to communicate the goals company-wide, to field e-mails and to respond to the enquiries of worried employees. Interchange programmes took place to make intercultural understanding easier, involving brief information visits, shared projects, seminars or even longer stays abroad. Daimler–Chrysler sought to clarify from the outset that this was a genuine merger of 'equals'. It kept two bases: one in

Auburn Hills, USA, and one in Stuttgart, Germany, and the respective CEOs, Robert Eaton and Jurgen Schrempp, led the company together. Both companies were equally represented at board level with equal rights and so avoided the victor/vanquished syndrome.

Of course, there were some negative aspects. Several high-profile former Chrysler executives left the new company. With those departures went valuable skills and personal knowledge. Nevertheless, many of the critical factors for a successful merger would seem to have been applied.

Sources: Various, including Guenther (2000).

Questions

1 What lessons might be learned about M & A from Daimler-Benz's first round of acquisitions?

2 Why does this study suggest that the merger with Chrysler appeared to have been a success shortly after its completion?

3 Suggest any pointers towards successful cross-border mergers from this study.

As already noted, a key strategic goal used to support M & A activity is that the combined entity creates positive net value (i.e. creates potential synergies). Of course, the *realisation* of any potential synergies will crucially depend on whether the *post-integration phase* really does permit the transfer of core competencies, from acquirer to target or vice versa. A study by Laurence Capron (1999) has examined this very issue and identified a number of strategic implications. In a survey of 253 companies in the manufacturing sector which merged horizontally between 1988 and 1992 across Europe and North America, some interesting results were obtained, as shown in Figure 8.11.

Figure 8.11(a) would suggest that the *potential* for synergies via M & A activity is considerable, as such integration is commonly followed by a transfer of competencies both to and from the target. For example, as regards 'sales networks', some 43% of respondents recognised that the *acquirer's* sales network was used to a substantial extent to distribute the target's products and 35% of respondents recognised that the target's sales network was used to distribute the acquirer's products.

Figure 8.11(b) is particularly relevant to the post-acquisition phase, with respondents asked to assess the extent to which the acquisition improved the performance of both the target and the acquirer. Four performance measures were used: general performance, cost savings (cost-based synergies), innovation capabilities (revenue-based synergies) and market coverage (revenue-based synergies). Only 49% of the respondents considered that the effect of the M & A activity has been to create positive net value (overall outcome) in terms of combined value though over half indicated a positive combined outcome in terms of specific objectives such as market share (56%), sales revenue (59%) and profitability (53%).

Interestingly, even for these horizontal acquisitions, less than half identified cost-based synergies as being realised in terms of either production costs (46%) or input costs (40%). However, from the perspective of revenue-based synergies, the results were more encouraging, with 64% of respondents acknowledging that acquisitions

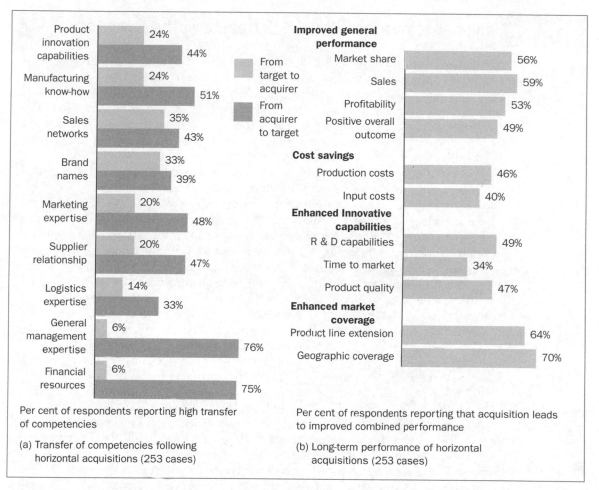

Figure 8.11 Impacts of horizontal acquisitions on target company and acquiring company
Source: Capron (1999). Reprinted with permission

broaden their product line and 70% reporting increased geographic market coverage. In similar vein, some 49% of respondents reported improved R & D capabilities, 47% improved product quality and 34% reduced time to market.

From a strategic perspective there would therefore seem to be a widely recognised potential for achieving synergies involving the transfer of competencies via M & A activity. However, the outcomes would seem to suggest that this potential has often failed to be realised, with net value actually falling and competencies lost. This would seem especially so as regards cost-based synergies, though the evidence is more favourable as regards revenue-based synergies. Particular attention should be paid to the post-merger phase to ensure that the identified potential is translated into reality.

Technological change and strategic choice

Case Study 8.4 below usefully reminds us that strategic choices are never made in a static environment but in dynamic, ever-changing environments. One of the key catalysts for such change is technology itself, which may then force a rapid re-examination of previous strategic directions.

CASE 8.4 How new monster plants will transform the industry

Sixty miles north of New York City, along the Hudson river, a manufacturing revolution is getting into full swing – one that could reshape the entire global semiconductor business. The manufacturing plant in East Fishkill, New York, is one of a new breed of outsized, multi-billion dollar chipmaking facilities. In 2002, the plant, run by International Business Machines, began to churn out silicon chips at a rate nearly three times that of older facilities, a speed that would have been unimaginable a few years ago.

This monster chip fabrication plant, or Fab, could produce more than $8 billion of chips a year, more than several medium-sized producers combined. 'When it's fully equipped, that's a new 5 per cent of global capacity,' says Ray Burgess, head of chip strategy at Motorola, one of IBM's biggest competitors. IBM's efforts to step up production are already contributing to an international realignment. Advanced Micro Devices and Nvidia, two leading US chip companies, recently signed up to have some of their own advanced chips produced at Fishkill. That has left a question hanging over their existing relationships with the world's biggest contract chipmakers, or foundries – Taiwan Semiconductor Manufacturing Corporation (TSMC) and United Microelectronic Corporation (UMC).

The shake-up among the 20-odd companies that dominate the global chip market is starting to gather momentum. Old alliances are changing and many industry executives are starting to talk about an inevitable consolidation that will leave only a handful of groups standing. It is a prospect that could cause international trade tensions to rise, given the strategic importance a number of countries such as South Korea have placed on building their own chipmaking industries.

Behind this upheaval lies a fundamental – and expensive – sea change in technology. It has come at just the moment when chipmakers can least afford it, after one of the most traumatic collapses seen in the chronically cyclical industry's 40-year history. The latest technology advances have come in two areas, Silicon wafers – the discs from which individual chips are cut – are getting bigger. Plants such as Fishkill work with dinner-plate sized wafers, 300mm in diameter. At the same time, individual chip sizes are getting smaller. Some elements on the most advanced chips are now only 90 nanometres across, or one-thousandth of the width of a human hair.

Taken together, these changes make it possible to produce nearly three times as many chips from each wafer. Manufacturers using older, 200mm wafers face unit costs that are about 40 per cent higher. In the past, the big technological leaps forward in chipmaking have all been justified by the industry's explosive growth rate. Revenues have grown by an average of 17 per cent a year since silicon chips were invented. But over the next five years the compound annual growth may be just 8 to 10 per cent, says the Semiconductor Industry Association, making it harder for 300mm Fab builders to recover their mushrooming capital investments.

'A large, integrated Fab costs $3 billion or more – easily double what it cost before,' says Bill Aylesworth, chief financial officer of Texas Instruments, the second biggest US producer. Texas Instruments is among the elite few that are building their own 300mm production facilities. Yet even these few may not all make it. 'Within the next few years, there will only be five independent chipmakers plus some large foundries with their own 300mm Fabs,' says Ulrich Schumacher, head of Infineon Systems, the second largest European chipmaker. Infineon also plans to stay in the game. But unless these new monster production facilities are operated at almost 90 per cent capacity, they will start to lose money at an alarming rate. For now, only Intel and Samsung have annual sales of more than $8 billion, suggesting that most will find it hard to fill their facilities.

The huge cost of building and equipping a 300mm facility is only part of the problem. Chipmaking remains as much an art as a science. The underlying technologies, which involve hundreds of chemical processes, take years to master. Indeed, skill at handling the manufacturing process is what gives the most successful chip companies their edge. Intel may be known to the world as the leading maker of PC microprocessors but that is a by-product of its real core competence; its ability to get very high yields from its manufacturing process. By producing more usable chips from each wafer and reducing waste, it has been able to lower its unit costs and outstrip rivals.

In the late 1990s, AMD, Intel's chief rival, was plagued by yield problems resulting in higher costs and lost business opportunities. 'Unless you have strong research and development, you won't be able just to jump into the next phase of advanced chipmaking; you need to have the technological base,' says Mr Schumacher.

IBM and Intel are considered the leaders in developing the complex and sometimes arcane manufacturing technologies that drive the global industry. While others had identified the potential advantages of using copper to replace aluminium in chips, it was IBM that first mastered the manufacturing process. Intel, meanwhile, continues to push the limits of chip manufacturing, recently demonstrating the world's smallest transistors, the basic component of all chips. It is also leading development efforts in using high-powered X-rays to create future generations of semiconductors.

This increasingly challenging production environment has left chipmakers with difficult choices. They can decide to forge ahead with their own 300mm Fabs but face considerable business and technological risks. They can form partnerships with others but risk the high failure rate that comes with joint ventures, particularly those done across national borders. Or they can contract out some or all of their manufacturing but risk being unable to secure enough production capacity during boom times when demand is high.

But the big guns of the industry realise they must own their own 300mm facilities. The companies so far to move in this direction include Intel, IBM and Texas Instruments in the US, Samsung in South Korea, TSMC and UMC in Taiwan, Infineon in Europe and Toshiba in Japan.

However, this strategy is not for the faint-hearted, particularly given the sector's terrible record in forecasting demand. At the end of 2000, the Semiconductor Industry Association, the leading trade group, predicted that global demand in 2001 would grow by 17 per cent to $240 billion. Instead the market plunged by nearly a third, to $140 billion. That $100 billion gap reflected the collapse in computer, communications and consumer electronics markets.

Source: Tom Foremski, Simon London and Richard Waters, *Financial Times*, 11 June 2003.

Questions

1 How do the international strategic approaches in either Figure 8.6 or Figure 8.7 relate to this case study?

2 In what ways is technological change in the semiconductor industry influencing new strategic directions?

Strategic alliances

We have already visited the issue of joint ventures and strategic alliances (Chapter 2). Here we are mainly concerned with the strategic choice between using M & A and forming such an alliance. Jeffrey Reuer (1999) suggests that the 'Four Is' of collaboration will crucially determine whether to enter into an alliance rather than acquire (Figure 8.12), namely infeasibility, information asymmetry, investment in options and indigestibility.

- *Infeasibility*. Alliances are more likely when acquisitions contain elements of infeasibility. For example, competition legislation may effectively prevent large corporate acquisitions or may impose conditions deemed unacceptable if they are to go ahead. Restrictions on inward fdi to some industrial/service sectors or countries may have the same effect.
- *Information asymmetry*. Alliances are more likely the greater the degree of (actual or perceived) information asymmetry. In other words, companies may be more likely to resort to alliances rather than acquisitions when one company knows more than some other company. Even after due diligence, the acquiring company may have reservations as to the true value of the assets to be acquired. In a large-scale analysis of US companies by Reuer and Koza (2000), the announcements of joint ventures and alliances led to higher rises in the stock market prices of the affected companies the greater the degree of information asymmetry perceived as existing between the proposed allies.

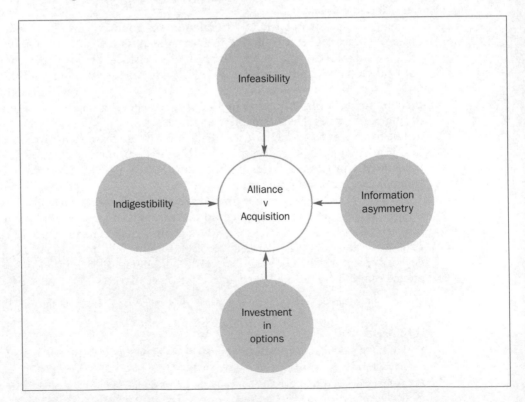

Figure 8.12 **The four 'Is' of collaboration**

- *Investment in options*. Alliances are more likely the greater the degree of uncertainty as to the future prospects of the combined activity. For example, alliances form a higher proportion of total linkages between companies in uncertain industrial sectors such as biotechnology. An alliance can develop into greater or lesser linkage between two or more companies depending on the degree of success actually achieved by the initial joint activity. This 'staged engagement' can be expressed in terms of *call options*: these confer the right, but not the obligation, for an allied party to expand its equity stake at a pre-specified price at some future date. Put another way, alliances are more likely the greater the perceived need to invest in call options rather than in an immediate equity stake.

- *Indigestibility*. Alliances are more likely the greater the perceived indigestibility of the potential target for acquisition. (This term arises from the need of an acquiring company to 'digest' the assets of the acquired company.) Such 'indigestibility' raises the anticipated transactions costs of acquisition (i.e. the post-acquisition integration costs). In such circumstances alliances will prove relatively attractive, giving the respective allies greater freedom to link *selected* assets only. As Reuer (1999) points out, Nestlé established a joint venture for breakfast cereals with General Mills in Europe, but the parties made no attempt to link any of their other businesses. The same happened with Nestlé allying its coffee and tea operations with Coca-Cola to make use of the latter's global distribution system.

Knowledge management

Before addressing this issue it will be helpful to begin with a definition of 'knowledge' itself. Knowledge is certainly not data, which are objective facts available to users without judgement. Nor is knowledge the same as information, which is merely data which have been categorised, analysed and summarised in order to give the data a context, i.e. a relevance and purpose. The following definition does, however, tell us something about what knowledge actually is.

> Information therefore is data endowed with relevance and purpose. Information develops into knowledge when it is used to make comparison, assess consequences, establish connections, and engage in a dialogue. Knowledge can, therefore, be seen as information that comes laden with experience, judgement, intuition and values. (Empson 1999)

Definitions such as this would question whether many IT-based 'knowledge management systems' are anything more than sophisticated information filing and disseminating systems. Figure 8.13 would, in this view, provide a more relevant breakdown of the key ingredients of a knowledge management system.

It may be useful to first consider the four knowledge 'labels' used in Figure 8.13:

- *explicit knowledge*: codified knowledge available in books, reports, online, etc.;
- *tacit knowledge*: knowledge embodied in human experience and practice;
- *individual knowledge*: the source of much tacit and explicit knowledge;
- *collective knowledge*: the outcome of corporate structures and processes for converting tacit and individual knowledge into explicit knowledge available for corporate use in process or product innovation.

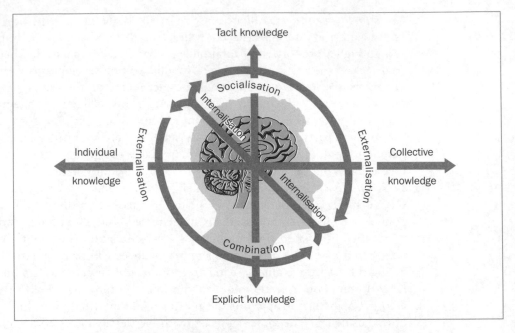

Figure 8.13 The knowledge-creating spiral

Source: Adapted from *The Knowledge Creating Company: How Japanese Companies Create the Dynamics of Innovation* by Ikujiro Nonaka and Hirotaka Takeuchi, © 1995 by Oxford University Press, Inc. Used by permission of Oxford University Press, Inc.

Nonaka and Takeuchi (1995) identify four interrelated processes *(see* Figure 8.13) by which knowledge flows around the organisation and is converted into different forms:

- *socialisation*: the process of communicating the tacit knowledge that resides within the individual human resource base of companies throughout the organisation;
- *externalisation*: the process of converting tacit knowledge into an explicit codified form accessible to others in the organisation both individually and collectively;
- *combination*: the process of analysing, classifying and integrating the explicit knowledge within the organisation into forms which can more readily be used in pursuing that organisation's objectives. Arguably these more usable 'forms' themselves constitute new explicit knowledge;
- *internalisation*: the process by which individuals absorb explicit knowledge so that it becomes a foundation from which new forms of tacit and explicit knowledge may subsequently emerge.

Nonaka and Takeuchi suggest five key mechanisms by which knowledge creation (seen from this perspective) can be encouraged.

1 *Intention*. Senior management must be committed to accumulating, exploiting and renewing the knowledge base within their organisations and to creating management systems compatible with this intention.
2 *Autonomy*. Individuals are the major source of new knowledge and they must be given organisational support to explore and develop new ideas.
3 *Creative chaos*. An internal 'culture' must be established which is willing to use new knowledge to challenge existing orthodoxies.

4 *Redundancy*. Knowledge should not be allowed to become 'redundant' via it being rationed to selected individuals only within the organisation. Instead knowledge exchange must be encouraged and supported throughout the organisation.

5 *Requisite variety*. The internal diversity within the organisation must at least match that of the external environment within which it operates.

Husenan and Goodman (1999) report that 78% of the major US companies surveyed claim to be 'moving towards becoming knowledge-based'. However, the authors themselves concluded that most of these companies are confusing 'information management' with 'knowledge management' and in their words, are 'nowhere near' devising a strategic framework to promote the agenda illustrated in Figure 8.13. A strategic imperative would seem to be to make as many as possible of the five conditions outlined above an integral part of the organisation's knowledge management system.

Of course, there are many other discrete areas of business activity in which strategic issues are playing an increasingly important part in a globalised economy. Some of these are touched on elsewhere in this book. Here we move on to consider some of the techniques which have been adopted by international businesses in an attempt to evaluate the external environment in which they operate and to devise specific strategies and counter-strategies to further their own objectives vis-à-vis those of their rivals.

Techniques for strategic analysis

Again, we must be selective. We consider in detail some of the more widely-used techniques for strategic analysis.

■ Game-based techniques

This approach has been widely used in highly-concentrated industries and markets dominated by a few large firms. The idea is to estimate for each proposed strategy the firm might adopt, the likely counter-strategies of the rival (or rivals). A variety of assumptions can be made as to how a firm views the likely counter-strategies to be adopted by the rival.

Decision rules

These assumptions are built into 'decision rules', two of which are widely adopted:

■ *maxi-min decision rule* – assumes that the rival (Firm B) reacts in the worst (for Firm A) way possible for each A strategy. Firm A then selects the best (maxi) of these worst (mini) possible outcomes.

■ *mini-max decision rule* – assumes that the rival (Firm B) reacts in the best (for Firm A) way possible for each A strategy. Firm A then selects the worst (mini) of these best (maxi) possible outcomes.

Of course, many other decision rules can be devised for such games. Box 8.2 shows an example of a market share game using the maxi-min decision rule.

Box 8.2 Two-firm zero-sum game

We might usefully illustrate the principles involved in game theory by a simple two-firm (duopoly) game, involving market share. By its very nature, a market share game must be 'zero sum', in that any gain by one player must be offset exactly by the loss of the other(s).

Suppose Firm A is considering two possible strategies to raise its market share, either a 20% price cut or a 10% increase in advertising expenditure (note that here each strategy involves only a single-policy variable). Whatever initial strategy Firm A adopts, it anticipates that its rival, Firm B, will react by using either a price cut or extra advertising to defend its market share. Firm A now evaluates the market share that it can expect for each initial strategy and each possible counter-strategy by Firm B. The outcomes expected by A are summarised in the pay-off matrix of Table 8.2.

Table 8.2 Firm A's pay-off matrix: market share game (%)

		Firm B's strategies	
		Price cut	Extra advertising
Firm A's strategies	Price cut	60*[†]	70[†]
	Extra advertising	50*	55

* 'Worst' outcome for A of each A strategy.
† 'Worst' outcome for B of each B strategy.

If A cuts price, and B responds with a price cut, A receives 60% of the market. However, if B responds with extra advertising, A receives 70% of the market. The 'worst' outcome for A (60% of the market) will occur if B responds with a price cut. If A adopts the strategy of extra advertising, then the 'worst' outcome for A (50% of the market) will again occur if B responds with a price cut rather than extra advertising (55% of the market).

If A expects B to play the game astutely, i.e. choose the counter-strategy best for itself (worst for A), then A will choose the price-cut strategy, as this gives it 60% of the market rather than 50%. If A plays the game in this way, selecting the best of the worst possible outcomes for each initial strategy, it is said to be adopting a 'maxi-min' decision rule or approach to the game.

If B adopts the same maxi-min approach as A, and has made the same evaluation of outcomes as A, it also will adopt a price-cut strategy. For instance, if B adopts a price-cut strategy, its 'worst' outcome will occur if A responds with a price cut; B then gets 40% of the market (100% minus 60%) rather than 50% as would be the case if A responds with extra advertising. If B adopts extra advertising, its 'worst' outcome will again occur if A responds with a price cut; B then receives 30% (100% minus 70%) instead of 45% (100% minus 55%) if A responds with extra advertising. The best of the 'worst possible' outcomes for B occurs if B adopts a price cut, which gives it 40% of the market rather than 30%.

In this particular game we have a stable equilibrium (a 'Nash' equilibrium – *see below*), without any resort to collusion. Both firms initially cut price, then accept the respective market shares which fulfil their maxi-min targets 60% to A, 40% to B. There could then follow the price stability which has been seen to be a feature of some oligopoly situations. In some games the optimal strategy for each firm may not even have been an initial price cut, but rather non-price competition (such as advertising). Game theory can predict both price stability and extensive non-price competition.

Box 8.2	Continued

The problem with game theory is that it can equally predict unstable solutions, with extensive price as well as non-price competition. An unstable solution might follow if each firm, faced with the pay-off matrix of Table 8.2 adopts entirely different strategies. Firm B might not use the maxi-min approach of A, but take more risk. Instead of the price cut it might adopt the 'extra advertising' strategy, hoping to induce an advertising response from firm A and gain 45% of the market, but risk getting only 30% if A responds with a price cut. Suppose this is what happens. Firm A now receives 70% of the market, but B only receives 30%, which is below its initial expectation of 45%. This may provoke B into alternative strategy formulation, setting off a further chain reaction. The game may then fail to settle down quickly, if at all, to a stable solution, i.e. one in which each firm receives a market share which meets its overall expectation. An unstable solution might also follow if each firm evaluates the pay-off matrix differently from the other. Even if they then adopt the same approach to the game, one firm at least will be 'disappointed', possibly provoking action and counteraction.

A number of other ideas are widely presented in game theory approaches.

- *Dominant strategy*. In this approach the firm seeks to do the best it can (in terms of the objectives set) irrespective of the possible actions/reactions of any rival(s).
- *Nash equilibrium*. This occurs when each firm is doing the best that it can in terms of its own objective(s), given the strategies chosen by the other firms in the market.
- *Prisoner's dilemma*. This is an outcome where the equilibrium for the game involves both firms doing worse than they would have done had they colluded, and is sometimes called a 'cartel game' because the obvious implication is that the firms would be better off by colluding.

There are different types of game to which these ideas might be applied.

One-shot game

The suggestion here is that the decision to be made by each firm is 'once for all'. We can illustrate this type of game using Table 8.3, which is a pay-off matrix that expresses the net gains for each of two firms in terms of daily profit, the first value being that for Firm A and the second value that for Firm B. The single policy variable shown here is output level, which can be set high or low, with the pay-off dependent on the rival's reaction. Clearly this is a non-zero sum game since the total daily profit for each combination of policies varies rather than remains constant (for example, total profit is £3,000 in the bottom right quadrant but £6,000 elsewhere).

Table 8.3 Pay-off matrix (daily profits)

		Firm B	
		Low output	High output
Firm A	Low output	£3,000; £3,000	£2,000; £4,000
	High output	£4,000; £2,000	£1,500; £1,500

Suppose, initially, that we treat this situation as a one-shot game.

- 'High output' would be the dominant strategy for each firm, giving both Firm A and Firm B £4,000 in daily profit should the other firm select 'low output'. However, if both firms follow this dominant strategy and select 'high output', they each receive only £1,500 daily profit.
- If each firm follows a maxi-min decision rule, then Firm A selects 'low output' as the best of the worst possible outcomes (£2,000 > £1,500), as does Firm B (£2,000 > £1,500). The combination (low output, low output) will then be a Nash equilibrium, with each firm satisfied that it is doing the best that it can in terms of its own objective, given the strategy chosen by the other firm (each actually receives £3,000).
- If each firm follows a mini-max decision rule, you should be able to show that both Firm A and Firm B will still select 'low output' as the worst of the best possible outcomes (£3,000 < £4,000 for each firm). The combination (low output/low output) remains a Nash equilibrium.

Even if one firm follows a maxi-min and the other a mini-max decision rule, the combination (low output/low output) will remain a Nash equilibrium in this particular game. We could reasonably describe this output combination (low/low) as a stable, Nash-type equilibrium.

Repeated game

However, should we view the pay-off matrix in Table 8.3 as part of a repeated game, then the situation so far described might be subject to considerable change. We might expect the respective firms to alter the strategies they pursue and the game to have a different outcome.

Suppose the firms initially establish the low output/low output 'solution' to the game, whether as the result of a 'Nash equilibrium' or by some form of agreement between the firms. Unlike the one-shot game, a firm in a repeated game can modify its strategy from one period to the next, and can also respond to any changes in strategy by the other firm.

- *Cheating.* If Table 8.3 is now viewed as the pay-off matrix for a repeated game, there would seem to be a possible incentive for either firm to depart from its initial 'low output' policy in the next period. Had the initial 'low output' policy been mutually agreed by the two firms in an attempt to avoid the mutually damaging high output/high output combination should each firm have followed its 'dominant strategy', we might regard such a departure as *cheating* on an agreement. By unexpectedly switching to high output, either firm could benefit by raising daily profit (from £3,000 to £4,000), though the loss of profit (from £3,000 to £2,000) by the other firm might provoke an eventual retaliation in some future time period, resulting in the mutually damaging high output/high output combination.
- *Tit-for-tat strategy.* Whether or not any 'cheating' is likely to benefit a firm will depend on a number of factors, not least the rapidity with which any rival responds to a breach of the agreement: the more rapid the response of the rival, the smaller any net benefits from cheating will be. Suppose, in our example, it takes the other firm five days to respond with higher output: then on each of these

days the cheating firm gains a first-mover advantage (*see also* p. 268) of an extra £1,000 in profit from breaching the agreement as compared with upholding the agreement. If the response of the rival were to be more rapid, say, in three days, then only £3,000 rather than £5,000 benefit would accrue as a first-mover advantage. Of course, once the rival has responded, both firms are damaged in Table 8.3 compared with the pre-cheating situation, losing £1,500 profit per day from the high output/high output combination. This may, of course, induce both firms to restore the initial agreement.

If it becomes known that rivals are likely to respond rapidly to any cheating on agreements (or even departures from Nash-type equilibriums) by adopting *tit-for-tat* strategies, then this may itself deter attempts by either firm to cheat. Provided that each firm believes the rival is sufficiently well informed to be aware of any change in its strategy, it will anticipate a tit-for-tat response that will ensure that any benefits from cheating are of shorter duration. When factored into the decision-making process, the anticipation of a lower profit stream may deter any attempt by either firm to cheat.

Sequential games

In the games considered so far, each firm has been able to make decisions at the same time (i.e. simultaneously). However, in a sequential game the moves and counter-moves take place in a defined order: one firm makes a move and only then does the rival decide how to react to that move. Table 8.4 is a pay-off matrix showing net gains as profit per period for each of two firms. The individual pay-offs depend on the price (low or high) selected by one firm and the price response of the rival, in this non-zero sum game.

The dominant strategy for both firm A and firm B is to set a low price (£3,000 profit), but if they both follow this strategy the outcome is mutually damaging (£1,000 profit each). You should be able to see that a maxi-min decision rule followed by each firm would lead to a low price/low price outcome in which the expectations of each firm are fulfilled given that they have adopted this decision rule.

Table 8.4 **Pay-off matrix (profit per period)**

		Firm B	
		Low price	High price
Firm A	Low price	£1,000; £1,000	£3,000; £2,000
	High price	£2,000; £3,000	£500; £500

pause for thought 3   What would the outcome have been had each firm adopted a mini-max decision rule?

First-mover advantages

If decisions can only be taken in sequence, an important issue is whether the firm making the first move can secure any advantage!

■ *Suppose firm A is in a position to move first.* It can choose 'low price', forcing firm B to choose between 'low price' (£1,000) and 'high price' (£2,000). Firm A might now anticipate that firm B will attempt to maximise its own return given the constrained situation (via A's first move) in which B finds itself. In this case firm B selects 'high price', and firm A receives £3,000 profit per period. The first move by A has given a net profit advantage to A of £2,000 (£3,000–£1,000) as compared to the previous low price/low price outcome.

■ *Suppose firm B is in a position to move first.* It can now choose 'low price' in the expectation that firm A will respond with 'high price' (£2,000 > £1,000) as firm A now seeks to maximise its own return given the constrained situation (via B's first move) in which it finds itself. In this case, firm B receives a pay-off of £3,000 profit per period and a net profit advantage of £2,000 via the first move.

Clearly this game does contain first-mover advantages, which lie in first anticipating the likely responses of the rival and then channelling those responses in a particular direction as a result of making the first move.

Case Study 8.5 indicates the use of game theory in designing the US airwaves auction. These ideas were instrumental in encouraging both the UK and German governments to use auctions in the allocation of broadband licences in 2000.

CASE 8.5 Game theory in action: designing the US airwaves auction

In 1993 the US Congress decided to auction off licences to use the electromagnetic spectrum for personal communication services. This involved selling off thousands of licences with different geographic coverage and at different spectrum locations.

Auctioning off the licences was a break with the tradition of direct licence allocation to those with a bigger 'need'. It required the Federal Communications Commission (FCC) to set up a mechanism capable of efficiently allocating licences to the bidder most valuing it. Game theory (and game theorists) played an important role in both the design of the actual auction mechanism used and in advising bidders on optimal bidding strategies.

Auctions are, a priori, an ideal method for allocating goods to those who place a higher value on them, as these people are likely to make the highest bid. However, research by game theorists has shown that the design of the auction matters, both for the efficiency of the allocation – does the good go to the person who values it most? – and the revenues earned for the seller. In this particular instance, Congress had asked the FCC to ensure that the spectrum was used in an efficient and intensive way, rather than simply to maximise auction income for the Federal government.

According to an account in the *Journal of Economics Perspectives*, by two of the economists involved in the design (Preston McAfee of Texas A & M and John McMillan of University of California, San Diego), the designers considered the existence of complementarities between the licences as the most important threat to efficiency in this particular context.

For the bidder, the value of each individual licence depends to a large extent on whether another licence has been obtained so that several licences can be grouped together to form a coherent region. The auction design needed to allow for the coherent aggregation of licences, so that a bidder would not find himself bidding for a licence as a part of a whole to discover that he is in fact awarded an incoherent entity of much smaller value to him or her.

Following the advice of several economic theorists employed by the bidders, including Stanford economists Paul Milgrom and Robert Wilson, plus McAfee and McMillan, the FCC opted for a novel design: a simultaneous ascending auction, in which the bidding for all the licences remained open as long as bidding in any of the licences remained active. The aggregation of licences was facilitated by the fact that bidding and the observation of the bids, were simultaneous.

For all its advantages, the simultaneous ascending auctions involved an important risk of implicit collusion between rival bidders. To avoid this problem, the identity of the bidder would remain hidden until the auction concluded. But it was still possible for a bidder to find ways to signal their intention in order to ensure allocation of the preferred licence at a low cost. In fact, as subsequent portions of the spectrum were auctioned off, complaints about this type of behaviour increased. For example, Mercury PCS, a US telecom operator, was accused of highlighting its interest in winning a specific licence by ending the bid amount in January 1997 with the postal codes of the particular city in which it was interested.

On the bidders side, the consultants to the bidders have not made public their recommendations. We can only speculate that game theory was used by bidders both to enhance the rationality of their bidding and to understand and influence the bidding behaviour of the rival bidders.

First, game theory could introduce a higher degree of rationality in the bidding process by helping to design optimal bidding strategies. For example, game theorists have long understood that in auction settings bidding as much as one would be actually willing to pay for a good could lead to what is known as the winner's curse: imagine that a licence will be in fact equally valuable to any firm, but that each firm has a different opinion about how valuable it is likely to be. Clearly the winning bid is most likely to be from the most optimistic firm. But the most optimistic firm's estimate of the value of the audio waves will be biased upwards – it will be too high. In fact, if the highest bidder wins without taking into account this effect, he will overpay, and winning will be a curse. Developing an algorithm for bidding that takes into account this curse requires the use of game theory.

Game theory could also be used by a bidder to understand the incentives of rival bidders and formulate strategies capable of altering their behaviour. In particular, if one could credibly commit to winning a licence, one could win the licence at zero cost, as the incentives for the rivals to bid when they know they are not going to win the licence, are likely to be low. An actual example of this could be the allocation in the April 1997 sale of wireless data frequencies, of the licences for several cities like Minneapolis, for $1.

To sum up, by identifying the individual incentives of each player in each auction design, game theory helped the designers and consultants in understanding the impact of the rules of the game on the behaviour of the actors. As McAfee and McMillan put it in their account: 'The role of theory is to show how people behave in various circumstances, and to identify the trade-offs involved in altering those circumstances.'

Source: Garicano (1999).

Garicano (1999) counsels against using game theory to 'solve' the game in terms of some type of equilibrium solution with a precise numerical answer. His arguments are that the possible solutions to the games are often too sensitive to the assumptions the modeller makes. These assumptions might involve:

■ the timing of the moves;
■ the information available to the players;
■ the rationality of the decisions taken;
■ the consequences of playing the game under changing 'decision rules'.

The major benefit of game theory analysis is arguably to focus attention on competitor behaviour and consequent implications for policy. For example, if British Airways understands that price warfare on Atlantic routes with Virgin is a 'prisoners dilemma' outcome, with both parties doing worse than need be the case, then remedial action can be sought. This may involve changing the 'rules of the game' (e.g. some kind of tacit collusion) in order to remove the incentives which induced both British Airways and Virgin to engage in such price warfare. It is guidance as to an appropriate type of strategic response that is arguably more important than any hypothetical (and unrealistic) numerical solution.

■ Strategic scenario analysis

Scenario analysis is another approach that is widely used to evaluate possible future outcomes of different courses of action (e.g. high, medium, low profitability scenarios). In more sophisticated treatments probabilities may be assigned to each outcome and expected values calculated. Arguably scenario analysis takes a broader perspective in terms of strategic direction than does game theory, the latter confining itself to competitor actions/reactions. Put another way, scenario analysis is more useful in dealing with broad based structural uncertainties, i.e. those stemming from changes in macroeconomic or industry-wide factors, whereas game theory is more useful in dealing with the strategic uncertainties related to rival reactions.

A scenario can be defined as an internally consistent view of the future, which often reflects a situation in which a large number of variables are seen as moving in a particular direction. (This is quite unlike 'sensitivity analysis', which often involves allowing a single variable to change and then assessing the impact of this single variable change on the whole system.) Gertner and Knez (2000) argue that the combination of scenario analysis with game theoretic approaches can create a still more effective technique for modelling the business environment. They term this technique 'strategic scenario analysis' and argue that it can help capture both structural and strategic uncertainties as a guide to policy formation. Case Study 8.6 outlines this approach in the context of new product development.

CASE 8.6   Strategic scenario analysis: AMD versus Intel

In 1997 Advanced Micro Devices (AMD) introduced its K6 microprocessor. Its aim was to capture leadership of the market for fast microprocessors, a position held at the time by Intel. The primary risk to AMD was that Intel would quickly introduce a comparable or superior chip and, with its brand equity, drive AMD out of the high-end chip segment.

The emerging cheap PC market dampened this risk for AMD, and is the focus of this case study. While the K6 chip was aimed at the high-end market, alternative versions (made in the same plant) could be sold in the low-end market. However, this low-end 'hedge' depended on Intel staying out of the low-end segment. Our strategic scenario analysis will focus on the low-end PC market and on the uncertainty surrounding Intel's decision as to whether or not to enter the low-end segment.

The key to strategic reasoning in general, and the application of strategic scenario analysis in particular, is for the decision-maker to take the perspective of other players in an effort to predict how they will behave. In this case, decision-makers at AMD needed to take Intel's perspective into account. So in what follows we develop a simple scenario game which seeks to capture the trade offs Intel had to make when deciding whether to enter the low-end segment. The results of that analysis in turn provide a foundation for the judgements AMD had to make about the likelihood of significant low-end market share.

In our game, Intel has to decide whether to bide its time as regards the low-end segment (i.e. 'wait'), with the option of introducing its low price Celeron chip at some later time, or to bring the Celeron chip into play without delay (i.e. 'introduce'). Besides Intel, there are two other sets of players: the competition (i.e. other chip makers) – AMD and National Semiconductor (NS), which will surely introduce low-end chips immediately; and the major PC manufacturers who purchase the chips – NEC, Compaq, IBM, Toshiba, DEC and others.

Intel faces many critical uncertainties in making its 'wait/introduce' decision. The most important are: (i) the demand for cheap PCs (and therefore the derived demand for low-end chips); (ii) the quality of its competitors' low-end chips; (iii) whether Intel's brand equity is strong enough to overcome its second-mover disadvantage if it waits.

Intel's uncertainties are linked to those faced by the PC manufacturers and the rival chip makers. The PC manufacturers will have to decide whether to buy the AMD/NS chips or Intel's. AMD and NS face capacity and pricing decisions that will depend on whether Intel has entered the low-end market.

For simplicity we focus on a single structural uncertainty – cheap PC demand – and a single strategic uncertainty – PC manufacturers' purchase decisions. The next step in any scenario analysis is to determine the minimum number of states that each scenario variable can assume. The idea is to choose as many states (scenarios) as will lead to qualitatively different outcomes. In many situations two or three states will suffice; 'average', 'more successful than expected', and 'failure' may capture the essence of the uncertainty.

So, while there is a continuum of alternative demand outcomes for cheap PCs, here we assume there are only two: 'high' or 'low'. Similarly, for the PC makers we assume a 40/60 versus a 60/40 split, where Intel retains either 40% or 60% of the market respectively. Note that the PC manufacturers have mixed motives in their

▶

purchase decisions. The demand for their product is likely to be higher if they use an Intel chip, but the price of competitors' chips is likely to be lower. The decision will come down to the price/performance trade-offs and the strength of Intel's brand equity.

The simplified description of the game generates eight initial scenarios, four under each of the two possible Intel actions – 'introduce' or 'wait' (Figure 8.14). The next step is to eliminate scenarios that are either implausible or internally inconsistent.

Beginning with those that arise under the Intel 'introduce' decision, scenarios 1 and 3 are relatively implausible. If Intel enters with a low-end chip that is comparable to the competition's low-end chip, Intel should be able to capture at least 60% of the market, whether demand is high or low. Hence, we can regard the 40/60 (Intel/other chip makers) scenarios 1 and 3 as implausible and we are left with two scenarios under 'introduce', whereby Intel gets 60% of either a large or small market for cheap PCs.

Under the 'wait' decision, all four scenarios are plausible, depending on how long Intel actually waits before introducing its low-end chip after observing the

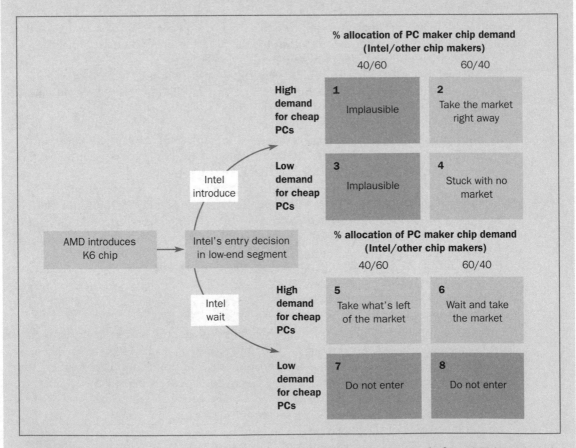

Figure 8.14 **Strategic scenario analysis of the low-end PC market by Intel after AMD introduced its K6 chip, % allocations (Intel/other chip makers)**

Source: Gertner and Knez (2000). Reprinted with permission level of demand for cheap PCs. However, it will not be optimal for Intel to introduce its low-end chips if demand for cheap PCs turns out to be low. Hence scenarios 7 and 8 are not internally consistent from a game theoretical perspective. This leaves us with two scenarios to consider under 'wait', whereby Intel gets either 40% or 60% of the low-end PC market under conditions of high demand.

Clearly this approach has eliminated scenarios 1, 3, 7 and 8 leaving scenarios 2, 4, 5 and 6 still in play.

From this simple scenario analysis we see that Intel's downside risk from an 'introduce' strategy is simply that the market for cheap PCs does not materialise – the 'stuck with no market' scenario. Of course, the upside is that the market does materialise – the 'take the market right away' scenario. If Intel follows the 'wait' strategy, the risk is that demand will be high and the PC manufacturers will commit to buying from the competition, which will give Intel a second-mover disadvantage – the 'take what's left' scenario. Alternatively, many PC manufacturers may switch to Intel as soon as it enters because of its brand equity – the 'wait and take the market' scenario.

As in most entry decisions, the benefit of waiting is the option value of observing whether demand is high or low before committing assets to enter. The value of this option depends on the degree of second-mover disadvantage. In Intel's case, that disadvantage is relatively low. It knows it will be able to capture significant market share with its brand equity (provided it has a price competitive chip). The question is to what extent profits will be dissipated through price competition.

The next step is to take the model beyond its role of explaining the strategic structure of the competitive environment and to use it to provide insights into the decision itself. The way to do this is to analyse each scenario in detail and determine pay-offs for each player. This can then be used to predict competitors' behaviour and to determine which course of action is most profitable.

In 1997 Intel in fact decided not to introduce a low-end chip for the emerging cheap PC market. Subsequently, the demand for cheap PCs grew rapidly. Intel was forced to introduce an underperforming chip in early 1998, leaving 80% of the low-end chip market to its competitors (mostly AMD). Andy Grove, the company's chairman, commented that the cheap PC boom was 'broader and more profound' than he had anticipated the previous autumn.

From AMD's perspective, Intel's delayed entry opened a critical window of opportunity. AMD had time to establish a strong position in the low-end market that could support its attempts to enter the more lucrative high end – Intel's dominant market. Ignoring the obvious criticism of hindsight bias, our simple strategic scenario analysis suggests that AMD had good reason to bet that Intel would delay, increasing AMD's expected pay-offs from introducing the K6 chip.

Source: Adapted from Gertner and Knez (2000).

Questions

1 Comment further on why Case Study 8.6 suggests that 'AMD had good reason to bet that Intel would delay'.

2 What might Intel be expected to learn from this experience? Consider any implications this might have for AMD's future use of strategic scenario analysis.

Useful websites

Now try the self-check questions for this chapter on the website at www.booksites.net/wall. You will also find further resources as well as the following useful weblinks:

Interesting material on global marketing and segmentation strategies can be obtained from:

www.marketing.week.co.uk
www.globalweb.co.uk
www.Virgin.com
Procter & Gamble's website is *www.pg.com*
Coca-Cola's website is *www.cocacola.com*
McDonald's website is *www.mcdonalds.com*

Useful key texts

Daniels, J., Radebaugh, L. and Sullivan, D. (2004) *International Business* (10th edn), Pearson Prentice Hall, especially Chapter 6.
Dicken, P. (2003) *Global Shift: Transforming the World Economy* (4th edn), Paul Chapman Publishing Ltd, especially Chapters 7 and 8.
Hill, C. (2003) *International Business: Competing in the Global Marketplace* (4th edn), McGraw-Hill Irwin, especially Part 5.
Morrison, J. (2002) *The International Business Environment*, Palgrave, especially Chapters 2 and 4.
Rugman, A. and Hodgetts, R. (2003) *International Business* (3rd edn), FT Prentice Hall, especially Chapters 8, 9 and 10.
Tayeb, M. (2000) *International Business: Theories, Policies and Practices*, Financial Times Prentice Hall, especially Chapters 5–8 and 14–15.
Woods, M. (2001) *International Business*, Palgrave, especially Chapter 5.

Other texts and sources

Ansoff, H.I. (1968) *Corporate Strategy*, Penguin.
Buckingham, L. and Atkinson, D. (1999) 'Whisper it … Takeovers Don't Pay', *Guardian*, 30 November.
Capron, L. (1999) 'Horizontal Acquisitions: the Benefits and Risk to Long-term Performance', *Mastering Strategy*, p. 202, Financial Times Prentice Hall.
Empson, L. (1999) 'Lessons from Professional Services Firms', *Financial Times*, 8 November.
Fuller, E. (2004) 'Mergers and Acquisitions in the Growth of the Firm', in *Applied Economics* (10th edn), Griffiths, A. and Wall, S. (eds), Financial Times Prentice Hall.
Garicano, L. (1999) 'Game Theory: How to Make It Pay', *Mastering Global Business*, Financial Times Prentice Hall.
Gertner, R. (2000) 'How Boards Can Say No to M&A', *Mastering Strategy*, Financial Times Prentice Hall.
Gertner, R. and Knez, M. (2000) 'Game Theory in the Real World', *Mastering Strategy*, Financial Times Prentice Hall.
Guenther, F. (2000) 'Critical Factors in M&A', Ashcroft International School of Management, APU.
Healey, N. (2004) 'The Multinational Corporation', in *Applied Economics* (10th edn), Griffiths, A. and Wall, S. (eds), Financial Times Prentice Hall.

Hornby, W., Gammie, B. and Wall, S. (2001) *Business Economics* (2nd edn), Longman, especially Chapters 10–11.

Husenan, R. and Goodman, J. (1999) *Leading the Knowledge: The Nature of Competition in the 21st Century*, Sage.

Kay, J. (1993) 'Economics in Business', *Economics and Business Education*, vol. 1, part 1, no. 2.

Mintzberg, H. and Quinn, J.B. (1991) *Strategy Process: Concepts, Contexts, Cases*, Prentice Hall.

Mitchell, M. and Lehn, K. (1990) 'Do Bad Bidders Become Good Targets?', *Journal of Political Economy*, vol. 98.

Nonaka, I. and Takeuchi, H. (1995) *The Knowledge-Creating Company: How Japanese Companies Create the Dynamics of Innovation*, OUP.

Porter, M.E. (1980) *Competitive Strategy*, Free Press, Collier Macmillan, New York.

Porter, M.E. (1985) *Competitive Advantage*, Free Press, New York.

Porter, M.E. (1986) *Competition in Global Industries*, Harvard Business School Press.

Prahalad, C.K. (1999) 'Changes in the Competitive Battlefield', *Financial Times*, 4 October. In *Mastering Strategy* (2000) Financial Times Prentice Hall.

Reuer, J. (1999) 'The Logic of Alliances', *Financial Times*, 4 October.

Reuer, J. and Koza, M. (2000) 'Asymmetric Information and Joint Venture Performance: Theory and Evidence for Domestic and International Joint Ventures', *Strategic Management Journal*, vol. 1.

United Nations Conference on Trade and Development (UNCTAD), *World Investment Report* (annual publication).

United Nations Development Programme (UNDP), *Human Development Report* (annual publication), OUP.

World Bank, *World Development Report* (annual publication).

International human resource management

By the end of this chapter you should be able to:

■ explain why it is so important to manage people effectively;

■ outline the key issues involved in international aspects of HRM;

■ describe the methods used and the particular problems faced by MNEs in managing human resources;

■ evaluate some strategic issues in international human resource management (IHRM).

Introduction

In order to create and distribute products (goods or services) every organisation needs people. Over time and in different places the ways in which people are being managed are constantly changing, though a general consensus has emerged that people are an organisation's greatest asset. This has led to an increasing interest in the way in which people are managed and how they are rewarded. After briefly reviewing the human resource management (HRM) function the emphasis shifts to defining the *international* context of that function and the problems and opportunities associated with it.

Human resource management function

Human resource management (HRM) is a concept that first emerged in the 1980s and concerns those aspects of management that deal with the human side of organisations. Armstrong (1999) defines HRM as: '… a strategic and coherent approach to the management of an organisation's most valued assets – the people working there who individually and collectively contribute to the achievement of its goals'.

This view is also advocated by Poole (1990) who adds a moralistic dimension and claims that: 'human resource management … regards people as the most important single asset of the organisation; it is proactive in its relationship with people; and it seeks to enhance company performance, employee "needs" and societal well being'.

Managing human resources is a central function within an organisation and its effective implementation involves combining the skills and knowledge of the human resource department with the expertise of line managers in other departments. The human resource function is a wide-ranging subject that covers, among other things: management/worker communications; elements of work psychology; employee relations, training and motivation; organisation of the physical and social conditions of work; and personnel management. In contrast with 'personnel management' – which deals purely with the practical aspects of recruitment, staff appraisal, training, job evaluation, etc. – HRM has a strategic dimension and involves the total deployment of all the human resources available to the firm, including the integration of personnel and other HRM considerations into the firm's overall corporate planning and strategy formulation procedures. It is proactive, seeking to continuously discover new ways of utilising the labour force in a more productive manner, thus giving the business a competitive edge.

For the purposes of this chapter, we shall adopt Brewster's and Hegewisch's (1994) model of HRM (Figure 9.1) which shows that the corporate strategies, HRM strategies and HRM practices are located within both an *internal environment* (which

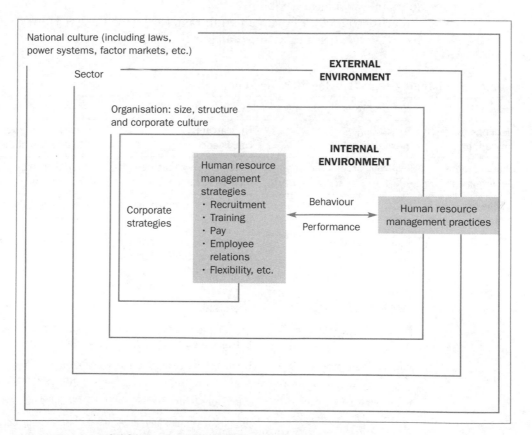

Figure 9.1 A model for investigating human resource strategies

Source: Adapted from Brewster and Hegewisch (1994). Reproduced by permission of Thomson Learning includes organisational features such as size, structure and corporate culture) and an *external environment* (which includes national culture, power systems, legislation, education and employee representation). The model shows how the human resource strategies and practices interact with, and are part of, the broader environment in which the company operates. The model may also serve as a reminder to practitioners that their human resource strategies must reflect the organisational and national cultures in which they are operating.

Human resource management has grown in importance over the past decades largely in response to the impacts of increasing internationalisation in fragmenting product and labour markets and creating the need for ever more strategic ways of managing people competitively. In the UK, prior to the 1980s, managing the workforce was largely the responsibility of the personnel department and focused on trade unions, the collective bargaining process and the handling of grievances and disputes. As a concept, HRM has arguably been imported into Europe from the United States. Its major differences with the former personnel departments being that it is more strategic, that management speaks more directly to employees rather than through the unions, and that it is underpinned by more scientific methods of measuring people's performance. Nevertheless, although more strategic in focus, HRM issues still involve functions and aspects such as recruitment, training, pay, employee relations, and workforce flexibility.

Oechsler (2000) drew up a useful framework (*see* Table 9.1) for examining how the HRM function and its aims and practices have changed over time.

Table 9.1 Changing aspects of the HRM function

	1950s–1960s	*1970s–early 1980s*	*Mid-1980s–1990s*
Management metaphor	**Structuring (providing order)**	**Fit, matching, consistency**	**Dynamic balance between dualities**
Nature of the environment	Relatively orderly and stable	Incrementally changing with increasing competition	Turbulent, complex, highly competitive
Focus of management attention	Structure and systems	Strategy and management processes	Innovation, flexibility, and organisational capabilities
	Planning systems	Strategic management: *matching* environmental threats and opportunities to internal strengths and weaknesses	Channelling entrepreneurship
	Budgeting systems	Organisation:	Focusing diversity
	Organisational structure	ensuring *consistency* between the 7 Ss	Integrating decentralised subsidiaries/business units
	Information systems	Human resource management:	Creating teamwork among strong individuals
	Job evaluation	*fitting* jobs to people	Planning opportunism
		Job design: matching technical and task specifications to social needs	Partnerships between competitors

As we can see, changes in the type of environment in which businesses operate have led to increasing diversity in the role of HRM. Innovation and flexibility are now key elements of that role, as are issues of diversity, teamwork, and partnerships. Increasing globalisation, as we shall see, has further increased the challenges faced by HRM managers.

In an attempt to investigate HRM issues in a wider environmental context, including that of internationalisation, a model of human resource management was developed by Beer *et al.* (1984) at Harvard University. According to this Harvard model, HRM strategies should develop from an in-depth analysis of (i) the demands of the various stakeholders in a business (e.g. shareholders, employees, the government, etc.) and (ii) a number of situational factors (e.g. the state of the labour market, the skills and motivation of the workforce, management styles, etc.). According to the Harvard researchers, both stakeholder expectations and situational factors need to be considered when formulating human resource strategies and the effectiveness of the outcomes should be evaluated under four headings: commitment (i.e. employees' loyalty), competence (i.e. employees' skills), congruence (i.e. shared

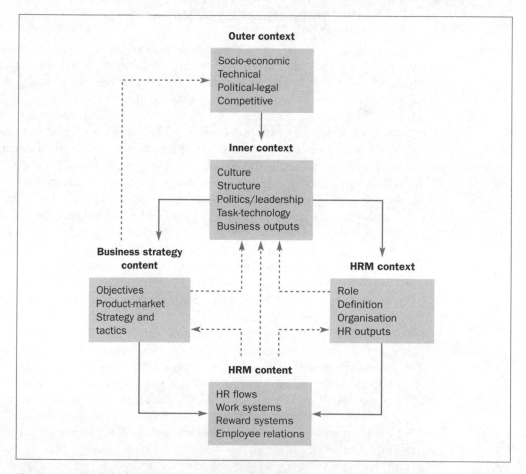

Figure 9.2 Model of strategic change and human resource management

Source: Hendry and Pettigrew (1990). http://www.tandf.co.uk/journals

vision of workers and management) and cost efficiencies (i.e. operational efficiency). The Harvard model suggests that human resource policies should be directed towards raising attainment levels for each of these four categories; for example, competence could be increased through the provision of extra training, adjustments to recruitment policy, different incentivisation schemes, and so on.

Hendry and Pettigrew (1990) offer an adaptation of the Harvard model (Figure 9.2) that attempts to integrate HRM issues with a still broader range of external societal influences (such as socio-economic, technical, political, legal and competitive issues) which may vary considerably in different international situations. These 'outer context' issues will influence HRM strategies and practices, as will a variety of 'inner context' and business strategic issues.

Before turning to the more obviously international aspects of HRM, it will be useful to see how both the internal and external environment impact on the human resource function in a specific firm. Case Study 9.1 below looks at this issue in the context of the Royal Bank of Scotland.

CASE 9.1 HRM and the external environment

A thorough understanding of the components of the external environment and their dynamic nature is crucial if an organisation such as the Royal Bank of Scotland (RBS) is to achieve long-term success. It has been said that the most important characteristic of today's business environment – and therefore the yardstick against which management techniques must be measured – is the new competition. This competition may be experienced within the domestic market or internationally. Due to increasing levels of competition within the financial services industry, organisations in this sector are striving to improve productivity. It is argued that one way of achieving this improvement is to manage human resources more effectively. The HRM department of the RBS could achieve this by empowering employees (i.e. allowing workers to make job-related decisions thereby increasing staff involvement), encouraging teamwork (in order to improve quality and efficiency) and introducing clear and consistently applied communication and assessment mechanisms (to enhance staff performance and increase awareness).

By introducing these initiatives into the workforce, it may be possible for the RBS to encourage employee involvement, thereby maximising the contribution made by employees. The direct effect of involvement in the organisation is expected to be an increase in the individual employee's commitment to the workplace or the job (one of the four important categories under the Harvard model). This commitment will be reflected in increased productivity, lower labour turnover and reduced absenteeism. For the RBS this empowerment of employees may also call for new skills on the part of both the managers and employees and it will be the role of the HRM function to try to successfully implement these changes. The HRM department will be involved in designing policies and procedures to encourage employee involvement in line with the overall strategic plan of the RBS. For example, managers may need training in the techniques of participative management if they have been used to a control management style, and employees may require confidence-building sessions and training in decision-making. This departure from a control culture which focuses upon close supervision can also have an impact on organisational structures; for example, the tall hierarchies with numerous reporting levels traditionally associated with companies like the RBS, may need to be replaced by the more modern, flatter structures which better facilitate empowerment.

A further component of the external environment that the RBS needs to consider involves the workforce and the changes that are occurring within it. For example, the British labour force is projected to increase by 1.6m people between 1995 and 2006 (i.e. from 27.8 to 29.4m), with an estimated 1.3m of this increase being women so that by 2006 women will represent 46% of the entire British labour force. These statistics arguably highlight the importance to the HRM department of the RBS of effectively utilising programmes for managing diversity among its workforce, whereby women and other minority employees receive support, recognition and the same opportunities as non-minority workers. The increasing proportion of women in the workforce may be attributed in part to socio-economic influences such as the social acceptability of women in employment and the growing availability of part-time work. These factors may oblige the RBS to adopt more open approaches to recruitment and to consider the necessity of providing more extensive training. It will be the role of the HRM department to proactively implement strategies to successfully manage diversity among the workforce. This may involve addressing stereotypes to ensure that a job does not become 'sex-typed' (i.e. deemed appropriate only for one gender) and developing gender-neutral job titles to encourage both male and female applicants. The HRM department might, for example, suggest that the RBS becomes involved in a government-supported national project, such as Opportunity 2000, which is specifically aimed at increasing the proportion of women in management.

The HRM department of the RBS must also undertake a thorough analysis of the internal environment in order for the organisation to retain its competitive edge. These internal influences may include: the company's strategy, objectives, and values; the leadership styles and goals of top management; the organisational structure, size, and culture; and the nature of the business.

An organisation's vision or mission statement is a brief explanation of its fundamental purpose and objectives and what it is striving to achieve. For example, the mission statement of the RBS includes: 'to provide financial services of the highest quality'. Organisations then develop objectives and strategies in an attempt to provide more focus and guidance for employees in seeking to achieve the company's mission. The role of the HRM department here will be to support the process of sharing an understanding about what needs to be achieved, and then managing and developing people in a way which will facilitate the achievement of these objectives. For example, in common with other companies in the financial services sector, the RBS is seeking to change from a culture that rewards performance using a 'slow' incremental pay system, into one that more closely relates pay to personal performance and achievement. The HRM department is therefore introducing new performance appraisal systems and incentive schemes in an attempt to help the company achieve its long-term strategic objectives. By introducing more beneficial

▶

bonus and profit sharing schemes, whereby pay is more closely related to individual and corporate performance, employees will arguably become more motivated to contribute to the achievement of the overall goals of the RBS.

A further internal factor that will influence the HRM function is the merger of the RBS with National Westminster Group. This merger will, of course, be of potential benefit to many employees by creating new opportunities and offering enhanced career prospects in the new, larger business. It will also place greater emphasis on the HRM function of the company and may even involve an expansion of the existing department and its operations. It will certainly be necessary to review the current HRM practices of the new and enlarged business and perhaps revise these in order to bring them into line with the objectives of the RBS. As well as increasing the activity of the HRM department in areas such as recruitment, selection, training and development, this expansion will inevitably also require the clear communication of the RBS's culture, values and strategy across a wider and more disparate cohort of employees. It is essential that the HRM functions of both businesses be closely integrated so that there is a well-defined, common goal for the new, expanded business.

Questions

1 Outline the strategic implications of this case study for the HRM function within an organisation.

2 Can you identify policies which might support the four outcomes identified in the Harvard model, namely commitment, competence, congruence and cost efficiencies?

International human resource management (IHRM)

The growth of business at an international level has led to an increase in the number of publications about international human resource management. However, what do we mean by this phrase? Boxhall defines IHRM as being:

> concerned with the human resource problems of multinational firms in foreign subsidiaries (such as expatriate management) or more broadly, with the unfolding HRM issues that are associated with the various stages of the internationalisation process. (Boxhall 1992)

Mark Mendenhall (2000) sought to be more specific by outlining a number of criteria relevant to a definition of IHRM.

1 IHRM is concerned with HRM issues that cross national boundaries or are conducted in locations other than the home country headquarters of the organisations within the study.

2 IHRM is concerned with the relationships between the HRM activities of organisations and the foreign environments in which the organisations operate.

3 IHRM includes comparative HRM studies; for example how companies in Japan, Thailand, Austria and Switzerland plan for increased employee commitment, upgrading of employee skills and so on.

4 IHRM does *not* include studies that are focused on issues outside the traditional activities inherent in the HRM function. In other words, topics such as leadership style, unless specifically linked to an HRM function (e.g. developing a selection programme to measure and select global leaders) do not qualify to be in the domain of IHRM. Such studies would arguably lie within the domain of *organisational behaviour*.

5 IHRM does *not* include studies of HRM activities in single countries. A study of personnel selection practices in Saudi Arabia, whether undertaken by an English, German or Canadian researcher, is still a study about domestic HRM in Saudi Arabia. Though such studies may have interest to those who work in international HRM issues, they are essentially examples of domestic HRM research.

■ IHRM and organisational structure

The type of international organisational structure adopted by the MNE will provide the context for many of the IHRM issues faced by the company. There are at least five widely recognised types of international organisational structures available to MNEs. There is no 'standard model' in this respect. A multinational enterprise may change from one type to another at different stages of the internationalisation process or as senior management perceives that emerging corporate needs are better served by one particular type.

The five readily identified 'types' of organisational structure include:

- international division structure;
- international geographic/regional structure;
- international product structure;
- international functional structure;
- matrix or mixed structure.

Figure 9.3 outlines the first four of these types.

- *The international division structure* is often used in the early stage of internationalisation with an 'international division' merely added to the existing divisional structures. As the activity within the international division grows (e.g. sales volume/value, number of overseas markets, etc.) then this division may itself need to be reorganised according to function, product or geographic area.
- *The international geographic/regional structure* involves separating out the different geographical/regional areas in which the MNE operates. Each geographic area may be given its own division with its own functional departments; MNEs with a wide variety of products in their portfolio sold across many geographic areas often adopt this organisational structure.
- *The international product structure* is where an MNE's divisions are established on the basis of related product lines rather than geographical area. Each product division is responsible for all functions relating to those items in that particular product portfolio – e.g. production, marking, finance and personnel relating to chocolate products for an MNE with confectionery interests. This structure is often adopted by MNEs with a variety of unrelated product lines (e.g. conglomerate MNEs).

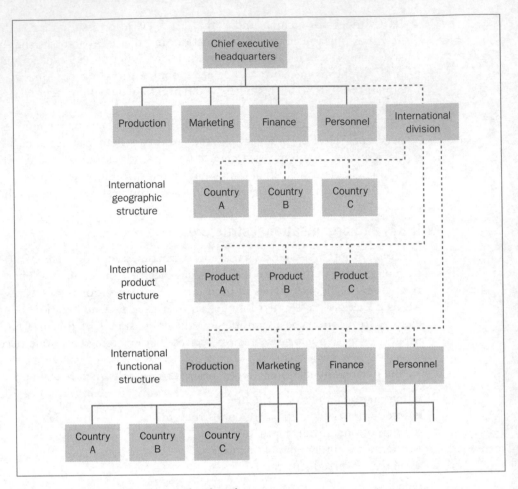

Figure 9.3 **International organisational structures**

- *The international functional structure* gives each functional department of the MNE (production, marketing, finance, etc.) responsibility for the international operations of that function.

Matrix (or mixed) structures bring together the functional, geographical and product structures and combine them in an attempt to meet the needs of a *specific activity or project*. Once that activity or project is completed, the 'team' is often disbanded and return to their original position within the divisional or other structures of the MNE.

International HRM approaches

When conducting business globally, organisations will also need to integrate HRM into their international strategy. How they do this will depend on the approach they adopt as regards HRM policies. Four approaches have been identified to describe the ways in which MNEs might conduct their international HRM policies (Dowling and Schuler 1990).

- *The ethnocentric approach.* In the ethnocentric approach, all key positions in the host country subsidiary are filled by nationals of the parent company. This approach offers the most direct control by the parent company over the host country subsidiary, and is often adopted when there is felt to be a need to maintain good communications between the headquarters of the MNE and the subsidiary. This ethnocentric approach is often followed in the early stages of internationalisation when the MNE is seeking to establish a new business or product in another country.
- *The polycentric approach.* Here, host country nationals are recruited to manage the subsidiaries in their own country. This allows the MNE to take a lower profile in sensitive economic and political situations and helps to avoid intercultural management problems.
- *The geocentric approach.* This approach utilises the best people for all the key jobs throughout the organisation, whatever their nationality or whatever the geographical location of the post to be filled. In this way an international executive team can be developed.
- *The regiocentric approach.* Here the MNE divides its operations into geographic regions and moves staff within particular regions, e.g. Europe, America, Asia, rather than between regions.

Choices between these different approaches will depend on the culture, philosophy and the local conditions in which the firm operates. Some international companies may adopt an ethnocentric approach in some countries and a polycentric approach in others. However a key element in this choice will involve the question as to how an international firm can manage a dispersed and diverse workforce responsively and effectively, retaining a measure of overall cohesion while being sensitive to local conditions.

Some firms have sought to resolve this dilemma by maintaining an international group of HRM managers with an ethnocentric orientation who can be moved in and out of the worldwide operations, yet at the same time devolving HRM responsibility down the line so that the firm can remain responsive to local developments. Finding the right balance between integration and decentralisation for IHRM is complex, and the mix will depend on the following factors.

- *Degree and type of internationalisation.* We have seen (*see* Chapter 2) that there is a range of options for international firms as to how they may expand, from exporting through to using wholly-owned subsidiaries. In general an integrated and more ethnocentric approach to HRM is often adopted for the wholly-owned subsidiary, with the MNE retaining centralised control over the way in which its employees are managed.
- *Type of industry and markets served.* Porter (1986) distinguishes the multidomestic industry, in which competition within each country is largely internal (retailing, distribution and insurance), from the global industry in which competition is worldwide (electronic equipment, branded food, defence products). Porter suggests that strategies for the global industry are more likely to involve the firm in integrating its activities worldwide, especially where strong brand images are involved. For the global industry, therefore, IHRM is more likely to be ethnocentric while for the multidomestic industry IHRM is more likely to be polycentric and to resemble that typically used in the particular country in which the subsidiary operates.

- *Characteristics of staff.* The types of employees may well influence the degree to which the IHRM function is decentralised. For example, if the employees of a subsidiary consist of highly skilled, experienced and fully committed staff, the IHRM function may be decentralised. Where, however, the employees mainly consist of unskilled and temporary staff (perhaps where the MNE has bought into a cheap labour market) then headquarters will usually wish to exercise a greater degree of control over the corporate foreign subsidiary.
- *Cultural preferences.* The degree of integration or decentralisation will also depend on the cultural preferences towards either of these approaches to management in both the organisation and in the country in which the subsidiary operates. The latter reflects Hofstede's idea of national 'cultural distance' (*see* Chapter 6), and is considered further in the context of Greece in Box 9.1.

> **pause for thought 1**
>
> Look back to Table 6.3 in Chapter 6. Which of these four approaches to IHRM might you expect an MNE which has Great Britain as its headquarters to adopt as regards an overseas affiliate in (a) Japan, (b) Canada?

Table 9.2 outlines some advantages and disadvantages of a decentralised approach to IHRM.

Figure 9.4 outlines a number of internal organisational influences which will influence the extent of integration or decentralisation of the IHRM function by MNEs.

Box 9.1 looks in more detail at the suggestion that national cultural attributes may also play a key role in an MNE's choice of a centralised or decentralised approach to IHRM.

Of course, corporate culture and national culture can exert separate, and sometimes opposing, influences. Morosini *et al.* (1998) suggest that specific absorptive mechanisms (such as job rotation, incentives, internal reporting systems and global coordination functions) involving people from different national backgrounds sharing a strong corporate culture can help to facilitate the cross-border transfer of routines and repertoires. Nevertheless, when national cultural characteristics are particularly strong and diverse these may dominate these internal absorptive mechanisms which seek to reinforce aspects of corporate culture irrespective of national identity. This would certainly seem to be indicated by Case Study 9.2, which considers the impacts on IHRM of theocratic (religious-based) cultures within Islamic countries.

Table 9.2 Advantages and disadvantages of a 'decentralised' approach to IHRM

Advantages	Disadvantages
Groups within the subsidiary can gain in status	Tendency to become 'exclusive'
Groups within the subsidiary become more cohesive, fostering group identity	Loss of central control, higher administrative costs as HRM function is sent 'down the line'
IHRM takes place within a culture appropriate to the local workforce and customers	Loss of organisational control and organisational identity

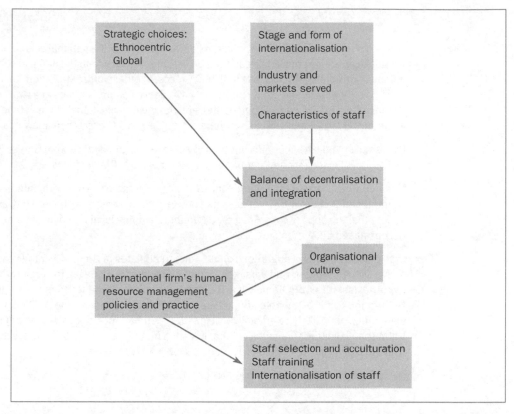

Figure 9.4 Impacts of internal organisational considerations on human resource management

---

Box 9.1   Greek national culture and decentralisation of the IHRM function

While the global nature of multinational activity may call for increased consistency, the variety of cultural environments in which the MNE operates may call for differentiation. Workplace values and behaviours are widely regarded as being influenced by national as well as corporate cultural characteristics. As Laurent (1986) claims, 'if we accept the view that human resource management (HRM) approaches are cultural artefacts reflecting the basic assumptions and values of the national culture in which organisations are embedded, international HRM becomes one of the most challenging corporate tasks in multinational organisations'.

Greece is clustered in the 'Mediterranean culture' sector of managerial models; native managers are assumed to be less individualistic and more comfortable with highly bureaucratic organisational structures in order to achieve their objectives. In Hofstede's terms, Greece is characterised by large power distance and strong uncertainty avoidance (*see* Figure 6.1, p. 174). Since the early 1960s, Greece has been the host country for many foreign firms, initially in manufacturing and more recently in services.

It is broadly accepted that management practices which reinforce national cultural values are more likely to yield better outcomes in terms of performance, with a mismatch between work unit management practices and national culture likely to reduce performance. The suggestion here is that multinationals, which have established their affiliates in Greece, will be more

> ### Box 9.1   Continued
>
> efficient if their management practices are better adapted to the national culture of Greece. Theory suggests that this adaptation will be better achieved where the national culture of the home country of the MNE is close to that of Greece. In other words, MNEs from collectivist, large power distance and strong uncertainty avoidance countries will be at a small cultural distance from Greece and will better integrate into the organisational culture of the Greek affiliate. The following hypothesis is therefore suggested by Kessapidou and Varsakelis (2000).
>
> Hypothesis: MNEs from home countries at a large cultural distance from Greece will prefer to employ local managers and permit more decentralised IHRM practices.
>
> This hypothesis would then predict that MNEs from home countries with national cultural characteristics of the individualist, small power distance and weak uncertainty avoidance variety (i.e. the opposites to Greece) will prefer to employ local managers and permit more decentralised IHRM practices.
>
> In their analysis of the operations of 485 foreign affiliates in Greece over the years 1994–96, Kessapidou and Varsakelis found considerable evidence to support this hypothesis. MNEs from home countries at a large cultural distance from Greece (e.g. UK, the Netherlands and USA, with cultural distance factors of 4.27, 4.03 and 3.47 respectively) were much more likely to employ local managers and adopt a decentralised approach to IHRM than countries at a small cultural distance from Greece (e.g. Italy, France and Spain, with cultural distance factors of 1.46, 0.99 and 0.58 respectively).
>
> *Source*: Adapted from Kessapidou and Varsakelis (2000)

CASE 9.2   Islamic culture and IHRM

Islam has grown enormously over the past three decades. In the countries where it is prevalent, from West Africa to the Lebanon, Malaysia to Indonesia, Muslims are returning to Islamic traditions, as a way of rediscovering their identity and as an alternative to the materialism and tensions of the twentieth century.

Islam is an all-encompassing creed, governing every aspect of public and private life. The Koran is regarded as containing the revealed words of God which can act as a guide and a steer. Nevertheless, humans are able to choose and intervene in their own destiny, and must be held responsible for the consequences of their deeds. The economic ideas of the Koran are quite close to those of the West, with the Koran advocating a system based on individual enterprise and reward. As for the Muslim individual, he or she should be guided by his/her conscience to treat employees and others responsibly. Individuals should pay a reasonable wage, charge a fair price and be restrained in the way in which they use any profits. They also have a responsibility for protecting the environment.

However, the way in which Islam is manifest is very different across nations. At the extreme end, the Taliban regime in Afghanistan does not allow women to work outside their homes, and girls do not attend schools or colleges. In Iran, however, while women have to follow a strict dress code at work and there is a policy of segregation on public occasions such as prayers, Iranian women are doing relatively well in public life. Women can go into most jobs and professions, and unlike their peers in Saudi, they can drive cars and vote.

The following work-related values of Islamic culture in Iran have been identified by Latifi (1997):

- equality before God;
- individual responsibility within a framework of cooperation with others;
- a view that people in positions of power should treat subordinates kindly, as if their subordinates are brothers or sisters;
- fatalism, but also a recognition of personal choice;
- encouragement of consultation at all levels of decision making, from family to the wider community.

Latifi closely observed a sample of Iranian managers and found traces of Islamic values in the HRM style. Iranian employees thought of their managers as sympathetic brothers and sisters or compassionate fathers and mothers. The family-like relationship seemed to have been extended to include social and teacher roles for the managers, and they were frequently involved in their subordinates' private lives and family matters. A high proportion of managers were willing to make their time and organisations available for high-school and university students who might wish to conduct a research project or acquire work experience as part of their courses. They viewed this as part of their responsibility to society and to the next generation of managers.

In Malaysia, Endot (1995) also found that Islam had filtered down to the HRM practices. One of the companies offers its employees interest-free loans for vehicle or house purchase, or for preparation for a wedding ceremony. Another organises Islamic study circles for managers. These are segregated, but help create cohesiveness of relationships among the members. Another company sends its employees on short courses in Islamic teachings, in order that the employees understand Islam and its values. Yet another organisation recruits individuals who have graduated in Islamic studies, only later exposing them to techniques of modern management.

In a study carried out in the Arab Middle East, decision-making and management–employee relationships were found to be characterised by a process of consultation, rooted in Islamic traditions. For example, the Koran asserts that those who conduct their affairs by consultation will receive favour. However, this does not take the form of the Western model of consultative decision-making. Rather consultation is used to avoid potential conflicts between executives and their subordinates: to please, placate or win over people who may be potential obstacles. It is also an information-gathering mechanism. So while consultation may occur, it usually involves only a few selected people and is not part of a hierarchical decision-making structure.

Questions

1 What type of approach to IHRM would you expect to be adopted if a Western MNE acquires an Iranian-based company which has been operating successfully for some time?

2 What results might you expect if the MNE were to use the Harvard model to evaluate the outcomes of the current HRM function within the Iranian firm? (Use commitment, competence, congruence and cost efficiencies.)

IHRM policies and practices

At this point it may be useful to consider in rather more detail some of the key elements within an IHRM programme.

■ Training and development in an international context

Obviously, training and development increases in complexity as MNEs move abroad. The type of training that takes place would usually depend on a number of factors:

- the degree to which management is centralised;
- the types of workers employed in subsidiaries or joint ventures;
- the importance of branding, and the extent to which employees are expected to reflect the brand;
- the cultural expectations of training.

In a global company, the training may well be centralised so that suppliers, employees and distributors are aware of the brand image that needs to be communicated. In Ford, for example, training programmes are set up centrally, and then translated and delivered to all main suppliers, subsidiaries and distributors. If, however, a more polycentric approach is taken, then the training may well be far more local, and more in line with the local culture.

Other problems may arise with teamworking. There has been a great deal of work done over the past three decades on how to train teams, and how to ensure that there is synergy in teamwork. Business psychologists such as Belbin, for example, have drawn up the types of characters that would make an ideal team, and have devised methods for testing the personalities of the team members in order that teams could be composed of a balance of types. In a cross-cultural context, it is not only the personality types that have to be taken into account, but also the very real cultural differences and approaches between team members. Attempts at cross cultural team training are becoming increasingly prominent in MNEs.

A further problem for MNEs is how to ensure that employees sent abroad (expatriates) are fully immersed in the foreign culture. Many MNEs run extensive training programmes for employees going overseas, designed to provide individuals with information and experience related to local customs, cultures and work habits so that they can interact and work more effectively with local colleagues. Indeed, such programmes may also be run for spouses and children.

Research shows that the following are the most popular:

1 environmental briefings used to provide information about such things as geography, climate, housing and schools;
2 cultural orientation designed to familiarise the individual with cultural institutions and value systems of the host country;
3 cultural assimilations to provide participants with intercultural encounters;
4 language training;
5 sensitivity training designed to help develop attitudinal flexibility;
6 field experience which sends the participant to the country of assignment to get them used to the emotional stress of living and working with people of a different culture.

The following case study looks at the implications for IHRM within the multinational enterprise of technical change, with particular reference to the growth of e-commerce.

CASE 9.3 IHRM implications of e-commerce

MNEs are increasingly adopting e-commerce as a new channel for commercial transactions worldwide. For example, it is estimated that by 2005, about 15% of US retail sales will be conducted by e-commerce compared to only 0.5% in 1997. This growth in e-commerce is altering the management systems of companies because more information is available to identify and support new business activities and the cost of gathering and processing this information is falling. Managers have to be able to develop the appropriate skills for both themselves and their subordinates in order to manage this information explosion to best possible effect. Moreover, 'virtual' world purchasing and selling operations require new systems to monitor and control activities. Many companies are engaged in merger and acquisition activities to develop their e-commerce capabilities, resulting in the rationalisation of organisations, with consequent implications for redundancies and for the redeployment and retraining of labour.

Implications for international human resource management

McDonald (2000) suggests that the widespread adoption of e-commerce has six main implications for IHRM. The magnitude and nature of these various impacts will need to be assessed in the individual country in which the affiliate operates:

1 many types of labour connected to traditional wholesaling and retailing activities will become redundant;
2 new distribution systems based on home deliveries and pick-up by customers from new distribution centres will require the development of a workforce that can fulfil these new jobs;
3 there will be a need to recruit labour with the skills to design, build, develop and maintain effective web pages that customers use to buy online;
4 labour will have to be trained and retrained to use virtual systems for taking, processing, and arranging for the delivery of orders;
5 mergers and acquisitions of Internet companies to provide new online services will lead to large-scale redundancies and redeployment of labour;
6 new types of management structures will emerge that will help companies to be more effective in the new information-rich environment.

Logistical systems are being revolutionised (*see also* Chapter 12) as distribution systems for products sold online will no longer be based on the large-scale storage of products in warehouses and shops. New logistical systems based on home deliveries and pick-up (by customers) from low-cost distribution centres will become more important. These developments may lead to radical changes to retailing outlets as large shops selling basic (and perhaps even elaborate) products lose their

▶

competitive advantage. Redundancies and redeployment of labour will inevitably follow. All companies that enter the world of e-commerce will have to train workers to use the techniques of the virtual world of online shopping. Technical staff who can 'work' and develop these new technologies will also have to be recruited. Given the expected rapid rise in the use of e-commerce systems and the general shortage of people with good IT skills, this could prove to be a difficult problem. E-commerce will lead to different types of customer relations problems that will require the development of appropriate recruitment, training and retraining of staff that can effectively deal with these problems. The development of e-commerce is also likely, in the long-term, to lead to a more competitive environment in both price and quality terms. This will require management staff to develop new attitudes and skills in areas related to providing value for money, customer satisfaction and cost control.

OECD study on e-commerce and the skills shortage

An OECD study on e-commerce (OECD 1998) projected significant increases in the demand for labour with high levels of IT skills. In 1996, 4.2m people worked in occupations that were directly IT-related, and the projection for 2006 was 5.6m. Moreover, there was evidence that lower-skilled labour was being displaced by people with good IT skills. This development followed the removal of layers of intermediation in industries such as banking and financial services and parts of the wholesaling and retailing industries. However, employment in transport industries, especially courier companies, was increasing. This, in part, appears to reflect the growth of home deliveries. The study found evidence that these trends were emerging in other developed countries.

IT skill shortages were reported by companies in the USA and in most Western European countries. In the USA in 1997 there were between 190,000 and 450,000 (depending on the source of the estimates) unfilled IT job vacancies. The figure for Germany was 60,000 and for the UK 20,000. The trend is towards rising demand for workers with high IT skills and to redeploy and/or retrain workers with poor IT skills. Nevertheless, the study found that in the USA, the median wages of computer scientists and programmers was not very different from the national median wage for other highly-skilled workers. A closer examination of the labour market found that in newly-emerging Internet companies there has been a very large increase in wages. In contrast, established IT companies, financial services and communications companies displayed a tendency to hire less-qualified staff, thereby suppressing the growth of wages. However, this often led to the delay or abandonment of projects when skill shortages became a problem. In the manufacturing sector and most retailing there was little evidence of any response to the developing skills shortage. This is likely to change very quickly as e-commerce systems develop in these sectors.

The study confirms that the development of e-commerce is, increasingly, leading to significant challenges for IHRM strategies. Developments in the USA indicate that skill shortages and significant changes in the pattern of jobs emerge rapidly when IT technologies are applied to buying and selling activities.

Implications for IHRM management teams

The management teams will have to devise and operate organisational systems that can overcome the many HRM problems that will arise from the widespread adoption of e-commerce. Once an e-commerce facility has been established, the management team will have to be able to make best use of the vastly increased flow of information that will become available on a national and international scale. This information will have to be processed into commercially valuable knowledge that can be used to help the company survive and prosper in the virtual world of e-commerce. It is not clear what the implications for management skills are of widespread access to low-cost and potentially commercially valuable information that can be easily disseminated throughout organisations. It can be expected that management systems for controlling and monitoring will have to change to prevent the loss of commercially valuable information. However, management systems that curtail the entrepreneurial activities of employees may lead to a failure to reap many of the possible benefits that the use of e-commerce makes available. Clearly the development of e-commerce will lead to significant challenges for the IHRM strategies and policies of those companies that become caught up in this new technology. These challenges include recruiting, redeploying, training and re-training of labour to provide the required IT skills. However, they also extend to the recruitment, training and re-training of management so that organisations are able to operate effectively in the new world of e-commerce.

Source: McDonald (2000).

Question

1 Consider some of the IHRM issues for an MNE with an extensive network of international affiliates that become heavily involved in e-commerce.

■ Pay and international employee relations

The way in which an organisation seeks to reward its employees may be critical to its success. As Hegewisch points out:

> the pay package is one of the most obvious and visible expressions of the employment relationship; it is the main issue in the exchange between employer and employee, expressing the connection between the labour market, the individual's work and the performance of the employing organisation itself. (Hegewisch 1991: 28)

As a result of competitive pressures, organisations are constantly looking to increase the 'added value' of their employees by encouraging them to increase their efforts beyond any minimal standard. The theoretical understanding of pay and other reward structures stems from theories of motivation.

To design an appropriate reward strategy for employees taking up an international position, may require a number of factors to be considered. These include a knowledge of the laws, customs, environment, and employment practices of the foreign countries; familiarity with currency relationships and the effect of inflation on compensation; an understanding of the allowances appropriate to particular countries, and so on.

The main method of drawing up a compensation package is known as the 'balance sheet' approach. This approach is, according to Reynolds (1986): 'a system designed to equalise the purchasing power of employees at comparable position levels living overseas and in the home country, and to provide incentives to offset qualitative differences between assignment locations'.

In order to achieve such 'balance', the organisation must take into account a number of factors when sending employees to a different country:

- income taxes incurred in both home and host country;
- housing allowances (which might range from financial assistance to employees to providing company housing);
- cost-of-living allowances (to make up any differences in prices between home and foreign country);
- contributions to savings, pension schemes, etc. while abroad;
- relocation allowances (including the moving, shipping and storage of personal and household items and temporary living expenses);
- education allowances for expatriate's children (e.g. language tuition and enrolment fees in the host country or boarding school fees in the home country);
- medical, emergency and security cover.

Appraisal

A formalised and systematic appraisal scheme will enable a regular assessment of an individual's performance, highlight potential, and identify training and development needs. A comprehensive appraisal system can provide the basis for key managerial decisions, such as those relating to the allocation of duties and responsibilities, pay, levels of supervision or delegation, promotion, training and development, and so on.

The benefits of a comprehensive appraisal system include the following:

- it can identify an individual's strengths and weaknesses, and show how these can be overcome;
- it can reveal organisational obstacles blocking progress;
- it can provide useful feedback to help improve human resource planning;
- it can improve communications by giving staff a chance to talk about expectations.

According to James (1988), performance appraisal has its roots in three key principles. People learn/work/achieve more when they are given:

- adequate feedback as to how they are performing;
- clear and attainable goals;
- involvement in the setting of tasks and goals.

Again, there are cultural factors which need to be taken into account when drawing up pay and appraisal schemes for workers in foreign countries. Table 9.3 highlights the cultural influences on appraisal systems with a key aspect being whether the country is regarded as 'low context' or 'high context' (see Chapter 6, Table 6.1).

Table 9.3 Cultural variations: performance appraisals

Dimension General	USA Low context	Saudi Arabia High context	Japan High context
Objective of performance appraisal.	Fairness, employee development.	Placement.	Direction of company/ employee development.
Who does appraisal?	Supervisor.	Manager several levels up. Appraiser has to know employee well.	Mentor and supervisor. Appraiser has to know employee well.
Authority of appraiser.	Presumed in supervisory role or position. Supervisor takes slight lead.	Reputation important (prestige is determined by nationality, sex, family, tribe, title, education). Authority of appraiser important.	Respect accorded by employee to supervisor or appraiser. Done co-equally.
How often?	Once a year.	Once a year.	Developmental or periodically once a month. Evaluation appraisal after first 12 years.
Assumptions.	Objective appraiser is fair.	Subjective appraiser more important than objective. Connections are more important.	Objective and subjective. Japanese can be trained in anything.
Manner of communication and feedback.	Criticism direct. Criticism may be in writing. Objective, authentic.	Criticism subtle. Older more likely to be direct. Criticism not given.	Criticism subtle. Criticism given verbally. Observe formalities in writing.
Rebuttals.	American will rebut appraisal.	Saudi Arabian will rebut appraisal.	Japanese would rarely rebut appraisal.
Praise.	Given individually.	Given individually.	Given to entire group.
Motivators.	Money and position. Career development.	Loyalty to supervisor.	Internal excellence.

Source: Adapted from Harris and Moran (1991)

CASE 9.4   IHRM and national cultures

A multinational European research group – the European Managerial Decision-Making Project – set out to explore the problem of cultural norms by identifying European national values directly related to typical organisational tasks mainly of the IHRM variety.

Four problem scenarios

The project's research methodology was developed in France and based on approximately 100 interviews with European managers. These semi-structured interviews identified four particularly troublesome problems: recruitment, promotion/job transfer, compensation, and workforce reductions.

Based on these problems and using the examples evoked by the interviewed managers, the project team developed four one-page scenarios, each centred on a specific problem. The respondents were asked to make and explain a choice on each specific problem. The four scenarios are summarised below.

- The *recruitment scenario* sets the problem of creating a position to service a growing market of international clients with both personal and small-business banking needs. The options for recruitment range from generalist, élite country national candidates to foreign, trilingual specialists. Hypothetical in-house managerial assessment test scores are assigned to each candidate.

- The *promotion scenario* sets the problem of creating a post to help an overloaded manager handle increasing business. The most important criteria are the source of the candidate for promotion (e.g. internal versus external), the performance criterion used to evaluate candidates (e.g. group service/loyalty versus individual performance), and age.

- The *remuneration scenario* concerns a bank that is becoming more sales-driven but has older generalist managers unwilling to adapt to a selling culture. A modification of the pay system is proposed to remedy the problem. Choices range from full salary with company-based bonus to at-risk pay with individual commission based on individual performance.

- The *staff reduction scenario* was developed using the intuitively reasonable criteria of age, seniority, performance and salary cost. The problem is a subsidiary that must reduce its workforce. A small department is being closed but only three or four of the employees can be placed elsewhere. One person must be selected to leave the firm. The family responsibilities of each choice are held constant at two children with no unusual problems. It is specified that none of the employees is a 'bad' employee. All have consistently average, above average or excellent performance ratings over the past five years. They range in age from 30 to 57 years, with salaries correlated with their ages.

Data were collected between 1994 and 1997 from more than 900 managers from 74 European banks. The banks were a representative sample of the industry in each of six countries (Austria, England, France, Germany, Italy and Spain) and included small, medium and large organisations. The banking sector was selected because few bank employees come into contact with 'foreign' expectations and therefore reflect more closely a 'pure cultural type' of manager.

Group logic and market logic

The results of the responses to each scenario are shown in Figure 9.5 where each country's responses are plotted between two opposing logics.

The first is called 'group logic'. Decisions immediately benefiting the group, rather than an individual, are characteristic of this logic. Concern about how a decision would affect the group was common among respondents. Even decisions such as who to promote or make redundant were sometimes discussed in terms of their group effects rather than the individual consequences.

The second logic is a type of economic rationality that the researchers call 'market logic'. Decisions based upon the perceived organisational needs arising from the marketplace are characteristic of this logic. For example, who should be hired for a new post primarily directed to servicing foreign clients – someone with foreign nationality and experience or someone local who matches the group's image?

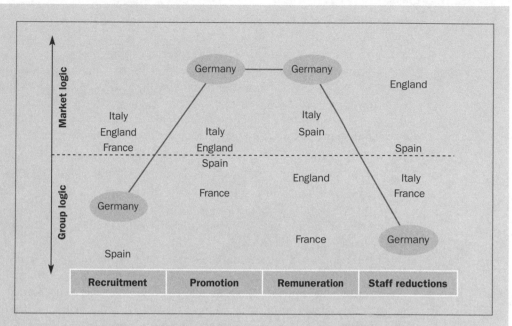

Figure 9.5 **Management decision criteria**

The results of the survey are summarised below.

■ In Italy, England and France respondents usually used market logic in hiring new managers. They more often chose to hire foreign, multilingual employees with an élite, generalist educational background. The German and Spanish managers followed the opposite strategy by hiring local managers with more technical training.

■ The German sample stood nearly alone in its concern for promoting managers on the basis of objective performance criteria. French managers were at the other extreme in basing promotion on seniority or group loyalty criteria.

■ The German sample again stood alone with its concern that remuneration should be based on measurable individual performance factors. Again, the French sample held the extreme opposite belief that remuneration should be based on group, not individual, performance.

■ English managers most often based staff-reduction decisions on the performance-to-salary ratio. More than 70% of the English respondents would have made redundant a middle-aged, high-salary manager with average performance.

■ In contrast, less than 10% of the German respondents would have discharged the same manager. They favoured discharging young managers who could find jobs more easily, thereby preserving social stability.

■ French respondents were not as concerned with the ratio of performance to salary as the Italians or Spanish. They usually made average-quality employees redundant but were more likely to choose a younger, average-quality manager than an older one.

■ It appears that the German companies in the sample have evolved a 'switching' model in their decision-making. Group logic is used to make decisions about entering or leaving a group. However, for group members, decisions related to promotion and salary are based on market logic. This means that individuals receive the full benefit of their efforts without sharing promotion opportunities or salary gains with lower-performance colleagues.

The challenge for human resources

The basic requirement of any international human resources integration programme is a very deep examination of the local cultural values relating to human resources policy. This is important because all cultures accumulate basic expectations about what employers and employees can or cannot demand from each other. Most international human resources managers will have experienced these expectation differences at first hand.

Unfortunately, while large sums are often spent on training and 'cultural change' programmes, few human resources managers are willing to commit much time, effort or money to understanding their own sets of expectations. For example, one large French multinational created an international management programme for young 'high potential' managers in its European network. An important goal was to create an international cadre of young managers who would help integrate the company's many recent acquisitions into a tightly organised pan-European organisation. Not only was the definition of 'high potential' different from country to country but despite detailed written guidelines those chosen were disappointing to the headquarters staff. During an eight-day training seminar in France many failed to understand what the programme was really all about. They maintained their normal expectations. Some felt that they were simply starting an expatriate assignment without all the perks. (There were no supplemental salary benefits during the two-year foreign assignment that was part of the programme.) Others saw themselves as 'high potentials' being groomed for higher posts in their home countries. They did not seem to grasp the idea that they were to be the backbone of a network of managers who should connect the various parts of the company.

Eight days was too short a time for the trainees to reconsider their expectations in light of the company's attempt to create an integrated organisation. A Dutch manager, after learning he would be assigned to France, publicly asked how he would be compensated for the loss of two holiday days. Approximately 80% of the expatriate assignments made during the first year were prematurely terminated. After three expensive years, the programme itself was ended.

The lesson is that integration programmes should be approached seriously because their success is often crucial to the success of the entire venture. Too often firms bring in 'cultural experts' to talk about different national values. These programmes are usually entertaining. But they ultimately fail because they do not require a firm's managers to examine their own values first. No quick fixes are available, as values are notoriously difficult to change. It is necessary to accept that certain national values will never be entirely amenable to change. But it is worth remembering that while national culture has a strong influence on personal values, it is but one among many factors.

It is possible to look for individuals within any society who have values more attuned to the culture that the integration programme is designed to create. Careful employee selection and promotion over a period of five to ten years can help firms effectively build the cultural values they want.

Source: Adapted from Segalla (1999).

Questions

1 What implications for IHRM can be drawn from Figure 9.5 above?

2 Does this case study have any bearing on the geocentric or regiocentric approaches (*see* p. 285) to IHRM?

Useful websites

Now try the self-check questions for this chapter on the website at www.booksites.net/wall. You will also find further resources as well as the following useful weblinks:

The human resource network has a number of brief guides on HRM issues: *www.hnetwork.co.uk*

Many human resources issues are covered at: *www.lpd.co.uk*
A wide range of motivational theorists are considered at: *www.westrek.hypermart.net*

Useful key texts

Daniels, J., Radebaugh, L. and Sullivan, D. (2004) *International Business* (10th edn), Pearson Prentice Hall, especially Chapter 21.
Hill, C. (2003) *International Business: Competing in the Global Marketplace* (4th edn), McGraw-Hill Irwin, especially Chapter 18.
Morrison, J. (2002) *The International Business Environment*, Palgrave, especially Chapters 1 and 5.
Rugman, A. and Hodgetts, R. (2003) *International Business* (3rd edn), FT Prentice Hall, especially Chapter 12.
Tayeb, M. (2000) *International Business: Theories, Policies and Practices*, Financial Times Prentice Hall, especially Chapters 19 and Part VI.
Woods, M. (2001) *International Business*, Palgrave, especially Chapter 10.

Other texts and sources

Armstrong, M. (1999) *A Handbook of Human Resource Management* (7th edn), Kogan Page.
Beer, M., Spector, B., Lawrence, P.R., Quinn Mills, D. and Walton, R.E. (1984) *Managing Human Assets*, Free Press.
Boxhall, P.F. (1992) 'Strategic HRM: Beginnings of a New Theoretical Sophistication', *Human Resource Management Journal*, vol. 2, no. 3, pp. 60–79.
Brewster, C. and Hegewisch, A. (1994) *Policy and Practice in European Human Resource Management*, Routledge/Thomson Learning, p. 6.

Dowling, P. and Schuler, R. (1990) *International Dimensions of Human Resource Management*, PWS-Kent.

Endot, S. (1995) 'The Islamisation Process in Malaysia', Ph.D. thesis, University of Bradford.

Foot, M. and Hook, C. (2003) *Introducing Human Resource Management* (3rd edn), Longman.

Harris, P.R. and Moran, R.T. (1991) *Managing Cultural Difference*, Gulf Publishing.

Hegewisch, A. (1991) 'The Decentralisation of Pay Bargaining: European Comparisons', *Personnel Review*, vol. 20, no. 6.

Hendry, J. and Pettigrew, A. (1990) 'Human Resource Management: An Agenda for the 1990s', *International Journal of Human Resource Management*, vol. 1, no. 1.

James, G. (1988) *Performance Appraisal*, Occasional Paper 40, ACAS Work Research Unit.

Kessapidou, S. and Varsakelis, N. (2000) 'National Culture, Choice of Management and Business Performance: The Case of Foreign Firms in Greece', in *Dimensions of International Competitiveness: Issues and Policies*, Lloyd Reason, L. and Wall, S. (eds), Edward Elgar.

Latifi, F. (1997) 'Management Learning in Natural Context', Ph.D. thesis, Henley Management College, cited in Tayeb, M. (2000).

Laurent, A. (1986) 'The Cross-cultural Puzzle of International Human Resource Management', *Human Resource Management*, 25.

McDonald, F. (2000) 'E-commerce: The Challenge for Human Resource Management', *British Economy Survey*, vol. 29, no. 2.

Mendenhall, M. (2000) *Mapping the Terrain of IHRM: A Call for Ongoing Dialogue*, Paper presented at 15th Workshop on Strategic HRM, Fontainebleau, France, 30 March–1 April.

Morosini, P., Scott, S. and Harbir, S. (1998) 'National Cultural Distance and Cross-border Acquisition Performance', *Journal of International Business*, vol. 29, no. 1.

OECD (1998) *The Economic Impact of Electronic Commerce*, OECD, Paris.

Oechsler, W.A. (2000) *Strategic Human Resource Management in an Age of Flexible Employment*, Paper presented at 15th workshop on Strategic HRM, Fontainebleau, France, 30 March–1 April.

Poole, M. (1990) 'Human Resource Management in an International Perspective', *International Journal of Human Resource Management*, vol. 1, no. 1.

Porter, M.E. (1986) *Competition in Global Industries*, Harvard Business School Press.

Reynolds, C. (1986)'Compensation of Overseas Personnel', in *Handbooks of Human Resource Administration* (2nd edn), Farnularo, J. (ed.), McGraw-Hill.

Segalla, M. (1999) 'National Cultures, International Business', in *Mastering Global Business*, Financial Times Prentice Hall.

United Nations Conference on Trade and Development (UNCTAD), *World Investment Report* (annual publication).

United Nations Development Programme (UNDP), *Human Development Report* (annual publication), OUP.

World Bank, *World Development Report* (annual publication).

International marketing

By the end of this chapter you should be able to:

- outline the principal activities of marketing;
- differentiate between international marketing and domestic marketing;
- conduct some basic international market research;
- outline the key stages in international marketing;
- specify the key elements in the international marketing mix and discuss how to balance them.

Introduction

Many people see marketing in terms of the advertising that accompanies products – such as that seen on advertising hoardings scattered throughout the world, or encountered on television, radio and the Internet. In fact, marketing is a far more sophisticated and complex activity and for many organisations can mean the difference between success and failure.

The Chartered Institute of Marketing (CIM) defines marketing as 'the management process responsible for identifying and satisfying customer needs profitably'.

The American Marketing Association's definition is: 'The process of planning and executing the conception, pricing, promotion and distribution of ideas, goods and services to create exchanges that satisfy individual and organisational goals.'

Hill and O'Sullivan (2003) describe marketing as: 'a business philosophy that regards customer satisfaction as the key to successful trading and advocates the use of management practices that help identify and respond to customer needs'.

Arguably at least three major elements are involved in the marketing role.

- *Customer orientation*. This sounds obvious, but in practice many organisations can become so preoccupied with manufacturing processes or technology, that they lose sight of what the customer wants, leaving themselves vulnerable to the activities of competitors who have a keener eye for customer needs.

- *Integrated effort.* A key role of marketers is to build bridges between the requirements of the customer and the capabilities of the organisation. For example, senior managers may not have a marketing orientation; they might focus on keeping costs down, as the route to success, when what is actually required might be more investment in research and design, or more stock on the shelves. 'Integrated effort' means a focus on marketing throughout the organisation.
- *Goal focus.* Many business activities can be focused on achieving short-term profit, rather than looking to the longer-term strategic aims of the organisation. Marketers may play a part in keeping these longer-term strategic aims in focus.

The principal activities of marketing

We have seen that marketing is an integrated activity that takes place throughout the organisation and seeks to align customer needs with the capabilities and goals of the organisation. We can therefore break marketing down into the following activities.

Analysis

Market analysis can itself be broken down into at least three elements.

1 *Environmental analysis.* This may involve scanning the environment for risks and opportunities, and seeking to identify factors outside the firm's control *(see also* Chapters 5–7).
2 *Buyer behaviour.* Firms need to have a profile of their existing and potential customer base, and to know how and why their customers purchase. Marketing seeks to identify the buyers, their potential motivation for purchase, their educational levels, income, class, age and many other factors which might influence the decision to purchase.
3 *Market research.* This is the process by which much of the information about the firm's customers and its environment is collected. Without such market research, organisations would have to make guesses about their customers. Such research may involve using data which already exist (secondary data) or using surveys and other methods to collect entirely new data (primary data).

Strategy

Once the environment has been scanned, then the organisation must develop a marketing strategy to give a sense of direction for marketing activity. The concepts of market segmentation and marketing mix invariably appear in such strategies.

Market segmentation

Major decisions need to be taken as to which *market segments* to target. A market segment is a group of potential customers who have certain characteristics in common, for example being within a certain age range, income range or occupational profile (*see* Box 10.1). Some of these market segments may be identified as more likely to purchase that product than others. When these segments have been identified, the organisation needs to decide whether one segment or a number of segments are to be targeted. Once that strategic decision is made, then the product can be positioned to meet the particular needs or wants which characterise that segment. The task here is to ensure that the product has a particular set of characteristics which make it competitive with other products in the market.

Box 10.1 Market segmentation

Producers tend to define markets broadly, but within these markets are groups of people who have more specific requirements. Market segmentation is the process by which a total market is broken down into separate groups of customers having identifiably different product needs, using characteristics such as income, age, sex, ethnicity and so on.

Occupational profile

There are many different methods of segmenting a market. One widely-used technique is to classify people according to the occupation of the head of the household as shown in Table 10.1 below, since market research suggests that consumer buying behaviour changes as individuals move from one such group or 'class' to another.

Table 10.1 Occupation of head of household

Group	Description	% of population
A	Higher managerial and professional	3
B	Middle management	11
C_1	Supervisory and clerical	22
C_2	Skilled manual	32
D	Semi-skilled and manual workers	23
E	Pensioners, unemployed	9

Interestingly BSkyB reported in mid-2000 that the 'old' analogue TV system attracted 46% of ABC_1 users, whereas the 'new' digital TV system was attracting 52% of ABC_1 users. The suggestion here was that digital TV appealed to a more 'up-market' audience because it allows users to access home shopping and other interactive services as well as the Internet.

VALS framework

Originally developed by Arnold Mitchell in the US in the 1960s, this framework has been much refined and is increasingly used by national and international marketers. It focuses on psychological, demographic and life-style factors to segment consumer groups.

The latest version of VALS segments the English-speaking population aged 18 or older into 8 consumer groups.

- *Innovators* – High self-esteem, take charge, sophisticated, curious. Purchases reflect cultivated tastes for up-market, niche products and services.
- *Thinkers* – Motivated by ideals, mature, well educated and reflective. Purchases favour durability, functionality and value.

▶

> ### Box 10.1 Continued
>
> - *Believers* – Strongly traditional and respect authority. Choose familiar products and established brands.
> - *Achievers* – Goal-oriented lifestyles centred on family and career. Purchase premium products that demonstrate success to their peers.
> - *Strivers* – Trendy and fun-loving. Purchase stylish products that emulate the purchasers of higher income groups.
> - *Experiencers* – Unconventional, active and impulsive. Purchase fashionable products and those related to socialising and entertainment.
> - *Makers* – Practical, responsible and self-sufficient. Purchase basic products, reflecting value rather than luxury.
> - *Survivors* – Lead narrowly-focused lives with few resources, seek safety and security. Purchase low-cost, well-known brands (i.e. exhibit brand loyalty) and seek out available discounted products.

Segmentation has allowed the growth of small specialist or 'niche' markets. As people have become more affluent, they have been prepared to pay the higher price for a product that meets their precise requirements. The growth of niche markets has also been important in supporting the existence of small firms. In many cases the large firm has found many of these segments to be too small to service profitably.

| *pause for thought 1* | Explain what is meant by the following terms: benefit segmentation; behaviour segmentation; geodemographic segmentation; lifestyle segmentation. |

Marketing mix

Strategy will also involve selecting a suitable *marketing mix*, which will take into account the following factors:

- the product itself (what particular defining characteristics should the product have?);
- price (what pricing strategies might be pursued?);
- promotional activity (how do we make consumers aware of this product?);
- place (is it available to key customers?).

These four elements are often referred to as the '4 Ps' and are considered in more detail in the context of international marketing strategies (*see below*). However, they can also play a part in the shorter-term action/reaction patterns ('tactics') of firms as Hill and O'Sullivan (2003) point out in the context of marketing responses to the product life cycle (Table 10.2).

Tactics

The tactics to be used are a shorter-term and more detailed extension of the marketing strategy. Many of these 'tactics' can involve individual elements of the '4 Ps'.

Table 10.2 **Marketing responses to the product life cycle**

	Introduction	Growth	Maturity	Decline
Marketing emphasis	Create product awareness Encourage product trial	Establish high-market share	Fight off competition; generate profits	Minimise marketing expenditure
Product strategy	Introduce basic products	Improve features of basic products	Design product versions for different segments	Rationalise the product range
Pricing strategy	Price skimming or price penetration	Reduce prices enough to expand the market and establish market share	Match or beat the competition	Reduce prices further
Promotional strategy	Advertising and sales promotion to end-users and dealers	Mass media advertising to establish brand image	Emphasise brand strengths to different segments	Minimal level to retain loyal customers
Distribution strategy (Place)	Build selective distribution outlets	Increase the number of outlets	Maintain intensive distribution	Rationalise outlets to minimise distribution costs

- *Product tactics* may involve attempts to utilise or modify the various stages (introduction, growth, maturity, decline) of the 'product life cycle'. For example, attempts may be made to extend the 'maturity stage' by finding new markets for existing products, new uses for the products and/or modifying the product.
- *Price tactics* may involve selecting particular pricing approaches for the product. For instance, 'price skimming' may be adopted whereby the price is initially set at a high level to 'skim' as much revenue and profit out of the product as possible. Alternatively, 'price penetration' may be used whereby a low price is set in order to reach as large a market as possible in a short period of time. 'Discriminatory pricing' may also be considered where the same product is priced lower in some markets than in others (e.g. lower price in those market segments with a higher price elasticity of demand – *see* Box 10.2, pp. 321–2).
- *Promotion tactics* may involve the degree of emphasis given to personal selling, advertising, public relations, sales promotion, etc. 'Push' tactics might focus on the producer offering incentives to key players in each distributional 'channel' to promote their products (e.g. the firm may offer incentives to wholesalers so that they 'push' the firm's products to retailers, etc.). 'Pull' tactics focus on the final consumer, the idea being to stimulate consumer demands which will then stimulate ('pull') retailers/wholesalers into stocking the firm's products.
- *Place tactics* might involve placing a particular emphasis on one or more *distributional channels* for the products in question. For example pre-eminence in distributional policy might be given to distributional channels such as direct selling, producer to retailer, producer to wholesaler or franchising.

■ Planning and management

These various marketing activities need to be integrated throughout the organisation, and this can only be done through careful planning and managing of the whole process.

Planning is the process of assessing market opportunities and matching them with the resources and capabilities of the organisation in order to achieve its objectives. However, planning is not just a one-off exercise. It needs to be integrated into the ever-shifting environment of the firm so that new issues are constantly addressed and met. Forecasts made at this stage will have a major effect on production, financial decisions, research and development and human resource planning.

Managing the process can involve many aspects. For example, in order for the planning to be ongoing, the whole process needs to be monitored to ensure that customer needs are being met effectively. This may involve measuring the outcomes of marketing strategies against objectives that may have been set at the strategic stage, for example, checking whether specific targets have been met for individual products. Customer surveys may also be used to audit the quality of the services delivered. Whatever the method, it is important that monitoring is built into the plan, so that major or minor adjustments can be made. Managing may also involve *organising* the marketing function, for example allocating different tasks to different individuals or different departments.

International marketing

We have outlined the general activities of the marketing process, but how do these apply to international markets? While the basic activities remain the same, the picture is far more complex. International marketing can simply be defined as involving marketing activities that cross national borders. However, such marketing activities can take place at different levels.

- Firms exporting to international markets but which have the majority of their sales in the domestic market. Here the international market is considered secondary to the domestic market.
- Multinational enterprises which have operations and sales worldwide and which regard the home or host country as but one of many equally important market environments.
- Firms (usually MNEs) which seek to adopt global marketing strategies. The basis of global marketing is to identify products or services for which similarities across several markets enable a single, global, marketing strategy to be pursued. Examples today might include Coca-Cola, Heinz, Kellogg's, McDonald's, Marlboro, etc. All the examples given are of consumer products but the potential for globalisation in industrial markets is also great, in particular where there is little or no need to adapt a product to local needs. Thus, a global market exists in areas such as telecommunications, computers, pharmaceuticals, construction machinery, bio-engineering, etc.

pause for thought 2   Can you list some of the differences between domestic marketing and international marketing?

A global branding approach may even be adopted by the firm itself on behalf of all its product portfolio. Case Study 10.1 looks at BP Amoco's global rebranding initiative which was launched in 2000.

CASE 10.1 Global rebranding of BP

In recent times the image of oil-based products has hardly been positive. Fossil fuels have been linked to CO_2 emissions and therefore to problems such as global warming and the emission of other hazardous substances. This is one of the factors which led BP Amoco to try to differentiate itself from the rest of the oil sector by looking for more environmentally-friendly solutions to providing energy, such as cleaner fuels, solar power and hydrogen cell technology. In addition, the company has changed dramatically over the past two years through a series of mergers and acquisitions, totalling $120 billion, which have brought together the former British Petroleum, Amoco Corporation, Atlantic Richfield Corporation (ARCO) and Burmah Castrol. Chief Executive Sir John Browne plans to spend £100 million over the next two years on a new unified global brand – including a new logo – a makeover for its petrol stations and a media advertising blitz. The new logo has been named the Helios mark after the Greek sun god and is designed to signify dynamic energy from oil to gas and solar and its initial advertising campaign carried the slogan 'Beyond Petroleum'.

Although these were the official reasons for this rebranding given by the company's Britannic House headquarters, some believe that Sir John also has ambitions outside of the energy field, and that the new logo would aptly cover a growing product portfolio such as an office cleaning company or a supermarket chain as much as a hydrocarbon group. In fact, a mini supermarket chain is on the way because BP has plans to open up convenience outlets at all its major petrol stations as part of ambitions to increase retail revenues by 10%. The BP Connect stores will feature in-store e-kiosks where customers can check weather and traffic conditions and shop online and in-store cafés offering freshly-made pastries, made-to-order hot snacks and freshly-ground gourmet coffee. Even solar panels have been embedded in the transparent canopies above the pumps to generate clean electricity directly from light to power the pumps and lights.

Probably the most important reason, however, is an acceptance that the traditional image of the oil company has become a negative one in the hearts and minds of the consumer. Petrol prices are high and are meeting consumer resistance and there is also a growing demand throughout the business sector for a social and ethical dimension in all that is done.

Further, customers believe that one petrol is much the same as another, making it almost impossible to build brand loyalty, as indicated by the fact that BP was 58th in a recent survey by consultant Interbrand on globally-recognised product names.

Such rebranding is good business practice, and is being done by every truly successful brand around the world, says Robert Jones, a director at consultant Wolff Olins. Brands such as Starbucks, Disney or Virgin are despised by a few but liked by millions. In a market filled with coffee bars, Starbucks stands for sociability as

▶

well as beverages. Disney stands for much more than cartoons and theme parks. It stands for fun – while Sir Richard Branson's Virgin is nothing if not youthful and irreverent. It can sell anything its founder comes up with – records, airlines, financial services, mobile phones and even energy.

So BP is not mistaken in spending all that cash on rebranding, but it does raise the question of whether the 'Beyond Petroleum' line it included in the initial advertising was correct. It points people in an interesting direction but does not explain what BP stands for, says Mr Jones. The challenge over the next few years will be to fine tune the message so that consumers understand what idea they are buying into – and, having set a new standard delivering on that, consumers do not like to be let down. Nike is seen as a brand that represents more than shoes; it represents winning. Allegations that it was using low-cost labour from poor countries damaged the company's name.

BP is engaged in some of the most politically sensitive countries in the world, such as Colombia, where it has been accused by charities of not doing enough to halt human rights abuses. The possibility that BP might drill in environmentally sensitive areas such as the Arctic National Wildlife Refuge, were it opened up for exploration, have also led to protest at its annual general meeting from green-fingered shareholders. But BP has so far managed to walk the tightrope between making spectacular financial gains and being seen by the wider community as a company that cares for both customers and employees. Although it has made large numbers of redundancies after taking over first Amoco, then Arco and then Burmah Castrol, it has done so by awarding generous financial packages.

Sir John Browne stresses that the bright new green and yellow logo is as much geared to inspiring people inside the organisation as outside. He has raised expectations that must be met.

Questions

1 Why has BP undertaken such global rebranding?

2 Comment on the prospects for the success of this strategy.

Reasons for international marketing

Obviously international marketing activities at all these levels involves additional risks and uncertainties as compared to selling in a domestic market only. It may be worth briefly reviewing the reasons why firms commonly seek to extend the geographical scale of their marketing activities.

■ *Increasing the size of the market.* Developing new markets abroad may permit the firm to fully exploit scale economies (*see* Chapter 8), which is particularly important when these are substantial for that product. In some cases the minimum efficient size for a firm's production may be greater than the total sales potential of the domestic market. In this case the firm's average costs can only be reduced to their lowest level by finding extra sales in overseas markets.

- *Extending the product life cycle*. Finding new markets abroad may help extend the maturity stage of the product life cycle. This can be particularly important when domestic markets have reached 'saturation point' for a product.

- *Supporting international specialisation*. In an attempt to reduce overall production costs, separate elements of an overall product may be produced in large scale in different geographical locations worldwide. For example, labour intensive components will often be produced in low-cost labour locations, whereas capital intensive components are more likely to be produced in high-technology locations. The final product, once assembled, must by definition be marketed internationally to achieve the huge sales volumes which are a pre-requisite for international specialisation.

- *Establishing first mover advantages*. From a less cost and more market-oriented perspective, being the first entrant within an overseas market may be an advantage. By becoming a 'first mover' a firm may make it difficult for new entrants to compete. For example, advantages include established customer loyalty, greater choice in terms of suppliers and the experience that comes with being the first entrant. The UK cider producer HP Bulmer, became a first mover when they decided to produce cider in Qufu, China. The company established a joint venture with the Chinese firm San Kong Brewery in the knowledge that they would be the first foreign company to produce cider in China.

- *Helping reduce investment pay-back periods*. Finding overseas markets helps achieve high volume sales early in the product life cycle, thereby reducing the pay-back period needed to return the initial capital outlay and making many investment projects more attractive. This may help to compensate for modern trends towards shorter product life cycles which are tending to inhibit investment expenditure.

- *Reducing stock-holding costs*. Overseas markets may provide new sales outlets for surplus stocks (inventories), thereby reducing warehousing and other stockholding costs.

Decision-making and international marketing

It is often said (e.g. Hollensen 2000) that at least five decisions must potentially be made by those involved in the international marketing process (*see* Figure 10.1), namely:

- whether to internationalise;
- which foreign market(s) to enter;
- how to enter these foreign markets (market-entry strategies);
- what international marketing mix to adopt (the 4 Ps);
- how to implement, coordinate and control the international marketing programme.

International marketing research can be regarded as a support activity, providing evidence and analysis of patterns and trends to support these five key decisions. We might usefully review each of these decisions and support mechanisms, some of which are considered in rather more detail elsewhere in this book.

Figure 10.1 Major international marketing decisions

Source: Tayeb (2000). Reprinted with permission

■ International marketing research

This function supports all five 'phases' outlined in Figure 10.1 providing vital information and analysis to underpin the decisions associated with each phase. A key aim of market research is to reduce the risk involved in taking effective decisions in these five phases. This is particularly important where the environment in which the firm is operating is unfamiliar. Market research can be divided into two types: desk research which means using information which has already been gathered for another purpose (secondary data), and field research, which involves obtaining information specifically directed towards a particular marketing issue and which is usually original (primary data).

From Figure 10.1 we can see from the 'Information needed' column that data will be required on both a macro level (e.g. GNP, demographic changes, inflation, exchange rates, etc.) and a micro level (e.g. firm sizes, productivities, cost structures, competitor reactions, consumer buying patterns, distribution channels available, etc.).

Desk research

There are numerous sources of secondary information available to the international marketer.

■ *International organisations*. The OECD, UN, EU, IMF and World Bank all collect large volumes of mainly macro data on an annual basis for both developed and developing countries. For example, the EU, apart from its many statistical publications, has established over 300 'European Documentation Centres' around the UK (and similar centres in other member countries). These centres are regularly updated with documents (often originating from the European Commission and Parliament) which impact on the single market.

■ *National publications*. In the UK National Statistics (formerly the Office for National Statistics (ONS)) publishes detailed annual (sometimes monthly or quarterly) data on most types of economic and socio-economic indicator. Similar information is available in most advanced industrialised economies.

■ *National Trade Associations and Chambers of Commerce* (or equivalents). These business agencies in the various countries can be invaluable in providing up-to-date market information.

■ *Trade journals*. These often provide up-to-the minute profiles of various aspects of industries, countries or specific market sectors.

■ *Financial Press*. The various FT indices and ratios (and their equivalents elsewhere) provide an invaluable source of up-to-date information on firms and industrial sectors.

■ *Internet*. Finally, of course, there is the Internet, though information found here is only as good as the researcher who is using it. Remember that many of the Web pages are commercially-based, and companies will not reveal any secrets that they feel might be useful to their competitors.

The major problems with secondary data are that it is available to competitors, it may be of limited value in terms of comparability between countries, and there may be large gaps in statistical coverage in certain countries. However, it is quick, easy to access, and may save valuable time as compared to field research.

Field research

Primary data may be obtained from a variety of sources. The main advantage of field research is that it is customised to the firm and is unavailable to competitors. However, it is expensive and time consuming and may present particular problems, such as collecting data in some national cultures which have little experience of using scientifically-based research methods. Survey methods that assume a high level of literacy, certain education levels, access to telephones, or a willingness to respond by those surveyed, may need to be reassessed in some international situations.

■ *Research agencies*. In most countries there are many enterprises that are specialists in research. Companies can specify the type of data they are interested in and the agency will carry out the research on their behalf.

■ *Company networks/personnel*. Original data may be obtained from company networks (e.g. suppliers who also work for rival firms). Sometimes members of a company are sent to investigate the nature of specified markets through 'shopping trips' which, while not rigorously scientific, can help the organisation 'get a feel' for the types of markets they may enter.

Market selection

The first two of the five phases for the international marketer in Figure 10.1 involve the decision on whether or not to internationalise and the decision on which markets to enter. The first of these decisions has already been considered in some detail in Chapter 2 of this book. Here we focus on the market selection decision (Phase 2 in Figure 10.1).

■ Segmentation and targeting

As in domestic marketing, once the larger market has been identified, the potential market has to be segmented as the firm's products are unlikely to appeal to the entire market. Segmentation, as we have seen, is the grouping together of customers with similar needs and characteristics. In international marketing, this means grouping countries with similar wants together or looking for similarities between specific groups of customers in different countries.

Accessibility/actionability

The viability of a particular market segment is determined to a large extent by issues of 'accessibility' and 'actionability' which arguably are even more important in the international context.

- *Accessibility*. This refers to the ability of the firm to reach the potential foreign customers with promotional and distributional techniques and channels. Market segmentation involves identifying groups of customers with common characteristics, but even where such groups exist they may be particularly difficult to access when they cross national borders. For example, finding a media source to host a promotional campaign that is equally effective in reaching high-income female professionals in London, Frankfurt and Milan may prove difficult, as indeed it may in finding a distribution channel to actually supply product to this market segment. It may be that adjustments will have to be made (e.g. narrowing down the intended market segment) because of such accessibility problems for the international marketer.
- *Actionability*. This refers to the ability of the firm to increase its scale of operations to match (with no diminution in efficiency) the now enlarged total market. All too often firms encounter logistical problems in raising capacity which, in effect, prevent the firm from realising the benefits of these new market opportunities. For example, various diseconomies of scale (*see* Chapter 8) may raise average costs or adversely affect product quality. One of the methods firms often use in seeking to overcome this problem of 'actionability' is to seek out alliances and collaborative agreements with existing players in overseas markets (*see* Chapter 8).

PEST analysis

The whole external environment is particularly important when selecting viable overseas markets. Firms often resort to PEST analysis to broadly evaluate the potential of markets for entry. Of course, these various political, economic, sociocultural and technological (and some would add ecological/environmental and legal) factors may be still more uncertain in an international context. Chapters 5–7 have already looked at these factors in some detail.

Targeting strategies

Having selected some potentially attractive international market segments, the firm will often adopt one of three possible targeting strategies: concentration, undifferentiated (or mass) marketing, differentiated marketing.

- *Concentration.* This refers to targeting a single market segment and developing an appropriate marketing mix for it. In international terms, this means concentrating marketing efforts on one or a small number of market segments to maximise the use of resources. For example, Rolls-Royce has targeted the luxury segment of the car market. Brand value may be crucial to successfully using concentration targeting strategies.
- *Mass (global) marketing.* This is where a single marketing mix is used worldwide. Very few companies attempt this because enormous resources are required to exploit world markets. It also assumes that markets are relatively homogeneous and that customers will respond to promotions in uniform ways.
- *Differentiated marketing.* This involves developing a different marketing mix for each of the market segments identified. Here, there is an assumption that the market is heterogeneous with consumers likely to respond in different ways and to different types of products.

Segmentation and targeting take place within a dynamic, ever-changing world business environment. No longer can organisations assume that things will stay the same for any significant period. Segmentation decisions often seek to identify sectors with high and growing levels of demand, but they must also focus on the trading environment that prevails. Any attempts at overt or covert protectionism by individual countries or regional trading blocs can have major impacts on market selection decisions. Indeed, the growth of regional trading blocs has led to 'insiderisation' with companies seeking a presence within a protected market through joint ventures with domestic firms or through founding a subsidiary company providing jobs and tax revenues within the host country. The strength of the competition also needs to be taken into account when deciding which markets to target. Organisations do not want to be crowded out by existing competitors who already have entrenched positions in terms of price, quality or consumer allegiance.

Market-entry strategies

The third decision phase in Figure 10.1 involves deciding how to enter the foreign market. Figure 10.2 outlines a number of possible methods which might be chosen.

These methods are by no means mutually exclusive: firms may be using one or more of these methods for market entry. Figure 10.2 suggests a broad spectrum ranging from minimum risk/minimum reward methods (e.g. indirect exporting) to maximum risk/maximum reward methods (e.g. foreign direct investment). These have already been discussed in some detail in Chapter 2. However, Figure 10.3 shows how Starbucks has tended to use a variety of joint ventures and licensing arrangements with local partners to move into new overseas markets as well as increasing its penetration within these markets. Its 'capital light' market entry strategy is clearly towards the minimum risk/minimum reward end of the spectrum of Figure 10.2.

Figure 10.2 **Market-entry methods**

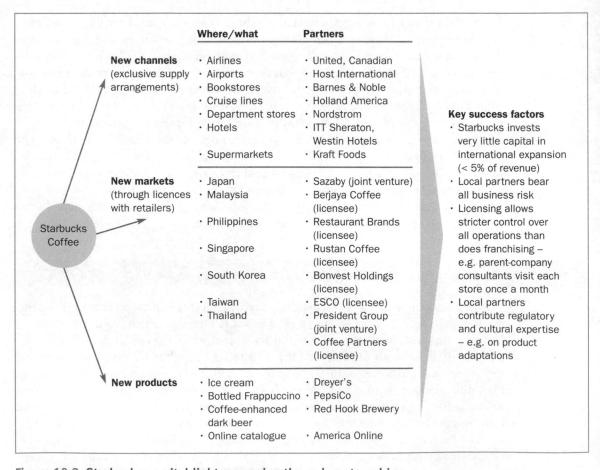

Figure 10.3 **Starbucks: capital-light expansion through partnerships**

International marketing mix

The fourth decision phase in Figure 10.1 involves the international marketing mix. The marketing mix of the 4 Ps can take on additional characteristics when viewed from an international perspective. This point is illustrated by Case Study 10.2 which shows how the importance of the various elements in the international marketing mix can vary between countries and regions.

CASE 10.2 Variations in the international marketing mix

International businesses are increasingly aware of consumer differences between countries and regions, even when these consumers otherwise have similar profiles (e.g. in terms of age, income, occupation). As a result, businesses which aspire to a global marketplace, are devoting more resources to identifying these differences before selecting the appropriate international marketing mix for that country or region.

Regina Maruca (2000) has reported on some research led by Dawn Lacobucci of Northwestern University's Kellogg Graduate School of Management. This research tries to get behind the cultural differences that might skew consumer responses to identical surveys in different countries. In other words, the research seeks to identify differences in consumer behaviour that are 'real' rather than 'apparent' as between nations and regions. In a recent test of their model, the researchers found important differences between consumers in four major geographical market segments (namely Asia, Latin America, northern Europe and southern Europe) in rating the products and services of a given company:

- price was seen as a key indicator of quality in Asia, northern Europe and southern Europe, but not in Latin America;
- product quality was seen as driving a company's repeat purchases in Asia, northern Europe and Latin America, but not in southern Europe;
- product after-sales service was seen as influencing repeat purchases in Asia, Latin America and southern Europe, but not in northern Europe;
- product 'value for money' was only seen as driving repeat purchases in Latin America;
- promotion was seen to have most impact on repeat purchases in Latin America and Asia, and least impact in northern Europe and southern Europe. (Here the number of sales representatives was used as a proxy variable for promotion in the sales of a given product in the different areas.)

Lacobucci concluded that 'companies that probe deeper to figure out what their global customers are thinking and feeling stand to create smarter branding strategies'.

Questions

1 If you were devising a marketing mix for selling the company's products used in the survey in northern Europe, where might you place the emphasis?

2 What other factors might play a part in adjusting the marketing mix between different nations and regions?

■ Product

This is the fundamental component of the marketing mix, since price, promotion and place are usually related in various ways to the characteristics which the product itself offers consumers. A key issue in international marketing is the extent to which a standard or differentiated product should be provided.

Standardised or differentiated?

There are good business reasons for trying to make a standard product acceptable to as many customers as possible – for example, it can help reduce average costs in design, production, promotion and distribution. Theodore Levitt of the Harvard Business School contends that tastes and preferences in many cultures are becoming more homogeneous due to the increased frequency of world travel and improved worldwide telecommunications. He claims that when marketers appreciate the fact that consumers' share basic interests they can market the same product worldwide and achieve economies of scale. A global marketing strategy is one that maintains a single marketing plan across all countries and yields global name recognition. Coca-Cola and McDonald's are examples of companies that use a global approach to market their products in different countries. Even when arguments for standardisation are strong, those who follow this path may still make subtle variations – for example, McDonald's uses chilli sauce in Mexico instead of ketchup, while in India it serves the 'Maharaja Mac' which features two mutton patties. The motto 'Think global, and act local' symbolises a patterned standardisation strategy which involves developing global product-related marketing strategies while allowing for a degree of adaptation to local market conditions. Some product types would appear more suitable for standardisation than others. Office and industrial equipment, toys, computer games, sporting goods, soft drinks are usually standardised across national borders.

On the other hand, arguments can also be advanced in favour of *product differentiation*. Where international market segments differ from one another, even when some group characteristics are held in common, then a more differentiated product strategy may be advisable. For example, if high-income households in Spain display different wants and needs from high-income households in Germany, products may have to be adapted in an attempt to sell to both groups of consumers simultaneously. Where products are highly culturally conditioned (as with many types of food, some types of drink, clothing, etc.), differentiated products and marketing strategies are commonplace. Table 10.3 outlines some of the factors supporting internationally standardised products and some of the factors supporting differentiated products.

As most companies are looking for some standardisation, they will often use a *modular product* design that allows the company to adapt to local needs while still achieving economies of scale. Car makers are beginning to adopt this form of production, with a basic body shape forming the shell around which different features are built (e.g. windscreen designs, sun roofs, etc.).

Branding

A brand is an element or group of elements that help distinguish the product of a particular supplier or (as we saw in Case Study 10.1) the image of the supplier itself. When attempting to set up brands, organisations need to consider whether the brand

Table 10.3 Factors supporting product standardisation or product differentiation

Factors supporting standardisation	Factors supporting product differentiation
Rapid technological change, reducing product life cycles (places a premium on rapid global penetration)	Slow technological change, lengthening product life cycles
Substantial scale economies	Few scale economies
International product standards	Local product standards
Short cultural distance to overseas market	Large cultural distance to overseas market
Strong and favourable brand image	Weak and/or unfavourable brand image
Homogeneous consumer preferences (within a given group characteristic, e.g. high income)	Heterogeneous consumer preferences (within a given group characteristic, e.g. high income)
Global competition	Local competition
Centralised management of MNE operations	Decentralised management of MNE operations

should be local (developed for a specific market), regional or global. Branding can sometimes extend into a communication that is separate from the product itself. Kotler and Armstrong (1994) make a distinction between the *utterable brand* (a name like Persil or Guinness) and the *unutterable brand* (a symbol, logo, colour scheme, or even typeface in which the name of the brand appears – such as Coca-Cola). Because of the difficulties of translation into words, the unutterable brand often works best at international level.

Many brand names do not travel well. There are a large number of examples of companies that have adopted a standardised approach to their branding, but have not researched the implications of translation when launching a brand into another country. For example, Coca-Cola when they first launched in China realised the name translated as 'bite the wax tadpole'. Fortunately, Estée Lauder was quick to notice their proposed export of Country Mist make-up to Germany could experience problems. This is because 'mist' in Germany is slang for 'manure'. Subsequently the product became Country Moist in Germany.

Very often brand names are changed in order to follow a standardisation strategy. For example, in the UK the following products have changed names to fall in-line with the same product in other countries. Starburst was formerly Opal Fruits, Cif formerly Jif, and Snickers formerly Marathon. Mars (the manufacturers of Snickers and Starburst) decided the sweets should be called the same name in the UK as they are in the rest of the world. Reasons for having one universal brand name can be attributed to cost savings by producing a single global advertising and marketing campaign for all countries. Also, with increased travel, consumers are able to recognise a brand abroad. Usually companies adopt expensive advertising campaigns advising of the name change. This needs to be done in a positive way to ensure the brand image maintains its current position in the mind of the consumer.

Corporate branding

Traditionally new drugs in the pharmaceutical sector are given new names to indicate a departure from previous alternatives available. The downside of this strategy is that large corporate investment in branding previous drug products is disassociated from the new products and may be regarded as largely wasted. Corstjens and Carpenter (2000) suggest that pharmaceutical companies might be well advised to consider *corporate branding* as a replacement for individual drug branding. In this way they suggest that company loyalty embedded in consumer allegiance to earlier products can then be transferred to successor products. They suggest that 'a customer looking for a treatment of allergies, for example, would not look for Claritin but for the latest Shering-Plough medicine'.

Positive marketing may even help turn disadvantages of individual drugs into brand benefits. For example, it was noted that Zyrtec, an anti-histamine drug developed by Pfizer induced rather more sleepiness in users than alternative therapies. Rather than allow rivals to use this as a negative, Pfizer sought to stress the positive benefits of drowsiness in increasing the likelihood of a good night's sleep and in reducing the itchiness which often accompanies the use of such drugs.

Case Study 10.3 reviews the debate on whether consumer tastes are consolidating, to the benefits of global brands, or fragmenting, requiring a more segmented approach by marketers.

CASE 10.3 · Global brands

The manifesto for global brands appeared in 1983 when the *Harvard Business Review* published an essay by Theodore Levitt, 'The Globalisation of Markets'. It was a hymn to homogenisation. Technology, by spreading mass transport and communication, was creating a world in which different cultural preferences and national tastes would disappear, Prof Levitt declared. The result was 'a new commercial reality – the emergence of global markets for standardised consumer products on a previously unimagined scale'. It was goodbye to the multinational and hello to the global company. 'The multinational corporation operates in a number of countries and adjusts its products and practices in each – at high relative cost – whereas the global company operates as if the entire world (or major regions of it) were a single entity: it sells the same things in the same way everywhere.'

When the Berlin Wall fell in 1989, Prof Levitt's theory was put into practice. And for at least two reasons, American companies were best placed to lead the way. One was that they had deep pockets. John Quelch, professor of business administration at Harvard Business School, says: 'The decade following the fall of the Berlin Wall was extraordinarily favourable for American muscle to go anywhere and everywhere in the world faster than their smaller competitors.' Another was that the principal brand attribute of America was freedom, a concept that had a magic resonance for those previously denied it.

Sure enough, once the trade barriers had gone, US brands poured into the world's newly opened markets and consumers lapped them up. The brand owners' share prices soared as investors savoured the prospects for seemingly limitless growth. In 1997 Procter & Gamble boasted that the number of consumers within its reach had shot up from 1bn to 4.5bn in a decade, saying its growth opportunities were 'literally unprecedented'.

Even before the decade had ended, however, the brand bubble had begun to burst. People in once-closed markets were happy to celebrate their freedom by tasting the forbidden fruits of American brands. But once the novelty wore off, a backlash set in. Consumers developed a pride in their national identity and started expressing a preference for local products, which, thanks to the introduction of western business methods, were simultaneously showing a big improvement in quality.

It turned out that Theodore Levitt's thesis was just plain wrong. Far from consolidating, consumer markets were in fact fragmenting. People did not want to become part of a homogenous mass, deprived of choice and force-fed standardised products. They wanted to be individuals expressing preferences and proclaiming their identity through what Sigmund Freud once called 'the narcissism of small differences'. In one of those 180-degree turns that periodically make a mockery of management theory, the big US brand owners realised the global approach was doomed and set about returning to the old multinational model in which local managements met local preferences with local products.

Fragmenting consumer tastes have made life much more challenging for global brand-owners. Before it launched Diet Coke in 1982, Coca-Cola had been a one-product company for nearly a century. Now it manages a portfolio of more than 200 brands, most of them local, and the number increases each year. Even so, its net profits have yet to regain their 1997 peak. McDonald's too, is varying its menus to suit national tastes. It has also experimented with diversification by investing in other food retailing chains such as Chipotle Mexican Grill in the US and Britain's Pret A Manger. Yet in 2002 it recorded the first net loss in its 37 year history as a stock market listed company.

'For many years in many of the most valuable product sectors, you really only had to say that something was American and life was unfairly easy for you,' says Simon Anholt, an adviser to government bodies on country branding. Many products around the world, such as Italy's Brooklyn chewing gum, adopted US-sounding names even though they had no connection with America. Views about America are now becoming more contradictory and ambivalent: some remain positive but, as the Pew research shows, uneasiness or outright hostility to America's position as sole superpower and global hegemon is creating more negative perceptions.

Big American brands such as Coca-Cola and McDonald's are not about to disappear but, to the extent that America's brand equity declines, they may lose some of the advantage they once enjoyed over products from other countries. And as that equity turns negative, they may have to work harder than other countries' brands just to stand still. Already, it is becoming difficult to imagine a new supplier of products or services adopting an American-sounding name in the hope that it will confer an automatic advantage. Of the 200-plus brands invented or acquired by Coca-Cola – from almdudler and Bibo to Tian Yu Di and Youki – hardly any have American associations and their ultimate ownership is often disguised by omitting Coca-Cola's name from the can or bottle.

Like Coca-Cola, other big US brand-owners may hope to counter the effects of declining American brand equity by acquiring local brands. But the trend also opens up an opportunity to China, India, Mexico and other emerging markets, many of which are hoping to follow the example of Japan, Taiwan and South Korea by transforming the image of their products and getting them on to the world stage.

▶

'Emerging countries are now getting very serious about creating brands that are not just domestic but global; and you will increasingly see them sharing the same space as, and competing with, American brands,' says Jagdish Sheth, professor of marketing at Emory University's Goizueta Business School in Atlanta. (The school is named after Roberto Goizueta, the late Coca-Cola chairman and chief executive.)

Amid a shift in tastes and fashions towards the ethnic and the authentic, western consumers are attracted as never before to the cultures and products of distant lands: 'The directions in which culture flows are multiplying and becoming more complex and other voices are beginning to be heard,' says Mr Anholt. 'People want exotic products with unusual stories to tell, partly because they're sick of brand America and partly because these products are just more interesting. The days when it was briefly fashionable to appear as global or monocultural as possible are well and truly over.'

The new cola war: one symptom of the anti-US consumer backlash is the appearance of a range of new soft drink brands catering for Muslims and others who no longer want to drink Coke or Pepsi. In the past few months, France has seen the launch of at least three brands: Mecca-Cola, Arab Cola and Muslim-Up. In Britain, a company has launched Qibla-Cola with plans to expand it overseas. Iran has increased exports of its Zam Zam Cola drink to the Middle East and Europe.

These drinks are not aimed solely at Muslims. 'The feeling against the American administration is not just a Muslim feeling: it's a world feeling,' says Mawfik Mathlouthi, founder of Mecca-Cola. The drink is now sold in 22 countries, mainly in Europe, and Mr Mathlouthi is preparing to launch a chain of fast-food restaurants in Europe and North Africa called Halal Fried Chicken or HFC, to take on the US-based KFC (formerly Kentucky Fried Chicken) chain.

Source: Richard Tomkins, *Financial Times*, 27 March 2003.

Questions

1 Examine the case for suggesting that consumer tastes are fragmenting rather than consolidating.

2 What are the strategic implications of the trends identified for both marketers and the companies they work for?

3 How might marketers respond to the growing anti-American sentiment alleged in the case study?

■ Price

Price in any marketing context is governed by competition, production costs and company objectives. International pricing decisions will reflect these aspects and will also need to take into account market differences between countries, exchange rates, difficulties of invoicing and collecting payment across borders, the effects of tariffs and purchase taxes on competitiveness, governmental regulations of the host country and the long-term strategic plan of the company in the different markets in which it operates.

Listed below are some of the major issues faced by those setting prices in different countries.

Market differences

Clearly some overseas markets are more attractive for a particular product than others in terms of population size, standard of living (e.g. real GNP per head), age profile, purchasing patterns, etc. Of particular interest in terms of international price setting is the possibility and profitability of setting different prices in different geographical markets. When the same product is priced higher in one (international) market than another, this is termed price discrimination.

For this to be possible, there must be barriers preventing purchase in one country at the lower price and resale in another country at the higher price (transport costs, tariff barriers, etc.). For this to be profitable, there must be different 'price elasticities of demand' in the different geographical markets. Where consumers in one country are more responsive to changes in price (i.e. have a higher price elasticity of demand), it can be shown that a firm can earn higher profits by charging a lower price in that country (see Box 10.2).

Box 10.2 Price discrimination

This involves charging different prices for an identical product.

In Figure 10.4 the firm faces two international markets, Market A with a relatively inelastic demand and Market B with a relatively elastic demand. To maximise profit the marginal cost of total firm output to both markets (MC_{A+B}) must equal aggregate marginal revenue from both markets (MR_{A+B}). This occurs at output Q_I, giving overall marginal cost of C. Now the conditions for maximum total profit is that the marginal cost of total firm output (C) must equal marginal revenue in each separate market.

i.e. $MC_{A+B} = MR_A = MR_B$ i.e. Q_A and Q_B respectively

No other allocation of output Q_I can raise total profit for the firm.

e.g. 1 more unit sold in market A, 1 less unit sold in market B.

Q_I unchanged, therefore TC unchanged (ignoring distributional costs).

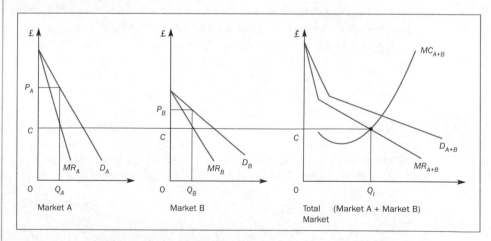

Figure 10.4 International price discrimination

> ### Box 10.2 Continued
>
> *TR* rises by ‹ *C* in market A   *TR* falls by *C* in market B
>
> i.e. *TR* falls net so that *TP* (= *TR* − *TC*) also falls
>
> OR
>
> 1 less unit sold in market A, 1 more unit sold in market B.
>
> Same outcome, *TR* falls net and with *TC* unchanged, *TP* (= *TR* − *TC*) also falls.
>
> The implication then must be that the profit-maximising price is lower in market B for which demand is more price elastic than in market A for which demand is less price elastic.

Exchange rates

When exchange rates fluctuate this can change the potential profitability of international contracts. For example, marketers must be alert as to any potential movements in the exchange rate between the date of quotation/invoicing and the date of payment so that the profit margin is not eroded. Price may have to be adjusted to cover adverse exchange rate movements. To reduce the impact of such problems currencies may be purchased on futures markets (*see* p. 129), or products may be priced in 'harder', more stable currencies. Of course, when both parties have a single currency, such as the euro, these problems will be avoided.

Cross-border payments

In contracts for internationally traded products it is important to specify exactly what a price covers. For example, does it cover cost, insurance and freight?

Tariffs and other taxes

Increases in tariffs (purchase taxes) on overseas sales can force a firm to raise the quoted price of its exports in order to retain its profit margin. Whether it will be able to pass these taxes on to the consumer as a higher price will, of course, depend on the price elasticity of demand for the product. The less price elastic the demand, the more of any tax increase can be passed on to the overseas consumer. Tariffs and taxes can have other impacts on trade issues. In an attempt to avoid such tariffs (and sometimes to overcome currency problems) there has been a growth in countertrade, namely the barter of goods and services between countries. Some 5% of all international trade has been estimated as being of this type. Further, any increases (or differences between countries) in *profit related taxes* (e.g. corporation tax) can result in MNEs adopting a policy of 'transfer pricing'. Here firms sell products on to subsidiaries within another country at prices which bear little relation to the true costs incurred at that stage of the overall production process (*see* p. 356).

Government regulations

As well as taxes, overseas governments may influence the firm's price-setting policies by regulations, perhaps setting maximum or minimum prices of products or minimum quality standards for particular products.

Strategic objectives

Overseas price setting may, of course, be influenced by the strategic objectives of the firm. For example, where market share or revenue maximisation are primary objectives, then prices will tend to be lower (e.g. penetration pricing) than they might be under, say, a profit-maximising objective.

■ Promotion

This is one of the most challenging areas of international marketing, since it is particularly affected by technological, sociocultural and regulatory factors. Promotion may involve press and media campaigns, direct mail, exhibitions or direct selling. When planning international campaigns, companies will need to ask the following questions:

- *What is the technological infrastructure of the country?* This will influence the prospects for reaching the final consumer. For example, in most industrialised countries over 90% of households own a TV, but this is often only a minority in the developing countries. If using direct selling by telesales, what proportion of the target market in that country possesses a telephone? If planning a poster campaign, what are the panel sizes available in different countries? Panel sizes are different, for example, in France and the UK, which can be important given the high costs of preparing and printing panels of varying sizes.
- *What appeals culturally in the advertisement?* English advertisements quite frequently use humour; French ones use erotic imagery, while in Germany the advertisements tend to be very factual. Great attention therefore needs to be paid to style and content in terms of the cultural impact of the campaign. If using direct selling, what type of sales force will be acceptable? For example, should we use local salespeople, an expatriate sales force or nationals from third countries?
- *What are the regulations on advertising in this particular country?* The UK, Belgium, the Netherlands and Denmark ban TV commercials for tobacco products but allow press adverts. In the UK any advertisement for tobacco products must carry a health warning. Are there any legal restrictions on the use of direct marketing (such as the use of information stored on computer databases)? Are there any legal restrictions on sales promotions? (Some countries do not allow certain types of free offers to be made; for example, money-off coupons are not allowed in Norway.)
- *What are the different media habits of the country?* For example, the current circulation figures per 1,000 of population of women's weekly magazines is around 29 in Germany, compared to 15 for the UK and 5 for Spain. Similar figures for TV guides are 37 for Germany, 10 for the UK and 7 for Spain.
- *What type of packaging do we use to retain the brand image yet meet country requirements* (e.g. ecological requirements demanded in Germany)? Do we need special types of labels? How much information needs to be presented about the content of the product?

We can see from these questions that international marketing is not an easy proposition. It requires an intimate knowledge of the market in each country. As market segmentation analysis becomes ever more sophisticated, this too can impact on promotion/advertising strategies.

Psychographic factors and promotion

Attempts are being made to segment markets in terms of psychographic factors, i.e. in attitudinal and behavioural characteristics resulting from cultural differences. For example, Roper Starch Worldwide (a leading market research company) claimed to identify four distinct shopping styles worldwide after surveying around 38,000 consumers in 40 countries, namely 'deal makers', 'price seekers', 'brand loyalists' and 'luxury innovators' (Shermach 1995). To the extent that such psychographic segmentation is shown to be reliable, companies can only adopt global promotion/advertising campaigns to clearly defined groupings across various countries. Cultural differences will prevent a more comprehensive advertising approach.

The FCB (Foote, Cone and Belding) two-by-two grid can be used to categorise a product in terms of its consumer orientation, using two key dimensions (*see* Figure 10.5):

1 an 'involvement' spectrum, with the *higher involvement* products reflecting those which are generally believed by consumers to further their personal objectives or have important personal consequences, as opposed to the *lower involvement* products;
2 a 'think-feel' spectrum, where *think products* possess characteristics which are primarily associated with functional outcomes and *feel products* with emotional outcomes.

Only where a product falls in a clearly defined quadrant in all its international markets can a global promotion campaign be applied with any confidence.

Ethnographic factors and promotion

Companies are increasingly sending their market researchers to live in consumers' homes to understand better their consumption patterns and perceptions of products. This practice, known as *ethnography* is based on the study of anthropology and the idea that you get more detailed and accurate information by immersing yourself with the subject (here the consumer). It is an attempt to overcome the known distortions that regularly occur when consumers fill in diaries or questionnaires, where sub-

Figure 10.5 **Consumer–product relationships**

consciously respondents often write what they think the researchers want to read. Brewers, for example, have found that men typically overstate how much they actually drank whereas women understate the true quantities. More accurate figures, arguably require researchers to live alongside the consumer and record what, and how often, they actually do drink.

The *Octagon Study* was conducted in 2002 by using an in-depth ethnographic survey of 11 households. Commissioned by Orange, Virgin and Pace, it sought to identify the behaviour of those households in responding to and using various new and established technologies, including mobile phones, the Internet and television. Orange's marketing research manager noted that the main beneficiaries of the study were the new product development team, the brand team and the advertising team as they gained rare and valuable insights into the responses and perceptions of actual users. In a separate ethnographic study, BT, Unilever, Cadbury, Centrica and Vodafone commissioned the 'Moby Study' to investigate the behaviour that makes consumers respond positively to certain brands, products and services and to certain types of advertising.

'Buzz' marketing and promotion

In some ways this is an attempt to promote with minimal expenditure on conventional promotional media. 'Buzz' marketing involves getting the trendsetters in any community themselves to convey the key message of the brand, creating interest in the product with little overt promotion or advertising. The message may be conveyed physically (the avant garde seen with the product), verbally (spoken about in conversation) or virtually (via the Internet). Ford used this approach to promote its new Focus. Having identified 120 people in six core markets as trendsetters (e.g. local DJs), each was given a Focus to drive for six months and promotional materials to distribute to interested acquaintances. Red Bull has also used this approach. For example in its eight US sales areas, representatives identify the bars and clubs visited by trendsetters and offer the owners branded refrigerators and other free goods along with their first order.

■ Place (distribution)

This is one of the major challenges for the international marketer, and mastery of this aspect can give the firm an edge over its competitors. A common problem in international marketing is for the firm to concentrate too much on the channels closest to the producer rather than channels closest to the customer. Some of these logistical issues involving type of channel selected are considered in more detail in Chapter 12.

The following aspects will influence the type of channel selected:

- the value and type of product;
- the cost and speed of alternative types of transport;
- the ease with which a channel can be managed;
- what the competitors are doing.

It is more difficult to control these channels from outside the overseas country itself. The type of distribution channel selected will also depend on the type of market entry a company has pursued. If it is operating from subsidiaries in that country (internalisation) then the subsidiary itself will often handle the distribution. If, however, products are simply being imported, then a third party such as a local agent may be employed to ensure that the quickest, cheapest and safest method is used. The company must adapt itself to local conditions, using strategies such as employing local distributors or buying such distributors and using them as part of the firm's internal operations, as appropriate to each circumstance.

CASE 10.4 Love in a warm climate

Nestlé's early chocolate experiences in India melted before its eyes. The Swiss manufacturer did not reckon on India's heat and poor distribution. Its chocolates were suitable for Europe, not India, where they were sold in tiny shops, sitting in direct sunlight without air-conditioning. Traders joked that Nestlé's chocolate ended up being sold as a drink. 'I told colleagues "if our chocolates become liquid why don't we sell them as liquid",' says Mr Carol Donati, Nestlé's boss in India.

Nestlé launched Chocostick, a liquid chocolate somewhere between a chocolate bar and a drink. Two years later, Chocostick and Chocki, a rival from Cadbury, are the fastest-growing chocolate brands, with a tenth of India's Rs7.2bn (£97m) chocolate market. Although demand for the innovative liquid product is slipping, Mr Bharat Puri, head of Cadbury in India, says: 'Ultimately, liquid chocolate is the product that can overcome our biggest barriers – weather and the related problem of distribution, and affordability.'

Liquid chocolates may have expanded the market, but they still only form a small share of the total. Most sales by value and volume come from old, solid, chewy favourites such as Cadburys Dairy Milk and Nestlé's Kit Kat. So while Coca-Cola hotfoots to communities of fewer than 10,000 people, Cadbury which has a two-thirds share of the market, and its closest rival Nestlé, will continue to target cities and small towns with its old favourite chocolate bars – and will continue to be at the mercy of weather, distribution and affordability.

Average summertime temperatures reach 43 degrees Celsius in India. Chocolate melts at body temperature of 36 degrees. India does not have controlled, refrigerated distribution. Air-conditioned supermarkets are rare. This is the environment in which chocolate is transported and sold, and the cost is high. Cadbury loses 1.5 per cent of annual sales of Ra6.85billion to heat damage; Nestlé loses 0.3–0.5 per cent of Ra5billion sales each year.

Both revise ingredients to make chocolate withstand heat. European chocolate makers use more vegetable fat, which produces a smoother chocolate. Indian manufacturers are banned from using vegetable fat by law and use less milk fat to produce a heat-resilient chocolate. Sugar is crystallised for long periods to make it harder. Indian chocolates are more resilient to heat than European chocolate by a factor of 2 degrees.

But the long-term answer to heat is a cold chain network. Its absence is a drag on growth. Ferrero Rocher sells a small quantity of its premium European brand to urban Indians each year, and wants to, but cannot, expand because non-refrigerated distribution would ruin its brand equity. It takes three to five years to build up a successful distribution system, a challenge that scares many foreign companies.

India's retailers are skillful improvisers. In north-west India one favoured cooling method is to place chocolates on a wet towel over a sales dispenser that is cooled by evaporation. These days, such techniques are used alongside coolers or fridges. Nestlé and Cadbury either supply coolers or loan small sums to retailers to buy fridges. But the result can be disappointing. To hold down power costs, distributors and retailers switch off air conditioning or fridges at night. When the cooling is switched on in the morning, the cocoa fat solidifies and turns white, presenting a bizarre, unsellable white on black form.

Nestlé has 350,000 mostly small retailers. Cadbury's 475,000 retailers are expanding by 48,000 a year. Even if distributors and retailers behave responsibly, chocolate companies face another hurdle: pricing. Chocki and Chocostick, for example, may be the right product, but even at Rs2 (less than 5 pence) they need to come down by 75 per cent to win rural consumers. More than half Cadbury's sales come from products that cost less than Rs5 each, an indication of how much more acute pricing will become if and when the company penetrates rural India.

For millions of poor rural (and poor urban) Indians, a typical transaction means buying one boiled sweet at a time. Each year Cadbury sells 895m Eclairs (a sweet confectionery) in 895m individual transactions at Rs1 each. The challenge is how far can manufacturers lower prices for a market that is not just vast, but where consumers regard anything brown, sweet and chewy like toffee as a chocolate surrogate.

Source: Kozem Merchant, *Financial Times,* 24 July 2003.

Questions

1 What are the problems for marketers of chocolate products reaching the vast, largely untapped Indian market outside the major towns and cities?

2 What possible solutions might there be to these problems? How feasible are these solutions?

3 What aspects of the marketing mix other than 'place' are highlighted by this study?

International marketing planning

The fifth and final phase of the international marketing approach, outlined in Figure 10.1, involves implementation, coordination and control.

Implementation does, of course, presume that there is an international marketing plan to implement! The nature of that plan will depend on some of the issues already discussed, for example, whether the product is standardised or differentiated, the stage of the product life cycle reached in different countries, the national regulatory environment, whether prices are to be uniform internationally or whether price discrimination is to be pursued, the nature of the distributional channels selected, and so on. Of course, such an international marketing plan must be consistent with the key corporate objectives.

Implementation of the international marketing plan, whatever its characteristics, will depend in part on the corporate structure of the firms in question. For example, when a firm grows from exports into international alliances such as those involving joint ventures, licensing or the establishment of subsidiaries it will often create an international division. This can be organised by geographical area or by product and can even take the form of an independent subsidiary. Such divisions usually specialise in international areas of marketing, manufacturing, finance, personnel and research, with responsibilities for the overall planning and control of these international activities. The degree of centralisation of the marketing function will usually depend on the strength of the particular brand. Strong brands need centralised marketing to preserve the integrity of the brand, but for weaker brands there will usually be a great deal of local adaptation so that marketing decisions will also tend to be localised.

International market planning, coordination and control faces a number of particular problems:

- despite technological advances, the market intelligence available for many international operations may be of poor quality and incomplete, especially in the developing/transitional economies;
- few tried and tested models of international marketing exist and those that do are often based on North American constructs which may have little relevance to many international markets.

Useful websites

Now try the self-check questions for this chapter on the website at www.booksites.net/wall. You will also find further resources as well as the following useful weblinks:

Interesting information on product launches, modifications, etc. can be found at:
www.mad.co.uk

The Business Owners Toolkit has a section on pricing and elasticity:
www.toolkit.cch.com

www.bized.ac.uk has information on the marketing strategies of various companies.

Information on market issues including objectives can be found at:
www.brandrepublic.com
www.keynote.co.uk
www.euromonitor.com

Interesting material on global marketing and segmentation strategies can be obtained from:
www.globalweb.co.uk

The Market Research Society can be found at:
www.bmra.org.uk
www.marketresearch.org.uk

Useful key texts

Daniels, J., Radebaugh, L. and Sullivan, D. (2004) *International Business* (10th edn), Pearson Prentice Hall, especially Chapter 16.

Dicken, P. (2003) *Global Shift: Transforming the World Economy* (4th edn), Paul Chapman Publishing Ltd, especially Chapters 7 and 17.

Hill, C. (2003) *International Business: Competing in the Global Marketplace* (4th edn), McGraw-Hill Irwin, especially Chapter 17.

Rugman, A. and Hodgetts, R. (2003) *International Business* (3rd edn), FT Prentice Hall, especially Chapter 11.

Tayeb, M. (2000) *International Business: Theories, Policies and Practices*, Financial Times Prentice Hall, especially Chapter 16.

Woods, M. (2001) *International Business*, Palgrave, especially Chapter 8.

Other texts and sources

Corstjens, M. and Carpenter, M. (2000) 'From Managing Pills to Managing Brands', *Harvard Business Review*, March–April.

Healey, N. (2004) 'The Multinational Corporation', in *Applied Economics* (10th edn), Griffiths, A. and Wall, S. (eds), Financial Times Prentice Hall.

Hill, E. and O'Sullivan, T. (2003) *Marketing* (2nd edn), Longman.

Hollensen, S. (2000) 'International Marketing Planning', in *International Business*, Tayeb, M. (ed.), Financial Times Prentice Hall.

Incandela, D., McLaughin, K. and Smith Shi, C. (1999) 'Retailers to the World', *McKinsey Quarterly*, no. 3.

Kotler, P. and Armstrong, G. (1994) *Principles of Marketing*, Prentice-Hall, Englewood Cliffs, NJ.

Maruca, R.F. (2000) 'Mappimg the World of Customer Satisfaction', *Harvard Business Review*, May–June.

Shermach, K. (1995) 'Portrait of the World', *Marketing News*, 28 August.

United Nations Conference on Trade and Development (UNCTAD), *World Investment Report* (annual publication).

United Nations Development Programme (UNDP), *Human Development Report* (annual publication), OUP.

World Bank, *World Development Report* (annual publication).

Chapter 11

International accounting and finance

By the end of this chapter you should be able to:

- discuss the background to accounting and its two main divisions;

- identify the main users of accounting information and the key financial statements;

- outline (and understand the reasons for) the differences of accounting treatment followed by various countries;

- assess the need for international harmonisation of accounting practices;

- examine some of the key issues facing the firm in the management of international finance and when operating under different financial and fiscal regimes (e.g. transfer pricing);

- identify some of the financial instruments used in the finance of foreign trade.

Introduction

The first part of this chapter looks at the role and nature of accounting – its main divisions, key financial statements and the regulatory frameworks which govern it. It also contrasts the differing accounting principles used within certain groups of countries, which might produce misleading results if used for comparative purposes.

There is a growing trend towards international harmonisation and in particular more use of International Accounting Standards (IASs). Over time it is expected that 'national' accounting regulations will be of less importance than agreed worldwide frameworks, and there is continuing pressure from international stock markets and organisations such as the European Union for the introduction of more unified and cohesive financial reporting standards.

The second part of this chapter looks at some of the key issues in international financial management and some of the instruments used in the finance of foreign trade. The broader international financial environment (both institutions and markets) has already been considered in Chapter 4.

The background to accounting

■ What is accounting?

Accounting has been defined as: 'the process of identifying, measuring and communicating economic information about an organisation or other entity, in order to permit informed judgements by users of the information' (American Accounting Association 1966).

The key aspects of accounting are therefore identifying, measuring and communicating:

- *identifying* the key financial components of an organisation, such as assets, liabilities, capital, income, expenses and cash flow;
- *measuring* the monetary values of the key financial components in a way which represents a true and fair view of the organisation;
- *communicating* the financial information in a way that is useful to the users of that information.

The identification of key financial components is universally based on a recording system, double-entry bookkeeping, which has been in use by businesses for many hundreds of years, but there is no global agreement regarding the way in which accounting information is measured or communicated. Analysis and appraisal can be distorted by national differences in accounting procedures and there is a growing movement to harmonise the accounting treatment for specific areas of difficulty. Regulatory frameworks have been developed within national and international contexts to help ensure commonality of approach, and large organisations are expected or required to observe *accounting standards*. These standards impose common procedures for specific accounting difficulties with the aim of avoiding inconsistencies between companies and improving the quality and usefulness of accounting statements.

■ Branches of accounting

Accounting is split into two key branches: financial accounting and management accounting.

Financial accounting is that part of accounting which records and summarises financial transactions to satisfy the information needs of the various user groups such as investors, lenders, creditors and employees. It is sometimes referred to as meeting the external accounting needs of the organisation.

Management accounting is sometimes referred to as meeting the internal accounting needs of the organisation, and is designed to help managers with decision making and planning. As such it often involves estimates and forecasts, and is not subject to the same regulatory framework as financial accounting. One professional body, the Chartered Institute of Management Accountants (CIMA), defines management accounting as:

'an integral part of management concerned with identifying, presenting and interpreting information used for:

- formulating strategy
- planning and controlling activities
- decision taking
- optimising the use of resources
- disclosure to shareholders and others external to the entity
- disclosure to employees
- safeguarding assets

The above involves participation in management to ensure that there is effective:

- formulation of plans to meet objectives: (strategic planning)
- formulation of short-term operation plans: (budget/profit planning)
- acquisition and use of finance (financial management) and recording of transactions (financial accounting and cost accounting)
- communication of financial and operational information
- corrective action to bring plans and results into line (financial control)
- reviewing and reporting on systems and operations (internal audit, management audit).' (CIMA 2000)

The CIMA definition is deliberately all-embracing, and there are some obvious infringements on what financial accountants might see as their 'territory'. It reinforces the notion that there are overlaps between financial and management accounting, particularly in the recording, interpreting and communicating aspects.

Users of accounting information

In the United Kingdom, an Accounting Standards Board (ASB) was set up in 1990 with the aim of improving standards of financial accounting and reporting. In 1999 it produced a Statement of Principles for Financial Accounting, which set out certain fundamental guidance for the preparation and presentation of financial statements. The Statement of Principles identified the seven groups of users of financial information (*see* Table 11.1), together with the information which they need from the financial statements.

We could also add an eighth group – the management of the organisation – as these people are the 'stewards' of the organisation and need to have reliable financial information on which to base their decisions.

Major financial accounting statements

There are three key accounting summaries produced by financial accountants:

- the profit and loss account (or 'Statement of Income');
- the balance sheet;
- the cash-flow statement.

Table 11.1 User groups and information needs

User group	Information needs
Investors	Investors need to assess the financial performance of the organisation they have invested in to consider the risk inherent in, and return provided by, their investments
Lenders	Lenders need to be aware of the ability of the organisation to repay loans and interest. Potential lenders need to decide whether to lend, and on what terms
Suppliers and other trade creditors	Suppliers need to take commercial decisions as to whether or not they should sell to the organisation, and if they do, whether they will be paid
Employees	People will be interested in their employer's stability and profitability, in particular that part of the organisation (such as a branch) in which they work. They will also be interested in the ability of their employer to pay their wages and pensions
Customers	Customers who are dependent on a particular supplier or are considering placing a long-term contract will need to know if the organisation will continue to exist
Government and its agencies	Reliable financial data helps governments to assemble national economic statistics which are used for a variety of purposes in controlling the economy. Specific financial information from an organisation also enables tax to be assessed
The public	Financial statements often include information relevant to local communities and pressure groups such as attitudes to environmental matters, plans to expand or shut down factories, policies on employment of disabled persons, etc.

Source: ASB, London (1999). Reprinted with permission

The profit and loss account (or 'Statement of Income')

This is the statement which summarises the income and expenditure of a specified period, disclosing whether the organisation has made a profit or loss. Under accounting conventions, all income and expenses for the specified period are included, whether or not cash has been received or paid. This is an important principle as otherwise the summary would fail to reflect the impact of all relevant transactions and financial events. For example, the decline in value (depreciation) over the lifetime of the organisation's fixed assets (e.g. buildings, machinery and computers) is estimated and included as an expense, even though no related cash outflow results in the period. 'Accruals and prepayments' are calculated – these are adjustments to ensure that all relevant expenses are included, not just the cash paid in the period – and adjustments for unsold stock are also made.

Taxation charges and dividend distributions are deducted from the organisation's operating profit to arrive at a retained profit which increases the accumulated reserves of the company.

Table 11.2 is an example of a profit and loss account.

Table 11.2 **Tesco plc: group profit and loss account**

52 weeks ended 22 February 2003		2003 £m	2002 £m
Sales at net selling prices		28,613	25,654
Turnover including share of joint venture		26,530	23,804
Less share of joint ventures' turnover		(193)	(151)
Group turnover excluding value added tax		26,337	23,653
Operating expenses	■ Normal operating expenses	(24,777)	(22,273)
	■ Employee profit sharing	(51)	(48)
	■ Integration costs	(4)	(–)
	■ Goodwill amortisation	(21	(10)
Operating profit		1,484	1,322
Share of operating profit of joint ventures and associates		70	42
Net loss on disposal of fixed assets		(13)	(10)
Profit on ordinary activities before interest		1,541	1,354
Net interest payable		(180)	(153)
Profit on ordinary activities before taxation		1,361	1,201
Profit before integration costs, net loss on disposal of fixed assets and goodwill amortisation		1,401	1,221
Integration costs		(4)	(–)
Net loss on disposal of fixed assets		(13)	(10)
Goodwill amortisation		(21)	(10)
Tax on profit on ordinary activities		(415)	(371)
Profit on ordinary activities after taxation		946	830
Minority interest		–	–
Profit for the financial year		946	830
Dividends		(443)	(390)
Retained profit for the financial year		503	440

The balance sheet

This statement summarises the assets, liabilities and shareholders' equity of the organisation at the end of the 'financial period'. Assets are usually divided between:

■ *fixed assets*, which are significant items likely to be owned by the organisation for at least a year, such as land, buildings, machinery and computers. These examples are all tangible fixed assets, meaning they are 'physical' assets, but organisations may also own intangible fixed assets of great value such as patents, trademarks and also the price paid for 'goodwill' (the value of a reputation) when buying other businesses; and

■ *current assets*, which are items which tend to change value rapidly during a financial period, being used in day-to-day trading. These include stock, debtors and bank and cash balances.

Liabilities are divided between:

- *current liabilities*, such as trade creditors, taxation and dividends owing and short-term indebtedness such as bank overdrafts; and
- *long-term liabilities*, such as loans due for repayment after more than one year from the balance sheet date.

Table 11.3 is an example of a balance sheet.

Table 11.3 Tesco plc: balance sheets (group and company)

22 February 2003	Group		Company	
	2003 £m	2002 £m	2003 £m	2002 £m
Fixed assets				
Intangible assets	890	154	–	–
Tangible assets	12,828	11,032	–	–
Investments	59	69	7,820	6,704
Investments in joint ventures	266	232	158	156
	14,061	11,503	7,978	6,860
Current assets				
Stocks	1,140	929	–	–
Debtors	662	454	1,012	3,060
Investments	239	225	–	5
Cash at bank and in hand	399	445	–	–
	2,440	2,053	1,012	3,065
Creditors: falling due within one year	(5,372)	(4,809)	(1,961)	(4,707)
Net current liabilities	(2,932)	(2,756)	(949)	(1,642)
Total assets less current liabilities	11,129	8,747	7,029	5,218
Creditors: falling due after more than one year	(4,049)	(2,741)	(3,772)	(2,609)
Provisions for liabilities and charges	(521)	(440)	–	–
Total net assets	6,559	5,566	3,257	2,609
Capital and reserves				
Called up share capital	362	350	362	350
Share premium account	2,465	2,004	2,465	2,004
Other reserves	40	40	–	–
Profit and loss account	3,649	3,136	430	255
Equity shareholders' funds	6,516	5,530	3,257	2,609
Minority interest	43	36	–	–
Total capital employed	6,559	5,566	3,257	2,609

The cash-flow statement

Even profitable business can fail due to their inability to find enough cash to pay their creditors, so a third statement is produced which concentrates on changes in the *liquidity* of the company during the financial period. Liquidity is the ability of a company to access enough cash and bank resources to meet liabilities as they fall due, and the statement focuses on the overall change in cash balances during the financial period. The cash-flow statement usually breaks down information into cash flows from operating activities (e.g. trading), investing activities (e.g. buying and selling fixed assets) and financing activities (e.g. issue of shares, raising or repaying loans).

Table 11.4 is an example of a cash-flow statement.

Table 11.4 Tesco plc: group cash-flow statement

52 weeks ended 22 February 2003	2000 £m	1999 £m
Net cash inflow from operating activities	2,375	2,038
Dividends from joint ventures and associates		
Income received from joint ventures and associates	11	15
Returns on investments and servicing of finance		
Interest received	37	44
Interest paid	(253)	(232)
Interest element of finance lease rental payments	(2)	(4)
Net cash outflow from returns on investments and servicing of finance	(218)	(192)
Taxation		
Corporation tax paid (including advance corporation tax)	(366)	(378)
Capital expenditure and financial investment		
Payments to acquire tangible fixed assets	(2,032)	(1,877)
Receipts from sale of tangible fixed assets	32	42
Purchase of own shares	(52)	(85)
Net cash outflow for capital expenditure and financial investment	(2,052)	(1,920)
Acquisitions and disposals		
Purchase of subsidiary undertakings	(419)	(31)
Net cash at bank and in hand acquired with subsidiaries	33	–
Received from/(invested in) joint ventures	(43)	(46)
Net cash inflow/(outflow) from acquisitions and disposals	(436)	(96)
Equity dividends paid	(368)	(297)
Cash outflow before use of liquid resources and financing	(1,054)	(830)
Management of liquid resources		
Increase in short-term deposits	(14)	27
Financing		
Ordinary shares issued for cash	73	82

Table 11.4 Continued

52 weeks ended 22 February 2003	2000 £m	1999 £m
Increase in other loans	774	916
New finance leases	249	–
Capital element of finance leases repaid	(73)	(24)
Net cash inflow from financing	1,023	974
(Decrease)/increase in cash in the period	(45)	171
Reconciliation of net cash flow to movement in net debt		
(Decrease)/increase in cash in the period	(45)	171
Cash inflow from increase in debt and lease financing	(950)	(892)
Cash used to increase liquid resources	14	(27)
Loans acquired with subsidiary undertaking	(178)	–
Amortisation of 4% unsecured deep discount loan stock	(8)	(14)
Other non-cash movements	(19)	(12)
Foreign exchange differences	3	18
Increase in net debt	(1,177)	(756)
Net debt at 22 February 2002	(3,560)	(2,804)
Net debt at 22 February 2003	(4,737)	(3,560)

Published accounts

Large corporations will publish financial information, usually as a requirement of a specific stock exchange or due to national legislation. For example, in the UK, Acts of Parliament require all limited companies to publish financial statements. Although there is no equivalent in the USA of the UK's Companies Acts, major US companies will be registered with the Securities and Exchange Commission (SEC), which sets out detailed requirements for audit and the rules of financial reporting. For smaller UK companies, only a brief summary of their finances is required, but for the largest companies, including all plcs (public limited companies), an 'annual report' must be prepared (often at great expense) which is sent to all shareholders and Companies House, which is the UK government's 'storehouse' of company information. The public have a right of access to the information – see the website http://www.companies-house.gov.uk for details. UK companies whose shares are listed on the Stock Exchange will also publish an abbreviated interim statement showing their results for the first six months of the financial period.

pause for thought 1 Can you identify any differences in the frequency of reporting between the UK and the USA?

Many corporations regard their annual report as an opportunity to show off the best of their company, in effect treating it as a public relations exercise. The glossy photographs of the company's products and exotic locations of major contracts can give some reports the style of a travel brochure. Many large mainland European companies not only produce corporate reports in their 'home' language but also produce English-language versions for wider circulation. An example can be found at http://www.bmw.com (click on 'investor relations', then 'publications').

A key feature of UK and other EU published profit and loss accounts and balance sheets is that they have to follow specific formats of presentation. These formats were devised to ensure a degree of uniformity across the European Community, as they apply to all member countries. Although there is a small amount of flexibility allowed (for example a company can produce statements in either a 'vertical' or 'horizontal' format), virtually all UK companies follow the 'vertical' style format as shown in Tables 11.1 and 11.2 above.

pause for thought 2	What are the key sections of an annual report?

CASE 11.1 Pearson plc

Look at the three extracts from the annual report of Pearson plc shown below, then answer the questions which follow.

Table 11.5 **Pearson plc: consolidated profit and loss account**

All figures in £ millions	2002 Operating activities	Other items	Total	2001 Operating activities	Other items	Total
Sales (including share of joint ventures)	4,331	–	4,331	4,240	–	4,240
Less: share of joint ventures	(11)		(11)	(15)		(15)
Sales	4,320	–	4,320	4,225	–	4,225
Group operating profit	496	(302)	194	444	(424)	20
Share of operating (loss)/profit of joint ventures and associates	(3)	(48)	(51)	19	(86)	(67)
Total operating profit/(loss)	493	(350)	143	463	(510)	47
Share of operating profit of associates	71	–	71	51	–	51
Loss on sale of fixed assets and investments		(13)	(13)		(12)	(12)
Loss on sale of subsidiaries and associates		(27)	(27)		(63)	(63)
Profit/(loss) on sale of subsidiaries and associates by an associate		3	3		(53)	(53)
Non operating items		(37)	(37)		(128)	(128)

Table 11.5 Continued

All figures in £ millions	2002 Operating activities	Other items	Total	2001 Operating activities	Other items	Total
Profit (loss) before interest and taxation	493	(387)	106	463	(638)	(175)
Amounts written off investments	–	–	–	–	(92)	(92)
Net finance costs	(94)	(37)	(131)	(169)	–	(169)
Profit before taxation	399	(424)	25	294	(730)	(436)
Taxation	(131)	67	(64)	(100)	133	33
Profit after taxation	268	(357)	(89)	194	(597)	(403)
Minority interests	(27)	5	(22)	(24)	4	(20)
Profit for the financial year	241	(352)	(111)	170	(593)	(423)
Dividends			(187)			(177)
Loss retained			(298)			(600)
Adjusted earnings per share			30.3p			21.4p
Loss per share			(13.9)p			(53.2)p
Diluted loss per share			(13.9)p			(53.2)p
Dividends per share			23.4p			22.3p

Table 11.6 Pearson plc: consolidated balance sheet

All figures in £ millions	2002	2001
Intangible assets	3,610	4,193
Tangible assets	503	542
Investments: joint ventures	7	7
Investments: associates	106	893
Investments: other	84	84
Current assets	2,542	2,522
Creditors due within one year	(1,363)	(1,368)
Net current assets	1,179	1,154
Total assets less current liabilities	5,489	6,873
Creditors due after more than one year	(1,794)	(2,661)
Provisions for liabilities and charges	(165)	(239)
Net assets	3,530	3,973
Capital and reserves	3,338	3,797
Equity minority interests	192	176
	3,530	3,973

Table 11.7 Pearson plc: consolidated cash-flow statement

All figures in £ millions	2002	2001
Net cash inflow from operating activities	529	490
Dividends from joint ventures and associates	6	25
Interest received	11	31
Interest paid	(151)	(187)
Debt issue costs	–	(1)
Dividends paid to minority interests	(1)	(9)
Returns on investments and servicing of finance	(141)	(166)
Taxation	(55)	(71)
Purchase of tangible fixed assets	(126)	(165)
Sale of tangible fixed assets	7	36
Purchase of investments	(21)	(35)
Sale of investments	3	22
Capital expenditure and financial investment	(137)	(142)
Purchase of subsidiaries	(87)	(128)
Net cash acquired with subsidiaries	1	83
Purchase of joint ventures and associates	(40)	(26)
Sale of subsidiaries	3	41
Net cash disposed with subsidiaries	(1)	–
Sale of associates	920	1
Acquisitions and disposals	796	(29)
Equity dividends paid	(181)	(174)
Net cash inflow/outflow before management of liquid resources and financing	817	(67)
Liquid resources acquires	(65)	(48)
Collateral deposit reimbursed	22	47
Management of liquid resources	(43)	(1)
Issue of equity share capital	6	20
Capital element of finance leases	(5)	(7)
Loan facility repaid	(507)	(521)
Bonds (repaid)/advanced	(167)	507
Collateral deposit reimbursed	17	–
Net movement in other borrowings	(7)	3
Financing	(663)	2
Increase/(decrease) in cash in the year	111	(66)
Reconciliation of net cash flow to movement in net debt		
Decrease/(increase) in net debt from net cash flow	111	(66)
Decrease in net debt from management of liquid resources	43	1
Decrease in net debt from other borrowings	664	11
Decrease in finance leases	5	7
Acquired with subsidiary	24	–
Debt issue costs	–	1
Other non-cash items	(1)	(6)
Exchange differences	132	(24)
Movement in net debt in the year	978	(76)
Net debt at beginning of the year	(2,393)	(2,317)
Net debt at end of the year	(1,415)	(2,393)

Source: Pearson plc Annual Report and Accounts 2002.

Questions

1 Look at Table 11.5. What was Pearson's total operating profit in 2002? By how much had it increased or decreased compared with the previous year?

2 Look at Table 11.6. What was the total net assets utilised by the company at the end of 2002 and 2001 respectively? Look back at Table 11.5's operating profit and calculate this as a percentage of the total net assets for each year. What does this tell you about the company's performance in this period?

3 Look at Table 11.7. Had cash funds increased or decreased in 2002 and by how much? How much debt did the company have at the end of 2002? By what percentage had it increased or decreased during the year?

Differences of approach in different countries

The practical implications of countries adopting differing accounting procedures can be seen in the two extracts below which appeared on the same day in an accounting magazine.

■ Extract 1: 'Rover trouble was avoidable'

'Sacked BMW chairman Bernd Pischetsrieder might have retained his job if he had persuaded colleagues not to impose harsh German accounting policies on Rover when the company bought the British car maker in 1994, analysis by *Accountancy Age* has shown. Though the British company is now widely blamed as jeopardising BMW's future as an independent business, Rover's results compiled under British accounting standards, quietly filed at Companies House, paint a picture quite different from the enduring story of huge losses that ultimately led to Pischetsrieder's downfall.

As shown in the table below, figures reveal that Rover made a profit of £147m between 1994 and 1997. Headline figures from consolidated accounts published by BMW, which took the company over in March 1994, however, show Rover making a loss of £363m in the same period. It is these figures that the press, analysts and indeed BMW's board have pounced on as proof of the British car maker's inefficiency.

(Losses in brackets)	Rover net profit using British accounting rules £m	Rover net profit using German accounting rules £m	Difference £m
1994	279	Unpublished	–
1995	(51)	(163)	−112
1996	(100)	(109)	−9
1997	19	(91)	−72
Total	**147**	**(363)**	**−216**

German accounting policies are notoriously harsh. Investments are depreciated faster, there are more possibilities for making provisions and different rules for valuing stocks. All these have the effect of depressing profits.'

Source: Accountancy Age, 18 February 1999. Reprinted with permission.

■ Extract 2: 'UK standards add £200m to British Airways results'

'Differing international accounting systems are affecting airlines' reported profit levels by hundreds of millions of pounds each year, according to an aviation industry expert. Using an analysis of the results of British Airways, Richard Shaylor, a financial analysis lecturer with Signal Training, says the differences are confusing investors. The airline publishes its results according to UK standards and has no plans to move to an international standard. But, because it has shares listed on both the London and New York Stock Exchanges, it also includes a revised profit and loss account constructed according to US generally accepted accounting practice in its annual report. As the table below shows, one of the larger distortions arises from BA's 1996 figures. Under UK rules, it made a profit of £473m, whereas using US rules the figure was £267m.'

	BA net profit using British accounting rules (£m)	BA net profit using US accounting rules (£m)	Difference (£m)
1994	274	145	−129
1995	250	297	+47
1996	473	267	−206
1997	553	548	−5
1998	460	654	+194
Totals	**2,010**	**1,911**	**−99**

Source: Accountancy Age, 18 February 1999. Reprinted with permission.

 pause for thought 3   Comment briefly on how the issues raised in these two articles have implications for international business.

Case Study 11.2 addresses the issue of a standardised international approach.

CASE 11.2 VW switches accounting model

'Volkswagen, Europe's largest car maker, plans to adopt International Accounting Standards or GAAP, the US financial reporting code, as early as 2001 in an attempt to become more shareholder-friendly.

The plan is expected to enhance VW's reported profits and bolster its share price. Last year, VW was the weakest performer in Germany's Dax 30 index of blue-chip stocks; its shares have halved in price since mid-1998 ... Volkswagen is the only Dax 30 constituent that still uses German HGB accounting standards. The standards allow companies to understate their earnings using measures such as rapid depreciation of their assets, heavy provisions and low valuation of assets and liabilities.

The move coincides with growing nervousness in Germany about foreign takeovers following Vodafone AirTouch's bid for Mannesmann.

Volkswagen's market capitalisation is dwarfed by international car makers such as Toyota, whose market value of roughly h176.3 billion ($174 billion) is more than ten times Volkswagen's h14.4 billion.

For the time being, however, Volkswagen is protected by the state of Lower Saxony, which holds a 18.65% stake and has no intention of selling.'

Source: *Financial Times*, 21 February 2000.

Questions

1 Why did VW want to move away from German accounting standards?

2 Why was the choice of accounting standards seen as a means of avoiding a takeover?

3 State two advantages which may have been gained by VW using German accounting standards.

■ Historic reasons for dissimilarity of accounting approach

As seen in the extracts above, major industrialised nations have developed their own specific accounting regulations. This rarely has a major impact when applied to domestic companies within those countries, but may have dramatic implications when international investment decisions have to be made. There are many reasons why countries developed dissimilar procedures, including those summarised in Table 11.8.

As stated previously, there is a strong movement to harmonise the international regulatory framework; indeed, from 2005 the published group accounts of EU listed companies must comply with international accounting standards. Eventually International Accounting Standards may become the universal framework on which multinationals base their financial reports, though national standards will still apply for domestic purposes.

Table 11.8 Reasons for different accounting standards

The legal system	Some countries (e.g. France and Germany) have all-embracing sets of rules and regulations which apply to businesses, whereas countries such as the UK and the USA have more general statute laws backed up by case law, allowing more flexibility for individual companies. For example, in the USA, individual companies decide the rates at which assets depreciate, but in Germany the government decides what are appropriate.
Types of ownership patterns	Countries with wide share ownership (e.g. UK, USA) have developed strong independent professional accountancy associations to provide reliable financial data to shareholders. Those countries with predominantly small, family-run businesses (e.g. France) or with banks owning most shares of large companies (e.g. Germany), have had less need for providers of independent financial information.
The accounting profession	Strong independent professional associations of accountants developed in those countries (e.g. UK, USA) with the most liberal company laws and widest share ownership. Countries with restricted patterns of business ownership and rigid company statutes (e.g. France, Germany) had weak groupings of accountants, and sometimes the governments themselves controlled the profession.
Conservatism	Financial statements produced by independent accountants should ideally show a 'true and fair view'. This is open to many interpretations, not least being the problem of asset valuation. Should assets be valued at original cost, what they might be sold at today, what it would cost to replace them or a depreciated value based on usage, wear and tear, etc.? US practice is conservative – don't revalue, but depreciate on a reasonable basis over the asset's lifetime. German practice is also conservative – don't revalue, but depreciate on a basis decreed by the government. UK practice is liberal – allowing companies either to revalue at intervals or show assets at cost, and depreciate on a reasonable basis.

Global accounting standards

For some time there has been support for a single set of accounting standards and practice all over the world to remedy some of the problems already noted. A particular complaint has been that while auditing and accounting rules are national in origin, today's capital is global in origin. This view has been reinforced by concerns as to the alleged inability of accounting rules and procedures to do more in preventing major corporate failures such as Enron and WorldCom in 2001/2. All this has resulted in increased pressure from the business community for a single set of global accounting rules, which ultimately might allow companies to list on any stock market in the world using one set of accounts, reducing the cost of capital for corporations everywhere.

Even a partial movement to a more uniform set of accounting standards is, however, by no means likely to be painless as is readily illustrated in the Japanese context in Case Study 11.3.

CASE 11.3 An end to make-believe accounting

FT

When Tomen, a second-tier Japanese trading house revealed in 2000 that it would record ¥407 billion (£2.4 billion) in losses and would need to ask creditors to forgive ¥200 billion in debts, investors were shocked. As its shares plunged below book value, fears spread through the market about hidden losses elsewhere.

The fate of Tomen showed how apparently arcane amendments in accounting principles that come into effect this month are forcing huge changes on corporate Japan. Tomen had decided to write off huge investments from the late 1980s before it had to, but other companies will soon follow.

All listed Japanese companies will now be required to record their saleable property assets and securities at current market value, and disclose the value of any shortfall in their pension liabilities. Next year, cross-shareholdings will be valued at market prices, and companies will have to write down the losses if the current market value is 30% lower than the value at which they are held in balance sheets.

The consequences could be momentous. 'Tomen is just the tip of the iceberg. They are just the first to admit they are in trouble', says Timothy Marrable, analyst at Warburg Dillon Read. Blue-chip Japanese companies such as Nissan Motors and Toshiba, the electronics group, have already announced billions of dollars of provisions to cover underfunded pension liabilities.

These changes – which analysts say make Japanese accounting standards among the toughest in the world – are intended to satisfy demands from international investors for greater transparency. The hope is that investors will be encouraged to place money in Japanese companies once they are sure that corporate balance sheets are sound.

But the new principles will also expose problems that have been hidden for years in many companies. 'The new accounting standards make it much more clear who are the winners and losers', says Craig Chudler, chief strategist at Nikko Salomon Smith Barney in Tokyo. 'Once the accounting rules are in place, and people understand the impact of them, investors can re-rate companies.'

Moody's Investor Services, the US credit rating company, is watching the transition carefully. 'If something comes out that we did not know about, or if the size of the surprise is larger than we expected, then we may have to make a certain adjustment in our credit opinion', says Yoshio Takizawa, a Moody's managing director.

Some sectors are likely to be hit particularly hard. Trading companies – diversified industrial groups – and construction companies could be most vulnerable because some invested heavily in property in the late 1980s. Analysts predict that more than 40% of Japan's big construction groups could have liabilities in excess of their assets under the new rules.

Atsushi Takagi, analyst at Morgan Stanley, expects the accounting changes to trigger consolidation in the construction industry. 'We are going to see a lot more debt forgiveness plans', he says. 'There will be huge unemployment as a result.' This is no small matter, since the Japanese construction industry employs 6 million people, or about 10% of the country's workforce.

The new rules will benefit some companies. Kathy Matsui, equity strategist at Goldman Sachs, estimates that non-consolidated, pre-tax earnings at non-financial

▶

companies on the first section of the Tokyo stock exchange could rise by 38% next year because companies will be forced to record previously unrealised gains on property and securities.

Analysts say the changes have largely been taken into account by the stock market. 'These companies are trading so cheaply anyway that any further fall is unlikely to affect the major indices', says Mr Chudler. Nonetheless, the standards will place pressure on Japanese managers to improve efficiency. 'In the past, you could always hide behind the cushion of latent gains on securities and property', says Ms Matsui. 'Without it, you have to live in the world of real, rather than make-believe, accounting.'

For Tomen, the new world has proved painful. The group, which has chemicals, machinery and food operations, had tried to cut costs before the accounting changes. But executives admit that they were unaware of the scope of the problems they faced until they saw accounts prepared on the new basis.

'We did anything and everything, and invested anywhere – that was the definition of a Japanese trading company', says one senior Tomen executive. The investments ranged from property development to semiconductors to airline leasing. Tomen also bought shares in its trading partners that have since plunged in value.

As well as forcing efficiency gains on companies, the new rules will encourage a wave of mergers and acquisitions, accountants say. They predict the unwinding of cross-shareholdings that have for decades held together the keiretsu business groupings. 'If cross-shareholdings diminish, then there is a lot of chances for aggressive M & A', says Aki Fujinuma, partner at Showa Ota, an affiliate of accountant Ernst & Young.

That could provide unprecedented opportunities for foreign groups that have wanted to make acquisitions but have found that the lack of financial transparency has prevented them from valuing potential targets accurately. Daimler-Chrysler, for example, backed away from an investment in Nissan Motor in February 1999 after it realised the extent of Nissan's hidden liabilities.

Given the potentially disruptive effect of the changes, Japan is taking a bold step by implementing them now. The economy has slipped back into recession, and corporate profits are in the doldrums. In spite of this, regulators have imposed the changes in an effort to bring balance sheets closer to reality before the gap between past and present values widens further.

'We are taking collective action to restore public confidence in Japanese companies', says Mr Fujinuma. 'Historical cost accounting is no longer appropriate.' The accounting changes will be tough for many companies in the short-term – and potentially fatal for some – but they provide longer-term hope for Japan's corporate sector.

Source: Alexandra Harney, *Financial Times*, 5 April 2000.

Questions

1 Which types of Japanese company are most at risk by these accounting changes?

2 Comment on the potential benefits and risks to Japanese companies and patterns of industrial organisation of implementing these accounting changes.

■ Redesigning accounting standards

The International Accounting Standards Board (IASB) has, as noted in Case Study 11.4 below, taken a lead role in seeking global standards for accounting procedures and practices. A major issue is the extent to which the role of auditor should be ring-fenced against a possible conflict of interest when the same accounting firm also acts as management consultant to its client. The main impetus for change in the UK is coming from audit committees of the FTSE 100 companies, which are increasingly seeking evidence of auditor independence when assigning non-audit (e.g. consultancy) work. This has major implications for the large accounting firms which currently earn three times as much from non-audit, tax advice and consultancy work for their FTSE 100 clients as they do from their audit work.

Case Study 11.4 reinforces the need for care in redesigning the accountancy rules and procedures on both national and global scales, taking the highly topical issue of setting agreed standards when accounting for pensions.

CASE 11.4 A sting in the tail: pension treatment may be strict

In Britain, many companies are issuing alarming figures showing deficits in their pension funds. The sobering financial transparency provided to UK employees may soon spread to other countries. The International Accounting Standards Board is seeking a global convergence on an agreed standard for accounting for pensions – and is modelling its proposals largely on rules recently introduced in the UK.

Sir David Tweedie, IASB chairman, wrote FRS 17, as the UK rule is known, when he was head of the UK Accounting Standards Board. In the 20 months since it came into force, some companies have blamed it for forcing the closure of their relatively generous defined benefit pension schemes. But Sir David has no regrets. 'I think it is one of the best things we have done,' he says.

Like the IASB's standard on financial instruments, the new rule on pensions is expected to put a heavy emphasis on 'fair value' accounting. As a result, it may run into opposition. Under FRS 17, the measurement of the assets in a defined benefit pension scheme should reflect their fair or market value. FRS 17 also tells accountants how to arrive at the present value for future liabilities; it tots them up and discounts back at an interest rate equal to that on AA-rated corporate bonds.

According to WM Company, a performance measurement consultancy owned by State Street, the US bank, British pension funds lost about £100bn ($160bn) in 2002. Morgan Stanley says the gap between pension liabilities of companies in the FTSE 100 index and assets available to meet them widened to £85bn at the end of January 2003. Credit ratings agencies are responding to FRS 17 by downgrading the debt of companies such as BAE Systems, the defence group, where they have concerns about pension deficits. 'They have got the same problems in America – funds in deficit,' Sir David argues. '[But] it is not visible.'

Many UK employers, however, argue that FRS 17 is misleading: although a pension shortfall is presented as a liability, it is not one about to come due in full any

▶

time soon. Companies have used FRS 17 since mid-2001, after stock markets began falling. If stock markets start rising, the gaping holes in many pension funds will be reversed; indeed, a rise in interest rates may have a similar impact.

Sir David refutes the idea that the deficit or surplus in a pension scheme has only limited utility because it is a snapshot at the end of a company's fiscal year. He highlights how under FRS 17 companies are required to put figures in their annual reports that set out the scheme's trend position over five years.

He also challenges companies to assert that deficits are a temporary blip. 'If it is not, you are going to have to take cash – which might have gone on dividends and investments – and put it into your pension fund. People should know that.'

Sir David's successor at the UK Accounting Standards Board decided last year to delay bringing FRS 17 into full force pending the outcome of the IASB's deliberations on a new global standard on pensions. The move followed an intensive campaign against the accounting rule by employer organisations and trade unions and pressure from the UK government.

But the sting in the tail is that the international rule may turn out to be even tougher than FRS 17: the IASB voted in January to ban the practice of reflecting projected rates of returns on pension fund assets in income statements. At present, companies are allowed to reflect anticipated gains in the profit and loss statement. Some US companies in particular use estimates viewed as recklessly optimistic. FRS 17 does allow some leeway: the IASB may be stricter.

Source: Norma Cohen and Andrew Parker, *Financial Times*, 10 March 2003.

Questions

1 Outline the case for and against the FRS 17 rule on pensions in the UK.

2 Why might a similar rule under consideration by the IASB create still more problems?

Corporate governance and international business

A number of major corporate failures in the US occurred in 2000–02 linked to alleged accounting irregularities, such as those involving Enron and WorldCom. As a result the Sarbanes-Oxley Act came into US law in late 2002 under which a variety of corporate activities would now be subject to criminal law. Executives who breach the accounts certification measures (*see* Box 11.1) face up to 20 years in prison and a $5 million fine. However in a global economy, these US laws will also affect international business worldwide.

Box 11.1 Sarbanes-Oxley Act 2002

Which companies does the act apply to?

Any that have securities registered in America. About half the FTSE 100 companies, for example, have a secondary listing for their shares in the US, while hundreds of other British companies have issued American Depositary Receipts (ADRs) and corporate bonds.

Do chief executives have to swear to the truth of their company accounts?

Yes, and finance directors. But the consensus of legal opinion is that for non-American companies, only annual reports will have to be certified. American companies have to provide a sworn statement even with quarterly accounts. Some British companies may, however, choose to certify their quarterly reports to show American investors that they are whiter than white.

What if the accounts are later proven to be wrong?

If officers of the company are proven to have intentionally filed false accounts, they can be sent to jail for up to 20 years and fined $5m.

When does the act come into force?

The requirement to swear the truth of accounts came into effect on July 29th 2002. A second, more onerous, requirement, which will ask companies to prove they have the correct processes in place to guarantee the accuracy of reports, came into effect at the end of November 2002.

What will it mean for more junior executives?

Some American companies have already started pushing responsibility further down the corporate ladder. Chief executives are asking divisional heads to sign similar statements pledging that the figures from their areas are accurate.

What else should companies look out for?

Sarbanes-Oxley contains a number of other corporate governance requirements. These include:

- executives will have to forfeit bonuses if their accounts have to be restated;
- a ban on company loans to its directors and executives;
- protection for corporate whistleblowers;
- audit committees made up entirely of independent people;
- disclosure of all off-balance-sheet transactions.

Is there any chance UK and other businesses may escape these provisions?

Possibly. In some cases Congress has given the Securities and Exchange Commission (SEC) discretion to grant exemptions, and some legal experts think this will be used to spare companies from outside America some of the Act's more draconian demands.

In the UK the Higgs Committee in 2002 sought to improve corporate governance in the wake of the bitter experiences for shareholders and investors from the collapse of Enron, WorldCom and other high-profile companies. The Higgs proposals include the following.

■ at least 50% of a company's board should consist of independent non-executive directors;
■ rigorous, formal and transparent procedures should be adopted when recruiting new directors to a board;
■ roles of Chairman and Chief Executive of a company should be separate;
■ no individual should be appointed to a second chairmanship of a FTSE 100 company.

International financial management

A number of issues involving international financial management are discussed in other parts of this book, as indicated below:

■ *sources of international finance* (Chapter 4, pp. 128–32), including the use of various international money, bond and equity markets as sources of funds and the various financial instruments associated with these markets;
■ *management of foreign exchange risk* (Chapter 4, pp. 123–8), including the use of options, swaps and futures markets to 'hedge' against unpredictable changes in exchange rates.

Here we look in rather more detail at some further aspects of international financial management.

Attempts and techniques to reduce corporate risk in the individual areas of risk exposure outlined in Figure 11.1 are covered in various parts of this book. Here our main concern is with strategic issues in risk management, and especially with the new possibilities of 'integrated' or 'enterprise' risk management. The suggestion here is that, via the identification and assessment of all the collective risks, the company can then implement a company-wide strategy to manage them.

Methods of integration

Lisa Meulbroek (2000) suggests that there are three ways of implementing integrated risk management objectives: modifying the company's operations, adjusting its capital structure and employing targeted financial instruments. Managers assess the advantages and disadvantages of each method before identifying the most appropriate mix for their particular enterprise.

■ *Modifying the company's operations*. The strategy adopted here will depend on the nature of the company's operations. Microsoft has chosen to use a higher ratio of temporary to permanent staff than is typical for activity within its sector. By reducing the fixed overhead of a more permanent workforce, it seeks to reduce the risks to its permanent workforce of unexpected and adverse shifts in demand, technology or regulation in an intrinsically volatile industry.

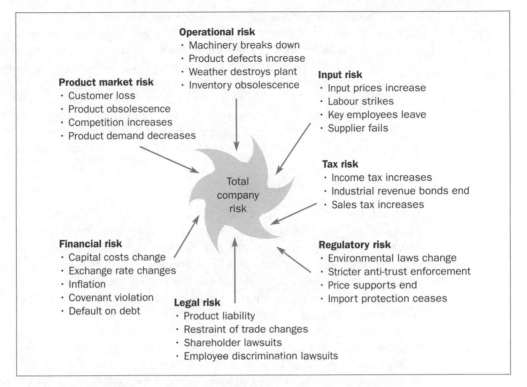

Figure 11.1 Integration of ways to manage risk
Source: Lisa Meulbroek, *Financial Times*, 9 May 2000.

■ *Adjusting the company's capital structure.* Managers cannot always predict the magnitude of a particular operational risk or indeed any specific risk. However, they can adjust the company's capital structure to give a general reduction in risk exposure, as for example by reducing the debt to equity ratio. Such low levels of leverage policies are practised by Microsoft, which in early 2000 has no outstanding debt, thereby using equity as a risk cushion.

■ *Employing targeted financial instruments.* Here companies seek to focus on a specific risk and to hedge against it at the lowest feasible cost. This method is, of course, only feasible where financial instruments exist for the specific risk the company seeks to target. The development of liquid markets for a broad set of financial instruments has greatly helped this method in recent years. Although its figures are now in doubt, Enron, the Houston-based power and industrial group, bought and sold options and forwards (*see* Chapter 4) in the electricity and gas markets to reduce its risk exposure. In contrast, Microsoft will, arguably, find that few of its major risks are correlated with existing financial instruments and must depend on the other two methods of risk management control.

■ Finding the appropriate mix

The essence of an integrated approach is to combine elements of these three methods to minimise the aggregate net exposure to risk from all sources. By aggregating risk, some individual risks within the company will partially or completely offset each other. Thus by concentrating on covering the (lower) aggregate net risk instead of each risk separately, an integrated approach to risk management can add value to the company by reducing costs. The technology products group Honeywell purchased an insurance contract in 1997 that for the first time covered a company's aggregate losses. By aggregating individual risks and then insuring the total net risk, Honeywell was able to make a 15 per cent saving on its previous contract. Since such an integrated approach to risk management clearly requires a thorough understanding of the company's operations and financial policies, it must be implemented by senior management only. It cannot be delegated to managers of functional areas.

■ Alternative risk transfer (ART)

Traditionally companies have used the capital and money markets to raise much of their finance and the *insurance markets* to cover many of the individual risks to which they are exposed, with the two market types being quite distinct. However, a vast array of new financial products are now available from both market types which, together with the impact of the Internet, is causing considerable convergence between these previously separate markets. This broad trend is often referred to as 'alternative risk transfer' (ART) and is reflected in Figure 11.2.

One driving force behind ART has involved the provision of financial instruments which can now be broken down into their smallest constituents, giving opportunities to price different bundles of risks in entirely new ways. The ability to identify and strip out individual risks and devise specific financial instruments to cover even the most complex bundle of such risks, is arguably a revolutionary development. So much so that the term *'nuclear financial economics'* has been applied to this process of stripping down any complex situation into its constituent 'risk particles' which

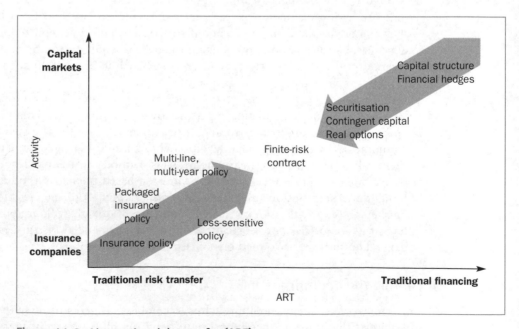

Figure 11.2 Alternative risk transfer (ART)

can then be priced. Many insurance companies are now able to diversify into providing financial instruments to cover foreign exchange and other contracts that were previously only available from the more traditional capital and money markets.

As can be seen from Figure 11.2, just as some insurance companies are developing financial instruments, which were once the preserve of the capital markets, the capital markets are themselves developing a variety of risk-related financial instruments, involving options, futures markets and swaps. The net result is a vast array of traditional and non-traditional instruments from all market sources able to meet the particular circumstances ('finite risk contract') of almost any corporate client. For example, since September 1999 the Chicago Mercantile Exchange has traded weather-linked securities (derivatives) whose value varies with the temperature, measured by an index of warmth in four large cities in the USA.

Such financial instruments can be the basis of 'contracts' to cover situations which previously would be regarded as entirely unpredictable and beyond mankind's control. Of course, the fears of such haphazard future contingencies often deterred firms from entering into a project, especially so the more risk-averse the firm's senior management. Now firms can take such risks explicitly into account and insure against them. For example, British Aerospace paid some $70 million in 1999 for an insurance policy that helped take £3 billion of aircraft-leasing risks off its balance sheet. Within six weeks of taking out the policy British Aerospace shares had outperformed the market by some 15 per cent, the argument being that its future profitability now depended on its skill in operating its core business of building aircraft rather than on haphazard events (involving leasing issues) outside its direct control.

Box 11.2 briefly defines some of the terms used for both traditional and non-traditional financial instruments.

Box 11.2 Financial instruments and international trade

The following is a brief review of some traditional and new financial instruments associated with the finance of international trade.

- *Bills of exchange*. An exporter may send this to an importer ordering the importer to pay a certain sum of money to the exporter on receipt of the bill or at a specified date in the future (often three months). The exporter (seller) is the '*drawer*' of the bill and the importer (buyer) the '*drawee*', the exporter's bank is the '*remitting bank*' and the importer's bank the '*collecting bank*'. The bill of exchange must be '*accepted*' (endorsed) by the foreign importer (*drawee)* before it becomes a 'negotiable instrument' – i.e. once accepted the bill can be sold to a third party for less than the face value (i.e. discounted) if the exporter needs immediate cash or held for the full three months, etc.

- An '*avalised bill of exchange*' carries a guarantee from the importer's bank that the bill will definitely be honoured. If the bill is not avalised, then the exporter's bank will expect the exporting company to repay the loan itself should the importer default. '*With recourse financing*' is a term used whenever a bank can demand compensation from an exporter should the importer default.

- *Forfaiting*. For large-scale (and often long-term) finance a company may issue a bundle of bills of exchange, each one maturing on a different date (e.g. six months, 12 months, 18 months, 24 months, etc.) up to the completion of the project. Once 'accepted', these bills can be sold in their entirety to the company's own banker should immediate cash be required.

| Box 11.2 | Continued |

- *Letters of credit*. These may be required by exporters who wish to have proof that they will be paid before they send their products abroad. Such letters are an order from one bank to a bank abroad authorising payment to a person named in the letter of a particular sum of money or up to a limit of a certain sum. Letters of credit are not negotiable but can be cashed at the specified bank. A 'confirmed' letter of credit is one which has been guaranteed by a bank in the exporter's own country; the confirming bank has no claim on the exporter should there be any default. Normally the exporter is paid by the confirming bank which then collects the money from the foreign bank issuing the credit. Almost all letters of credit are 'irrevocable', i.e. they cannot be cancelled at any time by the customer (importer).

- *Factoring*. Here the debt is sold on to another company for a price (usually well below the face value of the debt), with the new company now responsible for collecting the original debt.

- *Invoice discounting*. Similar to factoring, except that the exporter retains responsibilty for debt collection and for an agreed proportion of bad debts. However, the exporter does receive a cash payment (loan) from the invoice discounter issued to customers.

- *Securitisation*. The process of converting any existing (non-tradable) loan into a security which is tradable. The seller of the asset (security) guarantees payment of interest in the new bundled security, which now becomes more liquid than the assets it replaces.

- *Options, futures and swaps. See* Chapter 4, pp. 129–30.

A second driver behind ART has been the rapid development in telecommunication and computer-related technologies. Clearly the Internet has reduced search costs and times close to zero as regards finding the lowest price for various products. Intelligent automated asset managers (*see* Chapter 12, p. 383) are progressively able to seek out the financial instruments that best fit an investor's particular risk-profile. The availability of these technologies is clearly aiding the unbundling process, enabling providers to parcel risks into different classes of security on which prices can be readily quoted.

Centralised versus decentralised financial decisions

The financial decisions taken by MNEs reflect a variety of influences, such as choosing the types and sources of financing, the need for foreign exchange management, the short- versus long-term goal orientation of the company, the financial reporting requirements of different nations, tax, interest rate, inflationary and other financial considerations, and so on. Nevertheless, an important issue is whether the MNE seeks to take such decisions centrally or to direct many of these decisions to the management of affiliates in host countries. The facts would suggest a tendency towards centralisation: for example around 57 per cent of fund raising by MNE affiliates took place in host country financial markets in 1989, but this figure had fallen to below 45 per cent by the late 1990s.

We might usefully review some of the arguments for and against such centralisation.

Centralised financial management

A number of arguments support this approach.

1 *Minimising cost/maximising return*. The rapid growth in type and source of financial instrument already considered suggests a global rather than local approach to financing. Specialist financial managers with a global perspective can help the MNE borrow funds wherever in the world they are cheapest and invest them wherever the expected returns are highest.

2 *Flexibility*. Only centralised control can permit a rapid corporate response to changed conditions. For example, moving cash away from nations with high projected rates of inflation/currency depreciation and towards nations with high projected rates of economic growth/currency appreciation, etc.

3 *Scale economies*. Large-scale centralised borrowings can secure lower interest rates from lenders and reduce transaction costs per pound/dollar borrowed. Similarly, large-scale centralised deposits of cash surpluses can secure higher interest rates from borrowers.

4 *Professional expertise*. Higher paid and more expert financial managers can be expected to better appraise the vast array of financial alternatives open to the MNE. Specialisation in such operations can be expected to further develop these skills.

5 *Synchronisation*. Centralised control permits a more uniform approach across all affiliates with regard to financial matters, one more likely to be consistent with stated corporate objectives.

Decentralised financial management

A number of counterarguments can be used to support a more decentralised approach.

1 *Generality*. The financing requirement of particular foreign affiliates may be overlooked by managers at headquarters who focus on more global needs. Pump-priming and other longer-term objectives of foreign affiliates may be sacrificed if funds are unavailable for new developments. Headquarter financial management may be unaware of the particular circumstance of local financial markets, so that low-cost sources of funds are overlooked.

2 *Motivation and morale*. These may be diminished among employees within the foreign affiliate as they perceive a lack of control over their own financial destiny.

3 *Conflicts*. Headquarter policy may conflict with policy deemed appropriate by host countries to firms operating there. For example rationalisation of production involving unemployment in foreign affiliates where host governments are seeking to expand output and employment. Similarly, only affiliate financial managers may be able to appraise which financial reporting, control and cash management systems are appropriate to accurately reflect their local operations.

4 *Inflexibility*. Local financial managers may experience delays in receiving the go-ahead for new initiatives from an overburdened and bureaucratised headquarters.

In practice most MNEs centralise some of the financial management decisions and decentralise others, the extent of such decentralisation sometimes depending on the host country in which the affiliate operates.

■ Transfer pricing

We have already noted in Chapter 5 that multinational enterprises are well placed to take advantage of any differences in national tax and subsidy regimes. One particularly important aspect of international financial management involves attempts to reduce the corporate tax burden by 'transfer pricing', that is by adjusting the pricing of internal transactions between international subsidiaries of the multinational enterprise.

Multinationals are widely accused by governments of arranging intra-company transactions in order to minimise their tax liabilities, effectively forcing countries to compete to provide the lowest tax regime. Healey (2004) considers a simplified example in which a multinational's production is vertically integrated, with operations in two countries. Basic manufacture takes place in country A and final assembly and sale in country B (*see* Table 11.9). In country A, the corporate tax rate is 25%, while in country B it is 50%. Suppose the company's costs (inputs, labour, etc.) in country A are $40 million and it produces intermediate products with a market value of $50 million; if it were to sell these intermediate products on the open market, it would declare a profit of $10 million in country A, incurring a tax liability of $2.5 million in that country.

However, suppose the products are actually intended for the parent company's subsidiary in country B. In Scenario 1, the 'transfer price' (i.e. the internal price used by the company to calculate profits in different countries) is set at the market price of $50 million in country A for the intermediate products which are now to be 'shipped' to country B for $100 million, thus the subsidiary will declare a profit of $10 million and incur a tax liability of $5 million. The company as a whole will face a total tax liability of $7.5 million in countries A and B taken together.

Consider an alternative scenario (Scenario 2), in which the company sets a transfer price above the market price for the intermediate products manufactured in the low-tax country, A. With a transfer price of $60 million rather than $50 million and the same costs of $40 million the subsidiary in country A incurs a higher tax liability (25% of $20 million), but this is more than offset by the lower (in fact, zero) tax liability incurred by the subsidiary in country B. Because the latter is now recording its total costs (including the cost of the intermediate products 'bought' from the subsidiary in country A) as being $100 million rather than $90 million, its profits and tax liability fall to zero. As a result, the total tax liability faced by the company on its international operations is only $5 million, rather than $7.5 million.

The basic issue is that the multinational has earned a total profit of $20 million on its vertically integrated operation, i.e. $100 million actual sales revenue in B minus $80 million costs in A + B. However, by setting transfer prices on intra-company

Table 11.9 Multinational tax avoidances

	Scenario 1		Scenario 2	
$m	*Country A*	*Country B*	*Country A*	*Country B*
Costs	40	90	40	100
Sales	50	100	60	100
Profit	10	10	20	0
Tax liability	2.5	5	5	0
Total tax		7.5		5

sales and purchases of intermediate products appropriately, the company can 'move' this profit to the lowest tax country, thereby denying the higher tax country (in this case, country B) the tax revenue to which it is entitled. Such transfer pricing can, of course, only succeed when there is no active market for the intermediate products being traded. If the tax authorities in country B can refer to an open market price for the intermediate product, the inflated transfer price being paid can be identified. However, to the extent that many multinationals internalise cross-border operations because they have ownership-specific advantages (e.g. control of a specific raw material or technology), it may be that comparable intermediate products are not available on the open market. For this reason, high-tax countries may find they lose tax revenues to lower-tax centres as business becomes increasingly globalised. This creates, in turn, an incentive for countries to 'compete' for multinational tax revenues by offering low tax rates; the result of such competition is a transfer of income from national governments to the shareholders of multinational companies.

Useful websites

Now try the self-check questions for this chapter on the website at www.booksites.net/wall. You will also find further resources as well as the following useful weblinks:

International Accountings Standards Board:
www.iasb.org.uk

Accounting Standards Board (UK):
www.asb.org.uk

An excellent site giving many accounting related links:
www.icaew.co.uk

Company websites include:
www.pearson.com/investor/ar2002
www.tesco.com/corporateinfo/

A site giving information on Alternative Risk Transfer:
www.artemis.bm/artemis.htm

A site giving information on Transfer Pricing:
www.transferpricing.com

Useful key texts

Daniels, J., Radebaugh, L. and Sullivan, D. (2004) *International Business* (10th edn), Pearson Prentice Hall, especially Chapter 19.
Hill, C. (2003) *International Business: Competing in the Global Marketplace* (4th edn), McGraw-Hill Irwin, especially Chapters 19 and 20.
Rugman, A. and Hodgetts, R. (2003) *International Business* (3rd edn), FT Prentice Hall, especially Chapter 14.
Woods, M. (2001) *International Business*, Palgrave, especially Chapter 6.

Other texts and sources

Accounting Standards Board (1999) *Statement of Principles for Financial Reporting*, London.

American Accounting Association (1966) *Statement of Basic Accounting Theory*, AAA, New York.

Black, G. (2004) *Introduction to Accounting*, Financial Times Prentice Hall.

Choi, F., Frost, C. and Meek, G. (2001) *International Accounting*, Financial Times Prentice Hall.

CIMA (2000) *Management Accounting: Official Terminology*, London.

Healey, N. (2004) 'The Multinational Corporation', in *Applied Economics* (10th edn), Griffiths, A. and Wall, S. (eds), Financial Times Prentice Hall.

Meulbroek, L. (2000) 'Total Strategies for Risk Control', *Financial Times*, 9 May.

Nobes, C. and Parker, R. (2002) *Comparative International Accounting*, Financial Times Prentice Hall.

Chapter 12

International operations management and logistics

By the end of this chapter you should be able to:

- assess the relevance of operations management and logistics to international business competitiveness;

- examine international operations management approaches to both manufacturing and service activities, including recent developments in flexible specialisation, integration and modularity;

- explain the meaning and application of key logistical concepts such as the square root law, logistical cost trade-offs, time compression and the postponement principle;

- evaluate the contribution to international business success of factors such as freight transport, storage, inventory management, materials handling and order processing;

- assess the possible impacts on operations management and logistics of recent patterns and trends, such as Internet-related developments, extensions to geographical sourcing, application of mass customisation and quick response philosophies, etc.

Introduction

Both international operations management and international logistics involve the coordination of a set of interrelated activities directed towards the efficient production and supply of goods and services. Although there is some overlap between them, for the purposes of this chapter we deal with each approach separately.

International operations management

Operations management can be regarded as one of the key managerial roles within any organisation and has been defined as 'the management of a system which provides goods or services to or for a customer, and involves the design, planning and control of the system' (Harris 1989). The systems theory approach to operations management is based on the view that an organisation can be seen as a network of interconnected components, each performing a role or function. Each component within this system is influential to the extent that if one component were absent or ineffective in some way, then the behaviour of the whole system would change. These basic relationships involved in systems theory can be expressed diagrammatically in terms of inputs and outputs, as in Figure 12.1.

Although this systems approach is commonly applied to manufacturing, it can equally be used in the context of distributive activities, such as transport operations or warehousing. However, for purposes of illustration we first illustrate a 'traditional' approach to operations management within manufacturing before extending the scope of the discussion to consider its changing role within a globalised economy.

■ Operations management: a manufacturing perspective

Operations management is concerned with managing the transformation process whereby input resources are converted into outputs. Five general approaches can be used for managing the transformation process within manufacturing, namely project processes, jobbing processes, batch processes, mass processes and continuous processes. Each of these methods involves utilising different approaches to organising and managing the manufacturing activities, depending on the different volume and variety of products required, as can be seen from Figure 12.2.

- *Project processes.* These are traditionally used to produce highly customised, one-off items such as the construction of a new building, the production of a cinema film or the installation of a computer system (i.e. low-volume, high-variety products). There is a sequence of operations, but this sequence can be uncertain, may require alteration during the production process itself and is not usually repeated. With this type of process, the resources necessary for transformation will usually be allocated in a manner specific to each product.
- *Jobbing processes.* These involve the manufacture of a unique item from beginning to end as a result of an individual order. Products subjected to jobbing processes are usually of a smaller stature than those subjected to project processes and may include handmade shoes, restored furniture and individualised computer systems. As with project processes, this type of process is also characterised by low volume,

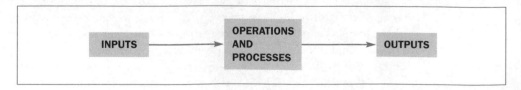

Figure 12.1 **The operations management system approach**

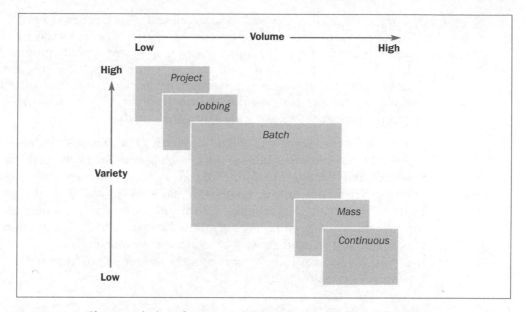

Figure 12.2 Characteristics of some traditional methods of manufacture

high variety and low repetition, but the transforming resources involved in job processes are typically shared between several products. The main features of jobbing processes are the high set-up costs, flexible multi-use equipment required, skilled and versatile labour required, high worker motivation and a high-priced product. Advantages include creating a unique product to the exact specifications of the customer, for which a premium price might be charged. Disadvantages include the limited opportunities for economies of scale.

■ *Batch processes*. These involve the manufacture of a number of similar items whereby a batch of products is processed through a given stage before the entire batch is moved on to the next stage in a well-defined sequence. Examples of batch production include car components, machine tool manufacturing and the production of clothes. Batch processes are typically characterised by larger volumes but a narrower variety of products than are produced by project or jobbing processes. The larger output provides some opportunity for scale economies, resulting in lower costs per unit than jobbing processes. The main features of batch processes are less skilled labour required, use of more specialised but flexible machinery, the possibility of repeat orders, some standardisation of product and the ability to supply a larger market.

■ *Mass processes*. These involve the use of a mass-production line whereby the product moves continuously from one operation to another without stopping. Mass processes typically produce goods in larger volumes but are less varied in terms of their design characteristics. Examples of mass processes include motor vehicle manufacturing, food preparation in fast-food restaurants and the production of compact discs. The operations involved in mass production processes are largely repetitive, highly predictable, very efficient but rather inflexible.

■ *Continuous processes*. These can be considered as a variation of mass processes in that goods are produced in even larger volumes and are often highly standardised in their design, such as petrochemical refineries, beer, paper and electricity production. The operations involved in continuous processes are usually more automated and standardised than mass processes and are often literally produced in an endless flow. The main features of mass or continuous (flow) processes are high capital investment, a greater proportion of unskilled and semi-skilled labour; specialised plant and equipment with little flexibility; highly automated production and the huge economies of scale which are available.

Some mass production manufacturing systems have adopted the 'just-in-time' (JIT) philosophy that aims to minimise stock-holding costs by planning the arrival of raw materials and components just as they are needed. This requires a highly efficient ordering system, normally computerised, that is linked directly to the suppliers, who, in turn, must be highly reliable. Customers orders 'pull' production and stocks through the manufacturing process, thus eliminating the need for large stock holdings and driving down the costs of production. Although this can reduce significantly the stock-holding costs, it also increases the danger of production disruption due to non-arrival of stock supplies.

pause for thought 1	Why, historically, have mass and continuous processes become a predominant form of manufacture in the past few decades?

In more recent times there has been considerable focus on slimming down 'mass production' processes into more flexible or 'lean production' approaches to manufacturing (*see* Box 12.1)

Box 12.1 Lean production

The Japanese have adopted a 'total approach' to removing anything that does not add value to the final product. The term lean production has been applied to this approach which aims to produce more by using less, and is to be achieved by:

- involving both management and workers in the decision-making and suggestion-making process;
- minimising the use of key resources such as materials, manpower, floor space, capacity and time;
- introducing just-in-time (JIT) materials handling in order to lower stock-holding costs and to minimise the need for buffer stocks;
- encouraging worker participation in quality circles where improvements can be suggested and discussed;
- introducing preventative maintenance;
- using multiple purpose machines for flexible production;
- employing and training multi-skilled operatives;
- encouraging teamwork.

This approach slimmed down 'mass' production into a flexible or 'lean' production system. Advantages claimed for this approach include:

- an increase in quality of product and after-sales service;
- shorter product development time;
- faster reaction to changes in consumer preferences;
- a reduction in unit costs of production without sacrificing quality;
- a better trained and more motivated workforce.

■ Operations management: a non-manufacturing perspective

In addition to the manufacture of goods, operations management is also concerned with the provision of services. Processes are equally relevant in both manufacturing and service delivery systems but the technologies for delivering services are clearly quite different from those used in manufacturing. As a result of this distinction, Slack *et al.* (1998) identified three process types specific to service operations namely, professional service, service shops and mass services, ranging from low volume/high variety to high volume/low variety respectively. Some writers argue that the five general process types applied to manufacturing are also appropriate to service operations.

Case Study 12.1 looks at the use of operations management techniques to an essentially non-manufacturing operation. This involves the marketing of handicraft products in the context of new, global opportunities.

CASE 12.1   Operations management system: Khan Handicrafts

Some of the key operations management issues can be illustrated in the context of Khan Handicrafts, which is a medium-sized co-operative located in Dhaka, Bangladesh. Khan Handicrafts currently serves three different segments of the market, namely foreign tourists (who buy 10% of products at a premium price), local 'ex-patriates' (who buy 40% of products at an above average price), and middle/upper class Bangladeshi's (who buy 50% of products at a lower 'local' price). The higher profit margin derived from the first two of these market segments has prompted Khan to concentrate on the tourist and ex-patriate markets, although this has involved increased amounts of quality control and design input. However, Khan is currently experiencing both a declining home market (reductions in aid agencies) and greater competition within that market. As a result, the organisation is reconsidering its strategic plan for the next decade. One option under active consideration involves moving into the export business.

Figure 12.3 summarises the current system in terms of systems theory. The co-operative's major systems input can be considered to be the workers within its 53 member societies. These societies are made up of poor rural men and women who utilise their woodwork, pottery, sewing, weaving and basket-work skills. Further inputs to the system include finance/capital, storage facilities, raw materials (e.g.

dye, wood, clay, etc.) and the equipment necessary to produce the goods. There is also an element of design input, whereby products are produced in accordance with specific customer requirements. Design might be subsumed within the 'information' heading, which might also include advice given by Khan to its member societies to remain solvent in terms of cash flow management.

The transformation stage of the system takes these inputs and uses them, together with the skills of the workers, to produce the desired outputs. The major output of the Khan organisation is obviously not only the goods produced but also their successful marketing. In other words, the outputs are both goods produced and a range of services which include distribution of the goods directly through Khan's own outlets and as an intermediary in using the outlets of others. In some ways the transformation process for Khan involves acting as an intermediary between producers (its member societies) and the consumers (currently foreign tourists, local expatriates and middle/upper-class Bangladeshis).

A more detailed systems diagram (Figure 12.4) can be used to express the operations of the Khan organisation incorporating the fact that its primary activity is to market the goods produced by the member societies of the co-operative. These goods are marketed either directly through one of Khan Handicraft's own marketing outlets or, more usually, through other outlets. At the central warehouse, the products are subjected to a rapid quality check, labelled with a Khan tag and securely stored until they are dispatched in batches to retail outlets. Khan also uses its extensive market knowledge to influence the design process of individual societies.

The influence of the environment on the transformation process is of particular importance when using the systems theory approach to operations management. It is important to understand that the organisation is embedded in its external environment and any changes in these factors, such as political, economic, social or technological changes, may result in changes in the system or one of its components. For example, it can already be seen in the case of Khan that the restrictions on aid missions imposed by the government is affecting a key market segment, namely the demand for its products by home-based expatriates. In attempting to develop existing and new market segments (e.g. export) in response to this environmental change, Khan will need to factor into its operations management system appropriate mechanisms for dealing with the new requirements for quality, flexibility, timeliness, capacity, etc. An important element in dealing with the environment involves the introduction of physical or organisational 'buffering' techniques wher-

Figure 12.3 **The operations management system of Khan Handicrafts**

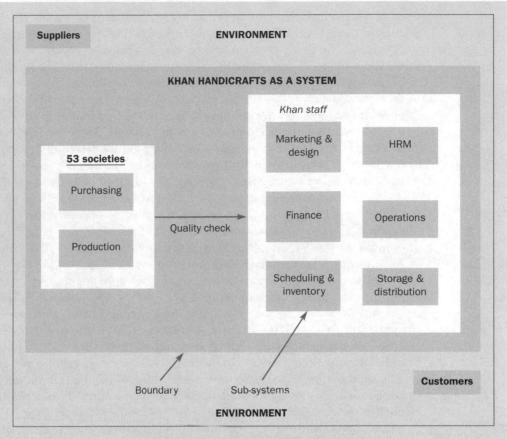

Figure 12.4 **A more detailed systems diagram of Khan Handicrafts**

ever possible as a means of minimising the impacts of unforeseeable 'environmental' disruptions, whether on the side of supply or demand.

One of the problems of the systems approach involves precisely delineating the boundaries between the operation function and other functions involved in the production of goods and services. A broad approach is adopted for the Khan systems analysis. A further problem involves modelling the hierarchy of operations appropriately, in particular the treatment given to internal customers and suppliers as compared to external customers and suppliers. Indeed, a network of micro operations, each involved in transforming inputs into outputs, are often key components of the overall macro operation. The fulfilment of customer needs will require the successful integration of all these operations.

Current operations management issues

If the organisation is to successfully achieve its objective of moving into the export business, there are various operations management issues that must be considered.

■ *Design*. The current design system utilised by Khan involves little input from its constituent societies. The Khan staff control the design activity as they feel they are more aware of the needs of customers within the market and therefore more able to design products that will satisfy those needs. As competition increases within the current market and Khan seeks to become established in the export market, the design element of the products will become increasingly important. It will be vital for Khan to identify exactly what its customers require from the product in terms of features, colour, fashion, etc. so it can meet, if not exceed, these requirements in order to gain a competitive edge. Changes to the traditional design specifications of products may require the workers to be retrained so that they have the skills to produce exactly what is required to a high standard. Khan may also need to alert workers to the fact that in export markets product design will often supersede functional aspects in terms of buyer behaviour. The company may also consider revising its current policy and encourage design input from the workers who may be able to contribute new ideas, thereby improving the quality of products and the efficiency of the system as a whole. If Khan is to succeed in breaking into the export market, it may also consider consulting its clients to request their input in terms of design features and technical aspects of the products.

- *Manufacture.* The manufacture of the products can continue to take place locally but a stronger emphasis must now be placed on improving the quality of the goods produced for a more discriminating export market. Obviously, if the possibility of entering the export market is to be a realistic option, Khan is going to have to seriously rethink its quality control procedures. Given the problems it currently experiences in producing goods of the standard needed by the foreign tourists segment of its market, dramatic improvements will be required. To achieve a higher quality of output, a better and more standardised quality of input (e.g. dyes) will be required. This could be done by introducing a degree of centralisation in supplying raw materials to the individual groups for the manufacturing process. There will also need to be greater quality control at various stages of manufacture, not least to control costs, e.g. if dyeing of spotted or cracked wax occurs in the batik work, this expensive process will have been wasted. It will be important for workers to inspect their own work for errors at each phase of the production process. This may involve additional training but should significantly reduce the need for quality inspections when the finished goods arrive at the central warehouse.

- *Distribution.* This will be a key component of the operations management system. Orders may be made in bulk by foreign purchasers and will often involve an element of product modification. Khan will need to ensure that these features are embodied in the design of sufficient numbers of products supplied to the central warehouse. Khan may also have to oversee the incorporation of higher quality raw materials (sometimes provided by customers themselves) into the manufacturing process, replacing previous sources of domestic supply. Flexibility will be an important element in such adjustments as, for example, in having to meet specialised and higher quality bulk orders, as compared to simply providing products, as made, in smaller batches to customers imposing less onerous time requirements.

- *Capacity.* Khan may need to expand capacity in order to cope with demand from both home and export markets, especially when the latter may involve bulk ordering. This is likely to involve larger warehousing facilities and more careful attention to demand estimation and production possibilities in order to ensure that orders are met and capacity is not exceeded. Even though, at present, some spare capacity is available, implementation of the new strategy is likely to require the purchase or leasing of additional storage space. The location of this warehousing capacity may need to be reviewed, e.g. ease of access to ports or airports may now become an important factor. Associated with enhanced capacity may be an extra requirement for labour input, as, for example, in support of additional quality control and stock handling activities.

■ *Stock (inventory).* Stock levels must be more carefully monitored in order to avoid 'stock-out' costs and resulting lost orders. Systems will be needed to handle the warehouse dispatch and location within the warehouse of the more differentiated products required by the export market. While sufficient stock must be held to meet urgent orders and provide adequate numbers of sample items on request, too much stock can result in excessive stock-handling costs. Improvements in inventory management will be an important component of any move into the export market.

■ *Purchasing.* The current policy regarding purchasing is that the individual societies purchase their own raw materials as required. Central purchasing may be an important element in ensuring the higher quality based products required by the export market. In fact bulk purchase of such inputs at discounts may also lead to the benefit of reducing the cost of purchasing for both domestic and overseas markets, thereby raising profit margins. However, the need for extra storage space already mentioned may absorb part of any additional profit. Some purchasing may now be undertaken under the direction of the clients themselves as they seek to ensure a better quality product.

■ *Scheduling.* This will also be a key component of the operations management system. Any delay in receipt or dispatch of stock may endanger future orders, by adding to movement and delivery time. Efficient scheduling of inputs and outputs will also help reduce average stock levels and associated stock holding costs.

■ *Employees.* A further operations management issue that will need consideration is that of the workers and the effect any changes made to current procedures will have on them. Khan may experience resistance from the workers in trying to implement the changes necessary to successfully enter the export market. For example, the majority of rural workers are only part-time and will have difficulty displaying the flexibility required to meet delivery dates due to their other commitments. The special training required might also cause problems as it will involve trying to change ingrained concepts (as to quality and design features for example) which may take years to modify and standardise.

It is important to understand that all of these elements are interrelated; for example, the decision to enter the export market will affect the production process selected, the skills and training requirements of the labour force, the layout of facilities, the warehousing capacity required, etc. These linkages highlight the need for a feedback loop within the overall system so that the elements can be monitored, controlled and any necessary changes made. The combination and interaction of these elements clearly have important implications for the organisation's overall operations management strategy.

Question

1 If Khan is to broaden its market base (for example, by moving into the export market segment), what strategic issues might be involved?

Flexible specialisation

The growth of world markets and the increasing and more rapid availability of detailed information on consumer characteristics and behaviour patterns in segmented markets are posing strategic challenges for operations management, for instance in choosing whether and to what extent to adopt a flexible specialisation approach to manufacture.

Flexible specialisation is a term that is often applied to new methods of manufacturing that attempt to produce 'an expandable range of highly specialised products' (Lowson *et al.* 1999). The strategy of flexible specialisation has emerged as a result of the globalised and information intensive environment within which firms operate and the increase in demand for products that are custom-made and more varied in nature.

This method of manufacturing has been considered as representing a departure from the more traditional approaches outlined above, and its principles have even been described as the reverse of those of mass production (or 'Fordism') which relies on producing large quantities of products as cheaply as possible in an attempt to maximise the return on investment. Mass production processes typically have very low unit costs because of the increased scale of production, the use of highly specialised machinery and the use of low-skilled, easily trained labour. However, the demand for such standardised goods is limited and the inflexibility of the mass production process means that it cannot efficiently adapt to situations where demand is more turbulent, as in the case of changes in fashion or design requirements.

This lack of flexibility experienced by the traditional manufacturing methods has led to the emergence of a more flexible process whereby 'the new flexible firms, reacting to rapidly changing market demand, seek to generalise the skills of workers so that they can adapt to a wide range of tasks' (Lowson *et al.* 1999). Attempts to achieve such generality in employees' skills arguably conflicts with the central aim of Fordism, namely to achieve maximum economies of scale and specialisation among the workforce in order to produce highly uniform products. It has even been suggested that the term 'flexible specialisation' implies a return to the fundamentals of the system of craft production whereby the output is unique and very variable. The flexibility that craft producers can achieve and their ability to modify their ideas to suit customer requirements are the main aims of a strategy of flexible specialisation.

At least for larger enterprises, the more traditional methods of operation have tended to be 'scale-based' and 'focused', involving the mass production of standardised goods using capital-intensive processes with low levels of mainly unskilled labour, and consequently high levels of recorded labour productivity. Costs are typically low, giving successful companies the opportunity to reduce prices and capture substantial market share of mature markets. Of course, this rather stylised approach has already undergone considerable change, with techniques such as 'continuous improvement' being adopted in many large-scale processes to raise quality. For example, tightly knit cross-functional groups have been established within many volume-manufacturing processes to improve performance, raise quality, reduce waste, etc. However, this is not the same as flexible specialisation, which in its more modern guise can be seen as underpinning 'flexible-scope-based' and especially 'quick response' approaches to meeting changes in consumer demand. Perhaps the 'mass customisation' approach best captures the key ingredients of flexible specialisation, namely an approach, which emphasises the primacy of carefully utilising selected packages of short-run processes ('modules') to meet specific customer requirements.

Implications of flexible specialisation

One implication of the flexible specialisation approach is to render less useful the idea of the learning or experience curve in contributing to productive efficiency, whether for the provision of goods or services. As indicated in Figure 12.5, costs per unit are regarded as varying inversely and exponentially with *cumulative output*, reflecting the importance of learning by experience. Such a relationship had been identified as early as the 1930s when studies suggested that a doubling of the cumulative production of airframes was accomplished by a 20% reduction in unit labour costs (Griffiths and Wall 2000). Initially such decreases in costs were related to the ability of workers to improve performance of a task through repetition and of workers and management discovering more effective methods of undertaking such tasks through experience. Arguably some of the benefits from continuous improvement

Figure 12.5 Experience or learning curve: declining average costs as a function of cumulative output

techniques can be attributed to such factors. However, such experience curve relationships depend on product and process standardisation, which are characteristics conspicuously absent from flexible specialisation approaches.

In a similar way, flexible specialisation shifts the focus away from various internal economies of scale as a major source of competitive advantage. Conventionally, increased efficiencies become available to the firm from higher volumes of output, as for example via the technical economies of higher productivity resulting from increased specialisation of labour and capital inputs. These, together with economies from increased dimensions (material inputs increase as the square, capacity as the cube) and linked processes (lowest common multiple for dovetailing separate processes being a high volume of output), combine to generate substantial reductions in technical costs of production from higher output. Under flexible specialisation such considerations become largely redundant. Instead the focus shifts towards the external economies of scale available from siting clusters or networks of small-scale producers and suppliers in geographically adjacent areas. Of course, the more recent developments of information technology may allow such networks to develop at greater geographical distance.

The focus under flexible specialisation shifts rather to issues such as economies of scope, whereby the product mix becomes an important aspect of cost reduction. Here firms may benefit from the joint use of inputs such as management, administration, marketing or storage facilities across two or more products, bringing cost savings for all the products produced.

It has been suggested that flexible specialisation and mass customisation techniques can only be successfully implemented by radically overhauling the organisational and cultural context in which goods and services are provided. For example, the tightly knit, cross-functional teams so appropriate to continuous improvement must become more loosely organised 'dynamic networks of relatively autonomous operating units' (Pine 1993). These groups or 'process modules' must continuously strive to increase their capability of performing an ever-expanding set of tasks, giving greater scope for the company to incorporate them into the provision of a wide array of customised goods and services. This is rather different from the situation under continuous improvement, where the assumption is that the objective of the group is to better achieve a specified task which has a well-defined role in developing the overall product. With flexible specialisation the overall product is continually changing at the behest of consumer demand and the key ingredient is to develop multi-faceted process 'modules' which can readily adapt to a wide variety of demand configurations. Of course, a pre-requisite for the success of such a 'quick response' approach is that some 'architecture' exists which is capable of rapidly converting specialised customer requirements into an appropriate combination of process modules capable of meeting those requirements. This is likely to involve sophisticated but reliable information-technology systems. For example, in the USA, Bally Engineering Structures Inc. uses a computer-driven intelligence network (CDIN) whereby sales personnel can directly input design specifications that have been agreed with customers for industrial refrigeration units and the system can, in real time, devise a combination of process modules capable of delivering the desired output. Case Study 12.3 below looks at some recent information technology based developments which are supporting the application of 'quick response' techniques.

Integration versus modularity

An important contemporary debate involving aspects of operations management is whether to remain integrated in the sense of retaining centralised control of the entire design and production processes, or whether to move in a modular direction. A 'modular product' has been defined as 'a complex product whose individual elements have each been designed independently and yet function together as a seamless whole' (Sako and Murray 1999). As we shall see, the role of 'enterprise resource planning' has played a part in this debate.

■ Enterprise resource planning (ERP)

This term refers to the wide variety of company-wide information systems that are increasingly replacing the more fragmented, stand-alone IT systems in many companies. Such ERP systems provide centralised real time data on all elements of an organisations operations, no matter how globalised they might be. Manufacturing strategy ceases to involve a sequence of discrete decisions which 'lock' the enterprise into a certain mode of manufacture or operation. Rather it involves the continuous application of intelligence to operational processes which at the same time may open up new product and service opportunities. The increased availability of data may permit the introduction of new and more efficient operational processes (e.g. the introduction of worldwide benchmarking standards) as well as refined and enhanced products more closely attuned to customer requirements.

■ Modular strategies

Globalisation has been a driving force for modular strategies, since these can help companies engage in large worldwide investments without a huge increase in fixed costs and with fewer of the problems typically associated with managing complex global operations. Modular strategies can embrace production, design and/or use (Figure 12.6).

■ *Modularity-in-production* (MIP). This provided the initial impetus to adopt modules in the car industry. Here production activities are broken down into a number of large but separate elements that can be carried out independently, with the finished vehicle then being assembled from these large sub-assemblies. Such modular production systems can help reduce the fixed capital overhead required for production, especially where selected modules are outsourced. Specialisation of labour and management on smaller, independent modules can also result in productivity gains and lower variable costs.

■ *Modularity-in-design (MID)*. There may be more problems in establishing modularity in the design process. This will be particularly true where the finished product embodies systems as well as sub-assembly components. For example, a finished vehicle offers climate control and vehicle safety 'systems' which, to be provided effectively, require design input into a whole range of sub-assembly module operations. Modularity-in-design may therefore require that boundaries be carefully drawn so as to capture as many interdependencies as possible within the modular groupings.

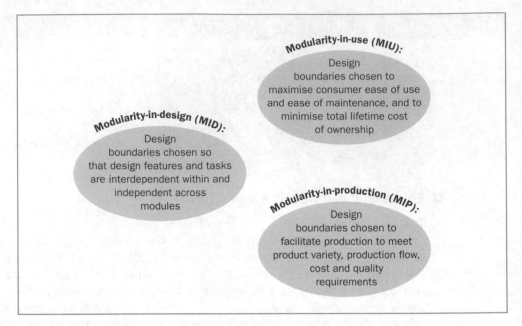

Figure 12.6 **Three arenas of modularisation**

- *Modularity-in-use (MIU)*. This was the main reason for the introduction of modularity in the computer industry. It became increasingly obvious that consumers required computer-related products that were both compatible and upgradeable. Much effort was therefore expended in standardising interfaces between different elements of the product architecture to give these desired user attributes. The then leader, IBM, found that the electro-mechanical system could be disaggregated without adversely affecting performance.

Of course, creating a modular product in any or all of these ways may have organisational consequences, not all of which may be foreseen. For example, a module product architecture may result in modular business organisation. This has certainly been the case in the computer industry. It can also stimulate certain types of organisational practice, such as outsourcing and shift power relationships between companies. For example, IBM's decision to outsource the development and production of its operating system to Microsoft and of its chip components to Intel was an important factor in shifting power away from the overall product architecture to these designers and producers of modular systems elements.

International logistics

Logistics is a term that has long been associated with military activities, and in particular with coordinating the movements of troops, armaments and other supplies to specified locations in the most efficient ways technically feasible. When first applied to business some 30 years ago the term was mainly used to refer to the total flow of finished products downstream from the plant to the customers. In more recent times it has been extended further to include the major part of the total flows of materials (finished and unfinished) and information both downstream and upstream. Activities such as transport, storage, inventory management, materials handling and order processing are commonly included within the 'logistics' heading. Indeed, over the last decade the term 'supply chain management' has sometimes been used interchangeably with 'logistics'. This still broader perspective includes the management of the entire chain from supply of raw materials through manufacture and assembly to distribution to the end consumer. As we shall see, when logistics is viewed from this broad perspective it increasingly becomes a strategic as well as an operational issue.

■ Logistical principles

Before turning to some specific areas of logistical concern for international business, it may be useful to review a number of logistical principles which are of general relevance. Many of these principles touch on the costs associated with holding stock (inventory), which are briefly reviewed in Box 12.2.

- *Square root law.* The amount of safety stock required will decline by a fraction whose denominator is the square root of the reduction in number of stock-holding points in the logistical system. For example, a reduction from 17 separate warehouses to a single separate warehouse will lead to an approximate reduction of $1/\sqrt{16} = 0.25$ or 25% in the safety stock required, which in turn implies an approximately pro rata reduction in stock-holding cost.
- *Logistical cost trade-offs.* It will often be the case that logistical changes will reduce certain specified costs but only at the expense of raising other costs. Such changes will only be applied where the net outcome is positive, i.e. the logistical cost trade-off is 'favourable'. For example, while the reduction in number of separate warehouses reduces stock-holding costs it may well have other impacts. On the positive side, the larger scale of warehousing operations may further reduce inventory and associated materials handling costs. On the negative side there may be additional transport costs incurred by distributions from a fewer number of larger warehouses to local customers. Only if the overall reduction in inventory and material handling costs more than compensates for any increases in transport related costs will this logistical trade-off be deemed 'favourable' to the enterprise. More generally MNEs must address such logistical trade-offs whenever they consider centralising production in factories/plants to create scale economies and reduced average production costs while simultaneously incurring additional transportation costs and lengthened lead time to customers.
- *Time compression.* This refers to the various attempts to accelerate the flows of materials and information in logistical systems. It is sometimes extended to cover a variety of techniques and approaches, such as just-in-time (*see* p. 362), quick response (*see* p. 368), lead-time management, lean logistics, process mapping techniques, and so on. The idea behind many of these techniques has been to reduce the expenditure of time within various aspects of the supply chain, with particular attention paid to eliminating slack time and time used in non-value adding activities. Even here, however, the logistical trade-offs will often apply. For example, saving time within large, highly automated and synchronised centralised

warehousing systems may be at the expense of incurring more time by lengthening the geographical supply chain to the final customer.

- *Postponement principle.* The company will benefit by postponing decisions as to the precise configuration of customised product until as late a stage as possible within the supply chain. This implies that companies should hold stock in generic form for as long as possible before deciding how to extend the product range by reconfiguring that stock into the separate 'stock-keeping units' (SKUs) which correspond to customised products. The application of this 'postponement principle' reduces the volume of inventory in the global supply chain and the costs associated with under-supplying (stock-out costs) or over-supplying (stock handling costs) a particular market with a customised product. However, the logistical cost trade-off principle can be expected to apply yet again, since the reduction in overall inventory costs may be at the expense of incurring additional costs associated with extending the global supply chain (e.g. transport/distribution costs).

Box 12.2 Inventory (stock) costs and control

There are three broad categories of costs involving inventories. The cost of holding stock (carrying costs), costs of obtaining stock (ordering costs) and the costs of failing to have adequate stock (stock-out costs).

Inventory costs include the following:

- *Holding or carrying costs.* These might include insurance, storage costs (staff, equipment, handling, deterioration, obsolescence, security). These might also include opportunity costs, i.e. the financial cost in terms of alternatives foregone (e.g. interest) through having capital tied up.
- *Order costs.* These occur when obtaining stock and might include the costs of clerical and administrative work in raising an order, any associated transport costs and inspection of stock on arrival, etc.
- *Stock-out costs.* These are difficult to quantify but might include the following:

  Stock-out of raw materials and work-in-progress, which may result in machine and operator idle time and possibly the need for overtime payments to catch up on missed production.

  Stock-out of finished goods, which may result in:

  (i) missed orders from occasional customers;

  (ii) missed delivery dates resulting in a deterioration in customer/supplier relations;

  (iii) penalty clauses incurred for late delivery.

  Stock-out of tools and spares, which may result in an increase in downtime of machinery and loss of production.

Stock carrying costs can be expected to rise as the order size increases, for reasons already discussed. However stock ordering costs can be expected to fall as the order size increases (*see* Figure 12.7).

If we ignore stock-out costs which are notoriously difficult to quantify, then total (inventory) costs can be regarded as the sum of the carrying and ordering costs. These will be at a minimum for the following value of Q (output).

Box 12.2 Continued

Economic order quantity

$$Q = \sqrt{\frac{2 \cdot C_o D}{C_c}}$$

Where   Q = economic order quantity
Co = ordering costs for one order
D = annual demand for stock
Cc = carrying cost for one item p.a.

A firm uses 100,000 components per annum in its manufacturing process each of which cost the firm £10 to purchase from its supplier. The carrying costs of stocking these components is estimated as 15% per annum of the purchase price. The ordering costs are estimated at £10 per order. Find the economic order quantity.

Solution

$$EOQ = \sqrt{\frac{2 \cdot C_o D}{C_c}}$$

Where   Co   = £10 per order
D   = 100,000 units p.a.
Cc   = £10 x 0.15 = £1.50 per item per annum.

i.e. $EOQ = \sqrt{\dfrac{2 \cdot (10) \cdot (100,000)}{1.50}}$

i.e.   EOQ = 1,155 units

Of course, more complex inventory control situations with variable usage rates, variable lead times and gradual (rather than instantaneous) replenishment may be encountered by firms.

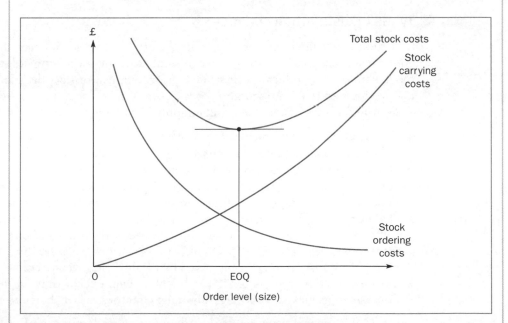

Figure 12.7 Finding the economic order quantity (EOQ)

International distribution systems

International business might, at one extreme, pay little heed to the logistical aspects of delivery by exporting on an ex-works basis. The responsibility in this case would be on the overseas purchaser to arrange for the collection of the goods and to bear all the insurance and freight costs. This rarely happens in practice, with the result that sellers and buyers must make an agreement as to their respective responsibilities and duties in trade, with the range of possibilities often referred to as 'incoterms'.

■ Incoterms

The International Chamber of Commerce has drafted standard definitions of export delivery terms to clarify these issues:

■ *ex works* (EXW): customers collect goods from the exporters premises;
■ *free on board* (FOB): customers only take responsibility after the goods are loaded onto the ship in the exporters country;
■ *free carrier* (FRC): as for FOB, but applies to any form of carrier, ship or otherwise;
■ *cost, insurance and freight* (CIF): customers only take responsibility after the goods have reached a named foreign destination (i.e. exporter bears all transport and insurance costs to that point);
■ *delivered at frontier* (DAF): customers only take responsibility after the goods have passed through a named frontier;
■ *delivered duty paid* (DDP): customers only take responsibility after the goods have reached their premises. This is increasingly becoming the standard approach for export sales.

■ Types of distribution channel

'Distribution channel' refers to the route the product takes from producer to the final consumer. Such channels must fulfil a number of functions, including the physical movement of the products, their storage prior to transit or sale, the transfer of title to the products and their presentation to the customer.

Four main types of channel are commonly identified:

■ *direct system*: no intermediaries involved, with orders sent directly from a factory or warehouse in the home country to the overseas purchaser;
■ *transit system*: exports sent to a transit (or 'satellite') warehouse/depot in another country. This then acts as a 'break bulk' point, with some items despatched in bulk over long distances and others in smaller units to more local destinations;
■ *classical system*: here each foreign country has its own separate warehouse/depot. Exports are sent to these and then distributed within that national market. Such warehouses/depots both 'break bulk' and perform a stock-holding function, with nationals of that country being served by locally held inventories;
■ *multicountry system*: as for the classical system, except that the separate warehouses/depots may serve several adjoining countries rather than one country only.

Table 12.1 summarises some of the advantages/disadvantages of each of the four types of distributional channel.

Table 12.1 International distribution systems

Types of system	Advantages	Disadvantages
1 Direct	■ No need for foreign warehouse ■ Greater inventory centralisation/ Lower inventory level	■ Longer order lead time ■ Less load consolidation/higher transport costs
2 Transit	■ Permits breaking of bulk ■ Greater load consolidation, so lower transport costs ■ Less packaging and administration	■ Extra handling costs in foreign markets
3 Classical	■ Permits breaking of bulk ■ Greater load consolidation, so lower transport costs ■ Less packaging and administration ■ Shorter order lead times ■ Local stock availability ■ Lower import dues	■ Incurs full warehousing cost ■ Decentralisation of inventory increases total stockholding
4 Multicountry	■ Higher degree of inventory centralisation and lower unit warehousing costs than 3	■ Longer lead times to customers ■ Higher delivery costs ■ Difficult to coordinate with nationally based sales organisation

Source: Adapted from Tayeb (2000). Reprinted with permission

■ Choice of distributional channel

In practice a few key factors will determine the choice of distributional channel:

- *foreign customer base*: the direct system is more likely to be used where a small number of large overseas purchasers are involved;
- *export volumes*: the use of 'break-bulk' or stockholding warehouses/depots will only be economically viable when export volumes exceed certain 'threshold' levels;
- *value density of product*: those products with a high ratio of value to weight/volume (i.e. high value density) are more suited to direct systems since they can more easily absorb the higher associated transport costs;
- *order lead times*: where direct systems are inappropriate (e.g. low value density) yet where customers required rapid and reliable delivery, stock may have to be held locally (i.e. classical or multicountry systems).

Recent evidence suggests a rise in *direct*, *transit* and *multicountry systems*. The rise of e-commerce is increasing direct systems use with international and personalised delivery via parcel networks (e.g. 'just for you', J4U delivery). Transit and multi-country systems have also been increasing, with many MNEs consolidating warehousing in a few large 'pan-European' distribution centres. Sony, Rank Xerox, Philips, Kellogg's, Nike and IBM have moved in this direction and away from the classical system previously adopted. Some of these choices of distribution channels may be influenced by opportunities for 'economies of scope' (*see* p. 251).

■ Transport

Transport issues are implicit in the choice of distributional channels and in other locational decisions for the multinational organisation. In traditional heavy industries the location chosen will often depend on whether the operation is 'bulk forming' or 'bulk reducing'. Bulk-forming operations, such as in furniture manufacture, need to be close to their markets in order to cut transport costs. However, for bulk-reducing operations, such as in the steel industry, the main need is to be close to the heavy raw materials used as inputs. Modern industries increasingly use lighter raw materials so that they, together with the service industries, tend to be more 'footloose'.

For any firm, access to rail, road, sea and air links is important, both for the inward movement of inputs and the outward movement of outputs (goods and services). New electronic technologies are reducing the importance of distance in some product areas such as books, CDs and software but in many other areas of economic activity transport costs still increase with distance.

Of course, the transport mode chosen will depend not only on cost but on the relative importance for that product or service of: speed of delivery, dependability of delivery, quality deterioration issues, transport costs, route flexibility. As shown in Table 12.2, Slack *et al*. (1998) suggest the ranking of the different modes of transport as regards these factors.

We noted in Chapter 2 that transport costs can be a factor in influencing MNE decisions as to whether to export or to produce abroad. However, transport issues can also influence other organisational and strategic decisions in international business, as indicated in Box 12.3.

Of course, the siting and location of depots/warehouses can provide similar benefits in terms of economies of scope.

■ Centralisation versus decentralisation

There has been much debate over the years of the logistical benefits and costs of centralised versus decentralised distributive systems. Certainly the predominant trend in logistics has been towards the centralisation of inventory holding in both national and international business, taking advantage of the 'square root law' previously discussed (*see* p. 373). We saw that moving from a decentralised system of 17 warehouses to a completely centralised system of one warehouse would cut the

Table 12.2 The relative performance of each mode of transport

Operation's performance objective	Mode of transport				
	Road	Rail	Air	Water	Pipeline
Delivery speed	2	3	1	5	4
Delivery dependability	2	3	4	5	1
Quality	2	3	4	5	1
Cost	3	4	5	2	1
Route flexibility	1	2	3	4	5

Source: Slack *et al*. (1998). Reprinted with permission

| Box 12.3 | Economies of scope and the transport sector |

Economies of scope refer to cost benefits from changing the mix of production, as, for instance, when a number of related commodities or services are produced using common processing facilities. The potential for such economies of scope can be found in the transport industry. For example, the deregulation of the aircraft industry in the USA after 1978 resulted in significant changes in the structure of carrier operations. Instead of a large number of individual routes between various cities, the carriers redesigned the route system into a hub and spoke system reminiscent of a bicycle wheel. Travel was routed from, say, a city positioned at the end of one 'spoke' through a 'hub' or central airport, then out again to another city at the end of another spoke.

For example, in Figure 12.8 (a) we have five point-to-point direct links from cities A to B, C to D, E to F, G to H and I to J respectively. If these are replaced by ten services from each of the cities to a hub airport, as in Figure 12.8(b), the number of city pairs that can be served rises sharply from five to 55. The total number of city pairs that can be served is given by the formula $n(n+1)/2$, where n is the number of spokes (cities served) emanating from the hub

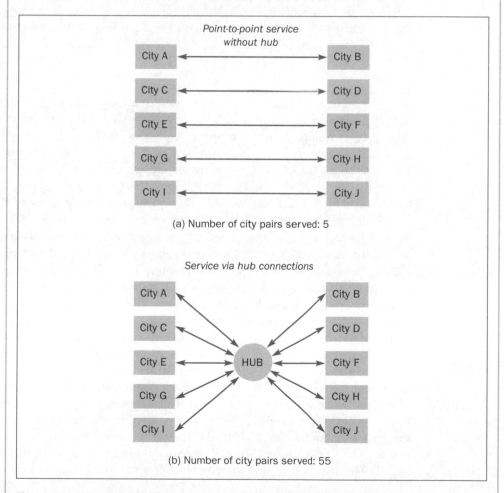

Figure 12.8 **Economies of scope and US aircraft routing operations**

Box 12.3 Continued

airport. It follows that if the number of spokes from the hub rises to 50, then the number of city pairs that can be linked rises to 1,275. This system has advantages, because all the passengers destined for a city at the end of one spoke will be collected at the hub airport from all the other cities at the end of the other spokes. This means that there will be many more passengers per flight, allowing definite economies of density: i.e. larger aircraft can be used, with associated savings in costs. On the marketing side, the hub system also facilitates more departures to a larger number of cities, making the marketing of a more integrated service network a more attractive proposition.

In this way economies of scope are realised. By serving a large number of city-pair markets through the hub, a carrier also provides many different products or combinations of products not previously available. These lead on to further economies as, for instance, airlines are now able to meet travel demands that have different characteristics from those previously met. In this case business and vacation travel can use a single network of flights instead of a variety of interconnecting networks of flights. The hub might permit still further 'common carriage' and cost reductions: for example, business-oriented routes might become still more cost-effective now that there is a greater chance (with a larger number of spokes) that vacation visitors might also wish to use these business-oriented routes.

required amount of safety stock by one-quarter. It has generally been perceived that the resulting savings in stock-holding costs outweigh any increases in transport and related costs resulting from a geographically extended distribution system. Certainly Buck (1992) provided case study support of this 'favourable' logistical cost trade-off for a Dutch manufacturing company. By closing one warehouse in each of the UK, Germany, the Netherlands, Denmark, France, Belgium, Switzerland, Italy and Spain (nine closures in total), and completely centralising warehousing in Rotterdam, the company reported an overall distribution cost saving of over $4 million per annum. Some $3 million of this annualised cost saving being attributed to savings in 'inventory costs' and much of the remaining cost savings to 'inbound freight' ($0.66 million) and 'labour' ($0.30 million) savings. The only rise in costs being attributed to 'outbound delivery' ($0.26 million) as transport linkages to the markets in the respective nine countries became geographically extended, but this rise being overwhelmed by the cost savings elsewhere.

There has been a similar tendency towards centralisation in productive systems as MNEs operate on an increasingly global scale and seek to achieve scale economies wherever possible, even if some parts of other overall productive processes are geographically located in different international countries. This again places greater strain on the logistical system in terms of delivering rapidly and efficiently to the final consumer. Christopher (1998) has pointed to the fact that the presumption in this case of a 'favourable' logistical trade-off (i.e. cost-reducing benefits of large-scale production outweighing the cost-increasing impacts of a more transport intensive and slower distribution system) may be over-optimistic in many cases.

Information technology: logistical and operational implications

We have already touched on some of the implications for logistical and operational decisions of developments in new technologies. Here we look in rather more detail at the particular impacts of some Internet-related technologies. Certain developments in outsourcing and in a variety of business-to-business e-commerce are important in this respect.

■ Outsourcing

We noted in Chapter 1 (p. 3) the increasing tendency for 'footloose' multinationals to relocate parts of a vertically-integrated global production network into geographical areas with lower cost configurations. Case Study 1.2 (p. 18) focused on a further and related aspect of locational decision making by cost-conscious MNEs, namely *outsourcing* by both manufacturing and service-sector firms. A key element in these outsourcing decisions has not only been the cost factor but also the continued improvement in the information and communications technology systems helping companies to better manage and coordinate the outsourced operations and functions. Case Study 12.2 focuses on the outsourcing potential within the IT sector itself and associated business processes.

CASE 12.2 Trend towards 'bundled' services

The breathless expansion of the outsourcing industry is leading to a rapid change in the scale and ranking of the leading providers. Historically, the industry arose from the dissatisfaction of companies with their cash-hungry information technology departments, which too often failed to deliver the desired outcomes within the necessary time-frame. To overcome the difficulty, some began – more than 20 years ago – to buy in IT solutions, contracting with hardware and software suppliers, such as IBM or Unisys, to provide the technology solutions, and overcome the glitches.

The success of this business strategy – particularly when some kind of 'transformation' or quantum leap in the quality or nature or services was involved, has led to the gradual expansion of the range of services companies are prepared to buy in. Ian Watmore, UK managing director of Accenture, the consulting group, that has become a leading outsourcing player, identifies three distinct phases in the development of the industry, beginning with IT services.

As trust grew between buyers and IT suppliers, companies began to outsource not just the supply of technology, but the process itself. For example, Unisys, which was historically strong in supplying the IT technology used by Britain's banks to process cheques, found itself taking on the complete process, as an outsourced provider.

Hence, there emerged the second kind of outsourcing: business process outsourcing, or BPO. Once the idea took root that it was possible to outsource not merely IT, but other non-core processes, such as finance, human resources, and so on, new providers, with new skills, were drawn into the market.

▶

More recently, companies have begun to seek fewer outsourcing providers to handle a far wider range of tasks. We are now witnessing, says Mr Watmore, the development of a third trend, called 'bundling' that will increasingly require broadly-based providers capable of supplying multiple outsourced functions, from IT systems to payroll and staff selection.

Thanks to their head start in the industry, their widening scope, and the accelerating up-take of outsourcing as a solution to the IT challenge, IT suppliers remain in the industry's vanguard. According to reports from analysts IDC and Gartner Dataquest, the clear leader in European outsourcing remains IBM, which secured more than $13.3 billion of deals in 2002 in the IT outsourcing market alone, with 11 of the 100 biggest deals. From its roots in manufacturing computers, IBM Global Services has grown to become the world's largest IT and consulting services company, with revenues of more than $36 billion last year. Its largest rival is Accenture, which announced outsourcing revenues of $828 million in the second quarter, ahead 33 per cent year on year. Outsourcing now generates 29 per cent of the group's total revenues, and is one of its main target areas for growth.

The scale and pace of growth at IBM and Accenture reflects the mounting demand by vanguard companies for their outsourcing providers to offer a broad spectrum of business process solutions.

When the London Stock Exchange ran into trouble modernising its computerised trading systems, it handed the job over to Accenture lock, stock and barrel. The result was that Accenture not only built the exchange's SETS trading system, but now runs it – and operates trading for the Johannesburg stock exchange on it, as well.

Similarly, it struck a landmark deal to take over the financial functions of BP in Aberdeen almost two decades ago, and subsequently assumed responsibility for the human resources function at BT, the UK telecoms leader. That, in turn, provided a platform and expertise for the sale of similar outsourcing services to other telecoms groups, including Cable & Wireless in the UK and Telecom Italia. More recently Accenture has signed two deals to run customer services, including call centres, for AT & T, the US telecoms group, and has taken over logistics and procurement functions for Thames Water, the utility, in a modest deal that will provide experience in a new area.

Another European group ploughing the same furrow from IT, through consulting to outsourcing services, is Cap Gemini Ernst & Young, which is particularly seeking to export experience gained in the vanguard UK market elsewhere. Other IT outsourcing pioneers remain leading players, particularly EDS, which reacted boldly to the UK government strategy, now two decades old, of requiring competitive tendering of many state-provided services. Today, EDS processes $80 billion of medical care benefits a year for US health insurance providers, and is the world's largest mortgage processing outsourced supplier, handling 2.3 million mortgages a year.

Its long-time rival, Unisys, has recently also branched into mortgage processing in the UK and Australia – a logical evolution according to its UK chief, Phil Heggie, who says that $1.5 billion of group annual revenues of $6 billion are now derived from outsourcing.

The growth of outsourcing is generally an evolutionary process for both buyer and supplier, he says. 'As you build a relationship, and trust develops, you are invited to take on more and additional things that are within your capabilities.' Thus, the group's systems expertise has led it to become Britain's biggest life and pension policy administrator.

A fourth trend, clearly identified by Gartner analyst Susan Cournoyer, is a 'dramatic' increase in offshore outsourced services, which, particularly in the IT arena, can deliver exceptional cost-savings. One such deal was that announced last October between Prudential Securities and Exigen, a US-based provider that gets much technical work done in Latvia, Lithuania and Russia.

The Indian IT industry now generates $11 billion a year of revenues in this way. According to Rajdeep Sahrawat, UK regional director of Tata Consulting Services (TCS), the biggest Indian IT outsource provider, using offshore staff for technical work can generate 60 per cent cost savings for UK companies. With annual revenues of more than £100 million last year, TCS now employs 1,100 UK staff serving British clients, as well as 1,300 servicing them from its low-cost base in India.

Source: Ross Tieman, *Financial Times*, 30 June 2003.

Questions

1 Identify the different states that outsourcing has gone through.

2 What are the advantages and disadvantages of outsourcing to the firm?

3 Why do IT firms dominate the outsourcing industries?

■ Business-to-business developments

By 2004 it has been estimated that some $2,700 billion worth of business-to-business (B2B) transactions will be conducted via the Internet, according to Forrester Research, a US market-research group. Large-scale online marketplaces are evolving in many industrial and product-specific sectors which involve integrating existing computer applications with new Web-based procurement systems (*see* Case Study 12.3). Competitive Internet auctions are bringing buyers and sellers together, as in multi-product websites such as eBay or more product specific websites such as E-Steel (steel products) or Chemdex (laboratory supplies). Access to better information on price and product availability is estimated to be bringing down the cost of raw material and other inputs by between 5 per cent and 15 per cent.

CASE 12.3 Rise of the agent economy

The term 'shopbots' refers to the widely used variety of software agents by which buyers automatically search the Internet to find the lowest price for a particular product. Now we have the rise of 'pricebots' by which online sellers themselves seek to undercut the price of rival sellers. These pricebots use price-comparison software that automatically adjusts the sellers' prices to lie a given percentage below the lowest priced rival. Such pricebots are essentially pursuing a market share strategy for the seller. However, more sophisticated (second-generation)

▶

pricebots are now available to replace these first-generation pricebots and these can be programmed to set the sellers' price according to a range of competitor information which includes not only their current prices but also information on the buyers' price sensitivity and other market characteristics. These pricebots can be programmed to seek out the price that sellers should charge to maximise profit rather than market share. For example, pricebots can now apply a short-term optimisation approach (dubbed 'myoptimal' for myopically optimal) which calculates the price that will maximise profits under the assumption that competitor prices remain unchanged.

Kephart and Greenwald (2000) reported on the outcome of investigations using shopbots to set seller prices using 'trial and error' methods (i.e. raising or lowering prices incrementally in an attempt to maximise profits) or using the more sophisticated 'myoptimal' method discussed above. If all the pricebots adopt 'trial and error' methods, the outcome has been found to be high prices and high profits. However, if one of the pricebots adopts a 'myoptimal' method, then it gains high profits as a first-mover advantage. Unfortunately, if all the pricebots adopt 'myoptimal' methods, the outcome has been found to be an endless price war. The pricebots continually undercut each other's price until some 'lowest price' is reached, at which point they re-establish a higher price before embarking once more on a new round of price warfare. Each pricebot is found to be worse off than if they all had maintained a 'trial-and-error' approach. This points to tacit collusion being a possible outcome of a 'prisoners dilemma' type of game (*see* Chapter 8). However, when all the pricebots are myoptimal, the greatest profits accrue to the one with the most up-to-date information.

Questions

1 Why might pricebots be described as 'essentially pursuing a market-share strategy for the seller'?

2 Comment on what is likely to happen to the seller's profit if first-generation pricebots are used and demand is relatively unresponsive to price (price inelastic demand).

3 What other implications might follow from the use of pricebots?

What these investigations do suggest is that, except in the unlikely event of tacit collusion being maintained over time, the use of pricebots, shopbots or other software agents will continually seek out lower priced sources of supply. In logistical terms this suggests a premium on flexibility regarding supply chain linkages. It may be that companies will have to continuously appraise whether established supply chain patterns and linkages are truly cost effective and whether the benefits from changing those linkages more than offset the costs of reconfiguration.

Case Study 12.4 looks at some recent developments in information technology which are driving forward the more widespread application of quick response/mass customisation techniques.

CASE 12.4 Build-to-order systems and quick response techniques

'Build-to-order' (BTO) (or 'order-to-delivery') systems are about to be introduced in the car industry. Currently some 90% of US purchasers and 80% of EU purchasers must wait three months or more between order and delivery of anything other than the most standard of cars. However, BTO may be about to change all that, being based on a Dell Computer system by which customers will be able to order customised cars online or via a freephone number. The customised car will then be assembled and sent on its way to the purchaser within days. Car manufacturers believe they will be able to reduce the order-to-delivery time to less than 14 days. They also believe that they will be able to charge premium prices for such cars, increase customer loyalty in terms of repeat purchases and keep costs down by basing the customised vehicle around standardised chassis and other body parts.

General Motors installed a B70 system in 2003 in the USA, Toyota has also developed the system for its plants in Ontario, Canada. Via the Internet, a customer can select a preferred package of features for the customised car. Within a few seconds of real time the central database of the car maker checks that the features selected correspond to an approved design. The car is then scheduled for assembly at the earliest time the various parts can be received by the car maker. Harold Kutner, head of purchasing for General Motors, states that 'I'd consider myself a failure if I don't take 50% out of overall inventory in this process'. Since General Motors is estimated to carry some $20bn of parts at any point in time to support its varied assembly activities, some several hundred million dollars of inventory-related savings can be anticipated by GM each year via this system.

Questions

1 What advantages do BTO systems offer to car makers (and other manufacturers)?

2 What logistical implications might follow the widespread adoption of such systems?

pause for thought 2   Using the business/financial press, find three examples of Internet-related developments which are likely to have future logistical implications for manufacturing or service firms.

Useful websites

Now try the self-check questions for this chapter on the website at www.booksites.net/wall. You will also find further resources as well as the following useful weblinks:

Explore the site *www.bised.ac.uk* which has several worksheets and many Web links on operations management topics.

The resources section of Dun and Bradstreet has reports on stock control:
www.dnb.com
Information on 'quality' issues can be found on:
www.qualitydigest.com

You can find the Institute of Operations Management at:
www.iomnet.org.uk
Also see the Kaizen Institute's website at *www.kaizen-institute.com*

Useful key texts

Daniels, J., Radebaugh, L. and Sullivan, D. (2004) *International Business* (10th edn), Pearson Prentice Hall, especially Chapter 18.

Dicken, P. (2003) *Global Shift: Transforming the World Economy* (4th edn), Paul Chapman Publishing Ltd, especially Chapter 14.

Hill, C. (2003) *International Business: Competing in the Global Marketplace* (4th edn), McGraw-Hill Irwin, especially Chapter 16.

Rugman, A. and Hodgetts, R. (2003) *International Business* (3rd edn), FT Prentice Hall, especially Chapter 10.

Tayeb, M. (2000) *International Business: Theories, Policies and Practices*, Financial Times Prentice Hall, especially Chapter 17.

Woods, M. (2001) *International Business*, Palgrave, especially Chapter 9.

Other texts and sources

Buck, R. (1992) 'Choosing a Distribution Strategy', *Site Selection Europe* 9: 60–3.

Christopher, M. (1998) *Logistics and Supply Chain Management*, Financial Times Prentice Hall.

Griffiths, A. and Wall, S. (2000) *Intermediate Microeconomics: Theory and Applications* (2nd edn), Financial Times Prentice Hall.

Harris, N. (1989) *Service Operations Management*, Cassell.

Healey, N. (2004) 'The Multinational Corporation', in *Applied Economics* (10th edn), Griffiths, A. and Wall, S. (eds), Financial Times Prentice Hall.

Kephart, J. and Greenwald, A. (2000) 'When Bots Collide', *Harvard Business Review*, July/August.

Lowson, B., King, R. and Hunter, A. (1999) *Quick Response: Managing the Supply Chain to Meet Consumer Demand*, John Wiley & Sons.

Pine, B.J. (1993) *Mass Customisation: The New Frontier in Business Competition*, Harvard Business School Press.

Sako, M. and Murray, F. (1999) 'Modular Strategies in Cars and Computers', *Financial Times*, 6 December.

Slack, N., Chambers, S., Harland, C., Harrison, A. and Johnston, R. (1998) *Operations Management* (2nd edn), Financial Times Prentice Hall, especially Part 5.

United Nations Conference on Trade and Development (UNCTAD), *World Investment Report* (annual publication).

United Nations Development Programme (UNDP), *Human Development Report* (annual publication), OUP.

World Bank, *World Development Report* (annual publication).

Answers and responses

Answers and responses to the 'pause for thought' sections are outlined below. Answers and responses to the Case Study questions have been placed in the Instructor's Manual to accompany this book.

Chapter 1

■ Pause for thought 1

Many possible examples here. Volkswagen recently announced plans to double car production in Changchun, Northern China, by 2007 and raise it by 75% in Shanghai. Case Study 1.1 (p. 9) shows Dyson, the vacuum-cleaner firm relocating production from the UK to Malaysia. Case Study 1.2 (p. 18) provides other production and service sector examples, as with BT and other companies relocating call centre and other back-office functions to India.

■ Pause for thought 2

France has total labour costs per hour some $3.4 per hour less than in the Netherlands but a productivity of labour some 6.5 points (based on UK = 100) higher than the Netherlands. On this evidence France would seem the most attractive. However quality of output, transport and distributive infrastructure, host government incentives and many other factors might also be important in determining production location.

■ Pause for thought 3

'Losers' might include airlines, travel- and tourist-related activities (hotels, restaurants, theatres etc.), among others; 'beneficiaries' might include providers of security equipment and security personnel among others.

■ Pause for thought 4

While there is an ageing demographic profile in many advanced industrialising economies, in many developing economies the demographic profile is becoming progressively younger – with implications for labour supply and consumption patterns. The scourge of HIV in some countries may have important implications for MNEs, reducing labour supply, impoverishing the country (lower increases or even falls in real income per capita) and reducing demand, and so on. Many possibilities here.

■ Pause for thought 5

Certainly there is greater interconnectedness – with terrorism, real or threatened, in one part of the world having impacts elsewhere. So shrinking space and time and disappearing borders would seem to be implied, which are related to the idea of globalisation as a new phenomenon. We noted earlier that global GDP is projected to be growing around 1 per cent per annum less than estimated before 9/11.

■ Pause for thought 6

There are many possibilities here. For example the brands Kit Kat, Yorkie, After Eight Mints, Polo and Quality Street within the product group *confectionary* are all owned by Nestlé. The brands Ariel and Daz Automatic within the product group *washing powders* are owned by Procter & Gamble, and so on.

Chapter 2

■ Pause for thought 1

Many possibilities. Saturation of demand in domestic market; overseas customers may help extend the product life cycle (if in maturity or decline phase at home); extra output may yield scale economies (lower average cost), to the benefit of both domestic and overseas markets; having consumers in different geographical areas is a useful risk-reduction method; overseas markets may be higher income/growing more rapidly/have less competition than domestic market, etc.

■ Pause for thought 2

Services are increasingly important globally and most patents refer to industrial applications. Copyright, trademarks and other more service-related means of protecting intellectual property rights are increasingly important.

■ Pause for thought 3

Pressure for greater transparency and compliance with WTO rules should help non-Chinese businesses to operate in China, as it becomes more open and 'rules based'. Entry into the WTO should further stimulate the Chinese economy, making it a still more attractive market for overseas firms.

■ Pause for thought 4

(a) Conglomerates have a diversified portfolio of products: many examples could be used, such as Virgin with its interests in transport (airlines, railways), entertainment (records etc.), electronic products (e.g. mobile phones), foodstuffs (cola) and many other product groupings.

(b) Benefits include risk-reduction since not all product areas are likely to experience adverse conditions at the same time. Other benefits include enterprise scale economies, e.g. being able to raise capital more cheaply because of the high valuation of the whole enterprise.

(c) In recent times there has been a trend towards focusing on core competencies: the belief being that management can become overstretched by having to deal with too diversified a portfolio of products (i.e. 'sticking to the knitting'). Many recent de-mergers (e.g. Hanson group, ICI) point to this changing perspective.

◼ Pause for thought 5

There are many possibilities here. Reuters has outsourced its own back-office activities to separate service providers in India (as has BT) and many other MNEs. General Motors has set up its own financial arm to lend money to customers buying cars. Ford, Daimler-Chrysler and others have done the same. Ford, the world's second biggest car maker, earns more from lending money than selling vehicles.

Chapter 3

◼ Pause for thought 1

(a) An export of 250 videos by A would now only give imports of 500 CDs instead of the previous 750 CDs. The new 'post-specialisation and trade' consumption point of 550 videos and 500 CDs is now inside A's production possibility frontier. In other words it could do better by being self-sufficient than by engaging in specialisation and trade according to comparative advantages.

(b) An export of 750 CDs by B would now only give imports of 75 videos instead of the previous 250 videos. The new 'post-specialisation and trade' consumption point of 250 CDs and 75 videos is now inside B's production possibility frontier. In other words, it could do better by being self-sufficient than by engaging in specialisation and trade according to comparative advantages.

(c) 1 CD : 0.2 videos equals 1 video : 5 CDs.

(d) Neither would be better or worse off by specialisation and trade according to comparative advantages. They would be in exactly the same situation as they would be had they chosen to be self-sufficient.

◼ Pause for thought 2

When there was complete protection, this area was *producer surplus* to domestic suppliers with the domestic price P_D. Now there is free trade, the world price for the product P_W is the same as the domestic price and this area is now *consumer surplus* to domestic purchasers. In other words, this area is neither gained nor lost as a result of free trade: it simply *transfers* from being producer surplus to being consumer surplus.

■ Pause for thought 3

There are many possibilities here. *Architecture*: The Body Shop, PizzaHut, McDonald's and many other MNEs are well known for using contractual relationships (e.g. franchising) to further their businesses. *Innovation*: Microsoft has a well-established reputation for innovative approaches to home and business uses of its software systems. *Incumbency advantages*: BP has acquired interests in oil fields all over the world, some dating back to the early twentieth century and the easy access then available to the oil fields in the Middle East via British colonialism.

■ Pause for thought 4

From a *national* perspective, the major reductions in global GDP noted in Chapter 1 (some 1% lower growth per annum) means that for most countries 'demand conditions' will be less favourable, with possible adverse consequences for 'factor conditions' and 'related and supporting industries'. Of course nations with competitive advantages in particular sectors (e.g. defence, security industries) may be relatively better placed than others.

■ Pause for thought 5

Export prices of the UK products in the euro-zone would fall in terms of the euro and import prices in the UK (from euro-zone countries) would rise in terms of sterling. For example, an item priced at £1,000 in the UK would have a euro-zone equivalent price of €1,600 before the sterling depreciation but only €1,500 after. An item priced at €1,600 in the euro-zone would have a sterling equivalent price of £1,000 before the sterling depreciation but £1,066.7 after.

Chapter 4

■ Pause for thought 1

For localisation: supports local output and employment; protects smaller firms and nations from the pressures of the larger (multinational) firms and nations; avoids allegedly unfair current rules of world trade; supports national sovereignty; etc.

Against localisation: lose any gains from global specialisation and trade; consumers may face higher prices since loss of scale economies (therefore lower real incomes); may be a reduction in global output and employment; involves imposing regulations on national governments; etc.

■ Pause for thought 2

We have seen that quotas, which form the basis of borrowing rights (e.g. reserve and credit tranches) are allocated in proportion to a member country's share of world trade. As a result, the richer countries get the higher quotas and borrowing rights when arguably they need them least. This same allocation principle also applies to Special Drawing Rights (SDRs) with most going to the richer countries. However, the many borrowing facilities (*see* p. 116) have been used to help the disadvantaged countries, as have many of the various stabilisation programmes, though many recipient countries have complained that the conditions required for such help have been too strict and too deflationary.

■ Pause for thought 3

- Shift (increase) in demand to the right of *D*. This might be caused by more overseas residents wanting to buy the UK's exports, demanding sterling to pay for them. Alternatively, more overseas firms (or individuals) might want to invest in the UK, demanding sterling to finance this investment.
- Shift (decrease) in supply to the left of *S*. Less expenditure by UK residents on imports into the UK and less investment by UK firms (or individuals) overseas, will result in less sterling being supplied in order to buy foreign currencies.

Chapter 5

■ Pause for thought 1

Mandatory labour benefits legislation (e.g. EU Social Chapter directives) and currency appreciation might figure highly. Other future possibilities include future risks of inflation, increased taxation and campaigns against foreign goods and perhaps violence (e.g. if Northern Ireland peace process is disrupted, etc.). Expropriation/confiscation and civil wars are highly implausible.

■ Pause for thought 2

Many possibilities here. Be careful in interpreting individual factors – for example, once established in a country, import restrictions (item 20 in Table 5.2) may benefit the MNE in excluding competitors rather than hinder it in excluding part of its supply chain.

Remember that political risk is only one of the relevant perspectives. Even if there is greater political risk, the MNE may choose that location if the potential economic or strategic benefits are deemed overwhelming. The decision also depends on how 'risk averse' the MNE management is.

■ Pause for thought 3

Imperfect information: some buyers or sellers know more than others, and knowledge is power in a marketplace. *Non-competitive market structures*: monopoly power may give undue influence to some firms in setting higher prices (exploit consumers) or offering lower wages (exploit workers); etc. *Externalities*: negative externalities imply that social cost is higher than private cost e.g. firms polluting the environment and not having to pay for it – tends to result in more output than society might want.

■ **Pause for thought 4**

A stronger euro against the US dollar means that euro-zone exports become more expensive in the US and US exports to the euro-zone become cheaper. The same will be true for China, which should find it even easier to penetrate the EU market now that its (low cost) exports are even cheaper in the euro-zone.

Chapter 6

■ **Pause for thought 1**

Australia and Denmark both score relatively highly for 'individualism' but relatively lowly for 'power distance'. This suggests that managers and employees will tend to focus on their own and other individuals' interests and to be somewhat critical of those in authority. Both (especially Denmark) are towards the weak end of the spectrum for 'uncertainty avoidance', suggesting that change will be viewed rather positively. However, Australia scores much higher in terms of 'masculinity' than Denmark, suggesting that socially-orientated goals are more acceptable in Denmark than Australia where a more acquisitive and assertive outlook is usually adopted (at least vis-à-vis Denmark).

Japan and Singapore are both towards the 'collectivist' end of the spectrum with more focus on group interests. They both more readily accept authority (larger power distance) than Australia and Denmark. However, whereas Japan strongly favours structure and a consistent routine (strong 'uncertainty avoidance'), Singapore will more readily accept change and look for new opportunities (weak 'uncertainty avoidance'). Japan more readily accepts values associated with material possessions (high 'masculinity') than Singapore with its more socially-orientated values (weak masculinity/high femininity).

These different national characteristics clearly have important implications for many aspects of management including organisational structures, methods of incentivisation, human resource management issues and so on, many of which are considered in Chapters 8–12 of this book.

■ **Pause for thought 2**

Individualism. The more individualist approach may result in greater focus on outcomes and individual contributions to these outcomes rather than team and group 'success'. Relationships may be neglected, causing confusion and a lack of goal-congruence between the collaborating companies.

Long-term orientation. The company placing more emphasis on this aspect may be looking at longer-term goals (e.g. market share) rather than shorter-term goals (e.g. profits, shareholder value). Again, there may be problems in establishing goal congruence.

■ **Pause for thought 3**

Many possibilities here. For example the founders of some companies (e.g. The Body Shop, Virgin) can have a major influence on their values and culture.

Chapter 7

■ Pause for thought 1

Various possibilities exist. For example, MNEs from western nations may resist various types of hospitality/gift-giving as akin to bribery, when in *guanxi* relationships of MNEs from East and South-East Asian nations it is an accepted way of doing business (*see* Chapter 6).

■ Pause for thought 2

What is deemed unethical under one set of national cultural values may be deemed acceptable under others. The *guanxi* relationships of giving which are part of a complex set of social networking in many Asian countries may be viewed as bribery in western-orientated countries, etc.

■ Pause for thought 3

There are many possibilities here, e.g. the *Forest Stewardship Council* sets the standards for sustainable forestry.

■ Pause for thought 4

There are many possibilities here, for example Nestlé introduced an 'ombudsman system' in 2002, allowing its employees to blow the whistle on any unethical marketing of baby milk formula to mothers in developing countries.

Chapter 8

■ Pause for thought 1

Horizontal diversification involves new products in new markets, where those new products broadly correspond to the *existing stage of production* in which the initiating company currently operates and which have some relationship to the current product range. For example, a clothing manufacturer introducing a new range of clothing into, say, the niche, higher priced/quality designer market having previously operated in the mass, low price/quality standardised garment market.

Vertical diversification involves *different stages of production*. This can be 'backward' towards the source of supply (e.g. a retail outlet starting to make some of the products it sells) or 'forward' towards the retail outlet (e.g. a manufacturer starting to retail some of its products).

All the above types of diversification were regarded by Ansoff as 'related'. *Conglomerate diversification*, however, is 'unrelated', involving new products which have little or no relationship to the existing product range. Virgin moving into car retailing might arguably be an example here.

■ Pause for thought 2

Many possibilities here. For example, in terms of supermarkets ('multiple grocers'), Safeway prior to being taken over by Somerfield might have been regarded as a 'marginal' firm and Tesco is certainly a market leader. Tesco has developed competitive advantage over its rivals in terms of 'incumbency advantages' (scale economies, reputation, etc.), 'innovation' with new kinds of club cards, new services (e.g. financial) and 'operational efficiencies' (check-out facilities, just-in-time delivery techniques), etc.

■ Pause for thought 3

Firm A: low price; best outcome for A is firm B adopting high price (£3,000).
Firm A: high price; best outcome for A is firm B adopting low price (£2,000).
Mini-max for A is high price (worst of best possible outcomes).
Firm B: low price; best outcome for B is firm A adopting high price (£3,000).
Firm B: high price; best outcome for B is firm A adopting low price (£2,000).
Mini-max for B is high price (worst of best possible outcomes).
Mini-max outcome is high price: high price – both disappointed.

Chapter 9

■ Pause for thought 1

(a) There is considerable 'cultural distance' between Great Britain and Japan in terms of the four cultural dimensions shown in Table 6.3. To bridge this cultural distance, a more decentralised and polycentric approach is perhaps more likely than an integrated and ethnocentric approach.

(b) With Canada there is much less 'cultural distance' with Great Britain so that any of the IHRM approaches would appear feasible, depending on the MNE's needs and objectives. Certainly there is more likely to be an integrated and ethnocentric approach to IHRM for Canada as compared to Japan.

Chapter 10

■ Pause for thought 1

- *Benefit segmentation* looks at the benefits consumers want from the product. Thus, toothpaste may be bought to obtain white teeth or a fresh-mouth taste. A drink may be bought because it has a great taste or less calories.

- *Behaviour segmentation* is based on individuals' behaviour patterns and consumption habits. Thus some people will only buy clothing from speciality men's or women's shops, while others will use departmental stores or discount stores. These shopping habits may be used as the basis for segmentation.

- *Geodemographic segmentation* is used where there are noticeable differences in peoples habits based upon geography. For example, urban versus rural, hot versus cold or North versus South.

- *Lifestyle segmentation* is based upon how individuals spend their time and money. Many magazines segment their market by lifestyle. These magazines provide other firms who wish to reach the same segment with the opportunity to advertise to, and reach that target market.

Pause for thought 2

Some of the following points might be listed.

Domestic marketing	International marketing
Main language	Many languages
Dominant culture	Multi-culture
Research relatively straightforward	Research complex
Relatively stable environment	Frequently unstable environment
Single currency	Exchange rate problems
Business conventions understood	Conventions diverse and unclear

Chapter 11

Pause for thought 1

In the USA, quarterly reports are expected from large companies, as well as the main annual report.

Pause for thought 2

An examination of the typical elements that make up a company report reveals a mixture of statutory items, requirements of the accounting profession, additional Stock Exchange requirements and voluntary disclosures. The most important items within annual reports are the following:

- Chairman's review
- Director's report
- Balance sheet
- Profit and loss account
- Statement of total recognised gains and losses
- Note of historical cost profits and losses
- Notes to the accounts (including statement of accounting policies)
- Cash-flow statement
- Auditors' report
- Historical summary

Much of a company's annual report is narrative rather than numerical. For example, the 'chairman's report' contains a general view of the company's past period's performance and its prospects for the future period.

■ Pause for thought 3

A standardised international approach to accounting practice would certainly help investors interpret reported data. In some cases it would also help senior executives and management avoid damaging and selective reporting in the press. Under British accounting standards, Rover's trading situation was much healthier than it appeared under German accounting standards. In the case of British Airways, the reported net profit varied upwards or downwards due to the fluctuating effects of UK or US accounting standards in specific periods.

Chapter 12

■ Pause for thought 1

Substantial economies of scale available (*see* Chapter 8), reducing average production costs substantially. When the minimum efficient size (MES) of the production unit is very high, the only way to be competitive with rivals may be to use these processes.

■ Pause for thought 2

Many possibilities here, including developments in WAP-related technologies involving mobile telephony, with implications for educational/entertainment and a host of other sectors and products.

Index

Athletic Ability
& the Anatomy

Rolf Wirhed

Translated by
A. M. Hermansson

M Mosby-Wolfe

London   Baltimore   Bogotá   Boston   Buenos Aires   Caracas   ...rk   Philadelphia   St. Louis   Sydney   Tokyo   Toronto   Wiesbaden

Copyright © Rolf Wirhed, Harpoon Publications AB
    Orcbro, Sweden, 1984
Copyright © Wolfe Medical Publications Ltd, 1984
Published by Wolfe Medical Publications Ltd, 1984
Reprinted in 1995 by Mosby–Wolfe, and imprint of
    Times Mirror International Publishing Ltd.
Printed by Butler & Tanner Ltd, Frome, England
ISBN 0 7234 0854 8 Cased edition
ISBN 0 7234 1540 4 Paperback edition

Reprinted 1987, 1988, 1991, 1992, 1994, 1995

Originally published in Sweden, under the title
'Anatomi och rörelsclära inom indrotten' 1982
(Samspråck Förlagsaktiebolag)

For a full list of other titles published
by Mosby–Wolfe, please
write to the publishers at: Times Mirror International Publishing Ltd
Lynton House, 7–12 Tavistock Square,
London WC1H 9LB, England.

A CIP catalogue record for this book is available from the
British Library.

CONTENTS

PREFACE

I have taught the subject of Kinetics (or the Theory of Motion) at the Örebro College of Physical Education (GIH) for a number of years. This subject deals with the mechanical laws that govern the technical execution of various exercises. During recent years, sportsmen have become increasingly interested in analysing the different aspects of, above all, technical kinds of sports (athletics, gymnastics, racket sports. . .). For example, instructors who train people in keeping fit are becoming more aware of the need to teach correct movements in order to increase the effect of training and reduce the risk of injury. Exercises designed to prevent injury are now an important feature of almost every sportsman's general training.

My own concern for these things was aroused by my keen interest in sports and the training I received in atomic physics which required, among other things, a knowledge of mechanics. I also studied anatomy in Uppsala so that I would better understand the mechanisms that govern the human body when it performs various movements.

This book takes up ideas that are usually summarized under the heading "Biomechanics". The lack of suitable literature has resulted in a dearth of anatomical and mechanical knowledge among sports leaders and the majority of them have felt the need for suitable literature and special sports associations have clearly expressed their desire that this need be met.

It is my hope that the readers of this book (including sports leaders, physical education teachers, physiotherapists) will find that examples contained in and ideas taken from this book will be of substantial practical value. The book may be used as a textbook for prospective physical education teachers, sports leaders and youth recreation leaders, and it may form the base for adult education classes. Students of the natural sciences at the upper secondary school level may find the book interesting as extra reading or may be inspired by it when working on special projects. It is my hope that after having read this book, you will have acquired a sound knowledge of the position and function of muscles, forces, the movement of force, the centre of gravity and the moment of inertia, and that you will find it easier to judge how and what to train. Hopefully, the general knowledge of anatomy and mechanics contained in this book will help you to gain new ability to analyze and understand the kind of sport you are interested in.

Rolf Wirhed
University Lecturer in Biomechanics

INTRODUCTION

This book deals firstly with general characteristics of bones, joints and muscles and it provides general guidelines for flexibility and strength training. Thereafter, the anatomy and function of the different parts of the body are described.

The main stress has been laid upon the analysis of movement, i.e. the biomechanical aspects of the exercises sportsmen perform to train a special part of the body. In the last section, such different types of movements as take off, rotation, flight, landing, etc., are dealt with. In the cases where the latin name is usual, it is given in brackets.

If you read the book on your own, you should always try to perform the movements or exercises. Feel the muscles that are described. Even if the book is read in a class, the exercises and movements should be carried out, at least to the extent that the situation allows. Anatomy and kinetics should be experienced in practice — they are not solely theoretical concepts.

Get to know your body! You have only got one and it must last your entire life.

GENERAL ANATOMY OF BONES, JOINTS, AND MUSCLES

A. The Skeleton

The aim of this general section on the bones of the human body is to provide the reader with the basic knowledge needed to benefit from the literature on sports injuries, and also to aid him in analysing how the bones react to the stresses and strains to which they are subjected in different training exercises.

The skeleton of the body is made up of a variety of bones which are classified as follows:

short bones (e.g. bones of the ankle and wrist),
long bones (e.g. bones of the hand and forearm, thigh bone) and
flat bones (e.g. bones of the skull, breastbone).

The process of bone formation is called ossification. The flat bones (e.g. the bones of the skull) are developed in one stage from connective tissue. This developmental process is called direct ossification (intramembranous ossification). The bones of the skull are not fully formed in the newborn baby. The areas of incomplete ossification, the so-called fontanelles, can be felt with the fingers. Most of the bones of the skeleton are formed by indirect ossification (intracartilaginous or endochondral ossification). A cartilaginous model of the future bone is developed in the embryo and is later dissolved and replaced by bone.

Short bones are formed by indirect ossification. The cells at the centre of the growing cartilaginous model die. The so-called osteoblasts (os = bone, blast = immature cell) migrate from the membrane which surrounds the cartilage (periosteum) to the spaces left by the wasted cells. These osteoblasts gradually transform into bone cells (osteocytes). Not all the cartilage ossifies, some parts of it remain in the form of articular cartilage.

Articular fluid — which is found in the cavity of synovial joints — provides the articular cartilage with nourishment. The blood vessels which lie inside the bone tissue beneath the plates of articular cartilage also supply nourishment to the cartilage. The nutrients diffuse through the cartilage cells (being pressed or massaged through) and are not transported through small blood vessels (capillaries). Thus, if the joints are subjected to suitable all-around stress during the formative years of childhood, they will be well supplied with nourishment. This in turn leads to a thickening of the cartilage, thereby providing better protection against the kind of injury caused by excessive stress. A joint which is not subjected to any kind of stress, or is not fully used in all possible directions, reacts in an opposite manner; that is, the cartilage thins out.

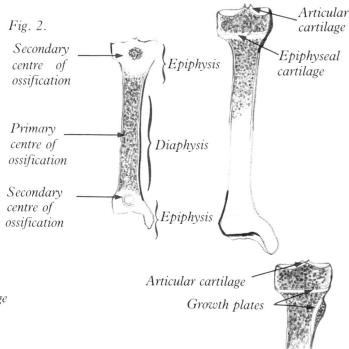

Fig. 2.

Secondary centre of ossification

Epiphysis

Articular cartilage

Epiphyseal cartilage

Primary centre of ossification

Diaphysis

Secondary centre of ossification

Epiphysis

Articular cartilage

Growth plates

Fig. 2. This shows the growth plates situated at the proximal (towards the centre of the body) end of the shin bone shaft just beneath the insertion of the knee extensor muscles.

Fig. 1.

Articular cartilage

Bone

Articular cartilage

The long bones are also formed by indirect ossification, but here several so-called ossification centres can be found. In the formation of these bones, articular cartilage and growth plates (epiphyseal cartilage) are left between the shaft (diaphysis) and each extremity (epiphysis). The epiphyseal cartilage usually ossifies in the late teens or when a person is fully-grown. The so-called epiphyseal cartilage can be located in a youth with the aid of an X-ray.

Pathological changes at the growth plates are often due to hormonal disturbances. They can also be a consequence of incorrectly loading or overloading the skeleton. Compared with the rest of the body the skeleton grows very quickly during the first few years of life and during adolescence. Athletically active young people should therefore refrain from *extreme* strength training during puberty. A good recommendation is that the child, while still undergoing the changes of puberty, use only his or her own weight as a load when training. Thus, only the postpubertal child should include weights and equipment in his or her strength training routines.

A rather common complaint among children between the ages of 10 and 16 years is Osgood-Schlatter's disease. This condition results from excessive tension in the knee extensor's insertion on the small prominence of the shin bone (tibial tuberosity). The growth plates are irritated and the ensuing growth may be accelerated. The enlargement can be seen with the naked eye when the affected leg is compared with the healthy one. The afflicted child may have difficulty in kneeling on hard surfaces.

Figure 3 shows the fully-grown bone in detail. Microscopically small bone cells (osteocytes) lie embedded in a tissue consisting of collagen fibres which are highly resistant to force, inorganic salts

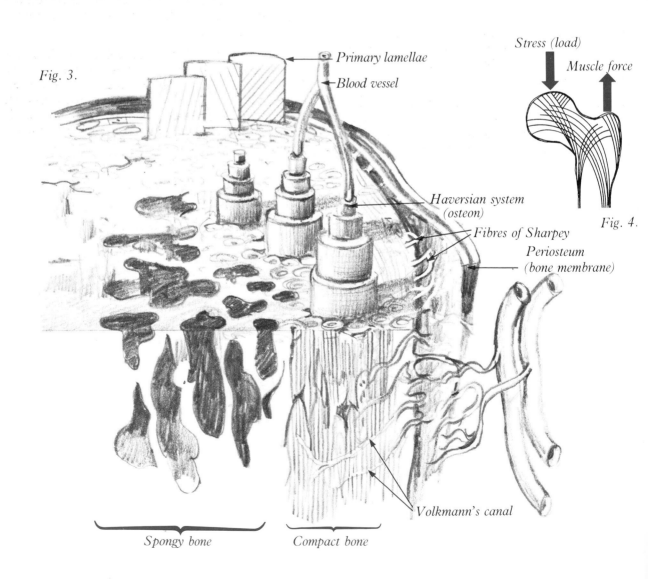

Fig. 3.

Primary lamellae

Blood vessel

Stress (load)

Muscle force

Haversian system (osteon)

Fibres of Sharpey

Periosteum (bone membrane)

Fig. 4.

Volkmann's canal

Spongy bone   Compact bone

(giving the bone its hardness) and organic salts (giving the bone its elasticity). The ratio between the inorganic and organic salts is 1 : 1 at birth, but changes to 7 : 1 by the time the body is 60 - 70 years old. This explains the skeleton's elasticity in youth and its frailty in old age. Also shown in Fig. 3 is how the bone cells are arranged circularly in several layers around a so-called Haversian canal through which a small blood vessel runs. This blood vessel supplies the many layers with nourishment. Such a system is called a Haversian System, or osteon.

The outer layers of the bone form a system of longitudinal lamellae. The tough collagenous fibres run in different directions in each layer, which considerably enhances the strength of the bone. The bone within the lamellae is made up of osteons. Farthest in towards the medullary cavity, the compact bone becomes so-called spongy tissue. Between the compact and spongy tissues are reinforcing bars or braces which give the bone its great strength.

Figure 4 shows how these bars are constructed in the neck of the thigh bone (femoral neck) in order to withstand the considerable stress to which this part of the bone is subjected.

The muscle tendons and ligaments are attached to the bone by collagenous fibres growing through the bone membrane and into the compact bone tissue. When subjected to severe stress a tendon may hold, but its attachment to the bone may give way. A bit of the bone may thus be torn off or avulsed.

Where the muscle's tendon of attachment passes through the bone membrane — which is rich in nerve and blood vessels — an unfavourable stress can irritate the membrane and lead to periostitis (inflammation of the periosteum) (see p.61).

In the deeper layer of the bone membrane there are many bone-forming cells (osteoblasts) which are responsible for the repair of broken bones (fractures). The bone is supplied with nutrients by the vast number of blood vessels which penetrate the compact tissue via the bone membrane. The vessels then ramify and reach the different parts of the bone through the Haversian canals. The ability of the bone to repair itself is directly dependant upon the adequacy of the blood supply to the injured area. For example, when one of the bones of the hand (metacarpals) is injured it often takes a long time to heal as there are few blood vessels in the area and, moreover, those that do exist are usually injured in the fracture.

Scientific investigation has revealed that the number of capillaries supplying muscles and bone increases if the muscles and bones are regularly subjected to stress (training). This could explain the observation that injuries sustained by well-trained people heal much faster than those sustained by untrained people.

B. Joints

The different parts of the skeleton are connected either by attachments such as membranes or by joints.

Attachments (membranes, ligaments, discs)

Between the the shin bone (tibia) and the calf bone (fibula) there is a uniting membrane (interosseous membrane) formed of collagenous fibrous tissues. It has two functions: (1) it serves as an origin for many of the muscles of the lower leg (see p.60), and (2) it transmits stress from the shin bone to the calf bone. For example, when landing from a jump, force is exerted on the ankle bone (talus) and up through the tibia, but is then transmitted via the membrane to the fibula. (The tibia is relieved of stress.)

Fig. 5.

Interosseous membrane
Shin bone (tibia)

Calf bone (fibula)

Ligament
Ankle bone (talus)

The tibia and fibula are also united by two strong bands of fibrous tissue at the ankle (inferior tibio-fibular joint — a syndesmosis). Such powerful, clearly distinguishable bands are called ligaments.

If the foot is violently pressed up against the lower leg (extension or dorsiflexion) the talus may wedge in between the fibula and tibia with such force that the anterior of the two ligaments may tear (rupture). The lower part of the membrane may also rupture.

Fig. 6.

Thigh bone (femur)

Posterior crossed ligament (cruciate)
Anterior crossed ligament (cruciate)

Lateral ligament
Medial ligament

tibia

fibula

The knee viewed from the front (without a kneecap)

Other examples of clearly distinguishable free ligaments are the crossed, or cruciate, ligaments which cross each other inside the knee joint.

Another type of ligament provides reinforcement in the capsule which encloses a joint. This ligament is responsible for blocking those movements whose deviations are too great. It also restricts movements in certain directions.

The strongest of all the ligaments in the body (iliofemoral ligament) is a thickened band of fibres situated on the anterior aspect of the hip capsule. It restricts excessive backward swings of the legs. The strength of a ligament or tendon can be 5000 – 10000 N/cm². The above-mentioned ligament in an adult person can withstand a stress of 3000 N.

Another type of attachment can be found between the vertebrae of the spinal column. It is composed not only of collagenous fibres, but also of cartilage cells; and in its centre is a soft nucleus. It is called a secondary cartilaginous joint. A further example of this type of cartilaginous joint is the symphysis pubis connecting the pubic bones of the pelvis.

Additional examples of joint types are that of the epiphyseal cartilage (a primary cartilaginous joint) (see p.7), and the fibrous joint between the flat bones of the skull (sutures).

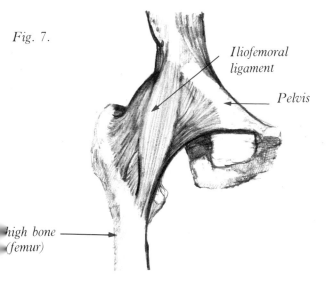

Fig. 7.

Iliofemoral ligament

Pelvis

high bone (femur)

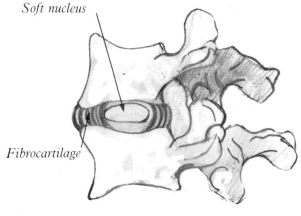

Fig. 8.

Soft nucleus

Fibrocartilage

Fig. 10.

Suture

Fig. 9.

Symphysis pubis (fibrocartilage)

Joints (synovial joints)

The parts of the bones of a synovial joint are always enclosed in a joint capsule and they are always covered with articular cartilage. The outer layer of the capsule is formed by collagen fibres which are highly resistant to force. The powerful reinforcements of the capsule wall are called ligaments (see Figure 7). They receive their names according to their position or according to the bones they connect.

In the inner layer of the capsule there are cells that produce a fluid containing albumin. This fluid acts as a lubricant and provides the cartilage cells with nutrients. It is also called synovial fluid and the membrane which lines the capsule is called the synovial membrane. The inner and outer layers are separated by a thin layer of fat (Figure 11).

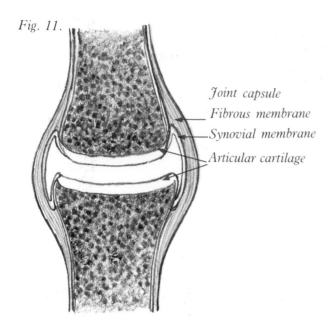

Fig. 11.

Joint capsule
Fibrous membrane
Synovial membrane
Articular cartilage

Fig. 12.

Suprapatellar bursa

Bursa

Bursa

The thickness of the cartilage of a joint depends on the stress to which it is normally subjected. The cartilage is able to absorb certain substances from the synovial fluid and swell temporarily. If we measure the size of the articular cartilage after a period of warming up, we would find that it had thickened. The thickening is only temporary, lasting for 10–30 minutes after the activity has ceased. Prolonged training causes the cartilage to thicken by the formation of additional cartilage cells. Severe or uneven stress can wear the cartilage down, resulting in seriously restricted movement at the joint.

Little sacs of synovial fluid (bursae) are found associated with certain joints; they are formed in the same way as the joint capsule (Figure 12).

The bursa's inner layer (synovial membrane) causes it to form a displacement cushion with very low friction.

The bursa's task is, above all, to prevent wear of the different structures which glide against each other. However, it also produces synovial fluid in those cases when it is connected with a joint.

The largest bursa of the body (the suprapatellar bursa) is situated between the thigh bone (or femur) and the knee extensors (the quadriceps muscle). When the knee is subjected to severe stress, the bursa becomes sore. It reacts by producing extra quantities of synovial fluid. This leads to a swelling of the knee which prevents further stress (water on the knee).

Bursae can be found in many different places in the body. For example, between muscles, between tendons and muscles, and between tendons and bone, i.e. wherever wear and tear is likely.

The bones that make up a joint generally fit together well. Usually one of the bones is convex (the head) and the other is concave (the socket or depression). If, however, the bones do not fit together well, the irregularities are evened out by extra layers of fibrocartilage. These inclusions are called menisci if they only partly subdivide a joint cavity. If the joint is completely partitioned into two separate parts, the layer of fibrocartilage is called a disc.

Fig. 13.

Disc

Meniscus

In sports injuries, reference to menisci usually refer to those of the knee, although one can also find menisci between other bones of the body. For example, between the collar bone and the shoulder blade (Figure 13).

Different types of joints

The function of joints is usually described with the aid of mechanical models. However, there is not always such a close resemblance between mechanical models and the actual joints of the human body. The diagrams below show different types of joints along with the parts of the body where they can be found. In addition, illustrations are given of the type of movement allowed by these joints.

Fig. 17.

Condyloid joint (movements round two axes)

Flexion   Adduction
Extension Abduction

Fig. 14.

Hinge joint (movement in one plane only)

Stretching   Bending
(extension)   (flexion)

Fig. 18.

Ball and socket joint (movement round three axes)

Extension   Flexion

Inward rotation   Outward rotation

Adduction   Abduction

Fig. 15.

Pivot joint (movement round one axis only)

Inward rotation   Outward rotation
(pronation)   (supination)

Fig. 16.

Saddle joint (movements round two axes)

Flexion   Abduction (movement away from
Extension   the midline of the body)
            Adduction (movement towards
               the midline of the body)

Fig. 19.

Gliding joint (multiaxial)

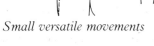

Small versatile movements

Because the capsular ligament around a gliding joint is almost always taut, the movements allowed at such joints are described as small but multidirectional (hence multiaxial).

Many of the body's joints cannot be compared with any of the above models. Instead, a combination of two models or one of the models with some modification is used for descriptive purposes. For example, the knee joint is a combination of a hinge and pivot joint. At that joint, flexion and extension are possible as well as inward and outward rotation of the lower leg, but the leg can only be rotated when the knee is bent.

The knuckle joints are modified ball and socket joints. The head of one bone and the socket of the other correspond almost exactly to the ball and socket model, but the capsular ligament prevents certain movements and there are no muscles for rotating the finger.

shown that even a completely torn heel or Achilles tendon heals if the ankle is set in such a position that the parts of the tendon lie against each other.

A ligament can be made slack and unstressed by taping. The aim of taping a joint is to prevent movements that can strain a weak or injured ligament. Taping in athletics is defensible after injury has been sustained or as part of an effort to prevent injury when it is known that the risk of injury is high (e.g. in vigorous football training, or other competitive situations). However, an athlete should avoid the habitual use of taping during training as this could lead to an injury of the skin. Moreover, the unloaded ligament becomes accustomed to external help after a while, and is thus weakened.

Fig. 20.

30-35° 45-50°

Of all the muscles that protect the joint from injury, the muscles directly surrounding it are the most important. A strong and supple musculature is always the best protection against joint injuries. Violent physical activity can lead to different kinds of muscle injuries. Muscles can be overstretched, partly ruptured (partial rupture) or even completely ruptured. When a ligament is stretched, it usually returns to its original length and function after some weeks of rest.

If the same ligament is repeatedly stretched, the result can be a slack non-functional ligament. The joint then only fits loosely together, which can lead to serious injury. Such a ligament should be shortened by surgery. Ligaments that are completely torn should be sewn together. Partially torn ligaments can be operated on, i.e. sewn together, but if the torn parts are in contact they can heal if the affected area is kept still. In such cases the joint should be set. In recent years it has been

C. Muscles

There are three different types of muscles in the body: smooth muscle, cardiac muscle and skeletal muscle. This book will only deal with the last of these, which is also called striated or striped muscle.

A skeletal muscle is surrounded by a layer of connective tissue. The connective tissue is built up in the same way as the outer layer of a joint capsule (see p.12). Its task is to provide a surface against which the surrounding muscles can glide, and it gives a muscle its form.

The layer of connective tissue is also called the muscle's fascia or epimysium. The connective tissue is formed mainly of collagen fibres. Looking at a section of a muscle with the naked eye, we see that it is made up of small cell bundles (fasciculi). Each of these is surrounded by a thin layer of connective tissue whose latin name is perimysium. In this layer of connective tissue — which is made up of both collagenous and elastic fibres — the nerve and blood vessels branch off before finally reaching the actual muscle cells. Under the microscope we can see that each fasciculus consists of a number of muscle cells.

Each cell is surrounded by a very thin layer of connective tissue which is called endomysium (endo = final, mysium = muscle).

The muscle cell is also called a muscle fibre, thus a muscle fibre consists of a single cell. The structure and function of muscle cells is described very thoroughly in the majority of books on physiology. The following account is therefore brief.

When examined under the microscope, the muscle cell is seen to be composed of small components called muscle fibrils or myofibrils (fibril = little fibre). The fibrils lie in parallel and give the muscle cell a striated appearance. This is because the fibrils are made up of smaller components, myofilaments (filaments = smaller than fibrils), which are regularly aligned.

Myofilaments are chains of protein molecules. The striated appearance is due to the presence of two types of myofilament, namely, actin (which is thinner and therefore more transparent) and myosin (which is thicker and is responsible for the darker bands).

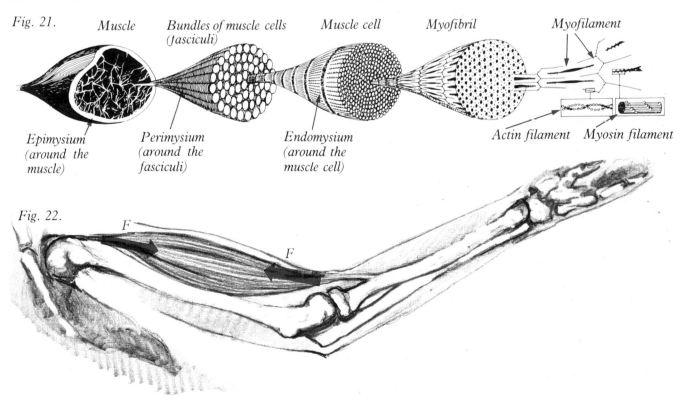

Fig. 21.

Muscle — Bundles of muscle cells (fasciculi) — Muscle cell — Myofibril — Myofilament

Epimysium (around the muscle) — Perimysium (around the fasciculi) — Endomysium (around the muscle cell)

Actin filament   Myosin filament

Fig. 22.

F

F

When the muscle contracts, the actin filaments move between the myosin filaments. As a consequence, the myofibrils shorten and thicken.

The connective tissue surrounding the muscle extends and is continuous with the muscle's tendon. When a muscle contracts, it produces a force *(F)* which affects the origin and insertion of a muscle equally, but in opposite directions.

The muscles of the body have very different shapes. Figure 23 shows the most common variations.
A muscle can develop a maximal force of about 50 N/cm^2 of the muscle's cross section. The cross section referred to here is physiological, and it is defined in the following way: if the cells of a muscle run longitudinally, the geometrical cross section of the muscle *(A)* will provide a measurement of how many actin and myosin filaments are contained in the muscle. If the area is 6 cm^2, the maximal force of contraction will be 6 x 50 = 300 N. If the muscle cells run diagonally in relation to the muscle's longitudinal direction, then the areas A_1 and A_2 must be measured in order to arrive at the total number of actin and myosin filaments contained in the muscle.

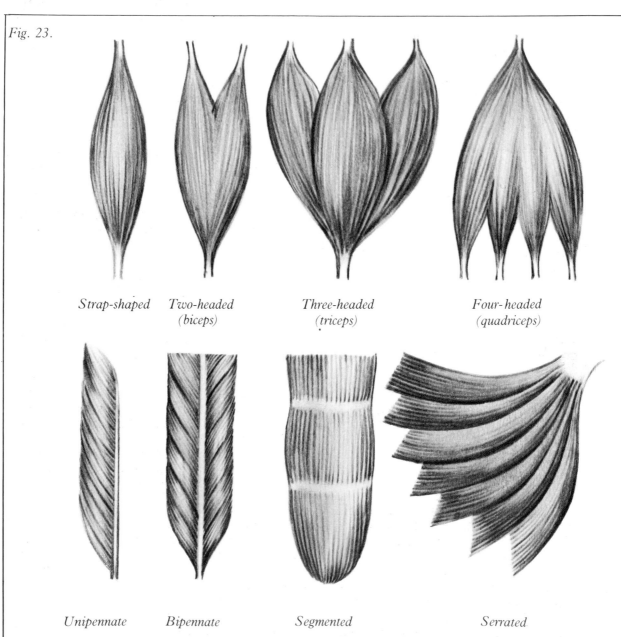

Fig. 23.

| Strap-shaped | Two-headed (biceps) | Three-headed (triceps) | Four-headed (quadriceps) |

| Unipennate | Bipennate | Segmented | Serrated |

Fig. 24.

Strap-shaped   *Pennate-shaped*

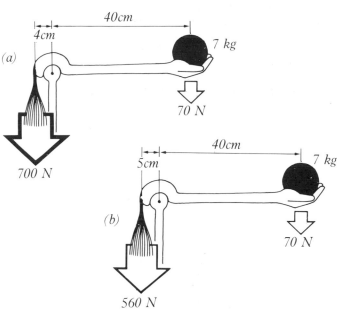

Fig. 26.

(a)

40cm

4cm

7 kg

70 N

700 N

(b)

40cm

5cm

7 kg

70 N

560 N

A_1 + A_2 gives the muscle's physiological cross section. If A_1 = 8 cm^2 and A_2 = 4cm^2, the muscle's physiological cross section will be 12 cm^2. The muscle's maximal strength is 12 x 50 = 600 N. This muscle is thus considerably stronger than the strap-shaped muscle, even if both muscles have equal mass. A muscle cell can shorten its length by about 50%. The strap-shaped muscle can therefore be shortened over a greater distance than the pennate muscles.

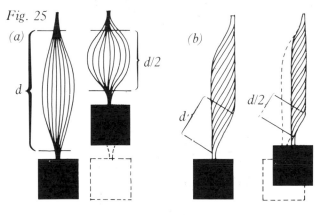

Fig. 25

(a)

d

$d/2$

(b)

d'

$d/2$

The strap-shaped muscle is found in places where it is necessary to execute large ranges of movement quickly. Pennate muscles, on the other hand, can be found where movements over a small range but of great strength are required.

The force of a muscle is dependent on its physiological cross section. Its ability to contract depends on the length of its fleshy part measured in the direction of the cells. In order to assess the effect of a muscle we must also know where it is attached in relation to the joint.

The diagrams above show that if a muscle is attached 4 cm from the joint axis, its force must be 700 N if it is to support a weight of 7 kg located 40 cm from the joint (70 x 4 = 7 x 40). If, instead, the same muscle were attached 5 cm from the joint, then its force need only be 560 N (56 x 5 = 7 x 40). The ability of a muscle to lift a heavy object is thus dependent on two factors: its physiological cross section and its position in relation to the joint. A muscle's strength is more adequately described when we know its ability to develop the moment of force *(M)* as well as its force of contraction. (The concept "moment of force" is described on p.30.)

In order to analyse a movement, it should be known that a muscle's force of contraction depends on its contracted length as compared to its length at rest. Suppose we want to investigate the ability of a muscle bundle to contract. The muscle bundle's resting length is d_0 cm. The muscle bundle is attached to two plates which are connected to a gauge. The gauge shows the force with which the plates are drawn towards each other.

If the distance between the plates is d_0, then the force is 0 (F_0). (The beginning of the broken-lined curve in Figure 32). If the muscle bundle is drawn out, the indicator will respond. This is because the elastic components of the muscle manifest their natural tendency to remain at rest d_0. The broken-lined curve below shows the magnitude of the force with which the muscle would return to its original resting length when it is stretched. (The muscle is passive, i.e. it does not contract.)

17

Fig. 27. F_0

If the muscle is drawn out slightly beyond its resting length and thereafter stimulated electrically, it will be seen that its ability to contract will be greater than it is at d_0, i.e. F_2. This greater value is due to the combination of elastic forces and the forces brought into action by the electrical impulse. The maximum value (F_4) is reached when the muscle is extended to about 120% of its resting length.

Fig. 28. F_1

If the distance between the plates is extended to d_1, then the force will be F_1.

Fig. 31. F_4

In order to examine which forces are developed when a muscle contracts, we do the following: via an electrical impulse, we incite the muscle cells to contract, and the force is gauged.

If the electrical impulse is given when the distance between the plates is d_0, then the force will measure F_2 (the absolute value will depend on the thickness of the muscle bundle).

If the distance between the plates is less than d_0, then the muscle force (F_3) which could be exerted on the plates, would be less than F_2.

Fig. 32.

Fig. 29. F_2

If the distance is reduced to about 50% of the muscle bundle's length (d_0), then during contraction the origin and insertion will only just reach the plates, i.e. the force will be 0.

If the muscle is drawn out more than 120%, then its force of contraction decreases again. This is because the actin and myosin filaments are pulled so far apart that the muscle's capacity for voluntary contraction decreases more than the elastic force of contraction increases.

When we want to obtain the maximal strength of a movement, a "good technique" for doing this involves working the muscles under the most favourable conditions possible.

The hip muscle that is engaged when the leg is pushed forcefully backwards is the large buttock muscle (gluteus maximus).

When a person walks on level ground he does not need to push off from the ground with excess force, but if he encounters a steep ascent, he automatically bends forward. Thus, the muscle is lengthened so that the force developed is greater (120% as shown above).

Fig. 30. F_3

Fig. 33.

Fig. 35.

Think about what a person does to increase his speed when skating, running or cycling. In order to give a football a mighty kick, for example, the hip must start from a position well back as an important knee extensor muscle (p.49) passes over the hip joint. If the muscle is required to develop much force, then the distance between its origin and insertion must be greater than d_0.

Different types of muscular work

When observing the way muscles work, it is usual to distinguish between dynamic and static work.

Dynamic work means that the origin and insertion of a muscle are forcefully affected by changes in muscle length. If the muscle force causes the origin and insertion to move towards each other, we say that the muscle works concentrically (the muscle is shortened, contracted). If the muscle force is exerted while the origin and insertion are receding from each other (i.e. the muscle tries to halt a movement in a joint), the muscle is said to work eccentrically (although the muscle tries to shorten, it is actually lengthened by external forces).

When a muscle contracts without any movement taking place in the joint, it is said that the muscle works statically (or isometrically).

Fig. 34.

For efficient throwing it is necessary to lengthen an important group of muscles, namely, the pectoralis major (p.82). It is stretched in relation to the arm, when the trunk rotates fully in the opposite direction. At the same time, the chest is expanded by inhaling deeply.

Fig. 36.

When lowering oneself, the elbow flexors work eccentrically

When pulling oneself up, the elbow flexors work concentrically

When hanging still, the elbow flexors work statically

19

Fig. 37.

Upward

Concentric work for the arm extensors

Downward

Eccentric work for the arm extensors

Stationary

Static work for the arm extensors

Fig. 39.

1

2

3

4

Figure 38 shows a training exercise that provides concentric work for the lumbar muscles (the movement takes place mainly at the small of the back), and static work for the neck and chest muscles. During descent, the lumbar muscles work eccentrically in an effort to halt the movement. (For the back muscles, see p.68.)

Fig. 38.

Figure 39 shows what happens when a person sits up from a lying position.
1–2. Concentric work primarily for the straight abdominal muscle (p.71).
2–3. Static work for the abdominal muscles, concentric for the hip flexors (p.43).
3–4. Almost no work for the abdominal muscles. Concentric work for the hip flexors.
4. Static work for the back extensors.

It is easier to analyse the exercises that are used in human motion, competitive sports, strength training, flexibility training, etc., when we know the origin and insertion of muscles. Physiological studies have shown that if a muscle is trained concentrically, its ability to work statically and eccentrically is not appreciably increased. We can assume that the reason for this lies in the fact that the muscle's ability to work is dependent partly on its mass, and partly on its supply of nerve impulses. Both these functions must operate for the muscle to be effective. A good athlete or trainer ought to be capable of analysing his particular branch of athletics and designing exercises to meet the demands of the movements involved.

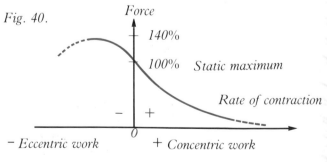

Fig. 40.

Force

140%

100% *Static maximum*

Rate of contraction

− +

0

− *Eccentric work*   + *Concentric work*

+ *Means that the point of origin pulls towards the point of insertion (concentric work).*
0 *Means unchanged distance between origin and insertion (static work).*
− *Means that the point of origin is pulled away from the point of insertion (eccentric work).*

When we investigate a muscle's ability to develop force, we see that the muscle becomes up to 40% stronger when made to work at its eccentric maximum compared with its static maximum. Its concentric ability to develop force decreases as the velocity with which it must work increases.

Thus, to build up high tension in a muscle, we would force the muscle to halt a movement that actually requires the muscle to stretch (also called negative work). The following experiment demonstrates this function.

1. Stand still with your arms hanging vertically at your sides. Bend your knees at a 90° angle. Starting from this position (without swinging your arms or rocking), jump straight up and estimate the height you reach.

2. Stand with your arms hanging at your sides and your knees straight. First make a get-ready movement which will take you to the starting position of exercise 1, and then jump straight up. In this way you will jump higher. This is because, in the position where you changed direction (which is exactly the same as the starting position of exercise 1), the muscles used in the jump were already "charged" by having been forced to work eccentrically when halting at the 90° angle.

Fig. 41.

Thus, both jumps start from the same position but involve different muscle tension. An effective movement has a certain rhythm, i.e. pattern of movement, which eccentrically charges the different muscle groups taking part in the movement. It is said that a tennis serve, or a volleyball smash, requires "timing". Here, timing means that the entire pattern of movement is such that each group of muscles being used by the player works optimally.

Almost all well-balanced movements begin with a perfect counter-movement (get-ready movement). The muscles that are thus activated are extended beyond their resting position length (120%) and are eccentrically charged (up to 140% of the static maximum force) in accordance with the principle of muscle physiology outlined above.

Knowledge of a muscle's origin, insertion and function, as well as external forces which can affect it (force of gravity, friction), allow us to analyse and understand the exercises used in athletics.

Muscles — Nervous System

The muscle's protective reflexes

There are two types of nerve cell that protect a muscle against unnecessary injuries: muscle spindles and tendon spindles. The muscle spindles are connected in parallel to different muscle cells throughout the muscle. The muscle spindles passively follow the movements of their adjacent muscle cells.

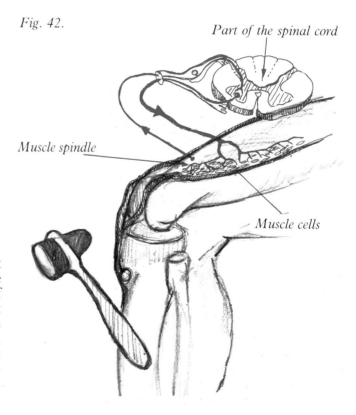

Fig. 42.

Part of the spinal cord

Muscle spindle

Muscle cells

When the muscle cells stretch, so do the muscle spindles. If the muscle stretches so much as to run the risk of being ruptured, the muscle spindle responds by sending a signal to the muscle to contract. This keeps the muscle from being injured. This protective mechanism is called the stretch reflex.

When a doctor taps the ligament directly below the kneecap (ligamentum patellae) with his rubber mallet, the muscle cells in the knee extensor muscles stretch (see p.49). The muscle's reaction to this unexpected stretching is to protect itself by contracting — i.e. the knee jerks a little. The period of delay between the tap with the mallet and the kick is an indication of the time it takes the nerve impulse to travel from the muscle spindle to the spinal cord of the central nervous system (CNS) and back again to the muscle cells.

of the neck). The head is held upright — despite its natural tendency to tilt forward — by the tension maintained by the muscles of the neck (see p.24). When a person falls asleep in a sitting position, the muscles of his neck relax, and his head falls forward. The muscle spindles stretch unexpectedly, which causes him to jerk his head up. This protective mechanism has probably saved the lives of many a tired motorist and kept many a bored listener awake.

The protective mechanism of the muscle spindle responds when the muscle spindle is stretched unexpectedly, but it does permit voluntary stretches which are not too sudden. The head may be allowed to fall forward–downward without the reflex being evoked. It has been shown that if a muscle first contracts and then stretches slowly, it can be made to extend a little further. These principles should be carefully adhered to when training flexibility and movement. They are described in more detail on page 24.

Fig. 43.

Cg

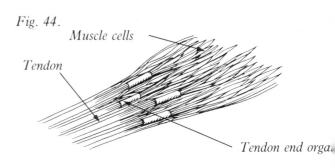

Fig. 44.

Muscle cells

Tendon

Tendon end organ

Tendon organs keep the CNS informed of the muscles' tension. If the tension is too high (and there is a risk of rupture) an impulse is sent from the tendon organs to the CNS and back to the muscle. The impulse inhibits the muscle from contraction which would lead to increased tension. This impulse is called the inhibitory impulse. Thus, the muscle relaxes and the tension decreases.

If a long-jumper stakes too much on his approach, the tension in his calf muscle can be too high. This may be caused partly by external forces, and partly by the contraction of the calf muscle. The muscle is inhibited and the jumper runs straight ahead — despite the fact that he is consciously charged for the jump.

Muscle spindles and tendon organs are a part of the body's most significant defence mechanisms. If they cease to function satisfactorily, the risk of injury increases considerably. This is particularly the case when an athlete is not warmed-up or is fatigued, as

The centre of gravity of an adult's head lies above and in front of the joint which is anterior to the upper cervical vertebra (i.e. the uppermost vertebra the protective reflex signals travel at a much slower rate then than when he is rested.

Motor unit

In order to judge the value of different strengthening exercises, one should be aware of the ·following.

A muscle is made up of a large number of muscle cells. These are an integral part of so-called motor units. Thus, the motor unit is composed of a nerve cell which has connections to the brain and which branches off into fine filaments terminating in the muscle. Each of these branches terminates in a single muscle cell. The number of cells in a motor unit depends on the degree of precision required from them. The muscles that are responsible for the movement of the eye, for example, contain five to ten cells in each motor unit. By comparison, the large muscle that forms the fleshy part of the buttock (p.39) is estimated to contain several thousand cells in each unit.

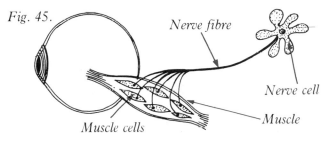

Fig. 45.

Nerve fibre

Nerve cell

Muscle

Muscle cells

When the motor unit is put to work, all the cells that comprise it contract with maximal force. If a muscle is compelled to contract with a certain force, the work is carried out by a certain number of motor units. If the force of contraction is to increase, more motor units have to be engaged. It is always the same motor units that are used for coping with a light load, and it is always the same units that, thereafter, are engaged when the load increases. It is always the same motor units that are ultimately engaged when the work load becomes maximal.

Light work loads train only the muscle cells in the motor units that are first engaged. If we want to train the entire muscle, we must subject it to maximal stress.

There are two different types of muscle cell. They are called slow (type I) and fast (type II) muscle cells. The slow cells are characterised by the fact that they are supplied with energy via oxygen in the blood. The fast cells use mainly the energy stored in the muscle (as glucose) which can be transformed into mechanical energy without oxygen. A by-product of this process is lactic acid. Different people have different percentage distributions of these cell types. The usual proportions are 50% type I fibres and 50% type II fibres. There are, however, great individual differences. Moreover, different muscles have different compositions of fibre types.

In recent years it has been revealed that it would be appropriate to divide the type II cells into two sub-groups: type IIa and type IIb. Special training can change the character of type IIa cells in such a way that they become more like type I cells, i.e. they are supplied with energy via oxygen and are thus capable of greater endurance.

It has been shown that when a muscle is required to exert force the cell types are engaged in the order, type I cells, type IIa cells and, finally, type IIb cells. When little force is required, only the type I cells are trained.

Fig. 46.
Type I cells are characterised by endurance and little force.

Force

Time

Type IIb cells are characterised by the great force they exert for short periods.

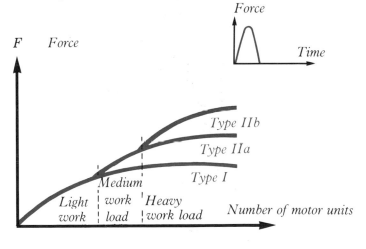

Force

Time

F   Force

Type IIb

Type IIa

Type I

Medium

Light   work   Heavy

work   load   work load

Number of motor units

Type IIa cells have the best qualities of both the other types, i.e. great strength and good endurance. Knowledge of the above is important when we wish to train for a special type of sporting event. However, it should be made clear that the designation "slow" does not mean that the muscle cells contract so slowly that they do not contribute to the movements of sports. Such "fast" movements as a golf swing and tennis smash are actually very slow compared with the speed with which the type I cells contract.

D. Flexibility Training

Different types of stretching

In order to maintain the natural flexibility of the joints and reduce the risk of injury in athletics, the training programme should always contain suitable, and correctly executed flexibility exercises. A muscle that is only trained for strength becomes shorter. This, in turn, means that its range of movement is restricted, which in practice decreases its ability to utilize its increased force resources correctly. Exercises that are designed to train the strength of a group of muscles, should always be followed by stretching exercises for the same muscle group.

Elastic stretching is used here to denote the activity of rhythmically swinging an arm or leg towards its most outer position. This swinging action has nothing to do with stretching the muscles. Elastic stretching has been used, and should be used, when warming and limbering up.

On the other hand, stretching exercises are those designed to lengthen the muscle groups involved quickly, which in turn, increases the range of motion in the joints. Thus, both stretching exercises and elastic stretching exercises are used to promote general agility.

Assume that a person wants to increase the range of movement of his arm so that he can draw it back as far as possible (swimmer, thrower, gymnast).

Fig. 47.

(a) If the arm is swiftly swung back, it could perhaps reach position *a*. What happens is that the muscles situated behind the shoulder give the arm its speed, but the arm is halted before it reaches an outer position. This halting is caused by the spindles in the muscles at the front of the joint and endings in the joint itself which send warning signals to the CNS. The CNS, in turn, sends contraction signals to the same muscles in order to prevent injury of the cells. Instead of stretching, the muscles on the fore side of the joint are forced to contract to protect themselves. This type of elastic stretching may produce eccentric strength but it certainly does not train flexibility. When elastic stretching is performed forcefully by a person who is not warmed-up, the risk of minor ruptures is obvious. However, easy elastic stretching is a good way of toning the muscle.

(b) If, instead, the arm is slowly drawn back as far as it will go, the position it reaches will generally be farther than that of the swinging arm described above. Just how far back depends on the suppleness of the muscles at the front of the joint, and the strength of the muscles which pull from the back of the joint. This method is called active stretching. Work is actively being done by the antagonists (the muscles on the other side of the joint) to the muscles we want to stretch. However, we try as far as possible to relax the actual muscles that are to be stretched.

(c) In passive stretching the arm is pressed backwards further with the help of external forces (i.e. not the muscles at the back of the shoulder). This could be done, for example, with the aid of a friend, or the hand could be held against a wall and pressed, thereby utilising the force of the legs. Passive stretching is always more effective than active stretching in reaching the outermost position.

(d) The best results will be obtained, however, by first extending the arm as far as possible by the passive stretching method. (The muscle group that is to be stretched should be as relaxed as possible.) Next, try to contract the muscle group for a few seconds (6 s) while the external force (friend, legs, wall) prevents any movement occurring at the joint. The muscle tension is thus static, which implies that the muscle belly is somewhat shortened and the collagenous fibres of the tendons are somewhat extended.

Fig. 48.

Examples of flexibility training

The example below is designed to demonstrate further how a muscle group can be stretched effectively, i.e. the flexibility of a particular joint improved. Good flexibility in the hip joint is of great importance to nearly all athletes. The group of muscles that are easily injured and which impede effective movement patterns, are the muscles of the groin (the adductors). These originate from the pubic bone and are inserted into the thigh bone (see p.41). When sitting on the floor with the soles of the

Fig. 50.

By relaxing again (2–4 s), after which passive stretching is again exercised, the arm could reach even farther. The method of contracting a muscle with the aim of increasing its ability to stretch, is called the PNF-method (Proprioceptive Neuromuscular Facilitating). The PNF-method is used by physiotherapists when they train an injured muscle in an effort to restore its natural length. It is also called the contraction–relaxation–stretching method.

Contraction affects the tendon organs of the muscle so that they send out inhibitory signals to the muscles during the ensuing relaxation. The limb should be close to the outermost position the whole time, and any movements should be slow and easy so that the muscle spindles are prevented from sending contraction signals to the muscle.

Fig. 49.

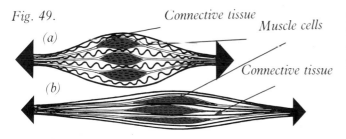

Figure 49 (a) shows what happens when one tries to stretch a contracted muscle. The external force acting on it affects only the muscle cells, and consequently only minor muscle ruptures can result.

Figure 49 (b) shows that when the muscle is relaxed, it is the fibres of the connective tissue that are stretched. Connective tissue is rigid and can resist swift stresses (jerks, elastic stretching) but yields to prolonged stress (remain in the outermost position for about 30 s).

feet together and as close as possible to the body, it will be seen that the length of the groin muscles will determine just how far the knees can be pressed to the floor.

Fig. 51.

When, in the same position, the knees are bounced up and down, the activity corresponds to that described in (a) on p.24. Further, if the knees are pulled down using the muscles of the outer side of the hip (abductors, p.39), the activity corresponds to the method described in (b) on p.24, i.e. active stretching of the groin muscles. Pressing the knees down with the hands corresponds to the method described in (c) on p.24, i.e. passive stretching of the groin muscles. The most effective method, i.e. the PNF-method (method (d) on p.24), is practised in the following way.

Press down with your hands holding back with your knees (approx. 6 s), relax (2 s), press down with your hands again (10 s), hold back once again (6 s), relax (2 s) and finally press with your hands for about 10 s with relaxed groin muscles.

The straight knee extensor muscle (rectus femoris, p.24) can be stretched using the PNF-method in the following way. Take your foot in your hand. Bend your knee maximally and try to keep your hip as straight as possible. Next, try to extend the knee joint holding back with your hand for about 6 s (the thigh muscle thus contracts statically).

Fig. 52.

6 s

Next, relax for 2 s. Then slowly press your hip forward a little and stand still for about 10 s. Repeat this several times.

It has been shown that the number of muscle injuries in, for example, football has been radically reduced when flexibility exercises were introduced as a regular part of the training programme. A properly executed stretching exercise following the PNF-method, takes about 20 s. A ball player should

perhaps work through five different muscle groups about three times on each training occasion in order to obtain good results: 20 x 5 x 3 = 300 s. Thus, no more than 5 min are required each time he trains. Many trainers claim that they have no time for flexibility training; but better knowledge of how to perform this type of training, as well as its benefits, should dispel such arguments. However, a prerequisite for this is that the trainer acquires in-depth knowledge of the origin, insertion and function of muscles. Suitable positions for stretching exercises are shown with the aid of diagrams after each part of the body has first been described anatomically and also in Chapter 7.

E. Strength Training

It is customary to distinguish between different types of strength.

Fig. 53.

Static maximum strength
Static endurance

Dynamic maximum strength
Dynamic endurance

Concentric

Eccentric

In addition, dynamic strength is divided into concentric and eccentric strength (p.19).

The majority of cells in the body are capable of reproducing themselves. This, however, does not apply to the striated muscle cells to any great extent. Their number is largely determined by genes. When training strength, the muscle cells are thus not increased. Instead, there is an increase in the number of myosin and actin filaments, which are responsible for muscle contraction. A certain division of cells takes place. Like the majority of cell types, the muscle cells follow the principle of overcompensation. According to this principle, training breaks down parts of the stressed structures. The body compensates for this by producing new fibrils, the number of which is somewhat greater than the number of broken down fibrils. The athlete should begin his next training session at the time when overcompensation has reached a maximum.

Fig. 54.

Muscle mass

Time

Training   Rest   Training   Rest

When the training sessions are too close together, or the training too vigorous without extra long pauses, the regeneration of fibrils never reaches the previous level. The athlete thus slowly wears down his body; he "becomes overtrained".

As a general rule we can say that recovery normally takes about 24–48 h. (After extremely vigorous training, about 72 h.) Thus, an athlete should train relatively vigorously three times a week in order to increase his strength quickly.

Strength decline is first noticeable after 5–6 days without training. About one session a week should therefore suffice for an athlete to maintain the strength he already has.

As mentioned earlier, youths should not train with loads exceeding their own bodyweight before or during puberty. Because children younger than 11 or 12 years find complicated movements difficult, they should avoid exercises demanding coordination. Training with light weights aims at accustoming young people to the equipment as well as training the correct technique.

On the basis of what has been said about motor units (p.23), strength should be trained by using heavy work loads (all the motor units must be activated). A common target for an athlete is 80–95% of what he can maximally manage. In this way he improves his ability to work at a dynamic maximum. If he wishes to improve his dynamic endurance, he should work with loads that correspond to 20–25% of his maximal capacity. Endurance training has the effect of decreasing both the maximal strength and speed of the muscle group in question. Training for speed is undertaken with a work load of 50–80% of the maximum that can be managed by the athlete.

There are two main types of muscle cell: white and red (see p.23). They have received their names from the colour they assume when they are specially treated to be examined under the microscope. The fast muscle cells (type II) described on p.23, are the white cells, and the slow muscle cells (type I) are the red. White muscle cells contain many actin and myosin filaments (see p.15). Red muscle cells contain relatively few but, on the other hand, have more energy-supplying components.

These conditions result in strong, fast white cells that tire quickly; and red cells that are characterised first and foremost by their endurance. Both red and white fibres are contained in the same muscle. A muscle's composition is determined by genes, but it can, in part, "be changed" by specific training.

Different sporting events require different types of strength, so athletes and trainers should choose exercises with care. Weight-lifting is dependent on strong, fast muscles. Weight-lifters training should, therefore, involve few exercises that are designed for dynamic endurance. It has been shown that pure endurance training considerably reduces both the strength and speed of the trained muscles.

The concepts "set" and "repetitions" (reps) are often used in descriptions of strength training. A set contains a particular exercise that is repeated a certain number of times. A set can, for example, consist of six consecutive repetitions. (Various scientific investigations indicate that the quickest increase in strength is acquired with 6 reps.) Several reps with a light work load promotes endurance. Fewer reps with a heavier work load develops maximal strength.

If we take, as an example, an exercise that strengthens the pectoralis major (the largest chest muscle), then a weight should be chosen that can be lifted and lowered six times with slightly bent arms (to avoid straining the elbow joint). This should be

followed by a period of rest (2–3 min). During the pause, a completely different muscle group (e.g. the knee extensors) can be trained in the same way. The exercise for the chest muscle is then repeated, i.e. a second set with its 6 reps. An instruction which reads "5 sets x 6 reps" means a total of 30 lifts with five 2–3 min pauses after each set.

The work load can be varied as the amount of arm flexion varies. (See the mechanics section on levers, p.34.) A muscle is stronger when it works eccentrically than when it works concentrically. This is easily verified by slowly lifting a weight; it feels easier to lower than to lift. If the aim is to train eccentric strength, the athlete should keep his arms almost straight while lowering weights, and bend them while lifting.

A curve which presents an approximation of the number of times a movement can be performed has been developed experimentally. This number depends on the ratio of work load to the maximal load the muscle group in question can manage.

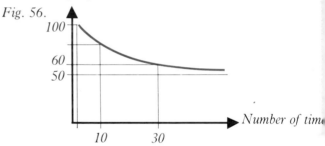

Fig. 56.

Another curve (Rhomerts curve) shows how many minutes an isometric contraction can take if it falls short of the isometric maximum of a muscle group.

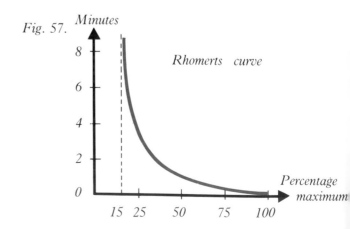

Fig. 57.

Fig. 55.

28

A method for quickly building up the strength of muscles is the so-called pyramid system. For each set the work load (weights) is increased and the number of reps is decreased so that the effort exerted in the final set is maximal.

Set 1: 6 reps with 70% of the maximum weight that can be lifted 6 times.

Set 2: 5 reps with 75% of the maximum weight that can be lifted 5 times.

Set 3: 4 reps with 80% of the maximum weight that can be lifted 4 times.

Set 4: 3 reps with 85% of the maximum weight that can be lifted 3 times.

Set 5: 2 reps with 90% of the maximum weight that can be lifted twice.

Set 6: 1 rep with 95–100% of the maximum weight that can be lifted once.

It should be pointed out that the strength of muscles increases faster than the strength of tendons, ligaments and cartilage. Extremely vigorous training can, therefore, injure muscle attachments and joints.

The table below give approximate work loads together with the number of times exercises should be carried out in order to develop different types of strength. Exercises for developing strength are described in each section of the book where the anatomy of different parts of the body is dealt with (e.g. the knee joint, p.50).

	Endurance	Speed	Maximal strength
% of max.	25–50	50–80	80–100
No. of reps	more than 40	approx. 10	1–6
No. of sets	5	4	3

BASIC RULES OF MECHANICS

In order to understand how the skeleton is constructed and how the muscles affect a particular part of the body, we must familiarise ourselves with certain properties of force as well as what is meant by the concept "moment of force".

A force (F) is represented by an arrow which indicates its size and direction.

Fig. 58.

If an object weighs 5 kg, it is said that the gravitational force acting on it is 50 Newtons (50 N).

Fig. 59.

5 kg

50 N

Fig. 60.

d

F

If a force is applied to a body at a certain distance (d) from a given point, it may happen that the force causes a certain angular motion at that point. This tendency toward angular motion is called the moment of force and is represented by M. The moment of force is calculated by multiplying the magnitude of the force by the length of the distance (d) between the force and the point.

Thus, $M = F \times d$.

The magnitude of the moment of force tells us just how much the object is striving to turn. Thus, the moment of force is a number which depends on two factors at the same time; in particular, the same force can have different turning effects depending on its point of application.

In the examples below, the force is the same but the moment of force varies such that it is least in example 1, and most in example 3. Suppose that the force is 50 N and the lengths are: $d_1 = 0.20$ m, $d_2 = 0.30$ m and $d_3 = 0.50$ m. The moment of force is then, according to the formula $M = F \times d$.

Fig. 61.

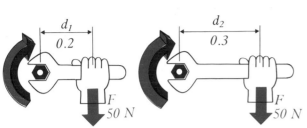

$M_1 = 50$ N x 0.20 m
$= 10$ N m

$M_2 = 50$ N x 0.30 m
$= 15$ N m

$M_3 = 50$ N x 0.50 m
$= 25$ N m

The numbers 10, 15 and 25 show how much the wrench handle tends to turn. The moment of force of 25 Nm can be obtained in many different ways. An alternative to example 3 would be to apply a force of 100 N at a distance of 0.25 m from the bolt. $M_4 = 100$ x $0.25 = 25$ Nm.

Fig. 62.

Example 5. If a mass of 5 kg is placed 2 m from the centre of a seesaw, the moment of force with respect to that point would equal 100 Nm, i.e. $M = 50$ x 2 $= 100$ Nm.

Fig. 63.

Example 6. The moment of force of 100 Nm can also be achieved by placing a 10 kg load 1 m from the centre.
$M = 100$ x $1 = 100$ Nm.

Fig. 64. Example 6.

Example 7. If weights are placed on each side of the seesaw's centre as in example 7, then the seesaw is in equilibrium. It is said that the moments cancel out (seesaw principle). 100 x 1 = 50 x 2.

Similar reasoning can be applied to the way in which muscles affect different parts of the body.

Fig. 65. Example 7.

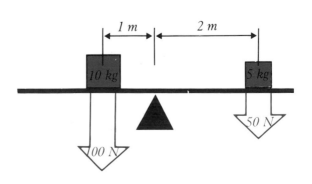

Example 8.
F_m = Muscle force.
d_m = The muscle's lever arm to the centre of the joint.
F = The force of gravity acting on the ball.
d = Distance to the centre of the joint.

Fig. 66. Example 8.

[cf. Fig. 26(a) and (b)]

The elbow joint can be compared with a seesaw where the external force (F) acts on one side and the internal force (F_m) acts on the other. The arm is held still if $F_m \times d_m = F \times d$.

Example 9. The body is in equilibrium when $F_m \times d_m = F \times d$. If $F_m \times d_m$ is greater than $F \times d$, the body accelerates upwards (rises even further on its toes). If $F_m \times d_m$ is less than $F \times d$, the body will not be able to hold its position and will sink. The numbers refer to a person of mass 80 kg.

Fig. 67. Example 9.

80 kg

800 N

F_m

If $F_m \times d_m = 800 \times d$, he will stand still

d_m d

800 N

800 N

Example 10. The weight of the trunk (30 kg) is counterbalanced by the traction force of the back muscles. If the trunk's weight lies three times as far in front of the vertebrae as the back muscles lie behind them, then the traction force of the back muscles must be three times greater than the trunk's weight.

Fig. 68. Example 10.

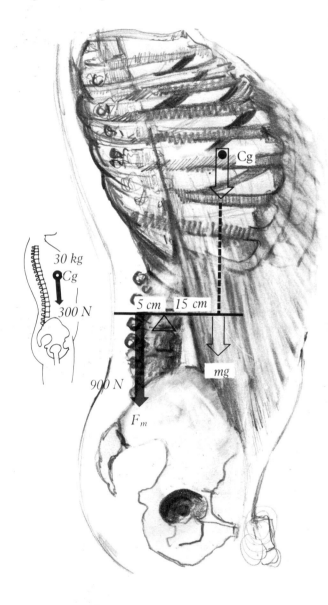

Cg

30 kg
Cg

300 N

5 cm 15 cm

mg

900 N

F_m

In general, the part of the body in question will accelerate in the direction where the moment of force is greater.

Fig. 69. Example 11.

F_m

d_m

d

mg

Fig. 70. Example 12.

F_m

d_m

d

mg

Fig. 71.
Example 13.

F_m

d_m

d

mg

In the three examples above, the force of gravity and the force of the muscle are both located on the same side of the joint, but pull in different directions. F_m x d_m = mg x d can be applied to all three.

33

Fig. 72. Example 14.

The forearm (1 kg) is acted on by a gravitational force of 10 N. If the centre of gravity lies 20 cm from the joint, then the moment of force will be equal to 10 x 20 Ncm. If the "muscle" that bends the elbow is attached at a point 5 cm from the joint, then F_m x 5 must equal 10 x 20 if the arm is to be held still.

The diagrams illustrate different types of joints and the way in which the body has solved the problem of resisting (or creating) movements.

If the point of insertion of the arm's most important flexor differs in two people (A and B), then these two people will differ greatly in the strength and speed of their arms.

Example 15. Suppose the muscle of A is attached at a point which gives a lever arm of 4 cm when the elbow is bent at a 90° angle.

Fig. 73. Example 15.

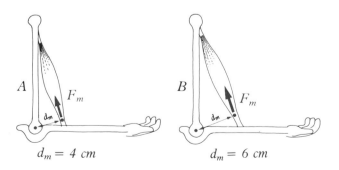

The muscle of B is attached at a point further from the joint, which means that the perpendicular distance to the muscle force is, say, 6 cm when the elbow is bent at a 90° angle.

If the muscle force (F_m) is equal for both people, the moment of force (strength) will be 50% greater for B than for A. Thus, B is stronger than A.

If the muscle is shortened by 3 cm in both cases, the forearm of A will move through a greater angle than the forearm of B. Thus, A is faster than B (Figure 74).

Fig. 74.

The ability of a muscle to develop force (F_m) can be influenced by strength training, but a muscle's attachments cannot be changed. In other words, we are constructed in such a way that we are particularly suited to certain activities and less suited to others — at least so far as top performance is concerned.

Tendon and ligament forces are passive (1; Figure 75). This means that they are brought about by external forces (2; Figure 76) or the muscles (3; Figure 77).

If we consider a small part of a taut tendon, we can understand that it strives to stretch. Thus, we can draw an arrow indicating force either in the direction of muscle pull or in the direction of tendon (muscle attachment) resistance (1).

Suppose a person is standing with knees slightly bent and that one of his knee extensors is contracted with a force of 1000 N. The force acting on its origin is then 1000 N (a) and is directed toward the knee. A force of 1000 N (c) is acting on the kneecap and is directed toward the thigh. A bundle of connective tissue somewhere in the muscle stretches with a force of 1000 N (b). The tension in the tendon extending between the kneecap and the shin bone is also about 1000 N. The force acting on the apex of the kneecap, the tendon's attachment and a point on the tendon is, according to Figure 79, 1000 N.

1 *Fig. 75.*

2 *Fig. 76.*

mg

3 Fig. 77.

Fig. 78.

(a)
1000 N
(b)
1000 N
(b)
1000 N
(c)
1000 N

Fig. 79

1000 N

1000 N

1000 N

The above explanations of how to draw force arrows, and how to calculate muscle forces with the aid of the seesaw principle, are applied to the descriptions of the body's structure in the following chapters.

Chapter 3
ANATOMY AND FUNCTION OF THE LEG

In order to analyse different types of movement correctly, we must first study the anatomy of the area concerned. Here, we will examine the origin, insertion and function of the larger muscles. In addition, we will look at the joints' potential for movement and their limitations.

A. The Hip

The majority of muscles responsible for moving the hip joint originate from the pelvis; some originate from the spinal column. Some of them also pass over the knee joint. Thus, we must acquaint ourselves with the parts of the skeleton shown in Fig. 80.

Fig. 80.

The pelvis is the collective name given to a ring formed by the two hip bones and the sacrum. The sacrum consists of five vertebrae which are fused together in the adult to form a wedge-shaped bone. Four terminal vertebrae are fused in the same way to form the coccyx.

36

Fig. 81.

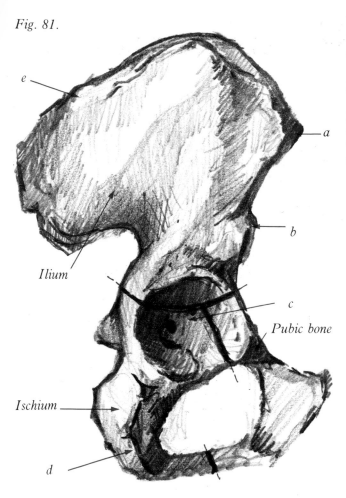

Right hip bone, external view.

The hip bone has developed from three separate centres of ossification, which is why the following distinction is made.

1. Ilium.
2. Ischium.
3. Pubis.

All the cavities, outgrowths and spines have different names. Those that are directly connected with important muscles are given here.

(a) Anterior superior iliac spine.
(b) Anterior inferior iliac spine.
(c) Acetabulum.
(d) Ischial tuberosity.
(e) Iliac crest.

The hip joint is a so-called ball and socket joint which means that it can move in all directions (p.13). There are certain extra-capsular structures that give strength to the joint and, in particular, prevent the leg from swinging outwards and backwards. Backward swinging is impeded by the powerful ligament which is attached to the iliac part of the hip bone and which passes downward to the thigh bone (a) iliofemoral ligament. Outward swinging is restricted by (b) pubofemoral ligament.

Fig. 82.

The diagrams below demonstrate actions that demand great flexibility of the hip.

It has not been shown that any injury is sustained when a person stretches in the directions mentioned above. If, on the other hand, a person compensates for a poor ability to swing his leg backwards by overstretching the lumbar region of his back, he would in probability be literally "making a rod for his own back". Overstretching the lumbar area often leads to pain of a more or less serious character.

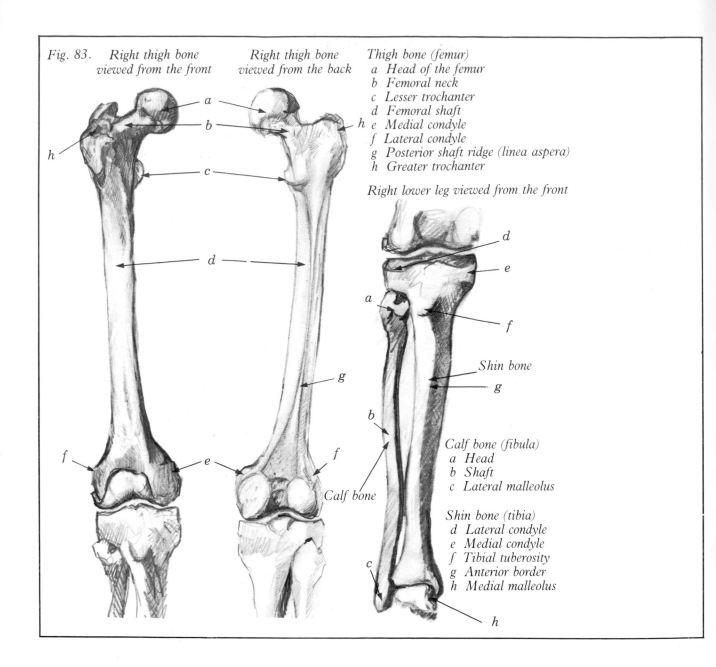

Fig. 83.   Right thigh bone
           viewed from the front

Right thigh bone
viewed from the back

Thigh bone (femur)
a Head of the femur
b Femoral neck
c Lesser trochanter
d Femoral shaft
e Medial condyle
f Lateral condyle
g Posterior shaft ridge (linea aspera)
h Greater trochanter

Right lower leg viewed from the front

Shin bone

Calf bone

Calf bone (fibula)
a Head
b Shaft
c Lateral malleolus

Shin bone (tibia)
d Lateral condyle
e Medial condyle
f Tibial tuberosity
g Anterior border
h Medial malleolus

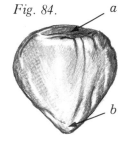

Fig. 84.

The kneecap (patella) has (a) a base that is directed upwards and (b) an apex that points downwards. The inside of the kneecap is covered with a 6-7 mm thick layer of cartilage whose surface articulates with the cartilage-covered condyles of the thigh bone.

B. Hip Muscles

The following are the most important muscles that pass over the hip joint.

1. Buttock muscles.
2. Groin muscles.
3. Hip flexors.

1. Buttock muscles

(a) Large buttock muscle (gluteus maximus).
(b) Intermediate buttock muscle (gluteus medius).
(c) Small buttock muscle (gluteus minimus).

Fig. 85.

Fig. 86.
(a) Large buttock muscle (gluteus maximus).

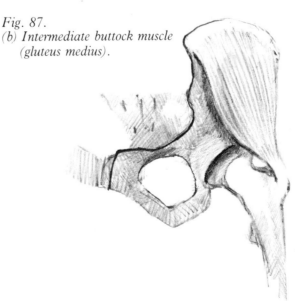

Fig. 87.
(b) Intermediate buttock muscle
(gluteus medius).

Two of the three muscles are attached to the greater trochanter. The intermediate and small buttock muscles have such a large area of origin that they can move the thigh bone in all directions except inward towards the midline of the body (adduction). These muscles are activated by walking and running. They have the important task of stabilising the hip joint when the corresponding foot only is in contact with the ground. This stabilisation is necessary in order to prevent the upper body from falling to the opposite side.

The buttock muscles are subjected to great stress when a person runs uphill (the large buttock muscle is responsible for the powerful backward drive of the leg) or downhill (medius and minimus stabilise the hip). The medius and minimus then work

Fig. 88.
(c) Small buttock muscle (gluteus minimus).

The large buttock muscle can work with greater force if the body is bent forward at the hip. This is because the distance between its origin and insertion becomes greater (see p.18).

Fig. 90.

Large buttock muscle

Iliotibial tract

eccentrically, i.e. they restrain the upper body so that it does not fold inwards at every step (Figure 85).

Examples of exercises for the buttock muscles: running; jumping on one leg; and, while standing on one leg, lowering and raising the opposite side of the pelvis. Further exercises for the medius and minimus are: (a) lying on one side and lifting the upper leg and (b) lifting the upper part of the body as far as possible while the legs are fixed (Figure 89).

Fig. 89.

(a)   (b)

The large buttock muscle (gluteus maximus) is used to swing the leg backwards powerfully, and it can help to keep the knee straight. This is possible because a part of the muscle is attached to the surface of the thigh bone (gluteal tuberosity; straightens the hip) and a part is inserted into a very strong, thick tendon band on the outer side of the thigh (iliotibial tract). This tendon band passes, in turn, in front of the axis of motion of the knee and is inserted into the lateral condyle of the shin bone. The tendon band is felt as a flat 3–4 cm wide tendon on the outside of the thigh directly above the knee joint.

The more force a person needs, the further forward he must lean. The best movements for training the large buttock muscle are those that simultaneously engage the knee and hip extensors.

Fig. 91.

The muscles which take part in swinging the leg backwards (hip extension) are — besides the large buttock muscle — those muscles originating from the ischial tuberosity. These muscles are all inserted into the lower leg which means that they flex the knee joint (see p.53).

2. The groin muscles (adductor muscles) swing the leg towards the midline of the body. They have received their names according to their area of origin, size and appearance.

Fig. 92.

Pubic bone

*"Comb" muscle
(Pectineus)*

Fig. 93.

*Slender thigh muscle
(Gracilis)*

Fig. 94.

*Long adductor
(adductor longus)*

All these muscles originate from the pubic bone (os pubis) and are inserted into the posterior surface of the thigh bone via the roughened ridge extending the length of its shaft (linea aspera). These muscles work powerfully when, in running, the foot leaves the ground and begins to swing forward. During the forward swing, the leg rotates outwards in relation to the hip. This can be accomplished because the adductor muscles are inserted into the posterior surface of the thigh bone. Such overexertion as occurs in the forceful movements of broad side-kicks in football, bringing the free leg forward in skating, tough sprinter training, etc., leads to discomfort in the muscle's area of origin (groin injuries). Groin injuries can be avoided by developing muscular strength and, more importantly, flexibility (p.25). Some strength-developing exercises are shown in Figure 97.

Fig. 95.

Large adductor (adductor magnus)

Fig. 96.

Short adductor (adductor brevis)

Fig. 97 (a).

Fig. 97 (b).

Fig. 97 (c).

Eccentric

Concentric

Concentric training when the legs are brought together. Eccentric training when one leg is slowly drawn away from the other.

For static training, compress a ball with both knees.

a Trains the adductors, b trains the abductors.

Outward rotation is affected by a number of small muscles which originate from the inner parts of the pelvis [Figure 98(a)]. They pass behind the thigh bone and are inserted into its outer surface at the greater trochanter. They are used a great deal in such an activity as ice-skating.

Fig. 98

(a)

(b)

(c)

Example of dynamic training of the outward rotators.

Example of static training of the outward rotators.
Lie on your stomach and try to "squash" the ball with your feet.

3. Hip flexors

The haunch muscle (iliacus) and great lumbar muscle (psoas major) are responsible for powerful flexion at the hip joint. They have different points of origin, but a common insertion point. They are often described under the collective name of the iliopsoas.

Fig. 99.

Large lumbar muscle (psoas major)

Haunch muscle (iliacus)

(b)

(a)

(c)

(a) Origin of iliacus (iliac crest).
(b) Origin of psoas major (lumbar part of the vertebral column).
(c) Insertion of both (lesser trochanter).

The following can occur when the iliopsoas contracts.
(a) If the legs are fixed, the trunk will move towards them as, for example, in the last phase of a sit-up [Figure 104 (a) and (b)].

Fig. 100.

(a)

(b) If the trunk is fixed, the legs will move towards it as, for example, when hanging from a bar and trying to bring the knees up towards the chest [Figure 104 (c), (d), (e) and (f)].

Fig. 101.

(b)

The iliopsoas is incomparably the most powerful hip flexor. It is forcefully engaged in the following examples.

Fig. 102.

Hurdling   High jump   Running

Javelin throw   Sit-ups

It is not necessary to train the iliopsoas for everyday use since it is sufficiently trained in such activities as walking, running, climbing stairs, etc. Athletes must realise that the stress they subject this muscle group to when they train it for strength affects both the insertion and origin (e.g. lumbar vertebrae) to

the same extent. Thus, the spine tends to sway forwards which subjects the discs between the vertebrae (p.64) to great stress. This action is counteracted by the abdominal muscles which hold the spine in place. The abdominal muscles are capable of correcting a sway of the lumbar spine by their contraction. Thus, the iliopsoas should not be subjected to greater stress than the abdominal muscles are capable of "parrying". Training ought to be aimed primarily at building up the abdominal muscles (p.71).

Fig. 103.

Straight abdominal muscle

After building up the abdominal muscles, the hip flexors can be specially trained. Here are some examples of exercises which specifically train the hip flexors of athletes whose abdominal muscles are well-trained: (prophylactic training of the abdomen is dealt with on on p.74).

Fig. 104.

(a) Sit-ups with bent knees. Weights (2 kg, 5 kg, . . .) may be held against the chest to increase the work load. The first three-quarters of the sit-up is pure abdominal muscle training (p.74). The rest of the movement concentrates on the hip joint and thus trains the iliopsoas for strength.

(b) If the legs are kept straight, then the exertion will be even greater due to the resistance offered by the muscles at the back of the thigh.

(c) Lie on a slanting plane or hang from a bar and lift your knees towards your hands, or

(d) (for greater stress) lift your legs as high as possible, keeping them straight. For eccentric training, resist the movement on the way down.

(e) Stand by a wall and have a friend provide external resistance to your thigh as you try to lift your knee.

(f) Tie a band of rubber around your foot and pull your knee up in quick movements.

(g) The hip muscles can be trained statically in the following way. Lie on your back with a 90° angle at your hips and have a friend take a hold of the lower part of your shin. By making large movements in different directions, he should try to make you change the angle between your legs and upper body.

In order to stretch the iliopsoas, the distance between its origin and insertion must be lengthened as much as possible while the muscles are relaxed. One way to stretch them is to kneel in the manner shown in Figure 105, i.e. the stress is placed on the leg in front and the legs are separated as much as possible. If the iliopsoas is short and strong, but the muscles at the back of the thigh are weak, then the body tends to tip forward at the pelvis. This leads to mild back-aches and a posture resembling that of a person with a "beer belly".

Fig. 105.

Another stretching exercise that has an effect on the iliopsoas is the following. Stand on one leg. With your hand pull your free leg back behind an imagined line passing vertically through the centre of your body. Let the backward movement take place at the hip and not in the lower back. Keep a wide angle in the knee joint, otherwise the movement will be resisted by another muscle, namely the straight thigh muscle (rectus femoris, p.49).

Fig. 106.

A third stretching exercise is shown in Figure 106. A friend lifts your leg upwards and backwards at the same time as he holds your pelvis still (thereby blocking any movement of the lumbar spine). This exercise should only be carried out by people who have received their instructions from a medically qualified trainer.

Fig. 107.

The tailor's muscle (Sartorius) is the longest muscle in the body (Figure 107). It extends from the anterior superior iliac spine (spina iliaca anterior superior) and passes down the thigh in a slightly S-shaped curve to the inner side of the knee where it is attached to the internal condyle of the tibia (Condylus medialis tibiae).

This muscle has so many different functions that it is difficult to place it in any particular muscle group. The tailor's muscle received its name from the fact that its functions allow a person to sit on a table with crossed legs as tailors once did. Thus, this muscle bends, abducts and rotates the hip outwards, and bends the knee and rotates it inwards.

C. The Knee Joint

The knee joint is a very complicated joint which needs detailed study. The movements produced at the knee joint are bending (flexing) and straightening (extending), and inward and outward rotation of the lower leg. The last-mentioned movements can only occur when the knee is bent. The more the knee is bent, the easier it is to rotate the lower leg and the foot. We can think of the knee as flexing either by:

Fig. 108.

(a) the thigh bone (femur) rolling back on to the shin bone (tibia) or by (b) the thigh bone gliding on the same spot on the shin bone.

In reality, both types of movement occur. Movement (a) takes place until the anterior of the two crossed ligaments (anterior cruciate ligament) is completely stretched, after which movement (b) is brought into action.

Thus, the anterior cruciate ligament prevents movements when the lower leg is moved forward in relation to the thigh. A common injury in football is rupture of the anterior cruciate ligament when a player receives a powerful kick on the back of his lower leg. The posterior cruciate ligament is injured when the lower leg is pressed backwards or when the knee is severely overstretched.

Fig. 109.

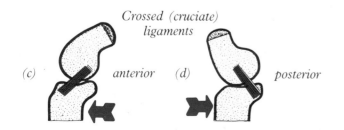

Crossed (cruciate) ligaments

(c)   *anterior*   *(d)*   *posterior*

The function of the two side (or collateral) ligaments is to prevent sidewards bending of the knee. They are taut when the knee is stretched (e), and slack when the knee is bent (f). This means, for example, that the lower leg can be rotated outwards until the ligaments are again taut. The lower leg usually cannot rotate as much inwards as it can outwards because the cruciate ligaments in the joint "twist" around each other during inward rotation and thereby block the movement (see Figure 20).

Fig. 110.

Lateral ligaments

(e)   *(f)*

The lower end of the thigh bone is ellipsoid and the upper extremity of the shin bone is flat. Therefore, there would be very little contact between their surfaces if the cartilage were not so thick and the so-called menisci were not shaped to receive the end of the thigh bone. The underside of the menisci is plain like the surface of the shin bone. Consequently, the stress to which the knee is subjected can be distributed over a relatively large area.

Fig. 111.   *Right shin bone viewed from above.*

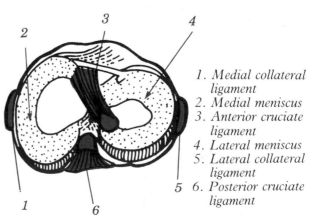

1. Medial collateral ligament
2. Medial meniscus
3. Anterior cruciate ligament
4. Lateral meniscus
5. Lateral collateral ligament
6. Posterior cruciate ligament

In flexion and extension of the knee joint, the menisci glide to suit the form of the condyles of the thigh bone. Because the medial meniscus fuses with the medial collateral ligament, it is very easily injured by being subjected to excessive stress while in "strange" positions.

Injury to the menisci due to rotational strain on a bent weight-bearing knee is very common. If there is a sudden pitching in the knee joint during outward rotation of the lower leg, the medial ligament stretches and can thereby tear the meniscus, which is locked between the thigh and shin bones. Because of this fact, movements of the following type should be avoided: (a) crow hopping or walking like a duck and (b) lying in the hurdle position to train flexibility.

Fig. 112.

(a)

(b)

D. Muscles of the Knee Joint

Knee extensors

The straight thigh muscle (rectus femoris) originates from the pelvis and bends (flexes) the hip joint. It is inserted into the kneecap and can — via the powerful tendon which extends from the kneecap to the shin bone — straighten the knee.

Fig. 114.

(a) *The muscle maximally stretched*

(b) *the muscle maximally shortened*

(a) is by far the best position for stretching the straight thigh muscle in accordance with the PNF-method.

Fig. 113.

Spine (anterior inferior) of the ilium

Straight thigh muscle

Kneecap

Ligament of the kneecap

Tuberosity of the shin bone

You can test how the straight thigh muscle works in the following way: stand on one leg with your body in the vertical plane and lift your free leg to the horizontal plane [Figure 114 (b)]. Can you manage to lift your leg? Are the muscles at the back of your thigh (p.53) flexible enough to allow you to straighten your leg? How long are you capable of holding that position? Very soon you will feel a smarting pain in the straight thigh muscle. The pain is a sign of the insufficient oxygen supply which quickly results from static activity.

Three other large muscles are inserted into the knee joint. They are also extensors of the knee. They are termed the vasti muscles (vastus = extensive, far-reaching). The four diagrams of Figure 115 show the extensors in the right leg viewed from the front.

Fig. 115.

(a) *(b)* *(c)* *(d)*

Origin:

(a) The straight thigh muscle (rectus femoris).
   Origin: Anterior inferior iliac spine.
(b) The external vast thigh muscle (vastus lateralis).
   Origin: Thigh bone ridge (linea aspera).
(c) The central vast thigh muscle (vastus intermedius).
   Origin: Anterior thigh bone shaft.
(d) The internal vast thigh muscle (vastus medialis).
   Origin: Thigh bone ridge (linea aspera).

Insertion:
Some of the fibres of the internal thigh muscle are inserted into the kneecap. The remaining muscles attach via a tendon into the kneecap. This is, in turn, attached to the tubercle of the shin bone (tibial tuberosity) via the kneecap ligament (patellar ligament) (Figure 113).

Function:
Straightens the knee when working concentrically. Impedes flexing of the knee joint when working eccentrically.

The collective name for the three vasti muscles and the straight thigh muscle is the four-headed thigh muscle (quadriceps femoris). Their action is to straighten the knee and to stabilise and guide the kneecap so that it correctly glides in the depression

formed by the condyles of the thigh bone (p.52).

The exercises shown in Figure 116 use the quadriceps femoris.

Fig. 116.

(a) *(b)*

(a) Sit with your back against a wall with a 90° angle between your hip and knee joints. The muscle works statically.

(b) Stand with your weight on your left foot and place your right knee directly behind the tendon of your left heel. You will notice a distinct difference if you stand completely still in this position (static stress), or if you bounce lightly up and down (short periods of relaxation allow the blood to be supplied to the muscle).

(c)

(d)

(c) Start walking with long strides followed by elastic stretches accompanying each stride. Your bodyweight should be placed far out over your left foot. The halting movement trains the muscle eccentrically.

(d) Step up and down from a bench or part of a vaulting horse and — if your back is sufficiently strong — you could even carry a load on your shoulders. This exercise provides dynamic (mostly concentric) training.

Fig. 116.

(e)

Fig. 117.

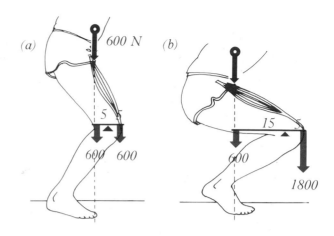

(a) 600 N (b)

(e) Jump up (concentric work) and down (eccentric work) on the spot. You must halt the movement before bending your knees too much (not more than a 90° angle at the knee joint, see Figures 117 and 118).

The work load in exercises (a)–(e) is greatest when the knee is flexed. The deeper you descend, the greater the work load will be. The muscles are subjected to large but harmless stress. However, the cartilage at the back of your kneecap will be subjected to harmful stress if you bend your knees too much. An explanation follows. (See p.18 for diagrams and descriptions of how the origin and insertion of muscles are affected by muscle forces.)

With extreme bending of the knee a muscle force of 4–5 times the force of gravity (bodyweight) may be required. The force that pulls the kneecap over the thigh bone (femur) can thus amount to 3000 N. Consequently, the kneecap is subjected to forces that together press it against the thigh bone with a force that, at small angles, is almost double — i.e. 5000 N according to Figure 118. If exercises of this type are repeated frequently, the athlete runs a great risk of tearing the cartilage. The rule of thumb: "never" bend too deeply at the knees while they are subjected to stress (in the form of extra weights, speed, short stopping distance, etc.), is really worth following!

The calculations above show that the stress to which a straight knee is subjected is almost zero. They also show that the deeper you bend, the greater the stress will become.

Fig. 118.

3000 N

5000 N

3000 N

Examples of stress produced in the knee joint

(a) When standing on one leg (with slightly bent knee and centre of gravity 5 cm behind the axis of motion of the knee joint), the knee extensors (quadriceps femoris) must contract with enough force to keep the body from collapsing and sitting down. According to the seesaw principle, the force of the muscle must equal that of gravity if the muscle's lever arm is also 5 cm.

(b) If the knee is flexed at a lesser angle than in (a), the distance between the vertical line [Figure 117 (b)] and the axis of motion of the knee will become 15 cm; although the muscle's lever arm will remain unchanged at 5 cm. In example (b) the muscle force must be 3 x 600 N because its lever arm is three times less than that of the gravitational force.

With the help of an EMG (electromyography = the recording of muscle activity), it has been shown that the internal thigh muscle (vastus medialis) is most active during the final extension of the leg. In order to train this part of the quadriceps, it is necessary to construct exercises that put the greatest stress on the leg when the knee is fully extended. None of the exercises described on p.50 are of this type.

In the following exercises (Figure 119) the extended knee is subjected to intense work loads (force to overcome).

Fig. 119.

In all three exercises the work load is greatest when the knee is fully extended (the knee remains extended for static stress). These exercises particularly strengthen the internal vast thigh muscle, a muscle which is particularly important for the stability of the knee. The thigh bone and the shin bone form a certain angle with each other. The kneecap is acted upon primarily along the direction of the thigh (rectus femoris and the medial and lateral vasti), but the depression in which the kneecap glides, lies on a vertical line (see Figure 120).

The muscle whose job it is to guide the kneecap correctly, so that it is not drawn outwards and "scrape" against the external or lateral condyle of

the femur, is the internal vast thigh muscle (vastus medialis). Its direction of pull is shown by the arrows in Figure 120. This muscle is weakened extremely quickly when the knee is injured. For this reason, a special training programme in which the extended knee is subjected to stress should be given top priority after the knee has been in a cast for a time. The diagrams below (Figure 121) illustrate some relatively easy exercises that are aimed at building up strength after an accident. Their goal is to place the greatest work load on the extended knee.

Fig. 120.

Fig. 121.

a)

(a) The four-headed thigh muscle must overcome the weight of the lower leg. Its work load can be increased by placing a sandbag on the foot or by wearing a weighted shoe.

Fig. 121.

(b)

(b) If the leg is lifted while straight, the weight of the lower leg still subjects the four-headed thigh muscle (quadriceps femoris) to stress. This exercise is more demanding than (a) because the muscles at the back of the thigh stretch and strive to flex the knee joint. Thus, the extensor has to work harder than in example (a).

Fig. 121.

(c)

(c) When a body sits, the pelvis tips forwards, which does not happen if it lies as shown in example (b). This causes the muscles at the back of the thigh to stretch even further. Thus, exercise (c) is heavier than exercise (b). Furthermore, it also subjects the flexors of the hip to stress.

A well-trained elite high jumper, for example, could aim at being able to sit and lift a straight leg 45° above the horizontal plane with a load of 15 kg on his foot.

Knee flexors

When judging the value of different exercises designed for the knee extensors, one must take account of their antagonist, i.e. the muscles situated at the back of the thigh. The collective name for these muscles is the hamstrings. They originate from the lowermost part of the hip bone (ischium) and run towards the knee. There are three in all.

Fig. 122

(a)

Ischial tuberosity

Semi membranosus muscle

Semitendinosus muscle

Two-headed thigh muscle (biceps femoris)

Head of the calf bone (or fibula)

Internal or medial condyle

The pelvis and femur seen from behind

All three originate from the ischial tuberosity. The two-headed thigh muscle (biceps femoris) is inserted into the head of the calf bone (or fibula). It can rotate the lower leg so that the foot points outwards. The semitendinosus and semi-membranosus muscles are inserted into the internal or medial condyle of the shin bone (tibia); therefore they can rotate the lower leg inwards.

This group of muscles is called the hamstrings because their tendons can easily be felt at the back of the thigh. The distance between the origin and insertion of these hip extensors and knee flexors vary greatly depending upon the angle of the hip and knee joints.

Fig. 122 (b).

Biceps femoris

Shortened muscles at the back of the thigh result in a stationary hip. When a person is unable to tip his pelvis forward, he tries to compensate for this by bending forward at his lumbar spine. Back trouble often results from the hamstrings being too short.

(a)

(b)

Fig. 123.

(a) Maximally contracted (b) Maximally stretched

Flexibility exercises for the knee flexors

The following diagrams (Figure 124) demonstrate stretching exercises for the knee flexors using the PNF-method (p.25).

Fig. 124.

(c)

Fig. 124 (a).

(a) Assume this position [Figure 124 (a)] without bending forward at your lumbar spine, and keep your back straight. Tip your pelvis as far forward as your thigh muscles will allow.

(c) Lie on your back and pull one leg — held straight — towards your chest.

Strength-developing exercises for the knee flexors

The exercises below are examples of different strength-developing exercises for the back of the thigh.

Fig. 125.

(a)

Figure 125 (a). A friend (or weighted shoe or rubber hose) should provide just enough resistance to allow you to bend your knee with even movements backwards (eccentric work for the muscles) and forwards (concentric work). The resistance should not be so great that you are forced to bend at the hip in order to perform the movements.

(b)

(b)   *Incorrect*

(b) Stand with your knees bent and your hands touching the ground. Then stretch your knees until you feel a comfortable tension at the back of your thigh. By supporting your hands on the ground you are taking the load off your back. If you straighten one leg at a time, the lifted leg will further unload your back. This exercise is best suited for those who already have relatively long hamstrings.

(b) By bending at the hip using the iliopsoas (i.e. tip your pelvis forward) the origin of the hamstrings (the ischial tuberosity) will move further away from your lower leg. Thus, you stretch your flexors and thereby increase their strength (p.18). This means that you subject your lumbar spine to stress in an unfavourable position, and this could lead to pain. Thus, you ought to press your hip down and not strain it more than is necessary to perform the movement with your hips touching the ground.

Fig. 125.

Keep your back flat

(c) The same strength-developing apparatus that was used to train the knee extensors can be used to train the knee flexors.

(d) The following exercise is demanding. Kneel on a soft surface with your lower legs fixed. Then let your upper body fall slowly forward and thereafter pull it back: Keep your hips straight. It is advisable to begin with small movements. This exercise subjects the muscles to great stress and can easily lead to a tendency for cramps if one is untrained. Here, it is the body's own weight that subjects the muscles to stress. The further the body's centre of gravity is placed in front of the knee joint, the greater is the moment of force the knee flexors must cancel. When the trunk is lowered, the muscles act eccentrically; when it is raised to the vertical position they are acting concentrically.

In order to train the muscles at the back of the thigh for coordination and speed you can run with short quick strides; sprint and try to kick your buttocks; or cycle quickly (in first gear).

E. Lower Leg and Foot

A muscle group which is very important for jumping and running is the calf muscle (triceps surae) [Figure 126 (a) and (b)]. This muscle has three parts: (a) the "twin" calf muscle (gastrocnemius) with its two heads of origin (one from each of the condyles of the thigh bone) and (b) the "flounder" muscle (soleus) (a flat muscle originating from the back of the lower leg). Together the three parts form the heel tendon (tend Achilles) which is inserted into the heel bone (calcaneum).

The gastrocnemius bends (or flexes) the knee and the ankle so that the body can be raised on its toes (plantarflexion). The soleus muscle acts only on the ankle joint.

Fig. 126.
(a) Twin calf muscle (gastrocnemius)
(b) Flounder muscle (soleus)

Heel tendon
(Achilles tendon)

Heel bone
(Calcaneum)

(c) Place the balls of your feet against something that will raise them 5 cm above your heels. Stand on your toes, and then return to your original position. This exercise can be done quickly many times (dynamic endurance) or with a heavy weight five or six times (maximal strength training) (p.29). When pressing upwards the muscles are trained concentrically and when descending they are trained eccentrically. For a very short period — when the heel is in contact with the ground — the muscle can relax in its extended position. This has a certain stretching effect.

If you want to stretch only your calf muscles, you can do the following exercise. Stand against a wall (d) or bent forward (e) with support for your hands. Then, move one leg as far as possible behind you keeping your heel on the ground.

The muscle can be activated with the PNF-method by pressing the ball of your foot against the ground for a few seconds. Another good way is to plant the ball of your foot against a tree and pull yourself carefully forward with your arms so that the calf muscles are stretched (f). If your knees are straight, then you will also be stretching your gastrocnemius, (d), (e) and (f). If your knees are bent, the soleus is stretched (g). The latter is often neglected. When it is, the calf muscle still feels stiff and sore.

Fig. 126.

Fig. 128.

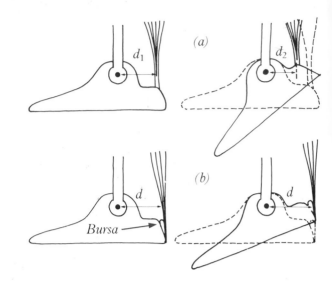

The foot

When the calf muscle is too short, the foot tends to assume a position with downward-pointing toes (Figure 127). The muscles which hold the foot up (situated at the front of the lower leg between the shin and calf bones, p.60), are thus forced to work constantly with raised tension (tone) in order to hold the foot in its normal position. Such tension may lie behind the pain which is experienced in the lower leg when an athlete trains too much at one session, or runs on hard surfaces, etc.

However, the heel tendon is attached to the heel bone near its base, which means that the lever arm (d) remains about the same length regardless of whether the whole foot is firmly planted on the ground or whether the body is standing on its toes.

Fig. 127.

When we take a closer look at how the heel tendon is attached to the heel bone, we can easily understand how mechanically correctly the muscles of the body are arranged. If the heel tendon were attached as shown in Figure 128 (a), below, then its lever arm (i.e. ability to turn the ankle) would have less and less affect the more the body is raised on its toes (d_1 would be reduced to d_2).

Fig. 129.

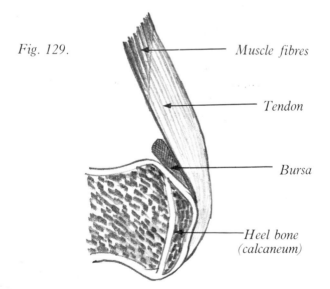

Muscle fibres

Tendon

Bursa

Heel bone (calcaneum)

The tendon is protected from scraping against the heel bone by a bursa which is situated between the tendon and the bone.

Movements of the foot

The foot can move around two axes. The movements around axis 1 are called flexion and extension. Movements around axis 2 are called supination and pronation.

Fig. 130.

1

Extension

Flexion

Pronation   *Supination*

2   *2*

Skeleton of the foot

The skeleton of the foot is divided into ankle bones (tarsus), bones of the foot (metatarsus) and the bones of the toes (phalanges).

Extension and flexion take place between the ankle bone itself (talus) and the lower leg bones (i.e. tibia and fibula). This joint is called the ankle joint.

Supination and pronation take place between the talus and the "boat-shaped" tarsal (the navicular) bone and the heel bone (the calcaneus). This joint is known as the subtalar joint.

Fig. 131 (b).
   Ankle bones

   a Heel bone (calcaneus)
   b Ankle bone (talus)
   c Boat-shaped tarsal bone (navicular)
   d , e, f Wedge-shaped bones (cuneiforms)
   g Cube-shaped bone (cuboid)

Supination and pronation take place simultaneously between several articulating surfaces which together form the subtalar joint.

Movements of the ankle and subtalar joints are independent of each other. The movements of the foot at these joints are controlled, as usual, by the muscles. If the muscles are unable to prevent movements that are too great or too sudden, the joint is still protected by the ligaments of the foot.

The ankle ligaments arise from the prominent lower ends (the malleoli) of the shin and calf bones (the tibia and fibula) and spread out down towards the articulating ankle bones. Thus, the internal or medial ligament of the ankle arises from the medial malleolus of the shin bone (tibia) and is inserted into the calcaneus, talus and navicular bones. It is called the deltoid ligament.

Fig. 131 (a).

Bones of the toe (phalanges)

Bones of the foot (metatarsal bones)

Ankle bones (tarsal bones)

Ankle joint

Subtalar joints

There are three separate ligaments making up the external or lateral ligament. They all arise from the external or lateral malleolus of the calf bone (fibula). One of them extends forward and is inserted into the talus, one passes downward to be attached to the calcaneus, and the third one extends backward towards the back part of the talus.

Fig. 132.

(a) Internal or medial ligament
Deltoid ligament

(b)

External or lateral ligament
1. Posterior talofibular ligament
2. Anterior talofibular ligament
3. Calcaneofibular ligament

The origin of the deltoid ligament corresponds to the axis of motion ⊙ of the ankle joint. Thus it is always taut. The origin of the external lateral ligament is situated below the axis of motion. Hence, its posterior part is taut when the foot points upwards and the anterior part is taut when the ankle is stretched. When injured, the ligament either suffers a partial rupture or is completely torn. In many cases the ligament remains intact but the malleolus is broken off.

Muscles of the foot

The most important flexors (see p.57) are the calf muscles (triceps surae). They are, however, assisted by other muscles whose tendons can be felt and seen behind the malleoli. The most important extensors

(1, 2, 3, in Figure 133) are found at the front of the leg between the shin and calf bones. Their tendons can easily be felt on the top of the foot at the base of the shin bone. Pronation is brought about by the two muscles whose tendons can be felt beneath the external or lateral (calf bone) malleolus (4, 5). Supination is produced mainly by the three muscles whose tendons pass behind and beneath the internal or medial (shin bone) malleolus (7, 8, 9). Figure 133 (b) shows their locations in relation to the different axes of motion.

Fig. 133.

(a)   (b)

Flexion

Extension

Supination

Pronation

The numbers in the diagrams refer to the following muscles. (They are also dealt with on the facing page.)

1. Anterior shin bone muscle (tibialis anterior).
2. Long great toe extensor (extensor hallucis longus).
3. Long toe extensor (extensor digitorum longus).
4. Long calf muscle (peroneus longus).
5. Short calf muscle (peroneus brevis).
6. Three-headed calf muscle (triceps surae).
7. Long flexor of the great toe (flexor hallucis longus).
8. Long toe flexor (flexor digitorum longus).
9. Posterior shin bone muscle (tibialis posterior).

When describing the structure and function of the foot it is useful to review the concept of *"arches"*. There are three types.

I Internal (medial) longitudinal arch (movement arch).
II External (lateral) longitudinal arch (support arch).
III Transverse arch (or anterior arch).

Fig. 134.

Running subjects the external arch to stress. Notice how a running shoe wears down at the outer border of the heel and under the great toe. The other arches — which are supported by *ligaments*, the *wedge-shaped construction of the bones* and the *muscles* — give the foot its elasticity. Departures from the normal appearance can either lead to an arch that is too high (not very common) or too low (flatfoot). The latter may be due to the ligament being stretched which, in turn, could be the result of subjecting the foot to severe stress (running on hard surfaces without arch support) or imbalance of muscle strength between the different muscles. The structures which affect the internal arch are listed below. The structures marked with a + have a tendency to raise the internal arch and those marked with a − tend to lower it.

Fig. 135.

(a) Calf muscles −
(b) Extensors −
(c) Foot stress −
(d) Ligaments of the sole
   of the foot +
(e) Muscles of the sole
   of the foot +

The most common foot injuries are those sustained by the external or lateral ligament of the ankle joint. These injuries are caused by lopsided gait. The majority of injuries can be avoided by wearing appropriate shoes. Shoes that are worn down on one side only (on the outside of the heel) are usually the culprit. Another common cause of foot injury is a surface that provides so much friction that the shoes stick at the slightest contact. The muscles which

simultaneously rotate the foot outwards and pronate (i.e. lift the outer border so that the shoe does not become firmly fixed on the ground too soon) are the long and short calf muscles (peroneus longus and brevis, 4, 5). It is very important that these muscles are strong and can react quickly. The calf muscles and their antagonists (7, 8) can be trained with "toe push-ups".

If you stand (a) on your toes with the sole of your foot pointing inwards as shown below (Figure 136) and push up balancing on the outside of your foot, you will be engaging 7, 8 and 9. If you stand (b) on your toes with the sole pointing outwards, 4 and 5 will be engaged.

Fig. 136.

(a)   (b)

Coordination and speed can be trained by standing and balancing on an unstable object.

You can both control and train your ability to finely adjust your foot position in the following way: stand on one leg with a bent knee keeping your arms by your sides and eyes shut. It is always considerably more difficult to balance on one leg if that leg has recently been injured as it takes time to retrain fine motor ability. The risk of new sprains is obvious if rehabilitation is not hastened.

Fig. 137.

Periostitis

A problem facing athletes sooner or later is inflammation of the membrane covering the bones, i.e. periostitis. The muscles responsible for lifting the foot (1, 2, 3) are situated at the front of the leg between the shin and calf bones. They are enclosed in a fascia (tough connective tissue, Figure 133). The inner part between the shin and calf bones (interosseous membrane) serves as a direct point of origin for some parts of the muscles. The rest of the muscles grow directly out of the bone walls and pass through the bone membrane which has intimate contact with the fascia.

The bone membrane (periosteum) may be detached from the bone due to the force of the muscle contraction or high tension in the muscle fascia which is inserted into the bone through the bone membrane. Small haemorrhages and inflammations appear in the microscopic cavities which form between the detached membrane and the bone.

As mentioned earlier, athletes who train by running a great deal often sustain periostitis. The healing process will be delayed if they continue to run, as by doing so the worn tissues are not given time to heal. Pain can also be caused by changing the running surface or suddenly increasing the amount of training. The muscles — which are confined within the muscle fascia — swell (fill with blood) more than the fascia will permit. The tension that then builds up leads to a pain resembling periostitis pain. Such increased pressure in a muscle compartment is referred to as "closed compartment syndrome".

A successful surgical method for treating severe cases of increased pressure is to cleave the muscle fascia by making a longitudinal slit between the shin and calf bones on the fore side of the leg. In this way the tension of the anterior muscle compartment will be reduced.

Running on hard surfaces can lead to a complaint similar to periostitis. The sudden and excessive stresses to which the leg is subjected at each stride can, at worst, give rise to microscopic small splits in the outer lamella of the bone. This type of complaint heals with greater difficulty than the more common periostitis.

The wearing of unsuitable shoes when running on hard surfaces causes the internal arch to fall at each stride. The anterior shin bone muscle (1) which is attached to the arch (Figure 138) will fall and thus pull on its origin with a great deal of force. This is especially the case when the whole foot is planted on the ground instead of the heel striking first. The shoe should be built up at the arch to give it support.

Fig. 138.

Chapter 4
ANATOMY AND FUNCTION OF THE TRUNK

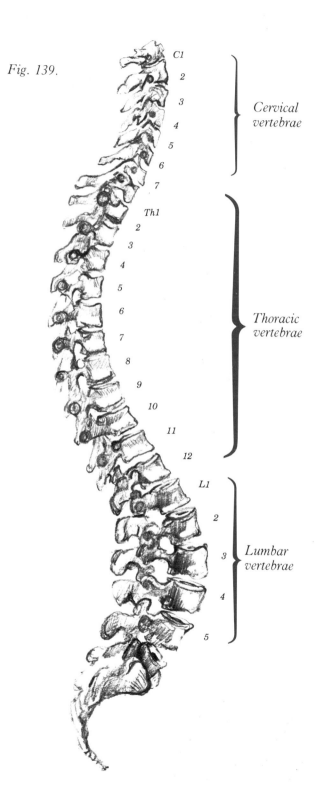

Fig. 139.

Cervical
vertebrae

Thoracic
vertebrae

Lumbar
vertebrae

The vertebral column consists of seven cervical (of the neck) vertebrae which are numbered and usually written as C1, . . ., C7; 12 dorsal (or thoracic i.e. of the chest) vertebrae Th1, . . ., Th12; and five lumbar vertebrae L1, . . ., L5 (Figure 139).

Between the vertebrae there are intervertebral discs made up of an outer layer of fibrocartilage (annulus fibrosus) (1) and a more pulpy centre (nucleus pulposus) (2). Thus, the disc, with its tough fibrocartilage rim and soft, pulpy, highly elastic centre, acts as a shock absorber. Discs make up about one-third of the height of the vertebral column (Figure 140).

When two vertebrae are placed on top of each other, there is a substantial space between the stalks or pedicles of each vertebra; this is called the intervertebral foramen (3). It is through this space that the nerves pass from the spinal cord (4) and reach out to all the different parts of the body.

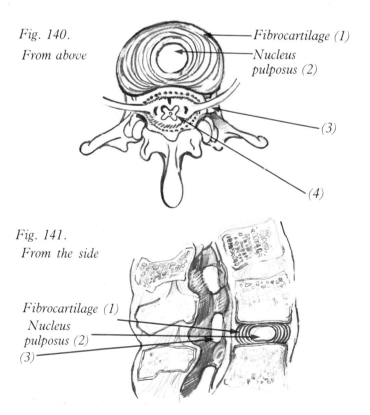

Fig. 140.
From above

Fibrocartilage (1)
Nucleus pulposus (2)
(3)
(4)

Fig. 141.
From the side

Fibrocartilage (1)
Nucleus pulposus (2)
(3)

Fig. 142.

From above

From the side

The following characteristics of a vertebra can be distinguished in Figure 142.

(a) Body.
(b) Neural arch.
(c) Vertebral opening.
(d) Transverse outgrowth or process.
(e) Spinous outgrowth or process.
(f) Articular outgrowth or process.

We are prevented from leaning too far back by the spinous processes and the tension of long ligament (1) which runs down the front of the spinal column (anterior longitudinal ligament) (Figure 143).

Fig. 143.

Forward bending is restricted partly by the back muscles, partly by the elastic ligament (3) which runs between the posterior parts of the neural arches (ligamentum flavum), and partly by the ligament which runs down the back of the vertebral bodies (i.e. in the anterior part of the vertebral opening). This ligament (2) is called the posterior longitudinal ligament.

The back complaints of athletes are often due to the spine being subjected to excessive or uneven stress, or the body being subjected to sudden movements while it is in an unfavourable position.

The back complaints of non-athletes are often due to poorly trained back muscles (even poorly trained muscles of the legs and abdomen), the wear and tear of lifting objects in a lopsided manner, sitting still, or working in a position where the body is tilted forward.

The pressure inside a disc varies according to the position of the body and external stress. The position which the body can assume to ensure that the least amount of pressure is placed on the lumbar spine is shown in Figure 144. Thus, lie on your back and support your lower legs on, say, a chair so that the iliopsoas does not pull (and thereby increase disc pressure) on your spine (see Figures 149 and 150). Sitting positions produce greater disc pressure than standing positions; a fact that is unknown to many!

Fig. 144.

This is because the back muscles must work harder (static work) when the body sits. Disc pressure is due to the bodyweight (mg) acting on the disc from above, and the contraction force (F) of the surrounding muscles (Figure 145).

The total pressing force in Figure 145 will be $mg + F$. Pressure (P) is calculated by dividing the force by the area of the disc. The L3 vertebra of an adult has an area of about 10 cm^2. The disc of a young person can withstand a stress of 800 kg, i.e. 8000 N. The ability of the discs of an older person to withstand stress is reduced to half of this. A young healthy disc can thus withstand a pressure of 800 N/cm^2. Compare these figures with those given on p.67.

Fig. 145.

mg

F

F

When a person carries something heavy the disc pressure is, of course, increased. Asymmetrical stress produces greater pressure than symmetrical stress (p.67). "Hanging" from a bar reduces the pressure on the discs and thereby unloads the back. At the same time the back muscles are stretched. For best results, "hang" with bent hips and support for your feet, (relaxed iliopsoas = straight back).

Fig. 146.

Incorrect   *Correct*

As a matter of curiosity it can be mentioned that if the stress is of long duration, or very great, a certain amount of fluid can be pressed out of the nucleus and we can actually measure a shortening of body height. A weight-lifter may be several centimetres shorter after a heavy training session.

If we measure disc thickness after a night's rest, we will find that they are thicker than if we measure them after a short period of normal activity. Therefore, we are somewhat taller in the morning than at the middle of the day.

We become shorter as we get older because the vertebral discs shrink as the tissues degenerate.

There are many reasons for back pain. A common reason is that the fibrous part of the disc tears and its nucleus is pressed backward, stretching the ligament which runs posteriorly along the vertebral bodies in towards the spinal canal. If the ligament stretches, pain is felt via its pain-sensitive cells. (There are only a very few nerves to register pain in the torn disc.) This type of pain can disappear if the back ceases to be stressed by the lifting of heavy objects, leaning forward while working, or sitting still. If the nucleus bulges too far out (Figure 148), it can press against the nerve root which passes through the intervertebral opening. Pain is then felt from the muscles that are supplied by this nerve. Thus, pain can be felt in the shoulder when a cervical disc is injured. Tense muscles, small vertebral displacements, or worn-down intervertebral cartilage can put the same pressure on the nerves, thereby causing pain. If the pain is felt in the leg, the name sciatica is used to describe it since the irritated nerve in this case is called the sciatic nerve.

Fig. 147.

Some of the nerves which pass out from a central spinal opening and into a muscle can be drawn out a little further by stretching the muscle. This can cause the nerve to be pressed against a protrusion on the disc, producing severe pain in the leg. One way to examine a person to see if his sciatic nerve is irritated, is to place him on his back and lift his leg as shown in Figure 147. This test is called the Lasègués test. This type of pain must not be confused with that felt by stiff people who try to stretch their hamstrings (p.55).

65

The fibrous part of the disc consists mainly of collagenous fibres, which stretch if they are subjected to prolonged stress. Hernia is commonly caused by working in a position which subjects the disc to such a force for a long period of time. Lifting heavy objects increases disc pressure which causes pressure in the nucleus pulposus (1) to rupture the fibrous annulus fibrosus (2).

Fig. 148.

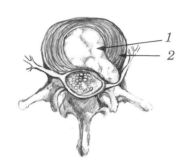

The increased pressure produced by simultaneously lifting something heavy and twisting the trunk (e.g. shovelling snow), is greatest in the posterior part of the disc which is not protected by extra ligaments (Figure 148). Such activities are therefore especially dangerous for those who suffer from back complaints.

Fig. 149.
When a person stands, a line from his centre of gravity to the ground (vertical mid line) passes about 5cm in front of the centre of disc L3, and his back muscles lie about 5 cm behind it. Hence, the muscle force must equal 400 N in order to prevent his upper body from falling forward. The force acting on the disc is 400 + 400 = 800 N.

Fig. 150.
When a person sits, his vertical midline passes about 15 cm in front of L3. The muscle's lever arm is 5 cm (as in standing). Therefore, a force of 1200 N is required for equilibrium to exist. The force acting on the disc will be 1200 + 400 = 1600 N.

Using the moment of force law (p.32), we can calculate which stresses the spinal column is subjected to in different positions, lifts and training exercises. The person in the example below weighs 80 kg, of which 40 kg lies above L3. Distance is measured in centimetres and force is measured in newtons. Thus, 40 kg corresponds to 400 N.

When lifting an object it is important to stand so that the external lever arm (the distance from L3 to the point where the force of gravity acts on both the body and the object) is as short as possible. In the example below (Figure 151), the upper body (40 kg) + load (10 kg) is equal to 500 N. The back muscles are at work about 5 cm behind L3. When a person stands correctly (a), his external moment arm is about 20 cm, compared with 30 cm when he stands and lifts incorrectly (b). When he lifts from a sitting position (c), even very small weights subject his back to great work loads.

$F_m \times 5 = 500 \times 20$
$F_m = 2000$ N

b)

30 cm

l

5 cm

F_m

$F_m \times 5 = 500 \times 30$
$F_m = 3000 \ N$

500 N

(c)

40 cm   5 cm

.d

$F_m \times 5 = 500 \times 40$
$F_m = 4000 \ N$

500 N F_m

According to the calculations above, the pressure to which the disc is subjected by the muscles in (c), is half of what it can tolerate in a healthy condition (8000 N, p.64). This is true even when a person lifts a "mere" 10 kg from a sitting position. The discs are, however, unloaded when a person instinctively tenses his abdominal muscles plus his diaphragm (p.77). By doing so, he builds up the pressure in his abdomen which has a piston effect in an upward and downward direction (preventing collapse). The disc — which is a part of the abdominal cavity's back wall — is thus protected. Hence, the pressure produced by the back muscles can be reduced by about 40%.

Fig. 152.

The calculations above show how important it is to have well-trained abdominal muscles to unload the back, and strong leg muscles in order to lift correctly, i.e. with bent knees.

If a load can be distributed symmetrically by carrying it with both hands, the stress to which the back is subjected is considerably reduced compared with carrying with only one hand.

In Figures 153 and 154, the body weighs 40 kg above L3. The load is 30 kg. The lever arm of the back muscles (for sideward bending) is 5 cm.

Fig. 153.
Symmetric lift

Cg

150   150
   400

Total work load
150 N + 150 N + 400 N = 700 N
(the reader should also take account of the discussion accompanying Figure 145).

Fig. 154.
Asymmetric lift

Cg

5 10

700
1400

Suppose the centre of gravity of the body plus load falls 10 cm to the side of L3 (note that their common centre of gravity lies to the right of L3, even if the body tilts to the left). The back muscles must then contract with a force of $F_m \times 5 = 700 \times 10$. $F_m = 1400 \ N$. Total work load is 700 N + 1400 N = 2100 N.

The back is heavily loaded when the iliopsoas (p.45) is forced to work. The muscles are forced to work statically to lift the legs straight out in front of a person who hangs from a bar. If he weighs 80 kg his legs weigh 30 kg, the centre of gravity of his legs lies 40 cm from his hip joint, and his iliopsoas works with a lever arm of about 5 cm, then the force can be calculated as follows (Figure 155):

About 1900 N of this force strives to increase the sway of the lumbar spine. The force pressing the discs together will be about 2200 N. If the abdominal muscles do not keep the back straight, then a force of 2200 N could greatly increase the pressure in certain parts of the disc (Figure 156).

Fig. 155.

F_m

5 cm

40 cm

300

$F_m \times 5 = 300 \times 40$
$F_m = 2400$ N.

Such an exercise is thus unsuitable for people with weak abdominal muscles. Some sporting events, however, subject the iliopsoas to considerably greater stress.

Fig. 156.

1100

2200   2400

Fig. 157.

By way of comparison we can examine the forces that are necessary to swing a leg forward during running, jumping, hurdling, etc. The weight and acceleration (for which the iliopsoas is responsible) of the leg may cause the force of muscle contraction to reach about 4000 N.

When we consider exercises that engage the back muscles, we must also take account of the stabilising effect of the abdominal muscles. The diagrams below illustrate the different types of back and abdominal muscles found in the body.

Muscles of the back (erector spinae)

The muscles of the back can be classified schematically as follows.

Long back muscles (pass at least seven vertebrae).
Back muscles of average length (pass two to six vertebrae).

Short back muscles (go to the nearest vertebra).

The long muscles lie outermost (Figure 158). They are called:

(a) iliocostalis (from the hip bone to the ribs);
(b) longissimus (from the spinous outgrowths to the transverse outgrowths and ribs) and
(c) spinalis (between spinous outgrowths).

Fig. 158.

a
b
c

The back muscles of average length (Figure 159) are:

(d) semispinalis (passes four to seven vertebrae) and
(e) multifidus (passes two to three vertebrae).

Fig. 159.

d

e

The short muscles passing from vertebra to vertebra (Figure 160) are:
(f) intertransversus (between transverse outgrowths);
(g) interspinales (between spinous outgrowths) and
(h) rotatores (between spinous and transverse outgrowths.

The muscles work together as a unit. The iliocostalis, however, is more adapted for taking part in sideward bending than the remaining muscles. The most important muscles for turning the trunk are the rotatores. A combination of bending and turning is important for all types of throwing.

Fig. 160.

It is believed that cramps of the short muscles — in particular the rotatores — are the most common cause of so-called lumbago. If a cramp is brought about in one muscle, the muscles surrounding it contract to prevent movements that could tear it. This, in turn, cuts off the blood supply to the area, causing cramps in other muscles.

Fig. 161.

The cramp condition can be relieved by taking the load off the muscles (bedrest) and inducing relaxation (warmth, massage, muscle relaxing medicine). A cramp may result from overexertion, unaccustomed movements or minor vertebral displacements caused by sudden stresses. The best protection is well-functioning back and abdominal musculature.

Exercises for the back

In the following exercise the rotatores are forced to work. Stand on all fours; then, simultaneously lift your right arm and left leg (Figure 162). This activates the diagonal muscles which prevent the right shoulder and left hip from falling downwards. You should remain in that position for a few seconds so the muscles can work statically. Next, change positions by lifting your left arm and right leg.

Fig. 162.

Fig. 163.

Additional exercises for the back are given below, along with the effect they are considered to have.

(a) This exercise should be done slowly. Well-trained young people can also turn sideways from the raised position in order to activate the rotatores. The work load to which the lower back is subjected can be increased by holding the arms stretched out in front of the body. Do not exaggerate backward bending of the neck. Do not go too far.

(b) Lift one leg at a time to train the hamstrings, the large buttock muscle and the lower back musculature. Do the exercise slowly. *Stop* in the raised position for static training. Do not combine exercises (a) and (b).

(c) Lie on a vaulting horse with your pelvis free as shown in the diagram. Keeping your back straight, pull yourself up until you reach the horizontal plane. You will be training all your back muscles statically; your hip extensors concentrically on the way up, and eccentrically on the way down. You can vary the work load with the help of your arms — little stress when your arms are by your sides, great stress when your arms are folded behind your neck. Light weights can be used.

Fig. 165.

(d) As in (c) except that you should roll up to the horizontal plane one vertebra at a time beginning at the lumbar spine. Your back muscles are then forced to work concentrically (in the order L5, L4, . . ., C1) while rolling up and eccentrically while rolling down (C1, . . ., L5).

The diagrams below (Figure 164) show how the back muscles can be stretched by leaning forward without subjecting the back to stress, so that the whole musculature can relax.

Fig. 164.

The above positions also reduce disc pressure by pulling on the back (traction).

When training the back muscles (Figure 165) one can (1) allow the trunk to fall forward — keeping the legs and back straight — until the horizontal plane is reached. Then (2) in an easy movement, bend further forward with flexed knees and back.

Next, (3) roll up one vertebra at a time, beginning at the lumbar spine. The first phase (1) stresses the muscles of the back statically. The work load increases as you approach the horizontal plane. You can increase the stress still further by making some "breast strokes" with your arms while you are in the horizontal plane. By doing so, you will be shifting the centre of gravity of your upper body even farther away from your hips. By falling forward beyond the horizontal plane, you can decrease the work load for your back muscles (the load will instead be borne by the posterior longitudinal ligament, p.64). People with back complaints and elderly people should avoid this.

Rolling up (3) forces the back muscles to work concentrically along the entire length of the spine [cf. Figure 163 (d)]. We are often told that rolling the trunk is a dangerous exercise, but there is no evidence that this is so. Moreover, trunk rolling exercises (Figure 166a) are often confused with hula-hula movements (Figure 166b).

Fig. 166.

Trunk rolling can be done by moving the upper body (trunk) in large circles while keeping the hips and legs still. If this movement is performed when the body is warmed-up and if the pace is controlled, then there is no risk associated with it. By the same token, it can hardly be claimed to have especially beneficial effects.

Hula-hula movements increase the flexibility of the hip joint. Here, the feet and head are kept still while the hips are moved around in a circle.

As far as the neck is concerned, so-called head rolls should be avoided. There is a certain risk of doing these too quickly and thereby subjecting the ligaments and cartilage to wear and tear. Figure 167 shows the approximate range of movement of the head. The head cannot bend as far backwards as it can in all other directions. The shaded regions of the diagram mark the dangerous areas which the head may be forced to pass if it rolls around quickly. However, if you roll slowly and under control, you may follow the outer limits of the cervical spine's range of motion without any problems.

Fig. 167.

Abdominal muscles

As we have seen when examining movements that strain the back, a well-functioning abdominal musculature unloads the back during lifting, and stabilises the spinal column (i.e. the abdominal muscles are antagonists to the back muscles). The examples given on p.66 show that the back muscles are always trained during lifting, standing, sitting, etc. The majority of people have abdominal muscles that are too weak in relation to their back muscles. Thus, general abdominal muscle training (Figure

Fig. 168.

168a) can be recommended for everyone. Athletes should strengthen their abdominal muscles with exercises which subject them to a heavy work load (Figure 168b). After that they should train their hip flexors (iliopsoas, rectus femoris) and back extensors for strength. (For such exercises, see p.45 and 69.)

In order to judge correctly which exercises to choose and how to execute them, we must first understand how the abdominal muscles function. It is also important to familiarise ourselves with the connection which exists between the back, abdomen and hip flexors.

There are four different kinds of abdominal muscle.

Fig. 169.

(a)

(a) Straight abdominal muscle The rectus abdominis originates from the apex of the breast bone and is inserted into the upper part of the pubic part of the hip bone. When it contracts the body bends forward at the lumbar and thoracic spines. If you lie on your back [as in Figure 168 (a)] and pull your upper body up as far as possible without tipping your pelvis forward (no movement at the hip joint), then you will maximally shorten your straight abdominal muscle.

(b) External oblique abdominal muscle The external oblique abdominal muscle arises from the anterior inferior part of the chest (lower ribs). This muscle becomes a tendinous expansion (or aponeurosis) which covers the straight abdominal muscle above, and below it is inserted into the crest of the hip bone and groin ligament. In the lower part of the abdomen the flat tendons of the two sides intersect.

Fig. 170.

(b)

Fig. 171.

(c)

(c) Internal oblique abdominal muscle The internal oblique arises from the hip bone and groin ligament, becomes a tendinous expansion passing under the straight abdominal muscle, and is inserted into the fibrous band which runs down between the pair of straight abdominal muscles.

Fig. 172.

The oblique abdominal muscles act to assist the straight muscle. In addition, they can turn the trunk. In diagonal sit-ups (Figure 172) the stress to which the oblique abdominal muscles are subjected will increase so that if the right shoulder is turned towards the left hip, the right external and left internal oblique muscles will be engaged.

Fig. 173.

(d)

(d) Transverse abdominal muscle The transversus abdominis is not connected with any movements. It only affects the figure (by pulling the abdomen in). It is also brought into action when the abdominal pressure is increased by so-called abdominal presses. All the abdominal muscles can, upon contraction, increase abdominal pressure (which would try to widen the abdominal cavity). In this way, the discs are unloaded during lifting (p.67).

Fig. 174.

Figure 175 shows a horizontal cross section of the body. From it we can detect the relationship between the back and abdominal muscles.

Fig. 175.

(a) *Straight abdominal muscle (rectus abdominis)*
(b) *External oblique abdominal muscle*
(c) *Internal oblique abdominal muscle*
(d) *Transverse abdominal muscle*
(e) *Square lumbar muscle (quadratus lumborum)*
(f) *Iliopsoas*
(g) *Back extensors (erector spinae)*
(h) *Broad back muscle (latissimus dorsi, p.84)*

Quadratus lumborum

Fig. 176.

Fig. 177.

Here, we should also mention the most important sideward flexor. Its name is quadratus lumborum. It takes part in sideward bending when the movement occurs at the lumbar spine. Compare this with the movements described on p.40 which take place at the hip and also engage the abductor muscles.

Fig. 178.

(a)

(b)

When a person lies on their back, there is a certain curvature on the lumbar spine which is due to the natural curvature of the spine as well as tension in the iliopsoas. The back can be pressed to the floor [Figure 178 (b)] by using the abdominal muscles (A), buttock muscles (B), and hamstrings (H) to tip the pelvis backwards. This would be found easier to do if the knees were bent slightly and the head lifted a little. Thus, the iliopsoas has been relaxed and a forward bending of the spine initiated.

Fig. 179.

If you lie on your back and lift your legs, keeping them straight, you will easily reach a position where your back curvature is considerably greater than it is in a standing position. This is because the force with which the iliopsoas lifts the legs also acts on the back in such a way that the curvature is increased (see p.68).

Fig. 180.

Incorrect

Correct

Exercises which require a person to lift straight legs, or give resistance to hip flexion (p.44), should only be undertaken if the abdominal muscles are capable of stabilising the back (tip the pelvis). Such exercises should be left to those who are relatively well-trained. Their aim, strictly speaking, is to strengthen the hip flexors. Nevertheless, there is a static training effect from which the abdominal muscles benefit.

If a person wants to train only their abdominal muscles, they should make sure that movement takes place at the spine and not at the hips. The most common exercise for strengthening the abdominal muscles is the sit-up. The best way to prevent a sit-up from procurring the aid of the iliopsoas is to be so bent at the hip that the muscle cannot contract with any degree of force. A common mistake is to bend the knees (with accompanying hip bending) at the same time as the feet are held under a wall-bar. In this position, the hip is not bent enough to disengage the iliopsoas and, because the feet are supported, the body can sit up without any great effort on the part of the abdominal muscles. If you assume the position shown in Figure 181 — without supporting your feet — you must roll up vertebra by vertebra (i.e. engage your abdominal muscles) before you can bend your hip and thereby pull yourself up.

Fig. 181.

The best way to train your abdominal muscles is by strongly flexing your hip, making sure that your feet are unsupported. It is then only possible to do half a sit-up (i.e. maximal contraction of your abdominal muscles) without bending your hips.

Fig. 182.

If you remain in the raised position and rotate to each side, you will be training your straight abdominal muscle statically as well as increasing the work load for your oblique abdominal muscles. You can vary the quantity of exercise by (1) keeping your arms straight by your sides (easy), (2) crossing your arms over your chest or (3) placing your hands over your ears (difficult) (Figure 182). The work load can be further increased by adding weights.

When we consider how the external stress increases during a sit-up (Figure 183), we see that the centre of gravity of the upper body lies some way from the hip joint at the beginning of the exercise, and that this distance decreases as the body rolls up vertebra by vertebra [Figure 183 (a)]. External stress (F_1) decreases as the abdominal muscles contract.

If a person lies on a sloping plane, the external stress will increase as he pulls himself up and as his abdominal muscles shorten (i.e. weaken). He would thus find this exercise very demanding [Figure 183 (b)].

Fig. 183.

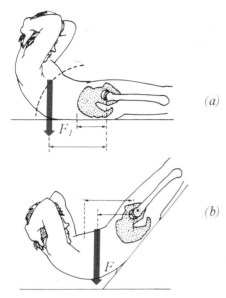

(a)

(b)

Which of the following is the most demanding: (1) sitting up on a slanting bench (45° slope) or (2) sitting up from the floor with 10 kg on your chest? Try them!

A person exercising on a slanting plane must have support for his feet. This means that he is tempted to use his iliopsoas at an early stage instead of rolling one vertebra at a time (i.e. working his abdominal muscles).

The four examples below are designed to illustrate the relationship between external forces (the weight of the legs and upper body) and internal forces (iliopsoas and abdominal muscles).

Fig. 184.

(1) A person who weighs 60 kg lies down as shown in Figure 184. The centre of gravity of his upper body, which weighs about 40 kg, is presumed to lie 30 cm above his hip joint. His legs weigh 20 kg. Their centre of gravity lies 30 cm below the hip. Thus, according to the formula, $M = F \times d$:
The moment of force of the upper body,
$$M = 400 \times 30 = 12000 \text{ Ncm.}$$
The moment of force of the legs,
$$M = 200 \times 30 = 6000 \text{ Ncm.}$$

Fig. 185.

(2) The iliopsoas (the main muscle group responsible for hip flexion) is presumed to be positioned so that its direction of pull in relation to the hip is 6 cm. If its contraction force reaches 1000 N, then the moment of force acting on the leg will be 1000 x 6 = 6000 Ncm (i.e. equal to the moment of force of the legs, according to Figure 184). He can thus begin to lift his legs. If the muscle force is even greater, he can lift his legs with greater speed.

Fig. 186.

(3) If his legs are fixed and the iliopsoas contracts with a force of 2000 N, then the muscle's moment of force will be 2000 x 6 = 12000 Ncm and he can lift his upper body (as shown in Figure 186).

Fig. 187.

(4) In order to sit up without supporting his legs, he must roll up one vertebra at a time using his abdominal muscles until the centre of gravity of his upper body lies 15 cm (instead of 30 cm) from his hip. The iliopsoas will now lift both his upper body and his legs. By bending a little further forward at the spine, he can sit up without moving his legs. If his legs are bent, and they are unsupported, his abdominal muscles will be forced to work over an even greater distance before his hips can be bent.

The diagrams below (Figure 188) present some variations of abdominal muscle training. You should make sure that movement takes place at your spine (easy forward bending) before possible movements take place at your hip joint. Never subject your legs to more stress than your abdominal musculature (whose job it is to hold your back slightly bent forward) can cope with.

Fig. 188.

(a)

(b)

(c)

(d)

There is rarely ever a need of stretching exercises for the abdominal muscles.

Respiratory muscles

Here we will consider the structure of the rib cage and function of the breathing musculature in outline only. The reader is referred to the literature on physiology for a deeper study.

The rib cage consists of 12 ribs (or costae). The first 10 (from the top) are attached directly (first seven) or indirectly to the breast bone (body of the sternum) via costal cartilages. Ribs numbers 11 and 12 have no anterior attachment and are therefore called floating ribs.

Fig. 189.

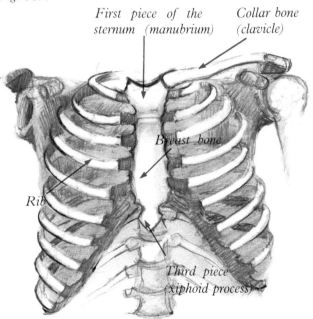

The chest and abdominal cavities are separated by the most important muscle of respiration, the diaphragm. This muscle arises from the lumbar vertebrae, from the lower ribs, and from the xiphoid process which is at the bottom of the sternum. It arches up like a dome into the chest cavity (Figure 190). When the muscle fibres (2) contract, they become less arched and thus cause the central tendinous part (1) of the dome to descend. During contraction, the volume of the chest cavity increases (inspiration) and the volume of the abdominal cavity decreases. The abdomen thus bulges out, which is why this type of breathing is called abdominal breathing (deep breathing).

76

Fig. 190.

Beside functioning as a breathing muscle, the diaphragm assists the abdominal muscles in increasing intra-abdominal pressure. This is important when it comes to lifting heavy objects (see p.73). The volume of the chest cavity can also be increased by raising the ribs. This is accomplished by the action of the muscles which are attached to the ribs. The direction of the muscle fibres is such that they lift the lower ribs up towards the upper ribs (3). These muscles are called external intercostal muscles. This latter type of breathing is called chest breathing. A number of muscles (back, chest, neck, etc.) may exert an influence on the rib cage during forced breathing.

ANATOMY AND FUNCTION OF THE ARM

The movements of the arm are controlled by many muscles. Three different muscle groups are responsible for the movements of the shoulder joint.

Fig. 191. A

B

Left shoulder blade viewed from the back

Group A. Muscles which have their origin on the shoulder blade and which are inserted into the upper arm.

Group B. Muscles which have their origin on the trunk and their insertion on the shoulder blade.

Group C. Muscles which have their origin on the trunk and their insertion on the arm.

The shoulder blade (scapula) is formed like a triangle. A sharp spine (1) (spine of the scapula) projects backward and forms two depressions on the posterior surface of the shoulder blade. The outer end of the spine forms a flat roof (2) (acromion) overhanging the shoulder joint. The anterior part of this roof articulates with the collar bone (3) (clavicle). This joint is the outer collar bone joint (4) (acromio-clavicular joint).

The inner collar bone joint (5) (sterno-clavicular joint) articulates with the manubrium of the breast bone (sternum) (6). The outermost part of the shoulder blade presents a shallow articular surface

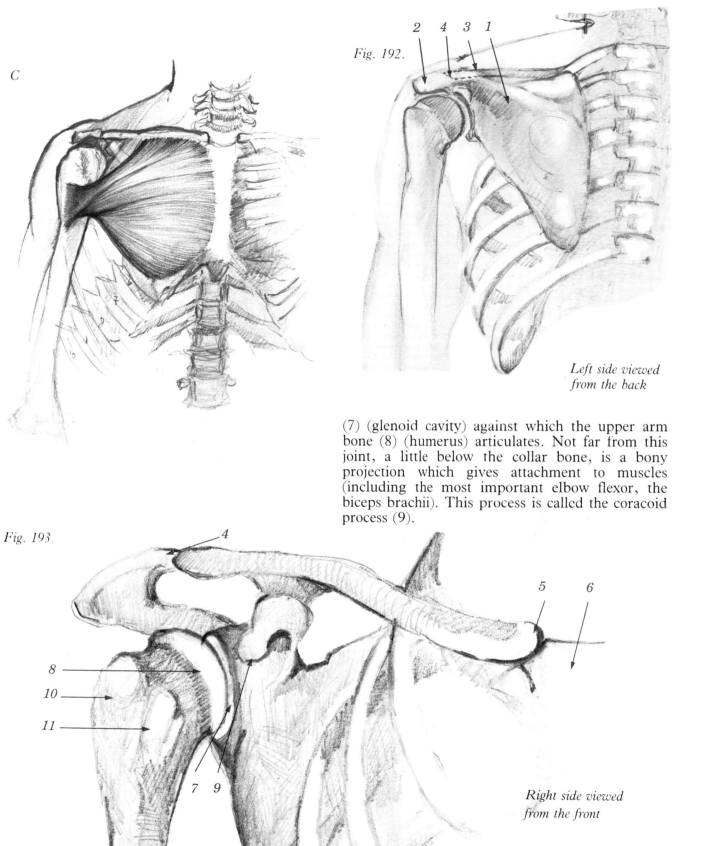

C

Fig. 192.

Left side viewed
from the back

(7) (glenoid cavity) against which the upper arm
bone (8) (humerus) articulates. Not far from this
joint, a little below the collar bone, is a bony
projection which gives attachment to muscles
(including the most important elbow flexor, the
biceps brachii). This process is called the coracoid
process (9).

Fig. 193.

Right side viewed
from the front

79

The arm articulates with the shoulder blade at a ball and socket joint, thus allowing movement in all planes.

(1) Forward and backward swings (flexion–extension).
(2) Outward and inward swings (abduction–adduction).
(3) Outward and inward turns (lateral and medial rotation).

Practically the whole of the shoulder blade functions as an area of origin for muscles. Between the neck and the shaft of the upper arm bone, we can distinguish two roughened projections of bone from which slight ridges run continuous with the shaft. The outer projection (10) (greater tuberosity) and the anterior projection (11) (lesser tuberosity), together with their ridges, will be referred to here simply as the external and anterior areas of attachment.

Many of the muscles of the shoulder blade have only Latin names. Translations of certain parts of the Latin words are therefore given in parentheses.

Group A

Group A consists of the following five muscles.

Fig. 194.

Left side viewed from the back

(1) Supraspinatus (supra = above, spina = spine) lifts the arm. It lies below the large muscle which give the shoulder its contour, the deltoid muscle (p.83) (Figure 194).

Fig. 195.

Left side viewed from the back

(2) Teres major (teres = rounded, major = greater). This large rounded muscle brings the arm to the side (adducts) and rotates it inwards. It works with the latissimus dorsi muscle (p.84) (Figure 195).

(3) Infraspinatus   (4) Teres minor

In the gap between the muscles described above, there are two muscles which together adduct the arm and rotate it outwards. These muscles are called infraspinatus (infra = below) and teres minor (minor = less, smaller) (Figure 196).

Fig. 196.

Left shoulder viewed from the back

(5) Subscapularis

Covering the inside of the shoulder blade (against the back wall of the rib cage) is a muscle which adducts the arm and rotates it inwards. Its name is subscapularis (sub = under, scapula = shoulder blade) (Figure 197).

Fig. 197.

Left shoulder viewed from the front

Fig. 198.

Group B

In order to move the arm with sufficient force, the articular surfaces of the shoulder blade must be positioned in such a way that the arm has an optimal starting point for its movement. The shoulder blade can be: (1) elevated–depressed (10-12 cm), (2) abducted – adducted (15 cm) and (3) rotated outwards and inwards.

Outward rotation means that the articular surfaces of the shoulder blade are directed outward and upward (Fig. 200).

The muscles which raise the shoulder blade are:

1. Levator scapulae (levator = "raiser")
2. Rhomboids (major and minor)

Lifting and a certain inward rotation occur simultaneously (Figure 198).

Both these muscles above are covered by trapezius.

3. Trapezius

Origin: Base of the skull and the spines of the cervical and thoracic vertebrae.

Insertion: Spine of the shoulder blade and external part of the collar bone.

Function: Raises and adducts the shoulder blade and rotates it outwards. Turns the head and bends the neck backwards (Figure 199).

Fig. 199.

3

Fig. 200.

Bends and turns the neck

Adducts or rotates the shoulder blade outwards

Fig. 201.

Attachment

Group C

The large, flat, muscles which arise from the trunk and pass to the upper arm. They are the most important muscles as far as strength and flexibility are concerned.

1. Greater chest muscle (Pectoralis major; pectoral = chest)

Origin (Figure 201): (1) Inner part of the collar bone, (2) manubrium and sternum and (3) part of the costal cartilage (of the ribs).

Insertion: External area of attachment of the upper arm.

Function: Forms the anterior wall of the armpit, and adducts the arm and rotates it outwards. It pulls a raised arm down and swings a lowered arm forward (flexion of the shoulder).

Exercises for the greater chest muscle (pectoralis major) are shown below.

Fig. 202.

Lie on your back on a bench with dumbbells in your hands (Figure 202). Lift the dumbbells and keep your arms slightly bent in order to avoid overexerting your elbows. The upward movement provides concentric training, and the downward movement provides eccentric training. You can vary the work load by varying the extent to which you bend your elbows. By keeping your arms a little straighter on the way down, you subject the muscle to a little more stress.

Fig. 203.

The same exercise as in Figure 202. This exercise trains only the upper part of the muscle (1) namely, that part which has its origin on the collar bone (i.e. prevents the arm from falling downwards). Other muscles taking part in the exercise are the deltoid muscle (Figure 207) and biceps brachii (see below) (Figure 217).

Fig. 204.

Bending and stretching the arms while the hands are well separated, activates pectoralis major (and triceps brachii, deltoid, serratus anterior and trapezius). Static training is provided when the palms of the hands are pressed together. The position of the hands in front of the body should be varied.

Fig. 205.   *Fig. 206.*

A good way to round off these exercises is to stretch the greater chest muscle following the PNF-method (Figures 205 and 206).

2. Deltoid muscle

Fig. 207.
(a)

Fig. 207.
(b)

3. Broad back muscle (latissimus dorsi)

Fig. 209.

Origin: Outer part of the collar bone, and along the entire spine of the posterior surface of the shoulder blade. (May even be assigned to group A.)

Insertion: Along the shaft of the upper arm (deltoid tuberosity).

Function: Since its origin arches around the shoulder joint, this muscle can take part in all the movements of the arms. Its most important function is to (2) lift the arm straight outwards and upwards (abduction). The parts of the muscle which arise from the posterior surface of the shoulder blade (1) swing the arms backwards and rotate it outwards. The parts which arise from the collar bone (3) swing the arm forward and rotate it inwards.

Fig. 208.

The deltoid is trained in almost all exercises which involve the arm. By lifting as shown in Figure 208, you can train the entire muscle. The work load should not exceed your ability to lift — with almost straight arms — the full distance six to eight times. Lift and lower your arms at the same pace (supraspinatus is also trained in this exercise, see Figure 194).

Origin: The spine of the lower half of the spinal column down to the sacrum and from it out to the crest of the hip bone.

Insertion: Anterior attachment area of the upper arm.

Function: Forms the back wall of the armpit and pulls the arm in behind the back (i.e. swings it backwards and rotates it inwards).

There is usually equipment for training the latissimus in the majority of bodybuilding gymnasiums. Using the special latissimus training apparatus, you should be able to cope with a work load of about six to eight exercises. (For maximal strength.)

By pulling yourself up so that your head comes in front of the bar [Figure 210 (b)], you will train exactly the same muscles as in (a), but with a greater work load (total bodyweight). The biceps brachii (arm bending), trapezius (shoulder blade positioning) and the pectoralis major (upper arm adduction) also take part in this exercise.

Fig. 210.

(a) (b) (c)

Fig. 212.

Inward rotation

Outward rotation

Figure 210 (c) shows how you can train the lattissimus dorsi by pulling on a suspended weight with a rubber hose. In general, this muscle does not need flexibility training. If you bend forcefully to one side and hold your arms outstretched above your head, you may possibly feel the latissimus blocking the movement.

The exercises below are examples of pure shoulder rotation.

Lie on your stomach on a bench with your elbows pointing outwards, and lift a dumbbell backwards (inward rotation) and forwards (outward rotation).

Anterior serrated muscle (serratus anterior)

This plays a very important role in stabilising the shoulder. It arises from eight, nine or even ten ribs, and passes backwards along the rib cage in behind the shoulder blade to be inserted into the medial border of the shoulder blade (should be assigned to group B).

Serratus anterior prevents the shoulder blade from being pressed backwards when the body supports itself on its arms [Figure 213 (a)]. It is trained in all types of exercises where the body is supported by the arms [Figure 213 (c)].

Fig. 211.

Inward rotation of the shoulder   *Outward rotation of the shoulder*

Fig. 213.

(a)

The main muscles helping to inwardly rotate are:

subscapularis,
pectoralis major,
latissimus dorsi,
teres major.

The main outward rotators are:

infraspinatus,
teres minor.

Flexibility of upper arm inward and outward rotation can be tested in the position presented in Fig. 212.

Figure 213 (b) shows how the shoulder blade moves when the serrated muscle contracts.

85

Fig. 213.
(b)

(c)

The two muscles shown in Figure 214 play no significant role in athletics but nevertheless contribute to stabilising the shoulder blade.

Fig. 214.

Figure 214 presents the location of (a) pectoralis minor (lesser breast muscle) and (b) coracobrachialis.

Elbow Joint

Elbow movements occur at three separate joints, namely:

hinge joint between the upper arm and ulna,
pivot joint between the ulna and radius and
ball and socket joint between the upper arm and radius.

Fig. 215.

Upper arm bone (humerus)

a

f

Hinge joint

Ball and socket joint

Pivot joint

g

b

d

e

Radius

Ulna

Right elbow viewed from the front (with the palm of the hand facing forward).

Fig. 216.

Upper arm bone

a

c

Ulna

Radius

Right elbow viewed from the back

The projections and articular surfaces concerned with the function of the elbow joint can be seen in Figures 215 and 216.

(a) Epicondyles give attachment to the muscles which move the hand at the wrist joint.
(b) Radial tuberosity gives attachment to the biceps brachii [Figure 217 (a)].
(c) Elbow outgrowth (olecranon process) gives attachment to triceps brachii (p.89).
(d) The articular surface of the upper arm bone at its hinge joint with the elbow (trochlea = pulley).
(e) Articular surface of the ulna at its hinge joint with the elbow (coronoid process = crown projection).
(f) Articular surface of the ball and socket joint (capitulum = small head).
(g) Head of the radius which forms the "socket" part of the ball and socket joint.

A relatively common difference between men and women can be seen in the elbow projection (c) and the hollow of the upper arm bone into which it is received when the arm is stretched. Because this projection and its corresponding hollow differ, women are more prone to overstretch their elbow joint than men.

Elbow flexion

The three most important flexors are the following.
(a) Two-headed arm muscle (biceps brachii)
    (Bi = two; ceps = head; brachii = upper arm.)

Origin:
1. Caracoid process ("short" tendon).
2. Upper rim of the shoulder blade's articular surface ("long" tendon).
Insertion:
3. Radial tuberosity (a roughened surface at the upper end of the shaft).
Function:
A. Flexes the elbow.
B. Turns the forearm so that the palm of the hand points upward (supination).
C. Swings the upper arm forward (flexion of the shoulder joint).

Fig. 217.

(a)

(b)

(b) **Upper arm muscle**
(brachialis)

Fig. 217.

(c) **Arm-radius muscle** (brachioradialis)
Flexes the elbow and helps control forearm rotation.

Fig. 218.

In order to develop strength in the elbow flexors, the barbell (or whatever) must be grasped with the palms of the hands turned upwards, since this is the only way the biceps can work with maximal strength.

In Figure 218 the girl's hands are supinated (they grasp the bar from underneath). Therefore all her flexors work maximally.

Fig. 219.

In Figure 219 the boy's hands are pronated (they grasp the bar from above), which means that his biceps cannot work maximally. Instead, he subjects his other flexors to a heavier work load. In general training, one should alternate between these two methods. Figure 220 shows arm pull-ups with (a) pronated forearm and (b) supinated forearm.

Fig. 220.

(a)

(b)

The long tendon of origin of the biceps [marked "2" in Figures 217 (a) and 221] passes through the shoulder joint and emerges from the joint capsule at its attachment to the upper arm bone where it descends in a groove between the anterior projection (lesser tuberosity) and the outer projection (greater tuberosity) (Figure 193). Because of this, the biceps contributes greatly to the stability of the shoulder joint. A person who has dislocated his shoulder has, therefore, good reason to build up the strength of his biceps muscle since by doing so he may help to prevent recurrent dislocations.

Biceps strength depends, amongst other things, on the position of the upper arm. If we consider the distance between the origin and insertion of the biceps muscle, we see that it is greater when the arm points straight upwards than when it hangs down.

Fig. 221.

Thus, the capacity of the biceps to bend the arm with force is greater when the arm is directed upwards. The numbers in Figure 222 give the approximate relationship between strength to carry, pull towards the body and lift oneself up.

A reasonable conclusion we can draw from Figure 222 is that the human body is better suited to hang in trees than to carry buckets.

Elbow extension

The elbow extensor (triceps brachii) is attached to the elbow outgrowth (olecranon). It has three heads. One arises from the shoulder blade and the other two from the posterior surface of the upper arm.

Its function is to straighten or extend the elbow and to swing the arm backwards.

A person's strength differs in different positions depending both on the length of his muscles (p.18) and the size of his moment arm into the elbow joint. Notice that the muscle is attached far back on the elbow outgrowth in order to allow the most favourable moment arm possible in all elbow joint positions.

Fig. 222.

Fig. 223.

In this figure the medial head is hidden behind the long head.

Fig. 224.

The extensor's lever arm is least (d_1) when the arm is fully flexed. At the same time, the force of the muscle is greatest. Strength (moment of force) is least when the joint is extended because the muscle force (F_2) is small. The strength of the muscle also depends on the way the arm is held in relation to the shoulder blade. If the arm is stretched out in front of the body, the long head of the triceps is in a worse position (shorter distance between origin and insertion) than if the arm is held straight above the body. Figure 225 shows the approximate relationship between the strength of the triceps brachii in downward, forward, and upward presses.

Fig. 225.

400 N

350 N

500 N

Fig. 226.

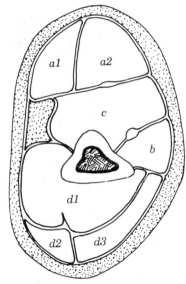

(a) Biceps brachii
a1. Short head
a2. Long head
(b) Brachioradialis
(c) Brachialis
(d) Triceps brachii
d1. Medial head
d2. Long head
d3. Lateral head

Figure 226 is a cross section to show the location and size of the muscles of the right upper arm.

Figure 227 gives suggestions for different exercises for developing strength in the triceps.

Fig. 227.

Wrist joint

The skeleton of the hand consists of eight carpal bones (bones of the wrist), five metacarpal bones (bones of the hand) and 14 phalanges (bones of the fingers).

The hand changes position by movement of the wrist which is a condyloid joint. It is formed by the articulation of three of the wrist bones with the radius.

Fig. 228.

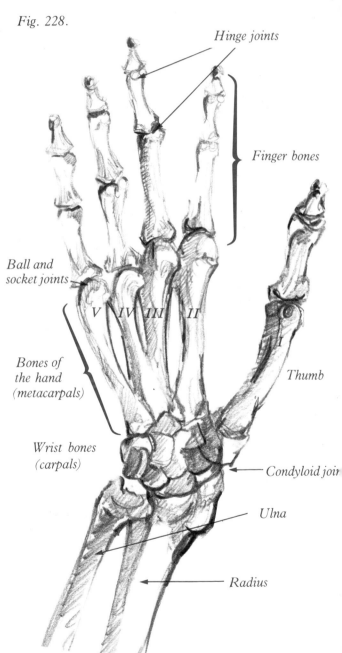

Right hand with palm turned forward [supinated according to Fig. 229 (f)].

The movements allowed at the wrist joint are (Figure 229):

(a) flexion (palms towards you),
(b) extension (palms away from you),
(c) abduction (flat hand tilted outwards) and
(d) adduction (flat hand tilted inwards).

Fig. 229.

The movements involved in turning the hand are called (Figure 229):

(e) pronation and
(f) supination.

Supination and pronation occur between the bones of the forearm (at the pivot joint formed by the ulna and radius, see Figure 215), and not at the wrist joint. The muscles which bring about rotation of the forearm, and thereby turn the hand, are called pronators and supinators. The diagrams below present the most important of these.

Fig. 231.
Pronator teres. Right elbow viewed as in Fig. 229 (f)

Fig. 230.

Fig. 232.

Pronator quadratus Right hand viewed as in Fig. 229 (f)

Supinator
Right elbow viewed as in Fig. 229 (e)

91

However, by far the strongest supinator of the hand is the biceps brachii (p.87).

The supinators are stronger (have a greater moment of force) than the pronators. This relationship has been taken into account in the manufacture of such things as screws. Thus, the thread is constructed in such a way that a right-handed person uses supinated movements to screw it into an object, and thereby allows his muscles to work concentrically. He can easy feel how the biceps brachii works with great force. If the screw is so troublesome that he cannot quite manage it, he locks his wrist (lets supinators work statically (or isometrically) — see the curve on p.20), and thus produces rotation by bending his elbow and rotating his shoulder joint outwards.

Of the 20 or so muscles responsible for the wrist's movements, the largest and most important are those attached to the epicondyles of the upper arm bone (humerus). The abductors and extensors of the wrist arise from the external condyle.

Fig. 233.

Right arm viewed from the back

Figure 233 shows some muscles that are brought into action when a person hits a backhand or lifts a hammer. The concept "tennis elbow" actually means that the area of origin of these muscles is injured.

The following can be seen in Figure 233:

(a) finger extensor (extensor digitorum),
(b) radial-wrist extensor (extensor carpi radialis); passes down the radius and
(c) ulna-wrist extensor (extensor carpi ulnaris); passes down the ulna.

The adductors and flexors of the wrist arise from the internal epicondyle. Adduction and flexion are the movements responsible for such actions as throwing or hitting a forehand smash. Injuries caused by overexertion in these types of activities are called thrower's elbow, golfer's elbow, etc.

All the muscles in Figures 234 and 235 arise from the internal epicondyle:

(d) finger flexor (flexor digitorum),
(e) radial-wrist flexor (flexor carpi radialis) and
(f) ulna-wrist flexor (flexor carpi ulnaris).

Fig. 234.

Right hand with the palm turned forward

For the prevention of such injuries as tennis elbow, strength should be trained in moderate doses. The exercises should subject the elbow to only light work loads. They should provide both static and dynamic training. Movements should be produced in all directions allowed by the wrist. Examples of suitable loads for these exercises are dumbbells, clubs and rackets.

Fig. 235.

Right hand with the palm turned forward

Fig. 236.

Towards the thumb (abduction)

Towards the little finger (adduction)

Bending (flexion)

Stretching (extension)

Fig. 237.

Inward rotation (pronation)

Lock your upper arm against your body

Outward rotation (supination)

The following movements can be recommended for limbering up the wrists and possibly stretching the wrist muscles.

Fig. 238.

(a) Lock your hands loosely and roll them around.

(b) Place your hands on the ground and press lightly. Keep your arms straight. Try to hold your wrists at right angles to your arms.

(c) As in (b), except that you could press the back of your hand against a wall, or use your other hand as shown in the diagram.

Notice that movements involving flexion (c) are somewhat less flexible than those involving extension (b).

Chapter 6

SPORTS MECHANICS

A basic understanding of the laws of mechanics is necessary for the study of movement. When we are familiar with these laws, we can more readily analyse and design suitable exercises. Unfortunately, when athletic performance is described with the aid of the laws of mechanics, the discussion tends to be too theoretical. In this section we will consider a few concepts that are directly applicable to the practical understanding of how and why exercises are performed in a certain way. The concepts I, force; II, centre of gravity; III, moment of inertia, will be described with the aid of diagrams (not formulae). The concept "moment of force" has already been defined on pp.30–35. In addition, it was used in a number of examples in the sections on anatomy (pp.51, 66, 67 and 75). Therefore, moment of force will only be illustrated in this chapter by providing some further examples.

I. Force

Fig. 239.

A force is represented by an arrow (vector). The magnitude of the force is indicated by the length of the arrow shaft and the direction of the force is indicated by the arrow head.

A distinction is made between internal and external forces. The external forces which must be taken into account when studying sports are (Figure 239):

(a) gravitational pull on a body (mg),
(b) force exerted on a body by the ground (called normal force, N),
(c) friction between feet and ground (F_μ) and
(d) air resistance (F_a).

Internal forces are:

(e) muscle forces (F_m) and
(f) tendon, ligament and connective tissue forces (F).

Fig. 240.

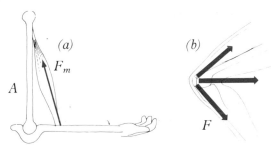

We will now look at some of the properties of these different types of forces.

External Forces
(a) Force of gravity

Fig. 241.

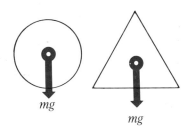

The force of gravity can be thought of as acting on a body at the exact centre of its mass (p.101). This force results from the action of the earth drawing all objects towards its centre. The size of the force depends on the weight or mass of the body being acted upon. Sixty kilogrammes corresponds to about 600 N. Kilogrammes are converted into newtons by using the following relationship: 1 kg = 9.81 N. This conversion factor is represented by the letter g. The gravitational force acting on a body weighing m kilogrammes is thus, m x g newtons, and is written mg.

Fig. 242.

(a) 60 kg *(b)*

70 kg

600 N

700 N

(b) Normal force (*N*)

Fig. 243.

60 kg

600 N

600 N

Normal force is exerted on a body when it comes in contact with the ground. If a person weighing 60 kg, stands still on flat ground, he will be exerting a force of 600 N on the ground. The reaction force exerted on his body by the ground will also be 600 N. Thus, these two forces are equal in size but act in opposite directions and on different objects. They constitute a so-called pair of co-linear forces, where one of the forces is called "action" and the other the "reaction". Some further examples of action – reaction forces are given on p.97.

The magnitude of the normal force depends on the force with which a person presses on the ground (i.e. how heavy he is) and to what extent he activates his hip, knee and ankle extensors. In taking off for a jump, swinging a leg forward while running and landing from a jump, the normal force can be as much as three to four times the body's own weight (*mg*).

Fig. 244.

(a) 1800 N *(b)* 4 mg

mg = 600 N mg

If a person stands and bounces up and down, the normal force acting on him will change. This can be explained by analysing how muscles work. To the skier bending and stretching his legs in Figure 245 the following applies.

His muscles work statically as long as he skis without bending. The normal force is then 600 N if he weighs 60 kg. From 1 to 2 he relaxes his muscles a little, with the result that less pressure is exerted on the ground (i.e. the normal force is reduced to, say, 400 N). From 2 to 3 he halts the downward movement which was present at 2. He accomplishes this by working his muscles eccentrically and

Fig. 245.

F (N)

800

600

400

Time

pressing more forcefully on the ground. From 3 to 4 his muscles work concentrically, and they still press forcefully on the ground (max. 800 N according to our example). At 4 the skier has such upward acceleration that he reaches 5 without pressing especially hard. He can even enjoy a moment's relaxation (400 N). From 5 onwards, he stands still again and his work load will once again be 600 N because his muscles work statically.

Fig. 246.

Fig. 247.

The normal force is also changed when a person swings his arms (Figure 246). Arm movements serve to load and unload the body during different activities. What is the significance of "arm swinging" in running, jumping, landing from a jump, clearing a bar, downhill skiing, kicking a football, vaulting, balancing, etc.? Examine an activity that you are familiar with, and think about the function of the arm movements (Figure 247).

In general, it can be said that a force is needed to change the velocity of the arm. The origin and insertion of the arm muscles are then acted upon by equal but opposing forces (i.e. the arm and the body are affected in different directions see Figure 248).

When the arm is accelerated or halted by, say, the greater chest muscle (pectoralis major) or the broad back muscle (latissimus dorsi), the body is affected

in the opposite direction. The arrows in Figure 249 show how the body is affected when the velocity of the arm changes. The black arrow represents the force acting on the arm and the red arrow represents the force acting on the trunk. The magnitude of the force is the same at the origin of a muscle as it is at its insertion.

Fig. 248.

Fig. 249.

(a)

(b)

If the arm:

(a) moves backwards but is halted,
(b) accelerates backwards,

(c)

(d)

(c) accelerates forwards or
(d) moves forwards but is halted,

then the body will be affected as shown by
the red arrows.

(a)

(b)

Fig. 250.

Normal force is also a part of the action of striking
(a football, golf ball, tennis ball). The normal force
acting on the ball is of the same magnitude as the
normal force acting on the foot [Figure 250 (a)]. It
is said that these normal forces are each others'
action–reaction forces. The force acting on the ball
increases to a maximum when the ball is maximally
compressed, and thereafter decreases to zero. The
situation is the same for the foot or the club.

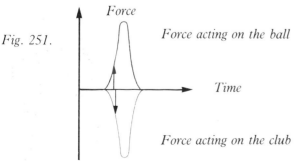

Fig. 251.

Force

Force acting on the ball

Time

Force acting on the club

(c) Friction

Friction is the resistance to motion of two moving
objects· or surfaces that touch. Friction is a force
which depends on the fact that small irregularities
between shoe and ground, racket and ball, skis and
snow, etc., must be evened out if the objects are to
glide against each other.

The magnitude of the force of friction depends on
the kind of materials in contact with each other (the
roughness of their surfaces, μ) and on how hard
the two surfaces are pressed together (N).

Fig. 252.

(a)

(b)

N

F_μ

N

F_μ

(c)

N

F_μ

Example 1 (Figure 253). If an object is exerting a
force of 100 N on the ground, and a force of 20 N is
needed to make it glide along the surface, it is said
that the coefficient of friction (μ) is 20/100 = 0.2.

Fig. 253.

100 N

10 kg

20 N

20 N

Example 2 (Figure 254). If a skier who weighs 60 kg
glides along a horizontal surface — the entire time
being resisted by a force of 30 N — it is said that the
coefficient of friction is 30/600 = 0.05.

Fig. 254.

600 N

30 N

If $\mu = 0$, then there is no friction.
If $\mu = 1$, then we may agree that the object is fixed.

97

(d) Air resistance (F_a)

Fig. 255.

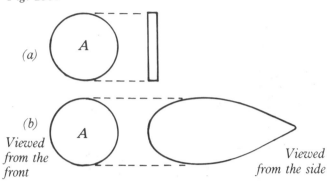

(a)

(b)

Viewed from the front

Viewed from the side

The resistance met by a body moving through air or water depends on the size of its surface area (A) directed forward, its velocity (v) and its form (c).

Two bodies a and b may have the same area when viewed from the front, but very different streamline forms when viewed from the side.

Fig. 256.

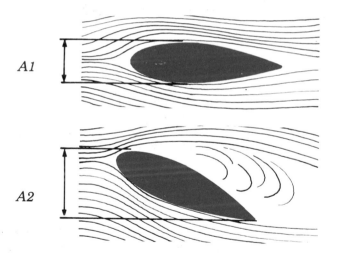

A1

A2

A change of body position often leads to a change in both A and c. The equation of air (water) resistance has been established by experiment: $F_a = A \times v^2 \times c$. Thus, if the area is doubled, the force of resistance will be doubled; doubling the velocity gives four times the force of resistance and improving the streamline form reduces the constant (c), i.e. less air resistance.

The aim in such sports as long jumping, ski jumping, skating and, in particular, downhill skiing, is to reduce air resistance. In swimming, it is especially important to reduce water resistance.

Fig. 257.

(a)

Both the area (A) and the streamline form (c) are greater in (a) than in (b).

(b)

Fig. 258.

(a)   (b)

The breast stroke kick assumes little area (A) while the heels are drawn in towards the buttocks.
Large area when the legs kick backwards.

Internal Forces
(e) Muscle forces

Muscle forces are counted among the so-called internal forces. In order to resist the forces of gravity and friction, or to increase the normal force, the body uses muscle forces. Muscle forces affect the origin and insertion of a muscle to exactly the same extent (Fig. 259), i.e. with equal but opposing forces. The size and structure (position of the centre of gravity) of the body parts A and B are the factors which determine what happens. Also important is whether A and B are free to move, or whether one of them is in some way "fixed".

Fig. 259.

Fig. 261.

Example 1 (Figure 259). If A and B are identical and both are free to move, they will come together much like a folding jack-knife. This is roughly what happens when a person jumps up with a straight back and flexes his hip joint. The iliopsoas muscle pulls his legs up and his trunk down. His legs are a little lighter than his trunk so they travel a longer distance. It is impossible to move the legs alone.

Example 3 (Figure 261). If the weight of the parts differ, the lighter of the two moves the farther. The diagrams below present different situations where both parts rotate in opposition to each other at a joint.

Fig. 262.

Figure 262. If the trunk is rotated in one direction, the skis try to turn in the opposite direction.

Fig. 260.

Example 2 (Figure 260). If B is held stationary, only A will move.

In pole-vaulting, the upper part of the body is lifted over the bar by extending the hip joint and kicking backwards with the legs.

99

Fig. 262.

(c)

(f)

To avoid knocking the bar off with the legs in the flop style high-jump, the hip joint is powerfully flexed once the legs have passed over the bar. By rotating his arms and legs backwards as far as possible, the high-jumper prevents the upper part of his body from rotating, and thus landing on his neck.

When preparing to throw (the discus, or whatever), the skilful athlete pulls his "non-throwing arm" well back as shown in Figure 262 (f). Before actually hurling the object this movement is blocked. The arm is thrust in the opposite direction in order to increase the rotation of the trunk which in turn increases the velocity of the throwing arm.

(f) Tendon and ligament forces

These are passive inner forces. They are brought about by muscle or external forces, i.e. the tendons and ligaments cannot themselves produce force. When subjected to severe stress from without, a ligament may rupture (Figure 263).

(d)

By thrusting his trunk forward and continuing the rotation of his arms, the long-jumper causes an opposing swinging movement of his legs in the landing phase of the jump.

Fig. 263.

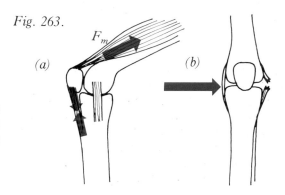

F_m

(a)

(b)

II. Centre of Gravity

The centre of gravity of a body is the point at which it could, in theory, be suspended and remain in equilibrium regardless of its position.

It is easy to discover the centre of gravity in a symmetrical body; it is more difficult to do so in an asymmetrical one. Nevertheless, a trainer should be able to discern just where the centre of gravity of an athlete's body lies in any given situation. By doing so, he can correctly instruct an athlete on how to execute exercises.

(e)

One way to avoid knocking the bar off with the trailing leg in the straddle style high-jump, is to pull the knee up by strongly flexing the hip joint once the body has cleared the bar.

Fig. 264.

Fig. 265.

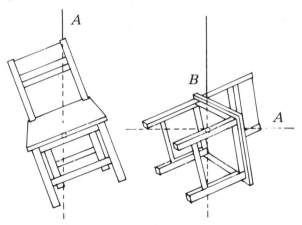

The centre of gravity of a rigid body can be determined by experiment in the following way: hang the body freely at an arbitrary point A. The centre of gravity will lie on the vertical straight line passing through A. Hanging the body from some other point B gives another straight line on which the centre of gravity lies. Clearly, the centre of gravity is the intersection of the two lines (Figure 265).

Fig. 266.

The centre of gravity of a human body standing in the anatomical position (Figure 266), lies approximately in line with the navel a few centimetres in front of the third lumbar vertebra. Naturally, the location of the centre of gravity changes with changes in body position (e.g. when an arm or leg is raised). If the centre of gravity in Figure 266 lies 100 cm above the ground it will rise about 4 cm when an arm is raised, 8 cm when both arms are raised, 8 cm if the body stands on its toes, etc. (see Figure 267).

Fig. 267.

Figure 267 demonstrates how the centre of gravity varies in relation to the ground.

If a person jumps up so that her centre of gravity reaches 150 cm above the ground (Figure 268), a change in body position will not affect the height of the centre of gravity in relation to the ground. Once the body has left the ground its position on the way up will not affect the maximal height of the centre of gravity.

Fig. 268.

Figure 268 shows that, although the centre of gravity reaches the same height in all four jumps, the height of the hand and head above the ground varies with the final position. If both arms are lowered, the body is raised 8 cm. If one leg is raised, the rest of the body will be lowered 8 cm (cf. diagrams overleaf). The explanation is quite simply that the muscle group which lifts the leg (e.g.

iliopsoas) affects the rest of the body with an equal but opposing force, i.e. pulls the body down.

Fig. 269.

The pattern of movement in such activities as the jump shot in handball, shooting in basketball, smash in volleyball, kick in football, clearing the bar in high jump and pole vault, hurdling, etc., is built on the principles outlined above.

Notice that by keeping the left arm and both legs straight at the moment of shooting, the right hand will be raised to a maximal height (Figure 269).

Fig. 270.

By holding both arms and right leg as high as possible, the left leg will reach the ground at the earliest possible moment, and the hurdler can begin to run again (Figure 270).

Fig. 271.

Figure 271 further illustrates variations in centre of gravity location. Hip flexion causes the centre of gravity to vary in three different ways depending on the situation.

Figure 272(a) shows where the centre of gravity lies in a certain part of the body expressed as a percentage of its length. For example, the centre of gravity of the arm lies at a point which — measured from the shoulder downward — corresponds to 40% of its length. The figures shown in (b) give the mass of each body part expressed as a percentage of total body weight. For example, the weight of the head is 7% that of the whole body.

Fig. 272.

The diagrams and calculations in Figure 273 show how we can make a total assessment of different exercises, once we know the location of the centre of gravity of a body, its moment of force and the function and position of its muscles.

Fig. 273.

Suppose a person hangs so that the centre of gravity of her legs (45% of the leg's length from the hip) lies 0.40 m directly out from her hip in (a), 0.30 m in (b) and 0.30 m in (c). If her legs weigh 25 kg (18.5% of her total body weight per leg), then the gravitational force acting on them will be 250 N. The moment of force of (a), (b) and (c), will then be:

(a) $M = F \times d$
  $M = 250 \times 0.40$
  $M = 100$ Nm.

(b) $M = F \times d$
  $M = 250 \times 0.30$
  $M = 75$ Nm.

(c) $M = F \times d$
  $M = 250 \times 0.30$
  $M = 75$ Nm.

Fig. 274

0.05

Suppose the iliopsoas is the muscle holding the legs, and that its lever arm is 0.05 m (Figure 274). Then,

(a) $F \times 0.05 = 100$
  $F = 2000$ N.

(b) $F \times 0.05 = 75$
  $F = 1500$ N.

(c) $F \times 0.05 = 75$
  $F = 1500$ N.

Fig. 275.

(b)

(a)

All those who have tried position (b) (Figure 273) know that it is almost impossible, despite the fact that the muscle force in (b) and (c) is the same according to the calculations. However, the iliopsoas is longer in (c) than in (b), and thus more capable of exerting sufficient force. In (b) the distance between the origin and insertion of the muscle is perhaps less than 50% of its resting length. This means that the muscle cannot develop any force at all (p.18). Another reason why it is

"impossible" to hold the legs in position (b) is that the hamstrings (p.54) are so drawn out that they try to pull the legs down with great force much like an elastic band strives to return to its resting length.

In the situations shown in Figure 275, the interplay between hip flexion strength and hamstring flexibility, is of decisive importance for the pattern of movement.

If the legs or upper body are folded forward too early, the legs cannot be held in the best position for landing. Instead, the body "opens" so that the feet land too soon.

The following observation is made to illustrate further the centre of gravity concept and its importance. When a person lifts an object, different muscles will be engaged depending on how he moves the object.

Fig. 276.

d

(a)   *(b)*   *d*

If he lifts as in Figure 276 (a), the work load to which his elbow flexors are subjected, will be less than if he lifts as shown in (b) (shorter lever arm *d*). The work load to which the shoulder joint is subjected is almost zero in (a) but very large in (b).

Fig. 277.

Training the elbow flexors for strength using a support for the upper arm (Figure 277), forces the elbow flexors to work the "heavy way" and, at the same time disengages the shoulder muscles.

Fig. 278.

Fig. 280.

Fig. 281.

In the forward swing on the horizontal bar (Figure 278), it is important to be so arched at the hip that the legs can be lifted quickly as the gymnast approaches the forward limit of his swing. Thus, his hips should be kept as straight as possible in positions 1-4. If his hips are piked at 1–2, then his legs will start falling (i.e. they will be on their way down when it is time for them to be lifted).

Fig. 282.

Fig. 279.

Fig. 283.

Because the centre of gravity of the head lies a few centimetres in front of the upper cervical vertebra (Figure 279), the neck muscles (F_m) are forced to work statically to hold it up. The centre of gravity of the upper body lies in front of the spine.

Therefore, the back muscles are activated. The full weight of the trunk is concentrated to a point which lies a little in front of the hip joint (varies greatly between individuals). Because of this, the buttock muscles are engaged. Quadriceps femoris counteracts the tendency of the body's weight to produce flexion at the knee joint. Soleus (with the help of gastrocnemius counteracts the body's tendency to fall forward at the ankle joint. The function of all these muscles is to maintain the body's upright position. They are called postural muscles (Figures 280 and 281).

When a particular part of the body is to be moved, it is very important to be aware of the location of the centre of gravity. When an object is to be swung or whirled around, it can be shown that it is easier to initiate the movement when the radius of rotation is small. A hammer whose wire has a radius of 0.5 m is easier to swing than one whose wire is, say, 1 m. A hammer with a 3 m long wire sling would be completely unmanageable.

If a person wants to swing his leg quickly forward while running, it is important that he keep the swing radius as small as possible (Figure 284). This can be accomplished by pulling the heel up towards the buttock (3) as soon as the foot leaves the ground (1). The leg is then swung forward with its centre of gravity as close as possible to the hip.

Fig. 284.

Sprinting　　　　　　*Long distance running*

This type of running is typical for sprinters. Long distance runners, on the other hand, do not waste energy by lifting the heel so high (which requires strength and speed of the hamstrings). Instead, they have time to allow the leg to swing forward aided by the force of gravity and the hip flexors.

The arm is bent in the initial stage of almost any throwing or hitting event (Figure 285). As long as the shoulder muscles are accelerating the arm, the centre of gravity of the arm should be close to the shoulder. When throwing an object, the muscle groups are activated in the order: abdomen, shoulder, elbow, wrist.

Fig. 285.

The pattern is the same when kicking a football (Figure 286). The muscles are then activated in the order: abdomen, hip, knee.

Fig. 286.

On p.99 it was pointed out that when two parts of a body of equal weight are brought together, they move symmetrically. This is only true when the distance between the centre of gravity and the joint is the same for both.

Fig. 287.

If this is not the case, the part whose centre of gravity is farthest away from the joint will move through a smaller angle. This phenomenon is often used in athletics.

Thus, for effective movement at a joint, the parts of the joint should be arranged in such a way that the centre of gravity of the part to be moved lies close to the joint, while the centre of gravity of the other lies far from it.

The following four examples [Figure 288 (a)–(d)] illustrate this principle when the legs are swiftly swung forward.

Fig. 288.

Example (a). By maximally flexing the knee, the centre of gravity of the leg is brought to a point near the hip joint. This makes the leg easy to swing forward. The centre of gravity of the upper body should, in principle, lie far from the hip joint, which implies that the arms should be relatively well flexed.

Example (b). Before swinging his legs forward a long jumper first bends them maximally behind him (Cg near the hips) and, at the same time, stretches his arms high above his head (Cg far above the hips).

Example (c). If a hurdler wants to make the most of the muscle force of his hip flexors, he should hold both his arms as far from his hips as possible (right arm straight, left arm bent). His right leg should remain bent on the way up and he should wait as long as possible before straightening it.

Example (d). When a footballer heads the ball, his whole upper body should be moving quickly. Here, the centre of gravity of his upper body should lie near his hips (arms by his sides). The moment the ball is hit, the centre of gravity of his legs should lie far from his hips (straight legs). Imagine how ineffective a header would be if made from a position corresponding to that shown in example (b), above.

The following five examples [Figures 289 (a)–(c) and 290 (a) and (b)] show how to arrange the body when making arm movements.

Fig. 289.

Example (a). If a person moves his arm in an arc in front of his body, his body will respond by rotating in the opposite direction. If his arm is bent, his body moves less. This and other similar effects can easily be observed with the aid of a mobile platform (turntable) or swivel chair.

Example (b). To roll his trailing leg (left) over the bar in the straddle style high jump, the high-jumper should pull his right arm in the opposite direction. Notice how the right arm changes position and rotates up behind the back in diagrams 2 and 3, below. The arm should be held straight and a long way from the body.

(c)

Example (c). A straight arm that counters the rotation of the body is more effective for throwing than a bent arm that merely pulls in towards the body.

Fig. 290.

(a)

Example (a). When landing, the action of pulling the arms backwards and downwards causes the body to rotate in the opposite direction (or, the arm movements reduce the body rotation).

As a result, the feet land further to the left in (a) than would be the case without arm movements.

(b)

Example (b). If the arms are pulled down in front of the body, the feet will land further to the right in (b). This is due to the opposing arm movement. The muscles that pull the arms down arise from the chest and therefore must draw the body up. If the arms are kept straight, the opposing movement of the body is greater than if the arms are bent. If the arms are pulled outwards and downwards the body's rotation is not affected.

III. Moment of Inertia

The previous examples show that the further out from the centre of rotation the centre of gravity of a particular part of the body lies, the greater is the force required of the muscles to set it in motion. Of course, the mass (weight) of the body part is also important. The more the body part weighs, the more force is needed to set it in motion (or stop it).

In physics, the term moment of inertia is used to describe not only the weight of a body but also how

Fig. 291.

Small moment of inertia	Large moment of inertia

(a)
(b)
(c)
(d)
(e)

far from the axis of rotation the centre of gravity of the body lies. The figures in the left-hand column in Figure 291 have less moment of inertia than their counterparts in the right-hand column.

In physics the letter I is used to symbolise moment of inertia. In order to determine the moment of inertia of a body we must know its mass (m) and its rotational radius (r). The moment of inertia is

$$I = mr^2.$$

Fig. 292.

(a)

$r = 3$ meter, $m = 5$ kg, $I = 5 \times 3^2 = 5 \times 9 = 45$ kgm^2

(b)

$r = 2$ meter, $m = 10$ kg, $I = 10 \times 2^2 = 10 \times 4 = 40$ kgm^2

$I = (5 \times 2^2) + (5 \times 2^2) = (5 \times 4) + (5 \times 4) = 40$ kgm^2

(c)

(d)

$I = 5 \times 0.2^2 = 5 \times 0.04 = 0.2$ kgm^2

(e)

$I = 5 \times 0.3^2 = 5 \times 0.09 = 0.45$ kgm^2

(f)

$I = 10 \times 0.3^2 = 10 \times 0.09 = 0.9$ kgm^2

The underlined numbers in Figure 292 give an idea of how great a force must be exerted in order to set the different bodies in motion.

If we want to calculate the moment of inertia of a body rotating about its own centre of gravity (which happens in all flights through the air), we do the following.

Fig. 293.

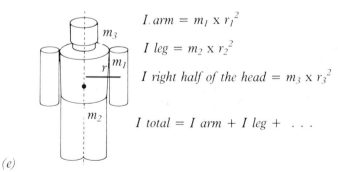

$I.\, arm = m_1 \times r_1^2$

$I\, leg = m_2 \times r_2^2$

$I\, right\, half\, of\, the\, head = m_3 \times r_3^2$

$I\, total = I\, arm + I\, leg + \ldots$

It has been shown with this type of calculation that the moment of inertia for rotation about a body's longitudinal axis varies as the body takes on different positions. In Figure 294 variations in body position are compared with the anatomical position (I).

Fig. 294.

The moment of inertia will increase as more body segments move away from the longitudinal axis of rotation, i.e. as the distance (r) to the axis increases.

The moment of inertia for forward and backward rotation (vault) varies roughly according to the following data.

Fig. 295.

It has been shown by experiment that when a body is made to rotate by some force and thereafter left to rotate without being influenced by other external forces, its rotational velocity (w) will depend on its position. It is said that moment of inertia x rotational velocity does not change. I x w = constant. This has the following consequences:

Fig. 296.

Example 1. If a person who is rotating with his arms by his sides (I) at a certain rotational velocity (w) lifts his arms out, he will reduce his rotational velocity by half (w/2). The moment of inertia will be changed from I to 2I by this change in his position.

If he sinks down to a half sitting position, I will be changed to 4I, and hence his rotational velocity (w) is reduced to a quarter (w/4). An example of such changes being brought about is the execution of a pirouette: jumping – pirouette – landing (Figure 296).

Fig. 297.

Example 2. In certain kinds of turns in skiing, the skier starts from a deep position (e.g. 4I) and stands during the swing (2I). He thus roughly doubles his initial rotation (Figure 297).

Fig. 298.

Example 3. When coming out of a turn, the skier can reduce his rotational velocity to about a half by dropping down to a deeper position (from 2I to 4I). Hence, he will find it easier to steer straight again (Figure 298).

Fig. 299.

Example 4. In the take off of the straddle style high jump, the body reaches a position of great rotational inertia about an axis which is parallel to the bar [Figure 299 (a)]. If the jumper cannot quickly change his position, he risks knocking the bar off with his trailing leg. This is because his rotation is very slow in this position. When he comes to straddle the bar with his trailing leg, it is important that his rotational velocity is at a maximum, i.e. the moment of inertia should be minimal. He does this by keeping his body straight and his arms close to his sides [Figure 299 (b)].

Fig. 300.

Example 5. The flop style high jumper rotates backwards with greater speed if he arches his back than if his body is straight. He has better stability against sideward rotation if he holds his arms out than if he keeps them close to his body (Figure 300).

Fig. 301.

Example 6. A thrower increases the total rotational velocity of his body (and thus the velocity of his throwing arm) in the following way. In the final phase of the throw, he rises from a relatively low position to one which centres all the parts of his body — except his throwing arm — around the rotational axis (Figure 301).

Fig. 302.

Example 7. A swimmer starts a front crawl flip turn by flipping his legs down against the water (which resists by pressing against him as shown by the arrows in Figure 302). His hands also press in the "wrong direction". By piking at the hip, he makes the water press against his back. These three measures have given him a certain rotational velocity (w). At this point, he folds up maximally, thereby doubling the rotational velocity he acquired.

Fig. 303.

(a)   (b)   (c)

Example 8. A gymnast who wants to rotate about a bar (wheel swing) has greater difficulty in swinging around if her body is kept completely straight [Figure 303 (a)] than if there is a slight piking at her hips (b). By piking slightly she shifts her centre of gravity to a place outside her body, i.e. near the bar. If she tries to swing around by pulling her head backwards, that is by arching slightly, her difficulties will only increase (c).

APPLICATIONS

This chapter concludes with an example of how we can analyse athletic performance when we are knowledgeable in anatomy and the laws of mechanics. On the basis of such an analysis, strength and flexibility training should be designed to suit the different needs of the individual athlete. The sports technique we will examine here as an illustration, is the long jump (Figure 304). We will consider in sequence: (a) run-up, (b) take-off, (c) flight and (d) landing. For each of these we will determine which muscles are active and how they work (concentrically, eccentrically, statically). We will also determine which muscles require a wide range of movement, i.e. ought to be trained for flexibility.

Fig. 304.

A. Run-up

Look at the way your foot strikes the ground. To minimise the risk of injury, the outer border of your heel should be the part of your foot which first makes contact with the ground. Make sure your foot is pointing straight ahead of you, in the direction you are running. In general, striking the ground with the whole foot or the front of the foot first while the foot is pointed slightly outward, leads to complaints of pain in the lower leg (periostitis, p.61). Strong knee extensors (quadriceps femoris, p.49) are essential for swinging the leg forward in running but above all, for the correct heel strike. In the swing phase, the hip extensors (gluteus maximus and hamstrings) should be so long and so relaxed that they do not prevent a proper forward swing, i.e. hip flexion with pelvis pressed forward. During the forward swing the body is supported in the forefoot of the stance phase foot, therefore the calf muscles (triceps surae, p.57) must be strong enough to prevent the body sinking "backwards" at the ankle while the knee and hip extensors work. The calf muscles work statically during part of the stance phase, and concentrically in the latter stages (Figure 305).

The heel should be pulled towards the buttocks as early as possible, [i.e. concentric work for the knee flexors (hamstrings, p.53)], during the swing phase. This also provides flexibility training for the knee extensors (quadriceps, p.49) and keeps the moment of inertia of the leg to a minimum during its forward swing. Thus, the speed of the forward swing is dependent on the strength of the hip flexors and the knee flexors, as well as flexibility of the knee extensors. According to the above, training ought to concentrate on: 1, strengthening the iliopsoas, hamstrings, quadriceps and triceps surae, and 2, stretching the iliopsoas and quadriceps.

Fig. 305.

(a)

(b)

111

B. Take-off

At take-off the body has maximal speed. For a body travelling at a certain speed to reach as far as possible in a long jump, its angle of take-off should theoretically be about 45° (Figure 306). In practice, however, the jumper must hold back, i.e. steal some of his approach speed, in order to project himself upwards. To reach a take-off angle of 45°, the force with which he gathers for upward thrust must be so great and directed so far back that his speed after take-off would be too low. The difficulty of taking-off effectively lies thus in obtaining sufficient height without losing too much horizontal velocity.

Fig. 306.

Theoretically, a jumper can take-off without reducing his speed only if the force of take-off is directed straight upwards. This would require a lightning swift upward thrust from a low position.

Fig. 307.

Short final stride.

In some take-off styles the jumper takes a long third "last stride" and in so doing lowers his centre of gravity. By making the final stride relatively short, he is able to plant his lift-off foot on the ground vertically from above (Figure 307). From that low position, there is even a possibility of projecting the body upwards *and* forwards.

Fig. 308.

Attempts to obtain height in this way — without losing speed — result in take-off angles of about 20–25° and — with a reduction in speed of about 30%. This style requires an explosive forward thrust of the hip, knee and ankle (Figure 308).

Fig. 309.

Long final stride.

The jumper may also obtain height by making a long final stride (Figure 309) and keeping his lift-off leg straighter than in the style outlined above. Now the muscles responsible for take-off are more hip extensor muscles (gluteal muscles, p.39) than knee extensors.

These styles of take-off in the long jump can be compared with the high jump styles. Dive Straddle (deep knee flexion and emphasised free arm and leg movements) and Fosbury Flop (greater speed of approach and bracing of the lift-off leg as strength of the hip is essential here).

We could also make comparisons between take-off styles in such sports as volleyball, football (to head the ball) and the like, when taking note of the speed of approach, i.e. the take-off styles requiring high approach speed compared with those requiring low approach speed.

C. Flight

Whatever the take-off style, the jumper usually has a certain forward rotation. This rotation can be "cancelled" by adopting certain in-the-air techniques such as [Figure 310 (a)] hang or (b) hitch-kick.

Fig. 310.
(a)

(a) If the jumper has a large forward rotation, he must lie outstretched in the air in order to avoid rotating so far that he arrives in an unfavourable position for landing. The speed of rotation is controlled by the body's moment of inertia (p.107). The more he folds together, the greater (faster) will be his rotation. The less rotation the jumper acquires from take-off, the sooner he can adopt a position that is advantageous for minimising air resistance.

(b)

(b) If the rotation is "too great", it must be countered by an opposing movement, i.e. the arms and legs should rotate in the same direction. If the arms move according to the arrow ➤ the body will move in the opposite direction at the shoulder joint, i.e. forward rotation is *"cancelled"*. A backward rotation of the legs according to the arrow ➤ causes the pelvis to tip in the other direction at the hip joint, i.e. forward rotation is "cancelled".

D. Landing

Landing requires good flexibility of the hamstrings and of the lower back. A maximal hip piking before touchdown requires long muscles at the back of the thigh in order to avoid striking the ground with the heels too soon.

Maximal jump length is obtained when the heels touch down at the point where the centre of gravity of the body would have landed (Figure 311). If the heel strike is too far in front of this point, the jumper will land on his buttocks. If his heels touch down too close to the take-off board, he will be seen to rotate forward at touchdown and, of course, his result will be poor.

Fig. 311.

In a perfect landing, the jumper is pressed together like an accordion, which subjects his knees to great stress. Therefore, his training must include deep knee flexion in order to prevent acute injuries.

Chapter 7
HINTS FOR STRETCHING

Examples of strength training and stretching exercises for different muscle groups accompany each section of the book, each of which describes a part of the body. The following diagrams summarise and complement these examples with positions that are designed to lengthen muscles and thereby increase the range of movement of a given body part. Sometimes several different positions are given for the same muscle group. It is up to you to choose the position (positions) that is (are) best suited to your particular needs. If you are "stiff" certain positions will be suitable, or if your body is already rather flexible others should be chosen. Test the methods to find those that best suit you.

Some variations of stretching methods, namely, elastic stretching, stretching and the PNF-method, were described on pp.24–26. It should be pointed out that all types of flexibility training aim at producing a more flexible body; i.e. reaching the outer limits of the body's range of movement is the ultimate goal. Stretching is excellent for restoring a shortened muscle (due to injury or incorrect training methods) to its normal length. When a muscle has regained its normal length, it can be "taught" to function correctly by submitting it to flexibility training consisting of flexibility and elastic stretching exercises.

Dancers have trained flexibility with elastic stretching for centuries; they provide excellent proof that this method of training yields good results. It cannot be stressed too strongly that it is essential to warm up before undertaking intensive exercise. Although a person can raise the temperature of particular muscles by static contraction (which is a part of the PNF-method), if he wants to raise his entire body temperature substantially and at the same time subject his joints to all-round stress, he should begin any athletic activity with a well prepared "running–gymnastics-programme"

1. Stretching exercises should be part of warming-up. Do not be afraid to make easy elastic stretches towards the outer limits of your range of movement, after you have first stretched in the ordinary manner for about 30 seconds. Muscle spindles (p.21) are sensitive to both position (stretching) and speed (elastic stretching); therefore muscles must become accustomed to moving towards the body's outer limits at a moderate speed.

2. Either stretching exercises or PNF exercises should be a part of special training sessions where the aim is to increase the length of a particular muscle group. Once he has been given suitable instructions, the athlete ought to be able to conduct these training sessions himself during periods (three times a week to increase flexibility; once or twice a week to maintain it) that do not interfere with such other training as team practice.

3. Stretching should be practised after heavy training sessions in order to avoid stiffness, soreness and muscular aches the following day. In this situation, stretching has the effect of lightly massaging the muscles.

Keep the principal objective in mind: a more flexible body.

Positions for stretching and elastic stretching exercises for muscles which pass over:

The front of the ankle (extensors, p.60)

Fig. 312.

(a)   (b)   (c)

Do you find it difficult to sit comfortably on your heels? If so, this is due to your knees. Therefore, you must not try to lower yourself by stretching elastically if your knees hurt!

Goal: Stretched, or somewhat overstretched ankle.

Back part of the ankle (flexors, p.57)

Goal: That the muscles at the back of the ankle shall not restrict the natural flexibility of the ankle. Short foot muscles may produce high tension in the muscles at the front of the lower leg which could easily lead to "periostitis".

Fig. 313.

(a)

(b)

(c)

Knee joint and front part of the hip (quadriceps femoris and iliopsoas, pp.49 and 43)

Goal: To be capable of initiating a forward swing (during sprinting or kicking a football, for example) of a leg whose starting position is well behind the body.

Fig. 314.

(d)

(h)

(e)

(g)

(f)

Knee joint and back part of the hip (hamstrings, p.53)

Goal: Sufficient flexibility to allow a person to "fall" forward at the hip and not tax his back unnecessarily by "bouncing". Short muscles at the back of the thigh generally lead to lower back pain.

Fig. 315.

Fig. 316.

Outer part of the hip (abductors, p.39)

Goal: To increase flexibility of the hip and at the same time stretch the tendon band which extends from the crest of the hip bone down to the outer surface of the knee (iliotibial tract, Figure 90). A tendon band that is too taut can lead to friction injuries of the outer condyle of the shin bone (tibia) in, for example, the long distance runner (runner's knee).

Fig. 317.

(a)

(b)

(c)

Inner part of the hip (adductors, pp. 41 and 42)

Goal: Increased flexibility for avoidance of groin injuries. Increased flexibility makes possible longer running strides, better forward swing in ice-skating, longer stopping strides when attacking in badminton or tennis, etc.

(d)

Back and abdomen (erector spinae and abdominal muscles, pp.68–73)

Goal: To increase flexibility of forward bending of the back. The diagrams (Figure 318) demonstrate positions that allow you to alternate between easy elastic stretching and relaxation.

(a)

(b)

Fig. 318.

(c)

(d)

(e)

(f)

(g)

(h)

(i)

The diagrams shown in Figure 319 demonstrate elastic stretching and positions suitable for sideward bending and rotation of the back.

Fig. 319.

Shoulder joint (pp.78–86)

Goal: Increased flexibility of the shoulder which is often necessary in such sports as badminton, tennis, golf, handball and swimming.

Fig. 320.

Fig. 320.

Wrist (p.91)

Goal: Dorsiflexion flexibility. Applies to racket sports.

Fig. 321.

Towel routine

It is easy to train strength and flexibility with the aid of a towel. The four exercises shown in Figures 322–325 provide an example of how you can work dynamically with elastic stretches in order to increase the strength and flexibility of your shoulders.

The position in exercise 3 is good for stretching the triceps brachii. There is seldom any need of stretching exercises for the muscles which pass over the elbow joint.

By using your imagination, you can easily develop your own exercises. It is a good idea to work in pairs. In that way you can both provide sufficient resistance to your partner in exercises that demand strength.

Fig. 322.

Exercise 1. keep the towel taut and "dry" the back of your neck. Make sure that your grip is such that you can pull one of your arms with the other and thereby increase its flexibility "a little bit" each time. Do 20–30 of these.

Fig. 323.

Exercise 2. Take a hold of the towel in such a way that your hands are far enough apart to allow you to move both arms over your head as you alternate between lowering the towel in front of your thighs and behind them. Keep your arms straight and the towel taut. Move your arms closer to each other as you become more flexible. Do the exercise 20–30 times.

Fig. 324.

Exercise 3. "Dry your back" Pull your right (bent) arm down with the aid of your left (straight) arm. After that, pull your straight arm up "a little bit further" with the aid of your bent arm. Do the exercise 10 times with bent right arm and 10 times with bent left arm.

Fig. 325.

Exercise 4. (a) Hold the towel with your hands so far apart that you can (b) move the towel alternately in front of and behind your body with straight arms. Swimming with "backstrokes" takes the towel to the behind-your-back position, and "forward strokes" takes it to its original position. Do the exercise 20 times for each arm.

REVIEW OF RELEVANT MUSCLES

Fig. 326

LIST OF NAMES OF THE MUSCLES SHOWN IN FIGURES
326, 327 and 328

1 Sterno-cleido-mastoid
2 Trapezius
3 Deltoid
4 Pectoralis major
5 Biceps brachii
6 Triceps brachii
7 Brachioradialis
8 Extensor carpi radialis longus and brevis
9 Extensor digitorum
10 Extensor carpi ulnaris
11 Flexor carpi ulnaris
12 Latissimus dorsi
13 Teres major
14 Infraspinatus
15 Teres minor
16 Supraspinatus
17 Rhomboid major
18 Rhomboid minor
19 Levator scapulae
20 Serratus anterior
21 External oblique
22 Rectus abdominis
23 Tensor fascia latae
24 Sartorius
25 Gluteus maximus
26 Iliopsoas
27 Pectineus
28 Adductor longus
29 Gracilis
30 Semitendinosus
31 Semimembranosus
32 Rectus femoris
33 Vastus medialis
34 Vastus lateralis
35 Biceps femoris
36 Gastrocnemius
37 Soleus
38 Peroneus longus
39 Peroneus brevis
40 Tibialis anterior
41 Extensor hallucis longus
42 Extensor digitorum longus
43 Tibialis posterior
44 Flexor hallucis longus
45 Flexor digitorum longus

Fig. 327

Fig. 328

1 2 3 4 5
6
12
12
20
20
21
22
25
23
24
26
27
28
29
35
32
33
35
34
40
23
24
26
27
28
29
30
31
32
33
36
37
43

125

Tables of the body's most important muscles, together with their origin, insertion and function. In the accompanying diagrams: the origin and insertion are marked.

Muscles which pass across the hip joint only (pp.39–46)

Muscle	Origin	Insertion	Function
Gluteus maximus (large buttock muscle)	Posterior part of the hip bone crest, the sacrum and coccyx and coccyx	Outer surface of the femur just below the greater trochanter and a strong tendon band on its outer side (iliotibial tract)	Straightens and adducts the hip, rotates the thigh outwards, and takes part in straightening the knee
Gluteus medius (intermediate buttock muscle)	Outer surface of the ilium	Greater trochanter	Primarily an abductor and rotator of the hip
Gluteus minimus (small buttock muscle)	Outer surface of the ilium immediately beneath and behind the intermediate buttock muscle	Greater trochanter	Same as the intermediate buttock muscle. Both are active during walking, and both stabilise the pelvis
Pectineus (comb muscle)	Upper border of the pubic bone	High on the posterior surface of the femur (pectineal line)	Adducts, flexes and rotates the hip outwards
Adductor brevis (short adductor)	Lower border of the pubic bone	Linea aspera	Adducts the hip and rotates it outwards
Adductor longus (long adductor)	Near the symphysis pubis of the pubic bone	Linea aspera	Adducts the hip
Adductor magnus (large adductor)	Two parts. One from the pubic bone and the other from the ischial tuberosity	Linea aspera and the medial condyle	Adducts the hip. Can also rotate it inwards
Psoas major (great lumbar muscle)	Side of dorsal vertebra 12 and lumbar vertebrae 1–5	These two muscles go under the common name of iliopsoas, which is attached to the lesser trochanter	Bends the hip. Rotates the leg outwards and can also bend the vertebral column sideways
Iliacus (haunch muscle)	Entire inner surface of the ilium		

Muscles which pass across both the hip and knee joints (pp.49–56)

Muscle	Origin	Insertion	Function
Rectus femoris (straight thigh muscle)	Anterior inferior iliac spine and margin of the acetabulum	Kneecap (patella) via quadriceps tendon	Straightens the knee and bends the hip
Gracilis (slender thigh muscle)	Pubic bone	As for semitendinosus	Adducts the hip and bends the knee and rotates it inwards
Tensor fascia latae (tensor of the fascia of the thigh)	Outer surface of the anterior superior iliac spine	Into strong tendon band of the thigh fascia (iliotibial tract)	Bends and abducts the hip and straightens the knee
Biceps femoris (two-headed thigh muscle)	Ischial tuberosity and linea aspera	Head of the fibula	Straightens (extends) the hip. Bends the knee and rotates it outwards
Semitendinosus	Ischial tuberosity	Top of the inner surface of the tibia	Straightens the hip. Bends the knee and rotates it inwards
Semimembranosus	Ischial tuberosity	Several sites on and around the internal condyle of the tibia	Straightens the hip. Bends the knee and rotates it inwards
Sartorius (tailor's muscle)	Anterior superior iliac spine	As for semitendinosus	Bends, abducts and rotates the hip outwards. Bends the knee and rotates it inwards

Muscles which pass across the knee joint only (p.50)

Muscle	Origin	Insertion	Function
Vastus medialis	Medial and posterior surface of the femur	Direct to the kneecap	Together with the straight thigh muscle, these muscles form the so-called four-headed thigh muscle (quadriceps femoris)
Vastus intermedius	Anterior surface of the femur	Kneecap via the quadriceps tendon	
Vastus lateralis	Posterior surface of the femur	Kneecap via the quadriceps tendon	The vasti muscles straighten the knee. The straight thigh muscle also bends the hip
Popliteus	Posterior surface of the lateral femoral condyle	Posterior surface of the internal condyle of the tibia	Bends the knee and rotates it inwards. ("Unlocks" the knee joint)

Muscles which pass across both the knee joint and the ankle (p.57)

Muscle	Origin	Insertion	Function
Gastrocnemius (twin calf muscle)	Posterior surface of the medial and lateral femoral condyles	Tuber calcanci (heel bone)	Bends the knee and straightens the ankle (plantarflexion)

Muscles which pass across the ankle only (p.60)

Muscle	Origin	Insertion	Function
Soleus (flounder muscle)	Head of the fibula and from the oblique line of the tibia	Heel bone. Joins with the twin calf muscle to form the three-headed calf muscle (triceps surae)	Standing on your toes (plantarflexion)
Tibialis anterior (anterior shin bone muscle)	Upper end of the tibia	Intermediate cuneiform and the 1st metatarsal bone	Dorsiflexion and supination
Extensor hallucis longus (long great toe extensor)	Fibula and the membrane situated between the fibula and tibia	Great toe	Dorsiflexion and pronation of the ankle. Straightens the great toe
Extensor digitorum longus (long toe extensor)	Membrane between the fibula and tibia as well as the fascia of the lower legs	All the toes except the great toe	Dorsiflexion and pronation of the ankle. Stretches the toes
Peroneus longus (long calf muscle)	Upper part of the fibula	Its tendon of insertion passes behind the external malleolus, crosses the sole of the foot and is inserted into the great toe and the internal cuneiform bone	Builds up the transverse arch. Dorsiflexion and pronation of the ankle
Peroneus brevis (short calf muscle)	Lower part of the fibula	Fifth metatarsal bone	Dorsiflexion and pronation of the ankle
Flexor hallucis longus (long flexor of the great toe)	Posterior surface of the fibula	Underside of the great toe	Plantarflexion and supination. Bends the toes
Flexor digitorum longus (long toe flexor)	Posterior surface of the tibia	Underside of the toes (excepting the great toe)	Plantarflexion and supination. Bends the great toe
Tibialis posterior (posterior shin bone muscle)	Posterior surface of the fibula and tibia	Underside of the naviculare	Plantarflexion and supination

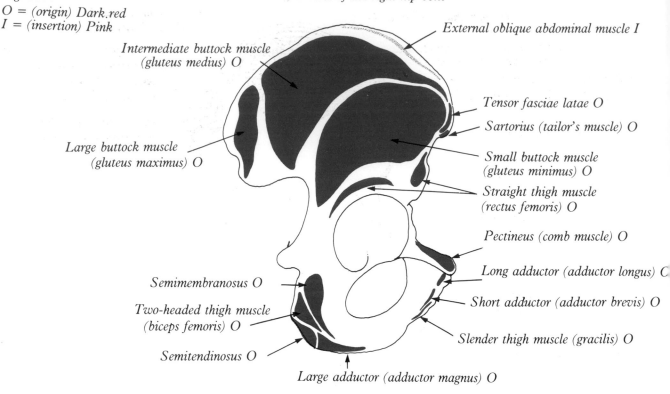

Fig. 329.
O = (origin) Dark.red
I = (insertion) Pink

External view of the right hip bone

External oblique abdominal muscle I

*Intermediate buttock muscle
(gluteus medius) O*

Tensor fasciae latae O

Sartorius (tailor's muscle) O

*Small buttock muscle
(gluteus minimus) O*

*Large buttock muscle
(gluteus maximus) O*

*Straight thigh muscle
(rectus femoris) O*

Pectineus (comb muscle) O

Long adductor (adductor longus) O

Semimembranosus O

Short adductor (adductor brevis) O

*Two-headed thigh muscle
(biceps femoris) O*

Slender thigh muscle (gracilis) O

Semitendinosus O

Large adductor (adductor magnus) O

Fig. 330.   (a) *Right thigh bone viewed from the front.*   (b) *Right thigh bone viewed from the back.*

Gluteus minimus I

Gluteus medius I

Vastus lateralis O

Iliopsoas I

Vastus lateralis O

Vastus medialis O

Pectineus I

Vastus medialis O

Adductor brevis I

Gluteus maximus I

Vastus intermedius O

Adductor longus I

Vastus intermedius O

Adductor magnus I

*Biceps femoris
(short head) O*

Vastus lateralis O

Gastrocnemius O

Adductor magnus I

Popliteus O

128

Fig. 331.

Internal view of the right hip bone.

Haunch muscle (iliacus) O

Square lumbar muscle
(quadratus lumborum) O

Transverse abdominal muscle
(transversus abdominis) O

Internal oblique abdominal muscle
(obliquus internus abdominus)

Internal oblique abdominal
muscle (obliquus internus abdominus) O

Broad back muscle
(latissimus dorsi) O

Sartorius (tailor's muscle)

Part of the deep-lying
back muscles (sacro-spinal) O

Pectineus (comb muscle)

Straight abdominal muscle
(rectus abdominus) I

Fig. 332. (a) Right lower leg viewed from the front.

(b) Right lower leg viewed from the back.

Biceps femoris I

Quadriceps
femoris I

Extensor digitorum longus O

Sartorius I

Gracilis I

Semitendinosus I

Tibial. ant. O

Peroneus longus O

Tibial. post. O

Peroneus brevis O

Extensor digitorum longus O

Tibialis posterior I

Flexor digitorum
longus I

Flexor hallucis
longus I

Semimembranosus I

Popliteus I

Biceps femoris I

Soleus O

Tibialis posterior O

Fibularis longus O

Flexor digitorum longus O

Flexor hallucis longus O

Fibularis brevis

Fibularis longus

Muscles whose origin is on the shoulder blade and insertion on the upper arm (pp.80 and 81)

Muscle	Origin	Insertion	Function
Supraspinatus (above-the-shoulder-blade-spine muscle)	Area above the shoulder blade spine (fossa supraspinata)	Greater external tuberosity of the upper arm bone (greater tuberosity)	Adducts and rotates the arm outwards
Teres major (greater round muscle)	Inferior angle of the shoulder blade (angulus inferior)	Anterior surface of the upper arm bone (medial lip of biceps groove)	Adducts the arm and rotates it inwards. (Assists the broad back muscle)
Infraspinatus (below-the-shoulder-blade-spine muscle)	A large part of the surface underneath the shoulder blade spine (fossa infraspinata)	Greater external tuberosity (greater tuberosity)	Rotates the arm outwards
Teres minor (lesser round muscle)	Outer border of the shoulder blade (margo lateralis)	Greater external tuberosity (greater tuberosity)	Rotates the arm outwards
Subscapularis (anterior shoulder blade muscle)	Entire inner surface of the shoulder blade (fossa subscapularis)	Lesser anterior tuberosity (lesser tuberosity)	Rotates the arm inwards
Coracobrachialis	Crow's beak projection	Inner surface of the upper arm	Swings the arm forward

Muscles whose origin is on the trunk and insertion on the shoulder blade (pp.81 and 82)

Muscle	Origin	Insertion	Function
Levator scapulae	Cervical vertebrae 1–4	Superior angle of the shoulder blade	Raises the shoulder blade
Rhomboideus	Cervical vertebrae 6 and 7, dorsal vertebrae 1–4	Inner border of the shoulder blade	Adducts and rotates the shoulder blade inwards
Trapezius	Base of the skull. Cervical and dorsal vertebrae	Shoulder blade spine and external part of the collar bone	Adducts and rotates the shoulder blade outwards. Turns the head bends the neck backwards
Serratus anterior (anterior serrated muscle)	Ribs 1–9	Inner border of the shoulder blade	Stabilises the shoulder blade when the hand presses against an object
Pectoralis minor (lesser chest muscle)	Ribs 3–5	Crow's beak projection (coracoid process)	Lowers the shoulder blade

Muscles whose origin is on the trunk and insertion on the arm (pp.82–84)

Muscle	Origin	Insertion	Function
Pectoralis major (greater chest muscle)	Inner part of the collar bone, breastbone and part of the costal cartilage	Greater external tuberosity (greater tuberosity and lateral lip of biceps groove)	Adducts the arm and rotates it inwards. Pulls the arm in front of the chest from any position
Deltoideus (deltoid muscle)	Outer part of the collar bone and the shoulder blade spine (spina scapulae)	Along the shaft of the upper arm (deltoid tuberosity)	Takes part in all movements of the upper arm
Latissimus dorsi (broad back muscle)	Dorsal vertebrae 6–12. Posterior part of the hip bone crest and ribs 9–12. Rump bone	Below the lesser anterior tubercle of the upper arm (floor of the biceps groove)	Swings the arm backwards and rotates it inwards

Muscles which pass across both the shoulder and elbow joints (pp.87 and 89)

Muscle	Origin	Insertion	Function
Biceps brachii (two-headed arm muscle)	(1) Coracoid process (2) just above the articular surface of the shoulder blade (supraglenoid tubercle)	Anterior surface of the radius (tuberositas radii). Is also connected to the ulna by way of a tendon band	Bends and supinates the elbow. Swings the shoulder joint forwards
Triceps brachii (three-headed arm muscle)	(1) Below the articular surface of the shoulder blade (infraglenoid tubercle), (2) posterior surface of the upper arm, (3) posterior surface of the upper arm	Elbow outgrowth (olecranon) and joint capsule	Stretches the elbow and protects the shoulder joint by keeping the capsular ligament taut

Muscles which pass across the elbow joint only (pp.87 and 91)

Muscle	Origin	Insertion	Function
Brachialis (upper arm muscle)	Greater part of the anterior surface of the upper arm	Coronoid process	Bends the elbow
Brachioradialis (arm-radius muscle)	External condyle of the upper arm (lateral epicondyle)	At the styloid process of the radius (styloid process)	Bends the elbow. Pronation or supination depending on the start position
Anconeus	Posterior surface of the upper arm	Posterior surface of the ulna	Straightens the elbow
Supinator	External condyle of the upper arm	Outer surface of the radius	Supinates the forearm
Pronator teres	Internal condyle of the upper arm	Outer surface of the radius	Pronates the forearm

Muscles which affect both the forearm and wrist (p.92)

Muscle	Origin	Insertion	Function
Extensor digitorum (finger extensor)	External condyle of the upper arm (lateral epicondyle)	Posterior surface of the finger bones (excepting the thumb)	Straightens the fingers, the wrist and finally the elbow
Extensor carpi radialis longus and brevis (long and short radial-wrist extensors)	At the external condyle of the upper arm	Posterior of the 2nd and 3rd metacarpals	Associated with extension and abduction of the wrist joint
Extensor carpi ulnaris (ulna-wrist extensor)	External condyle of the upper arm	Posterior surface of the 5th metacarpal bone	Associated with extension and adduction of the wrist
Flexor digitorum superficialis (superficial finger flexor)	Internal condyle of the upper arm and anterior surface of the radius	Middle row of the phalanges	Bends the elbow and fingers. Assists in flexing the wrist
Flexor carpi radialis (radial-wrist flexor)	Internal condyle of the upper arm	Anterior surface of the 2nd and 3rd metacarpals	Bends the elbow. When acting alone it flexes the wrist. Can also assist in pronating the forearm and hand
Flexor carpi ulnaris (ulna-wrist flexor)	Internal condyle and the inner margin of the elbow outgrowth (olecranon)	Pisiform, hamate bone and 5th metacarpal bone	When acting alone it flexes the wrist and, by continuing to contract, it bends the elbow

Fig. 333.

Right shoulder blade viewed from the back.

O = origin
I = insertion

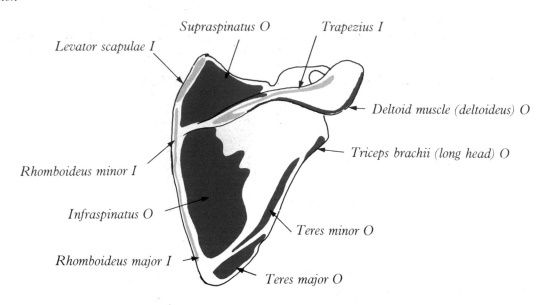

Supraspinatus O

Trapezius I

Levator scapulae I

Deltoid muscle (deltoideus) O

Triceps brachii (long head) O

Rhomboideus minor I

Infraspinatus O

Teres minor O

Rhomboideus major I

Teres major O

Fig. 334. (a) *Right upper arm viewed from the front.* (b) *Right upper arm viewed from the back.*

Infraspinatus I

Supraspinatus I

Teres minor I

Subscapularis I

Broad back muscle
(latissimus dorsi) I

Triceps brachii (lateral head) O

Teres major I

Greater chest muscle
(pectoralis major) I

Deltoid muscle (deltoideus) I

Deltoid I

Brachialis O

Coracobrachialis I

Brachioradialis O

Brachialis O

Brachioradialis O

Triceps brachii (medial head) O

Long radial-wrist extensor O

Short radial-wrist extensor O

Pronator teres O

Ulna-wrist-finger extensor O
and supinator

Anconeus O

Finger flexor and
radial-wrist flexor O

Ulna-wrist flexor O

Fig. 335   Right shoulder blade viewed from the front.

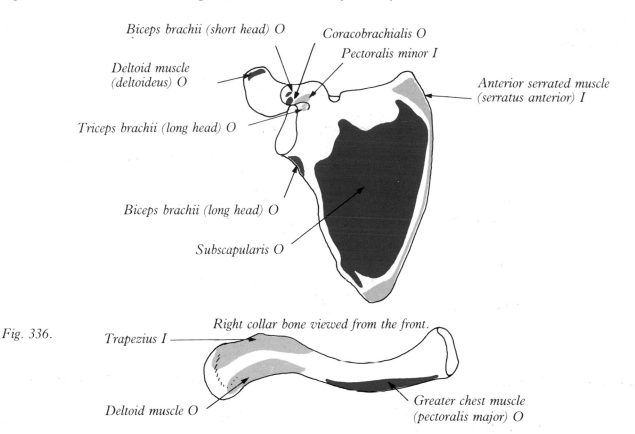

Biceps brachii (short head) O   Coracobrachialis O

Deltoid muscle   Pectoralis minor I
(deltoideus) O
                                       Anterior serrated muscle
                                       (serratus anterior) I

Triceps brachii (long head) O

Biceps brachii (long head) O

Subscapularis O

Fig. 336.
                        Right collar bone viewed from the front.
Trapezius I

                                       Greater chest muscle
Deltoid muscle O   (pectoralis major) O

Fig. 337.   (a) Right forearm viewed from the front.   (b) Right forearm viewed from the back.

                                                           Three-headed arm muscle
                                                           (triceps brachii) I

Pronator teres O   Ulna-wrist flexor O
Brachialis I   Ulna-wrist extensor O
Supinator O   Anconeus I
                                                           Superficial finger flexor O
Two-headed arm muscle   Supinator I
(biceps brachii) I

Supinator I   Abductor of the thumb O
                                                           Pronator teres I

                                                           Long extensor of the thumb O
Superficial finger flexor O

Thumb flexor O   Short thumb extensor O

Pronator quadratus O, I

Brachioradialis I

133

REFERENCES

Anderson B.	Stretching ISBN 0-9601066-1-8
Basmajian J.V.	Muscles Alive 4th ed (Illus) 1979 Williams & Wilkins Co, USA ISBN 0-683-00413-1
Biomechanics	International Series on Biomechanics, Volume I-VI University Park Press, USA ISBN 0-8391-1242-4
Dagg A.	Running Walking and Jumping Wykeham publications, London 1977 ISBN 0-85109-530-5
Doherty K.	Track and field omnibook ISBN 0-911520-73-2
Dyson G.	The mechanics of athletics University of London press Ltd 1962 SBN 340 08905 9
Eaves G.	Diving A.S. Barnes & Co, Cranbury N.J. USA NBN 99-042-1168-X
Ekstrand J.	Soccer injuries and their prevention Linköping University Medica Dissertations No 130 SBN 91-73-72-526-9
Frankel-Burstein	Orthopaedic biomechanics Lea & Febiger, Philadelphia 1970 ISBN 8121-0090-5
Harris R.	Kinesiology Houghton Mifflin Co, Boston USA 1977 ISBN 0-395-20668-5
Hay J.	The biomechanics of sport techniques Prentice-Hall INC. N.J. USA ISBN 0-13-035-139-3
Hjortsjö C-H.	Rörclseapparaten Spec. del. Gleerups, Lund 1967
Hochmuth	Biomechanik sportlicher Bewegungen Sportverlag, Berlin 1974 Lic No 140355-5-74-9004
Janda V.	Muskelfunktionsdiagnostik Studentlitteratur, Lund 1976 ISBN 91-44-11351-X
Liljedahl-Gillqvist	Idrottsskador Liber 1974 ISBN 91-47-01109-2
Petersson, Renström	Skador inom idrotten Sv. Riksidrottsförbundet 1977 ISBN 098-2034-X1
Styrka och Rörlighet	Sv. Riksidrottsförbundet/Utb. NBN 99-031-6079-8
Sölveborn S.	Boken om stretching Sölve Bok, Ystad 1982 ISBN 91-970392-0-9
Thompson C.W.	Manual of Structural Kinesology 1977 C.V. Mosby Co, St. Louis USA ISBN 0-8016-4939-0
Tittel K.	Beschreibende und funktionelle Anatomie des Menschen Gustav Fischer Verlag, Stuttgart
Tveit P.	Bevegelseslaere Universitetsforlaget, Norge ISBN 82-00-25923-4
Williams-Lissner	Biomechanics of Human Motion SBN 0-7216-9440-3
Williams-Sperryn	Sports medicine ISBN 0-7131-4275-8
Åstrand-Rodahl	Textbook of work physiology McGraw-Hill 1977 ISBN 07-002405-7